AF383166

BY HER HAND

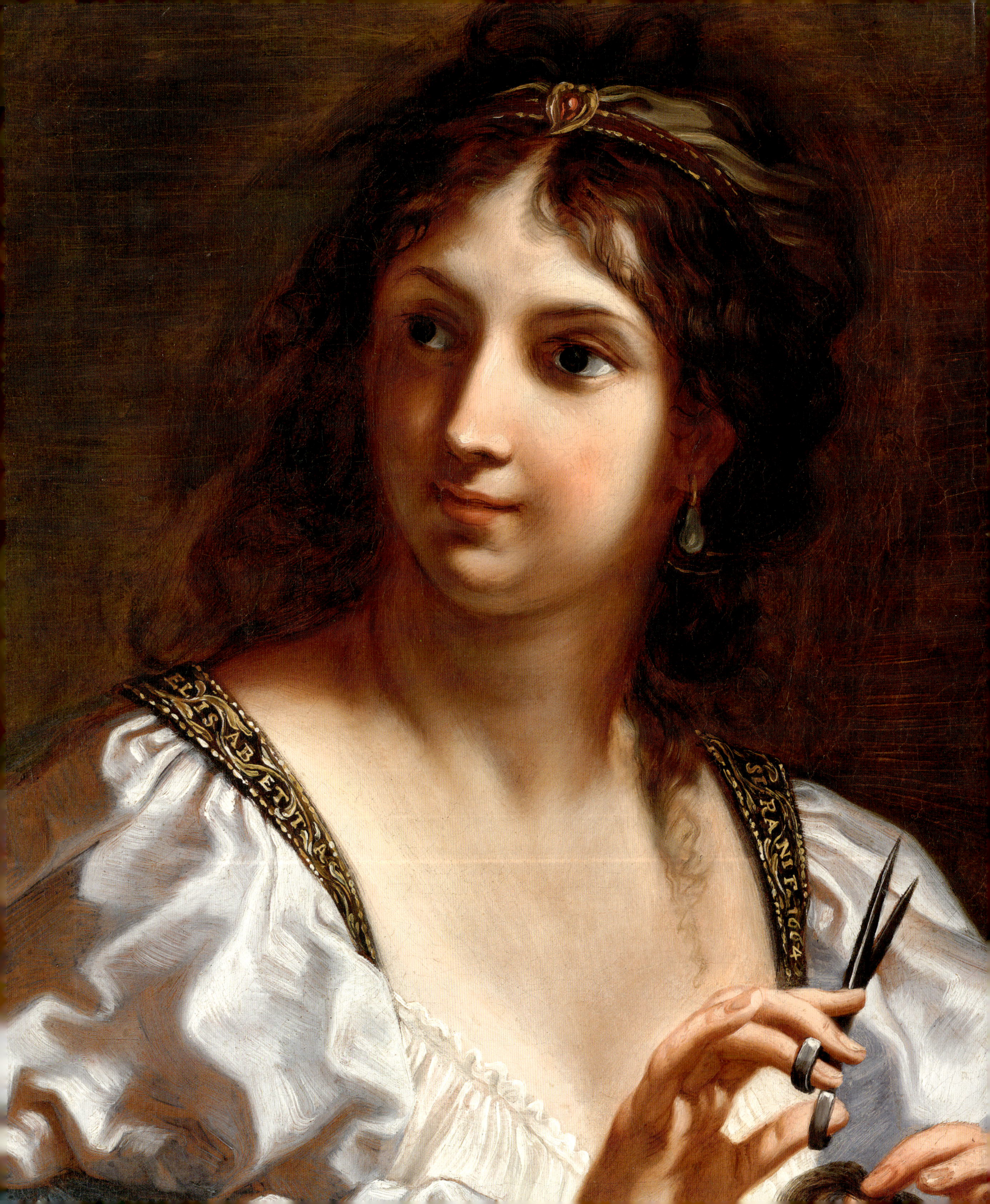
ELISABETTA
SIRANI F. 1664

EDITED BY **Eve Straussman-Pflanzer and Oliver Tostmann**

WITH ESSAYS AND ENTRIES BY Sheila Barker, Babette Bohn, Claude-Douglas Dickerson III, Jamie Gabbarelli, Hilliard Goldfarb, Lara Lea Roney, Joaneath Spicer, Eve Straussman-Pflanzer, and Oliver Tostmann

Wadsworth Atheneum Museum of Art
Detroit Institute of Arts

DISTRIBUTED BY Yale University Press, New Haven and London

By Her Hand: Artemisia Gentileschi and Women Artists in Italy, 1500–1800 is organized by the Wadsworth Atheneum Museum of Art and the Detroit Institute of Arts.

At the Wadsworth Atheneum Museum of Art, the exhibition is generously supported by the Cheryl Chase and Stuart Bear Family Foundation, JPMorgan Chase & Co., the National Endowment for the Arts, the Robert Lehman Foundation, the Gladys Krieble Delmas Foundation, the Tavolozza Foundation, the Private Art Dealers Association, the Samuel H. Kress Foundation, and the Dau Family Foundation.

At the Detroit Institute of Arts, major support is provided by the European Paintings Council, Masco Corporation, TCF Bank, Anne G Fredericks, and the Valade Family.

Additional support is provided by Jennifer Adderley, Peter and Carol Walters, Mary Ann and Robert Gorlin, MSU Federal Credit Union and the Desk Drawer Fund, Claudia J. Nickel, the Nancy S. Williams Trust and Sharon Backstrom, executor, Brenda Naomi Rosenberg, an anonymous donor, the Richard and Jane Manoogian Foundation, and the Robert Lehman Foundation.

Funding is also provided by Ann Berman and Daniel Feld and the Samuel H. Kress Foundation.

JP Morgan Chase & Co.

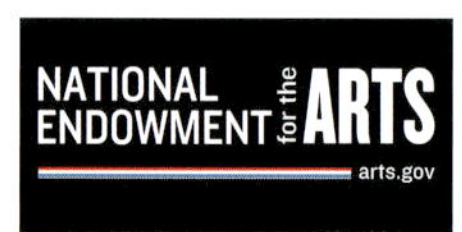

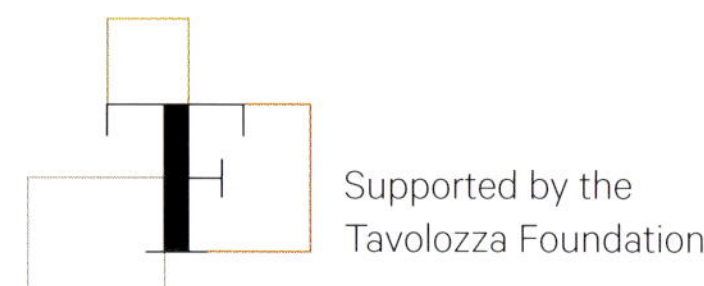

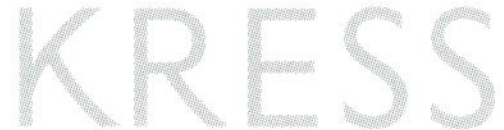

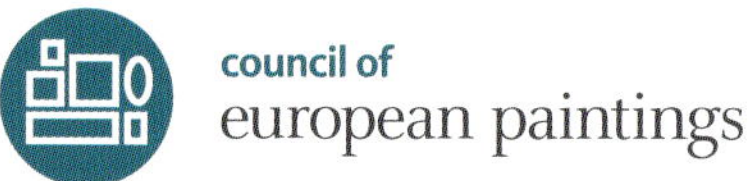

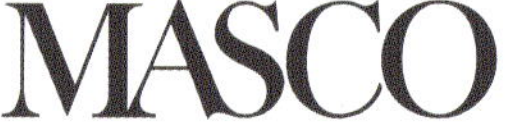

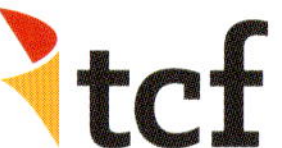

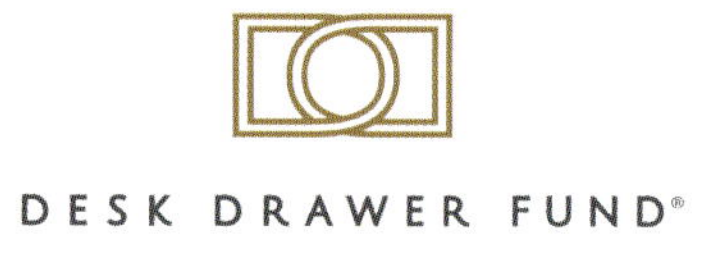

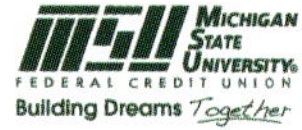

Arader Galleries

The Cleveland Museum of Art

Columbus Museum of Art

Cooper-Hewitt, Smithsonian Design Museum

Cornell Fine Arts Museum at Rollins College

Detroit Institute of Arts

Collection of Anne G Fredericks

Gallerie degli Uffizi

The John and Mable Ringling Museum of Art

Los Angeles County Museum of Art

Lowe Art Museum, University of Miami

The Metropolitan Museum of Art

Bart and Beatrice Moerman-Masereel

Montreal Museum of Fine Arts

The Morgan Library & Museum

Museo della Città di Bologna

Museum of Fine Arts, Boston

National Gallery of Art, Washington, D.C.

National Gallery, London

National Museum of Women in the Arts

Marnix Neerman

RISD Museum

San Diego Museum of Art

The Stephen K. and Janie Woo Scher Collection

Southampton City Art Gallery

Toledo Museum of Art

Wadsworth Atheneum Museum of Art

Walters Art Museum

Linda Cheverton Wick and Walter Wick

Worcester Art Museum

Yale University Art Gallery

By Her Hand: Artemisia Gentileschi and Women Artists in Italy, 1500–1800 is published in conjunction with an exhibition of the same title organized by the Wadsworth Atheneum Museum of Art and the Detroit Institute of Arts.

Wadsworth Atheneum Museum of Art
September 30, 2021–January 9, 2022

Detroit Institute of Arts
February 6, 2022–May 29, 2022

At the Wadsworth Atheneum Museum of Art, the exhibition is generously supported by the Cheryl Chase and Stuart Bear Family Foundation, JPMorgan Chase & Co., the National Endowment for the Arts, the Robert Lehman Foundation, the Gladys Krieble Delmas Foundation, the Tavolozza Foundation, the Private Art Dealers Association, the Samuel H. Kress Foundation, and the Dau Family Foundation.

At the Detroit Institute of Arts, major support is provided by the European Paintings Council, Masco Corporation, TCF Bank, Anne G Fredericks, and the Valade Family.

Additional support is provided by Jennifer Adderley, Peter and Carol Walters, Mary Ann and Robert Gorlin, MSU Federal Credit Union and the Desk Drawer Fund, Claudia J. Nickel, the Nancy S. Williams Trust and Sharon Backstrom, executor, Brenda Naomi Rosenberg, an anonymous donor, the Richard and Jane Manoogian Foundation, and the Robert Lehman Foundation.

Funding is also provided by Ann Berman and Daniel Feld and the Samuel H. Kress Foundation.

© 2021 Detroit Institute of Arts

All rights reserved. No part of this publication may be reproduced, transmitted, or utilized in any form or by any means, electronic or mechanical, including photocopy, digital recording, or any other information storage or retrieval system (beyond that copying permitted by Sections 107 and 108 of the US Copyright Law), without prior written permission from the Detroit Institute of Arts, except by a reviewer, who may quote brief passages.

First edition
Printed in China

ISBN: 978-0-300-25636-9

10 9 8 7 6 5 4 3 2

Library of Congress Control Number: 2021939461

Published by
Detroit Institute of Arts
5200 Woodward Avenue
Detroit, Michigan 48202-4094
www.dia.org

Distributed by
Yale University Press
302 Temple Street
P.O. Box 209040
New Haven, Connecticut 06520-9040
www.yalebooks.com/art

Produced by the Detroit Institute of Arts
Edited by Lisa Bessette, Ann Arbor, Michigan
Designed and typeset by Joan Sommers, Glue + Paper Workshop, Cushing, Maine
Production and project management by Amanda Freymann, Glue + Paper Workshop, Beverly Shores, Indiana
Proofread by Sheila Majumdar, Chicago, Illinois
Index by Jane Friedman, Evanston, Illinois
Photography research by Elena Berry, Detroit Institute of Arts
Separations by Professional Graphics Inc., Rockford, Illinois
Printing and binding in China through Asia Pacific Offset

Jacket front: Artemisia Gentileschi, *Self-Portrait as a Lute Player*, 1615–1617 (detail), oil on canvas. The Wadsworth Atheneum Museum of Art, Hartford, Charles H. Schwartz Endowment Fund, 2014.4.1 (cat. 24)

Jacket back: Artemisia Gentileschi, *Judith and Her Maidservant with the Head of Holofernes*, ca. 1623–1625 (detail), oil on canvas. Detroit Institute of Arts, Gift of Mr. Leslie H. Green, 52.253 (cat. 27)

Information on details can be found in the photography credits.

CONTENTS

9   Directors' Foreword   JEFFREY N. BROWN AND SALVADOR SALORT-PONS

11   Acknowledgments   EVE STRAUSSMAN-PFLANZER AND OLIVER TOSTMANN

13   Introduction   EVE STRAUSSMAN-PFLANZER AND OLIVER TOSTMANN

17   Why Have There Been No Exhibitions of Early Modern Italian
     Women Artists in Hartford or Detroit?   EVE STRAUSSMAN-PFLANZER

31   The Advantages of Painting Small: Italian Women Artists and
     the Matter of Scale   OLIVER TOSTMANN

43   Art as Women's Work: The Professionalization of Women Artists
     in Italy, 1350–1800   SHEILA BARKER

52   Catalogue   BABETTE BOHN, CLAUDE-DOUGLAS DICKERSON III, JAMIE GABBARELLI,
     HILLIARD GOLDFARB, LARA LEA RONEY, JOANEATH SPICER, EVE STRAUSSMAN-PFLANZER,
     AND OLIVER TOSTMANN

183 Exhibitions

186 Bibliography

204 Index

208 Photography Credits

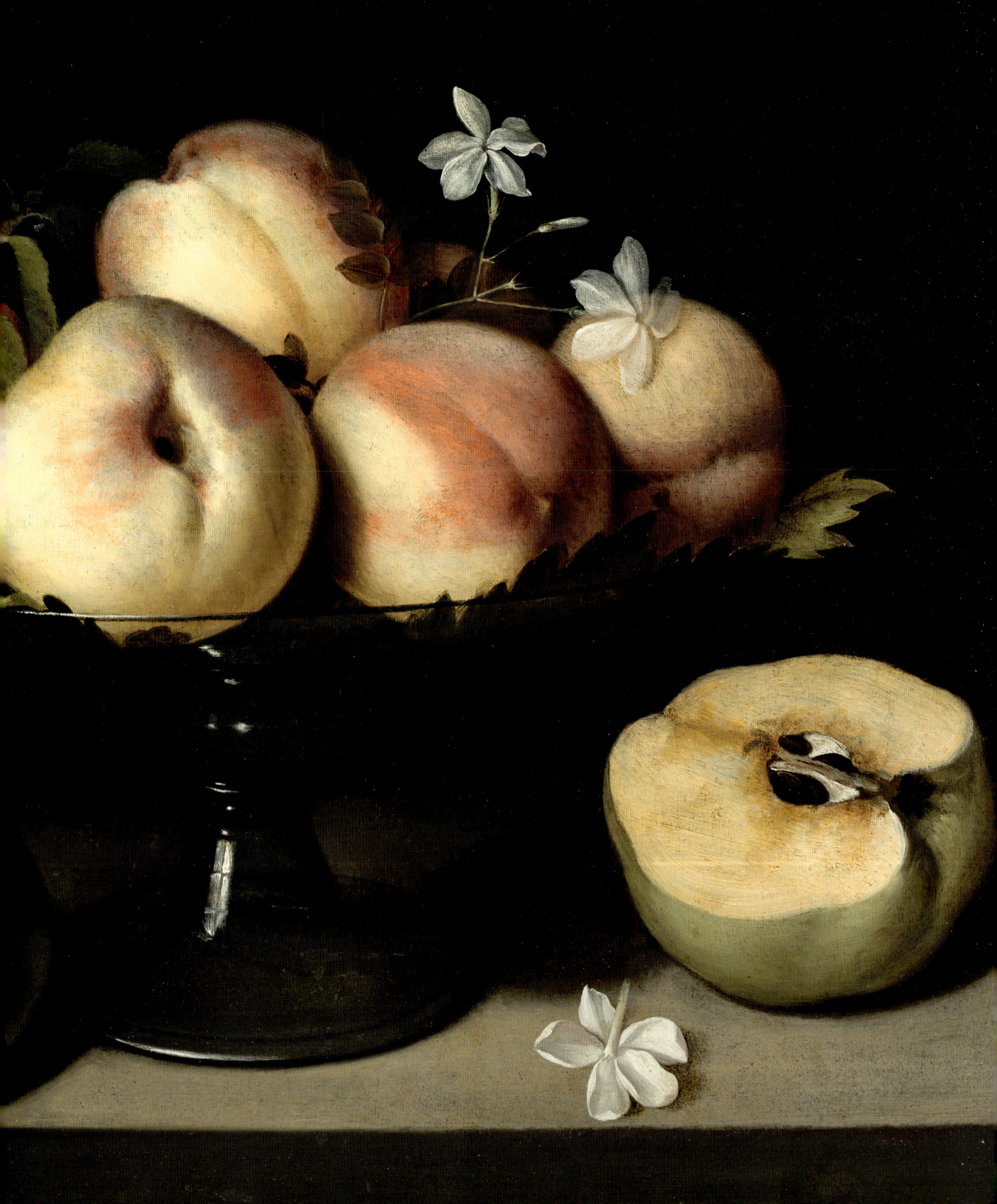

DIRECTORS' FOREWORD

CATALYZED BY TWO OUTSTANDING PAINTINGS by Artemisia Gentileschi—*Self-Portrait as a Lute Player* (1615–1617), in the collection of the Wadsworth Atheneum Museum of Art, and *Judith and Her Maidservant with the Head of Holofernes* (ca. 1623–1625), in the collection of the Detroit Institute of Arts—the groundbreaking and timely *By Her Hand: Artemisia Gentileschi and Women Artists in Italy, 1500–1800* brings together an unparalleled group of artworks. By doing so, we hope to engage critically with topics of keen public interest through the art of the past. In the following pages, leading scholars explore over sixty works of art by early modern women artists—overwhelmingly known for their talents as painters—from across the Italian peninsula and spanning three centuries of production. These women shared a drive to succeed as artists when the art world was dominated by men. Their paths to realizing that professional accomplishment and the road to fame associated with their creations are remarkably diverse and rich. Perhaps it goes without saying that such a sensitive and complete examination would not have been possible even a generation ago, as a brighter spotlight has come to shine on these artists since the turn of the century, and the foundational work to understand each more specifically is still emerging.

Both our museums are distinguished by important collections of Italian art of the early modern period. Indeed, both were trailblazers in promoting Italian art of this period: the DIA led by German-born Wilhelm Valentiner (1924–1945); the Wadsworth by A. Everett "Chick" Austin (1927–1944), and, later, Charles C. Cunningham (1946–1966). The work of women artists has been central to the Wadsworth's collection growth since the 1850s, but the museum did not acquire works by eminent women of the premodern era until later—buying a Margaretha de Heer in 1937, for example, and a still life believed at the time to have been painted by Fede Galizia (now attributed to the Master of Hartford Still Life) in 1942. In Detroit, Gentileschi's *Judith and Her Maidservant with the Head of Holofernes* joined the collection in 1952 as a gift from Mr. Leslie H. Green, the first major work by the artist to enter a civic museum in the United States; *Berenice* (ca. 1741), a pastel by Carriera, was acquired by gift in 1956. Yet, admittedly, the female authorship of these works may have been incidental.

The great majority of works by women artists housed today at our museums are by American painters, sculptors, ceramicists, printmakers, textile makers, and photographers. The more concerted collecting of pre-twentieth-century European women artists across all periods and geographies has risen as a higher priority and greater opportunity in the twenty-first century. The Wadsworth's Gentileschi was acquired only seven years ago, and during the last four years, the DIA has purchased works in different media by seventeenth-century women artists working in Italy, Portugal, and Spain. An interest in collecting the work of early modern women artists has flowered dramatically outside museums as well. More than a third of the works in this exhibition have been lent from private collections in the United States and Europe, including several fascinating, recently discovered paintings that have rarely been publicly displayed. We are grateful to all of the lenders—museums and individuals alike—who have enriched this exhibition through their generosity.

Our institutions share a long history of collaboration. *By Her Hand: Artemisia Gentileschi and Women Artists in Italy, 1500–1800* was conceived by Eve Straussman-Pflanzer, former Head of the European Art Department and Elizabeth and Allan Shelden Curator of European Paintings at the DIA (now Curator and Head of Italian and Spanish Paintings at the National Gallery of Art, Washington, D.C.), and Oliver Tostmann, Susan Morse Hilles Curator of European Art at the Wadsworth Atheneum. As you will see in the acknowledgments, the exhibition and catalogue were realized with the help of many dedicated colleagues. They would not have been possible without the generous support of our sponsors. At the Wadsworth Atheneum, we want to thank the Cheryl Chase and Stuart Bear Family Foundation, JPMorgan Chase & Co., The National Endowment for the Arts, the Robert Lehman Foundation, the Gladys Krieble Delmas Foundation, the Tavolozza Foundation, the Private Art Dealers Association, the Samuel H. Kress Foundation, and the Dau Family Foundation. At the DIA, we want to thank the European Paintings Council, Masco Corporation, TCF Bank, Anne G Fredericks, the Valade Family, Jennifer Adderley, Peter and Carol Walters, Mary Ann and Robert Gorlin, MSU Federal Credit Union and the Desk Drawer Fund, Claudia J. Nickel, the Nancy S. Williams Trust and Sharon Backstrom, Brenda Naomi Rosenberg, an anonymous donor, the Richard and Jane Manoogian Foundation, the Robert Lehman Foundation, Ann Berman and Daniel Feld, and the Samuel H. Kress Foundation.

Jeffrey N. Brown, Interim Director and CEO,
Wadsworth Atheneum Museum of Art

Salvador Salort-Pons, Director, President, and CEO,
Detroit Institute of Arts

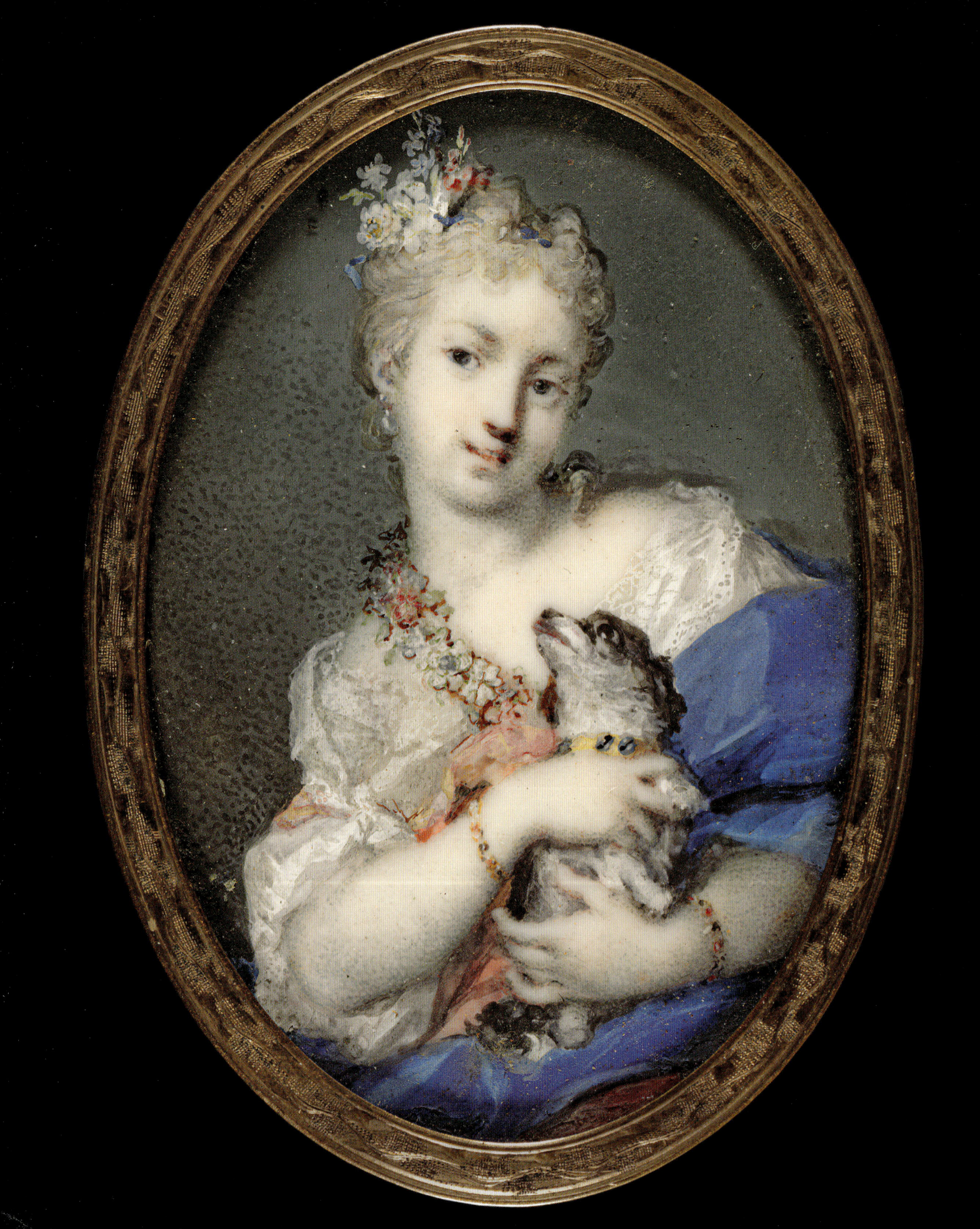

ACKNOWLEDGMENTS

THE CURATORS WOULD LIKE TO THANK the following colleagues and friends for their invaluable support of and contributions to this ambitious project.

It would not have been possible without the generous loans and support from the following institutions and colleagues: Accademia Nazionale di San Luca, Rome: Consuelo Lollobrigida, Francesco Moschini; Biblioteca Ambrosiana: Monsignor Marco Ballarini; Collezioni d'Arte e di Storia della Fondazione della Cassa di Risparmio di Bologna: Mirko Nottoli, Fabio Roversi Monaco; Chazen Museum of Art: Maria Saffiotti Dale, Amy Gillman; Cleveland Museum of Art: William Griswold, Cory Korkow; Columbus Museum of Art: Nannette V. Maciejunes, David Stark; Cooper Hewitt, Smithsonian Design Museum: Mir Finkelman, Julia Siemon, Yao-Fen You; Cornell Fine Arts Museum at Rollins College: Gisela Carbonell, Ena Heller; Davis Museum at Wellesley College: Mark Beeman, Lisa Fischman, Bo Mompho; Dumbarton Oaks Research Library and Collection: Thomas B. F. Cummins, Anatole Tchikine; Fondazione Musei Civici di Venezia: Gabriella Belli, Elena Marchetti; Frick Collection: Aimee Ng, Xavier Soloman, Ian Wardropper; Los Angeles County Museum of Art: Michael Govan, Leah Lehmbeck; Lowe Art Museum, University of Miami: Jill Deupi, Eugenia Incer; J. Paul Getty Museum: Julian Brooks, Jim Cuno, Timothy Potts; The Metropolitan Museum of Art: Andrea Bayer, Keith Christiansen, Max Hollein, Mark McDonald, Nadine Orenstein, David Pullins, Allison Rudnick, Femke Speelberg, Talia Steinman, Stephan Wolohojian; Milwaukee Art Museum: Tanya Paul, Marcelle Polednik; Montreal Museum of Fine Arts: Stéphane Aquin, Hilliard Goldfarb; Morgan Library and Museum: Colin B. Bailey, John Marciari, Zoe Watnik; Museo Nacional del Prado: Miguel Falomir; Museum of Fine Arts, Boston: Marietta Cambareri, Frederick Ilchman, Matthew Teitelbaum; National Gallery London: Gabriele Finaldi, Larry Keith, Letizia Treves; National Gallery of Art, Washington, D.C.: Jonathan Bober, Claude-Douglas Dickerson III, Kaywin Feldman, Ginger Hammer, Rena Hoisington; National Museum of Women in the Arts: Susan Fisher Sterling, Virginia Treanor; RISD Museum: Sarah Ganz Blythe, Jamie Gabbarelli (now at the Art Institute of Chicago), Jan Howard; John and Mable Ringling Museum of Art: Sarah Cartwright, Steven High, Elizabeth Robson; San Diego Museum of Art: Michael Brown, Roxana Velásquez; South Hampton City Art Gallery: Clare Mitchell, Rebecca Moisan; Walters Art Museum: Julia Marciari-Alexander, Joaneath Spicer; Toledo Museum of Art: Adam Levine, Lawrence W. Nichols; Worcester Art Museum: Matthias Waschek, Claire Whitner; Yale University Art Gallery: Laurence Kanter, Stephanie Wiles; Gallerie degli Uffizi: Cristina Gnoni, Eike Schmidt, Maria Matilde Simari.

We extend particular thanks to those private lenders who so kindly agreed to support this project, including Anne G Fredericks, Bart and Beatrice Moerman-Masereel, Marnix Neerman, Stephen Scher, Linda and Walter Wick, and those who prefer to stay anonymous.

We would like to thank everyone involved with the production of this catalogue, especially Sheila Barker, Babette Bohn, Claude-Douglas Dickerson III, Jamie Gabbarelli, Hilliard Goldfarb, Lara Lea Roney, and Joaneath Spicer, who contributed illuminating texts; and Lisa Bessette, who provided exceptional editing.

At the Wadsworth Atheneum, we are grateful to those who made this project a reality: Thomas J. Loughman, Cecil B. Adams, Angelina Altobellis, David Borawski, Joe Bun Keo, Mary C. Busick, Anne Butler Rice, Brandy Culp, Michael Dudich, Jon Eastman, Carrie Evans, Mark Giuliano, Patricia Hickson, Kim Hugo, Janna Israel, Jessica Kelley, Amy Kilkenny, Allen Kosanovich, Caroline Maddox, Erin Monroe, Alison Parman, Christopher Roque, Linda H. Roth, and Aviva Santopietro.

At the Detroit Institute of Arts, we thank Salvador Salort-Pons, Nancy Barr, Blair Bailey, Elena Berry, Terry Birkett, Judith F. Dolkart, Theodora Doulamis, Kim Dziurman, Carolyn Fenner, Christopher Foster, Rosemarie Gleeson, Caitlin Grames, Ellen Hanspach-Bernal, Nina Holden, Elizabeth Homberger, Jim Johnson, Presh Johnson-Arabitj, Everett Keyser, Christine Kloostra, Marc Langlois, Rachel Lewis, Ken Morris, Tracey Morton, Laticia Nelson-Clemons, Jennifer Paoletti, Melanie Parker, Clare Rogan, James Rotz, Andi Schreiber, Richard Scott, Aaron Steele, Eric Wheeler, and Erin Wilcox. We extend special thanks to Lara Lea Roney, research assistant for Italian Art, for her tireless and painstaking efforts on this project. We are grateful for her keen eye.

Eve Straussman-Pflanzer further thanks Kaywin Feldman and Franklin Kelly for allowing her to finish this project, as well as Gretchen Hirschauer and David Essex for their support and good cheer. Additionally, she expresses her gratitude to Victoria Sancho Lobis, Adam Thomas, Elizabeth Rothstein, Eileen Straussman, Emily Sosland, Yao-Fen You, Katherine Kasdorf, Cheryl Turski, Elizabeth Johnson, and Elizabeth Monti.

Oliver Tostmann extends his appreciation to Thomas Bruhn and Susan Talbott, and particularly to Margaret, Bertie, and Henning.

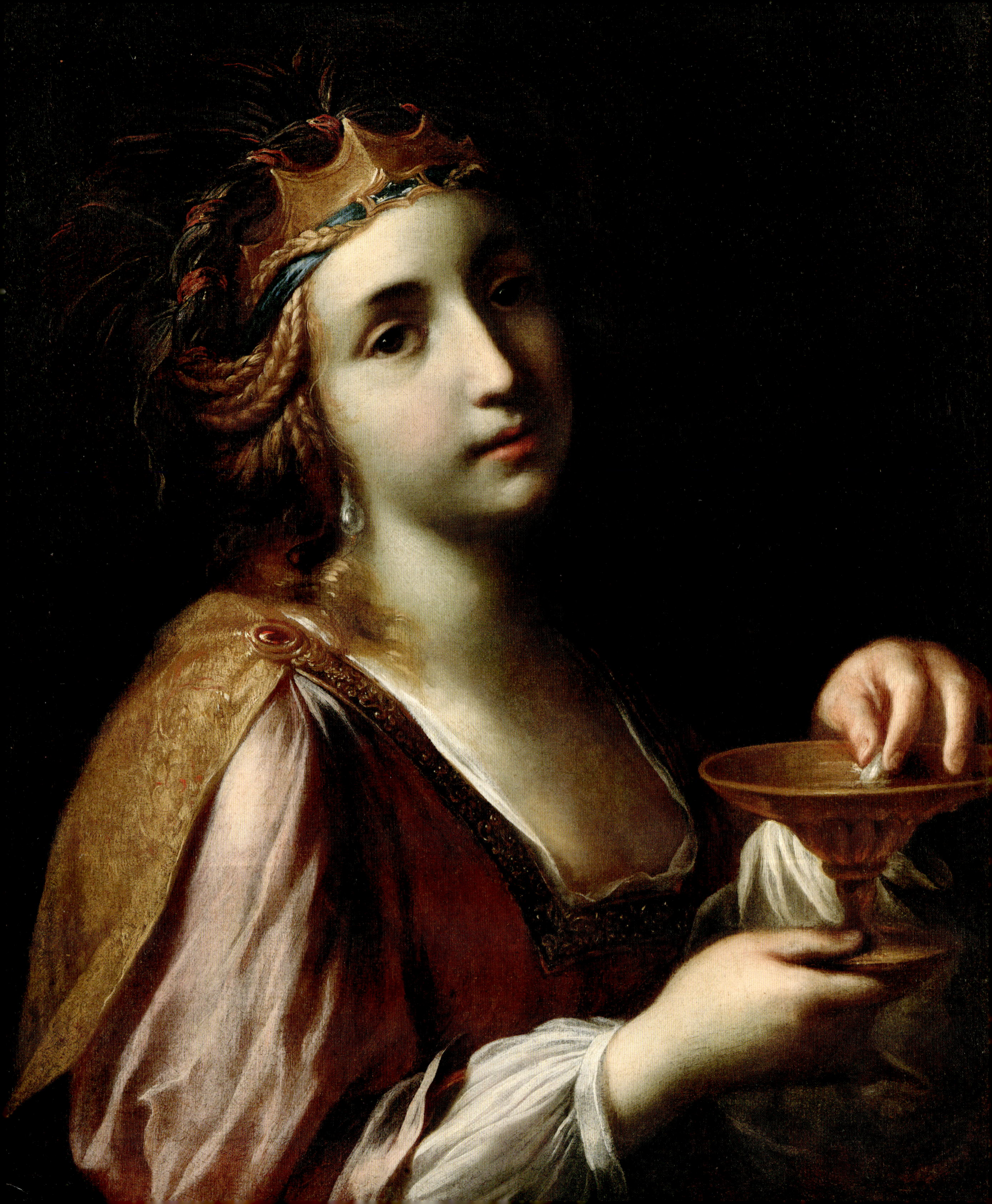

Introduction

THIS EXHIBITION MARKS A FIRST—it is the first occasion on which two of America's oldest civic art museums, the Wadsworth Atheneum Museum of Art in Hartford, Connecticut, founded in 1842, and the Detroit Institute of Arts in Detroit, Michigan, founded in 1885, have dedicated a special exhibition to early modern Italian women artists—those who practiced between roughly 1500 and 1800.[1] Beginning in the nineteenth century, museums like these set the tone for the type of art that would be collected in the United States, and the work of early modern European women artists was not favored. For this and several other reasons, it has taken well over one hundred years for a show on this subject to be mounted in these institutions. The moment has finally arrived to introduce wider audiences to these pioneering and captivating artists.

The history of scholarship on early Italian women artists has also contributed to their neglect. From the very beginning, they have not received the same attention as their male contemporaries. In artist and historian Giorgio Vasari's (1511–1574) influential *Lives of the Most Excellent Painters, Sculptors, and Architects* [*Le vite de' più eccellenti pittori, scultori, et architettori*], a collection of artist biographies first published in 1550, women comprise less than one percent of the artists discussed—a trifling figure. And when women artists are referenced, gender inequality is evident in the language used to describe them. The Bolognese sculptor Properzia de' Rossi (ca. 1490–1530), for example, the only Italian woman artist featured in the 1550 edition, is said by Vasari to be "a young woman talented not only in household matters . . . but also in innumerable fields of knowledge." Domestic duties are never mentioned in his discussions of male artists. Slightly later, other noted authors, such as the painter and writer Giovanni Baglione (1566–1643) and the painter, antiquarian, and biographer Giovanni Pietro Bellori (1613–1696), similarly offered little space in their texts to Italian women artists. Since then they have only occasionally been the recipients of scholarly interest, considerations that have taken a variety of forms—from the prosaic to the passionate and from the scholarly to the salacious.

By following in the footsteps of scholars like Vera Fortunati (Lavinia Fontana) and Mary Garrard (Artemisia Gentileschi), to name just two trailblazing examples, and continuing to place early modern Italian women artists at the center of the story, *By Her Hand: Artemisia Gentileschi and Women Artists in Italy, 1500–1800* counters the historical position of women artists as a secondary or peripheral topic. Reflecting the latest scholarship, and including newly attributed works and an introduction to artists that are known only to specialized scholars at present, the exhibition is another step towards the greater visibility of early Italian women artists and scholarship attuned to their vital contributions to the history of art.

This exhibition builds in several ways on the foundation of the groundbreaking 1976/1977 exhibition *Women Artists: 1550–1950*, co-curated by Ann Sutherland Harris and Linda Nochlin. First, it increases the number of women artists presented to the public, introducing, for instance, painters such as the Bolognese Ginevra Cantofoli (1618–1672) and the Venetian Marianna Carlevarijs (1703–after 1750) to museum visitors in the United States. Secondly, it enlarges the oeuvres of Italian women artists who are already well known, such as Artemisia Gentileschi (1593–1654 or later), whose recently discovered *Self-Portrait as Saint Catherine of Alexandria* from the National Gallery, London, and *Mary Magdalene in Ecstasy* from a private collection, are on display. It also features notable examples of the sizable quantity of works by Italian women artists that institutions and private collectors have purchased and amassed since the 1970s, many seen here publicly for the first time. Lastly, the show incorporates new conservation and technical information that leads to a deeper understanding of how these artists practiced.

Indeed, an important goal of the exhibition is to explore the different ways women worked as artists in Italy. The survey begins with Sofonisba Anguissola (ca. 1535–1625), one of the earliest women to be recognized as an artist during the Renaissance. It concludes with Anna Bacherini Piattoli (1720–1788), a painter working in Florence in the mid-eighteenth century. Both artists are best known for the self-portraits in this exhibition. While Anguissola shows herself as a young *gentildonna*, Bacherini Piattoli presents herself as a mature woman in her fifties. In the two-hundred years that elapsed between these two self-representations, an increasing number of Italian women chose to become artists and repeatedly depicted their own likenesses, arguably more often than their male peers. Like Anguissola, they often painted themselves at a young age, perhaps as a means to initiate and promote their careers. As becomes clear in this exhibition, self-portraiture was an important genre through which women explored their artistic identity across time periods. Artemisia Gentileschi, who often painted her likeness, famously played with her features in different guises, ranging from straightforward to allegorical self-portraits.

In early modern Italy, the artistic training of women differed fundamentally from that of men, and so did their professional trajectories. And yet, as the exhibition shows, women artists came up with inventive strategies to circumvent these practical challenges. Most young male artists had access to workshops and art academies where they learned to study the human figure, while women were usually prevented from taking advantage of the resources offered by these institutions. At a time when drawing the nude figure from male models was the backbone of a traditional art education, this meant women were fundamentally disadvantaged. Drawing thus seems to have played a different role for women artists. Even though some, like Lavinia Fontana (1552–1614) and Elisabetta Sirani (1638–1665), drew extensively, most seem not to have drawn at all, or to have done so infrequently. Even Fontana, who became famous for her portraits and paintings with complex historical subjects, created for the most part sensitively rendered drawings of heads, and few, if any, showing the whole human body. Women artists were trained in a variety of ways, from studying with their fathers, husbands, or brothers, to attending drawing classes or training with women outside their families. The field could benefit from greater study of the crucial topic of the early education of women artists.

This exhibition also explores the choices women artists had to make in the course of their careers. Partially due to their roles as wives, mothers, and managers of their households, a number made decisions about their specializations from the beginning. For some, still lifes and portraits were common subjects, while others became successful by painting large historical scenes, sometimes with a gendered twist, such as Artemisia Gentileschi and Elisabetta Sirani. Less than a handful of women worked as sculptors in this period, likely due to gender constraints. Working in small formats was a common gateway into the arts for women during the Renaissance and Baroque periods, and many focused on miniatures, diminutive paintings, and pastels—works that were ideally suited for the domestic sphere.

This exhibition also investigates the early reception of women artists among their contemporaries. Although they were often belittled and critiqued in literature on art, such as Giorgio Vasari's and Giovanni Baglione's *Lives*, there are instances in which peers recognized their artistic talents and merits. Portrait medals commemorated Lavinia Fontana and Artemisia Gentileschi during their lifetimes, while an elaborate catafalque celebrated Elisabetta Sirani on the occasion of her untimely death in Bologna. Other artists, like Virginia da Vezzo (1600–1638) and Maria Felice Tibaldi (1707–1770), little known today, were well-known painters in Rome and Paris during their lifetimes and were portrayed by their respective painter husbands, Simon Vouet (1590–1649) and Pierre Subleyras (1699–1749).

The catalogue essays explore these themes and questions further. Eve Straussman-Pflanzer examines the critical fortune of Italian women artists from the 1800s until today, investigating how feminism influenced scholarship on women artists and how art museums have responded to this growing discourse, primarily by mounting an increasing number of exhibitions devoted to them. Oliver Tostmann discusses the importance for women artists in Italy of small-scale works, which, as a largely unregulated niche in the art world, allowed them to practice, to experiment, and to challenge each other and their male peers without the restrictions and regulations applied to other genres. Finally,

Sheila Barker traces the professionalization of women artists in Italy, showing that while male artists practiced either as professional artists or as amateurs, these categories were more fluid for women and sometimes overlapped—a considerable number of women artists even resisted the confines of professionalizing and practiced in an "alternative scene" consisting of nuns and noblewomen.

Practical considerations required us to make difficult choices and to omit some fascinating artists and artworks. The Florentine nun Plautilla Nelli (1524–1588) and the Venetian painter Giulia Lama (1681–1747), each a captivating artist in her own right and deserving of further attention, could not be included in this survey. Likewise, Properzia de' Rossi, the most famous woman sculptor of her time, is not included in our survey. And though some Italian women artists, such as Sofonisba Anguissola, traveled outside of Italy, and others, such as Artemisia Gentileschi, found non-Italian patrons, we show only a few works created by Italian women artists outside of Italy. Nor do we show works by influential northern European women artists such as Levina Teerlinc (ca. 1520s–1576) and Caterina van Hemessen (1528–after 1565), even though, as the catalogue essays and entries make clear, some Italian woman artists were in contact with such European associates.

To invigorate connoisseurial debate, we decided to include artworks that have never been exhibited nor fully discussed and whose attributions, as a consequence, are open to debate. Questions of attribution often raise thorny issues in this still understudied field. Even for major artists such as Sofonisba Anguissola, there is much that is unknown about their practices, including the extent of their oeuvres. Rosalba Carriera (1673–1757), for instance, is best known as a pastel artist, while her miniatures are less studied. There is even greater uncertainty in the case of only recently investigated artists such as Ginevra Cantofoli and Marianna Carlevarijs. Orsola Maddalena Caccia (1596–1676), still too little known, is represented in this exhibition with two works, one of which was recently "discovered" on the art market.

A major challenge was deciding how to balance attention between artists like Sofonisba Anguissola and Artemisia Gentileschi, who left behind many works, and artists like Virginia da Vezzo, by whom few, if any, works have survived. We also had to contend with the reality that the works we have from any given artist may not fully represent her practice. Ultimately, we decided that we should focus on the major figures and include multiple works by important and prolific women artists, ideally done for different reasons, in a variety of genres and media. For Lavinia Fontana, we show a range of portraits and religious paintings. For Artemisia Gentileschi, we selected direct and disguised self-portraits, together with larger history paintings from her later periods. For Rosalba Carriera, we present miniatures as well as pastels. One consequence of these choices is that our exhibition reveals most about the artistic activity of women in Bologna, Florence, and Rome. Another is that it largely represents the taste of American collectors, either private or institutional, who acquired these works for different purposes within a timespan of roughly one hundred years.

More than ever, women and their artistic creations are one of the most fascinating and dynamic subjects not only in the history of Western art, but globally. By bringing together and celebrating drawings, miniatures, pastels, and paintings created by women artists in Italy from the 1500s to the 1700s—an unusually fertile period—we sincerely hope to spark conversation and inspire viewers and readers alike, while paving the way for a more just and equitable world for all.

NOTE

1. We have chosen to use the word "women" or "woman" in relation to artist, rather than the word "female." This is because the word woman applies only to humans, while female can apply to any species, particularly animals, and has been used historically to diminish women. For just one discussion of this debate, see Norris 2019.

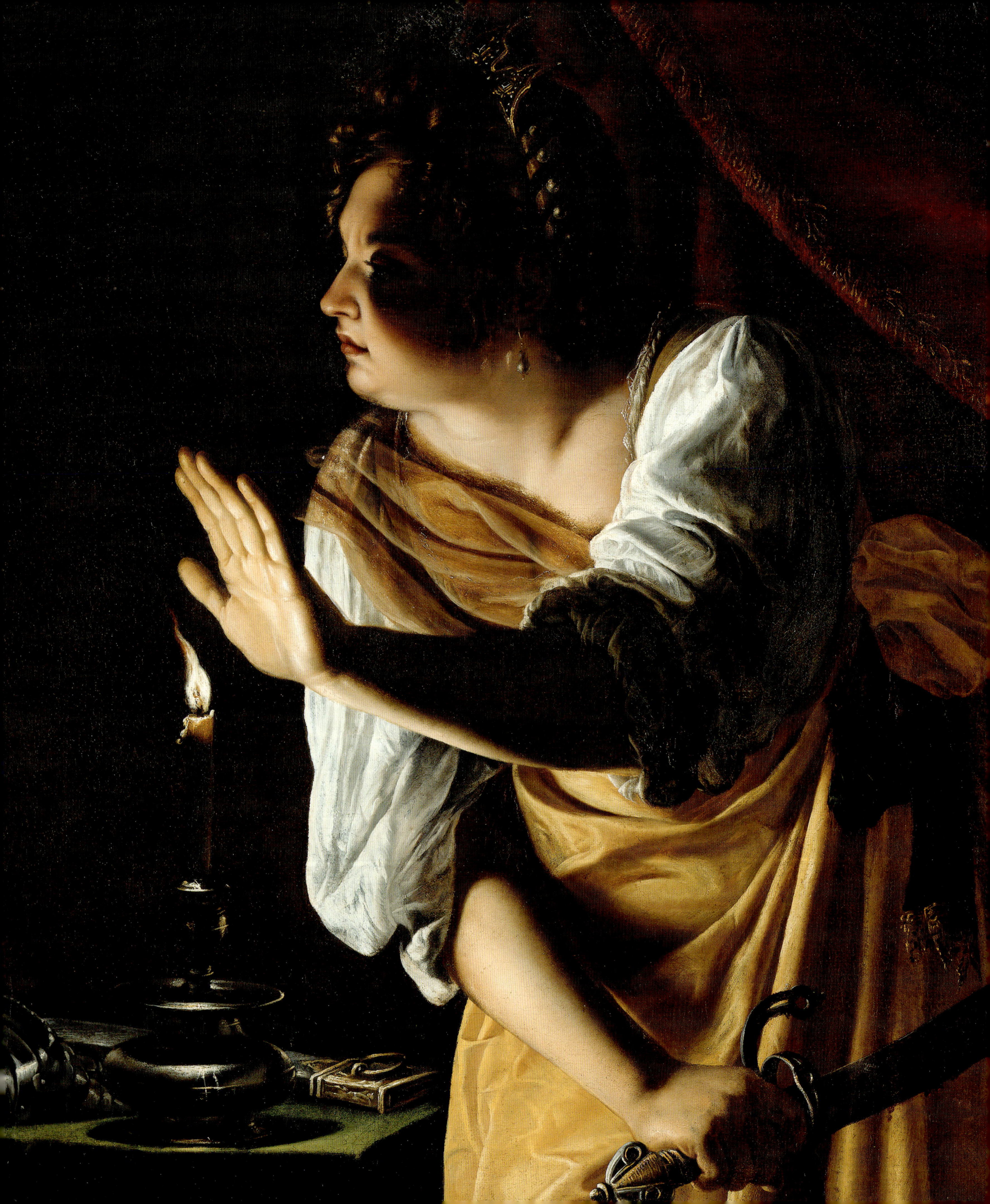

Why Have There Been No Exhibitions of Early Modern Italian Women Artists in Hartford or Detroit?

The fault lies not in our stars, our hormones, our menstrual cycles, or our empty internal spaces, but in our institutions and our education—education understood to include everything that happens to us from the moment we enter this world of meaningful symbols, signs, and signals. The miracle is, in fact, that given the overwhelming odds against women, or blacks, that so many of both have managed to achieve so much sheer excellence, in those bailiwicks of white masculine prerogative like science, politics, or the arts.—LINDA NOCHLIN, 1971[1]

WHY HAVE THERE BEEN NO EXHIBITIONS exclusively devoted to early modern Italian women artists in America's oldest civic museums?[2] This question echoes art historian Linda Nochlin's (1931–2017) leading query in her 1971 disquisition "Why Have There Been No Great Women Artists?"[3] As the feminist movement ushered in a new era of questions surrounding the roles of women in the Western world, Nochlin galvanized the next generation of scholars to examine the place of women artists in history, forever averting the discipline's gendered gaze. Drawing attention to the unquestioned hegemony of the "white Western male viewpoint," she called for a feminist reassessment of art history on "moral and ethical grounds." Her contributions to the field cannot be overstated. In her large body of scholarship, she scrutinized the foundations of art history in order to challenge them and find space for myriad critical approaches to art.[4] By probing intellectual assumptions, Nochlin paved the way for an art history—as well as other academic disciplines and popular culture—open to multiple perspectives, ushering in an era of inclusivity for marginalized groups beyond the confines of gender.[5]

Although the embrace of historically marginalized groups has progressed in academia, museums lurch forward at a slower pace, including in their approach to women artists. A study published in 2019 entitled "Diversity of Artists in Major U.S. Museums" found that in eighteen museums—among them the Detroit Institute of Arts—eighty-seven percent of objects in the collections are by men.[6] According to another study published the same year, from 2008 to 2018, only fourteen percent of all art exhibitions were either solo shows featuring women artists or group exhibitions in which the greater part of the works were by women artists.[7] This includes, of course, women artists from all time periods. Perhaps then it is not surprising that *By Her Hand: Artemisia Gentileschi and Women Artists in Italy, 1500–1800* marks the first time either the Wadsworth Atheneum Museum of Art (fig. 1)—the earliest civic fine arts museum in the United States, founded in 1842 and opened in 1844—or the Detroit Institute of Arts (fig. 2)—a stalwart among American art museums since 1885—has featured an exhibition devoted to European women artists before the twentieth century. There is much at stake in this exhibition, art historically and politically.

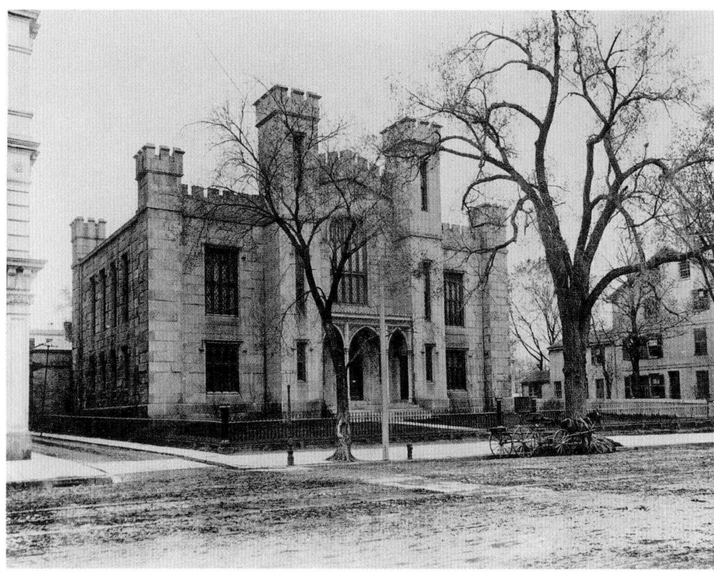

FIGURE 1 Wadsworth Atheneum facade, 1882. Photograph Collection, Wadsworth Atheneum Museum of Art Archives, Hartford, CT, RG9_1_F3551

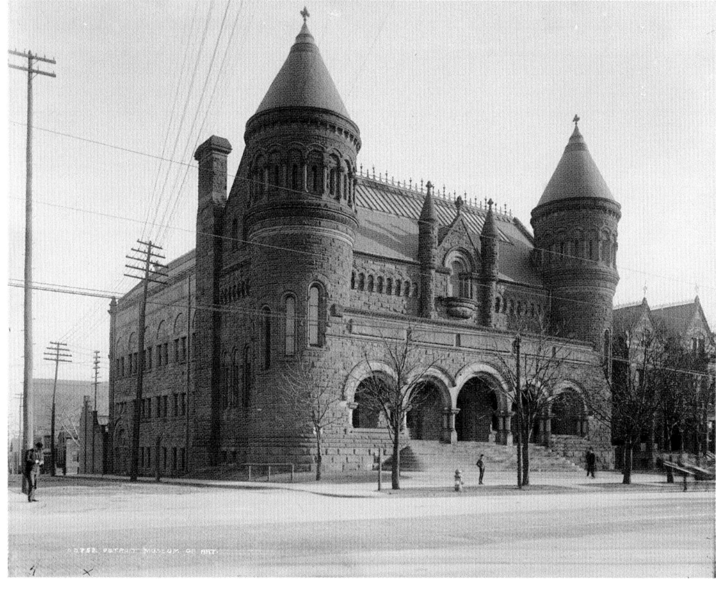

FIGURE 2 Detroit Museum of Art facade, between 1880 and 1899. Library of Congress, LC-DIG-det-4a03650

Given the focus in the United States on issues of race, religion, sexuality, class, and accessibility, there has been a wide-ranging re-examination of the role museums play in public life in recent memory. The Black Lives Matter movement in particular has left an indelible imprint, compelling many museums to think afresh about their biases and privileged perch. To whom should museums cater? Whose art hangs on the walls permanently or is featured in special exhibitions? Who are the curators of these shows?[8] The overwhelming conclusion—and I certainly tip my hat in this direction—is that a greater array of art must provide visual interest and meaning to increasingly diverse audiences. This exhibition is part and parcel of this push by museums, scholars, and curators to change the status quo.

This essay explores the critical fortunes of early modern Italian women artists and the state of research in this historically overlooked area of art history from the 1800s until the present. In this period art history was officially born as a discipline and the concept of feminism, as understood today, arose.[9] It begins with an examination of nineteenth-century and early twentieth-century sources on primarily Italian women artists. The next section considers the explosion of exhibitions devoted to early modern women artists, including those of Italian origin, beginning with the advent of what is called Second-Wave feminism in the 1970s. The final section charts the success, or lack thereof, of early modern Italian women artists on the global art market as a barometer of their value. In order to address the yawning gender gap still evident in museum collections, feminist art history and the global art market must continue to promote and propel interest in and study of Italian women artists.

Early Feminist Art History in Europe and the United States

Recent scholarship on women artists in the West has its roots in the modern feminist movement, which originated in 1848 with a two-day Women's Rights Convention in Seneca Falls, New York (fig. 3).[10] On the first day it was resolved "that woman is man's equal—was intended to be so by the Creator, and the highest good of the race demands that she should be recognized as such."[11] From around 1850 until around 1920, this first wave of feminism touched on all sectors of society in Europe and the United States.

In Italy the feminist movement was less robust and took shape a bit later, commencing after the unification of the country in 1861. Anna Maria Mozzoni (1837–1920)—often regarded as the founder of the women's movement in Italy—published *La donna e i suoi rapporti sociali in occasione della revisione del codice italiano* (*Woman and Her Social Relationships on the Occasion of the Revision of the Italian Civil Code*) in 1864. Mozzoni also translated into Italian John Stuart Mills' (1806–1873) foundational 1869 essay *The Subjugation of Women*. Many of the important figures involved in the nascent feminist movement in Italy contributed to or read the periodical *La Donna*, which was started in Padua by Gualberta Alaide Beccari (1842–1906) in 1868 and ceased publication in 1891 (fig. 4).[12] *La Donna* began as a "moral and instructive periodical. Compiled by Italian women."[13] Only in 1871, after publication of the journal transferred to Bologna, did it explicitly "promote women's rights."[14] Though more in-depth research needs to be done on this topic, it would appear that the nineteenth-century women's rights movement had more force in the United States than in Italy.[15] Subsequently, post-1970, the American focus on women artists in the history of art seems to have had more momentum as well.

Although the Seneca Falls Convention in the United States and other activities in Europe mainly addressed the social rights of women in the public sphere—such as suffrage—the ideas and energy fomented by the movements slowly trickled into other realms, including the arts. In this period art history—a discipline originating in nineteenth-century Germany—was also at a nascent stage of development in England, Western Continental Europe, and the United States. These two new disciplines—art history and the history of women—dovetailed in the second half of the nineteenth century in important and revealing ways. They did not reach their apex, however, until the end of the 1960s and beginning of the 1970s, with what today is recognized as the Second Wave of the feminist movement. What follows is an episodic rather than exhaustive review of the literature on women artists in art history, focusing—given the thrust of this exhibition—on early modern Italian women artists.

The German author Ernst Guhl's 1858 *Die Frauen in der Kunstgeschichte* (*Women in the History of Art*) was the first publication devoted to a general history of women artists. The volume encompasses women poets as well as painters, sculptors, and engravers, spanning from Western antiquity through the eighteenth century. Guhl, who was not trained as an art historian, sets out in his meandering and lackluster introduction to flatter women artists—and to put women as a gender on a pedestal—commenting:

> Raised by women's hands, I have always followed the examples of the most esteemed female worthies before my eyes and am still happy to confess, to find in my interactions with noble women the actual artistic appeal of life.[16]

In the July 1858 edition of the *Westminster Review*, an anonymous author appraised Guhl's book.[17] While largely an English summary of the German text, in a moment of true critique and insight the author summarizes the tension between the

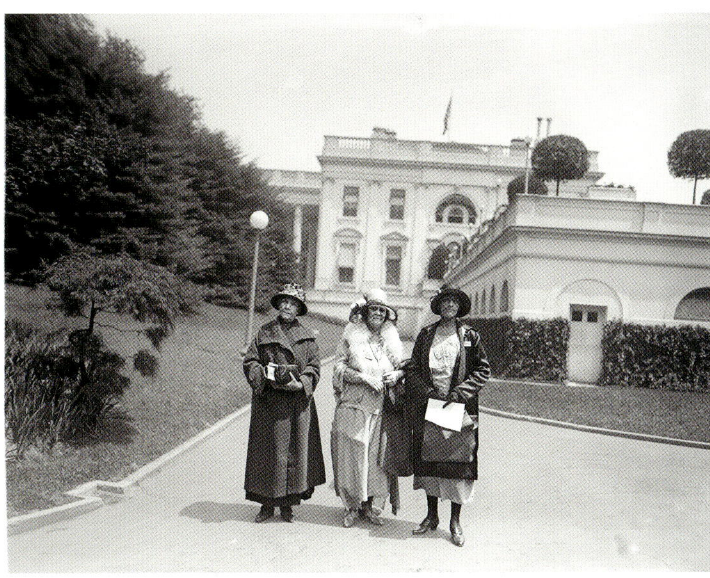

FIGURE 3 Attendees at International Council of Women, 1925. Library of Congress, LC-DIG-npcc-27027

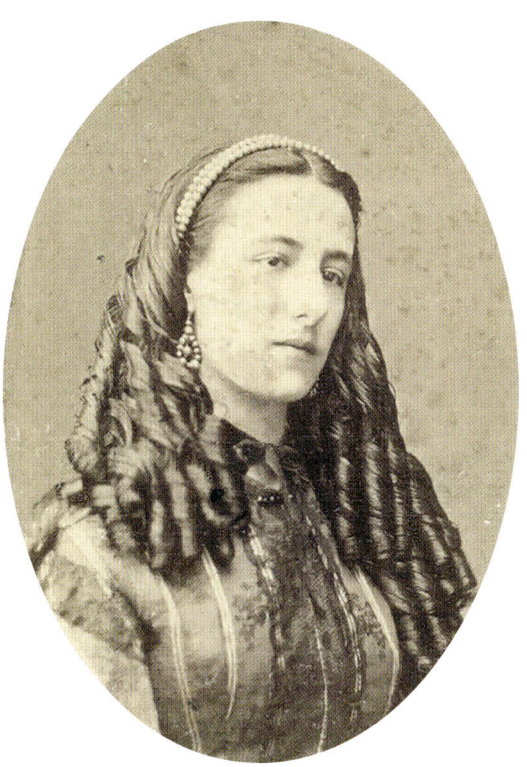

FIGURE 4 Gualberta Alaide Beccari. Municipality of Padua, Department of Culture, RIP III 5593

intellectual and artistic gifts of women and the low esteem in which society holds them:

> The social and political inferiority in which she has hitherto been held, cannot fail, they maintain, to have acted in a depressing manner on her intellectual nature, whatever its original force and vigour. In both these arguments there is a certain degree of plausibility. Perhaps the truth lies between the two.[18]

Where, indeed, does the truth about a women's artistic worth reside? Somewhere, this anonymous author shrewdly concludes, between a woman's abilities and the opportunities available in the society within which she must succeed as an artist.[19] The review offers a more incisive critique than the gendered, historical narrative compiled by Guhl. His volume is ambitious, and he should receive credit for being the first author of a tome on women artists. Ultimately, however, it lacks true perspicacity.

In 1859 the cause of women's contributions to the history of art was picked up by the American writer and poet Elizabeth F. Ellet (1818–1877) in *Women Artists in All Ages and Countries*. Ellet was the first woman since Christine de Pizan (1364–ca. 1430)—over four-hundred years earlier—to pen a work that focused on, or even included, women's contributions to the arts.[20] Her intent was not just historical. Ellet advises the reader:

> Should the perusal of my book inspire with courage and resolution any woman who aspires to overcome difficulties in the achievement of honourable independence or should it lead to a higher general respect for the powers of women and their destined position in the realm of Art, my object will be accomplished.[21]

Ellet's book absorbs Guhl's teachings, adding five chapters on women artists of the nineteenth century to bring the history up to the present. Albert Ten Eyck Gardner pithily captured her contribution when he described it as "an odd compound of literacy piracy, scholarship, and sentiment, braced with a mild grade of feminism."[22] In her "feminist re-view"—a popular strain of scholarship in the 1980s—of Ellet's 1859 volume, the art historian Sandra Langer astutely framed Ellet's historical perspective:

> As a biographer and historian, Mrs. Ellet had her prejudices; her work was not intended for art historians, nor was she interested in writing a scholarly and critical history of women in art. It was her intention to compile a much needed popular text dealing with the lives and art of women. Her value judgments are reflective of the state of art, if not criticism, at midcentury and reflect American taste of the period especially.[23]

While Ellet's work is a landmark in English on the history of women artists, it is also a pedestrian work, with no surprises in content, structure, or even rhetorical flourish, that reflects the mental tendencies of many mid-nineteenth-century authors.[24]

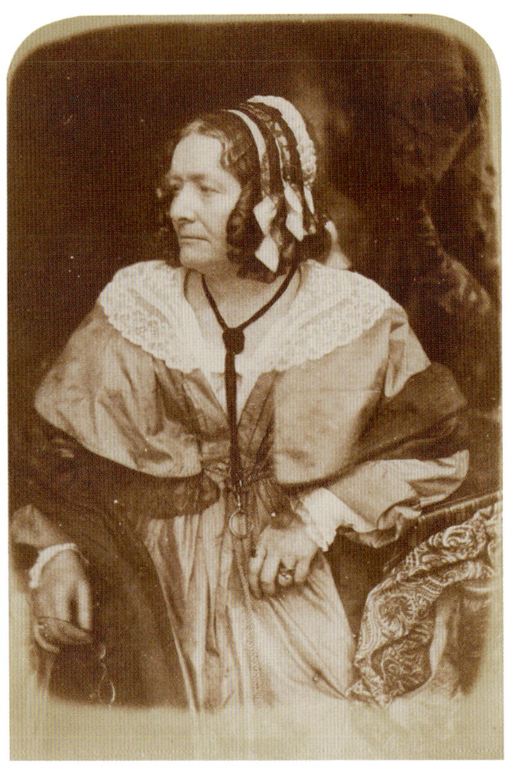

FIGURE 5 Anna Jameson. National Portrait Gallery, London

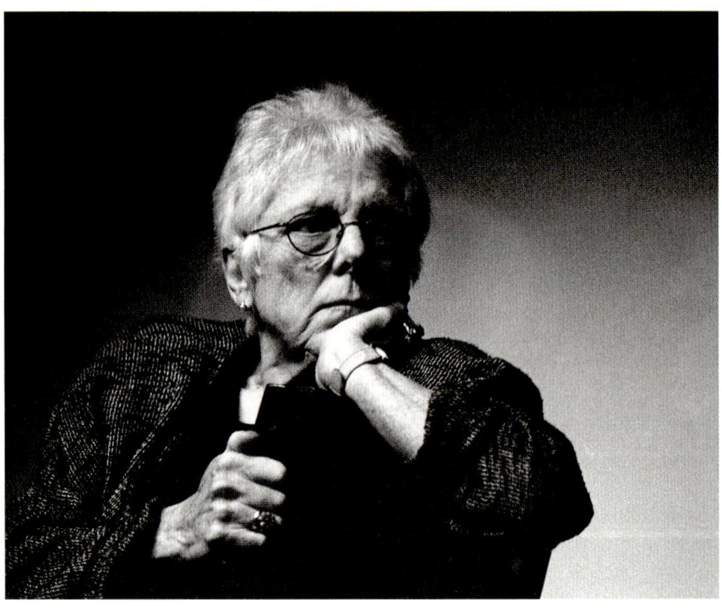

FIGURE 6 Linda Nochlin at the Los Angeles County Museum of Art, 2000. LACMA Archives

The writer and first Anglo-Irish art historian Anna Jameson (1794–1860) was an exception in every sense, shunning received norms on art in favor of a boldness of voice and perspective (fig. 5). The majority of her art writings predate the suffrage and women's rights movements in Europe and the United States. Though "popular" literature, they reveal a candor and originality of thought less rooted in her time. An extraordinary contribution to the history of art in general and the history of women artists specifically, Jameson's writings—both published and not—deserve greater study.

Born in Dublin in 1794, Anna Murphy was the eldest daughter of Denis Brownell Murphy (1755–1842), a painter in miniature and enamel. In 1798 the family moved to England, eventually settling in London. To make a living, Anna became a governess at age sixteen for the family of the Marquess of Winchester, and in 1825 she married Robert Jameson (1773/4–1854), from whom she was largely estranged by 1829. Between 1826 and 1864 she published twenty books,[25] and she counted Elizabeth Barrett Browning (1806–1861), Robert Browning (1812–1889), and George Eliot (1819–1880) among her circle of intimates.[26] By living a life on her own terms as much as was possible in the nineteenth century, Jameson challenged prevailing ideas about a woman's rightful role in society. These same societal norms are also challenged in the bulk of her writings, which touch upon literature, theater, and the fine arts. Often one finds a connective thread in her focus on representations of women, whether as protagonists or agents in their own right. As the art historian Adele Holcomb writes, Jameson "seems to have been alone in challenging through published argument the entrenched prejudices of women in the arts."[27]

Jameson's greatest exploration of women artists is found in a ten-page portion of her 1834 *Visits and Sketches*, which was based on tours in 1829 and 1833 of German museums, where, truth be told, there was not a wealth of works by Italian women artists to be seen. The exception is the spectacular room of Rosalba Carriera (1673–1757) pastels in the former Dresden palace, which inspired a tangent on women artists that made the author wish her "vagrant pen were less discursive."[28] For the purposes of this essay, I will only note the Italian artists, in the order presented: Rosalba Carriera; Marietta Tintoretto (ca. 1560–1590); Violante Beatrice Siries (1709–1783); Elisabetta Sirani (1638–1665); Lucia Anguissola (ca. 1537–ca. 1565), Europa Anguissola (ca. 1548–1578), and Sofonisba Anguissola (ca. 1535–1625); Lavinia Fontana (1552–1614); and Artemisia Gentileschi (1593–1654 or later).[29] Jameson concludes, "All those whom I have mentioned were women of undoubted genius; for they have each a style apart, peculiar, and tinted by their individual character."[30] Her use of the word "genius"—largely reserved for men historically—is noteworthy.[31]

Unfortunately, Jameson never completed the volume to be devoted to women painters, musicians, and performers. A letter dated August 30, 1841 to her close friend and contemporary Ottilie von Goethe (1794–1872)—daughter-in-law to the famous German writer Johann Wolfgang von Goethe (1749–1832)—with whom she hoped to collaborate on the project, gives us the fullest glimpse of the ambitions of this unrealized work:

> *Memoirs of celebrated female artists*—by artists I mean all women who have gained a livelihood (*une existence*) by the public exercise of their talents—whether as painters, engravers, musicians, dancers and actresses, considering the whole position of these women as regards society, how society has treated them, how they have influenced society—their former position in different countries—& their present & future (probable) position—the first volume will contain the female professors of painting & engraving—in Italy, Germany, &c—the second volume will contain musicians, singers, & dancers—& the third volume, actresses.[32]

Jameson meant to privilege women's accomplishments in the arts and consider "how society has treated them." If she had published these volumes, they would have been far ahead of their time.[33]

In 1905 Walter Shaw Sparrow (1862–1940), a Welsh writer on art and architecture, presented notable women painters in his *Women Painters of the World, from the Time of Caterina Vigri, 1413–1463, to Rosa Bonheur and the Present Day*, the first chapter of which was devoted to "Women Painters in Italy Since the Fifteenth Century."[34] Touted as the "first illustrated history of the Women Painters of the World," it sought to counter the assertion that "the achievements of women painters have been second-rate."[35] Sparrow, who included a sizable number of Italian women artists in his tome,[36] concluded that the fate of women artists was different in the Italy of an earlier era, stating, "The Renaissance was heralded by a long, troubled dawn; but it came at last, and its effects on the destinies of women were immediate and far-reaching."[37] Although this is perhaps a bit overstated, the early modern period in Italy, as this exhibition demonstrates, did usher in important cultural and social changes that gradually enabled more women to work as artists.

Laura Ragg's *The Women Artists of Bologna*, published in 1907, was the first book devoted solely to Italian women artists, and it was a milestone in the literature on them. In it, Ragg foregrounds the distinct contribution of women artists to this illustrious and liberal university city:

> No city of the world has produced more women of distinguished talent; none has been more prompt to further their achievements, more generous in crowning their success. We are not speaking, moreover, of ladies of exalted birth and exceptional opportunity, such as those who graced many of the Italian courts

of the fifteenth and sixteenth centuries, and who, betrothed in childhood, owed alike their unusual education and their subsequent influence to their husbands' power and position; but of women belonging to obscure and sometimes to poor families, who achieved a name and a fame by their own exertions, before or independently of marriage.[38]

Bologna is presented as a unicum—a utopia in which women of any class or social position could excel in the arts. As this show demonstrates, from the 1500s through the 1800s the city did have the highest concentration of women artists from a range of social classes, including Lavinia Fontana, Elisabetta Sirani, and Ginevra Cantofoli (1618–1672), but the story is more complex.[39] Even though these artists are noted in Italian primary sources in the seventeenth and into the eighteenth centuries, their critical fortunes began to decline with the rise of the discipline of art history in the nineteenth century.[40]

Except for a couple of earlier monographs on Rosalba Carriera, an article from 1916 devoted to Artemisia Gentileschi and her father Orazio Gentileschi (1563–1639) by Roberto Longhi, and an early monograph on Fede Galizia (ca. 1574–ca. 1630), historical Italian women artists did not get their due until the 1970s, thanks in large part to Linda Nochlin's revolutionary 1971 essay (fig. 6).[41] In addition to revealing biases and chauvinism, Nochlin sought to understand the exclusion of women from the history of art through a measured lens. In other words, she did not laud them beyond the merit she believed they were due as visual artists. In this often-cited quote, Nochlin states brazenly:

> The fact of the matter is that there have been no supremely great women artists, as far as we know, although there have been many interesting and very good ones, who remain insufficiently investigated or appreciated; nor have there been any great Lithuanian jazz pianists, nor Eskimo tennis players, no matter how much we might wish there had been.[42]

Scholars have vacillated wildly since. Some champion the merits of earlier women artists beyond all measure.[43] Some take the more deliberate approach of understanding the impact of context, training, and opportunity as often limiting—or mitigating factors of—their artistic excellence.[44] Whatever position one adopts, Nochlin's attempt to disentangle personal desire from historical reality—to create a nuanced and emancipated historical record, free of personal yearning—is key. It engenders clarity about the complexity of the subject of women artists—especially as art historians continue to explore what artistic success has and could look like for this heterogeneous group.

Arising from Nochlin's roots, recent scholarship on women artists has moved in myriad directions, a topic worthy of its own essay. Here I will point out the significant veins of investigation, which, to my mind, fall into three main categories—art historical

scholarship, art activism, and art criticism, with some overlapping among them. In terms of scholarship, as women artists and feminist art history became permissible—one might even use the word licit—subjects of research in academia, more scholars in Europe and the United States have devoted their energies to them, including, most notably, French feminists.[45] In the 1990s a new wave of art activism with a feminist bent materialized with the Guerrilla Girls, a collective of artists who don gorilla masks in public and use facts and provocative images to expose gender inequity in the arts. In more recent memory, art criticism has sought to reveal institutional biases against women and demand a more diverse body of works by women artists be acquired and displayed by galleries and museums.[46] An examination of how social categorizations such as race, class, sexuality, ability, and gender intersect—termed intersectionality—takes center stage in academia today.

This was not the case when Audre Lorde (1934–1992)—the self-described Black, lesbian poet—powerfully and presciently wrote in 1984, "It is a particular academic arrogance to assume any discussion of feminist theory without examining our many differences, and without a significant input from poor women, Black and Third World women, and lesbians."[47] She rightly concluded, "Only within that interdependency of different strengths, acknowledged and equal, can the power to seek new ways of being in the world generate, as well as the courage and sustenance to act where there are no charters."[48] At present, within this increasingly intersectional and ever more inclusive feminist art history, there is particular emphasis placed on Native American, Latinx, African American, and African diasporic women artists.[49]

This show on early Italian women artists is one part of a larger movement towards gender equity in the arts. These artists are but one strand of a rich and textured tapestry of global women artists being studied more thoroughly today. In order to grapple with gender disparity in the arts, it is imperative that museums display work by women artists from all backgrounds as well as devote exhibitions to their art.

Early Modern Italian Women Artists: An Exhibition Overview[50]

Exhibitions of the work of early modern women artists, Italian or otherwise, were rare before 1971, when Linda Nochlin's essay ignited a fire in art historians. A series of shows followed, both generalized surveys and specialized monographs (see Appendix). The first in the United States was *Women: A Historical Survey of Works by Women Artists,* which opened on February 27, 1972 at the Salem Fine Arts Center in Winston-Salem, North Carolina.[51] This survey of the contributions of seventy-eight largely

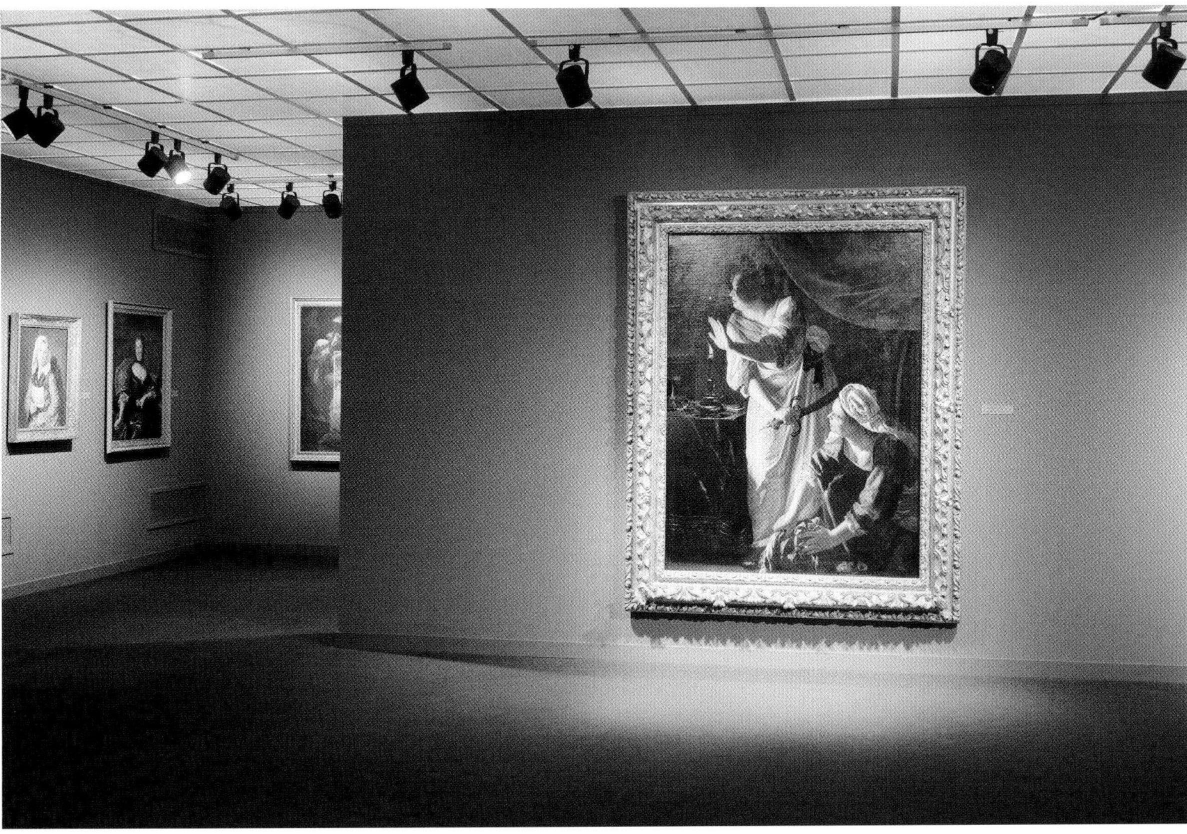

FIGURE 7 Installation view of *Women Artists: 1550–1950* at the Brooklyn Museum, 1977. Brooklyn Museum Archives, Records of the Department of Photography

American women artists was comprised of artworks "selected in an effort to show the variety of areas in which women painters and sculptors have worked, and their changing roles as artists."[52] Less than two months later, on April 17, 1972, the first exhibition devoted to early modern women artists opened at the Walters Art Gallery in Baltimore, Maryland. Entitled *Old Mistresses: Women Artists of the Past*, it featured thirty women artists from the early modern period to the present hailing from Europe and the United States. It would appear this forward-looking show was so hastily put together that the accompanying "catalogue" is an unpaginated photocopy of an exhibition checklist with no preface or introductory essay. An article by the exhibition's co-curators, Ann Gabhart and Elizabeth Broun, in the April 1972 *Walters Art Gallery Bulletin* provides the best portal into their exalted aspirations for this pivotal show:

> It is hoped that this exhibition will promote a serious consideration of the creativity of women. The issue is one of enormous complexity and it must be admitted that no one theory can explain the relative shortage of great women artists or the widely differing ways in which each woman represented here dealt with her situation.[53]

The dance between more general surveys and more specialized shows on women artists continues to this day.

Without question, the exhibition offering the most important historical overview of women artists was Ann Sutherland Harris and Linda Nochlin's 1976/1977 *Women Artists: 1550–1950*, organized by the Los Angeles County Museum of Art (LACMA), which traveled to the University Art Museum in Austin, the Carnegie Museum of Art, Pittsburgh, and finally to the Brooklyn Museum (fig. 7). The show, which was accompanied by an exhibition catalogue, was prompted by political activity. In 1971 the Los Angeles Council of Women Artists presented a proclamation to Kenneth Donahue, then director of LACMA, demanding the equal representation of women artists in the museum.[54] Donahue was receptive to the idea, and proposed an exhibition on Artemisia Gentileschi, who was among the most famous early modern artists at that time. This ultimately became *Women Artists: 1550–1950*, a historic exhibition of unprecedented breadth and importance that required six years of gestation and development to come to fruition.[55] In their preface to the exhibition catalogue, Sutherland Harris and Nochlin articulate an ambitious goal:

> Our intention in assembling these works by European and American women artists active from 1550 to 1950 is to make more widely known the achievements of some fine artists whose neglect can in part be attributed to their sex and to learn more about why and how women artists first emerged as rare

exceptions in the sixteenth century and gradually became more numerous until they were a largely accepted part of the cultural scene. Neither of us believes that this catalog is the last word on the subject. On the contrary, we both look forward to reading the many articles, monographs, and critical responses that we hope this exhibition will generate.[56]

Much additional scholarship on the women artists presented to the public—the majority for the first time—was engendered by this foundational exhibition. At the end of her introductory essay, Sutherland Harris proclaims: "This exhibition will be a success if it helps to remove once and for all the justification for any future exhibitions with this theme."[57] The stakes were set inordinately high.

The critical responses to this groundbreaking show ranged from laudatory to cautionary. Martha Alf captured the political urgency of the LACMA exhibition in the January 22, 1977 edition of *Artweek*, declaring in her opening salvo victory on the front lines: "If you don't give up the fight and the battle is worth it, winning often follows. *Women Artists: 1550–1950* . . . is the resplendent triumph of such a fight."[58] Art historian Mary Garrard, an Artemisia Gentileschi expert, was more staid and admonitory in her thoughtful and provocative review in *Burlington Magazine*:

> Dr. Harris is entirely correct in her conclusion that there is now no justification for future exhibitions with this theme . . . Now that they have been displayed as women, it is time to shift the emphasis and to examine their achievement as artists, shaped by a variety of personal experiences, not the least nor the most of which was being born female.[59]

This was, ultimately, wishful thinking. One exhibition did not—and cannot—reverse long-entrenched institutional misogyny in universities and museums, where women's voices, ideas, and art are suppressed or undervalued. Shows devoted to women artists trickled out in the latter part of the 1970s and into the 1980s and 1990s, but only since the 2000s has there been a steady stream of art exhibitions devoted to women artists in general, and to early modern women artists in particular.[60]

More exhibitions, by far, have focused on the work of Artemisia Gentileschi than any other early modern woman artist. Given her history of sexual abuse and the powerful women represented in her art, Gentileschi's life and professional ambition have captured the imaginations of contemporary audiences. Even those with very little interest in earlier Italian art have found ways to relate to her life, work, and perceived persona.[61] With all these factors, as well as the wealth of books, exhibitions, films, theater, and passing references devoted to her in all variety of media over three decades, she could now be considered equal in fame to Caravaggio (1571–1610), if not the most famous Italian artist of the seventeenth century. As testament to this, seven

exhibitions have been devoted to Artemisia Gentileschi in the last thirty years, with the first occurring at the Casa Buonarroti in Florence in 1991 and the most recent at the National Gallery, London, in 2020/2021.[62] In between was the formative 2001/2002 show *Orazio and Artemisia Gentileschi* at the Palazzo Venezia, Rome; The Metropolitan Museum of Art, New York; and the Saint Louis Art Museum. And while that show was dedicated to both artists, father and daughter, it provided American audiences with the best forum yet for viewing Artemisia Gentileschi's pictures.[63] A tremendous scholarly effort, it paved the way for all future exhibitions on Artemisia Gentileschi.

Solo or focused exhibitions on the artist took place in the next decade in Milan (2011), Paris (2012), Chicago (2013/2014), Rome (2016/2017), and London (2020/2021). In an effort to "abandon the narrow stereotype," a few of these exhibitions expanded her oeuvre with new attributions, some more probable than others. By focusing on widely accepted works as a stable platform for reflection, the 2020 show at the National Gallery, London, offered a distillation of lessons learned to bring us into the next decade of scholarship on Gentileschi. Although there is still more research to be done on this exceptional artist, one might ask whether the future of scholarship on Italian women artists is best served by monographic exhibitions, or by group exhibitions that introduce the public to a greater number of women artists, including those who are almost unknown, even to specialists.

In the last decade or so there has been an interest in group exhibitions celebrating women artists from the 1500s through the 1700s on both sides of the Atlantic, including *Italian Women Artists from Renaissance to Baroque* at the National Museum of Women in the Arts, Washington, D.C. in 2007, and *The Ladies of the Baroque* at the Museum of Fine Arts in Ghent, Belgium in 2018–2019. *By Her Hand* is an effort to introduce a broad public to eighteen early modern Italian women artists.[64] Pressing issues of scholarship include new or questionable attributions, how gender factors into interpretations of artworks, and investigations of the varied techniques these women used and the circumstances in which they practiced.

Valuing Italian Women Artists

The reasons early modern Italian women artists have not been given their due are complex. Their fate and their critical fortunes are inextricably tied to the appraisal of scholars and institutions as well as to the estimation of their work on the art market. In museums, both in terms of exhibitions and acquisitions, a significant reason for the historical oversight of early Italian women artists—or any woman artist—lies in their perceived value. In the 1768 edition of the lives of Genoese artists,

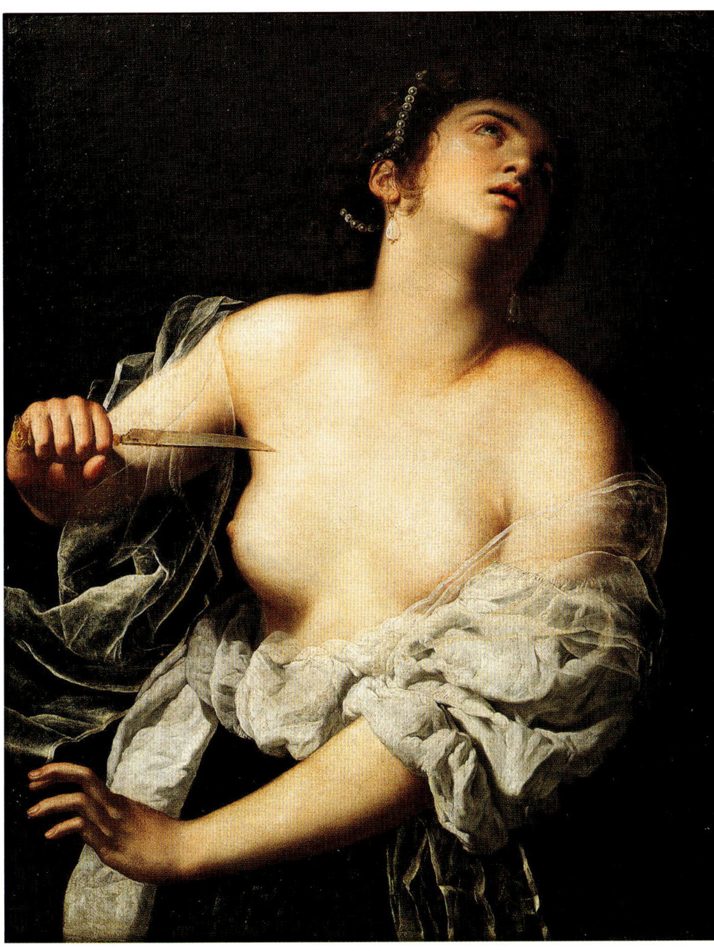

FIGURE 8 Artemisia Gentileschi, *Lucretia*, ca. 1630, oil on canvas, 38 × 29½ in. (96.50 × 75 cm). J. Paul Getty Museum, Los Angeles

Raffaele Soprani (1612–1672) and Carlo Giuseppe Ratti (1737–1795) describe Artemisia Gentileschi as "a female painter of much value [*valore*]."[65] Whereas for Gentileschi this is an exceptional distinction, contemporary male artists such as Annibale Carracci (1560–1609) and Caravaggio often received the accolade. As defined by the 1612 Florentine *Crusca Dictionary*, the Italian word *valore* encompasses both monetary and less tangible aspects of worth.[66] The primary meaning is given as price. The secondary meaning can be liberally understood as goodness and courage, attributes that enter the realm of the moral. Unlike their male peers, on these two levels Italian women artists, including Artemisia Gentileschi, have not always been deemed worthy of focus by scholars or museums. Both aspects of worth are reflected in the historically lower prices paid for works by Italian women artists and the hesitance with which many museums have collected them over the years.

The assessment of earlier Italian women artists continues to change. The wealth of exhibitions and scholarship devoted to Artemisia Gentileschi and to early modern Italian women artists in the last two decades has increased their value on the art market. Indeed, scholarship and the art market are a necessary—if sometimes reluctant on the part of curators and academics—partnership, and the market value of work by women artists goes virtually hand-in-hand with the number of publications and exhibitions devoted to them. Since the 1970s there has been a resurgence of interest in early Italian women artists among both private and institutional collectors. In recent memory it has increased precipitously, a swell that can be attributed to the changing role of museums and to the expanding interests of collectors, both striving to reflect a broader spectrum of history in which issues of gender and race are paramount.

Due to an interest in gender parity, paintings by Artemisia Gentileschi are particularly prized at present. As this essay goes to press it should come as no surprise that she holds the record for the highest price paid for a work by an early modern Italian woman artist.[67] At the November 13, 2019 sale at Paris's Artcurial auction house, a recently "discovered" painting of Lucretia was acquired for €4.7 million ($5.2 million) (fig. 8).[68] And in the past decade, a handful of works by Artemisia Gentileschi or attributed to her have garnered among the highest auction prices for any early modern women artist. In addition to the *Lucretia*, three works have sold in excess of a million dollars. These include another *Lucretia*, purchased at the Dorotheum auction house for €1.8 million ($2.1 million) in October 2018; *Self-Portrait as Saint Catherine of Alexandria*, on offer through Christophe Joron-Derem auction firm and subsequently acquired by the National Gallery, London, for £3.6 million from the London dealers Marco Voena and Fabrizio Moretti—who originally paid €1.8 million ($2.1 million) at the Parisian auction house (cat. 25); and a Mary Magdalene acquired at Sotheby's Paris for €865,500 ($1.1 million) on June 26, 2014 (cat. 28). Prices for works by other Italian women artists are rising as well, while the prices for many male artists have remained steady, with exceptional works by Leonardo da Vinci (1452–1519), Raphael (1483–1520), and Titian (1488/90–1576) still setting records.

That said, a 2017 article by behavioral economists concludes that auction prices for works by women artists across time and geography are significantly lower than those realized for works by male artists.[69] The team of four authors determined that:

> Using a sample of 1.5 million auction transactions between 1970 and 2013 in 45 countries for 62,442 individual artists, we document that auction prices for paintings by female artists are significantly lower than prices for male artists even after including country-fixed effects.[70]

Any biological imperatives at play are ignored—the authors argue that "since auction price differences are higher in countries with more gender inequality . . . the price difference identifies a pure effect of culture on economic outcomes for female artists."[71] This notion of a "pure effect of culture" on the economic realities of women artists resulted from several empirical studies, including asking the public to identify the gender of an artist simply by looking at a painting. The correct gender was guessed 50.5 percent of the time.[72] In other words, unsurprisingly, viewers are unable to determine the gender or sex of an artist simply by seeing their work. This lends further credence to the theory that cultural factors are at play in the financial inequity to which the majority of women artists and their artworks from the early modern period to the present have been and continue to be subjected.

Recently there has been a push by auction houses to promote early modern women artists. Is this primarily for economic gain? Or is there a nod to gender equity in this marketing scheme? For the Master Paintings Evening Sale on January 30, 2019, Sotheby's auction house held a sale called "The Female Triumphant." Élisabeth-Louise Vigée Le Brun's (1755–1842) *Portrait of Muhammad Dervish Khan, Full-Length, Holding His Sword in a Landscape* set the record for a work by a premodern woman artist when it sold for $7.1 million. The record for a modern woman artist is held by Georgia O'Keeffe's (1887–1986) *Jimson Weed/White Flower No. 1*, which sold for $44.4 million at Sotheby's New York on November 20, 2014. If one compares Vigée Le Brun's record with the world record at auction by a male artist, Leonardo da Vinci's *Salvator Mundi*, which sold at Christie's New York on November 15, 2017 for a staggering $450.3 million, we find a disparity in price between the two artists of over $443 million. Perhaps this equation and math are unfair, but the gulf symbolically represents the very real financial gap between artists of different genders. This is why, as the feminist art historian Maura Reilly has noted, "Not only do we need to ensure that women's work is purchased, we need to continue to curate women-only and feminist exhibitions as well as ones with gender parity."[73] *By Her Hand: Artemisia Gentileschi and Women Artists in Italy, 1500–1800* is one part of this vital effort to integrate the work of these overlooked Italian women artists into the history of art and into the culture more broadly.

In doing so, it also seeks to promote gender equity in museums. As Reilly cautions, "Sexism is still so insidiously woven into the institutional fabric, language, and logic of the mainstream art world that it often goes undetected."[74] Just as the historiography, exhibition history, and market value of early modern Italian women are deeply intertwined, they are also profoundly connected to how power manifests in universities, museums, auctions houses, and art galleries, including who gets to lead these institutions and how much they are paid. Only one woman leads a top ten art museum in terms of budget—Kaywin Feldman, director of the National Gallery of Art in Washington, D.C.[75] According to a 2019 *Washington Post* article, in 2017 "female directors at the top 25 largest museums earned on average about 76 cents for every dollar paid to a male director."[76] As Nochlin warned in her 1971 essay, "Those who have privileges inevitably hold on to them, and hold tight, no matter how marginal the advantage involved, until compelled to bow to superior power of one sort or another."[77] As the grip on power in the cultural sphere very slowly loosens to become more inclusive of a range of genders, races, sexualities, and abilities, the very fabric and structures of our institutions are gradually changing to become more all-encompassing. With hopes for the future, we must, as Nochlin urges, "leap into the unknown," where an equitable world full of women artists—indeed artists of any background or orientation—hopefully awaits.[78]

Appendix: Italian Women Artists Exhibition History

*denotes an accompanying exhibition catalogue

1972 *Old Mistresses: Women Artists of the Past*
Walters Art Gallery, Baltimore, Maryland

1972 *Women: A Historical Survey of Works by Women Artists*
Salem Fine Arts Center, Winston-Salem, North Carolina*

1973 *Les femmes peintres au XVIIIe siècle*
Musée Goya, Castres, France*

1975 *La femme peintre et sculpteur du 17e siècle au 20e siècle*
Grand Palais, Paris, France*

1975 *Women Artists: A Review of the Permanent Collection*
San Francisco Fine Arts Museum, California

1976–1977 *Women Artists: 1550–1950*
Los Angeles County Museum of Art, California; University Art
Museum, Austin, Texas; Museum of Art, Carnegie Institute, Pittsburgh,
Pennsylvania; Brooklyn Museum, New York*

1979 *Women Artists in Washington Collections*
University of Maryland Art Gallery, College Park*

1982 *Women's Art Show, 1550–1970*
Nottingham Castle Museum, England*

1983 *Frauen und Kunst im Mittelalter*
Städtische Galerie, Wolfsburg, Germany*

1983 *Women Artists: Selected Works from the Collection*
Herbert F. Johnson Museum of Art, Cornell University,
Ithaca, New York*

1991 *Artemisia*
Casa Buonarroti, Florence, Italy*

1994–1995 *Sofonisba Anguissola e le sue sorelle/Sofonisba Anguissola and
Her Sisters*
Santa Maria della Pietà, Cremona, Italy; Kunsthistorisches Museum,
Vienna, Austria; National Museum of Women in the Arts,
Washington, D.C.*

1995 *La prima donna pittrice Sofonisba Anguissola:
Die Malerin der Renaissance (um 1535–1625)*
Kunsthistorisches Museum, Vienna, Austria*

2001–2002 *Orazio and Artemisia Gentileschi: Father and Daughter Painters
in Baroque Italy*
Museo del Palazzo Venezia, Rome; Saint Louis Art Museum, Missouri;
Metropolitan Museum of Art, New York*

2004–2005 *Elisabetta Sirani "pittrice eroina"*
Museo Civico Archeologico, Bologna, Italy*

2007 *La donna nell'arte: Intorno a Rosalba Carriera*
Palazzo Ducale, Salone del Piovego, Venice, Italy; *Rosalba "prima
pittrice de l'Europa,"* The Giorgio Cini Foundation, Venice, Italy*

2007 *Italian Women Artists from Renaissance to Baroque*
National Museum of Women in the Arts, Washington, D.C.*

2007–2008 *L'Arte delle donne dal Rinascimento al Surrealismo*
Palazzo Reale, Milan, Italy*

2010–2011 *Autoritratte: "Artiste di capriccioso e destrissimo ingegno"*
Gallerie degli Uffizi, Florence, Italy*

2011–2012 *Artemisia Gentileschi: Storia di una passione*
Palazzo Reale, Milan, Italy*

2012 *Orsola Maddalena Caccia: Storia singolare di una monaca pittrice*
Fondazione Cosso, Castello di Miradolo, Pinerolo, Italy*

2012 *Artemisia: Pouvoir, gloire et passions d'une femme peintre*
Fondation Dina Vierny, Musée Maillol, Paris, France*

2012 *Di mano donnesca: Donne artiste dal XVI al XVII secolo*
Palazzo Venezia, Rome, Italy*

2013–2014 *Violence and Virtue: Artemisia Gentileschi's "Judith Slaying
Holofernes"*
Art Institute of Chicago, Illinois*

2014–2015 *Picturing Mary: Woman, Mother, Idea*
National Museum of Women in the Arts, Washington, D.C.*

2016–2017 *Artemisia Gentileschi e il suo tempo*
Museo di Roma, Italy*

2017 *Eighteenth-Century Pastel Portraits*
Metropolitan Museum of Art, New York

2017 *Plautilla Nelli: Arte e devozione sulle orme di Savonarola*
Gallerie degli Uffizi, Florence, Italy*

2018 *Dipingere e disegnare "da gran maestro": Il talento di Elisabetta Sirani
(Bologna, 1638–1665)*
Gallerie degli Uffizi, Florence, Italy*

2018–2019 *De dames van de barok: Vrouwelijke schilders in het Italië van de
16de en 17de eeuw*
Museum voor Schone Kunsten, Ghent, Belgium*

2019 *The Female Triumphant*
Sotheby's, New York*

2019 *Histórias das mulheres: Artistas até 1900*
Museu de Arte de São Paulo, Brazil*

2019–2020 *Historia de dos pintoras: Sofonisba Anguissola y Lavinia
Fontana/A Tale of Two Women Painters: Sofonisba Anguissola and
Lavinia Fontana*
Museo Nacional del Prado, Madrid, Spain*

2020 *"La grandezza del universo" nell'arte di Giovanna Garzoni*
Gallerie degli Uffizi, Florence, Italy*

2020–2021 *Artemisia*
National Gallery, London, England*

2021 *Le signore del Barocco*
Palazzo Reale, Milan, Italy*

2021–2022 *Fede Galizia: Amazzone nella pittura*
Castello del Buonconsiglio, Trent, Italy*

2021–2022 *By Her Hand: Artemisia Gentileschi and Women Artists in Italy,
1500–1800*
Wadsworth Atheneum Museum of Art, Hartford, Connecticut; Detroit
Institute of Arts, Michigan*

NOTES

1. Nochlin 1971, 25.

2. There have been shows that have included Italian early modern women artists, but no monographic or group shows that have been devoted exclusively to Italian early women artists. For instance, the 2001–2002 show in Rome, New York, and St. Louis, *Orazio and Artemisia Gentileschi: Father and Daughter Painters in Baroque Italy*, focused half on Artemisia Gentileschi and half on her father Orazio Gentileschi. The 2013–2014 *Violence and Virtue: Artemisia Gentileschi's "Judith Slaying Holofernes"* orbited around the loan of one picture by Artemisia Gentileschi from the Uffizi Gallery and representations of Judith by male artists of multiple nationalities.

3. Sheila ffolliott recently wrote the online piece "Do We Have Any Great Women Artists Yet?" ffolliott 2020.

4. As part of her embrace of many approaches to art history, Nochlin also called herself an "ad hoc" art historian, explaining, "Nor, in declaring myself to be an 'ad hoc' art historian, am I advocating a user-friendly eclecticism. In my experience, which has shaped this strongly held opinion, each concrete art-historical issue, problem or situation demands a different set of strategies." Nochlin 1999, 10. Beyond feminism, or often intertwined with her feminist approach to art history, Nochlin also tackled issues of religion, race, and sexuality. For issues of religion see Nochlin and Garb 1996. For questions of race see, for example, her review of the 1994 Whitney Museum exhibition *Black Male*, where she writes: "I believe in inclusiveness—in openness to other visions and articulations besides the mainstream ones approved by the purity police"; "Such worthlessly enshrined relics also remind us that we who have inherited that tradition must constantly revise, deconstruct and reconsider it in the light of present-day concerns and passions." Nochlin 2017. For issues of sexuality, see Nochlin 1972, 9–15.

5. This inclusivity has paved the way for African American, Latinx, Queer, and disability studies, among other avenues, in the history of art.

6. Topaz et al. 2019, 1.

7. The new analysis was done by Artnet, an art market information company, and "In Other Words," a weekly podcast and newsletter produced by Art Agency, Partners, an art advisory firm acquired by Sotheby's. It was reported in the *New York Times* on September 19, 2019, updated on September 25, 2019. See Jacobs 2019.

8. Reilly 2015. The Andrew W. Mellon Foundation, in partnership with AAMD (Association of Art Museum Directors) and Ithaka S+R, produced a 2018 study of the ethnicities and genders of museum staffs across the United States. This was a follow-up study to a 2015 survey that found "double the number of African-American curators—from 2 percent in 2015 to 4 percent in 2018, an increase of 21 positions. The number of women in leadership positions also grew four to five percentage points, from 57 percent in 2015 to 62 percent in 2018, and women continue to comprise some 60 percent of museum staffs." For this study see Andrew W. Mellon Foundation 2019. While the improvements between 2015 and 2018 are significant and show the importance of such studies as catalysts for change, there is still much work to be done to achieve gender and racial parity in museum staffing.

9. For an overview of the birth of art history, see Hatt and Klonk 2006, 21–64. As far as we know, the words *féminisme* and *féminist* in the Netherlands and France were first used in 1872 by the Dutch feminist pioneer Mina Kruseman (1839–1922) to the French writer Alexandre Dumas (1802–1870) in her *Lettre a M. Alexandre Dumas fils au sujet de son livre l'Homme-femme* (1872). For an overview of Mina Kruseman, see Praamstra 2010, 23–25.

10. The remarks of British feminist art historian Lisa Tickner about the importance of the feminist movement in England are applicable to the rest of Europe and the United States: "It cannot be a coincidence that a flurry of books devoted to women artists, the first exhibitions that grouped them together as women and the first opportunities for their serious education and employment all accompanied the rise and influence of the Victorian women's movement." Tickner 1988, 13.

11. *Report of the Woman's Rights Convention* 1848, 5.

12. Gazzetta 1995, 249–70.

13. "Periodico morale ed istruttivo. Compilazione di donne italiane." Gazzetta and Sega 2006, 144.

14. "Propugna i diritti femminili." Gazzetta and Sega 2006, 144.

15. In addition to *La Donna*, which is a later nineteenth-century periodical, it is important to note the publication in 1840 of the anonymously written *Delle donne illustri italiane dal XIII al XIX secolo*, which was an encyclopedia of entries on famous Italian women, including artists Anna Bacherini Piattoli, Lavinia Fontana, Artemisia Gentileschi, Antonia Bertusi Pinelli, and Elisabetta Sirani, among many others. *Delle donne illustri italiane* 1840.

16. "Von Frauenhänden erzogen, habe ich von jeher die Beispiele hohen weiblichen Werthes vor Augen gehabt und noch jetzt gestehe ich es gern, in dem Verkehr mit edlen Frauen den eigentlichen Künstlerischen Reiz des Lebens zu finden." Guhl 1858, 7–8. I want to thank Ellen Hanspach-Bernal for her refinement of my English translation.

17. A further condensed synopsis of "The Westminster Review" for the "general reader" can be found in *Cosmopolitan Art Journal* 1958, 47–48.

18. *Westminster Review* 1858, 92.

19. In his 1932 review of two shows of women artists at the Brooklyn Museum, Herbert Tschudy posits: "Sometimes I think that art has suffered immensely from this thing we call sex. We cannot solve the riddle of this preponderance of male art workers prior to the nineteenth century by hanging our deductions on the overworked biological consideration. Women did not enter the arts simply because their daily work, their interests, were directed to other things. There is nothing about creative art which finds its best interpreter in man or in woman." Tschudy 1932, 13.

20. Women artists are discussed in Christine de Pizan's 1405 *Book of the City of Ladies*. See Gaylard 2015, 287–318; Dabbs 2009, 2 and 36–38.

21. Ellet 1859, v.

22. Gardner 1948, 112.

23. Langer 1980–1981, 58.

24. Ellet 1904, xi. "In studying the subject of this book I have found the names of more than a thousand women whose attainments in the Fine Arts—in various countries and at different periods of time before the middle of the nineteenth century—entitle them to honorable mention as artists, and I doubt not that an exhaustive search would largely increase this number."

25. Johnston 1997, 1.

26. Johnston 1997, 4–7.

27. Holcomb 1987–1988, 16.

28. Jameson 1834, vol. 2, 121.

29. Jameson 1834, vol. 2, 114–20.

30. Jameson 1834, vol. 2, 119. She continues: "But all, except Gentileschi, were *feminine* painters," a quotation worthy of a separate essay!

31. Jameson qualifies her understanding of female genius: "I wish to combat in every way that oft-repeated, but most false compliment unthinkingly paid to women, that genius is of no sex; there may be equality of power, but in its quality and application there will and must be difference and distinction. If men would but remember this truth, they would cease to treat with ridicule and jealousy the attainments and aspirations of women, know that there never could be real competition or rivalry. If women would admit this truth, they would not presume out of their sphere." In other words, female "genius" is at a different level than male "genius." Jameson 1834, vol. 2, 120–21.

32. Holcomb 1987–1988, 16 n. 7.

33. In 1905 the art historian Anton Hirsch published *Die bildenden Künstlerinnen der Neuzeit*, which dealt with contemporary artists of his period. See Hirsch 1905.

34. Sparrow 1905.

35. Sparrow 1905, 12 and 11, respectively.

36. He included: Caterina Vigri (1413–1463); Sienese nuns of Santa Marta; Barbara Rangoni (dates unknown) and two other sister nuns; Plautilla Nelli (1524–1588); Barbara Longhi (1552–1638); Sophonisba Auguisciola (author's spelling); Artemisia Gentileschi; Maria La Caffa (likely Margherita Caffi, 1648–1710); Isabella del Pozzo (d. 1700); Felicità Sartori (ca. 1714–1760); Violanta [Violante] Beatrice Siries; Rosalba Carriera; Lavinia Fontana; Elisabetta Sirani; Sirani's "large class of girl art-students"; Diana Ghisi (Diana Scultori, ca. 1547–1612); Maria Felice Tibaldi (1707–1770); and Agnese Dolci (1659–1731). He describes Artemisia Gentileschi as attaining a "masterful and singular ruthlessness." Sparrow 1905, 28. For Sirani's students see Sparrow 1905, 30. Sparrow also includes three "contemporary" artists: Elisa Koch, Juana Romani, and Rosina Gutti. Sparrow 1905, 30.

37. "It is not easy to explain why the Italian towns and universities gave so much encouragement to the higher aspiration of girls." Sparrow 1905, 22.

38. Ragg 1907, 1.

39. See, most recently, Bohn 2021.

40. That said, the English author Dinah Craik (1826–1887) wrote a short prose piece on Elisabetta Sirani. See Craik 1853, 317–34. Craik notes, "The whole face of Elisabetta Sirani showed a combination of masculine powers and womanly sweetness . . ." and at the end, in a twist, her pupil Ginevra Cantofoli is credited with poisoning her! See Craik 1853, 318 and 332, respectively.

41. Among the handful of earlier sources are two books devoted to Rosalba Carriera: von Hoerschelmann 1908 and Malamani 1910. The earliest modern publication on Artemisia Gentileschi is Longhi 1916. French women artists received more attention earlier. See, for instance, Fidière 1885. An early monograph on Fede Galizia is Bottari 1965.

42. Nochlin 1971, 25.

43. Mary Garrard's sometimes feminist-oriented attributions of Artemisia Gentileschi come immediately to mind. The following two quotes encapsulate her approach: "But I believe that something else is involved, namely, a denial of Artemisia's core feminism, without which her oeuvre would indeed be incoherent."; "At its best Artemisia's art speaks for many women, and its anti-patriarchal expression stands as a powerful cultural statement on their behalf." Garrard 2001, 15 and 113, respectively.

44. The best general reference text on women artists is Gaze 1997. Greer 1979 is an important early title. See, as well, Chadwick 1990 and Heller 1987.

45. French feminist theory in the writings of Julia Kristeva, Luce Irigaray, and Hélène Cixous bring the notion of an *écriture féminine*, writing marked by the female body, to the subject. Lucy Lippard, Griselda Pollock, Sheila ffolliott, Sheila Barker, Babette Bohn, and Adelina Modesti, among a great number of other scholars, are worth naming in this context. Even those art historians who had never written on women artists prior felt so moved, including Keith Christiansen and Michael Cole.

46. The examples of art criticism are too numerous to cite here, so a handful will have to suffice. See, for instance, Jacobs 2019; Guzman 2019; Polonsky 2019; Eisner Eley 2017; Reilly 2015.

47. Lorde 2007, 110 (original essay 1984).

48. Lorde 2007, 111.

49. See, for example, Mannarino 2018, which is not meant to be representative or serve as an exemplar, but rather to alert readers to one of many articles and essays on the subject.

50. For a complete list of exhibitions with works by early modern Italian women artists, see the Appendix at the end of this essay. For a brief overview of this topic online, see Barker 2020b.

51. This show commemorated the 200th anniversary of the Salem College and Academy for Women.

52. Hill 1972, vii.

53. Gabhart and Broun 1972, unpaginated, 7th page into the periodical.

54. For this document see *Los Angeles Council of Women Artists* 1971.

55. Donahue originally asked Ann Sutherland Harris to curate an Artemisia Gentileschi show and she brought Linda Nochlin on board as co-curator for the later material.

56. Sutherland Harris and Nochlin 1976, 11.

57. Sutherland Harris 1976, 44.

58. Alf 1977, 19.

59. Garrard 1977, 532.

60. The 2007 National Museum of Women in the Arts exhibition in Washington, D.C., *Italian Women Artists from Renaissance to Baroque*, created the foundation upon which this exhibition arises, building upon their success in offering "a complete picture of the range of the art and the opportunities accessible to the early modern Italian *artista*." Larson 2007, unpaginated, 6th page into the catalogue.

61. Just the other day I was reading *Luster*, published in summer 2020, by Raven Leilani, in which the book's protagonist—a young African American woman artist in New York—proclaims, "There is a painting that I love by Artemisia Gentileschi, *Judith Slaying Holofernes*." Leilani 2020, 28.

62. The seven are: 1991: Casa Buonarroti, Florence, *Artemisia Gentileschi*; 2001–2002: Palazzo Venezia, Rome, Saint Louis Art Museum, Metropolitan Museum of Art, New York, *Orazio and Artemisia Gentileschi: Father and Daughter Painters in Baroque Italy*; 2011: Palazzo Reale, Milan, *Artemisia Gentileschi: The Story of a Passion*; 2012: Fondation Dina Vierny, Musée Maillol, Paris, *Artemisia 1593–1654*; 2013–2014: Art Institute of Chicago, *Violence and Virtue: Artemisia Gentileschi's "Judith Slaying Holofernes"*; 2016–2017: Museo di Roma, Rome, *Artemisia Gentileschi and Her Times*; 2020–2021: National Gallery, London, *Artemisia*.

63. At the Metropolitan Museum of Art the show was divided between Orazio Gentileschi and Artemisia Gentileschi and began with a room of overlap between father and daughter for her early years in Rome. Except for this room, it was like two separate monographic exhibitions. At the Saint Louis Art Museum, as Keith Christiansen kindly informed me, the artists' works were compared and intermingled throughout the exhibition space.

64. Of these eighteen artists, two—Virginia da Vezzo and Maria Felice Tibaldi—are represented in portraits by their husbands.

65. Soprani and Ratti 1768, 453.

66. *Vocabolario* 1612, 917.

67. There has not been, for instance, a systematic appraisal of Artemisia Gentileschi's period earnings. Sheila Barker has treated the financial reality of Artemisia Gentileschi in Florence in Barker 2017b, 59–88.

68. This is a high price for any early modern picture, as the prices for art of this period do not match those reached for modern and contemporary art.

69. Adams et al. 2017.

70. Adams et al. 2017.

71. Adams et al. 2017.

72. Adams et al. 2017.

73. Reilly 2015.

74. Reilly 2015.

75. McGlone 2019. For another article on this topic, see Sheets 2017.

76. McGlone 2019.

77. Nochlin 1971, 25.

78. Nochlin 1971, 70.

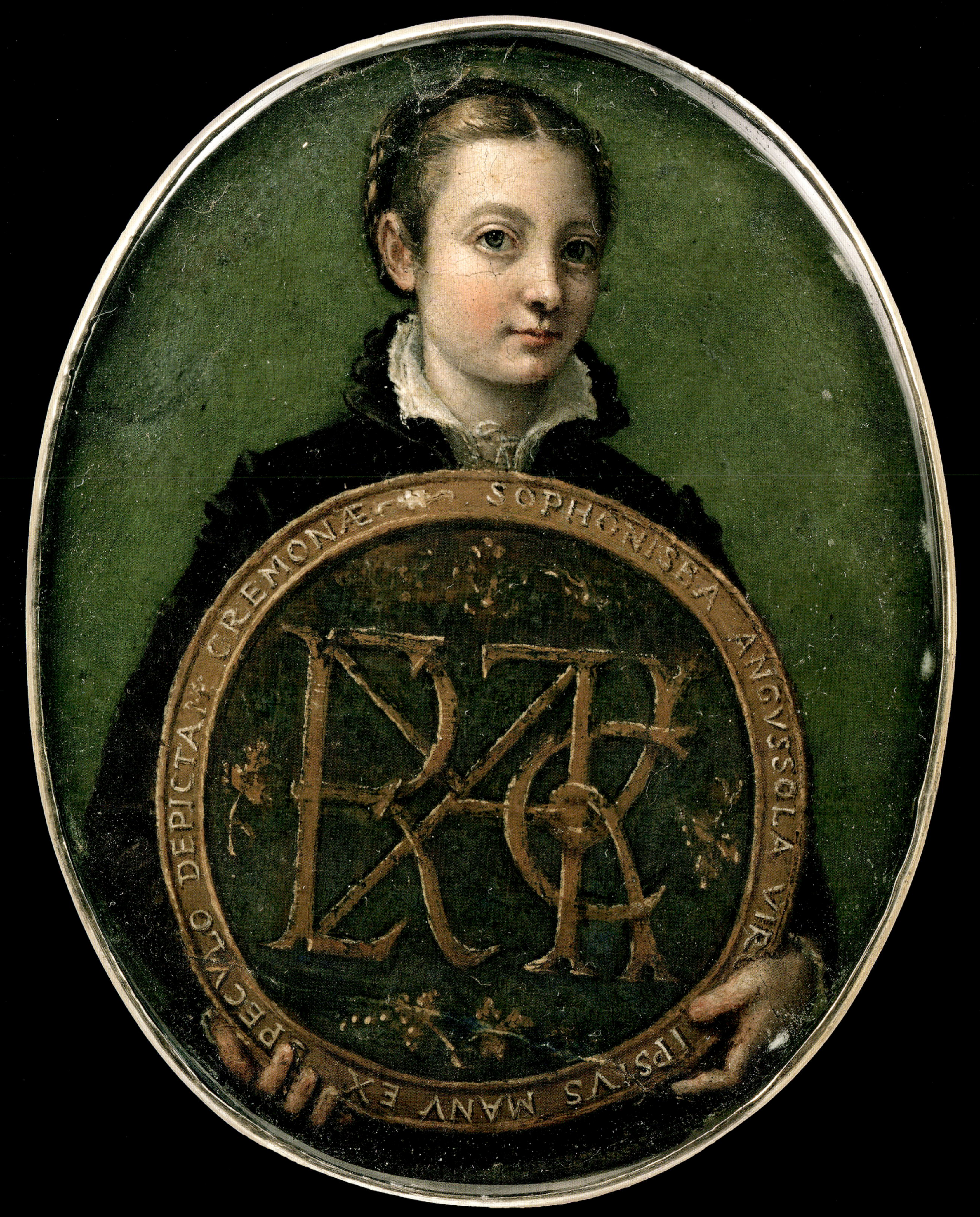

SOPHONISBA ANGVSSOLA VIR
IPSIVS MANV EX
SPECVLO DEPICTA CREMONAE

OLIVER TOSTMANN

The Advantages of Painting Small: Italian Women Artists and the Matter of Scale

IN 1554 THE TWENTY-TWO-YEAR-OLD Cremonese painter Sofonisba Anguissola (ca. 1535–1625) finished her earliest surviving self-portrait (fig. 1). At only $7^{11}/_{16} \times 5^{11}/_{16}$ in. (19.5 × 14.5 cm) it is modest in size, but it demonstrates her thirst for recognition and fame at a young age.[1]

As the earliest surviving independent self-portrait of any Italian woman artist, the painting is groundbreaking. Carefully groomed and elegantly dressed, Anguissola fixes her gaze on the viewer as she opens outward a small book—perhaps a collection of poems or prayers—held close to her chest; it is as if she has invited us to share an intimate moment of her life. Anguissola's signature in Latin on the book's recto, *Sophonisba/ Angussola/virgo/seipsam/fecit/1554* ("The virgin Sophonisba Anguissola made this in 1554"), refers to her authorship, virtuosity, and learnedness. In many ways, the small book, with its carefully rendered luxurious binding and minuscule writing, echoes the painting itself—the portrait can be held in the viewer's hand as easily as the book is held in the artist's. Even if Anguissola did not mean to indicate her place in history with her gesture, she points to the immense potential that small-format artworks offered to generations of women artists.

Like their male contemporaries, Italian women painters created a rich body of small and large works from the Renaissance to the Rococo period. Compared to their male peers, however, small works seem to have played a different role in the careers of women artists and served a different purpose for them. Like Anguissola, women often depicted themselves in small format works or showed themselves working on small-scale paintings, a motif that seems to have been far less common among men.[2] Although some male artists, such as the Italian miniaturist Giulio Clovio (1498–1578), became famous for small works, this was the exception rather than the rule. And while working in a small format was just one of many options for male artists, many women did not have this choice. As a result, women worked more consistently, broadly, and perhaps with greater urgency at small scale.

The importance of small-scale artworks by women has been marginalized in discussions of early modern artists. While small pictures have been considered in monographic works, a comprehensive study of the women working in this format remains to be written. One reason for this lack of critical study is a general disregard among art historians for small-scale works.[3] Those by women specifically have often been denigrated because of their size.[4] Already in his *Lives of the Most Excellent Painters, Sculptors, and Architects (Le vite de' più eccellenti pittori, scultori, et architettori)*, published first in 1550 and with an extended edition in 1568, the artist and author Giorgio Vasari

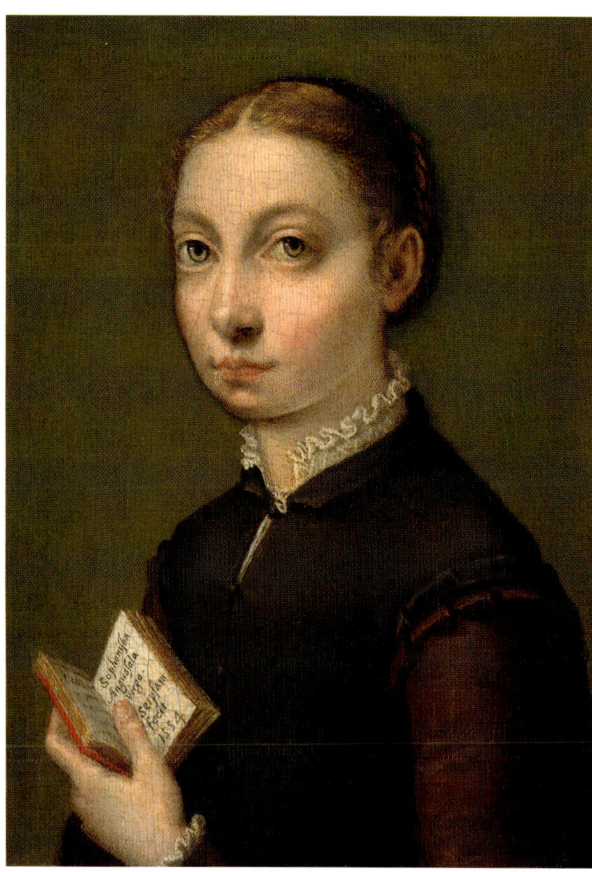

FIGURE 1 Sofonisba Anguissola, *Self-Portrait*, 1554, oil on panel, 7¹¹⁄₁₆ × 5¹¹⁄₁₆ in. (19.5 × 14.5 cm). Kunsthistorisches Museum, Vienna, GG285

(1511–1574) denigrated the works of women artists as being "small in scale and modest in ambition."[5] Indeed, scale played an integral role in the artistic hierarchy. Defined by male critics, such as Vasari, the so-called *gran maniera* or "grand manner" elevated large-scale figure painting and narratives to their very pinnacle. In short, this belief equated large works with greatness of quality in general.[6] Simultaneously, Renaissance and Baroque women artists were often encouraged by (male) teachers and writers, often their fathers, to work small.[7] To avoid reinforcing gendered hierarchies and values, scholars since the 1970s have focused on demonstrating how women artists competed with male peers in larger format works. But while they have embedded women artists in broader cultural frameworks, they have rarely offered an in-depth discussion of matters of scale.[8] This essay investigates how small works determined and shaped the careers of Italian women artists between 1500 and 1800.

Small Works: Terms and Issues

Today small pictures from the Renaissance to the Rococo are given scant attention and are often considered merely decorative objects; contemporaries, however, found them significant.

Small pictures in different media—oil paintings, watercolors, and pastels—were used in various ways: set into frames, they were displayed on walls; they were bound together; they were worn as jewelry, and often exchanged as gifts. Diminutive works were painted on supports as diverse as canvas, panels, and copper for paintings; vellum and ivory for miniatures; and paper for pastels. They required different paints and applications as well: oil colors, watercolors, and bodycolors were used for miniatures, and pastel colors were applied directly with crayons on paper. Such small pictures convey a sense of intimacy and an element of surprise, which carefully balances the private self with the public gaze.[9]

Although there is no firm definition of a small picture, it usually presents a subject considerably smaller than life-size. The objects evaluated in this essay range from two to twenty inches (less than five centimeters to about fifty centimeters).[10] Small pictures were often described in general terms such as *pitture in piccolo, tavolette,* and *quadretti.* Genres bore specific diminutives, such as *ritrattini* or *testini* for small portraits, but none of these were associated with specific dimensions.[11] For lack of a better definition, Vasari described small oil paintings as being made "quasi di minio" or "seemingly in red lead," referring to *minium,* a color commonly used in illuminations and miniatures, but not in oil painting.[12] In 1584 the painter and writer Giovanni Paolo Lomazzo (1538–1592) mentioned the art of the miniature painter Giulio Clovio and equated it with other media, but he did not point out the obvious differences in size and techniques among miniature, oil, and fresco painting.[13] Other writers, believing the term *miniature* to be a derivation from the Latin term *minimus,* meaning small, categorized all small works as miniatures. In 1585, for instance, the writer Tommaso Garzoni (1549–1589) defined miniatures by their size, but he did not associate them with a specific technique.[14] Similarly, by 1621, the Sienese doctor and author Giulio Mancini (1559–1630) described miniatures as synonymous with small paintings.[15] Others, however, defined miniatures "as a thing apart," noting they differed from paintings in their function and materials.[16] Still, a clear sense of scale and of different media was lacking.[17] With the growing popularity of pastels during the seventeenth and eighteenth centuries, a terminology analogous to that of miniatures developed.[18] A Neapolitan inventory from 1716, for instance, lists pastels by the Neapolitan artist Teresa del Pò (1649–1713) as "miniature di pastello."[19] In a letter to Rosalba Carriera (1673–1757) in 1720, the French art collector Pierre Crozat (1665–1740) stated that pastels and miniatures together make up the small arts.[20] By the end of the eighteenth century, women had become associated with small-scale works, but there was still no clear differentiation of small works by medium. As we will see, this lack of a definition afforded women artists broad liberties in the production of small works.

Precursors: Women Who Painted Miniatures

Women practiced painting in small formats well before the sixteenth century. According to the first-century Roman historian Pliny the Elder, one of the first and most famous women artists was Iaia from Cyzicus, later known as Marcia. Iaia became the highest paid artist in Rome in the first century BCE, specializing in small portraits painted on ivory.[21] In his collection of biographies of famous women, Giovanni Boccaccio (1313–1375), who had read Pliny, stated that she also painted a self-portrait on a panel with the help of a mirror (fig. 2).[22] It is likely that ancient stories such as Iaia's were a continuous source of inspiration for later women artists.

Even though few Italian women worked outside of convents at the beginning of the sixteenth century, the situation was different in the Netherlands.[23] The Low Countries had been the center of illumination in Europe and its artists exerted considerable influence across the continent. One of the most famous women artists was Susanna Horenbout (1503–1554), whose ability to paint excellent miniatures was "beyond belief," according to her Italian contemporary Lodovico Guicciardini (1521–1589).[24] Horenbout must have been something of a legend, because early in her career she had already attracted the praise of Albrecht Dürer (1471–1528). In 1521, while visiting Susanna's father, the illuminator Gherard Horenbout (ca. 1465–ca. 1541), Dürer saw one of her miniatures, admired it, and noted in his journal: "It is a great wonder that a woman should be able to do such work."[25] By mentioning Horenbout's accomplishment in the context of her gender, Dürer's praise is tinged with a prejudice rooted in the lack of opportunities for women to train as artists. Yet his encomium can also be seen as a harbinger of the greater opportunities that would arise in the course of the sixteenth century, when more women started to gain recognition as artists.

At Home: The Domestic Sphere

In 1577, at the outset of her career, the young Bolognese artist Lavinia Fontana (1552–1614) painted a striking self-portrait showing herself playing a spinet (fig. 3). The portrait was a gift to the artist's future in-laws and part of a broader marital strategy. Fontana does not present herself as a painter so much as an accomplished and self-assured woman, assessing the viewer with curious eyes. Joanna Woods-Marsden observed that her elegant red and white garments reference the Petrarchan colors of love.[26] Fontana's world is confined to a large but somber studio. She fashions herself as the mistress of her domestic sphere, reigning over a circumscribed space while exerting her artistic talents, accompanied only by her female servant. No church tower, neighboring house, or other sign of the outside world is visible through

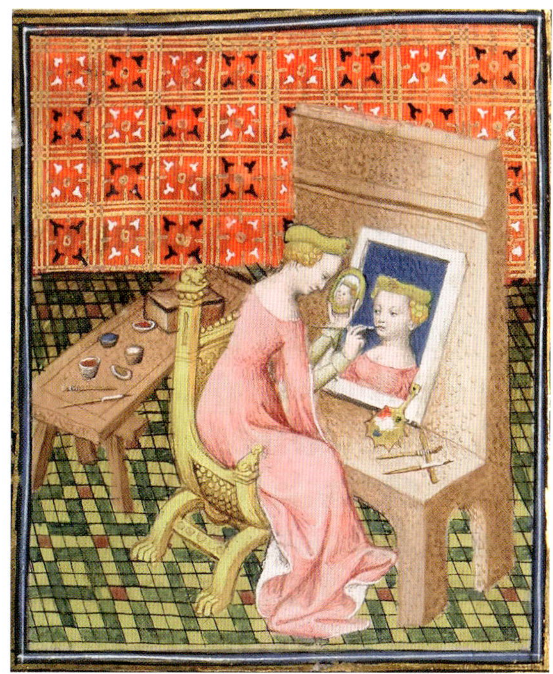

FIGURE 2 Unknown artist, *Marcia*, manuscript illumination from Boccaccio, *Des cleres et nobles femmes*, ca. 1402. Bibliothèque Nationale de France, Ms. français 12420, fol. 101v

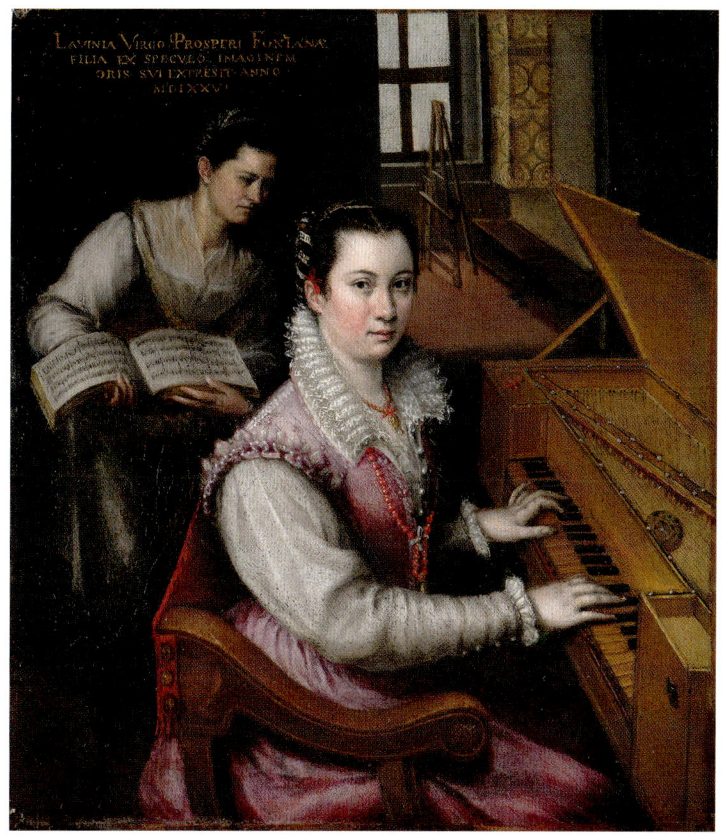

FIGURE 3 Lavinia Fontana, *Self-Portrait at a Spinet*, 1577, oil on canvas, 10⅝ × 9⅜ in. (27 × 23.8 cm). Accademia Nazionale di San Luca, Rome, inv. 743

the large window in the background—Fontana presents herself in splendid isolation, as was perfectly appropriate for a virtuous young woman of her time. Only the easel in the background, on which two small paintings rests, hints at her profession. The size of the paintings within the painting, combined with the small format of the portrait itself, indicate Fontana's predilection for small-scale work at the time.[27]

The portrait is also a microcosm of the conditions and practices of contemporaneous women artists. In early modern Europe women were largely bound to their homes and families, as daughters, wives, and mothers.[28] Reputable women managed the domestic sphere, avoided contact with men outside of their family, and, more broadly, were the guardians of family honor.[29] For artistically inclined women from middle- and upper-class backgrounds, working at small scale was convenient and inconspicuous: painting could be practiced from home, in private, and did not require large studios or assistants; costs for pigments and other materials were lower because smaller quantities were used; and small-format works did not require the use of ladders and scaffolds—miniatures, pastels, and small oils could be conveniently produced while seated at a desk or before an easel, as shown in the background of Fontana's self-portrait.[30]

Whitney Chadwick argues that the foremost contribution of women artists from this period was in so-called domestic genres, by which she means portraits, still lifes, and genre scenes.[31] While Chadwick does not focus on scale, many of the works she describes are well-suited to small formats. With notable exceptions, a small piece of ivory or parchment is not necessarily conducive to a multifigure historical scene or a landscape, and small works generally show complex multifigure scenes less frequently than large ones. Nevertheless, some women, such as Fontana, Giovanna Garzoni (1600–1670), and Teresa del Pò, painted small religious scenes comprised of multiple figures on such supports. Others copied famous paintings, often with multiple figures, in miniature.

Training

The training of women artists differed fundamentally from that of men. Traditionally, convents played a large role in women's artistic lives. During the Middle Ages, nuns worked in convents all across Europe, and some illuminated the manuscripts used for daily prayers. The most famous Italian nun practicing painting and illumination was Caterina Vigri (1413–1463). After her death a strong cult developed around her in Bologna, and she eventually became the local patron saint of artists. Her influence as a model for Bolognese women artists cannot be overstated, and it may have been one reason why the Emilian city produced the highest number of women artists in Italy from the sixteenth to the eighteenth century.[32] In Florence, another well-known

artist emerged from this tradition. Plautilla Nelli (1524–1588), a nun in the Dominican convent of Saint Catherine, produced both miniatures and large altar paintings in the mid-sixteenth century. The overall importance of convents in artistic training, however, began to wane during the Baroque and Rococo periods.[33]

From the late sixteenth to eighteenth centuries, most women received their earliest artistic education in family workshops. Lavinia Fontana, Artemisia Gentileschi (1593–1654 or later), and Elisabetta Sirani (1638–1665) came from such artistic lineages. A third, smaller group of women, often from elite families, trained with artists outside of convents or family workshops. Painters such as Sofonisba Anguissola, her sister Elena Anguissola (ca. 1536–ca. 1585), and Giovanna Fratellini (1666–1731) were trained in this way. Unprecedented at the time, the Anguissola sisters left their family home to train with the local artists Bernardino Campi (1522–1591) and Bernardino Gatti (ca. 1495–1576) during the second half of the 1540s. More than one hundred years later, the young Fratellini was introduced to the Medici court, which provided her with an education in writing, drawing, and painting.[34]

While the training of young male artists tended to take place in workshops, and later in academies, access to studios was limited for women, and it was difficult to practice at an art academy.[35] A few girls from elite families received drawing lessons at home, as it was part of the humanist education. Drawing served as the traditional entry into the arts for men, but such lessons were more difficult for women to obtain. Moreover, the most important training exercise—studying from a nude male model—could severely tarnish their reputations.[36] Exceptions, however, could be made for married women. The German miniaturist Maria Sibylla Merian (1647–1717) stated wittily that she had only married her husband to practice drawing with a nude model.[37] Elisabetta Sirani and Giulia Lama (1681–1747)— among the most prolific Italian draftswomen—frequently created drawings in which they explored human bodies in preparation for complex, large-format historical scenes.[38] They must have found ways to draw from life, probably using family members as models. Dated ca. 1700, a self-portrait by Rosalba Carriera shows the artist drawing a head with red crayons (fig. 4). In depicting herself as a draftswoman, Carriera shrewdly inserted herself into the tradition of highlighting one's artistic education popularized by male artists in the Renaissance and Baroque.[39] Whether Carriera received lessons in drawing and to what degree she practiced it, however, is a matter of speculation. Only about a dozen drawings are attributed to her today.[40]

If drawing from life was difficult to practice for young women artists, the so-called crafts may have offered a viable alternative. Stitching, embroidery, and calligraphy traditionally played a large role in the education of middle- and upper-class

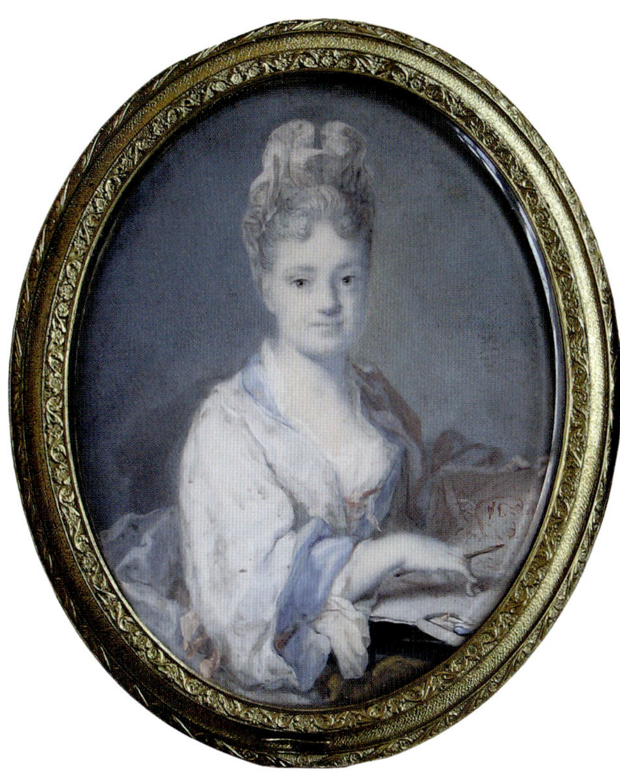

girls, and sometimes laid the foundations for later careers in the arts.[41] Many women who specialized in small works practiced weaving, stitching, and designing patterns in their early years. Such activities provided women artists with a steady source of income, critical during the early stages of their careers. Arcangela Paladini (1599–1622) and Giovanna Fratellini, for instance, stitched as young girls, whereas Rosalba Carriera assisted her mother in making embroideries. While the connection between needlework and the so-called major arts is still understudied, embroidery may have familiarized and prepared women to produce intricate objects, or, as Michael Cole put it, "One craft made it easier to learn the other."[42] Embroidering textiles could have taught the young artists valuable lessons about the sequencing of different patterns, the rhythmic arrangements of motifs, and, more generally, the beauty of lines; it was an intricate exercise not unlike decorating borders in illuminated manuscripts. This gender-related training may have set women artists apart from men, and it is possible that women who specialized in small paintings were not as reliant on extensive drawing lessons from life as artists who worked in larger formats.

Women artists, unlike men, commonly focused on small works, especially when they were young. Well-known examples in the late sixteenth century are Lavinia Fontana and Fede Galizia (ca. 1574–ca. 1630). After being trained by her father, Fontana painted numerous small portraits and mythological as well as devotional paintings, especially during the 1570s and '80s. Galizia started as a miniaturist before turning to small paintings. In the mid-seventeenth century, the Roman artist Plautilla Bricci (1616–1705), who developed her skills by producing miniatures and small paintings at the convent of Saint Joseph in Rome in 1664, eventually moved on to altarpieces and large frescoes.[43] Around 1700 the young Venetian Giulia Lama started with miniatures as well, before specializing in large religious paintings with multiple figures.[44] Other artists, such as Teresa del Pò, also began with small formats.[45] Del Pò started her career with small oil paintings of history scenes, and, according to her biographer Bernardo De Dominici (1683–ca. 1759), believing that she was not able to compete in this male-dominated field, she switched to miniatures and pastels, after which she quickly became successful.[46] Like del Pò, Carriera mastered multiple techniques and media. She painted miniatures early on, and she maintained this practice for most of her career. Eventually, in her early thirties, during the first decade of the eighteenth century, she began to experiment with and soon excelled in small-to mid-scale pastels, for which she is best known today.[47]

By manipulating and experimenting with different materials and techniques, women turned challenges inherent to the size of small objects to their advantage and were often lauded by contemporaries for their virtuosity and ingenuity. In the 1530s Properzia de' Rossi (ca. 1490–1530), a rare woman artist who sculpted, started her career by carving out of wood miniature objects resembling precious jewels. She was well known for carving from cherry, apricot, and peach pits.[48] A few decades later the English miniaturist Nicholas Hilliard (1547–1619) noticed the innovative techniques of female miniaturists from the Netherlands. In *The Art of Limning* from ca. 1600, he marvels about an excellent white color, referring to it as "this whit the women painters usse."[49] Giovanna Garzoni developed a stipple technique during the 1620s that she used to fill her still lifes meticulously with tiny dots, creating irregular patterns that enhance their naturalistic effects. Rosalba Carriera likewise experimented with miniatures. At the beginning of her career, she decorated snuffboxes made of ivory. Soon she began to remove the plates from the boxes, and she became the first artist to paint independent miniature portraits on ivory, so called *fondelli* or *ritrattini*,[50] developing a technique that fully exploited the warm, natural coloring of the white ivory plate. Many other miniaturists in the eighteenth century, men and women, followed her lead and started to paint portraits on ivory. After 1700 Carriera also systematically experimented with unusually small formats in pastel painting. Although small-scale pastel work was sporadically practiced before her, Carriera was the first artist to make intimately sized pastels internationally fashionable.[51] And because she practiced miniatures and pastels simultaneously for many years, she was lauded for her artistic range.[52]

Her contemporaries Giovanna Fratellini in Florence and Teresa del Pò in Naples also made small-scale pictures and pastels their trademarks, using these media in their rise to fame in Italy and beyond. These women not only practiced but excelled in the dynamic artistic field of small works.[53]

Small Works as Vehicles of Self-Promotion

During her stay in Paris from 1720 to 1721, Rosalba Carriera ironically lamented that she envied men for nothing except their ability to travel easily.[54] Although Carriera enjoyed the liberty of travel throughout her life, most women did not. Generally duty-bound to their homes, they were far less mobile than their male peers.[55] Working in small formats may have been a strategy in response to these restrictions, for not only were small works suited to home production, they were also relatively easy to dispatch across great distances, and thus became vehicles for establishing bonds between women and far-flung patrons.[56]

The first woman who fully exploited the portability and utility of small portraits was Sofonisba Anguissola.[57] In her enigmatic *Self-Portrait* from ca. 1556, now in the Museum of Fine Arts, Boston, the Latin inscription states that she painted the portrait "at Cremona" (cat. 2).[58] Because of this explicit mention of her hometown, Sylvia Ferino-Pagden's belief that the painting was meant for an outside recipient is likely correct.[59] This precious, small medallion must have stimulated vivid conversations about its subject when held in the hand or worn as a piece of jewelry. Indeed, contemporaries marveled at Anguissola's jewel-like portraits and referred to them as "marvelous oddities."[60] Anguissola used similar small portraits, offered as gifts, to introduce herself to potential patrons in North Italy and beyond.[61] During the 1550s she sent self-portraits to the courts of the d'Este in Ferrara, the Gonzaga in Mantua, and the Farnese in Parma and Piacenza, and her image campaign achieved its ultimate success when King Philip II (1527–1598) invited her in 1559 to join the Spanish court.[62] Anguissola's example clearly inspired other women artists. When Lavinia Fontana was asked by the Dominican friar and collector Alonso Chacón (1540–1599) to send him a small self-portrait in 1578, she explicitly referred to Anguissola's portraits in her correspondence with him.[63] Moreover, by choosing a small circular format and presenting herself as an elegantly dressed scholar in the painting she sent, Fontana closely emulated Anguissola's earlier self-portraits (fig. 5).[64]

Beginning around 1500, exchanges of portraits became more common among artists throughout Europe. One example is Sofonisba Anguissola's portrait of the miniaturist Giulio Clovio, whom she may have met in 1556 at the court of Ottavio Farnese (1524–1586) and his wife Margaret of Parma (1522–1586)

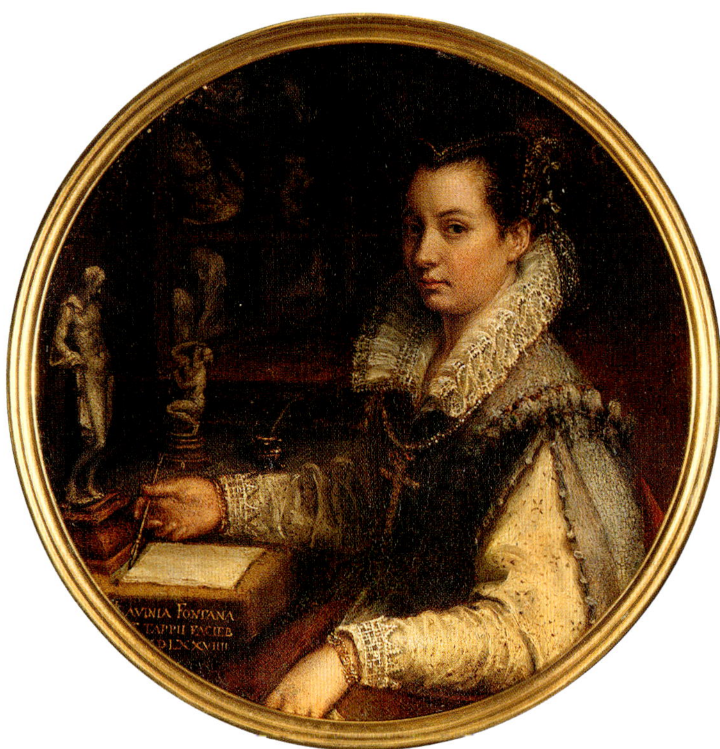

FIGURE 5 Lavinia Fontana, *Self-Portrait in a Studio*, 1579, oil on copper, diameter: 6⁵⁄₁₆ in. (16 cm). Gallerie degli Uffizi, Florence, 1890.4013

in Piacenza or Parma (fig. 6). In Anguissola's portrait, probably painted in 1556, Clovio sits at a desk and holds a thin brush in his right hand. In his left hand he presents an oval portrait miniature depicting a female figure, holding it in a way that emphasizes a bond of alliance and loyalty between himself and the sitter.[65] In the absence of any information about the painting's early provenance, it is difficult to determine the subject of the miniature portrait; some scholars suggest it is Clovio's friend the English court miniaturist Levina Teerlinc (ca. 1520–1576), and others argue for Anguissola.[66] From Clovio's inventory we know that both artists had given portraits to him, but none have survived. Specifically, an unfinished portrait of Clovio by Anguissola and a "little round box with a portrait of Livinia, miniaturist to the Queen of England" by Teerlinc were listed in Clovio's inventory.[67] Such gifts became critical tools for women to establish and cultivate artistic networks across Europe.

The Role of Courts

In 1621 Giulio Mancini considered miniatures and small paintings to be ideal presents for nobles.[68] Portraits, especially small ones, were particularly useful as they could be gifted by rulers to their peers and subjects.[69] Courtiers often wore medallions as jewelry, and they exchanged them as tokens of friendship. Initially such precious works were locked away in private chambers.[70]

Later they were increasingly displayed in public spaces.[71] The rising demand for small works that began in the fifteenth century attracted painters, illuminators, and miniaturists to courts across Europe.[72] The Tudor court in England, for instance, employed numerous artists, especially from the Low Countries, to produce small works. Among the most famous were Susanna Horenbout and Levina Teerlinc, who were highly paid and excelled at portraits of court members. From Teerlinc's arrival in England in 1547, she served various kings and queens from Henry VIII (1491–1547) to Elizabeth I (1533–1603).[73]

The Spanish court was more important to Italian artists. Due to dynastic connections across Europe, the ruling Habsburgs employed a vast group of international artists, several of whom were women who worked in small formats.[74] The most famous was Sofonisba Anguissola, who joined the court in 1559 at the invitation of King Philip II and served in the households of queens Elisabeth of Valois (1545–1568) and Anna of Austria (1549–1580). In Madrid Anguissola taught painting and completed numerous portraits, large and small.[75] Artists who specialized in small-scale works were highly regarded in Italian courts as well. The Medici in Florence, the Savoy in Turin, and the Della Rovere in Urbino all employed miniaturists. Numerous women artists became members of the Medici court throughout the seventeenth century.[76] Supported by the archduchess, the young artist Arcangela Paladini (1599–1622) came under the tutelage of Jacopo Ligozzi (1547–1627), a celebrated court painter and miniaturist.[77] Her first work for the Medici was a miniature, painted in 1612, using precious ultramarine pigment given to her by the court.[78] Other artists working in small format, such as Giovanna Garzoni, Camilla Guerrieri Nati (1628–after 1694), and Giovanna Fratellini, found employment at the Medici court in the following years.

At the same time, small-scale painting became a popular pastime among noblewomen at courts, where the boundaries between professional women artists and amateurs were remarkably fluid. Many aristocratic women collected, patronized, and painted small works—activities regarded as appropriate for women of honor.[79] Ulrika Eleonora, queen of Sweden (1688–1741), Marie Louise d'Orléans, queen of Spain (1662–1689), and Maria Christina, archduchess of Austria (1742–1798) (fig. 7), to name just a few, painted miniatures and pastels. This courtly practice greatly contributed to the fashion for small objects during the seventeenth and eighteenth centuries.

In addition to cultivating a taste for small precious objects, courts were intellectual forums in which the role of women in society and their equality to men were frequent points of discussion.[80] As Christina Strunck observed, these debates coincided with the employment of the first women artists in courts, starting in the mid-sixteenth century. According to Strunck, courts

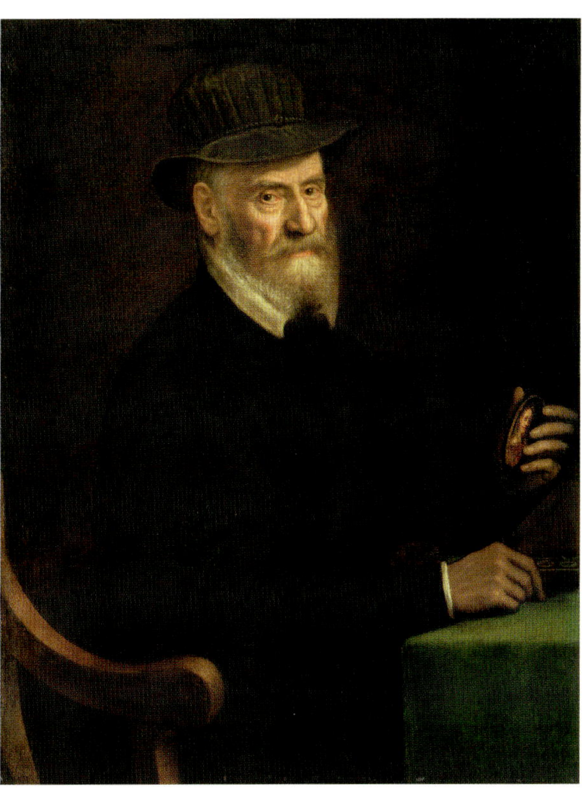

FIGURE 6 Sofonisba Anguissola, *Giulio Clovio*, ca. 1556, oil on canvas, 38½ × 29½ in. (98 × 75 cm). Private collection, Rome

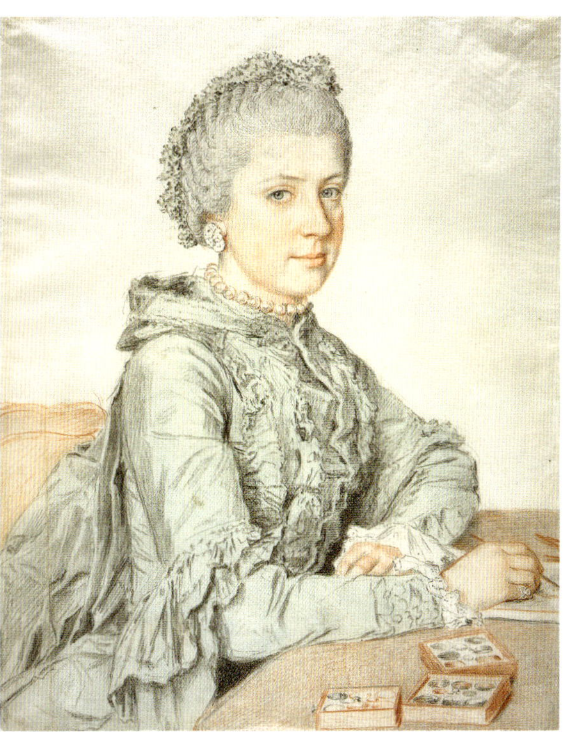

FIGURE 7 Jean-Étienne Liotard (Swiss, 1702–1789), *Portrait of Archduchess Maria Christina Habsburg*, 1762, black and red chalk, graphite pencil, watercolor, and watercolor glaze on thin paper, heightened with color on the verso, 12½ × 10¼ in. (32 × 26 cm). Musée d'Art et d'Histoire, Geneva, 1947-0038

had a positive influence on women artists in general and, we can add, especially on artists working in small formats.[81] Service at court helped women to avoid oversight by male dominated guilds. Nevertheless, many women were widely regarded as mere "ornaments" who contributed to the fame and reputation of courts.[82] All too often, their artistic aspirations were secondary to their duty to engage with their mistresses.[83] The most prestigious commissions at courts were traditionally reserved for male artists, and women often worked in genres that were considered less important, such as portraits, flowers, and still lifes.[84] Perhaps due to these limitations, some women, such as Rosalba Carriera, declined offers to join courts. Nevertheless, to a small group of female artists, courts offered valuable training, exposure, and connections to international patrons.

A Strategy for Success?

Contemporaries looked through gendered lenses at artists in early modern Europe, and scale played an important role in their judgments. With its vivid critique of one altar panel by Lavinia Fontana, Giovanni Baglione's (1566–1643) description of contemporaneous artists' lives, first printed in Rome in 1642, provides a case study for male bias.[85] While Baglione concedes that Fontana produced fine portraits, he forcefully criticizes her monumental *Stoning of Saint Stephen* altarpiece painted for the Roman church of San Paolo fuori le Mura (Saint Paul Outside the Walls) in 1604 (now destroyed).[86] According to Baglione, the painting suffered from severe weaknesses in the design of what must have been larger-than-life figures (cat. 19).[87] Baglione's condemnation of Fontana's ambitious work was echoed later by the critic Giuseppe Maria Mazzolari (1712–1786), who stated that Fontana's large history paintings are typical for a woman artist "who has left the usual path and all that which is suitable to their hands and fingers."[88] One term proved to be particularly effective in denigrating the work of women artists among contemporaries: *un mano donnesca* ("a womanly hand") was used by numerous critics to describe a delicate, diligently executed, and highly finished style, as discussed by Fredrika Jacobs.[89] It implies a slow working process, produced mechanically rather than spontaneously. The opposite is a vigorous style, painted with a loaded brush. Although both men and women could employ a "womanly style," the term was used by art critics to diminish the work of women in particular.[90]

Critics such as Baglione may have been incensed by the growing success of women in a realm that was traditionally controlled by male artists.[91] Large works of art presenting religious, mythological, and historical scenes intended to elevate the public stood traditionally at the pinnacle of the arts. Male critics and artists defended this type of painting as their territory. Small

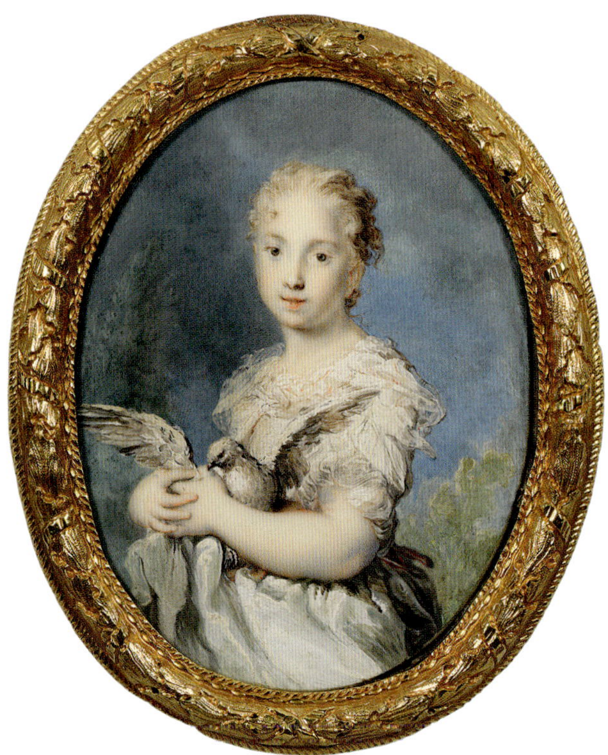

FIGURE 8 Rosalba Carriera, *Allegory of Innocence (Fanciulla con colombe)*, gouache and watercolor on ivory, 5⅝₁₆ × 3¹⁵⁄₁₆ in. (15 × 10 cm). Accademia Nazionale di San Luca, Rome

works in genres such as portraits and flower paintings, produced mostly for private enjoyment, were probably considered less threatening, and consequently were largely exempt from criticism. In 1568 the antiquarian Ercole Basso (dates unknown) described a "little picture" by Lavinia Fontana in his collection as being made "carefully" ("molto diligente"), and "as the work of a woman, praiseworthy."[92] Likewise, when Giambologna (1529–1608), the court sculptor of the Medici, saw Fontana's small painting *Vision of Saint Hyacinth* in Florence in 1599, he commented, "No painter, neither great or small, has failed to stop to see it . . . it has astounded and amazed everyone."[93] Despite its small size, he extolled its "great majesty." It seems that as long as women artists restricted themselves to small works, they were not criticized, and they were even celebrated for their patience, diligence, and grace.[94]

Indeed, small, polished, "jewel-like" works of art were considered a manifestation of self-control, and the virtues assigned to the creation of these objects may explain the success of the women who made them. When working on a small picture, the artist needed to keep not just the workspace tidy and clean, but herself as well, as dandruff, for example, could mar the wet surface of the work. The painting process needed to be methodical and thorough since correcting a mistake in a miniature is famously difficult, if not impossible. Moreover, the work required a high degree of coordination and control, as the artist needed to be keenly aware of her breathing when she set down the tip of a brush to paint a dot or tiny line. As laid out in numerous contemporaneous treatises, such perfect control of the body demonstrated a high degree of self-discipline and self-awareness, and to be in control of the self was one of the most respected virtues for men and women alike from the Renaissance to the Baroque period.[95] While small-scale works lack the fanfare and éclat of large-scale works, the very absence of these qualities may explain why women chose to work small. Such works exude a sense of privacy, discretion, and to a certain degree humbleness, traits that were perfectly aligned with larger societal expectations of women in early modern Italy and beyond.

Specializing in small works seems to have provided a solid pathway to success for women who sought official recognition. A comparison with memberships of leading art academies, which largely disadvantaged women, confirms this. Among the few women who were admitted to them, those who worked in small formats played an important, if not dominant, role.[96] According to its secretary Giuseppe Ghezzi (1634–1721), the Roman Accademia di San Luca admitted sixteen women as members from its inception until 1695.[97] About half of them worked in small formats.[98] In 1705, Rosalba Carriera was accepted as a full female member.[99] She had applied with her *Allegory of Innocence*, a miniature painted on a small piece of ivory, which was particularly admired by the president of the academy, the painter Carlo Maratti (1625–1713), who commented on the difficulty of the subject and the artist's innovative white-on-white technique (fig. 8).[100] In the following years, the artists Maria Felice Tibaldi (1707–1770), Veronica Stern Telli (1717–1801), Caterina Cherubini (1730–1811), and Theresa Concordia Maron (1725–1806), all miniaturists as well, joined Carriera as members of the academy.[101] By 1796, the academy had fourteen female members.[102] Remarkably, only women were listed as miniaturists, and the majority of female accademicians practiced at small scale.[103]

Diminutive work was a niche market in the arts from 1500 to 1800. During this time, especially in Italy, women contributed significantly to the production of small paintings, miniatures, and other types of small artworks, a largely unregulated segment of the art world. Such objects allowed women to practice, to experiment, and to compete with each other and with their male peers. One might even say that small works afforded women artists liberties they otherwise did not have. Small works produced by women did not openly question patriarchal hierarchies; instead, they subtly expanded female possibilities. Indeed, while coveted by collectors and lauded by art critics, such small works reinforced existing gender prejudices in the nineteenth century.

NOTES

*I would like to warmly thank Janna Israel for her steady assistance and her insightful contributions to this essay.

1. Sofonisba Anguissola probably gifted this portrait to Ercole II d'Este, the Duke of Ferrara (1508–1559). On the painting and its date see Cole 2019b, 166, cat. 14. On Anguissola's self-fashioning see the fundamental essay Garrard 1994, 556–622.

2. See, for instance, Caterina van Hemessen's *Self-Portrait at the Easel*, 1548, oil on oak panel, 12³⁄₁₆ × 9¹⁵⁄₁₆ in. (32.2 × 25.2 cm), Kunstmuseum Basel. The vast majority of Anguissola's self-portraits measure less than 20 inches (ca. 50 cm). The same is true for Lavinia Fontana's self-portraits. See also Artemisia Gentileschi's now-lost *Allegory of Painting*, ca. 1609, oil on panel, which according to Mann, who saw it, was about 8 to 9 inches. Illustrated and discussed in Mann 2016, 15. The young Giovanna Garzoni portrayed herself in small format as well; see her *Self-Portrait as Apollo*, ca. 1618–1620, tempera on vellum, 16½ × 13 in. (42 × 33 cm), Segretario della Repubblica, Palazzo del Quirinale, Rome, inv. ODP 758. For Rosalba Carriera see Sani 2007, who lists twelve self-portraits by the artist. While Carriera occasionally worked at life size, she painted the vast majority of her pastel self-portraits in small sizes of about 15¾ × 11¹³⁄₁₆ in. (40 × 30 cm). Jeffares lists some thirty pastel self-portraits by her, among them replicas and possible works by students. The popular motif of a woman working on a small subject occurs for the first time in self-portraits by Caterina van Hemessen (1528– after 1565) and Sofonisba Anguissola in the mid-sixteenth century. For later examples see Giovanna Fratellini, *Self-Portrait*, ca. 1720, pastel on paper, 28⅜ × 22⁷⁄₁₆ in. (72 × 57 cm), Gallerie degli Uffizi, Florence, 1890.2064 (Barker, "Art as Women's Work," fig. 4); Anna Bacherini Piattoli, *Self-Portrait at the Age of Fifty-Six*, 1776, oil on canvas, 30¹³⁄₁₆ × 23⅝ in. (78.2 × 60 cm), Gallerie degli Uffizi, Florence, inv. 1890 no. 2032 (cat. 62).

3. "Today we tend to look at small objects more casually than we look at larger but that habit is unhistorical since the creative process was essentially the same in both." Pope-Hennessy 1989, 21; Honig 2016, 4–5.

4. One of the roots of this prejudice towards small works can be found in Michelangelo (1475–1564), who stated that he preferred to work in fresco instead of oil painting, which he considered "women's work." See Cole 2019b, 67.

5. Quoted after Woods-Marsden 1998, 196.

6. Leon Battista Alberti (1404–1472) encouraged artists to work at life size. On Alberti and Vasari's term "gran maniera," see Smith 1964, 396. According to Antoine-Joseph Dézallier d'Argenville's *Abrégé de la vie des plus fameux peintres* (1781), a female friend advised Rosalba Carriera to give up painting large pictures in oil for miniatures, as they were "more appropriate for her sex." Dézallier d'Argenville, "The Life Story of Rosalba Carriera," trans. and ed. in Dabbs 2009, 344–47.

7. Contemporaneous miniature manuals often addressed a female readership. Catherine Perrot (ca. 1620–after 1693) dedicated her treatise to the Princess de Guimenée. Perrot 1693, frontispiece.

8. Germaine Greer offers an exception. See Greer 1979, 104–14. While he did not address matters of scale, Omar Calabrese raised the question of why there were so many self-portraits painted by women during the early phases of their careers. By pointing to the scale of many of these portraits, this essay hopes to give one answer. Calabrese 2006, 216. See also Woods-Marsden 1998, 187–222.

9. I follow Ann Bermingham in her case study of Elizabethan miniatures. Bermingham 2000, 21.

10. Bauman 1998, 37–42; Sani 1981, 385–417. Compare with entries "minutezza, minuzia, minute" in Grassi and Pepe 1994, 529.

11. Small objects were called *minuterie*. In the English-speaking world, the term "cabinet pictures" became popular during the seventeenth century.

12. Vasari used this comparison when he described a small oil painting. He also called the miniaturist Clovio "eccelente miniatore o vogliamo dire dipintore di cose piccole" (an "eccellent miniaturist or, shall we say, a painter of small things"). Both quotes in Smith 1964, 398 and 399.

13. "(. . .) la maniera del gran miniature D. Giulio Clovio, che l'ha fatta risplendere egualmente come la pittura (. . .)." Lomazzo 1844, vol. 2, 382. Quoted after Smith 1964, 395. See also Braesel 2009, 23.

14. Garzoni 1605, ch. 91, 669–76.

15. "Della miniature poi basta sol dire ch' è una pittura piccolo (. . .)" in Mancini 1956–1957, vol. 1, 84.

16. "Limning, a thing apart . . . which excelleth all other painting whatsoever." The English miniaturist Nicholas Hilliard used the term limning for painting miniatures in his treatise from ca. 1600. Quoted in Coombs 2005, 7. Similarly, the Italian art historian Filippo Baldinucci defined miniatures as different from oil paintings in 1681. According to him, they were small objects, painted with watercolors. "Miniare: Dipignere con acquerelli cose piccolo in su la cartapecora, o bambagina, servendosi del bianco della carta in vece di biacca, per i lumi della pittura." See Baldinucci 1975, vol. 2, 337.

17. For an excellent discussion of miniature painting in seventeenth- and eighteenth-century Florence, see Acanfora 2014, 23–37.

18. Sani 1981, 387.

19. The inventory of Nicola Cardinale, Naples, from 1716 lists seventeen "Miniature di pastello" by del Pò. See Jeffares 2020e.

20. Letter Pierre Crozat to Rosalba Carriera, January 20, 1720. Quoted and discussed in Sani 1981, 400.

21. Pliny the Elder 2004, 336.

22. See Giovanni Boccaccio, *De claris mulieribus*, written 1361–1362. On its influence on Renaissance women artists, see Schweikhart 1992, 125.

23. If women entered guilds and confraternities in the Low Countries, they were illuminators. See Reynolds 2003, 22.

24. Guicciardini 1588, 129.

25. "Ist ein gross Wunder, das ein weibs bild also viel machen soll." Quoted after van der Stighelen 1999, 34.

26. Woods-Marsden 1998, 216. Woods-Marsden also suspects that it was Fontana's future father-in-law who commissioned the picture. Fontana describes herself as a virgin in the inscription: "LAVINIA VIRGO PROSPERI FONTANAE/ FILIA EX SPECVLO IMAGINEM/ORIS SVI EXPRESIT ANNO/MDLXXVII."

27. Maria Teresa Cantaro noted that Fontana produced numerous small-scale paintings during the early part of her career. Cantaro 1993, 86.

28. Hufton 1998, 73.

29. Ajmar-Wollheim 2006, 152–53; Wiesner-Hanks 2016, 121.

30. Compare with Fontana's *Self-Portrait*, 1579, oil on copper, diameter: 6⁵⁄₁₆ in. (16 cm), Gallerie degli Uffizi, Florence (fig. 5).

31. Chadwick 1990, 104–26.

32. See Bohn 2004b, 240.

33. Hamburger 1997.

34. Fratellini offers a fascinating case study for artists who received an education at court. Miniature painting was exclusively taught to female members of the Medici court. Male artists who had specialized in small works played an important role in teaching and educating young women. In Fratellini's case, the Medici provided Ippolito Galantini (1627–1706), a skilled painter who taught Fratellini miniature painting. As noted by the contemporary critic Francesco Moücke— Galantini "strove to teach her [Fratellini/O.T.] the precepts not of a simple dilettante, but on the contrary to make of her an expert professional." Quoted in Dabbs 2009, 311.

35. Wassyng Roworth 1997, 43–45.

36. See Sutherland Harris 1976, 26.

37. Quoted in Gerhard and Simon 1901, 101.

38. Sutherland Harris notes that Lama drew from life models. Sutherland Harris 1976, 26–27. A large corpus of drawings by the Neapolitan painter Angela Maria Beinaschi (1666–1746) may have survived in Düsseldorf. See Grisolia 2019, 155–219.

39. Numerous male artists, including Titian (1488/90–1576), Baccio Bandinelli (1488–1560), and Alessandro Allori (1535–1607), represented themselves as draftsmen in their self-portraits. See Woods-Marsden 1998, 225–33. To my knowledge, only Lavinia Fontana preceded Rosalba Carriera, with her depiction as a draftswoman in 1579 (fig. 5).

40. On the role of drawings in Carriera's artistic practice see Sani 2007, 48. Sani lists thirteen surviving drawings in her catalogue of Carriera's works.

41. Merry E. Wiesner-Hanks points out that embroidery became increasingly identified as feminine between 1500 and 1800. Wiesner-Hanks 2016, 177–78. Compare with Speelberg 2015, 39–46.

42. Cole 2019b, 77. Sutherland Harris saw embroidery as nothing more than a "background to the later emergence of women painters." Sutherland Harris 1976, 17. This view is changing, however, and the intersection of embroidery and the arts has become more recognized. See Bauman 1998, 231–32, n. 57; Jacobs 1997b, 107.

43. Primarosa 2014, 145–61.

44. De Girolami Cheney 2017, 225–52.

45. Rabiner 1984, 16–22.

46. Bernardo De Dominici, "The Life Story of Teresa del Pò," trans. and ed. in Dabbs 2009, 257–59, esp. 257.

47. For Carriera's career and work, see Sani 2007.

48. For more about the artist, see Fortunati and Graziani 2008.

49. Quoted in James 2016, 295.

50. Falconi 2008, 19.

51. For an overview of the sizes of Carriera's pastels, see Burns 2007, 109, fig. 52. For the impact of Carriera's pastels in France, see Shelley 2011, 5.

52. See, for instance, Dézallier d'Argenville's description of Carriera's success in Paris 1720/21. Dézallier d'Argenville, "The Life Story of Rosalba Carriera," in Dabbs 2009, 344–47, esp. 346–47.

53. Male artists specialized in miniatures and pastels (and oil painting) as well during the eighteenth century. The best-known artists are the Swiss Jean-Étienne Liotard (1702–1789) and the German Anton Raphael Mengs (1728–1779).

54. "Je n'envie la condition des hommes que pour un seul point, c'est qu'ils peuvent voyager à leur gré." Quoted after Giovanni Vianelli in Gerhard and Simon 1901, 100.

55. Wiesner-Hanks 2016, 180.

56. Contemporaries noticed the mobile character of small artworks, as Giulio Mancini did for miniatures in 1621. See Mancini 1956–1957, vol. 1, 84.

57. Sofonisba Anguissola produced more self-portraits than any other artist after Albrecht Dürer (1471–1528) and before Rembrandt (1606–1669), as Sutherland Harris has noted. Sutherland Harris 1976, 27.

58. "Sophonisba Angussola vir(go)/ipsius manu ex (s)peculo depictam cremonae" ("The virgin Sofonisba Anguissola, depicted by her own hand, from a mirror, at Cremona").

59. Ferino-Pagden 1995, 62.

60. See King 1995, 387.

61. As the Anguissola family stemmed from the lower nobility, they could not introduce themselves directly to a princely family. Sending a gift was a shrewd way to circumvent these societal restrictions. On this strategy see Strunck 2017, 22–23.

62. See Madrid 2019, 139.

63. See letter Lavinia Fontana to Alonso Chacón May 1579, in Cantaro 1989, 306.

64. Unlike Anguissola, however, Fontana shows herself as a scholar and humanist in this self-portrait.

65. Cole 2019b, 37. Compare with Christadler 2000, 197.

66. There is no surviving portrait of Teerlinc. Nevertheless, Wied hesitantly identifies it as a portrait of Teerlinc. Wied 1995a, 81. On this discussion see most recently Docampo 2019, 123.

67. A picture of Saint Ursula by Anguissola was listed as well. See Docampo 2019, 123. For Teerlinc's relationship with Clovio, see also James 2016, 306–8.

68. Quoted in Barocchi 1979, 42.

69. Small portraits were also used in the construction of genealogical trees.

70. Pointon 2001, 48–71.

71. The Tribuna Gallery in the Uffizi in Florence is arguably the best-known example.

72. Strunck 2017, 20–37; Wiesner-Hanks 2016, 163–67.

73. In addition to painting portraits, Teerlinc may have composed the very first treatise on miniatures during her stay at the English court. James 2016, 287–333.

74. In addition to Sofonisba Anguissola, the Flemish artists Caterina van Hemessen and Caterine Haensen and the Spanish artist Isabel Sánchez Coello (1564–1612) worked at the Spanish court during the second half of the sixteenth century. They specialized in small paintings and miniatures.

75. Pérez de Tudela 2019a, 53–69.

76. On the taste for miniatures at the Medici court, see Meloni Trkulja 1979, 1167–71; Fumagalli 2020, 54–61.

77. On these artists see Goldenberg Stoppato 2016, 88; and Bauman 1998, 364.

78. Bauman 1998, 364.

79. For a comparison with Dutch amateur women artists, see Honig, 2001–2002, 31–39. See also the research of Charlotte Guichard on female amateurs, for instance, Guichard 2015, 80–89.

80. Wiesner-Hanks 2016, 157–67.

81. Strunck 2017, 24–27.

82. Strunck 2017, 25.

83. Anguissola, for instance, served as lady-in-waiting to the Spanish queens Elisabeth of Valois and Anna of Austria from 1559 to 1573. She primarily lived with the queen, traveled with her, and joined her for festivities. Soon after her introduction to the future queen in early 1560, Anguissola gave Elisabeth her first lessons in the arts. In the following years Anguissola painted numerous portraits of the royal family. See Pérez de Tudela 2019a, 53–69.

84. Strunck 2017, 26.

85. Baglione 1733.

86. "(. . .) E vi dipinse la Lapidazione di S. Stefano Protomartire con quantità di figure, e con una Gloria nell' alto, che rappresenta I Cieli apperti, be' egli è vero, che, per esser le figure maggiori del naturale, si conduse, e sì felicemente, come pensava, non riuscisse (. . .)." Baglione 1733, 136.

87. "(. . .) Poichè è gran differenza da quadro ordinario a machine di quella grandezza, che spaventano ogni grand' ingegno." Baglione 1733, 136.

88. Quoted in Jacobs 1997b, 91.

89. Jacobs 1997b, 85–122.

90. Sohm 1995, 759–808.

91. Over the course of her career, Fontana painted many religious pictures, large and small, without provoking negative judgments.

92. Quoted in Jacobs 1997b, 105.

93. Quoted in Jacobs 1997b, 95.

94. Sohm 1995, 793–98.

95. Elias 1969. Regarding the control of one's emotions in early modern Europe, see Matzat 2001, 151–64.

96. For example, the French Académie Royale admitted only fifteen women in the course of its history (1648–1793). About half of them worked in small formats, often having been trained as miniaturists. Baetjer 2016, 33–45.

97. For the list see Ghezzi 1696, 42.

98. The artists who worked occasionally or consistently in small formats are Lavinia Fontana, Virginia da Vezzo (1600–1638), Giovanna Garzoni (1600–1670), Anna Maria Vaiani (1604–ca. 1655), Teresa del Pò (1649–1713), Teresa Raimondi Velli (active 1690s). I was not able to find information about the works of Countess Laura Marescotti and Maria Rospigliosi, Countess of Zagarola. They may have been honorable members. Another list, Nomi delle SS. Pittrici Accademiche, undated, but written after 1706, includes the additional names of the otherwise obscure Sig. ra Oligiani miniatrice and Rosalba Carriera; see Lukehart 2020, 102–3.

99. On the different levels of membership at the Roman academy, see Lukehart 2020, 96–105, and S. Barker, "Art as Women's Work," in this volume.

100. Carriera was admitted as *accademica di merito*, a category that indicates her professional status. The back side of the *Allegory of Innocence* miniature bears an inscription written by Maratti, according to Sani 2007, 70; Johns 2003, 20–45. Christian Cole, Carriera's friend and agent, witnessed the moment and described it in a letter to Carriera. According to Cole, Maratti added "Guido Reni would not have been able to do better." See Johns 2003, 44, n. 25.

101. See Johns 2019, 167–71, on Maria Felice Tibaldi.

102. *Statuti* 1796, 52–54.

103. Compare this with other Italian academies, such as Florence's Accademia del Disegno, in which Giovanna Fratellini was listed as a miniaturist in 1706. See S. Barker "Art as Women's Work," in this volume.

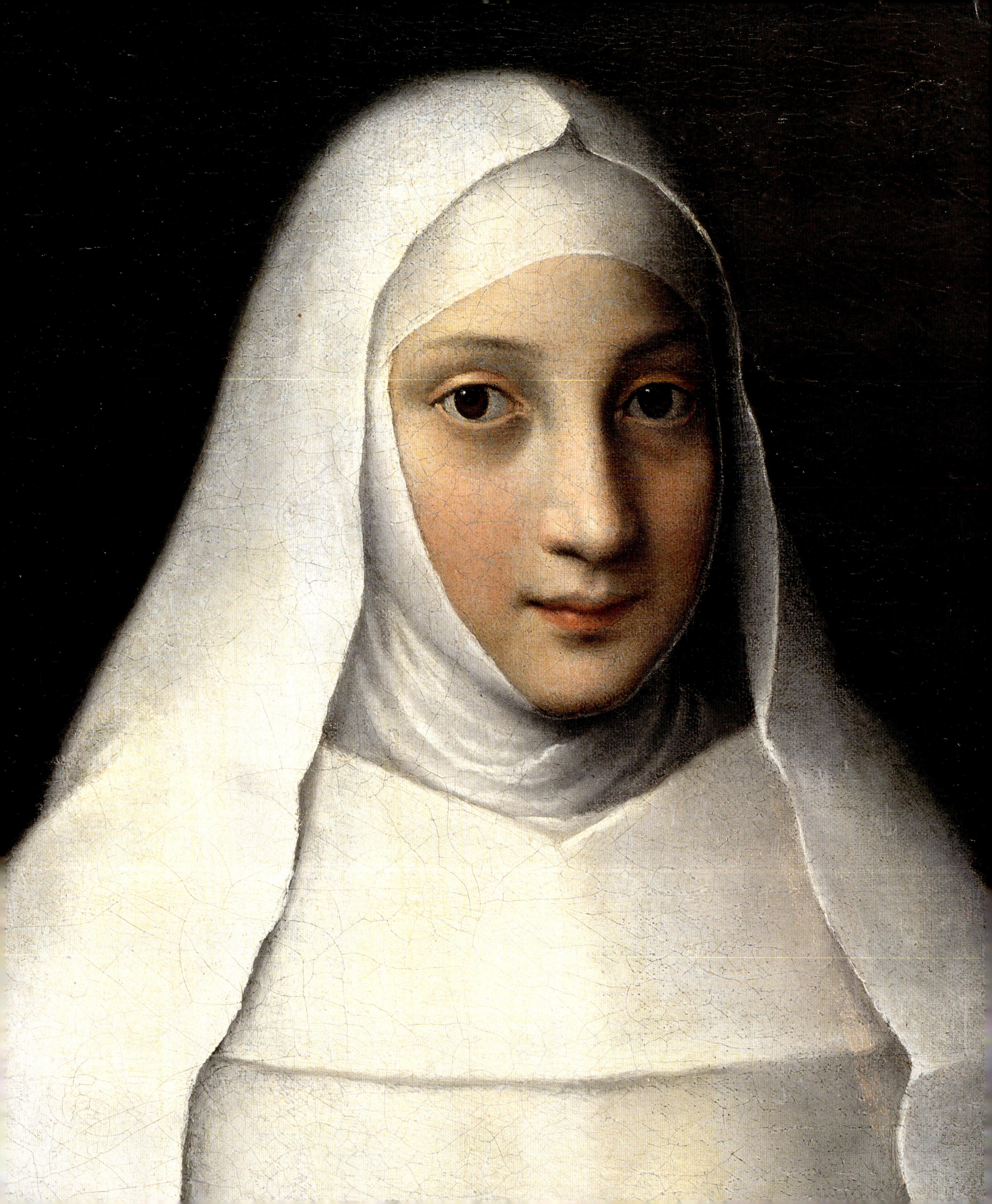

SHEILA BARKER

Art as Women's Work: The Professionalization of Women Artists in Italy, 1350–1800

Defining the Problem

In 1546 Francesco da Sangallo observed that "you must know how many women there are in Flanders and France, and in Italy as well, who paint so well that in Italy their pictures are much appreciated."[1] Indeed, many women made art in early modern Italy, yet only a few gained recognition as professional artists on par with men. When and how did women begin to enter the professional sphere? If few women made this transition, what were the alternative situations in which women made art? And what does the question of the professionalization of women artists mean for the study of early modern art?

Before approaching these questions, we should begin by defining "professional artist," the term on which this investigation hinges. Artists who practiced professionally in early modern Italy generally had attained all or most of the following four requisites: a standard repertory of skills, competencies, and technical knowledge of the sort transmitted in the course of an apprenticeship under a master artist; a workshop space with specialized tools, as well as regular access to art materials and, if possible, assistants to help with manual labor; legal and fiscal operability deriving from such intangibles as credit worthiness, guild membership, and legal autonomy; and, finally, a means of exchanging artistic products for economic benefits, whether in the form of a salaried position, reliable patronage, or access to an art market.

A Gamut of Professional Profiles

Artemisia Gentileschi (1593–1654 or later) met all the conditions of professionalization throughout her long career, both during her marriage and five pregnancies and during the decades that witnessed her estrangement from her husband and her independent widowhood. She received expert training from her father Orazio Gentileschi (1563–1639), himself a professional artist from a long line of artisans. By her early twenties she had her own customized workshop, first located inside her home and later at a significant distance from it. She employed factotums and skilled shop hands beginning in her late teenage years and continuing throughout her life. Based on her dowry (which she controlled, according to a special arrangement), her personal jewelry, and her father-in-law's economic status, Gentileschi enjoyed ample credit, which allowed her to employ assistants and purchase painting materials with flexible payment plans. Moreover, court records show that shortly after she joined the Florentine artists' guild in 1616, she began operating her business with fiscal and legal autonomy.[2] Finally, Gentileschi adroitly navigated the patronage system by making use of brokers and agents to promote her reputation across Europe.[3] In short, her vigorous and enterprising engagement with the business of art was fully in line with the practices of the most consummately professional artists of her era.

Letter writing was vital to the career of any professional artist, but women artists were much less likely to be literate than their male peers. Although as an adolescent Artemisia Gentileschi was reputed to have written love letters, it is certain that she did not receive a formal humanist education. Upon marrying and moving to Florence in 1613, however, she furthered her education by learning the literary hallmarks of the polite discourse that was an essential passkey to the Medici court.[4] In this endeavor she may have been helped along by her Florentine husband, an apothecary named Pierantonio Stiattesi (born 1584), or by one of her elite Florentine patrons, such as the playwright Michelangelo Buonarroti the Younger (ca. 1568–1646). By her mid-twenties Gentileschi had begun to apply herself in earnest to epistolary practices, recognizing them to be a tool for conducting business. Later in life, with patrons scattered around Europe, she relied on written correspondence to cultivate her clients' interest in new commissions, negotiate prices and terms, and obtain the help of intermediaries in making introductions and collecting unpaid debts.

Giovanna Garzoni (1600–1670) and Rosalba Carriera (1673–1757) also made extensive use of written correspondence to manage their affairs and communicate with agents and clients at courts across Europe.[5] Garzoni was even a practiced calligrapher, and the care with which she both composed and penned her letters demonstrates that she valued literacy not only as a pragmatic tool for conducting ordinary business, but as an indicator of the upbringing and gentility that made her suitable company for the highborn women from whom she sought commissions.[6] Two other professional women artists who took pains to be thought of as learned and literate are Lavinia Fontana (1552–1614) and Elisabetta Sirani (1638–1665). In their self-portraits, Fontana (Tostmann, "The Advantages of Painting Small," fig. 5) and Sirani (fig. 1) fashioned themselves as well-educated women by posing in the presence of books, writing materials, antiquities, and other symbols of culture. Both of these artists also painted subjects that exhibited their considerable knowledge of mythology, and Sirani, moreover, distinguished her oeuvre with highly esoteric histories drawn from the books of her father's extensive library.[7] In the eyes of Bologna's wealthy patrician class, this gloss of cultural refinement helped transform Fontana's and Sirani's artistic practices from mere occupational labor into admirable and virtuous displays of talent and intellect.[8]

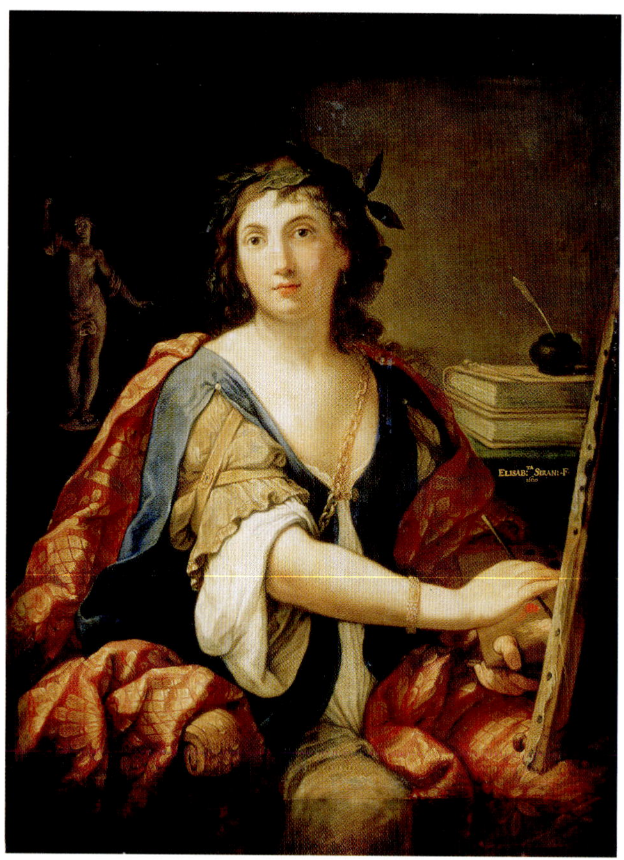

FIGURE 1 Elisabetta Sirani, *Self-Portrait as the Allegory of Painting*, 1658, oil on canvas, 49½ × 33½ in. (114 × 85 cm). Pushkin Museum, Moscow, inv. 70

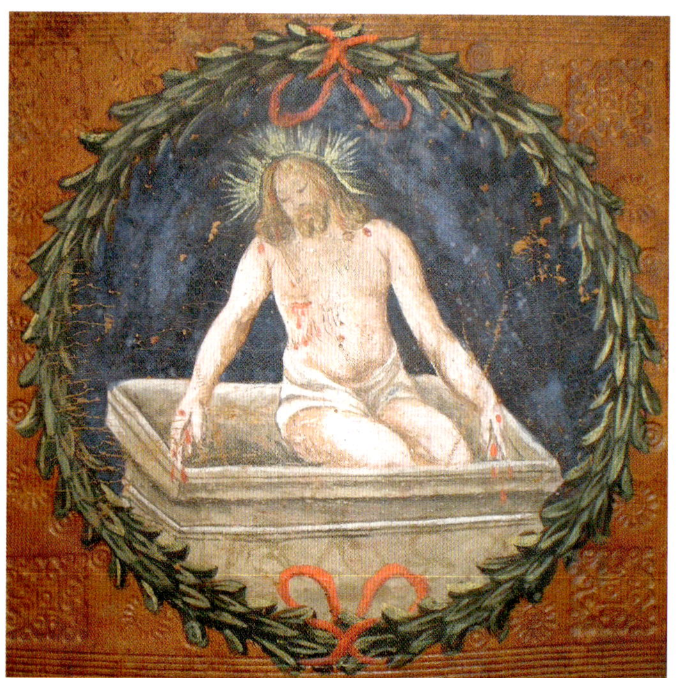

FIGURE 2 Anonymous candlepainter, *Man of Sorrows*, tempera on paper laid down on leather, diameter: 4 in. (10 cm). Archivio dell'Arciconfraternità di San Giovanni dei Fiorentini, Rome, Libri Mastri 385m–387

If literacy and access to European courts characterized several of the most successful professional women artists in Italy, at the other end of the spectrum were women lacking in cultural refinements and adhering only minimally to the professional profile while eking out a living with their art. Costanza Francini (1597–1654), whose name would surely have been forgotten had she not been Artemisia Gentileschi's friend during her youth, painted candles and perhaps book covers for the Roman archconfraternity of San Giovanni dei Fiorentini (fig. 2). She began this work in 1634, shortly after the death of her husband, a painter and miniaturist named Filippo Francini (before 1600–1632), and she continued it until the year of her death. In a groundbreaking study of this obscure artist, Julia Vicioso has suggested that Francini perhaps supplemented her meager annual earnings of two scudi as a candle painter either by serving as a studio model or by providing workshop assistance—something she may well have done in previous years for her husband or for her brother-in-law Agostino Tassi (1578–1644), or even, perhaps, for Artemisia Gentileschi in the 1610s.[9] Another professional candle painter, Sister Beatrice Camelli (active 1615–1616), was paid about one scudo a month by the merchant's court in Florence at the same time that Gentileschi was earning up to one hundred scudi for a single painting for the grand duke.[10] The example of Camelli reminds us that nuns, too, had a stake in the art market, particularly since the cheap and rustic devotional imagery they typically specialized in answered a cross-market demand for small artworks that inspired humility and piety, especially in the wake of the Counter-Reformation.[11]

Italy's First Women Artists: Natura non facit saltum *("Nature does not take leaps")*

In seeking the origins of professional women artists in Italy, we inevitably succumb to the influence of artist and historian Giorgio Vasari's (1511–1574) 1568 edition of the *Lives of the Most Excellent Painters, Sculptors, and Architects* (*Le vite de' più eccellenti pittori, scultori, et architettori*), a work that both illuminates and obfuscates the problem. For the second, updated edition of his popular artist-biographies, Vasari had expanded the sole *vita* dedicated to a woman artist in the previous 1550 edition, namely the Bolognese sculptor Properzia de' Rossi (ca. 1490–1530).[12] Specifically, he folded into her *vita* the short profiles of three additional women artists, each of whom belonged to Vasari's own era: Sofonisba Anguissola (ca. 1535–1625), Plautilla Nelli (1524–1588), and Lucrezia Quistelli (1541–1594).[13] On the one hand, by including the *vite* of these four female practitioners among those of celebrated and esteemed male artists, Vasari's best-selling publication brought unprecedented fame and honor to Italian women artists while firmly establishing their

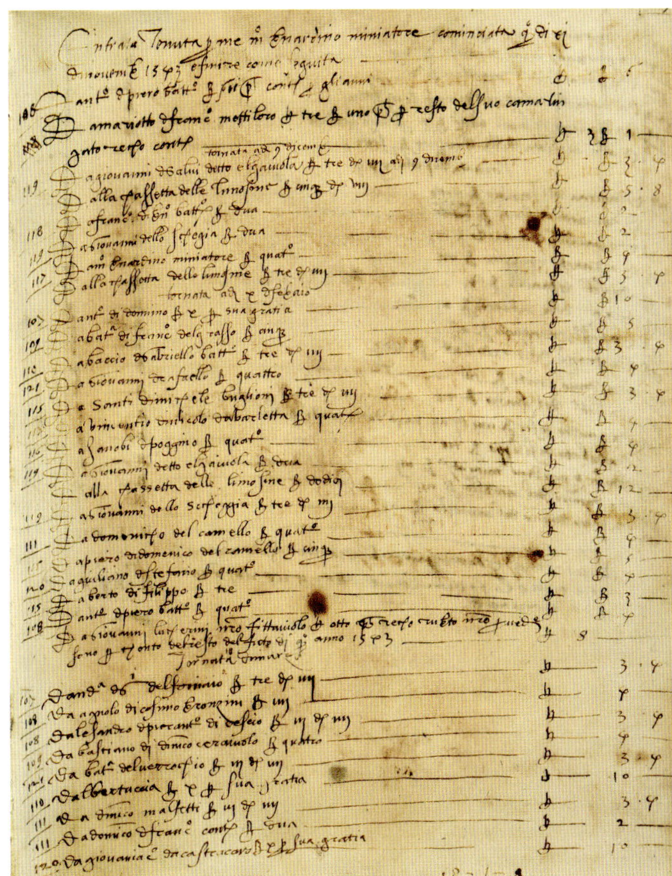

FIGURE 3 Archivo di Stato di Firenze, Accademia del Disegno 4, folio 25 recto

historiographic record for posterity. On the other hand, the publication unintentionally fostered the perception that the history of Italy's women artists began *ex nihil* in the sixteenth century with Properzia de' Rossi.

In truth, women artists had been part of the professional artistic landscape for at least a century and a half before Properzia de' Rossi's lifetime, if not longer. Evidence of this is found in the fourteenth-century statutes of the Compagnia dei Pittori di San Luca, a confraternity for professional painters, miniaturists, and wax-workers in Florence. These medieval statutes, first composed in 1339 upon the confraternity's founding, explicitly sanction the admission of both men and women ("huomini o Donne") to the Compagnia on the same condition, namely that they evince contrition and a willingness to go to confession.[14] Additionally, the confraternity's statutes establish that on the first Sunday of each month, new members would be admitted, with men paying three soldi annually for membership and women a mere two soldi.[15]

Although only a fraction of the matriculation records for the Compagnia dei Pittori di San Luca have survived, we find a woman's name, Albertuccia, listed among those who matriculated on March 10, 1544 (Florentine year 1543), just a few lines away from the record of the Medici court portraitist Agnolo Bronzino (1503–1572) (fig. 3). This Albertuccia is recorded to have paid ten lire "by her grace" ("per sua gratia"), whereas Bronzino paid the lower fee of four lire granted to sons and nephews of older members.[16] When the Florentine Accademia delle Arti del Disegno was established in 1563, women were not specifically mentioned in the founding charter. Nevertheless, their presence at the guild level of this organization can be detected in matriculation lists and other accounting records. For instance, the female doll maker ("fantucciaia") Lisabetta di Michele (dates unknown) matriculated into the Accademia del Disegno in February of 1605, and her payments continue through 1607.[17] Before di Michele officially matriculated, other women had been closely associated with the Florentine artists' academy. Isabella Soldani (dates unknown) gave money to the academy in 1603, as did Maria di Giorgio in 1604, two examples of many women who did so; although the purpose of their payments was not specified in the records, they paid exactly the same amount as male matriculants were charged for membership.

Artemisia Gentileschi, in other words, was not the first woman to gain entrance to Florence's artists' guild. In 1616, more than a decade after the matriculation of Lisabetta di Michele the doll maker, and longer still after the intriguing payments of Isabella Soldani and Maria di Giorgio, Gentileschi matriculated into the Florentine academy for a reduced fee—which, nevertheless, she does not seem to have ever actually paid.[18] She may have been reluctant to join the Florentine academy, for she had already been in the city painting professionally for three years before she visited the Accademia del Disegno, and she never joined the Roman artists academy at all.[19]

While women artists were apparently welcome to partake in the guild functions of Florence's Accademia del Disegno, they did not participate in the institution's governance in the sixteenth and seventeenth centuries, judging from the absence of their names from the lists (*bacheche*) of the votes taken by the regular male *accademici*. Finally, beginning in the second decade of the eighteenth century, professional women artists began to enter all the realms of the Florentine academy from which they had traditionally been excluded. A pathbreaker in this regard was the wellborn court portraitist of the Medici: Giovanna Marmocchini Cortesi Fratellini (1666–1731) (fig. 4). She had matriculated as a "miniatora," or miniaturist, in 1706, paying her annual taxes through 1730; in 1711 she was elected as an "accademico."[20] It is not entirely clear what privileges Fratellini enjoyed thanks to this elevation in status. We might note, however, that Fratellini's student Violante Beatrice Siries Cerroti (1709–1783) was elected "accademico" in 1733, on the day preceding her matriculation. Cerroti at first paid her annual taxes at the rate of her voting and governing male peers; indeed,

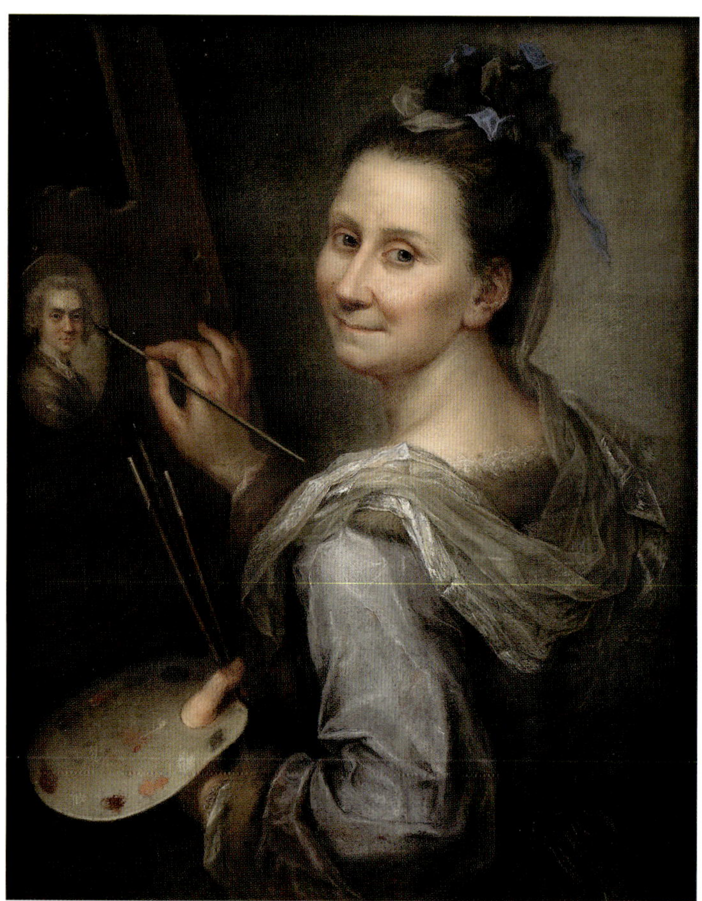

FIGURE 4 Giovanna Fratellini, *Self-Portrait*, ca. 1720, pastel on paper, 28⅜ × 22⁷⁄₁₆ in. (72 × 57 cm). Gallerie degli Uffizi, Florence, 1890.2064

she was allowed to cast her vote, too, as shown by the license she obtained for her husband to serve as her proxy in academy elections.[21] However, beginning in 1738, she started paying a lower tax rate for a type of membership that did not include the right to hold office, as indicated by the phrase "era inabile al godimento degl'uffizi" ("she was ineligible for the benefit of offices") next to her payments from 1738 through 1760.[22] It seems logical to assume that this change was in accordance with her own wishes, and that she preferred to renounce the option of holding office (if that option was ever in fact available to her) because it allowed her to save money.

Perhaps not coincidentally, Fratellini, Cerroti, and other Florentine women artists assumed their prominent standing in the Accademia delle Arti del Disegno at the same time that noblewomen like Marchesa Cassandra Capponi Riccardi (1653–1723) and Medici Grand Duchess Violante Beatrice of Bavaria (1673–1631) began lending their works to this institution's semi-annual art exhibitions. The works that Violante loaned to the exhibition of 1715 included the first by women artists to have ever been displayed in these public events. This important milestone was achieved with Violante's loans of paintings by the Lombard floral still-life specialist Margherita Caffi (1647–1710) that had been commissioned by a previous Medici grand duchess, Vittoria della Rovere (1622–1695), and three pastel portraits by Fratellini. Women artists were particularly well represented in the exhibition of 1729, which featured eighteen works by four women artists: one each by Rosalba Carriera and Maria Maddalena Gozzi Baldacci (1718–1782), four by Giovanna Fratellini, and eleven by a cloistered Florentine nun, Sister Teresa Berenice Vitelli (1687–1738).[23]

The situation of professional woman artists at the artists' academy in Rome, known as the Accademia di San Luca, developed along a somewhat different trajectory between its founding in 1577 and the eighteenth century. For one thing, there is a complete absence of matriculation payment records for professional women artists throughout the sixteenth and seventeenth centuries, suggesting they did not fall within the scope of the institution's guild-level functions. Nevertheless, quite early on, beginning in 1607, the Accademia di San Luca began officially granting women a nominal place in the institution as "accademiche di merito," perhaps in order to associate their collective body with such famous and successful women artists as Lavinia Fontana. This "accademica di merito" status was an honorific; it did not allow women to participate in the meetings, but it did give them unspecified "privileges of membership." In his recent study, Peter Lukehart hypothesized that the "accademiche di merito" status held by professional women artists at the Accademia di San Luca was probably similar to that of amateur noblemen who joined this association as "accademici d'onore," so perhaps women *accademiche* could attend lessons even though there is no specific evidence of this happening.[24]

What is notable under these circumstances is that Rome's professional women artists made voluntary donations to the Accademia di San Luca that were not tethered to any formally defined privilege, beginning in 1638 with Caterina Ginnasi (1590–1660) and followed by Giovanna Garzoni, Plautilla Bricci (1616–1705), Caterina Vaiana (dates unknown), Caterina Catani (active 1664–1672), and others.[25] More study is required to understand the motivations behind these women's voluntary donations, but at least in Garzoni's case, it seems that as a former court artist living alone with no surviving family and no workshop assistants, she used donations as a means of entering into rapport with a community of professional peers for the sake of friendships, support networks, and stimulating conversations.[26]

Although the matriculation of women artists into artists' guilds and confraternities is a strong indicator of their participation in the professional sphere, their absence from the matriculation records cannot be correlated with their alienation from the professional sphere. Archival research has proven the latter point: in 1427, for example, when no women artists were matriculated in the Florentine guild records, several were registered as painters ("pittrici") in that year's census (*catasto*).[27] From data like this, we may reasonably assume that many Italian women artists over the centuries worked professionally without matriculating in guilds.

The explanation of why this occurred speaks to the larger issue of women's labor history. Beginning in the fourteenth century, women's rate of matriculation in the artisanal guilds across Europe began to drop, yet women continued to work in similar numbers.[28] Whereas this decline was formerly attributed to efforts to cast women out of guilds through exclusionary tactics, historians now widely agree that late medieval and early modern women may have deliberately avoided joining guilds, probably to save money and time, and to skirt requirements that could cut into their profit margins, productivity, employment opportunities, and market shares.[29] In Italy, female artisans frequently viewed guilds and their strict codes as a threat to their business practices, and both they and the captains of industry regarded their unregulated labor as a great economic asset.[30] If economic concerns dissuaded many women artists from joining guilds and early art academies, they were not alone: male artists often shared their reluctance, although they were not always able to escape the legal reach of guild regulations. In Florence in the year 1632, for instance, only half of the city's male artists belonged to the Accademia del Disegno, and in Rome many male artists practiced professionally without joining the Accademia di San Luca.[31]

The Alternative Scene

Not only did women artists sometimes shun membership in professional guilds and art academies, many of them shunned professionalization entirely, especially religious women and noblewomen. Nevertheless, these last two categories are so integral to the history of women artists that we find them indicated on the well-known sheet of notes where Vasari planned out, probably around 1563, which artists he would add to the second edition of his *Lives*. On this sheet, he listed the names of some forty or so contemporary male artists, including Bronzino, Tintoretto (1518–1594), and Giambologna (1529–1608), followed immediately by:

> la cremonese
> la Monacha
> la contessa.[32]

These last cryptic entries refer to, respectively, Sofonisba Anguissola (a native of Cremona), Plautilla Nelli (a nun at Santa Caterina da Siena in Florence), and Lucrezia Quistelli (who was Countess Pietra by marriage), in other words, the three women

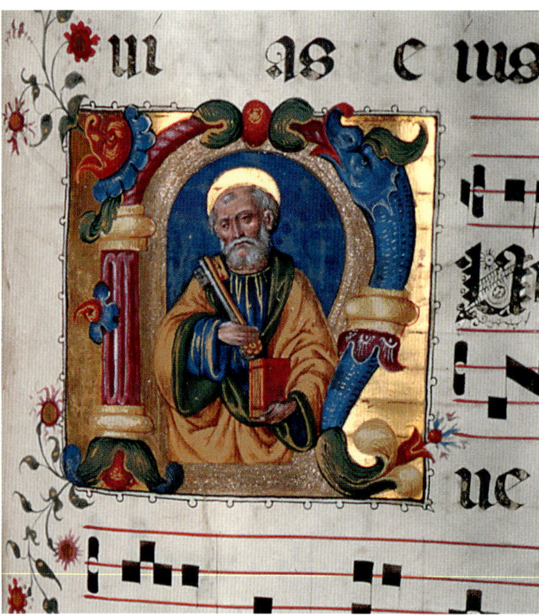

FIGURE 5 Sister Eufrasia Burlamacchi, *Saint Peter*, tempera on parchment. San Rafael, Dominican University of California, Archbishop Alemany Library, ms. 5, fol. 139r

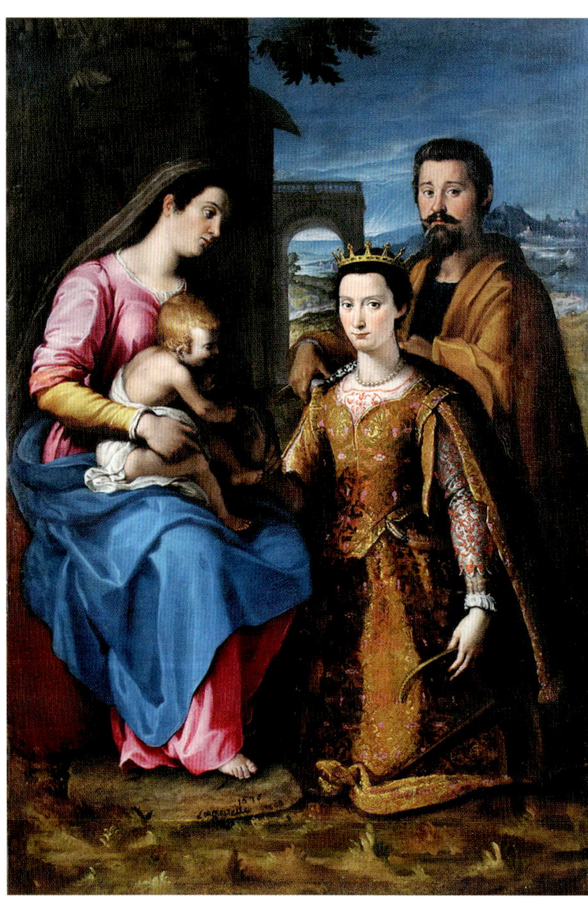

FIGURE 6 Lucrezia Quistelli, *The Enthroned Madonna and the Christ Child with Saint Catherine of Alexandria and an Apostle*, 1576, oil on panel, 70⅞ in. × 47¼ in. (180 × 120 cm). Silvano Pietra (PV), Italy, Church of Santa Maria e San Pietro

artists he added to his second edition, nested within the *vita* of Properzia de' Rossi. From his choice of women artists, and particularly from the monikers by which he categorized them, it appears that Vasari deliberately wished to include examples of what for him were three distinct types of women artists: a professional artist, a nun-artist, and an aristocratic amateur.

Sister Beatrice Camelli, the semi-professional nun-artist mentioned earlier, represents an exception to the pattern of nuns' production of art.[33] Generally speaking, nun-artists carried out their work entirely within the convent walls (especially after the conclusion of the Council of Trent in 1563). They worked as a collective, not for the sake of personal gain or glory, but as an aid to pious devotions and to ward off laziness.[34] But this does not mean that they did not have a good deal in common with professional artists. As writers like Fra' Serafino Razzi (1531–1613) and Cristoforo Bronzini (1580–1633) observed, Plautilla Nelli headed a very large and diversified workshop at Santa Caterina da Siena, which in all likelihood was the place where she was trained to paint miniatures in the 1540s.[35] Indeed, although it has sometimes been claimed that Lavinia Fontana was the first woman to run a painting workshop, she was certainly preceded by many nun-artists. Before Plautilla Nelli, for example, there were the Dominican nuns of San Domenico in Lucca, who operated the manuscript illumination workshop where Eufrasia Burlamacchi (1482–1548) acquired her impressive technical skills (fig. 5).[36] Nun-artists' knowledge of art and artistic materials no doubt came to them through the many sisters who had gained some hands-on experience and training as the widows or daughters of professional artists.[37] That the styles and techniques they practiced might be obsolete did not matter a great deal, since nuns often did not aspire to a mastery of their craft's most virtuosic aspects, preferring instead to answer a market demand for pious, humble, and inexpensive art. Notable exceptions to the latter tendency include Sister Plautilla Nelli's learned and highly accomplished altarpieces, Sister Ortenisia Fedeli's (active 1620) cycle of lunettes in the church attached to her convent; Sister Teresa Berenice Vitelli's botanical studies of natural specimens; and Sister Maria Luigia Raggi's (1742–1813) paintings of landscapes with classical ruins and other *capricci*.[38]

Aside from women religious, the other women artists who deliberately resisted professionalization were distinguished by their birth. Starting in the Renaissance, noblewomen began to receive artistic instruction because draughtsmanship was a component of the humanist education undertaken by the children, male and female, of Italian elites.[39] In a number of documented cases, they even attained proficiency thanks to lessons from professional artists—a role to which women professional artists like Anguissola and Sirani were ideally suited.[40] Decorum required them to eschew manual labor, and conduct codes barred them from selling their works; these are among the reasons they did not fully integrate into the sphere of professional artists.[41]

The best-studied example of an early modern Italian noblewoman who practiced art as an amateur is Lucrezia Quistelli, mentioned above. The daughter of a wealthy judge in Florence, Quistelli completed her humanistic education by undertaking the study of art at the age of fourteen, or perhaps earlier. The teacher hired to instruct her, Alessandro Allori (1535–1607), was perfectly suited to the role: not only had he learned to paint from Bronzino, but he had also studied literature under a Camadolese monk and writer of outstanding cultural sophistication, Silvano Razzi (1527–1611). Quistelli continued to paint even after her social status was exalted in 1557 through her marriage to the Lombard aristocrat Count Clemente Pietra (1521–1574), and Vasari dedicated laudatory passages to her in the 1568 *Lives of the Artists*, as noted above. Nevertheless, she and her family were reluctant to draw widespread attention to her talent because of its debasing associations with a manual profession. With a single exception (fig. 6), Quistelli never signed her paintings; similarly, the inscription composed by Quistelli's sons for her funerary monument omits all reference to her artistic practice.[42]

The near total obliteration of the record of Quistelli's paintings was a common fate among noblewomen who shared her reluctance to sign and to sell artworks. For instance, there is only one remaining trace of the various drawings and prints made by Eleonora Orsini (1571–1634) and the future queen of France, Maria de' Medici (1575–1642), both of whom studied under the Medici court artist Jacopo Ligozzi (1547–1627) in 1587. It consists of a woodblock print that Maria de' Medici designed and carved when she was fourteen years old, a surviving exemplar of which is at the Bibliotèque Nationale de France; the latter bears a handwritten notation by the artist Philippe de Champaigne (1602–1674) stating that the print was given to him by the queen herself on February 22, 1629, and that it was by her own hand ("faite da sa propre main") (fig. 7).[43] It has not been possible to trace any of the art made by Irene di Spilimbergo (1538–1559), a minor noblewoman of Friuli who studied first under the professional female artist Campaspe Giancarli (dates unknown) and then under Titian (1488/90–1576).[44] None of the wax statuettes, altar frontals, or paintings made by Camilla Orsini Borghese (1603–1685) have been identified; nor have the devotional artworks made by Maria Cristina de' Medici (1609–1632); nor the paintings on amber and silver made by Princess Maria Virginia Borghese Chigi (1642–1718).[45] Thanks to a prominent signature, a single work—a portrait of her sister Faustina del Bufalo from 1604—can be ascribed to Claudia del Bufalo (active 1604–1609) (fig. 8), a Roman noblewoman who also is documented to have

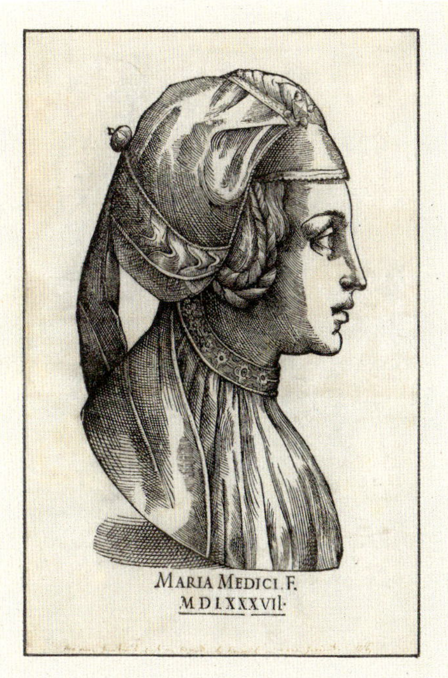

FIGURE 7 Maria de' Medici (possibly with Jacopo Ligozzi), *Portrait of a Woman Traditionally Identified as Maria de' Medici*, 1587, woodcut, 9¾ × 5⅜ in. (24.7 cm × 13.6 cm). British Museum

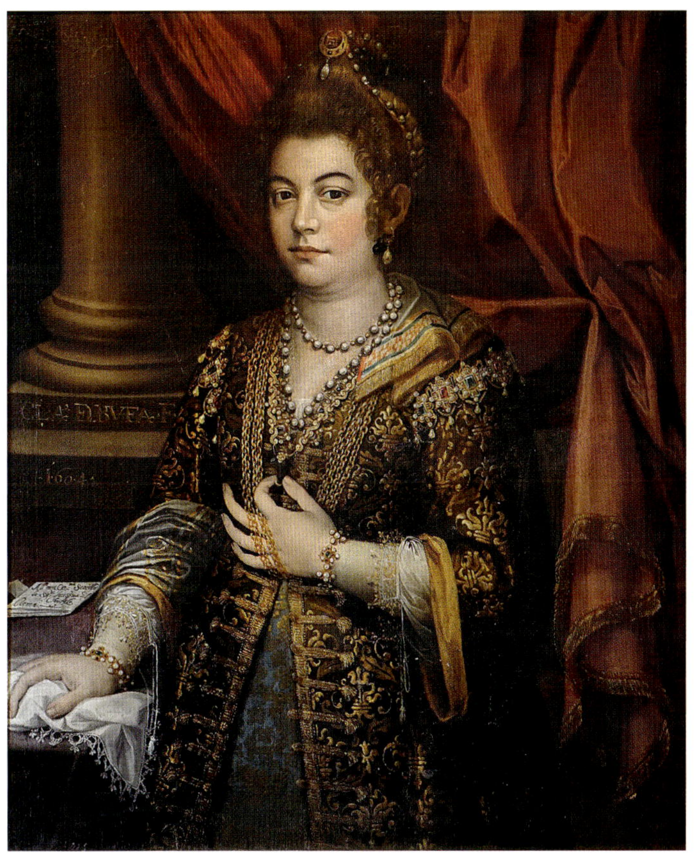

FIGURE 8 Claudia del Bufalo, *Portrait of Faustina del Bufalo*, oil on canvas, 41⁵⁄₁₆ × 34⅝ in. (105 × 88 cm). Dario del Bufalo Collection, inv. P127

made mythological paintings such as an image of Andromeda Chained to the Rocks.[46]

Final Reflections

While the first part of this essay traced out the profile of early professional women artists, the second half has been devoted to the substantial numbers of women who practiced art without meeting all the conditions for professionalization, including professional women artists who worked outside of guilds and women artists who sidestepped the professional sphere altogether by giving priority to either their religious vocation or their identities as nobles. All of these scenarios have been presented as if they were voluntary and free choices, and certainly in some cases they were. We cannot discount, however, the very real possibility that many of the women who sought alternatives to a fully professional status did so at least in part due to their perception that doing otherwise would bring them into conflict with forces beyond their control, including institutionalized sexism and the strictly differentiated gender roles of early modern Italian society that burdened women with the care of family members.[47]

Women who did seek full professionalization risked open friction with their male peers. Vasari himself acknowledged that, in the early sixteenth century, Properzia de' Rossi had been unfairly underpaid for her work at the stoneyard of San Petronio due to the antagonistic interference of Amico Aspertini (1474–1552), a rival sculptor.[48] In the seventeenth century, not only was Artemisia Gentileschi sexually assaulted by one of her father's colleagues while she was at work, but she was also paid less than male painters, who on at least one occasion stole her designs. Despite its downsides—economic risk, the loneliness of breaking with social norms, the hardship of entering a highly competitive field with disadvantages—professionalization remained an alluring goal for early modern women artists. It was a chance to compete head-to-head with men on the basis of talent, manual skill, and ingenuity, and for those at the very top, it was a chance to attain glory, fame, and wealth. When women artists did demonstrate their ability to equal and even surpass their professional male peers, they took a critical step in overturning their society's conventional notions of women's limitations.

NOTES

1. "Dovete sapere quante donne sono per la Fiandra e per la Francia e ancora in Italia, le quali dipingono in modo che in Italia i loro quadri di pittura sono tenuti in buon pregio," cited mistakenly as a quote from Giuliano da Sangallo in Fortunati and Graziani 2008, 31.

2. Barker 2017b.

3. Her agents included Michelangelo Buonarroti the Younger (ca. 1568–1646), Cassiano dal Pozzo (1588–1657), Galileo Galilei (1564–1642), and Fabio Gentile. On the latter see Nappi 2005, 97–98.

4. Solinas 2011; Locker 2017.

5. Nearly all of Garzoni's known letters are published in Casale 1991. For Carriera's letters see Sani 1985.

6. On Garzoni's calligraphy see Cosgrove 2020. On women's education as the privilege of elites, see Strocchia 1999, 25, 34. On the post-Tridentine education of women, especially in Bologna, see Modesti 2014, 59–62.

7. On Fontana see Madrid 2019, 213–29; on Sirani, see Modesti 2014, 9–11, 84–96.

8. On the example of Sirani, see Modesti 2014, 190–96.

9. Vicioso 2016, 99–120.

10. Barker 2015b, 122.

11. Turrill 2003; and Barker 2015b, 113–14, 134–38.

12. Giansante 2017.

13. In total, Vasari mentioned fifteen women artists in the 1568 edition. See Dabbs 2009, 46.

14. "Ordiniamo ke tucta quelli ke venghono o verranno a scriversi a questa compagnia huomini o donne sieno chontriti et confessi de' loro peccati o almeno con intendimento di confessarsi il più tosto ke potrà acconciamente." ASF, AD 1, 4 (modern numeration); a transcription is in Baldinucci 1845–1847, vol. 1, 240 (decennale V del secolo II). Just two years earlier the Florentine guild of bakers (*Fornai*) drew up statutes that similarly foresaw the matriculation of both men and women; see Morandini 1956, 3–45, esp. 5–6, 40, 42.

15. "Porre il descho fuori e scrivere quelli ke voranno entrare alla detta compagnia et fare pagare soldi tre per anno alli huomini et soldi due alle donne et raccordare che ae a pagare che paghi," ASF, AD 1, 5 (modern numeration); Baldinucci 1845–1847, vol. 1, 242 (decennale V, secolo II). The reason for the lower membership fee for women is not explained in the medieval Florentine statutes, however a parallel perhaps can be drawn with the early seventeenth-century statues for the Roman Accademia di San Luca, discussed below.

16. ASF, Accademia del Disegno 4, fol. 25r.

17. ASF, Accademia del Disegno 103, fol. 10 right: "ad dì 13 febbraio 160[5]. Da monna Lisabetta di Michele fantucciaia nella via de' Servi lire tre acconto di tassa reco Rinaldo Talani nostro provveditore." Her further payments are on ASF, Accademia del Disegno 103, 14 left, 15 right, 18 left, and 18 right.

18. Artemisia's matriculation is located in ASF, Accademia del Disegno 57, Stratto de' Matricole B, fol. 57r, and was first published in Bissell 1968, 154, n. 14.

19. On Artemisia's possible reluctance to join the Accademia del Disegno, see Barker 2017b, 86, n. 101. That she had no association with the Roman artists' academy is affirmed by Lukehart 2020, 99.

20. On Fratellini's status as court artist to the Medici, see Moücke 1752–1762, vol. 4, 209–21. The 1711 date for Fratellini's "accademico" status is reckoned here according to the modern calendar; according to the Florentine calendar it occurred on January 29, 1710 (ASF, Accademia del Disegno 13, fol. 61r). For her matriculation and taxes, see ASF, Accademia del Disegno 110, fol. 63; 129, fol. 117; 131, fol. 141; 132, fol. 62. For all these archival references I kindly thank Miriam Goodall.

21. ASF, Accademia del Disegno 88, courtesy of Miriam Goodall.

22. ASF, Accademia del Disegno 18, fol. 51r; 111, fol. 62v; 132, fol. 159; and 133, fol. 52. Many thanks to Miriam Goodall for these references.

23. It is noteworthy that a woman artist, Giovanna Fratellini, received the status of an "accademica" from the Accademia del Disegno in 1710, having already joined its guild in 1706; further research is needed to determine whether the latter title was merely an honorific or whether it came with full-fledged participation in the governance of the institution. On the Florentine academy's exhibitions, see Borroni Salvadori 1974, 1–166; and Barker and James 2020.

24. Lukehart 2020, 96–105. Perhaps these privileges included attending classes and participating in discussions, since we know that male amateurs could do these things; however there is no direct evidence of this; see Lukehart 2020, 98.

25. This is explained in Lukehart 2020, 99. The donation records are in the AASL, Libro del Camerlengo, vol. 42, and were published in Lollobrigida 2017, 184–86. Garzoni's donations are detailed in Lukehart 2020, 99–100.

26. See Lukehart 2020; Barker 2020d, 142–43; and Barker 2020e, 144.

27. Cohn 1998, 112, 115.

28. Zanoboni 2016a, 40.

29. This shift in explanation is discussed in Zanoboni 2016b, 64–68.

30. Zanoboni 2016a, 41–56. This mutual interest of the women laborers and the industrial leaders explains why Renaissance Florence was generally tolerant of women not belonging to the guilds; see Zanoboni 2016a, 59.

31. Fumagalli 2010, 174; Cavazzini 2008, 4, 19.

32. Casa Museo Vasari, Arezzo, Archivio Vasari 31, fol. 57v.

33. On the general conditions of Florentine nuns' production of art in the sixteenth and seventeenth centuries, see Barker 2015b, 105–39.

34. A similar pattern is described in Strocchia 2011.

35. On Nelli's early training, see Turrill 2017, 20–22; Barker 2017c.

36. On Burlamacchi see Tozzi 2005, 20–25; Vandi 2007, 19–39; and Vandi 2015, 89–104.

37. For several Florentine examples, see Barker 2015b, 121–22.

38. On Nelli's humanistic art, see Barker 2015b, 106–13; on Fedeli's lunettes see Goldenberg Stoppato 2016, 89; on Vitelli's botanical art, see Tongiorgi Tomasi 2008, 176–77; and Barker and James 2020, 318, 324–25; and on Raggi's landscapes, see Lollobrigida 2015, 191–98.

39. The role of drawing in a humanist cursus was first theorized in 1528 by Baldassare Castiglione; see Castiglione 1976, 96–98. On amateur artists and the humanist curriculum, see Middeldorf 1978; Dempsey 1980; Farago 1992, 123–24; and, with particular reference to women, Modesti 2014, 68; Barker 2015b, 124; and Barker 2016b, 75–76, n. 47.

40. On Anguissola's teaching of Spain's Queen Elisabeth of Valois (1545–1568), see Pérez de Tudela 2019a, 54–55; on Sirani's lessons to Bolognese nobles, see Modesti 2014, 68.

41. By way of comparison, Estefanía de la Encarnación (1598–1665), a Spanish nun of noble ancestry, complained that the manual component of art production demeaned her status in the convent. See Nancarrow 2003, 41–52.

42. On the life of Quistelli, see Barker 2016b.

43. Conigliello 1992, 196; and Chappell 2003.

44. On Spilimbergo's training see Jacobson Schutte 1991, 53 n. 42.

45. Barker 2015b, 132–33; Dunn 1997, 176; and Letter of July 20, 1658, Torquato Montauto to Giovanni Battista Gondi, in Archivio di Stato di Firenze, Mediceo del Principato 3384, fol. 67r, accessed in MIA (Medici Interactive Archive) as MAPdocID# 21000.

46. Cavazzini 2008, 43.

47. Following Nochlin 1971, additional studies of the obstacles that hampered women's professionalization include Fox Hofrichter 2005; Greer 1979; and ffolliott 2016, 15–27.

48. Fortunati and Graziani 2008, 13, 108.

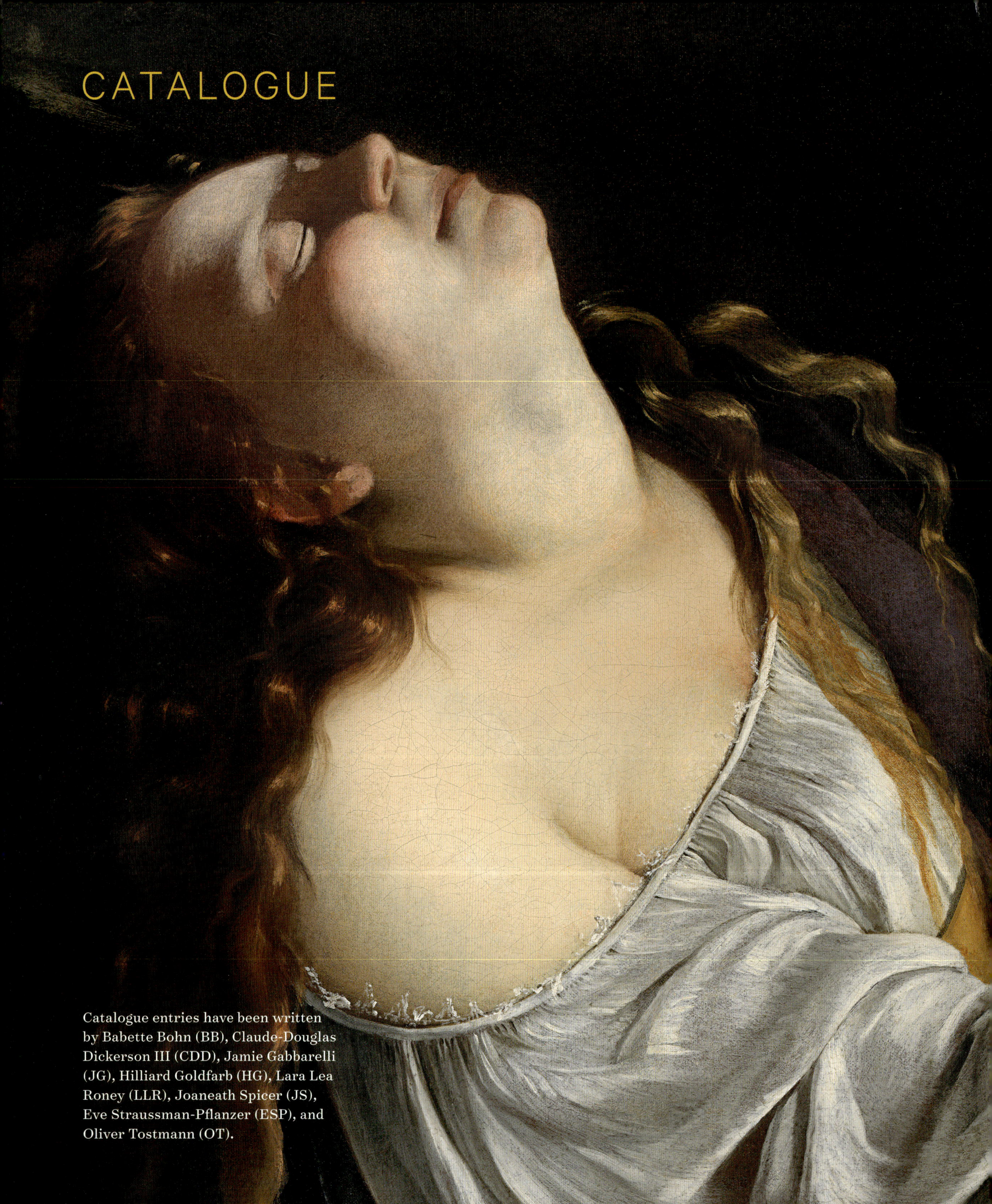

Catalogue entries have been written
by Babette Bohn (BB), Claude-Douglas
Dickerson III (CDD), Jamie Gabbarelli
(JG), Hilliard Goldfarb (HG), Lara Lea
Roney (LLR), Joaneath Spicer (JS),
Eve Straussman-Pflanzer (ESP), and
Oliver Tostmann (OT).

SOFONISBA ANGUISSOLA

Cremona, ca. 1535–Palermo, 1625

BORN INTO A MINOR NOBLE FAMILY, Sofonisba Anguissola received an unusually deep education in letters and the arts. Unprecedented at the time, she and her sister Elena (ca. 1536–ca. 1585) were sent outside of the family home to study with the painters Bernardino Campi (1522–1591) and Bernardino Gatti, called il Sojaro (ca. 1495–1576). Her sisters Lucia (ca. 1537–ca. 1565), Europa (ca. 1548–1578), and Annamaria (ca. 1554–1611) were artists as well. Due to numerous self-portraits and portraits, Sofonisba Anguissola became well known in Northern Italy and beyond in the 1550s. She was invited to join the court of King Philip II of Spain (1527–1598) in 1559, and there she became lady-in-waiting to Queen Elisabeth of Valois (1545–1568) and Queen Anna of Austria (1549–1580). In 1573 she left Spain for Sicily to live with her new husband. After his death she remarried and moved to Genoa, and then to Palermo, where she died at an advanced age. Thanks primarily to her sensitive portraits, Anguissola was a woman painter of unprecedented fame during her lifetime.

1

The Artist's Sister in the Garb of a Nun

1551
Oil on canvas, 27 × 21 in. (68.5 × 53.3 cm)
Inscribed (now missing, but reported first by Wey 1854): Sophonisba Angussola, Virgo M . . . teri Ago.ti Pinxit MDLI. [Sophonisba Anguissola, virgin, monastery of the Augustines, painted it 1551]
City Art Gallery, Southampton, 1979/14

BECAUSE OF ITS now lost inscription, *The Artist's Sister in the Garb of a Nun* is considered the earliest painting to survive by the Cremonese artist Sofonisba Anguissola. It is part of a small group of works that can be safely ascribed to her. With this painting's contemplative mood, quiet intensity, and fine detail, the young Anguissola demonstrates a remarkable maturity at the outset of her career. Such portraits of single sitters became a mainstay in her oeuvre.

The young nun gazes directly towards the viewer with a restrained smile, expressing a determination that is reinforced by the pristine shades of white of her clothing as she emerges from the dark background. She appears prepared to leave the secular world behind and consecrate her life to God. The inscription, now illegible, initially led scholars to identify the sitter as Elena Anguissola,

the only nun among the Anguissola sisters. Both Elena and Sofonisba Anguissola studied with the Lombard painter Bernardino Campi from 1546 to 1549. Before 1556 Elena entered the Dominican convent of San Vincenzo in Mantua,[1] where she was known as Sister Minerva, likely due to her humanist education; the luxurious book might allude to this. While serving in the order, she may have continued to paint.[2]

Whether the sitter belongs to the Dominican order, however, has been contested. Rossana Sacchi rightly pointed out that her immaculate white garb is more likely that of an Augustinian novice.[3] Moreover, the now missing fragmentary inscription can be interpreted as referring to "Monasteri Sancti Agostini," or Monastery of Saint Augustine. These arguments speak against identifying her as Elena Anguissola,

who was not in an Augustinian institution.[4] Nevertheless, the sitter's delicate features and large eyes bear a resemblance to those of the Anguissola sisters.[5] In addition, she appears to be a very young woman, which is consistent with Elena's age of about fifteen in 1551. While the sitter's apparent kinship and age make an identification with Elena Anguissola likely, the questions of the order and her status remain unresolved.

If Sofonisba Anguissola executed this portrait in 1551, she painted it during or shortly after her apprenticeship with Bernardino Gatti. His influence may be seen in the softened features of the girl's face and hands, the translucent whites of her tunic, and the harmonious interplay of light and shadows. Already in this early painting, Anguissola incorporated visual devices that she continued to use in her later works. An X-radiograph shows subtle changes that speak to her talent for including arresting details in her pictures (fig. 1). By extending the open white page of the book, she gave more space to the sitter's left thumb, thereby creating more depth. She also included details such as the creases on the left side of the veil and the right forearm. The intricate interplay between the sitter's hands, her book, and its ribbons foreshadows similarly observed details in later

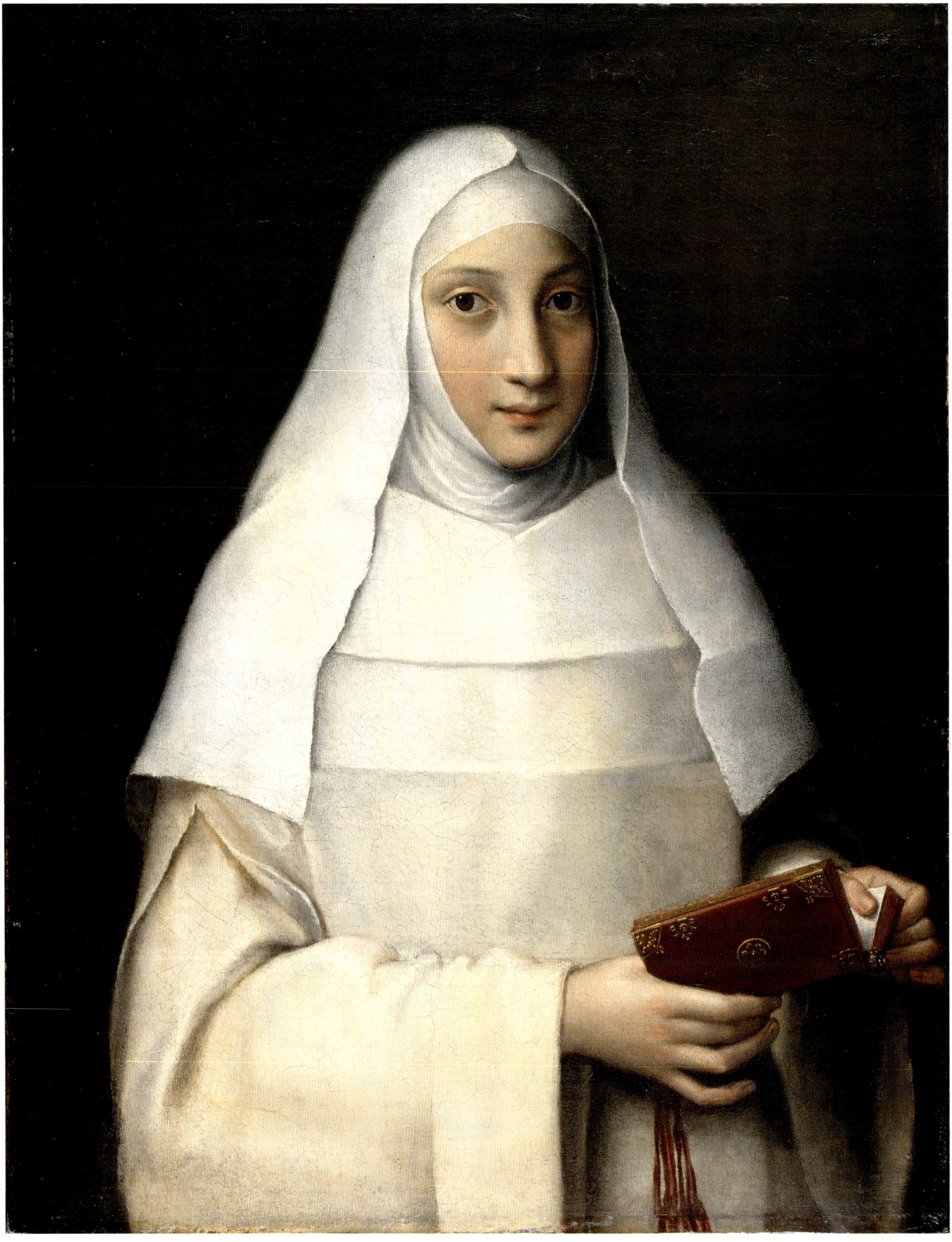

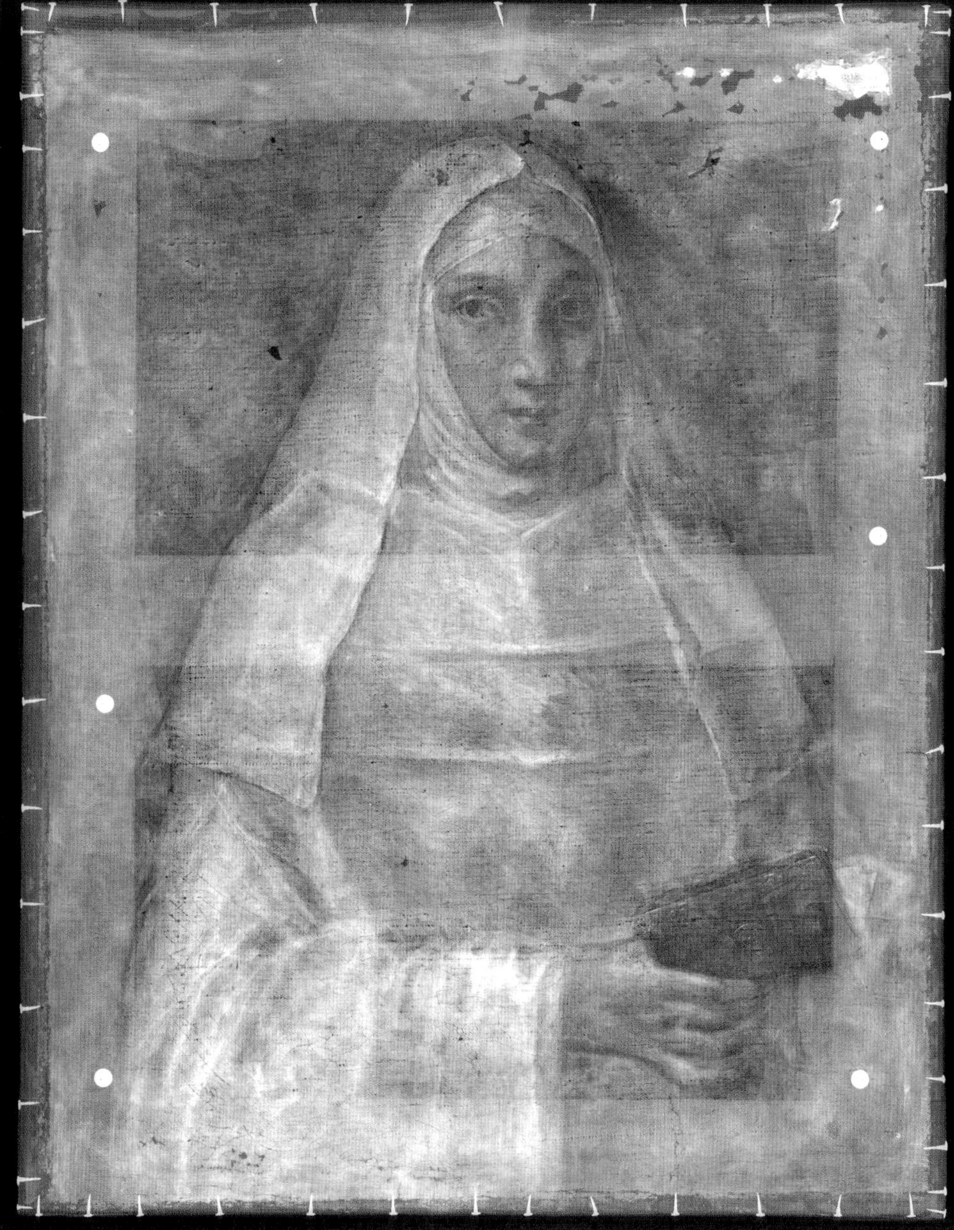

FIGURE 1 X-radiograph, Sofonisba Anguissola, *The Artist's Sister in the Garb of a Nun*, 1551. City Art Gallery, Southampton

works, such as the *Self-Portrait* from 1554 in the Kunsthistorisches Museum, Vienna (Tostmann, "The Advantages of Painting Small," fig. 1). Overall, the X-radiograph reveals the working process of an artist who is already remarkably self-assured. The carefully balanced and blissfully restrained *Artist's Sister in the Garb of a Nun* is a distinctive achievement for the young Anguissola and an important contribution to Northern Italian portraiture in the mid-sixteenth century. A later copy at the Istituto Madri Orsoline in Gorizia attests to its enduring success.—OT

NOTES

1. Gamberini 2019a, 109.

2. A portrait in the collection of the Borghese Gallery has been connected with Elena Anguissola: *Portrait of a Nun as Saint Catherine of Siena*, undated, oil on panel, 9⁷⁄₁₆ × 7¹⁄₁₆ in. (24 × 18 cm), Galleria Borghese, Rome, inv. no. 512. Discussed in Prohaska 1995.

3. Sacchi 1994a, 186.

4. Anastasia Gilardi, however, argued that Elena Anguissola was associated with the Augustinian order. Sacchi 1994a, 186.

5. Compare with Sofonisba Anguissola's *Self-Portrait*, ca. 1556, in the Museum of Fine Arts, Boston (cat. 2).

PROVENANCE

By 1850, Earls of Yarborough, then by descent; December 7, 1929, sold at (Christie's, London, UK), lot 7, to T. Ward; June 1936–present, purchased by the Southampton City Art Gallery (Southampton, UK).

SELECTED EXHIBITIONS

Royal Academy, London, 1962, no. 70; Wildenstein Gallery, London, 1970, no. 3; Centro culturale "Città di Cremona," 1994; Kunsthistorisches Museum, Vienna, 1995; National Museum of Women in the Arts, Washington, D.C., 1995; National Museum of Women in the Arts, Washington, D.C., 2007; Museum voor Schone Kunsten, Ghent, 2018–2019; Museo Nacional del Prado, Madrid, 2019–2020.

SELECTED PUBLICATIONS

Wey 1854, 293–95, no. 171; Waagen 1857, 65; Sacchi 1872, 6–7; Minghetti 1877, 34; Tufts 1974b, 22, 26, fig. 4; Caroli 1987, 24–26, 92–93, no. 1; Perlingieri 1992, 57–60, pl. 29; Cremona 1994, 18–19; Sacchi 1994a, 186, cat. 1, 187 illus.; Prohaska 1995, 99; Vienna 1995, 77, cat. 12, illus.; Washington, D.C. 1995, 14–15, 35, pl. 1; Murphy 2003, 201 n. 49; Washington, D.C. 2007, 106, 108, cat. 7, 109 illus.; Ghent 2018, 60, cat. 4, 61 illus.; Cole 2019b, 10, 164–65, cat. 12, 164 illus., fig. 8; Gamberini 2019a, 108 illus., 109, cat. 10.

2

Self-Portrait

ca. 1556

Oil (?) on parchment, 3¼ × 2½ in. (8.3 × 6.4 cm)

Inscribed (in frame of object): SOHONISBA ANGVSSOLA VIR[GO]/IPSIUS MAU EX [S] PEVLO DEPICTAM CREMONAE [The virgin Sofonisba Anguissola, depicted by her own hand, from a mirror, at Cremona]. On the disk the entwined letters ERMALCKI. Museum of Fine Arts, Boston, Emma F. Munroe Fund, 60.155

SOFONISBA ANGUISSOLA'S fame spread quickly from her hometown of Cremona across Italy and beyond, thanks in large part to numerous self-portraits painted during the 1550s. No artist, male or female, between Albrecht Dürer (1471–1528) and Rembrandt (1606–1669), produced as many self-portraits.[1] These pictures were gifted to potential patrons and fellow artists in an unprecedented and carefully orchestrated image campaign involving her family. Within just a few years Sofonisba Anguissola had become one of the most famous artists of her time, hailed by critics such as Annibale Caro (1507–1566), Giorgio Vasari (1511–1574), and Giovanni Paolo Lomazzo (1538–1592), and crowned by her appointment to the Spanish court in 1559.

In this outstanding portrait she created an ambiguous self-likeness that can be read in various ways, as if the intent were to play with the viewer's expectations. In the center, she holds a large disk adorned with multiple inscriptions, including entwined initials that remind Sylvia Ferino-Pagden of Amilcare, the artist's father's name.[2] If this is true, the disk may function as a heraldic device referring to the artist's family, who played a crucial role in launching her career. The letters may have additional meanings as well. Conceits in which letters are combined into harmonious figures to stimulate ambiguous readings were fashionable during the mid-sixteenth century.[3] The Latin inscription on the rim of the disk states: "The virgin Sofonisba Anguissola, depicted by her own hand, from a mirror, at Cremona." By explicitly mentioning the mirror in the inscription, Anguissola may mean to reference the famous ancient painter Iaia from Cyzicus (1st century BCE), later known as Marcia, who was said to have painted a self-portrait with this device.[4] Subtle distortions of the face, such as the enlarged eyes, make it plausible that she painted this portrait with the help of a mirror. She also refers to herself as a virgin, and Marcia reportedly preserved her virginity in order to devote herself completely to the arts of painting and sculpture. Anguissola painted this self-portrait as a token of her virtuosity. Her references to her humanist education and her beautified features can be understood as indicators of this quality, which was highly desirable for any woman, but especially for a noblewoman such as herself. As she also references Cremona on the rim, this portrait was likely painted for a recipient outside that city.[5]

Noting its miniature-like character, some scholars date this medallion around 1556, when Sofonisba Anguissola supposedly met Giulio Clovio (1498–1578), the most famous miniaturist of her time.[6] It should be cautioned, however, that she had already experimented with miniature-like techniques during the first half of the 1550s. The 1554 *Self-Portrait* in Vienna (Tostmann, "The Advantages of Paining Small," fig. 1) indicates an affinity with and perhaps knowledge of highly polished painting techniques.

Painted on parchment and set into a metal frame with a scroll mount, this small portrait may have been intended to be worn as a necklace.[7] The size of such medallions, which makes them accessible only to someone physically close, gives them a private character. With its entanglement of words and image, this medallion may have been used to encourage playful discussions. During the mid-sixteenth century, such works were highly fashionable, especially at courts. One of the most famous contemporaneous artists working in miniatures was the Flemish painter Levina Teerlinc (ca. 1520–1576), who excelled in this genre at the Tudor court in England. She was known in Italy, and it is tempting to speculate that Sofonisba Anguissola created this ambitious self-portrait as a response to the fame and success of her Flemish colleague.[8]—OT

NOTES

1. Sutherland Harris 1976, 27.

2. Ferino-Pagden cautioned, however, that this explanation excludes the letter "K" at the right. Ferino-Pagden 1995, 62.

3. Lozano 2019a, 95, refers to Giovanni Battista Palatino's *Libro nuovo d'imparare a scrivere*, 1540.

4. Iaia's life was widely known through Pliny the Elder (1st century), *Naturalis Historia*, Book 35, ch. 40. Later, Giovanni Boccaccio (1313–1375) included her life, under the name Marcia, in his compilation of famous women, *De claris mulieribus*, ca. 1362.

5. See Ferino-Pagden 1995, 62.

6. Sacchi 1994b, 196; Lozano 2019a, 95.

7. Proper miniatures are painted with bodycolors on parchment and other smooth supports. Whether this medallion was painted in oil is being questioned by the Museum of Fine Arts, Boston.

8. On the relationship between Sofonisba Anguissola and Levina Teerlinc, see in this catalogue Tostmann, "The Advantages of Painting Small," 36–37. There is a slightly larger copy of Anguissola's self-portrait on copper at the Victoria and Albert Museum, London (Dyce 103).

PROVENANCE

By 1801, collection of Richard Gough [1735–1809] (London, UK); July 21, 1810, sold at (Sotheby's, London, UK); by 1862, collection of Henry Danby Seymour [1820–1877] (Ashridge, UK); 1912–1928, by descent to the collection of Jane Margaret Seymour [1873–1943] (Knoyle, Wiltshire, UK); May 9, 1928, sold at (Sotheby's, London, UK), lot 61; November 9, 1959, sold at anonymous sale, "the property of a lady," at (Sotheby's, London, UK), lot 28, to (F. Kleinberger and Co., New York, New York); March 10, 1960–present, purchased by the Museum of Fine Arts, Boston (Boston, Massachusetts).

SELECTED EXHIBITIONS

Centro culturale "Città di Cremona," 1994; Kunsthistorisches Museum, Vienna, 1995; National

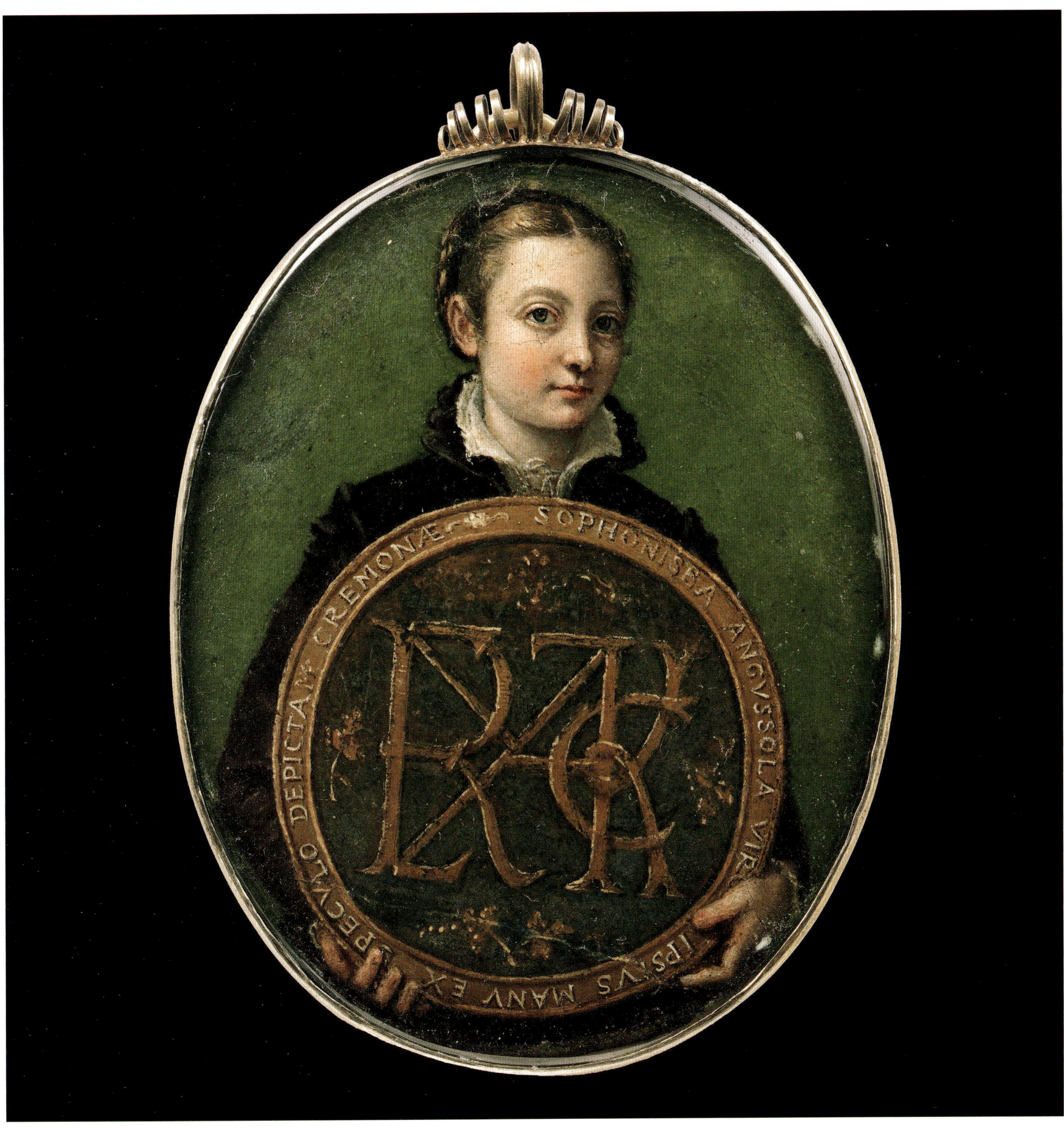

Museum of Women in the Arts, Washington, D.C., 1995; Metropolitan Museum of Art, New York, 2004; Museo Civico Ala Ponzone, Cremona, 2004; Museo Nacional del Prado, Madrid, 2019–2020.

SELECTED PUBLICATIONS
Sutherland Harris 1976, 27, fig. 3; Simon 1986, 117, 120, 121 n. 5, fig. 4; Caroli 1987, 96, no. 3; Perlingieri 1992, 60–65, pl. 33–34; Schweikhart 1992, 119–21; Bologna 1994, 39–41, fig. 2; Cremona 1994, 23; Garrard 1994, 604, 606, fig. 25; Sacchi 1994b, 196, cat. 6, 197 illus.; Ferino-Pagden 1995, 62, cat. 2, illus.; King 1995, 385, 389–90, fig. 8; Washington, D.C. 1995, 19, 22–23, 46, pl. 3; Borzello 1998, 24 illus., 26; Woods-Marsden 1998, 203, pl. 130; Costa 1999, 54–62, fig. 1; Christadler 2000, 221–32; Murphy 2003, 42, fig. 42; Cremona 2004, 200, illus.; New York 2004, 160, cat. 54, illus.; Washington, D.C. 2007, 106, 110 under cat. 8; Lacas 2015, 30, 67; Matthews-Grieco 2017, 26; Vullo 2017, 28–29, fig. 3; Antwerp 2018, 9–10, fig. 1; Barker 2018, 424–25, fig. 13; Ghent 2018, 52 under cat. 1; Cole 2019b, 17, 33–39, 156–57, cat. 2, 157 illus., figs. 9, 16; Lozano 2019a, 94 illus., 95, cat. 3.

3

Self-Portrait at the Easel

1554–1555
Oil on canvas, 9½ × 7¾ in. (24.1 × 19.7 cm)
Private collection, Connecticut

THIS ALLURING small portrait, exhibited here for the first time, is one of the earliest independent pictures showing a woman artist painting at an easel. The Flemish painter Caterina van Hemessen (1528–after 1565) preceded Sofonisba Anguissola by a few years with this subject, but in Italy it was new and groundbreaking.[1] Sitting close to the easel with a brush in her right hand and a mahlstick in the other, the artist turns toward the viewer as if just interrupted at her work. While Caterina van Hemessen shows herself painting a study of a head, Anguissola sits before a devotional painting of the Virgin and Child. By presenting herself as a practitioner of religious paintings, she includes herself in a well-established tradition of male painters in the guise of Saint Luke depicting the Virgin and Child, which became a popular motif in male self-portraiture beginning in the fifteenth century. For a woman painter, this choice was unprecedented.

Various versions and copies of this subject by Sofonisba Anguissola are known and they can be separated into two groups, divided by size. The best-studied version, now at the Museum Zamek in Łańcut, belongs to the group of larger works.[2] The Connecticut painting belongs to a group of several small versions, one of which (once in the Stirling collection, Keir, Scotland, and now in a private collection in Italy) is traditionally believed to be an autograph example (fig. 1).[3] There is no consensus on the attribution of the largely unknown Connecticut *Self-Portrait at the Easel* under discussion here. Mina Gregori and Andrea de Marchi endorsed its attribution to Sofonisba Anguissola.[4] Michael Cole, however, considers it to be a sixteenth-century copy.[5]

Self-Portrait at the Easel differs in numerous details from other versions, particularly the Stirling picture. While the Stirling version is painted on a panel, this version is on canvas. And in addition to different laced collars and cuffs, it shows the sitter with a striped sleeve. At least one other small portrait, sold in 2017 at Bonham's London, seems to derive from it.[6] That sitter wears a striped sleeve and a similarly laced collar. The Bonham version, however, considered a copy by the auction house, lacks this painting's delicacy and details, such as the animated cheeks and fine hair. In addition, this *Self-Portrait* (or its copy), rather than the Stirling version, was used by the British printmakers Thomas Worlidge (1700–1766) and William Baillie (1723–1810) for their undated prints.[7]

The painting shows the young Sofonisba Anguissola with blond hair, while it is

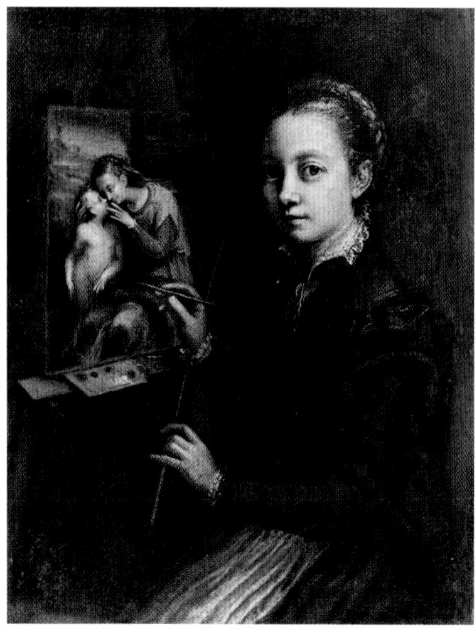

FIGURE 1 Sofonisba Anguissola, *Self-Portrait at the Easel*, mid-1550s, oil on panel, 9¹⁄₁₆ × 7¼ in. (23 × 18.5 cm). Private collection, Italy

chestnut colored in the Łańcut portrait. But the Łańcut version has been dated ca. 1556–1557, while this portrait of a slightly younger sitter could date to 1554–1555.[8] Its compelling quality and the numerous subtle derivations make it unlikely that it is a copy from the better-known Stirling version or any other portrait. Since we still know little about Anguissola's practice of painting multiple versions of one composition, her self-portraits could be revealing in this regard. This painting showcases her focus on producing small self-portraits based on successful prototypes, all created to widely distribute her image among potential patrons. By representing herself as a painter at work in multiple variations, she demonstrates her iconographical inventiveness, efficiency, and marketing acumen.—OT

NOTES

1. Caterina van Hemessen, *Self-Portrait at the Easel*, 1548, oil on oak panel, 12¹³⁄₁₆ × 9¹⁵⁄₁₆ in. (32.5 × 25.2 cm), Kunstmuseum Basel. Around 1550, male painters such as Titian (1488/90–1576) and Alessandro Allori (1535–1607) also started to portray themselves at work. See Woods-Marsden 1998, 225–37.

2. Sofonisba Anguissola, *Self-Portrait at the Easel*, ca. 1556–1557, oil on canvas, 25⅞ × 23¼ in. (65.7 × 59 cm), Museum Zamek, Łańcut.

3. Sofonisba Anguissola, *Self-Portrait at the Easel*, mid-1550s, oil on panel, 9¹⁄₁₆ × 7¼ in. (23 × 18.5 cm), private collection, Italy. See Sacchi 1994c, 198; Cole 2019b, 184–85, cat. 33. To my knowledge, this painting has only been reproduced in black and white images.

4. See Bob P. Haboldt & Co., object sheet, undated.

5. On this painting see Cole 2019b, 66–67.

6. After Sofonisba Anguissola, *Portrait of the Artist at Her Easel*, 17th century, oil on panel, 9¹¹⁄₁₆ × 7½ in. (25.8 × 19.8 cm), sale Bonhams Knightsbridge, Old Master Paintings, October 25, 2017, lot 00011.

7. Thomas Worlidge, *Portrait of Sofonisba Anguissola*, ca. 1750–1766, etching, 6¹⁵⁄₁₆ × 4¹⁵⁄₁₆ in. (17.6 × 12.6 cm), Courtauld Institute of Art, London, G. 1990. WL. 223; William Baillie, *Sofonisba Angusciola Pittrice*, ca. 1761–1786, mezzotint, 14 × 10 in. (35.6 × 25.4 cm), British Museum, London, 1870, 0813.572.

8. Compare with the dating of the Stirling version in Sacchi 1994c, 198. See also Policicchio 2018b, 54.

PROVENANCE

June 8, 2011, sold at (Christie's, New York, New York), lot 4; 2012–present, sold by (Bob P. Haboldt) to a private collection (Connecticut) as Sofonisba Anguissola.

SELECTED PUBLICATIONS
Cole 2019b, 66–67, fig. 46.

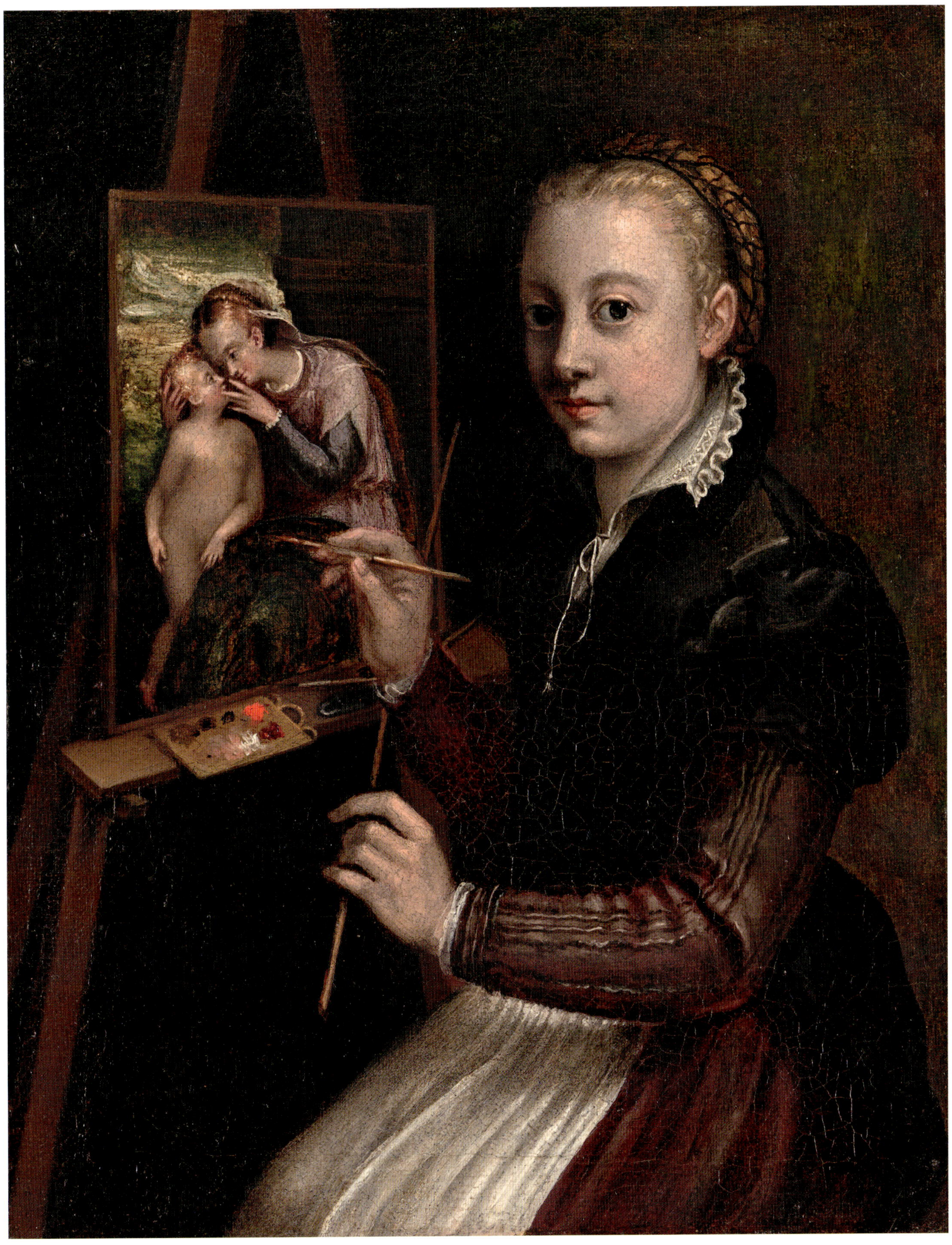

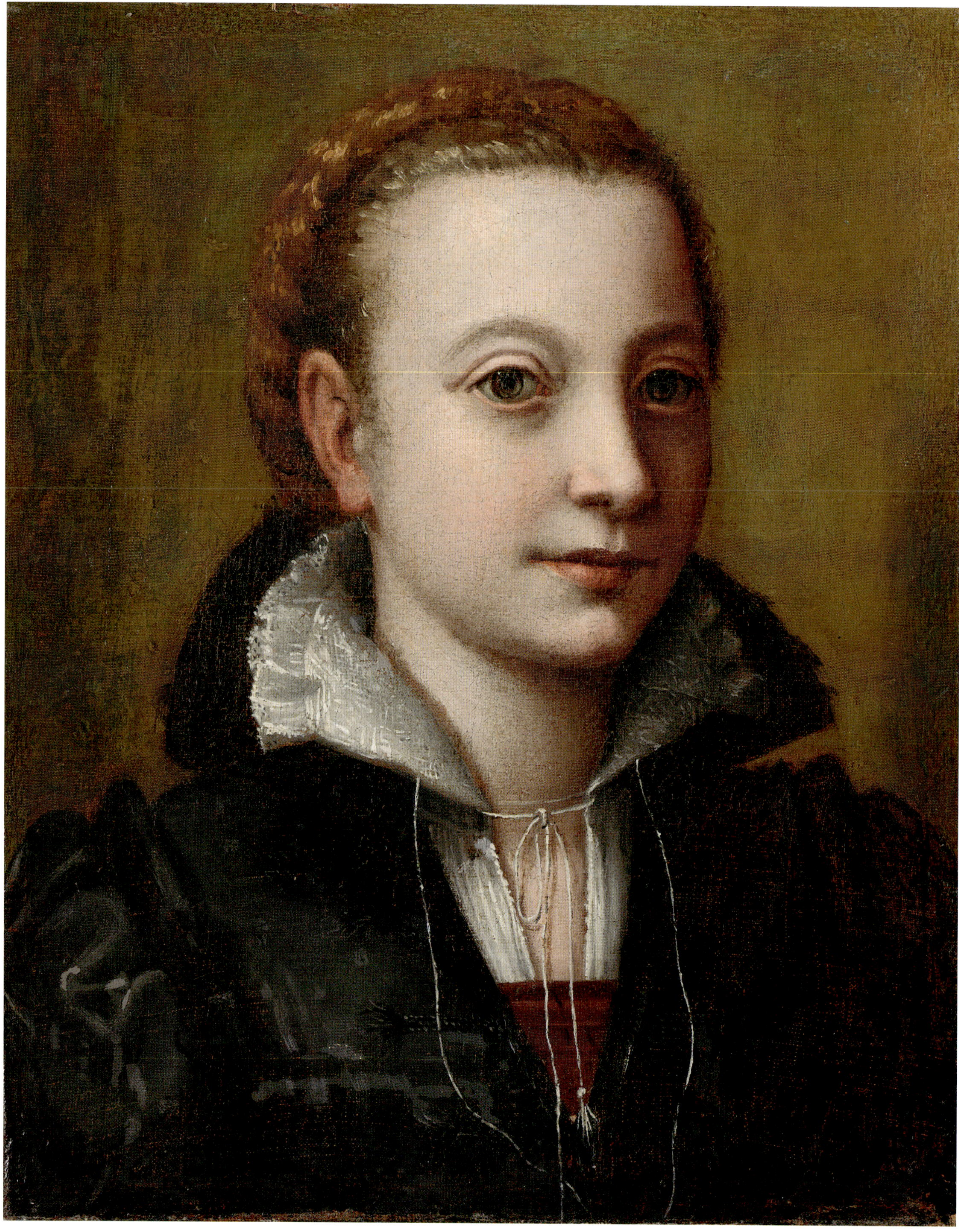

Self-Portrait

Late 1550s
Oil on canvas, 11¾ × 9½ in. (29.8 × 24.2 cm)
Private collection, Connecticut

THIS LITTLE-KNOWN PICTURE is part of a larger group of small-scale portraits by Sofonisba Aguissola and her sisters, all painted during the 1550s in Cremona. It leads us directly into the family's household, where, unique in Italy at the time, several women painters closely practiced alongside one another under the guidance of their father, Amilcare Anguissola (1515–1557), who was not an artist. The sisters particularly excelled in portraiture. To what extent they learned from, collaborated with, and perhaps challenged one another is still unknown. This portrait is a case in point.

Depicted in bust format and looking directly at the viewer, the sitter wears a high-necked collar in the Venetian style and a shirt with a lace collar; both indicate her distinguished style and high rank. Ilaria Bianchi was the first scholar to identify this painting as a self-portrait by Sofonisba Anguissola in 2007, with Mina Gregori concurring in 2009.[1] Michael Cole, however, considers it a portrait of Sofonisba Anguissola by an unknown male artist.[2] Calling it a derivation, he compares it negatively with Anguissola's *Self-Portrait* in the Colonna collection in Rome, painted in 1558 (fig. 1).[3] The Colonna portrait and this picture differ indeed in their quality. Here Anguissola's likeness lacks the marbleized appearance and depth of the Colonna portrait, and the hair is fairer. The complexion seems to have deeper colors, most noticeable in the ear and lips. Yet one should be cautious with comparisons. This portrait is considerably compromised by its abrasions, losses, and overpaint. Other versions attest to the success of this type in the second half of the 1550s and after.[4]

The handling of this portrait compared with pictures by Sofonisba Anguissola might also suggest it is by one of her sisters. Indeed, Gregori first identified it as a self-portrait by Lucia Anguissola (ca. 1537–ca. 1565), before changing her opinion to Sofonisba.[5] Lucia Anguissola's half-length *Self-Portrait* at the Castello Sforzesco in Milan employs a similar three-quarter perspective for the face.[6] Few paintings can be safely ascribed to her hand, and this portrait could be a possible addition to her little-known oeuvre. While the sitter's fair hair may indicate she is a younger Sofonisba, it may also indicate that this is one of the other Anguissola sisters, but not Lucia, who had dark brown hair.[7] Minerva Anguissola (1543–ca. 1564) was depicted with auburn hair, and a portrait of her, probably painted by Lucia Anguissola in 1554, now in the Poldi Pezzoli collection in Milan, has some similarities with this portrait.[8]

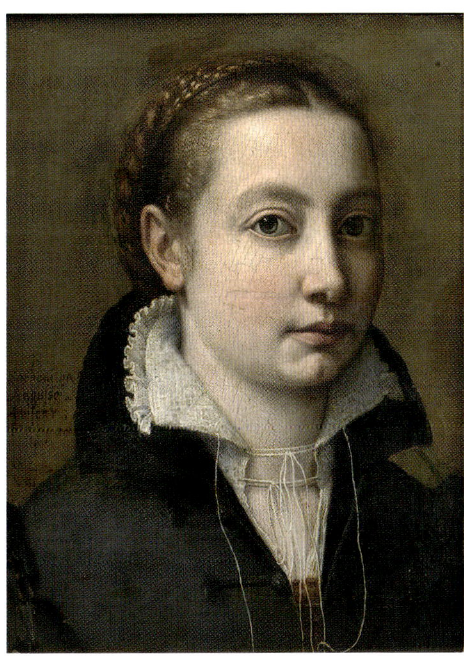

FIGURE 1 Sofonisba Anguissola, *Self-Portrait*, 1558, oil on paper mounted on panel, 9¹¹⁄₁₆ × 7½ in. (25.6 × 19.3 cm). Palazzo Colonna, Rome, inv. no. 268

While the portrait differs in the modeling, refined coloring, and sense of detail from undisputed early portraits by Sofonisba Anguissola, it has the artistic qualities found in portraits by the Anguissola family, and is a testament to their contributions to Cremonese portraiture during the 1550s.—OT

NOTES

1. Email from Elena Ishukova, Maison d'Art, to the author dated October 15, 2019.

2. Cole 2019b, 61.

3. Sofonisba Anguissola, *Self-Portrait*, 1558, oil on paper mounted on panel, 9¹¹⁄₁₆ × 7½ in. (25.6 × 19.3 cm), Palazzo Colonna, Rome, inv. no. 268.

4. For other examples of this bust format type, see Sofonisba Anguissola, *Self-Portrait* or *Portrait of Minerva Anguissola*, oil on canvas, 14³⁄₁₆ × 11⁷⁄₁₆ in. (36 × 29 cm), Pinacoteca di Brera, Milan, inv. no. 1309; Sofonisba Anguissola, *Self-Portrait* (the "Ashburnham Medaillion"), oil on panel, diameter: 5³⁄₁₆ in. (13.2 cm), Fondation Custodia (Lugt Collection), Paris, inv. no. 6607; Sofonisba Anguissola (?), *Portrait of a Woman*, oil on canvas, 13⁹⁄₁₆ × 11¼ in. (34.5 × 28.5 cm), private collection, Brescia; Sofonisba or Lucia Anguissola (?), *Self-Portrait* or *Portrait of Minerva Anguissola*, oil on canvas, 17⅝ × 13⁷⁄₁₆ in. (44.8 × 34.2 cm oval), Museo Poldi Pezzoli, Milan, inv. no. 322.

5. See Gregori 2005. According to Gregori, Rossana Sacchi shared her opinion.

6. Lucia Anguissola, *Self-Portrait*, 1557, oil on panel, 11 × 7⅞ in. (28 × 20 cm), Castello Sforzesco, Milan.

7. Ilyia Sandra Perlingieri suggested that Sofonisba Anguissola's hair color changed to a darker brown during the 1550s. Perlingieri 1992, 51–52.

8. The painting in the Poldi Pezzoli Collection, Milan, which shows the sitter with the characteristic reddish ear, has been traditionally identified as a self-portrait by Sofonisba Anguissola. More recently, various scholars have proposed Minerva Anguissola as its sitter, painted by her sister Lucia. For an overview of the different opinions, see Cole 2019b, 197 and 199, cat. 48. The portrait by Sofonisba Anguissola at the Pinacoteca di Brera, Milan, inv. no. 1309, has also been identified as a portrait of Minerva Anguissola by some scholars. See Cole 2019b, 160, cat. 7.

PROVENANCE

Collection of Sir Evelyn de la Rue [1879–1950]. 2009–present, sold at TEFAF Maastricht 2009 by (Maison d'Art, Monte Carlo, Monaco) to a private collection (Connecticut) as Sofonisba Anguissola.

SELECTED EXHIBITIONS

Maison d'Art, Monte Carlo, 2005; Palazzo Reale, Milan, 2007–2008.

SELECTED PUBLICATIONS

Gregori 2005, 40, cat. 7, 41 illus. (as attributed to Lucia Anguissola); Milan 2007, 74 illus.; Cole 2019b, 61, 242, cat. 158, illus.

La vecchia rimbambita muove riso alla fanciuletta (The Childish Old Woman Makes the Young Woman Laugh)

Jacob Bos (Dutch, active 1549–1580) after Sofonisba Anguissola

ca. 1560–1564

Engraving, 13⅝ × 17 in. (33.8 × 43.1 cm)

Signed (in plate, lower left): Iacobus Bos belga.incidebat [Jacob Bos from the Netherlands incised it]

Inscribed (in plate in margin below image): LA VECCHIA RIMBAMBITA MVUOVE RISO ALLA FANCIVLETTA/Opera di Sofonisba Gentildona Cremonese./Ant. Lafreri Sequani. Formis Impresse Roma [The childish old woman makes the young woman laugh/Work by the Cremonese gentlewoman Sofonisba Anguissola/Printed by Antonio Lafreri, French, in Rome]

Museum of Fine Arts, Boston, George Peabody Gardner Fund, 64.2039

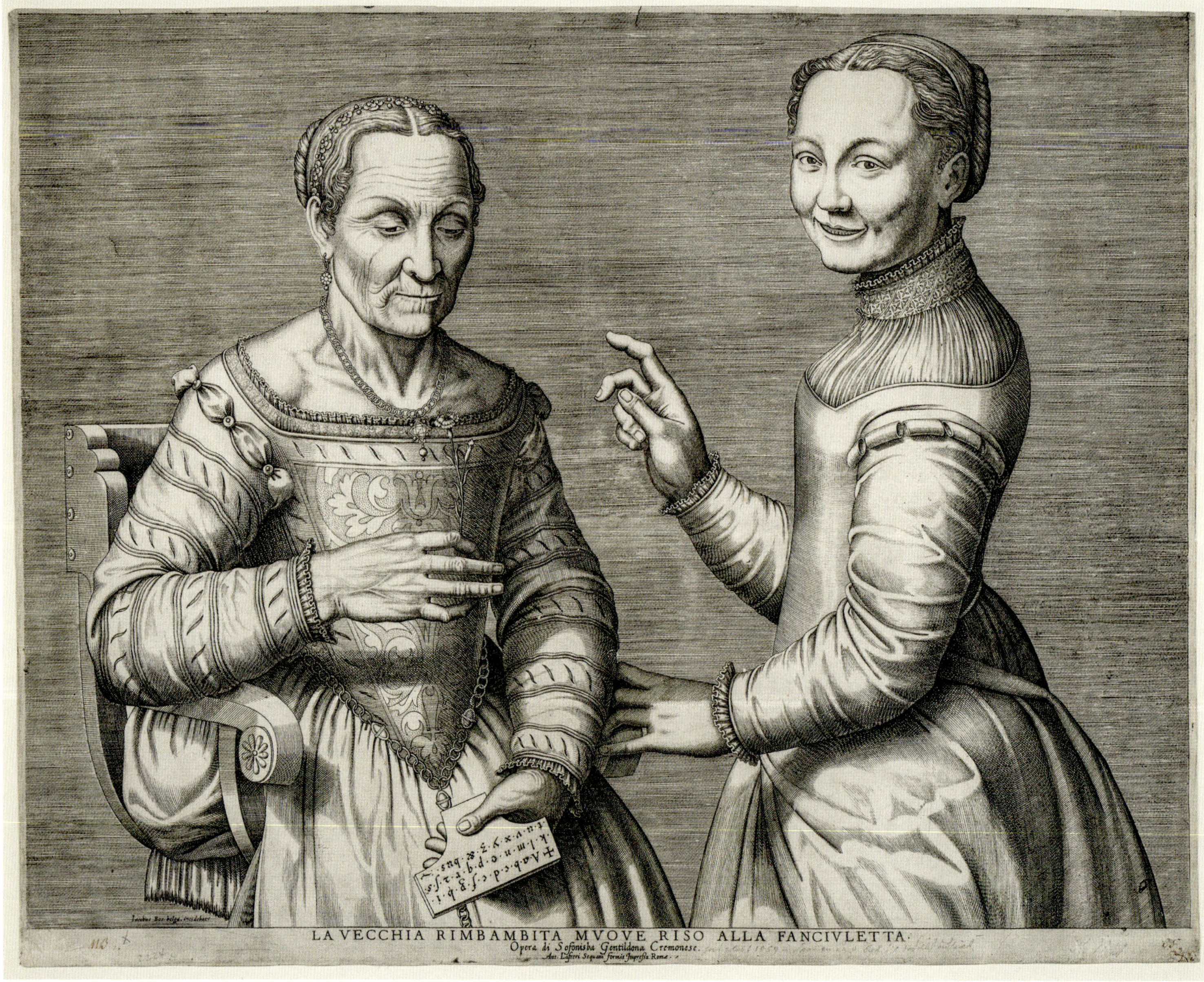

THIS PRINT AFTER A LOST drawing by Sofonisba Anguissola belongs to an important group of narrative scenes by the artist, all distinguished by their close observations from life. Like the best-known painting from the group, the 1555 *Chess Game* in the National Museum, Poznań, this engraving shows female figures experiencing various emotions.[1] An old woman holds a horn-book—a tablet commonly used by children to learn reading—while her young teacher turns to the viewer, smiling. This comical narrative is explained in the title of the print: the childish old woman makes the young woman laugh. Traditional roles are reversed: the young person is not only teaching the dotty old lady, but she is also bemused by her. The image was engraved by Jacob Bos, who specialized in maps and images of antiquities, and printed in Rome in the early 1560s. This is the only instance in which Anguissola's work was translated into a print in her lifetime.

Two surviving drawings by Sofonisba Anguissola with similar content may give us an idea of the now-lost drawing.[2] These works have been related to an artistic exchange between Anguissola and Michelangelo (1475–1564).[3] According to Michelangelo's student and friend Tommaso Cavalieri (1512–1587), after seeing a drawing of a laughing girl by Anguissola, Michelangelo challenged the young artist to draw a weeping figure. She responded with a drawing of her young brother weeping, together with a smiling girl (fig. 1).[4] This and a drawing by Michelangelo were sent by Cavalieri as gifts to the Grand Duke Cosimo I de' Medici (1519–1574) in 1562. About one hundred years later, the Florentine art critic Filippo Baldinucci (1625–1696) describes another drawing by Anguissola in which "she showed a girl who—mocking an old woman who with great concentration studies the abc's on a children's tablet—points at her with a happy laugh."[5] This now-lost drawing may have been the model for the print.

Exploring emotions and their comical side effects had a long history among artists in Northern Europe and Northern Italy,

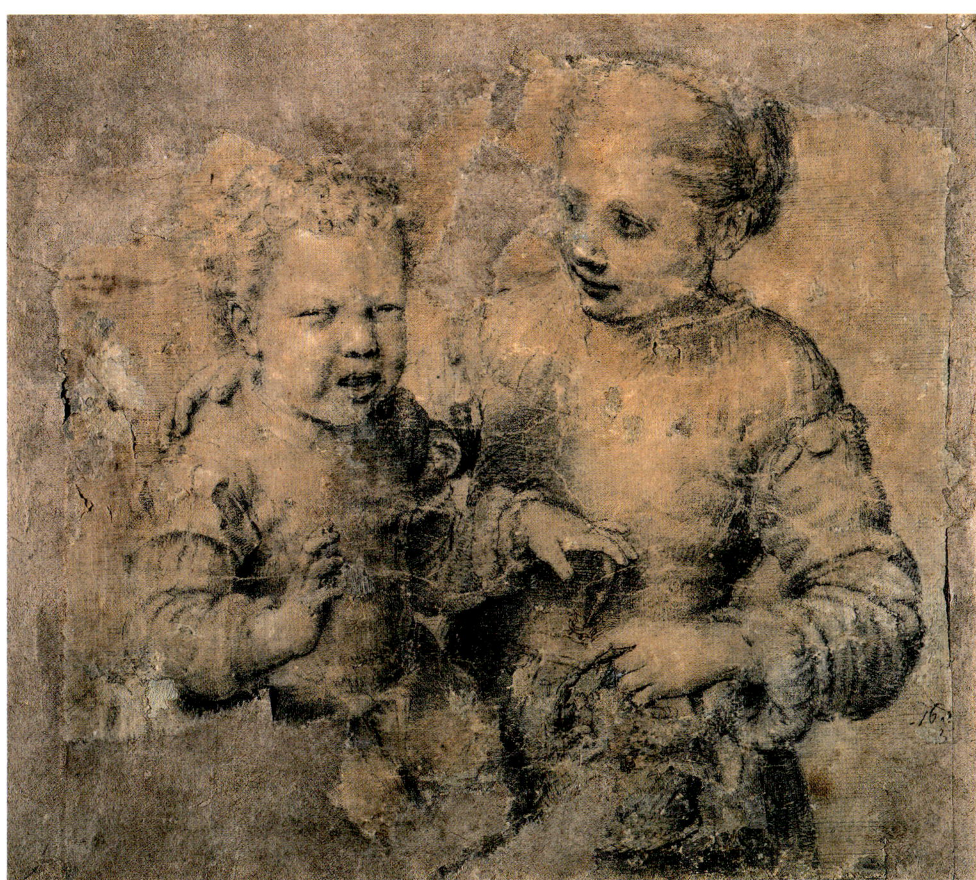

FIGURE 1 Sofonisba Anguissola, *Boy Bitten by a Crayfish*, ca. 1555–1558, black pencil and charcoal on paper, 12¹¹⁄₁₆ × 14¾ in. (32.2 × 37.5 cm). Museo di Capodimonte, Gabinetto dei Disegni e delle Stampe, Naples

most notably Leonardo da Vinci (1452–1519). In the early 1580s, the art critics Gabriele Paleotti (1522–1597) and Giovanni Paolo Lomazzo (1538–1592) described a new genre of paintings, the so-called *pitture ridicule*, defined by a comical motif with a laughing figure.[6] Sofonisba Anguissola's works in this genre allowed her to demonstrate once again her conceptual ingenuity as well as her fine sense of observation directly from life.—OT

NOTES

1. Sofonisba Anguissola, *The Chess Game*, 1555, oil on canvas, 28¾₁₆ × 38¾₁₆ in. (72 × 97 cm), Raczyński Foundation at the National Museum, Poznań.

2. Sofonisba Anguissola, *Old Woman Studying the Alphabet with a Laughing Girl*, ca. 1556–1558, black chalk on paper, mounted on canvas, 11⅞ × 13⁹⁄₁₆ in. (30.1 × 34.5 cm), Gallerie degli Uffizi, Gabinetto dei Disegni e delle Stampe, Florence; *Boy Bitten by a Crayfish*, ca. 1555–1558, black pencil and charcoal on paper, 12¹¹⁄₁₆ × 14¾ in. (32.2 × 37.5 cm), Museo di Capodimonte, Gabinetto dei Disegni e delle Stampe, Naples.

3. Cole suggests 1553 in Cole 2019b, 102.

4. Letter Tommaso Cavalieri to Cosimo I de' Medici, January 20, 1562, in Cremona 1994, 370.

5. Baldinucci 1845–1847, vol. 8, 228. I am using here the translation in Cole 2019b, 103.

6. For Paleotti see de Klerck 1994, 274–77; for Lomazzo see Meijer 1994, 272.

PROVENANCE

1964–present, sold by (C.G. Boerner, New York, New York) to the Museum of Fine Arts, Boston (Boston, Massachusetts).

SELECTED PUBLICATIONS

Baldinucci 1845–1847, vol. 8, 228; Meijer 1994, 272–73; Vienna 1995, 93; Christadler 2000, 158–59; Cole 2019b, 98–117; Madrid 2019, 118 under cat. 14.

Portrait of Marchese Massimiliano Stampa

1557

Oil on canvas, dimensions, including painted extensions around all four sides:
53⅛ × 28 in. (134.94 × 71.12 cm)

Inscribed (in a contemporary hand on the reverse of the original canvas in black paint): MAX.STA.MAR.SON.III-AET.AN.VIIII-1557 [Massimiliano Stampa, the third marquess of Soncino, in his ninth year, 1557][1]

The Walters Art Museum, Baltimore, bequest of Henry Walters, 1931, 37.1016

Detroit only

AS A PORTRAITIST, Sofonisba Anguissola demonstrated a rare sensitivity to children's moods as expressed in their body language, especially their faces. This was apparent in her early, often quite casual, portrayals of her younger sisters and brother.[2] This early masterpiece, painted when she was about twenty-five, is Anguissola's first formal full-length portrait.

Official state portraits of the period typically represent the subject wearing a mask of decorum, but stress permeates the downturned face of the wide-eyed young Massimiliano Stampa (1548–1601). In 1557, at the age of nine, he was thrust into the public realm by the death of his father, Ermete Stampa, the second marchese of Soncino.[3] As the inscription suggests, the Walters portrait was surely commissioned by the family to mark his investiture as the third marchese. Sofonisba Anguissola was likely introduced to the family by one of her teachers, both having carried out commissions from Ermete.[4] Four other versions of the Walters portrait, probably by Anguissola's sisters, who learned to paint from her, have been identified.[5]

In composing this portrait, Anguissola drew on structural and iconographic elements of Lombard portraiture by artists such as Giovanni Battista Moroni (1520/24–1579/80), but she infused it with the sympathy and intimacy of her earlier work (fig. 1). She fashions Massimiliano as a person of stature through his clothing, a ring appropriate to an adult nobleman, a miniaturized rapier, a "hunting dog," and his cultured pose. Architectural elements such as the column were commonly used in Moroni's portraits to provide support for the subject while suggesting an ease of belonging in a magnificent palatial setting. Here the scale of the pedestal has been manipulated to be proportionate to Massimiliano's height, subtly conveying his equivalence with adult counterparts.[6] There is, however, an approachability generally foreign to Moroni's male subjects, who commonly stand somewhat to the side with their feet more or less parallel to the picture plane. With no indication of their distance from the viewer, they remain in a world apart. Massimiliano is posed so that we take in his feet from above, as if he were standing before us, creating a palpable intimacy.[7] With its original dark glaze, the green rear ground would have added a vibrant surround found on several earlier portraits, but it stands in contrast to the neutral tones of her subsequent, more somber court portraits in Madrid.[8]

Portrait of Marchese Massimiliano Stampa is a pivotal work in Sofonisba Anguissola's career, not only because it surely contributed to her 1559 invitation to the Madrid court, but because it was followed by a turn towards the past. The fresh, modern sensibility of portraits painted before she was engulfed by court expectations would soon be put by.—JS

NOTES

1. Simon 1986, figs. 2–3.

2. Such as her well-known *Chess Game*, 1555, in the National Museum, Poznań, which features siblings Lucia, Europa, and Minerva Anguissola.

3. For the interesting life of the third marchese of Soncino, see Simon 1986, 120–21.

4. Sacchi 1994d, 206; Wied 1995b. See also Gamberini 2019b, 120, for family connections.

5. Sacchi 1994d, 206–7; Sacchi 1994e, 208–10.

6. Although the pedestal was drawn in rough perspective, its proportions relative to the column are awkward, as Wied has pointed out in Wied 1995c. Having studied portraiture privately with Campi rather than in a workshop environment, Anguissola was probably not trained in drafting architectural elements.

7. The same is true of Anguissola's informal portrait of her father and two siblings in the Nivaagaards Malerisamling, Nivå.

8. At some point the rear ground was overcleaned, largely eliminating the glaze.

PROVENANCE

Chantel collection (Lyon, France); (Galerie Trotti & Cie, Paris, France); James Jewett Stillman [1850–1918] (New York, New York); by descent to his son, Charles Chauncey C. Stillman [1877–1926] (New

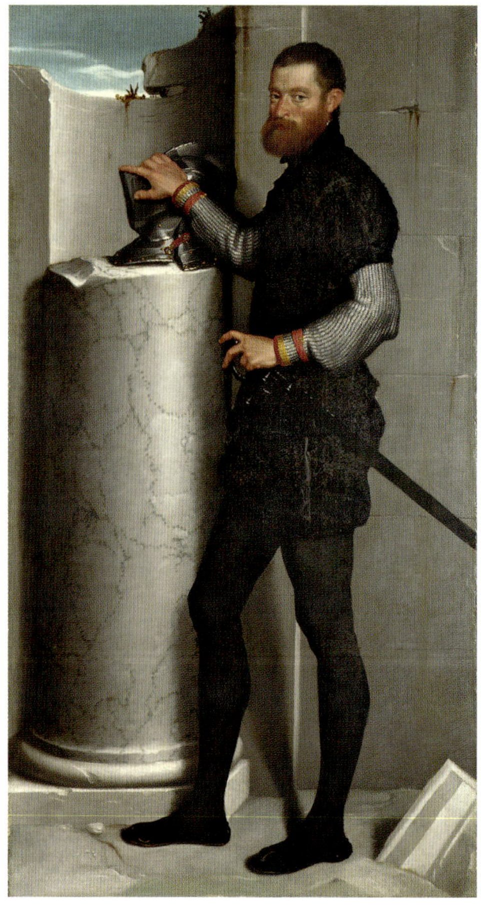

FIGURE 1 Giovanni Battista Moroni, *Portrait of a Gentleman*, ca. 1555, oil on canvas, 73⁵⁄₁₆ × 39⁵⁄₁₆ in. (186.2 × 99.9 cm). National Gallery, London

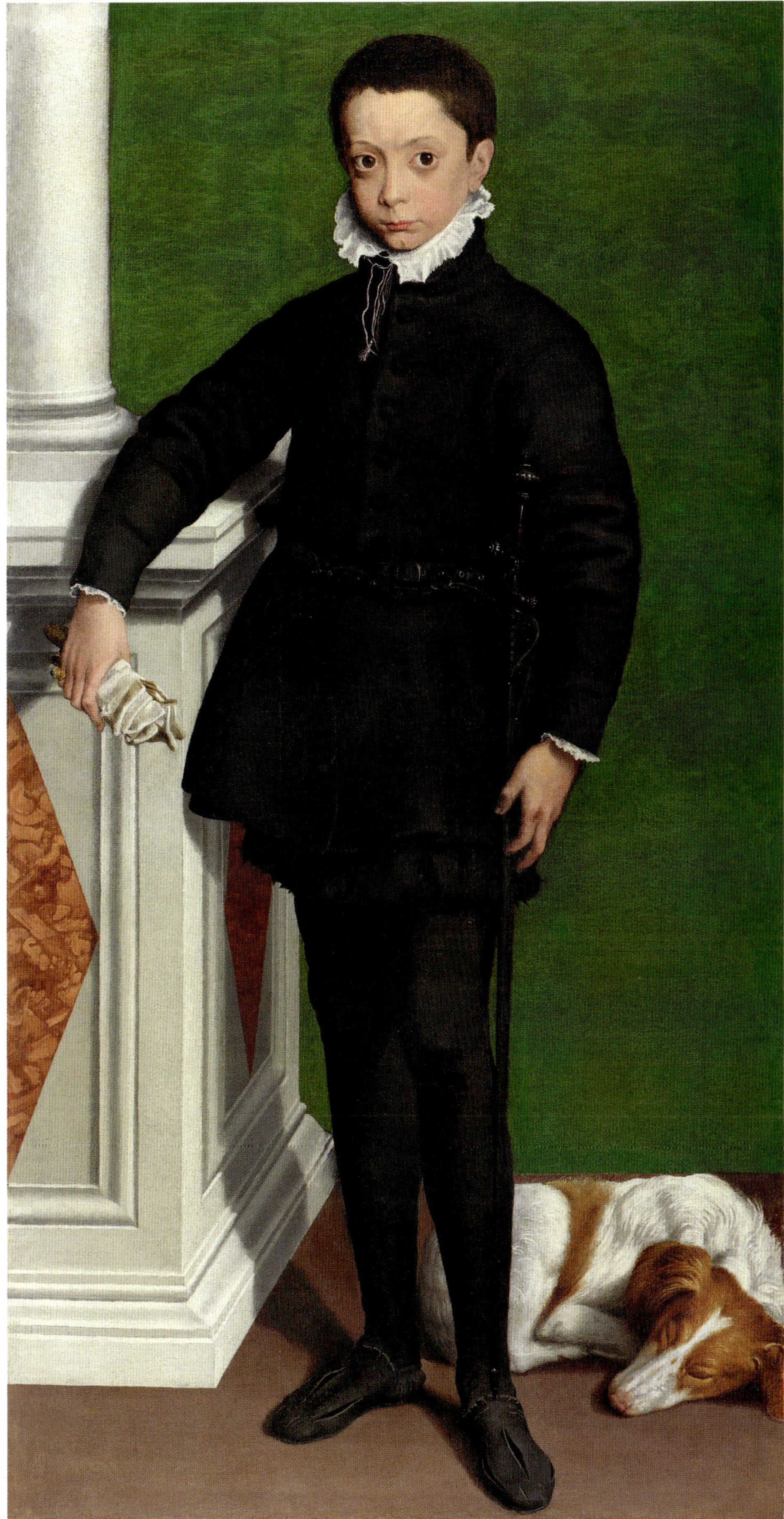

York, New York); February 3, 1927, sold at his sale through (American Art Galleries, New York, New York), no. 29, as *Portrait of a Young Prince of the Este Family* by G. B. Moroni, to Henry Walters [1848–1931] (Baltimore, Maryland); 1931–present, bequest to the Walters Art Gallery (Baltimore, Maryland), now the Walters Art Museum (Baltimore, Maryland).

SELECTED EXHIBITIONS

Metropolitan Museum of Art, New York, 1923; Walters Art Gallery, Baltimore, 1972; Centro culturale "Città di Cremona," 1994; Kunsthistorisches Museum, Vienna, 1995; National Museum of Women in the Arts, Washington, D.C., 1995; Walters Art Gallery, Baltimore, 1995–1996; Museo Nacional del Prado, Madrid, 2019–2020.

SELECTED BIBLIOGRAPHY

Borenius 1913, 195, under no. 172 (as attributed to Giovanni Battista Moroni); Burroughs, Breck, and Ivins 1923, 109, pl. 35 (as attributed to Giovanni Battista Moroni); *Important Paintings by Old and Modern Masters* 1927, no. 29, illus. (as attributed to Giovanni Battista Moroni); Berenson 1932, 23; Berenson 1936, 20; De Tolnay 1941, 114–16, fig. 1; Kühnel-Kunze 1962, 92–93, fig. 13; Berenson 1968, vol. 1, 13, pl. 1976; Tufts 1972, 50, 52 illus.; Tufts 1974b, 22, 28, fig. 6; Zeri 1976, vol. 2, 427–28, no. 298, pl. 205; Greer 1979, 252, illus.; Simon 1986, 117–22, fig. 1; Caroli 1987, 126–29; Perlingieri 1992, 79, 96, 99–102, 157–59, pl. 61; Cremona 1994, 33, 41, 125–26, 207 illus., fig. 9; Garrard 1994, 586–87, fig. 12; Sacchi 1994d, 206–7, cat. 11, 207 illus.; Baltimore 1995, 20, 38, illus., 72, illus.; Washington, D.C. 1995, 36–37, 46, pl. 7; Wied 1995b, 84, cat. 17, 85 illus.; Wied 1995c, 84; Hansen and Spicer 2005, 102, cat. 28, 103 illus.; Cole 2019b, 40–41, 139–40, 169–70, cat. 17, 169 illus., fig. 23; Gamberini 2019b, 120, cat. 15, 121 illus.

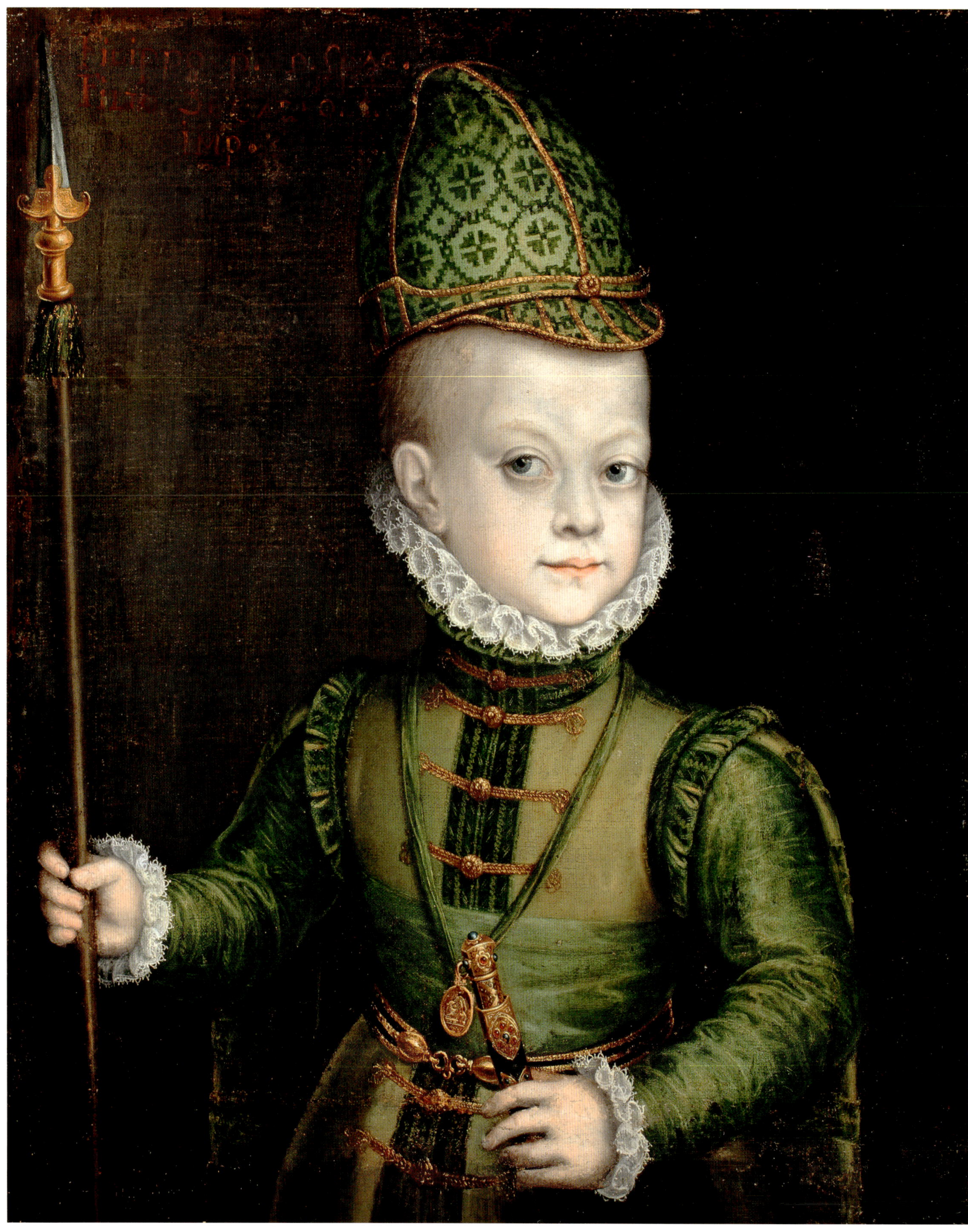

7

Portrait of a Spanish Prince, Probably the Infante Don Fernando

1573

Oil on canvas, 23¼ × 19 in. (59.06 × 48.26 cm)

Inscribed (upper left, perhaps by a later hand): Filippo p.di Spag./Filio Di Carlo/
iMP [Philip, Prince of Spain, son of Emperor Charles]

San Diego Museum of Art, 1936.58

UNTIL RECENTLY, most scholars believed this to be a portrait by the Spanish court artist Alonso Sánchez Coello (1531–1588), a painter who occasionally collaborated with Sofonisba Anguissola. In 2015, however, John Marciari ascribed it to Anguissola, and it now provides new insight into her time at the Spanish court (1559–1573), a period that is still far less understood than her preceding years in Cremona. This exhibition is the first occasion on which the portrait has been shown alongside her other work.

The painting is part of a larger group of five portraits of members of the royal family by Sofonisba Anguissola. At the invitation of King Philip II (1527–1598), she lived with the Spanish royal family from 1559 to 1573. Despite the inscription, the sitter cannot be the Infante Felipe, the future King Philip III (1578–1621). Marciari identified the boy as the Infante Fernando, born December 4, 1571; he was sworn in as heir to the Spanish throne on May 31, 1573, and the portrait would have been painted around that date. At the same time, Anguissola painted two portraits of Don Fernando's half-sisters, Infanta Isabella Clara Eugenia (1566–1633) and Infanta Catalina Micaela (1567–1597).[1] All three portraits are similar in size and follow the restrained fashion of Spanish state portraiture. They must be among the last works that she executed before leaving Spain in June 1573. Almudena Pérez de Tudela proposes that these three paintings, together with two portraits of Philip II and Anna of Austria (1549–1580), were painted "as a farewell to the Spanish court."[2] The three portraits of children bear similar inscriptions that were probably added at a later date, perhaps in Turin, when they were still together.

This likeness reveals an unusual sensitivity to the child's character by introducing a degree of intimacy into the strict formal requirements of a princely portrait. As a member of the Spanish royal household, Sofonisba Anguissola's primary responsibility was not painting, but service to the queen and, by extension, to the royal children. She had known the children since their births, and after the death of Queen Elisabeth of Valois (1545–1568), she was entrusted with the upbringing of the two infantas.[3] In 1570 Anguissola became a member of the household of the new queen, Anna of Austria, a position that allowed her to live in proximity to the two princesses and, after 1571, to the newborn Prince Fernando (1571–1578). This intimacy seems to have contributed to her nuanced rendering of the boy. According to records, he was often dressed in green, and he may have posed for Anguissola in the private quarters of the palace.[4]

The roughly two-year-old child is shown with thin blond hair, long eyelashes, and two clumsy hands playfully clasping a spear and small sword. Compared with contemporaneous portraits of Fernando, Anguissola adjusted and diminished the prince's protruding chin, a Habsburg family characteristic.[5] By turning his face to the viewer's right, and his body and eyes in the opposite direction, she created a dynamic composition that suggests the vivacious nature of the boy, who died only five years later. This rendering is visually enhanced by the calculated contrasts between the enamel-like flesh tones against the dark background. With her delicate and assured brushwork, Sofonisba Anguissola found an appropriate response to the artistic challenge of depicting the young crown prince. Thanks to her long-standing familiarity with the Spanish royal family, she was able to create carefully calibrated portraits that never fail to show the personality of, and an element of empathy for, the sitter.—OT

NOTES

1. Sofonisba Anguissola, *Infanta Isabella Clara Eugenia*, ca. 1573, oil on canvas, 22 × 18½ in. (56 × 47 cm), Galleria Sabauda, Turin; and *Infanta Catalina Micaela with a Marmoset*, ca. 1573, oil on canvas, 22 × 18½ in. (56.2 × 47 cm), private collection. Pérez de Tudela suggests March to April as the date for the portrait of Infanta Catalina Micaela in Pérez de Tudela 2019b, 156.

2. Pérez de Tudela 2019b, 156–57. See Sofonisba Anguissola, *Philip II*, ca. 1573, oil on canvas, 34½ × 28³⁄₁₆ in. (88 × 72 cm), Museo Nacional del Prado, Madrid, inv. no. 1036; *Queen Anna of Austria*, ca. 1573, oil on canvas, 33¹¹⁄₁₆ × 26⁹⁄₁₆ in. (86 × 67.5 cm), Museo Nacional del Prado, Madrid, inv. no. 1284.

3. Kusche 1995, 43.

4. For the dress see Pérez de Tudela 2019b, 156.

5. See, for instance, Alonso Sánchez Coello, *Infantes Diego and Felipe*, 1579 (?), oil on canvas, 67¾ × 40³⁄₁₆ in. (172 × 102 cm), Monasterio de las Descalzas Reales, Madrid.

PROVENANCE

By 1635, possibly in the royal collection (Turin, Italy). Perhaps taken from Turin to France during the Napoleonic occupation. Collection of Godfroy Brauer [1857–1923] (Paris and Nice, France); July 5, 1929, sold by Brauer through (Christie's, London, UK); purchased under the name "Ackroyd"; 1936, purchased from (Ehrich-Newhouse Galleries, New York, New York) by Anne R. and Amy Putnam; 1936–present, gift to the San Diego Museum of Art (San Diego, California).

SELECTED EXHIBITIONS

Albuquerque Museum, 2005.

SELECTED PUBLICATIONS

Andrews 1947, 74–75, 75 illus. (as attributed to Alonso Sánchez Coello); Gaya Nuño 1958, 297, no. 2566; *Fine Arts Society* 1960, 83–84 (as attributed to Alonso Sánchez Coello); Madrid 1990, 28 illus., 144 illus. (as attributed to Alonso Sánchez Coello); Dunn 1993, 137, illus. (as attributed to Alonso Sánchez Coello); Albuquerque 2005, 77–78, 120–21, cat. 12, pl. 12; Marciari 2015, 177–81, cat. 35; Cole 2019b, 200–201, cat. 52, 201 illus.; Pérez de Tudela 2019b, 156–57 under cats. 30–31, 157 illus.

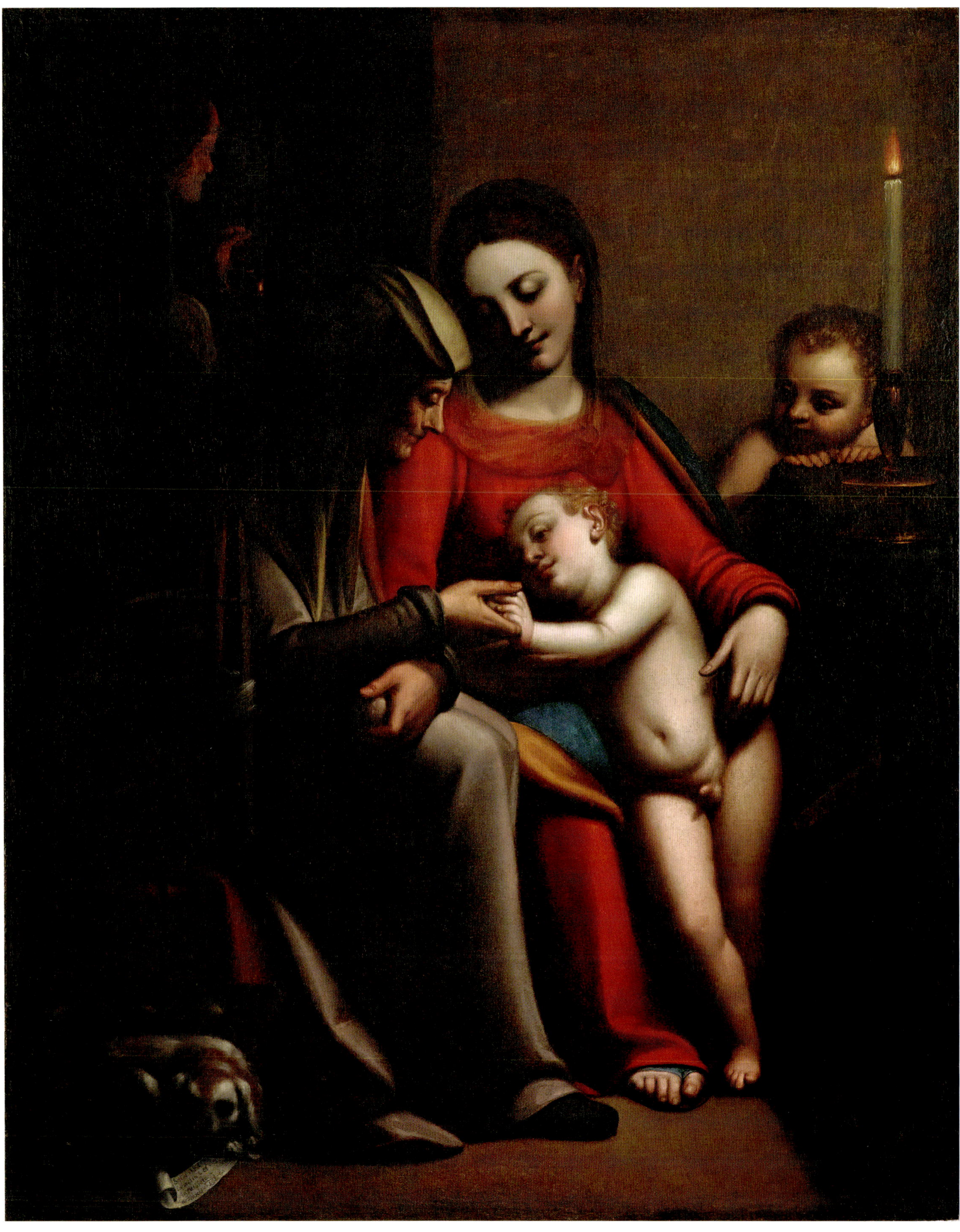

Holy Family with Saints Anne and John the Baptist

1592
Oil on canvas, $48\frac{7}{16} \times 42\frac{15}{16}$ in. (123 × 109 cm)
Inscribed (on *cartellino* at lower left): Sofonisba Lomelino et Anguissola pinsit 1592 [Sofonisba Lomelino and Anguissola painted it 1592]
Lowe Art Museum, University of Miami, Coral Gables/Miami, 52.003.000

EVEN THOUGH RELIGIOUS paintings form only a small part of Sofonisba Anguissola's oeuvre—about half a dozen examples are known—they played an important role in her career, as evidenced by her numerous self-portraits painting the Virgin and Child. She painted *Holy Family with Saints Anne and John the Baptist*—her last dated work—in Genoa, where she lived from about 1580 to 1615. The art critic Filippo Baldinucci (1625–1696) reported later that numerous Genoese princes and other nobles owned paintings by Anguissola, yet there is no information about the purpose and early provenance of this *Holy Family*.[1] Pietro Paolo da Ribera (dates unknown), another contemporary, wrote in 1609 that the Empress Maria of Austria (1528–1603), while on her way through Genoa in 1582, received a painting of the Virgin as a gift from Anguissola. That work has not been identified, but the episode illustrates the artist's interest in religious subjects during her late career.[2]

As exemplified by this picture, Sofonisba Anguissola favored Marian themes, which allowed her to explore the tender interplay between the Christ child, his mother, and other family members. Here, she chose an interior setting whose nocturnal scenery emphasizes the contemplative mood. Leaning against his mother, Christ silently plays with his grandmother Anne and a ball of yarn.[3] John follows the game from behind the table, while Joseph, in the background, is about to leave the room. By placing Christ close to the burning candle, which is precariously close to the edge of the table, Anguissola demonstrates her talent for painting a nude figure. Thanks to subtle contrasts of light, his body,

especially the neck, belly, and legs, are softly modeled. This tenderness in the execution of the child and the hazy light effects are reminiscent of works by Leonardo da Vinci (1452–1519), and particularly Antonio da Correggio (1489–1534).

As with her other religious paintings, here Sofonisba Anguissola has emulated works from well-known artists. In this case, she based her composition on paintings by Luca Cambiaso (1527–1585), the leading artist in Genoa during the second half of the sixteenth century. A work such as his *Madonna of the Candle* from 1575 may have inspired her with its simplified geometric order and interest in exploiting a nocturnal

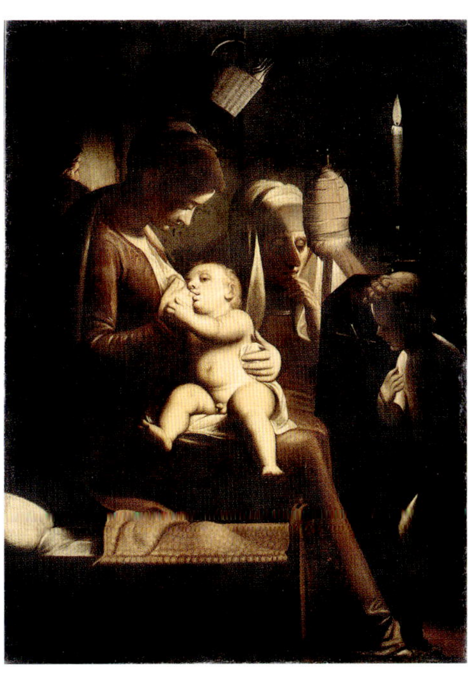

FIGURE 1 Luca Cambiaso, *Madonna of the Candle*, 1575, oil on canvas, 55 × $42\frac{13}{16}$ in. (140 × 109 cm). Palazzo Bianco, Genoa

scene (fig. 1). Anguissola, however, rendered her *Holy Family* in a softer light and added a sense of detail not shared by Cambiaso. The reposing lap dog, the metallic light reflections on the candlestick, and the *cartellino*, an illusionistically rendered strip of paper that is unique in her work, reveal her spirited interpretation of the subject.

By imbuing the well-known religious narrative with her own sensitivity for family scenes, interiors, and minute gradations of moods, Sofonisba Anguissola created with this *Holy Family* one of her most memorable and poetic works.—OT

NOTES

1. Baldinucci 1845–1847, vol. 2, 632. Quoted in Cole 2019b, 272 n. 14.

2. Three more religious paintings by Sofonisba Anguissola have survived from this late period, ranging in date from 1574 to 1592: *Pietà*, 1574–1585, oil on canvas, $17\frac{3}{16} \times 10\frac{1}{2}$ in. (44 × 27 cm), Pinacoteca di Brera, Milan; *Virgin Suckling the Infant Christ*, 1588, oil on canvas, $30\frac{3}{16} \times 24\frac{11}{16}$ in. (77 × 63.5 cm), Szépművészeti Múzeum, Budapest; *Mystic Marriage of Saint Catherine*, 1588, oil on canvas, 37 × $27\frac{9}{16}$ in. (94 × 70 cm), Museo de Bellas Artes de Bilbao. For Empress Maria of Austria's visit to Genoa, see Pietro Paolo di Ribera, *Le glorie immortali*, 1609, quoted in Cole 2019b, 149.

3. García-Frías Checa 2019, 200.

PROVENANCE

1952–present, gift of Mrs. Forbes Hawkes to the Lowe Art Museum, University of Miami (Coral Gables, Florida).

SELECTED EXHIBITIONS

Museo Civico, Cremona, 1985; Cornell Fine Arts Museum at Rollins College, Winter Park, 1991; Centro culturale "Città di Cremona," 1994; Kunsthistorisches Museum, Vienna, 1995; National Museum of Women in the Arts, Washington, D.C., 1995; Museo Nacional del Prado, Madrid, 2019–2020.

SELECTED PUBLICATIONS

Fredericksen and Zeri 1972, 10, 576; Cremona 1985, 178, cat. 1.16.11, illus.; Caroli 1987, 68–70, 142–43, no. 29; Winter Park 1991, 26, cat. 13, 27 illus.; Perlingieri 1992, 177–78, 183–84, pl. 104; Cremona 1994, 41–42, 268, cat. 36, 269 illus.; Vienna 1995, 137, cat. 51, 138 illus.; Washington, D.C. 1995, 88, 100–101, pl. 24, Jacobs 1997a, 190; Cole 2019b, 149–50, 159, cat. 5, illus., fig. 101; Madrid 2019, 200, cat. 50, 201 illus.

Young Man

Unknown Northern Italian artist (formerly attributed to Sofonisba Anguissola)
ca. mid-16th century
Oil on panel, 17 × 12⅛ in. (43.2 × 30.8 cm)
Detroit Institute of Arts, Bequest of Mr. and Mrs. Lawrence P. Fisher, 68.300
Detroit only

PURPORTEDLY BASED ON a 1928 authentication by Richard Offner, the attribution of this panel to Sofonisba Anguissola has received no further consideration since it was bequeathed to the Detroit Institute of Arts in 1968. Once assigned to "the artist's early period (about 1570),"[1] the *Young Man* demands a reassessment aligning with our current understanding of Anguissola's career and output.[2] Reopening the question of the attribution underscores the difficulties inherent in determining which of the many works that have been associated with Sofonisba Anguissola securely fit within the canon of her authorship.[3]

The unidentified youth in the DIA panel wears a black doublet with slashed sleeves revealing hints of a reddish-brown lining at the shoulders and cuffs. The ruffled edges of a white undershirt peek out at the collar and below the cuffs.[4] Technical analysis indicates his attire may originally have looked quite different, perhaps with red lower sleeves, as suggested in infrared reflectography (IRR), where the black of the doublet absorbs differently in the bottom section of the sleeves (fig. 1).[5] Is it possible the entire costume was once more colorful?[6] Was Anguissola inclined to make such drastic revisions directly on the painted surface? Little is known about her process, a factor complicating the work of attribution, but technical analyses have proven Anguissola could rethink a composition, as she did when she changed the position of the king's arm in her portrait of Philip II (ca. 1573, Museo Nacional del Prado, Madrid).[7]

More telling is the absence of Anguissola's usual attention to the minutiae of attire.

The gloves and white collar fail to equal the crisply defined cuffs of the sitter's gloves in her portrait of Massimiliano Stampa (1557, Walters Art Museum, Baltimore, cat. 6), or the fine description of the delicately patterned trim of his collar. Anguissola's brushwork could be both precise and loose—the stylistic disparities that exist even among her secure works pose a further challenge to recognizing her authorship[8]—but her efforts to describe texture and ornamentation overwhelmingly betray a meticulous hand. Though some articulate brushwork indicating the texture of the lower sleeves is visible in the IRR photograph, overall, when compared to even Anguissola's earliest

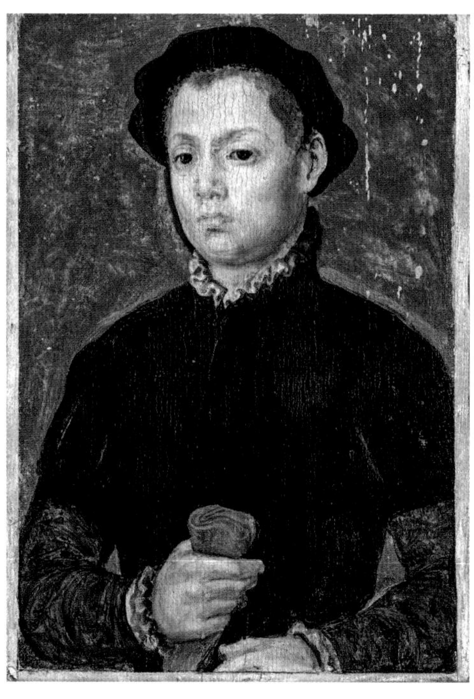

FIGURE 1 Infrared reflectogram (IRR), unknown Northern Italian artist, *Young Man*. Detroit Institute of Arts

Cremonese portraits, details of costume in the *Young Man* are more cursorily executed. Atmospheric subtleties—the soft modulation of light and shadow that give volume to the sitter's face in the Southampton portrait of a nun (ca. 1551, City Art Gallery, cat. 1), where transitions diffuse rather than demarcate figure from background—are likewise lacking in the Detroit panel.[9]

In its current state the painting's commonalities with Anguissola's secure works are superficial at best. Though she favored a green background in her early portraits, she was not unique among the Cremonese circle in doing so.[10] The eyes, though perceptibly enlarged, lack her characteristic delineation of the lid crease, and the austere black costume, while recurrent among her subjects, may have originally been more colorful.[11] Though seemingly made within the wide ambit of Northern Italy of the mid- to late sixteenth century, a more precise attribution for the DIA's *Young Man*—as with so many works linked, with varying credibility, to Sofonisba Anguissola—remains elusive.—LLR

NOTES

1. Heil 1930, 108.

2. It is, for a start, well established that in 1570 Anguissola was engaged at the Spanish court of Philip II (r. 1556–1598), a pinnacle in her career that most would now hesitate to call her "early period."

3. Cole 2019b provides a comprehensive catalogue of works associated with Sofonisba Anguissola, distinguishing between those that are securely attributed, nearly universally accepted, still debated, and previously attributed but now almost unanimously rejected, showing how widely scholarship has differed in the attempt to assemble a decisive corpus of her works.

4. A photograph found in the registrar's file at the DIA, possibly taken around the time of Offner's 1928 authentication, reveals a *Young Man* that differs markedly from its present appearance, with greater linear definition in the hair, eyes, and lips, and a more evenly toned face. The panel was cleaned in 1969, but the treatment is so briefly documented that it is difficult to ascertain whether this or a previous intervention is responsible for its present appearance. Curiously, while the 1969 "rehabilitation" report (accessible in the DIA's curatorial file for the object) ascribes the panel to an "Italian Artist about 1550," the Anguissola attribution was maintained when the painting was catalogued a year later in *Paintings in the Detroit Institute of Arts* 1970, 10. It is uncertain whether the photograph or what we see today captures more of the painting's original appearance.

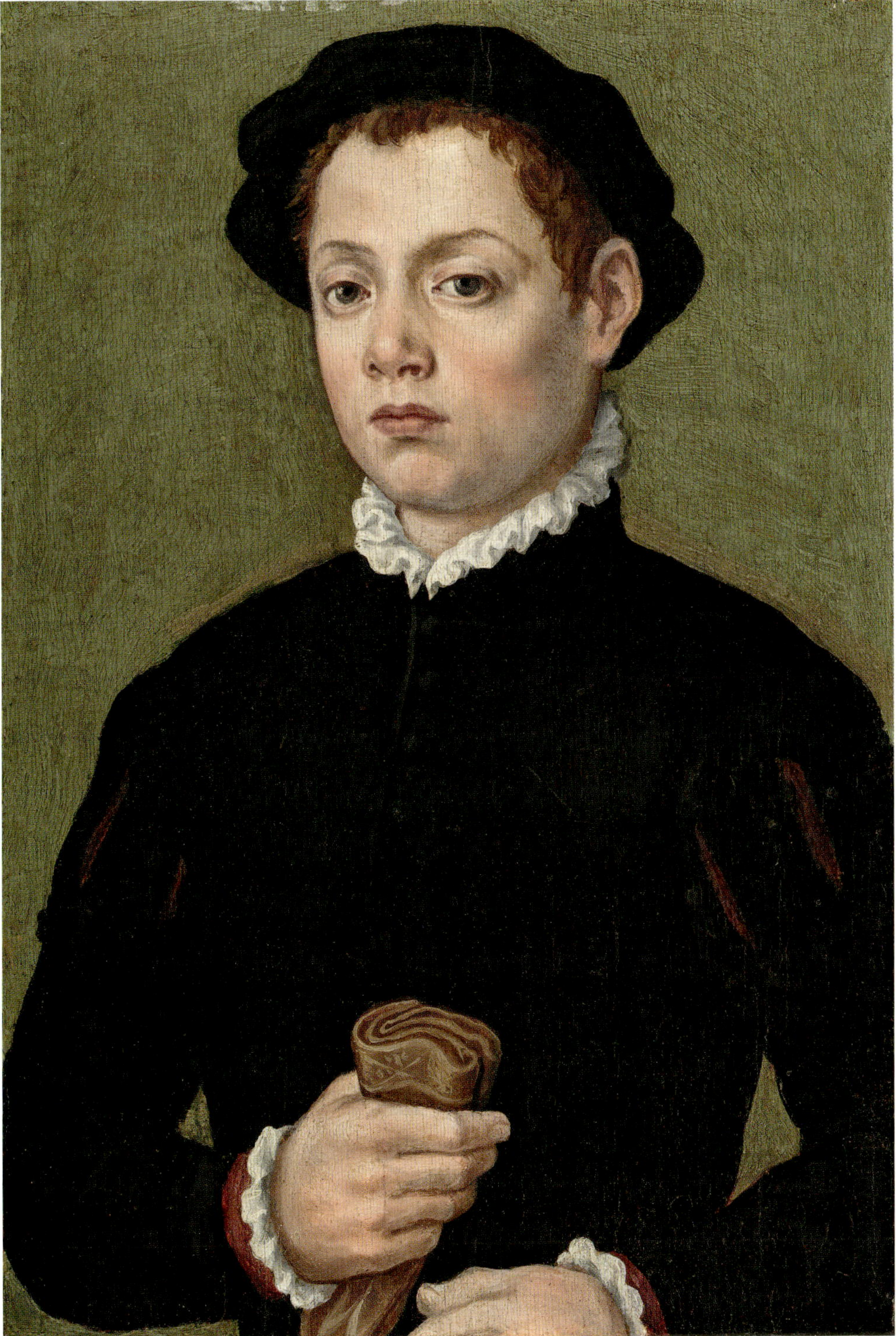

adopting the local technical practices in use by her contemporaries at court (see Jover de Celis, García, and Carcelén 2019, 71, 84–85), making direct technical comparisons with works that would pre- or post-date her time in Spain difficult.

8. Cole puts the issue in perspective, writing, "At one extreme, her painting has been difficult to distinguish from that of the fine, precise manner of Alonso Sánchez Coello; at the other, serious scholars believe that she may be the author of one or two flashily brushed paintings traditionally assigned to El Greco." Cole 2019b, 12.

9. Given the painting's uncertain history, however, we cannot preclude the possibility that such subtleties once existed but have since been obscured.

10. Green backgrounds prevail in the small group of portraits attributed in recent years to Antonio Campi (1523–1587) (see Tanzi 2019, 2–6), and are likewise found among those attributed to his brother, Giulio Campi (ca. 1508–1573), whose pupil Bernardino Campi (1522–1591) was Anguissola's own teacher, and whose extended family was foundational in forming the Cremonese school. Might the green background be more uniquely Cremonese than uniquely Sofonisba Anguissola?

11. The painting's support may be further cause to doubt the attribution to Anguissola, as the majority of her secure works are executed in oil on canvas. Among his catalogue of Anguissola's "documented works/works with uncontested signatures" and "attributions largely accepted by specialists," Cole lists only four works on panel, two of which are miniature and circular in format, and all of which are considerably smaller than the DIA panel. Works on panel the size of the DIA portrait are entirely foreign to her documented oeuvre.

PROVENANCE

1968–present, bequest of Mr. Lawrence P. Fisher [1888–1961] and Mrs. Dollie May Fisher [d. 1968] (Detroit, Michigan) to the Detroit Institute of Arts (Detroit, Michigan).

SELECTED PUBLICATIONS

Heil 1930, 46, 108; *Bulletin of the Detroit Institute of Arts* 1969, 19; *Bulletin of the Detroit Institute of Arts* 1970, 15; *Paintings in the Detroit Institute of Arts* 1970, 10.

5. Microscopic abrasions in the same area reveal a red lower layer, prompting the hypothesis that the lower portions of the sleeves may once have been red. I am deeply grateful to Ellen Hanspach-Bernal, conservator of paintings, and Aaron Steele, digital imaging specialist, at the Detroit Institute of Arts for their expert analysis and shared observations on this work.

6. The application of the topmost black layer of the doublet where it is painted in around areas such as the hands, gloves, and collar suggests that it may be a later addition. See Hanspach-Bernal's report, consultable in conservation at the DIA.

7. See Jover de Celis, García, and Carcelén 2019, 76–77. Their study was, in part, an update and expansion of Garrido 1990 (see especially 226–30, cats. 9–10 and 5). Published analyses have primarily concentrated on paintings from Anguissola's career in Spain, when she was not only adapting to the stylistic conventions of the court, but also likely

DIANA SCULTORI

Mantua, ca. 1547–Rome, 1612

THE ONLY SIXTEENTH-CENTURY ITALIAN woman artist to sign her prints, Diana Scultori is also known by the last names Ghisi, Mantuana, and Mantovana. Born in Mantua, she moved to Rome in 1575. That year she married the architect Francesco da Volterra (1535–1594) and received a papal privilege—a rare occurrence—that enabled her to profit from the sale of engraved prints after works by her husband and by artists in the papal workshop, including Giulio Romano (ca. 1499–1546). Trained by her father, she is one of only fifteen women artists mentioned in the second edition of Giorgio Vasari's (1511–1574) *Lives of the Most Excellent Painters, Sculptors, and Architects (Le vite de' più eccellenti pittori, scultori, et architettori)* (1568). Her first print dates to 1575 and her last to 1588, though she would live another twenty-four years.

10

Latona Giving Birth to Apollo and Diana on the Island of Delos, second state (?)

Diana Scultori, after Giulio Romano (ca. 1499–1546)
Prior to 1575
Engraving on laid paper
Plate: 10³⁄₁₆ × 14¹⁵⁄₁₆ in. (25.8 × 38 cm); sheet: 11¹⁵⁄₁₆ × 16⅝ in. (30.3 × 42.2 cm)
Inscribed and marked (lower left, in plate): DIANA; (lower left, below image in brown ink): [PMC.?]; (lower right, below image in brown ink): premiere Epreuve avant l'adresse d'Horatio Pacifico, et cette de DeRossi [first proof before the attempt of Horatio Pacifico, and that of DeRossi]
National Gallery of Art, Washington, D.C., Rosenwald Collection, 1943.3.4619

11

The Spinario, first state

Diana Scultori, after Cornelius Cort (Netherlandish, ca. 1533–1578)
Published by Claudio Duchetti (French, active in Italy, d. 1585)
1581
Engraving on laid paper
Plate: 12¹⁄₁₆ × 8³⁄₁₆ in. (30.6 × 20.8 cm); sheet: 21⁵⁄₁₆ × 16⅞ in. (54.2 × 42.9 cm)
Inscribed (lower left, in image): DIANA INCIDEBAT [Diana incised it]; (lower right, below image, in plate): Romae. Claudij. Ducheti. Formis. 1581 [Published by Claudio Duchetti in Rome in 1581]
National Gallery of Art, Washington, D.C., Ailsa Mellon Bruce Fund, 2009.100.1

DIANA SCULTORI provides a unique example of how a "woman could learn a trade in the arts, produce, circulate, and protect her authorial rights to signed images."[1] Trained by her father Giovanni Battista Mantovano (1503–1575), a sculptor and engraver for the Gonzaga family in Mantua, Scultori's earliest works were prints after drawings by her father, by Giulio Romano, or by other artists of the Gonzaga court. In 1575, the year her father died, she married the architect Francesco da Volterra and moved to Rome.[2] She arrived in the city with engraved copperplates after Giulio Romano and other artists who worked in Mantua, and on June 5, 1575, she obtained permission from Pope Gregory XIII (1502–1585) to make prints from these plates to sell.[3]

Based on a preparatory drawing by Giulio Romano for a painting now in Hampton Court Palace in England (fig. 1), *Latona Giving Birth to Apollo and Diana on the Island of Delos* was executed prior to 1575,[4] during Diana Scultori's early years in Mantua. Jupiter created the Island of Delos for Latona—pictured reclining at the center of the print—so she could peacefully give birth to twins Diana (being washed in the foreground) and Apollo (being hidden at right), away from his wife Juno's wrathful gaze.[5] As only the name DIANA is engraved at the bottom left of the print—evenly inked with full plate impressions intact—this is likely the second of five known states of the engraving.[6]

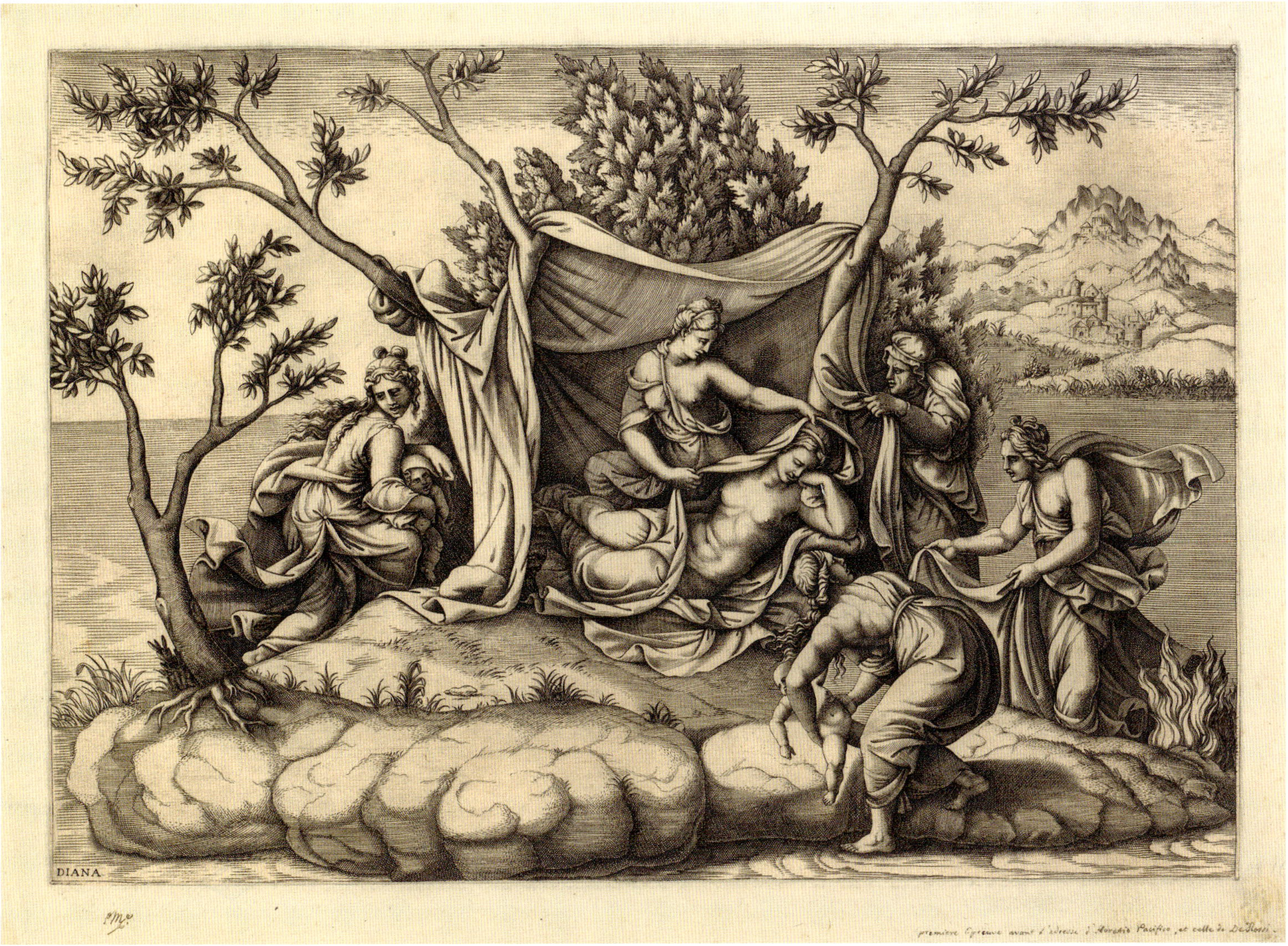

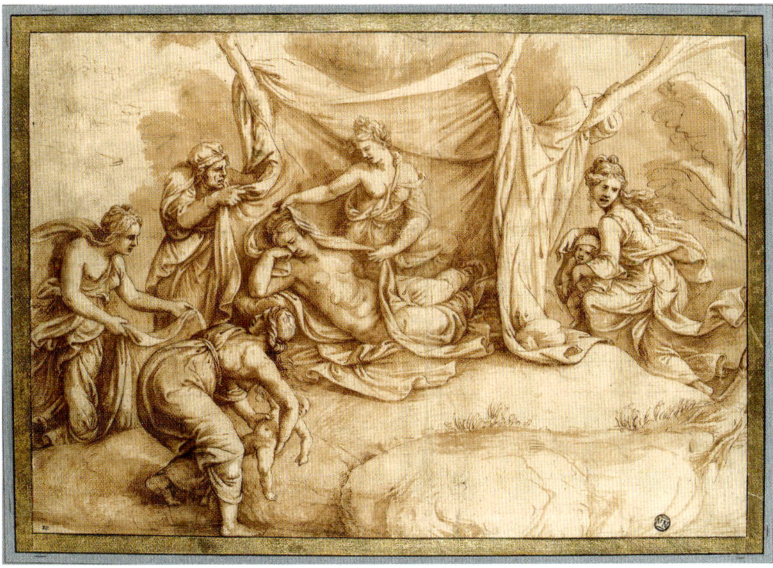

FIGURE 1 Giulio Romano, *Latona Giving Birth to Apollo and Diana on the Island of Delos*, ca. 1533–1534, pen, brown ink, brown wash, on beige paper, 12 × 17⁹⁄₁₆ in. (30.4 × 44.6 cm). Musée du Louvre, Paris, inv. 3500

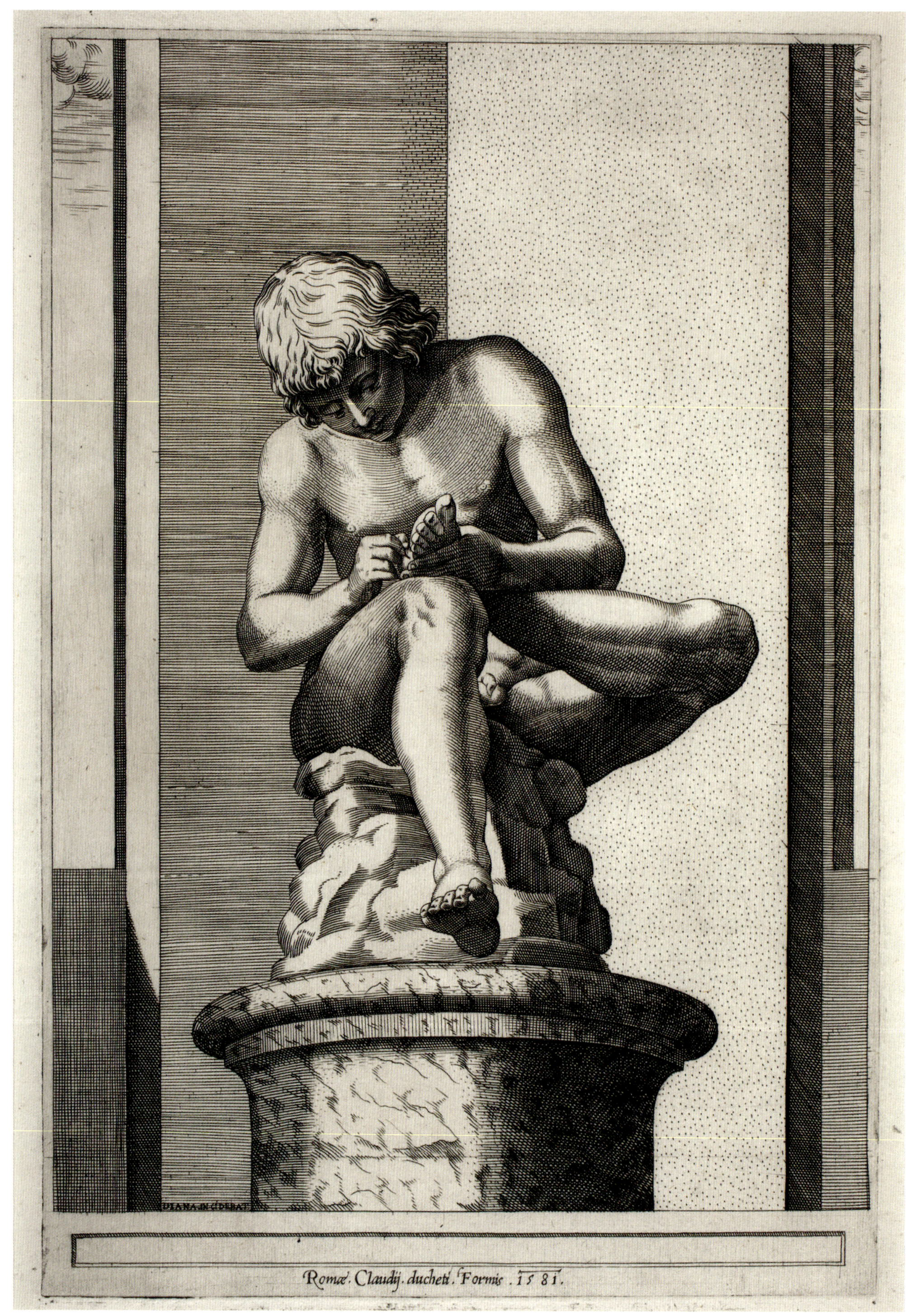

Romæ. Claudij. ducheti. Formis. 1581.

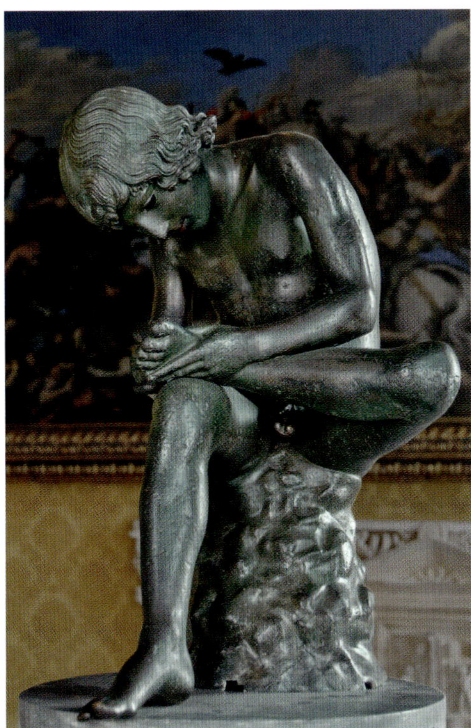

FIGURE 2 *Spinario*, 1st century BCE, bronze, height: 28¾ in. (73 cm). Palazzo dei Conservatori, Musei Capitolini, Rome, MC1186

THE BEAUTIFULLY PRESERVED first state of Diana Scultori's print after *The Spinario*—the iconic and often-reproduced Greco-Roman bronze sculpture of a boy removing a thorn from the sole of his foot (fig. 2), now in the Palazzo dei Conservatori, Rome—was copied by the artist after an engraving by the Dutch printmaker Cornelius Cort.[7] It demonstrates Scultori's awareness of the popularity and potential market value of a print of this famed bronze sculpture from antiquity.

In the second edition of Giorgio Vasari's *Lives of the Artists*, published in 1568, Diana Scultori is praised for her prints, which Vasari describes as "very beautiful," and as having rendered him "amazed."[8] It is not until the seventeenth century that an additional group of Italian women printmakers emerged that included Isabella Catanea Parasole (active 1585–1625) (cats. 22 and 23), Anna Maria Vaiani (1604–ca. 1655) (cat. 39), and Elisabetta Sirani (1638–1665) (cat. 48).[9]—ESP

NOTES

1. Lincoln 2006.

2. Lincoln 2006.

3. Bellini 1991, 30.

4. Some misidentified this subject as the Birth of Castor and Pollux. See, for example, Huber 1800, 143; Ticozzi, 1831, 170. The subject is identified correctly in Bartsch 1802–1821, 1813, vol. 15, 449.

5. The literary source of this print is likely the *Bibliotheca* of Apollodorus, also known as Pseudo-Apollodorus, a compendium of Greek myths and legends arranged in three books, most often dated to the first or second century. It describes how "Latona for her intrigue with Zeus was hunted by Hera over the whole earth, till she came to Delos and brought forth first Artemis, by the help of whose midwifery she afterwards gave birth to Apollo." *Apollodorus* 1921, vol. 1, 25.

6. For this print as the first state, see Bartsch 1802–1821, 1813, vol. 15, 449. For this print as the second version, see Bellini 1991, 174, no. 9. According to Bellini, in the second state, the letter "F" is removed and we only read "DIANA," which is what we see here.

7. The most complete entry on this print is Bellini 1991, 239–41, no. 50.

8. "Sono bellisime . . . stupefatto." The whole passage: "Una figliuola, chiamata Diana, intaglia anch'ella tanto bene, che è cosa marauigliosa, & io che ho veduto lei, che è molto gentile, e graziosa fanciulla; e l'opere sue, che sono bellissime, ne sono restate stupefatto." Vasari 1568, vol. 2, 559 (labeled 558).

9. Additional early modern Italian women printmakers include Teresa del Pò (1649–1713) and Sister Isabella Piccini (1627–1719). For a brief and incomplete overview of early modern Italian women printmakers, see Alexander 1997, 61–62.

Latona Giving Birth to Apollo and Diana on the Island of Delos

PROVENANCE

Emanuel Levy (New York, New York); Edward Duff Balken [1874–1960] (Pittsburgh, Pennsylvania); March 1940, gift to Lessing J. Rosenwald [1891–1979]; 1943–present, gift to the National Gallery of Art (Washington, D.C.).

SELECTED EXHIBITIONS

Antioch College, Yellow Springs, 1963–1964; National Gallery of Art, Washington, D.C., 1985; National Museum of Women in the Arts, Washington, D.C., 2007.

SELECTED PUBLICATIONS

Huber 1800, 143, no. 11 (as *The Birth of Castor and Pollux*); Bartsch 1802–1821, vol. 15, 449, no. 39; Ticozzi 1831, 170 (as *The Birth of Castor and Pollux*); Brulliot 1832–1834, vol. 3, 44, no. 287; Zanetti 1837, 482, no. 1316; D'Arco 1840, 76, no. 10 (as *The Birth of Castor and Pollux*); Le Blanc 1854–1858, 292, no. 34; Albricci 1975, 18, no. 25; Massari 1980, 91–93, 256–57; Boorsch and Spike 1986, 279, no. 39; Bellini 1991, 174–76, no. 9; Washington, D.C. 2007, 132, cat. 17, 133 illus.

The Spinario

PROVENANCE

June 4, 2009, sold at (Bassenge, Berlin, Germany), no. 5259; (C.G. Boerner, Inc., New York, New York); 2009–present, purchased by the National Gallery of Art (Washington, D.C.).

SELECTED PUBLICATIONS

Bartsch 1802–1821, vol. 15, 451, no. 42; Brulliot 1832–1834, vol. 3, 44, no. 287; Zanetti 1837, 478, nos. 1304–05; Le Blanc 1854–1858, 293, no. 38; Albricci 1975, 22, no. 49; Massari 1980, 108–9, 274; Boorsch and Spike 1986, 284, no. 42; Bellini 1991, 239–41, no. 50.

LAVINIA FONTANA

Bologna, 1552–Rome, 1614

A PROLIFIC PAINTER, LAVINIA FONTANA died just shy of her sixty-second birthday after a successful career. Her earliest efforts date to around 1575. Trained by her father Prospero Fontana (1512–1597) in the late Mannerist style and most famous for her portraits of noblewomen, Fontana also painted secular and religious subjects in a range of sizes, including altarpieces for churches, portraits of scholars, and mythological nudes—a rarity for women artists in the period. Also unlike many other Italian women artists, a number of sensitively rendered and naturalistic portrait drawings survive by her hand. In 1577 she married Gian Paolo Zappi (ca. 1555–1615), and supported the family, which included eleven children, not all of whom survived childhood, with her painting.

12

The Annunciation

ca. 1575

Oil on copper, 14⅛ × 10¹¹⁄₁₆ in. (35.88 × 27.15 cm)

Signed (on the base of the Virgin's chair): LAVINIA FONT. FA [Lavinia Fontana made it]

The Walters Art Museum, Baltimore, 37.1814

Detroit only

FEATURED IN THE FIRST KNOWN exhibition devoted to early modern women artists, which took place at the Walters Art Gallery in 1972,[1] this *Annunciation* by Lavinia Fontana is one of a handful of the artist's earliest works, all small-scale religious subjects on a copper or panel support intended for private devotion in the home.[2] As it is signed with the artist's maiden name alone, it must date prior to 1577, the year she married Gian Paolo Zappi and began signing her name "Fontana de Zappis" [Fontana [Wife] of Zappi]. Dates of ca. 1575 and early 1576 have been proposed for this work.[3]

Set in a spartan, domestic interior, this *Annunciation* is executed in a late Mannerist style, which Lavinia Fontana was taught by her father, Prospero Fontana. The elongated figures of the angel Gabriel and the Virgin, with lower bodies of sturdier stock that taper to a narrower torso and upper body, are characteristic of Mannerist art of the second half of the sixteenth century.

The portrayal of Gabriel's arms—the right holding a lily symbolizing Mary's spiritual and physical purity and the left pointing to a dove representing the Holy Spirit, said to have been present over the Virgin at the moment of conception—is also exaggerated.

The painting evidences the pared down *maniera devota*, or devout manner, of Counter-Reformation piety promulgated in Bologna by Cardinal Gabriele Paleotti (1522–1597), who in a 1582 treatise charged artists to paint Mary with "humility and modesty."[4] The choice of a somber palette characterized by darker blue and red tones is consistent with the restraint expected of religious pictures at the time. As Caroline Murphy notes, Lavinia Fontana "emphasizes Mary's humility by contrasting her simple costume and downcast gaze with a dazzling and exotically clad angel."[5] Before a painterly Venetian sky, Gabriel enters a portal, his gold-flecked robes aflutter, to inform Mary that she will give birth to God's son. Dressed in a simple smock, Mary receives this momentous news with reverent awe, her head bowed and arms crossed in a prefiguration of the fate that will befall her son on the cross.[6] Upon Gabriel's dramatic entrance, Mary has risen in haste from the prayer bench—a type often found in convents—her sewing and book of prayers abandoned at her feet.[7] Mary is often presented being interrupted either at

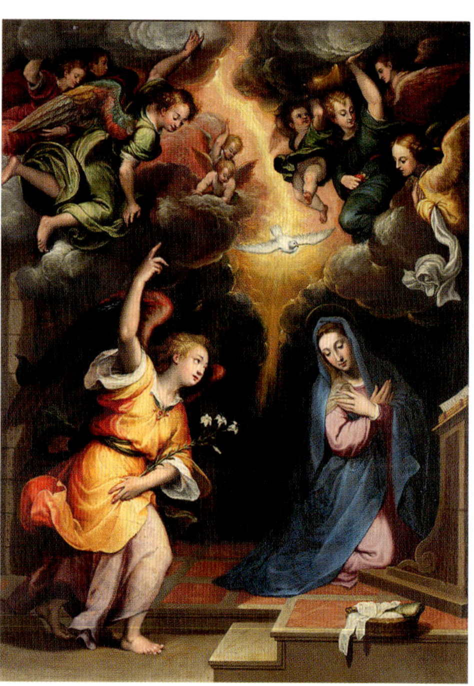

FIGURE 1 Denis Calvaert, *Annunciation*, last decade of 16th century–beginning of 17th century, oil on canvas, 41⁵⁄₁₆ × 30⁵⁄₁₆ in. (105 × 77 cm). Musei Civici d'Arte Antica, Collezioni Comunali d'Arte, Bologna

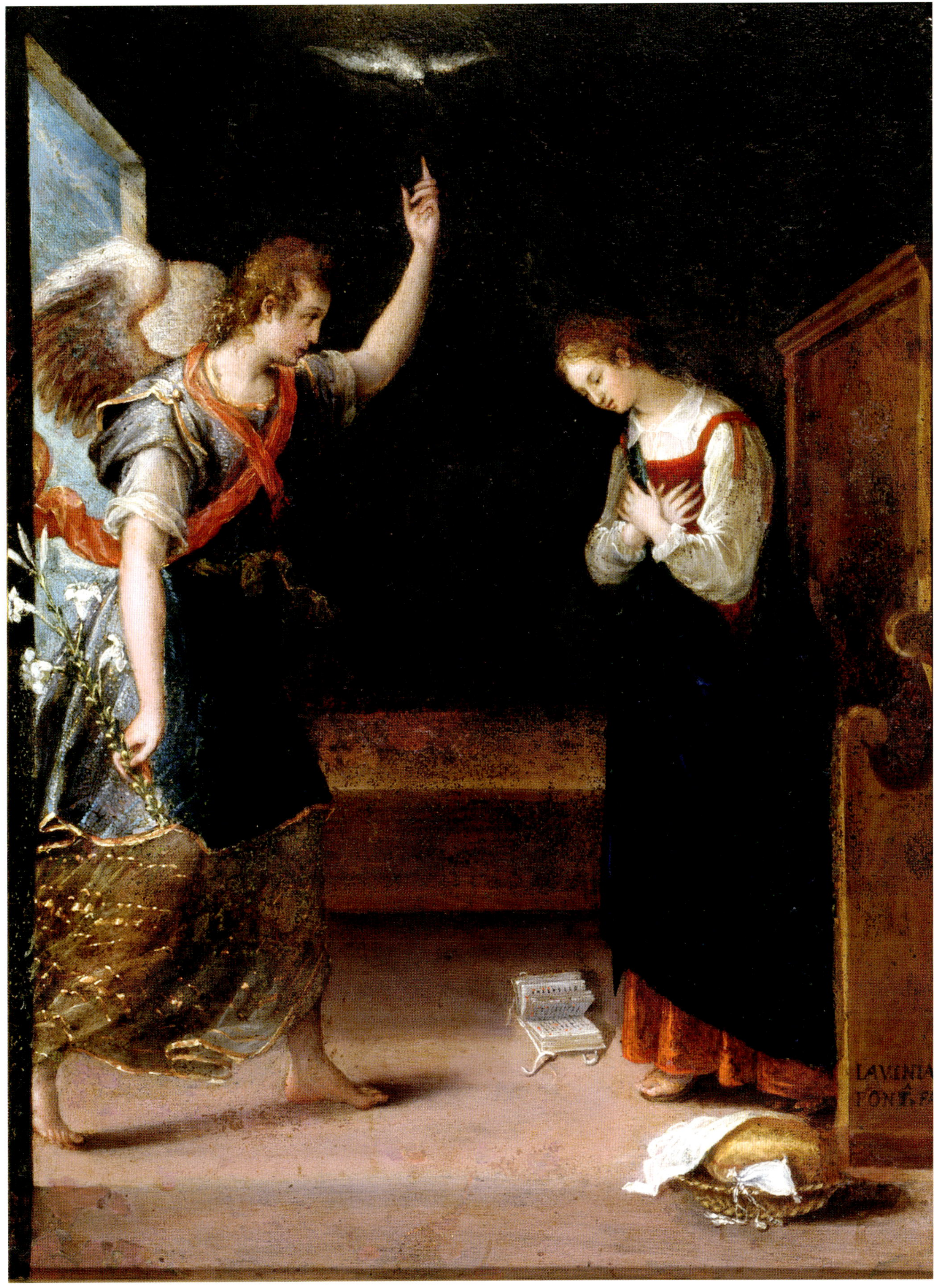
LAVINIA
FON. FA

her prayers or her sewing, but the conflation of the two is unusual; it does have a precedent in the Flemish-Bolognese Mannerist artist Denis Calvaert's (ca. 1540–1619) *Annunciation* (fig. 1).[8]

This work by Lavinia Fontana has suffered considerable abrasion over the years. It is, however, an important early record of her foray into devotional art.[9]—ESP

NOTES

1. Walters Art Gallery, Baltimore, 1972.

2. Fortunati 1998, 14–15.

3. Murphy 2003, 24 and 30; Cantaro 1989, 31.

4. For this quote from Cardinal Paoleotti, see Cantaro 1989, 67.

5. Murphy 1997a, 535.

6. Cantaro 1989, 67.

7. For the prayer bench, see Cantaro 1989, 67.

8. The similarities between this composition and two *Noli me tangere* paintings (Denis Calvaert, *Noli me tangere*, 1570s, Pinacoteca Nazionale di Bologna; and Lavinia Fontana, *Noli me tangere*, 1581, Gallerie degli Uffizi, Florence) by the two artists may suggest that Fontana was taught alongside Calvaert in her father's workshop, rather than independently by other Bolognese artists. At the very least it suggests that Lavinia Fontana had exposure to the work of Prospero's other pupils and did not work solely in isolation. Caroline Murphy also suggests that Fontana's use of a copper support may have been inspired by Calvaert's use of this material. According to Murphy, the Bolognese biographer Carlo Cesare Malvasia (1616–1693) "describes the demand in Bologna for Calvaert's copper paintings as gifts for noviciate nuns and young brides, and it is possible that Lavinia's own works were also made for this particular market." Murphy 2003, 30.

9. On the picture's condition, see Zeri 1976, vol. 2, 384. Packard notes: "The top and bottom corners on the left side are bent and damaged. Major losses in the Virgin's blue mantle, as well as numerous others throughout the picture, indicate serious cleavage between the paint and the copper support. The removal of darkened varnish in 1967 disclosed the shimmering colors of the angel's garments and the exquisite detail of the book and sewing basket on the floor. Except to the angel's mouth, the flesh tones are in good condition."

PROVENANCE

Until 1898, Marchese Filippo Marignoli (Rome and Spoleto, Italy); 1898–1899, Marchese Francesco Marignoli; 1899–1902, Don Marcello Massarenti Collection (Rome, Italy) [1900 cat. suppl., no. 36, as by Lavinia Fontana]; 1902, acquired with the Massarenti Collection by Henry Walters [1848–1931] (Baltimore, Maryland); 1931–present, bequest to the Walters Art Gallery (Baltimore, Maryland), now the Walters Art Museum (Baltimore, Maryland).

SELECTED EXHIBITIONS

Walters Art Gallery, Baltimore, 1972; Museo Civico Archeologico, Bologna, 1994; National Museum of Women in the Arts, Washington, D.C., 1998.

SELECTED PUBLICATIONS

Baltimore 1972, cat. 4; Zeri 1976, vol. 2, 384, no. 259, pl. 181; Tufts 1982, 132; Fortunati Pietrantonio 1986, vol. 2, 728, 742 illus.; Cantaro 1989, 31–32, 66–67, no. 4a.9, 66 illus.; Bologna 1994, 123 illus., 187, cat. 43; Fortunati 1998, 15; Washington, D.C. 1998, 50, cat. 1, 51 illus.; Murphy 2003, 24, 28, 30, 34, 167, fig. 29; Rocco 2017, 55–57, 78, fig. 2.2; Madrid 2019, 37 n. 100, 168 under cat. 35; Bohn 2021, 44–45, fig. 13.

13

Portrait of a Prelate

ca. 1580

Oil on copper, diameter: 5½ in. (14 cm)

Inscribed (on the reverse, in ink, partially illegible, perhaps): U.P. Coreggio/ fondatore d—[U.P. Correggio founder (of?) . . .]

The Metropolitan Museum of Art, New York, 62.122.141

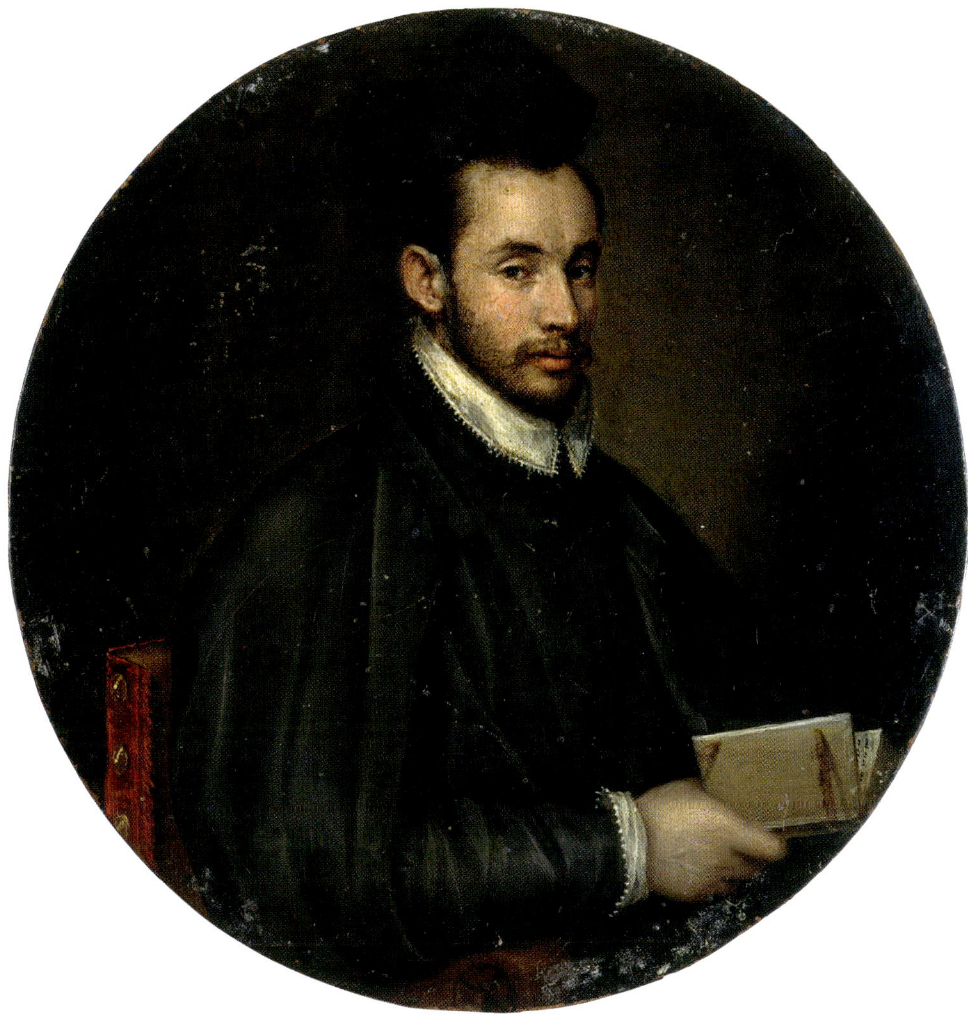

ALTHOUGH LAVINIA FONTANA was most celebrated for her numerous portraits of women, she also painted at least twenty portraits of men that are still known today. Caroline Murphy has shown that Fontana's portraits of male scholars, prelates, poets, and other professionals, beginning in the late 1570s, helped to launch her career, even before she was discovered by the noblewomen of her native city.[1] Within this group, the Metropolitan Museum of Art's miniature portrait is currently the only known example on copper, although Fontana probably painted others that may come to light. The work is similar to her portrait of the famous Bolognese historian Carlo Sigonio (1523–1584); only one portrait of this scholar is currently known (Museo Civico d'Arte, Modena, ca. 1578–1579), and it is on canvas, but she painted another on copper that is no longer traceable. Fontana was one of the earliest artists in Bologna to paint on copper supports, a practice that she evidently began around 1575, very early in her career.[2] Of her eighteen currently known paintings on copper,[3] most were small portraits of women, including her famous *Self-Portrait in a Studio* (Gallerie degli Uffizi, Florence; Tostmann, "The Advantages of Painting Small," fig. 5), which is signed and dated 1579. The present picture probably dates slightly later than that work, to about 1580, as other scholars have suggested.

The identification of the sitter as a prelate is based on his ecclesiastical robes and three-cornered hat (*beretta a corni*).[4] The young man is portrayed half-length, holding a small, open book, a device that appears in many of Lavinia Fontana's male portraits. He looks out quietly at the viewer as a strong light creates highlights on the left side of his face, white collar, black garments, and proper right hand. The man is seated in a red chair and silhouetted against an otherwise empty, dark background. The early inscription on the reverse of the portrait, always previously described as illegible, may read "Coreggio," and could be an early attribution to the famous sixteenth-century painter Antonio da Correggio (1489–1534), or it is perhaps the name of the sitter.[5]—BB

NOTES

1. Murphy 2003, 49–79.

2. Murphy 2003, 30–31.

3. See Bohn 2021, ch. 2.

4. Bayer 2003, 47.

5. I am grateful to Andrea Bayer, Dorothy Mahon, and Evan Read, all of the Metropolitan Museum of Art, who provided the high-resolution photographs, including infrared and ultraviolet, that enabled me to have some partial success at deciphering the inscription.

PROVENANCE

By 1943 (?)–1962, Mrs. Leopold (Millie Bruhl) Fredrick [1878–1962] (New York, New York) [Paine 1960 inv. no. 148]; 1962–present, bequest of Millie Bruhl Fredrick to the Metropolitan Museum of Art (New York, New York).

SELECTED PUBLICATIONS

Paine 1960, 19, no. 148; Cantaro 1993, 85–86, 99 n. 5, fig. 1; Baetjer 1995, 115, illus.; Bayer 2003, 47–48, fig. 32; Murphy 2003, 58–59, fig. 62.

14

The Dead Christ with Symbols of the Passion

1581

Oil, tempera on panel, 14¼ × 10⅝ in. (36.2 × 27 cm)

Signed and dated: Lavinia Fontana VIRGO/Faciebat MDLXXXI [Lavinia Fontana virgin made it 1576]

Cornell Fine Arts Museum, Rollins College, Winter Park, 1936.30

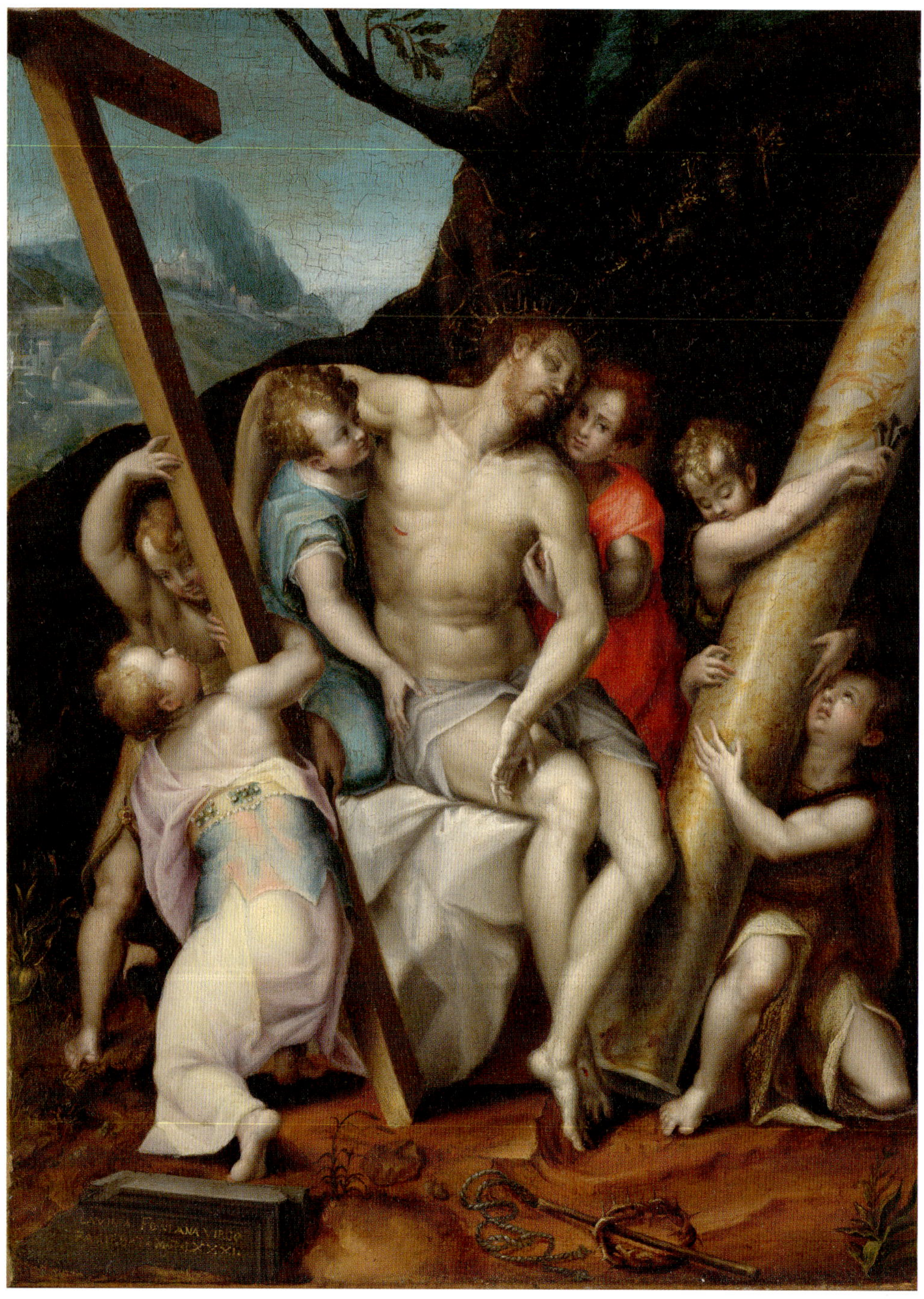

THE SMALL-SCALE *Dead Christ with Symbols of the Passion* was meant for private devotion. It is signed "Lavinia Fontana VIRGO/Faciebat MDLXXXI" ("Lavinia Fontana virgin made it 1576"). As the artist stopped including "virgin" in her signature after her marriage to Gian Paolo Zappi (ca. 1555–1615) in 1577, this inscription raises a number of questions, the most pressing of which is whether it is autograph.[1] All scholars believe the painting to be by Lavinia Fontana's hand.[2]

In all probability this work is a replica of Lavinia Fontana's 1576 signed and dated painting on copper of the same subject now in the El Paso Museum of Art, Texas—her earliest surviving signed and dated work (fig. 1). This is the sole instance of two nearly identical—save for the size of the crucifix in this version and the slightly varied tonalities of the cloths in this version—autograph pictures in her oeuvre. The two variants may be the result of a patron commissioning a replica, or they may reflect the popularity of the subject.

This work would have aided devotees in visualizing Christ's suffering, or Passion, as narrated in the Gospels.[3] The dead Christ is seated on a white cloth and supported by two small angels while two other pairs of angels support key instruments of his Passion: the cross on which he was crucified and the column on which he was flagellated. The wide array of poses and the range of arm gestures add what artist and historian Giorgio Vasari (1511–1574) called *variazione*, or variety, to an otherwise somber subject.[4] Before Christ are the crown of thorns and a staff, as well as the rope with which he was flogged—all tools for the viewer to meditate upon in their prayers as sanctioned by the Jesuit Saint Ignatius of Loyola's (1491–1556) *Spiritual Exercises* (1548) and Friar Minor Francesco Panigarola's (1548–1594) soon to be published 1585 tome, in which he declared "well-done paintings and images of the Passion of Christ . . . a remedy to increase within us our pain about Christ's death."[5]

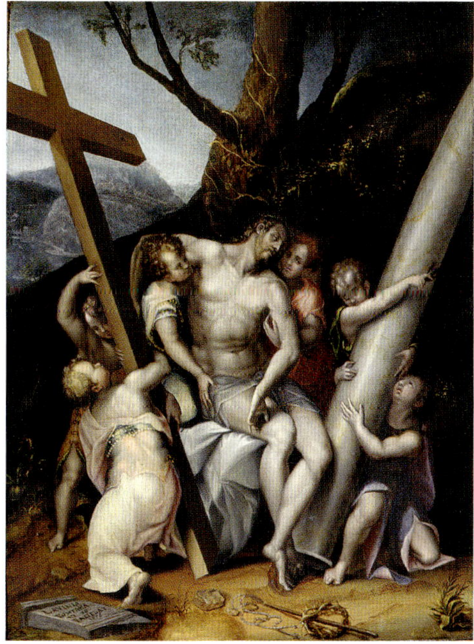

FIGURE 1 Lavinia Fontana, *Christ with the Symbols of the Passion*, 1576, oil on panel, 15¼ × 11⅞ in. (38.7 × 30.2 cm), signed "Lavinia Fontana Virgo." Gift of the Samuel H. Kress Foundation, Collection of the El Paso Museum of Art

Christ's elongated body, contorted left forearm, and the implausible crossing of his legs owe an allegiance to the Mannerist style of painting that Lavinia Fontana learned from her father Prospero Fontana (1512–1597). The almost balletic elegance of Christ's body responds to the languid lines of Taddeo Zuccari's (1529–1566) *Pietà* (1560s) from the Church of the Crucifix in Urbino (now Palazzo Ducale, Urbino) (fig. 2)—albeit in Fontana's painting, Christ's body exhibits a more ample and volumetric musculature. Michelangelo's (1475–1564) Florentine *Pietà* (ca. 1547), also called *Deposition*, originally intended for his own tomb, was the iconographic impetus for most sixteenth-century representations of Christ in the moments after he was crucified.[6] As the scholar Patricia Rocco aptly notes, Lavinia Fontana's "rendition combined Flemish fastidiousness with a mystical sense of nature, a landscape as part of God's *theatrum mundi*, creating what can be termed a 'contemplative icon' for meditation on Christ's suffering."[7]

This rare work in Lavinia Fontana's oeuvre—an oil on panel painting with two variants—is instructive. It offers a view into how she operated in the early years of her career as she tried to find her footing within the orbit of Post-Tridentine devotional painting.—ESP

NOTES

1. Two leading scholars of Lavinia Fontana, Vera Fortunati and Maria Teresa Cantaro, believe this signature to be spurious. See Fortunati Pietrantonio 1986, vol. 2, 728; Cantaro 1989, 71; and Winter Park 1991, 24, cat. 12, where Arthur R. Blumenthal raises the intriguing possibility that Fontana may have "wished to underscore the fact that she had been unmarried when she painted the original version of this most popular painting."

2. Fortunati Pietrantonio 1986, vol. 2, 728; Cantaro 1989, 71; Winter Park 1991, 24, cat. 12.

3. Mathew 27; John 19; Winter Park 1991, 24.

4. The crouching and contorted angel in the left foreground is reminiscent of Parmigianino's (1503–1540) *Cupid Carving a Bow*, ca. 1533–1535, oil on panel, 53⅛ × 25¹¹⁄₁₆ in. (135 × 65.3 cm), at the Kunsthistorisches Museum, Vienna.

5. Panigarola 1585, 13. Translated into English and quoted by Göttler 2013, 401.

6. Winter Park 1991, 24.

7. Rocco 2017, 64. The tree and rocky outcropping in the middle ground of the composition, as well as the lighter, meticulous landscape in the background, owe their inspiration to Flemish/Northern precedents.

PROVENANCE

1936–present, gift of General John J. Carty [1861–1932] and Mrs. John J. Carty to the Cornell Fine Arts Museum at Rollins College (Winter Park, Florida).

SELECTED EXHIBITIONS

Cornell Fine Arts Museum at Rollins College, Winter Park, 1991; Museum of Fine Arts, St. Petersburg, Fla., 1992; Cornell Fine Arts Museum at Rollins College, Winter Park, 1993–1996.

SELECTED PUBLICATIONS

Fredericksen and Zeri 1972, 71, 650; Shapley 1973, 71; Los Angeles 1976, 111 n. 2; Fortunati Pietrantonio 1986, vol. 2, 728, 741 illus.; Cantaro 1989, 70 illus., 71; Winter Park 1991, 24, cat. 12, 25 illus.; Winter Park 1993, 8, cat. 4, 9 illus.; Fortunati 1998, 30 n. 17; Murphy 2003, 30, 33, fig. 33; Modesti 2014, 180 n. 59; Rocco 2017, 54–55, 64, 123, fig. 2.1.

FIGURE 2 Taddeo Zuccari, *Pietà* from the Church of the Crucifix in Urbino, 1560s, oil on canvas, 111⁷⁄₁₆ × 60¼ in. (283 × 153 cm). Palazzo Ducale, Urbino

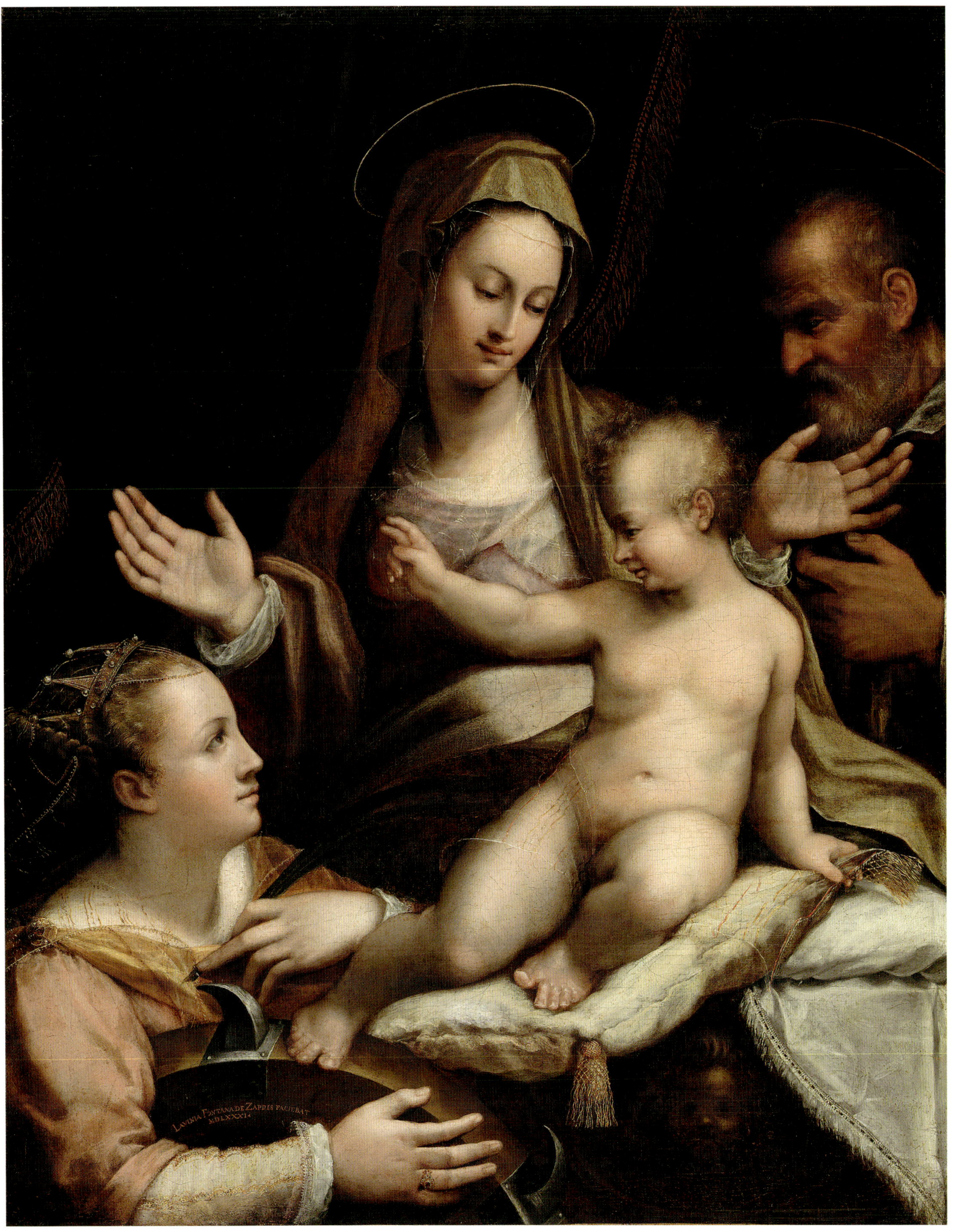

LAVINIA FONTANA DE ZAPPIS FACIEBAT
MDLXXXI

The Holy Family with Saint Catherine of Alexandria

1581

Oil on canvas, 43 × 34¾ in. (109.22 × 88.27 cm)

Signed and dated (on the rim of the wheel, lower left): LAVINIA FONTANA DE ZAPPIS FACIEBAT / MDLXXXI

[Lavinia Fontana (Wife) of Zappi made it]

Los Angeles County Museum of Art, Gift of The Ahmanson Foundation, M.2011.2

THIS *Holy Family with Saint Catherine* is signed with Lavinia Fontana's married name, Zappi. A devotional picture likely intended for a family's private chapel, an unspoken world of religious meaning and association unfolds through the subtle interplay of gestures and glances within it.[1] Pushed towards the picture plane, and thus the devotee, the Christ child occupies a substantial portion of the composition. He raises his right arm in a gesture of blessing that is received by the Virgin, who assumes the position of an *orante*, her arms outstretched in prayer, and by Saint Catherine of Alexandria, who kneels in devotion with her left hand at her breast, a symbol of supplication.[2]

An artist trained in the Mannerist tradition by her father, Prospero Fontana (1512–1597), Lavinia Fontana came to the fore in a Post-Tridentine Bologna led by the religious and artistic dictates of Cardinal Gabriele Paleotti (1522–1597), a close associate of her father. Paleotti promoted religious compositions that prioritized clarity and moved the viewer to devotion—a decisive shift away from Mannerist art, which often eschewed naturalistic and visually legible compositions.

A light from the upper right illuminates Christ, the Virgin, and Saint Catherine of Alexandria, who was executed under the Roman Emperor Maxentius in the fourth century, while Joseph occupies a secondary role in a more dimly lit position at back right. Saint Catherine, adorned with a jewel- and pearl-encrusted crown, wears a costly ring on her right hand, which clutches the wheel that is her common attribute. As Catherine, who serves as a proxy for the viewer, was invoked as a patron saint for maidens and girls, perhaps this image was commissioned to aid the prayers of an unmarried woman.

In orchestrating this devotional picture, Lavinia Fontana relied directly, or indirectly via printed sources, on aspects of compositions from the Renaissance masters Raphael (1483–1520) and Michelangelo (1475–1564). The Virgin's *orans* posture recalls that in Michelangelo's drawing of the *Pietà* (Isabella Stewart Gardner Museum, Boston) made for the Italian noblewoman and poet Vittoria Colonna (1492–1547). A 1546 engraving of the drawing by Giulio Bonasone (ca. 1510–after 1576) served as a model for the print by the Bolognese artist Agostino Carracci (1557–1602), which Fontana may have seen. Christ's elegant, semi-reclined position echoes his pose in Raphael's *Alba Madonna* (ca. 1510, National Gallery of Art, Washington, D.C.).—ESP

NOTES

1. Murphy 2003, 47.

2. For the most comprehensive text on this picture see Walsh 2019b, 76–77, no. 22, 97, 140. See also Cantaro 1989, 105. A related picture attributed to Pietro Candido (ca. 1548–1628) is presently with Altomani & Sons.

PROVENANCE

By 1757, Charles-Jean de Bertin [1716–1774], bishop of Vannes [1746–1774]. By 1868, James Edward Harris [1807–1889], 3rd Earl of Malmesbury; by inheritance to Lord Malmesbury (probably James Edward Harris, 5th Earl of Malmesbury [1872–1950]); May 4, 1925, sold at (Christie's, London, UK), lot 9, to (Fritze). November 9–12, 1966, sold at (Bukowski, Stockholm, Sweden), lot 139, to an anonymous buyer; 1967, given to a Swedish religious institution. November 26, 2009, sold at (Stockholms Auktionsverk, Stockholm, Sweden), lot 2275, to (Richard L. Feigen & Co., New York, New York); 2011–present, sold to the Los Angeles County Museum of Art (Los Angeles, California).

SELECTED EXHIBITIONS

Leeds General Infirmary, 1868.

SELECTED PUBLICATIONS

Leeds 1868, 29, no. 292; *Catalogue of Ancient and Modern Pictures* 1925, no. 9; Cantaro 1989, 36–37, 105, no. 4a.31, illus.; Walsh 2019b, 76–77, no. 22, 76 illus., 140–41.

16

Portrait of a Lady of the Gonzaga or Sanvitale Family

ca. 1584
Oil on canvas, 34⅝ × 44¹⁄₁₆ in. (88 × 112 cm)
Private collection, Connecticut

LAVINIA FONTANA, who is perhaps best known for her portraits of Bolognese noblewomen in elegant and highly-detailed attire, had a diverse portrait painting practice—from group to individual likenesses and from intellectuals to nobility—throughout her professional life. Her earliest signed and dated work, presently unlocated, is a portrait of a boy holding a carnation from 1575.[1] After her marriage in 1577, her work as a portrait painter expanded and she was often chosen to depict scholars at the University of Bologna.[2] Around 1584 she began to work for Bolognese nobility and to establish particularly strong bonds with noblewomen. Portraiture is the genre for which she is most famous today, and it was the foundation of her livelihood, allowing her to support her family of eleven children.[3]

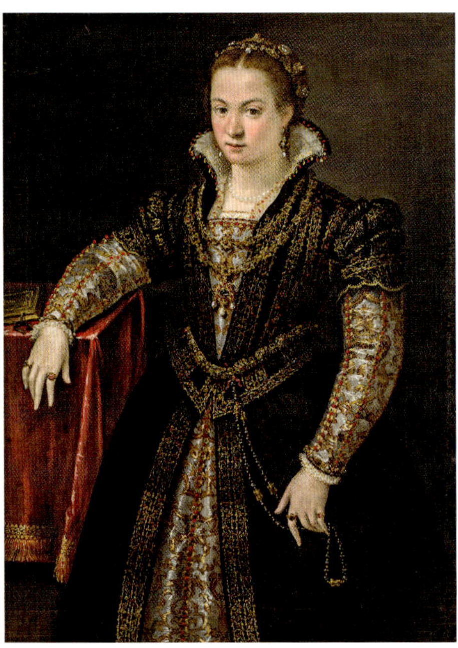

FIGURE 1 Lavinia Fontana, *Portrait of a Lady of the Gonzaga or Sanvitale Family,* ca. 1584, oil on canvas, 45¼ × 34¼ in. (115 × 87 cm). Virginia Museum of Fine Arts, Richmond

Here the sitter, believed to hail from the Gonzaga or Sanvitale family, is depicted at three-quarter length and at a three-quarter angle, as is characteristic of Lavinia Fontana's portraits of Bolognese noblewomen.[4] The portrait is often compared to one recently acquired by the Virginia Museum of Fine Arts that is nearly identical in size (fig. 1). Although the two paintings are thought to show the same figure at different points in her life, the physiognomies suggest two distinct sitters to this writer. The face in this portrait has slenderer proportions, a more aquiline nose, thinner lips, lighter and more refined eyebrows, and wider set and slightly lighter eyes—disparities that cannot be accounted for by changes in weight or age.

The sitter's arm rests on a table and a letter alerts the viewer to her literacy. The letter at one time carried a fragmentary inscription: "Laura Gonzaga, contessa of Sabbionetta," which was added to the portrait later in its history and removed in a conservation treatment. Gonzaga was born in 1547 or 1548 and entered a Benedictine convent as a nun in 1566, which is inconsistent with the 1580s date for this portrait.[5] In addition, the sitter holds a glove, which is often associated with marriage, as are the bands on the ring and pinkie fingers of each hand. The distinctive hammered gold and bejeweled marten's head was deeply connected to women's fertility in the Renaissance and evoked everything from chastity to childbirth (fig. 2).[6]

Maria Teresa Cantaro, a leading expert on Lavinia Fontana, identifies these pictures with two identically sized portraits in the eighteenth-century Sanvitale inventories, described as in the "manner of Girolamo Mazzola."[7] Our portrait was photographed

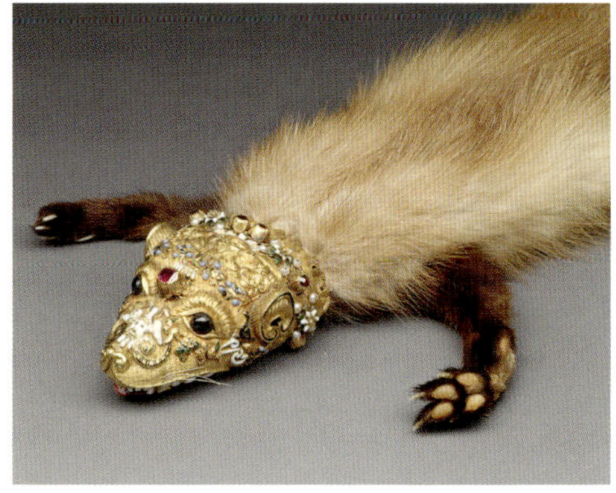

FIGURE 2 Umbrian artist, *Marten's Head,* ca. 1550–1559, gold with enamel, rubies, garnets, and pearls, 1⁵⁄₁₆ × 2¾ × 2³⁄₁₆ in. (3.4 × 7 × 5.5 cm). The Walters Art Museum, Baltimore, 57.1982

in the collection of Count Giovanni Sanvitale (1872–1951) at the Rocca di Fontanellato in 1931. In 1937 it was displayed in the exhibition *Mostra Iconografica Gonzaghesca* at the Ducale Palace in Mantua, with the catalogue noting the presence of a similar portrait, possibly the one now at the Virginia Museum of Fine Arts.[8]

The provenance of this portrait is either directly from the Sanvitale family, or perhaps from the Sabionetta or Bozzolo branches of the Gonzaga family, with whom it remained until the 1940s, when the family's collections were dispersed.[9] Cantaro has proposed that the sitter may be Isabella Gonzaga (1565–1637), who married Don Luigi Caraffa (1567–1630) in 1584—the date around which this portrait was executed and the period in which Lavinia Fontana's career as a portrait painter began to flourish.[10]—ESP

NOTES

1. Murphy 2003, 24.

2. "In the late 1570s and early 1580s, the portraits that she produced of and for a scholarly clientele were a critical step in positioning her on the next rung of the ladder of financial success and wider acclaim." Murphy 2003, 49.

3. For a concise overview of Lavinia Fontana and portraiture, see Murphy 1997a, 535. Only three of her children ultimately outlived her. Murphy 2003, 195–96.

4. For the best overview of this portrait and its history, see Ferrante and Simon 2019, 64–67, 100.

5. "Lavinia Fontana, Portrait of a Lady." Ferrante and Simon 2019, 64–67, 100.

6. This accessory is known as a *zibellino,* a word directly referencing a sable but employed for other

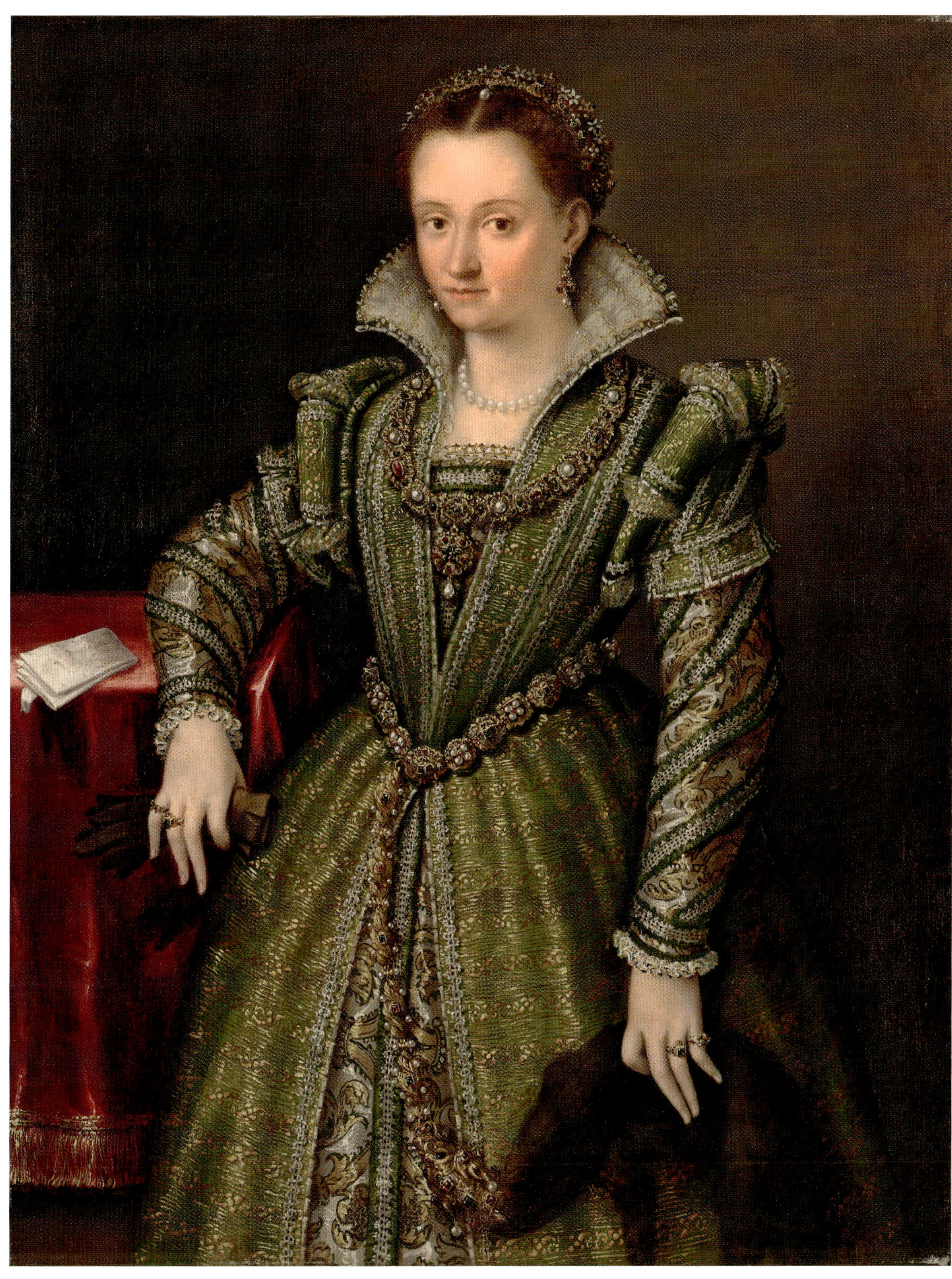

types of furs as well. For the importance and symbolism of weasels, including martens, see Musacchio 2001, 172–87.

7. Lollobrigida 2018, 96, cat. 19.

8. Mantua 1937, 70, no. 312: "Ritratto simile al presente trovasi anche nella sala d'armi della Rocca di Fontanellato." See also Ferrante and Simon 2019, 64–67, 100.

9. Ferrante and Simon 2019, 64–67, 100.

10. Ferrante and Simon 2019, 64–67, 100.

PROVENANCE

By 1931, collection of Count Giovanni Sanvitale [1872–1951] at the Rocca di Fontanellato (Fontanellato, Italy). 2012, with (Galerie Canesso, Paris, France); private collection (Connecticut).

SELECTED EXHIBITIONS

Palazzo Ducale, Mantua, 1937; TEFAF, Maastricht, 2012, with Galerie Canesso.

SELECTED PUBLICATIONS

Sorrentino 1931, 32 illus., 33; Mantua 1937, 70, no. 312 (as attributed to A. Mazzola); *Apollo* 2012, 10 illus.; *Burlington Magazine* 2012, unpaginated illus.; Lollobrigida 2018, 96; Ferrante and Simon 2019, 64–67, fig. 1; Findlen 2020, 18, 20, fig. 0.11.

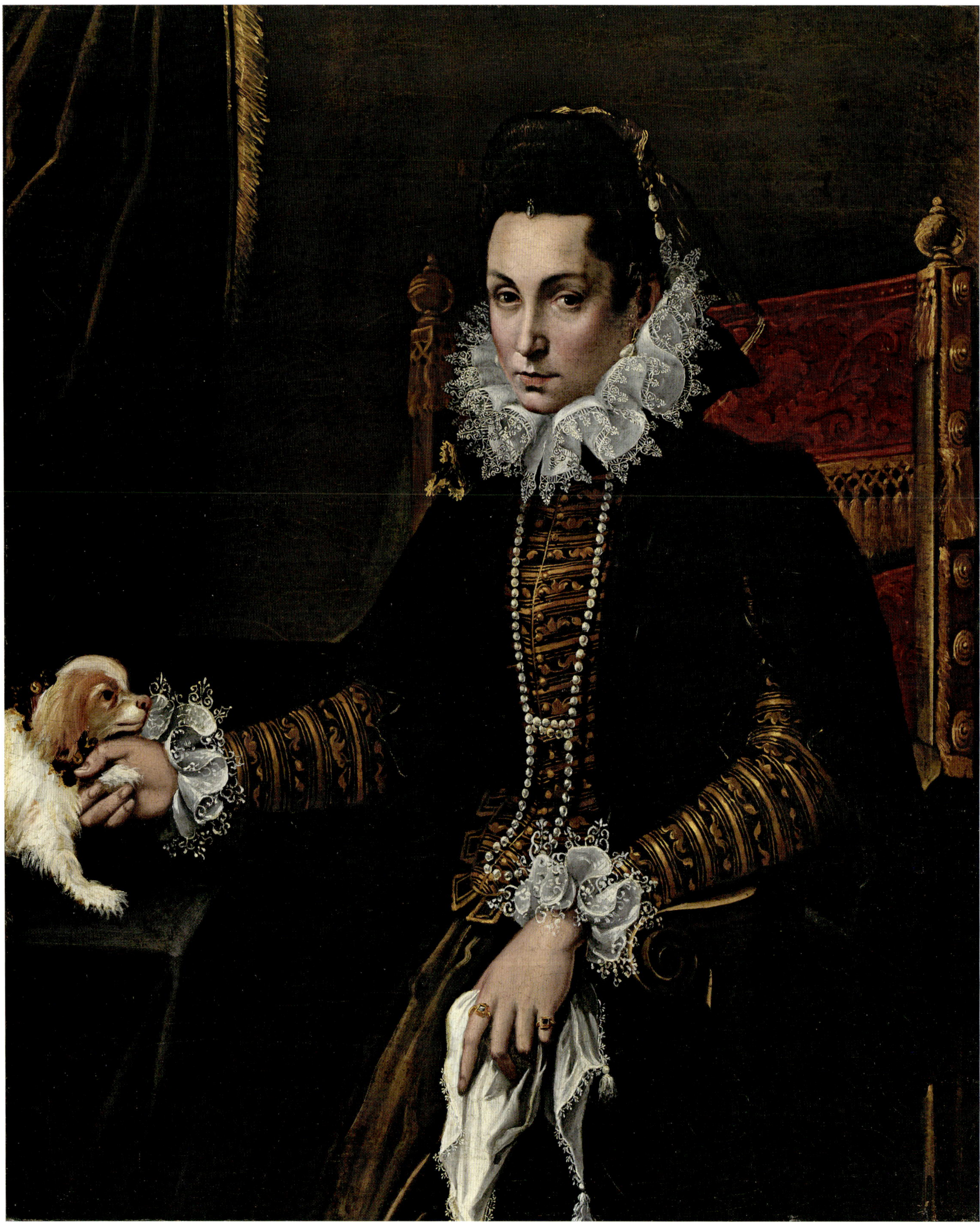

Portrait of Ginevra Aldrovandi Hercolani

ca. 1594–1595
Oil on canvas, 45¼ × 37⅜ in. (114.94 × 94.93 cm)
The Walters Art Museum, Baltimore, 37.1915
Detroit only

LAVINIA FONTANA was especially famous for her elegant portraits of noblewomen, both in her native city of Bologna and later in Rome. Her seventeenth-century biographer Carlo Cesare Malvasia (1616–1693) stated that they competed for the painter's attention, driving up her prices to levels that matched those of leading (male) portraitists such as Anthony van Dyck (1599–1641).[1]

Caroline Murphy was the first modern writer to connect this portrait with the work mentioned in a nineteenth-century guidebook as a portrait of Ginevra Aldrovandi Hercolani (dates unknown). An inventory of the Hercolani collection in Bologna in 1835 also describes the painting of a half-length woman with a dog by Lavinia Fontana.[2] Ginevra Hercolani was the daughter of one senator, Ercole Aldrovandi (dates unknown), and the wife of another, Ercole Hercolani (died 1593). Her husband came from a wealthy noble family that traced its origins in Bologna back to at least the early fifteenth century and that included many senators and government leaders.[3]

Murphy suggests that this work portrays the sitter as a widow. Fontana paints her in a black overdress with a richly embroidered silk bodice trimmed in gold bands over a brown velvet skirt. The sitter's white cuffs, collar, and handkerchief are all trimmed with lace, and she wears a long string of pearls, pearl earrings, a pearl-trimmed hair ornament, and two rings. The small (and expensive) dog who accompanies his mistress, like her rich costume and jewels, testifies to her wealth, but it also symbolizes her fidelity to her deceased husband. Other indications of the widow's wealth are provided by the fine red velvet chair trimmed with gold and the gold trim on the curtain behind her. Like several of Fontana's portraits of widows, the woman looks out directly at the viewer rather than modestly averting her gaze, as was typical of most such portraits by Fontana's contemporaries.

The date of this picture during the mid-1590s, prompted by the hypothesis that it was produced after Hercolani was widowed, is confirmed by the artist's sophisticated handling of facial features, fabrics, and jewels. The inscription on the reverse side of the canvas, reading "Lavigna Fontana Zappi," indicates a date after her marriage in 1577.—BB

NOTES

1. Malvasia 1678, vol. 1, 219–20; Malvasia 1841, vol. 1, 176.

2. Murphy 2003, 143; Bassani 1816, 205. The inventory, housed in the Archiginnasio, Bologna (B.4601), is published in Ghelfi 2007, 430.

3. Dolfi 1670, vol. 1, 288–96.

PROVENANCE

Hercolani collection (Bologna, Italy) [date and mode of acquisition unrecorded]; before 1881, Don Marcello Massarenti Collection (Rome, Italy) [details of acquisition unknown; 1881 cat., no. 194; 1897 cat., no. 180]; 1902, purchased by Henry Walters [1848–1931] (Baltimore, Maryland); 1931–present, bequest to the Walters Art Gallery (Baltimore, Maryland), now the Walters Art Museum (Baltimore, Maryland).

SELECTED EXHIBITIONS

Walters Art Gallery, Baltimore, 1972; Pinacoteca Nazionale di Bologna, 1986–1987; Museo Civico Archeologico, Bologna, 1994; National Museum of Women in the Arts, Washington, D.C., 2007.

SELECTED PUBLICATIONS

Galli 1940, 66; Baltimore 1972, cat. 3; Tufts 1974a, 63–64; Tufts 1974b, 32, 36, fig. 10; Los Angeles 1976, 113; Petersen and Wilson 1976, 27, fig. III.11; Zeri 1976, vol. 2, 384–85, no. 260, pl. 182; Tufts 1982, 130, 132, fig. 165; Bologna 1986, 134–35, cat. 46, 135 illus.; Fortunati Pietrantonio 1986, vol. 2, 733, 768 illus.; Cantaro 1989, 25, 45, 173 under no. 4a.74, 179 under no. 4a.78, 180 under no. 4a.79, 181–82, no. 4a.80, 181 illus., 183 under no. 4a.81, 186 under no. 4a.84, 221 under no. 4a.102, 233 under no. 4b.107M, 252 under no. 4c.119; Perlingieri 1992, 184, 186, pl. 106; Bologna 1994, 34, 119 illus., 188–89, cat. 46, 192 under cat. 52; Vertova 1995, 44, 46, fig. 3; Fortunati 1997, 696; Murphy 1997a, 535; Murphy 1997b, 134–37, fig. 5.8; Fortunati 1998, 27; Washington, D.C. 1998, 96, cat. 24, 97 illus.; Borzello 2000, 45 illus., 218; Murphy 2003, 112, 142–47, fig. 123; Hansen and Spicer 2005, 106, cat. 30, 107 illus.; Washington, D.C. 2007, 47, 66, 134 illus., 154, cat. 27, 155 illus.

Selections from *Album of Portrait Studies*

ca. 1577–1595

Morgan Library and Museum, New York, IV, 158a–s

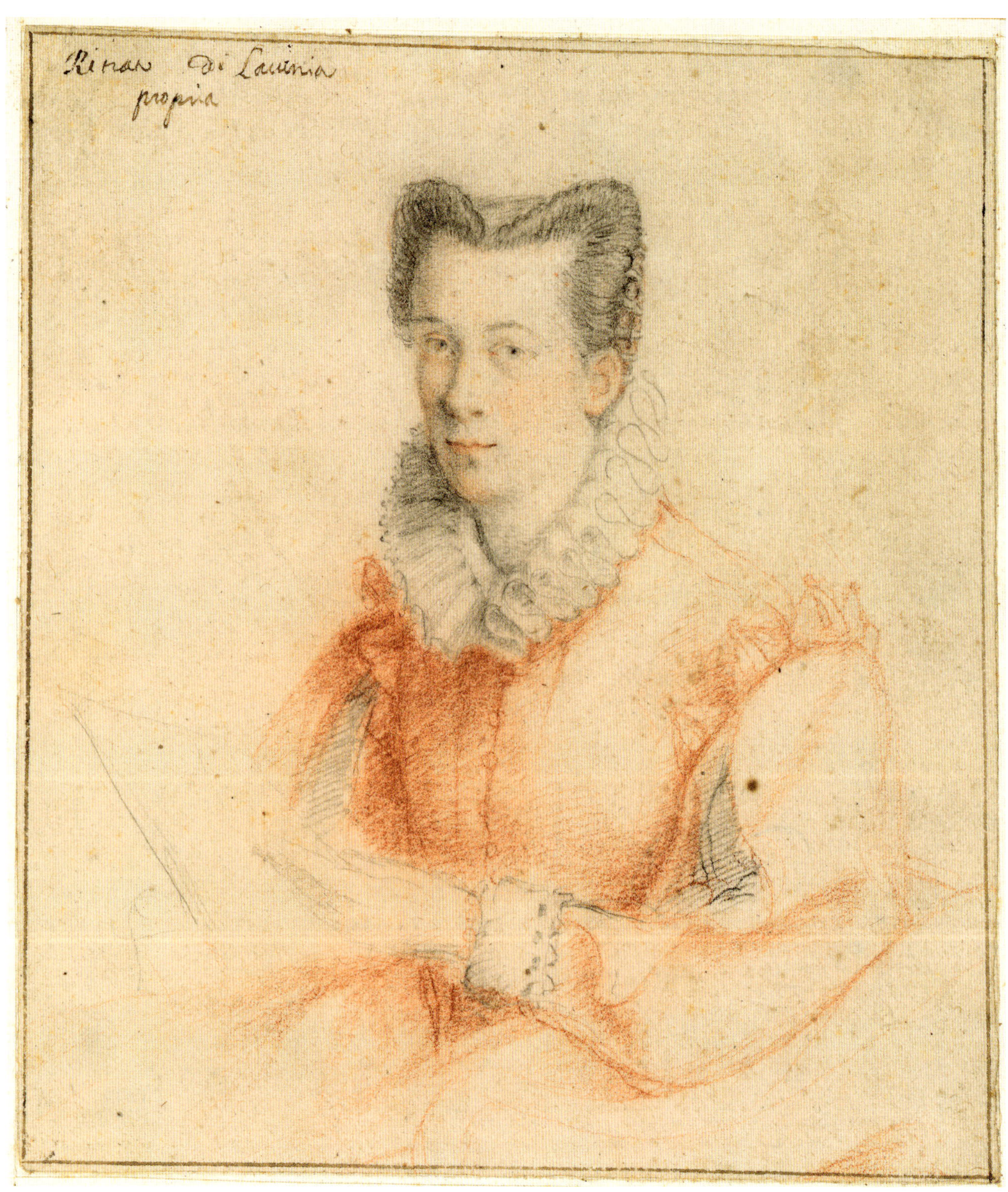

FIGURE 1 Detail of *Self-Portrait*, ca. 1579, drawing in red and black chalk, 6⁷⁄₁₆ × 5¹¹⁄₁₆ in. (16.4 × 14.5 cm), IV, 158b (exhibited in Detroit).

LAVINIA FONTANA is the first Italian woman artist by whom we have more than a dozen extant drawings; her work is known today in at least thirty sheets. To my knowledge, she is also the only Italian woman of the period by whom an album of drawings is known, if we exclude botanical studies such as Giovanna Garzoni's (1600–1670) album in the Dumbarton Oaks Research Library, Washington, D.C. This anomaly might suggest some early interest in collecting her drawings, but this hypothesis is not confirmed by other evidence. None of Fontana's early biographers even mentions her drawings, suggesting that she was not famous for her draftsmanship in her own day and for long afterwards. This conclusion is also borne out by the infrequency with which her drawings appear in early Bolognese inventories. Although many of Fontana's paintings are identified in such inventories during the seventeenth and eighteenth centuries, only one inventory, that of the Marchese Alessandro Facchinetti (dates unknown) in 1685, identifies a drawing by her.[1] Both the paucity of mentions of Fontana's drawings in early collections and the complete absence of early writings on the subject suggest they were not fully appreciated until long after her death. This may have more to do with a widespread disinclination to credit women with the capacity for invention during the period than with her undeniable skills on paper.[2]

Most of Lavinia Fontana's extant drawings, including all the sheets in the Morgan album, are chalk portrait studies. Some were likely preparatory studies for paintings, but whatever their original function, they were also probably intended from their inception as collectible objects. The collector who assembled this album of drawings is no longer known, but the binding, created between about 1705 and 1740, has been identified as the work of the Konstboeken-binderij in Amsterdam.[3] There is no evidence to suggest that the nineteen drawings it contains were produced as a series and no evidence to confirm exactly when before 1705–40 the group was assembled. Two of the drawings (IV, 158c, 158g) are not autograph, confirming

that the collection was probably created after the artist's lifetime.

The striking naturalism and sensitivity to facial expression of the seventeen autograph sheets suggest that they were drawn from life. Lavinia Fontana's handsome self-portrait, created from a mirror, seems less idealized than her two early self-portrait paintings of 1577 and 1579, to which different scholars have linked this drawing (fig. 1).[4] Since the paintings were probably based on drawings, whereas the drawings were created from life, this accounts for the discrepancy in naturalism and idealization. The process of direct observation from the living model also informs the two studies of fashionable young women in elaborate clothing (fig. 2).[5] Such drawings were presumably used in Fontana's activity as a popular portraitist for Bolognese noblewomen, and doubtless she created many more such studies that are no longer known. Fontana's extant paintings (over one hundred) are more than half portraits, and this was the type of picture for which she was most famous. Her seventeenth-century biographer Carlo Cesare Malvasia (1616–1693) remarks that noblewomen competed for the artist's attention, driving her prices up to levels that were

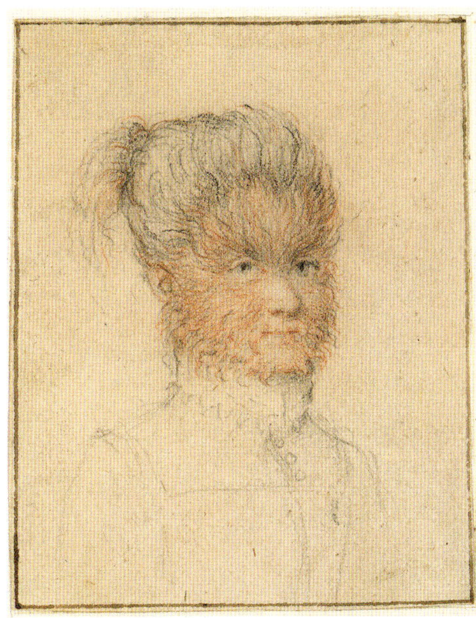

FIGURE 3 Detail of *Portrait of a Young Woman from the Gonzalez Family*, drawing in red and black chalk, 3¹¹⁄₁₆ × 3 in. (9.4 × 7.6 cm), IV, 158h.

comparable to those received by such eminent portrait painters as Anthony van Dyck (1599–1641).[6] The example illustrated was connected unconvincingly with Fontana's *Portrait of Isabella Ruini* (Galleria Palatina, Florence, 1593).[7]

One sheet portrays a young woman with hair covering her face (fig. 3).[8] The sitter is a daughter of Petrus Gonzalez (dates unknown) from the Canary Islands, and suffered from the rare genetic disorder of hypertrichosis, resulting in hair covering much of the body.[9] Fontana probably met the woman through Ulisse Aldrovandi (1522–1605), the famous naturalist at Bologna's university, who may have commissioned the drawing to support his studies of unusual biological phenomena. Although the even distribution of hair over the face suggests that Fontana somewhat idealized her sitter (in his notes, Aldrovandi remarks that the hair was of uneven length in various areas), the detail and immediacy of the woman's expression confirm the drawing's inception directly from the model.

A half-dozen drawings of monastic men and women are perhaps the liveliest portraits in the album (fig. 4).[10] The delightfully unidealized example illustrated here

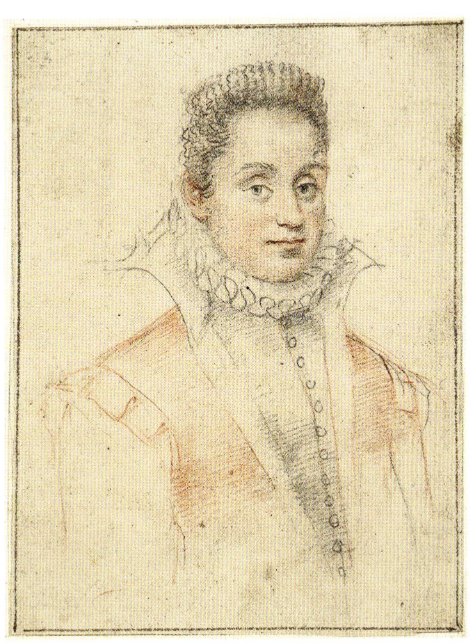

FIGURE 2 Detail of *Portrait of a Young Woman*, drawing in red and black chalk, 5⅛ × 4 in. (13.1 × 10 cm), IV, 158o.

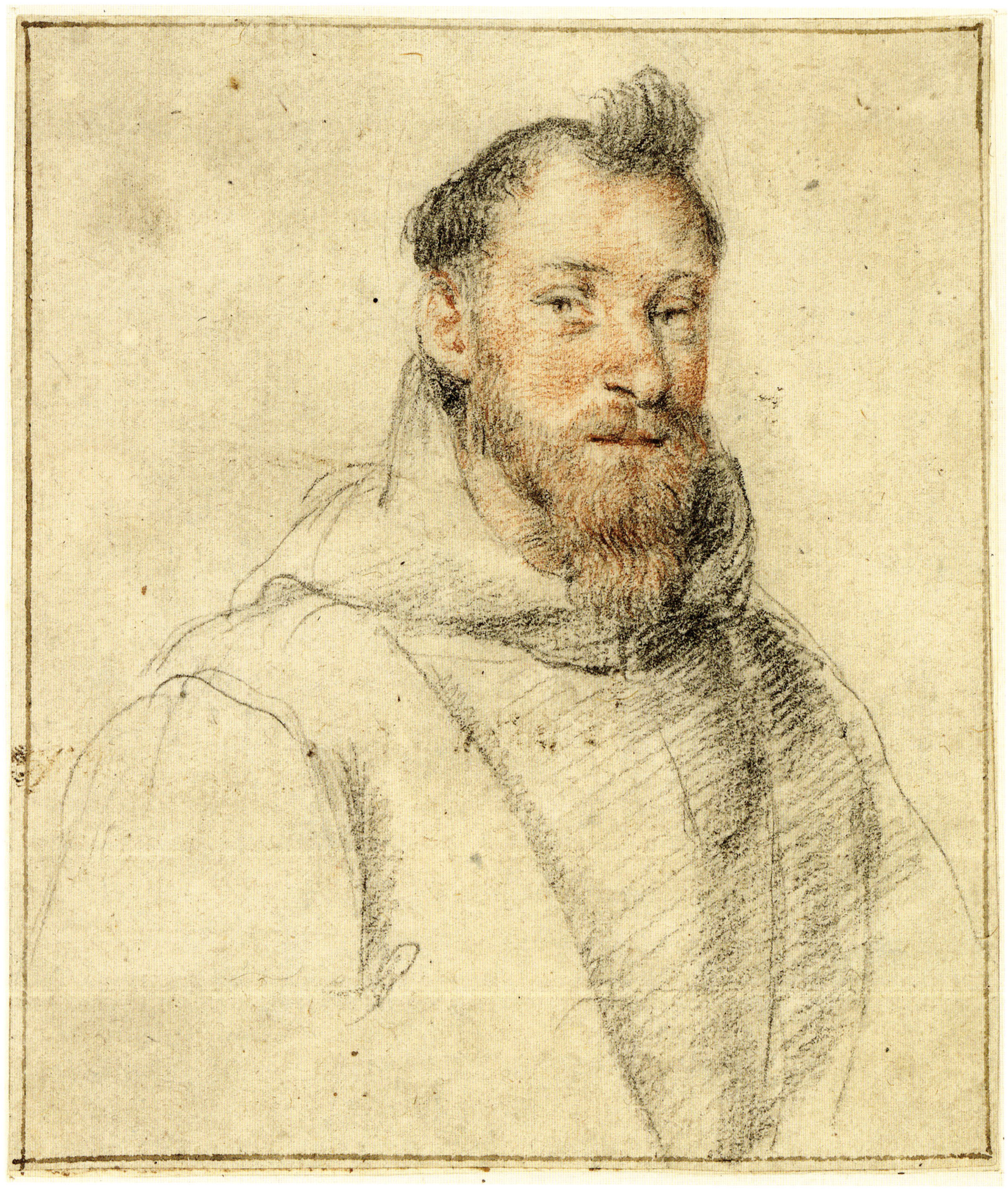

FIGURE 3 Detail of *Portrait of a Friar*, drawing in red and black chalk, 4 × 3½ in. (10.1 × 9 cm), IV, 158k (exhibited in Hartford).

portrays a young friar with a tuft of hair sticking straight up, as he looks out disarmingly. Fontana's painted portraits of friars (e.g., Galleria Estense, Modena, 1581, Cantaro no. 4a.33) seem more rehearsed and idealized than these charmingly unaffected drawings.—BB

NOTES

1. See Bohn 2021, app. 2.

2. See Bohn 2021, ch. 7.

3. Morgan Library and Museum website; https://www.themorgan.org/drawings/item/263862.

4. Inv. no. IV, 158b, red and black chalk, inscribed in ink upper left: "Ritrato di Lavinia / propria," $6\frac{7}{16} \times 5\frac{11}{16}$ in. (16.4 × 14.5 cm). Murphy 2003, 40–42; Bohn 2004a, 209; Bohn 2004b, 251–55.

5. Inv. no. IV, 158o, red and black chalk, $5\frac{1}{8} \times 4$ in. (13.1 × 10 cm). The other drawing referenced is inv. no. IV, 158q.

6. Malvasia 1678, vol. 1, 219–20; Malvasia 1841, vol. 1, 176.

7. See Cantaro 1989, nos. 4b.109E, 4a.68.

8. Inv. no. IV, 158h, red and black chalk, $3\frac{11}{16} \times 3$ in. (9.4 × 7.6 cm).

9. See Zapperi 2004 and Wiesner-Hanks 2009, 3–10.

10. Inv. no. IV, 158k, red and black chalk, $4 \times 3\frac{1}{2}$ in. (10.1 × 9 cm).

PROVENANCE

Second Viscount Palmerston [1739–1802]; April 24, 1891, sold at his sale at (Christie's, London, UK), lot 200, "A Volume of Portraits—in colours—by Lavinia Fontana," to Murray, for 4.17.6; Charles Fairfax Murray [1849–1919] (London, UK, and Florence, Italy); 1909, purchased from Murray through (Galerie Alexandre Imbert, Rome, Italy) by Pierpont Morgan [1837–1913] (New York, New York); by descent to his son, J.P. Morgan, Jr. [1867–1943] (New York, New York); The Morgan Library and Museum (New York, New York).

SELECTED EXHIBITIONS

Metropolitan Museum of Art, New York, 1965–1966; Museo Civico Archeologico, Bologna, 1994; National Museum of Women in the Arts, Washington, D.C., 1998; National Museum of Women in the Arts, Washington, D.C., 2007.

SELECTED PUBLICATIONS

New York 1965, 81, no. 149; Los Angeles 1976, 111 n. 7; Tufts 1982, 132, fig. 171; Cantaro 1989, 2, 4, 24, 49, 51, 164 under no. 4a.68, 204 under no. 4a.93, 227 under no. 4b.107, 233 under no. 4b.107M, 236–40, nos. 4b.109A–G, 237–40 illus.; Bologna 1994, 16, 47, 158–59 illus., 208–9, cat. 75, illus.; Fortunati 1998, 27; Washington, D.C. 1998, 35, 92, cat. 22, 93 illus., fig. 4.; Murphy 2003, 40–42, 128, 161–64, figs. 40, 112, 141; Bohn 2004a, 208–9, fig. 2; Bohn 2004b, 255–56, fig. 10; Washington, D.C. 2007, 150, cat. 25, 151 illus., 152 under cat. 26; Cantaro 2014, 105–6, fig. 9; Rocco 2017, 37, 39, fig. 1.5; Cole 2019a, 39–40, fig. 14; Bohn 2021, 176–78, figs. 91–95.

19

The Stoning of Saint Stephen, 1611, plate 1 of *Les Tableaux de Rome, Les Eglises Jubilaires*, 1607–1611, second state of three (Lieure)

Jacques Callot (Nancy, 1592–1635), after Lavinia Fontana
Engraving, sheet: 4⁷⁄₁₆ × 3¹⁄₁₆ in. (11.2 × 7.8 cm)
Inscribed (lower left): 1; (lower right): Callot fe. [Callot made it]
The Metropolitan Museum of Art, New York, The Elisha Whittelsey Collection, The Elisha Whittelsey Fund, 59.569.2

THIS PRINT BY THE FRENCH printmaker Jacques Callot is our only surviving visual record of Lavinia Fontana's last and most ambitious altarpiece, painted in Rome at the end of her career, when she was in her early fifties. This over-life-size commission for the Basilica of San Paolo fuori le Mura (Saint Paul Outside the Walls) depicting the Stoning of Saint Stephen was destroyed in a fire on July 16, 1823, that gutted the church.[1]

By all accounts, Lavinia Fontana was among the first women artists to produce a sizable number of large-scale altarpieces for churches.[2] On February 19, 1603, when her husband, Gian Paolo Zappi (ca. 1555–1615), signed the contract for this picture of an "*istoria* of Saint Stephen Protomartyr" in the presence of Girolamo Bernerio, Cardinal of Ascoli (1540–1611), and Don Angelo da Genova (Angelo Grillo) (1557–1629), abbot of the basilica, she was still in Bologna. So great was the altarpiece's size that on April 28, 1604, Virginio Roberto (dates unknown)—the Roman agent of Cardinal d'Este (very likely Cardinal Alessandro d'Este, 1568–1624) in Ferrara—sent the cardinal a request for the artist to use a larger room in the Roman Este Palace to complete the work.[3]

As the original altarpiece is no longer extant, we are left with only Callot's print and a less than favorable 1641 account by the painter and biographer Giovanni Baglione (1566–1643) to piece together an image of it.[4] The print, plate one of a series published by Lieure between 1607 and 1611, provides the best idea of the composition. It shows Saint Stephen kneeling at the lower right in his deacon's robes as an unidentified figure in Roman garb gestures to the story unfolding for the viewer. The narrative comprises fifteen figures in the foreground and around twelve in the background—a complex feat for any artist to achieve at over life-size.

Baglione was deeply critical of the finished altarpiece, explaining:

> Even though there were many good painters, the best masters who were then working were passed over and the work was given to Lavinia alone and she painted The Stoning of St. Stephen Martyr with many figures and a glory above, shown with the skies open; nevertheless it is true that because the figures are larger than lifesize, she became confused and did not succeed as well as she thought; because there is a big difference between an ordinary picture and machines of that size, which frighten every great intellect. She then made portraits, for which her talent suited her, and she made them quite well.[5]

This is a seventeenth-century instance of a woman being told in no uncertain terms to return to the genre perceived to be more suited to her gender—portraiture. Was Giovanni Baglione, as some have suggested, jealous because he did not receive the commission?[6] Was he resistant to Lavinia Fontana's late Mannerist approach to figures, which did not adhere to the tenets of naturalism practiced by early seventeenth-century Roman painters? It is likely her gender, his jealousy, and the *retardataire* mode of painting all factored into his assessment. Not all seventeenth-century commentators shared his opinion. In his 1625 guidebook for pilgrims visiting Rome for the Jubilee year, Ottavio Panciroli (1554–1624), described this altarpiece as "known for being excellent."[7]—ESP

NOTES

1. One of seven basilicas that every pilgrim to Rome endeavored to visit and still does. Cantaro 1989, 208.

2. Dated to around 1580, *Christ in the House of Martha and Mary* for the church of Santa Marta Zitella in Bologna (now, Conservatorio di Santa Marta) is the first recorded; it was most likely a collaboration with her father, Prospero Fontana. Lavinia Fontana's most prestigious altarpiece commission was executed at the behest of the Spanish King Philip II (1527–1598), who in 1589 commissioned the *Holy Family with Sleeping Christ Child and Infant Saint John the Baptist* altarpiece in the El Escorial Monastery and Palace, Madrid, for which she received the considerable sum of 1000 ducats, finally delivering it to Spain in 1593. For an overview of Lavinia Fontana's altarpieces, see Murphy 1997a, 537. In 1599 Fontana received her first commission for an altarpiece in Rome, *Virgin Appearing to Saint Hyacinth* for Cardinal Ascoli's chapel in the Church of Santa Sabina (in situ). Likely as a result of this commission, she moved to Rome in 1604. Murphy 1997a, 537.

3. For this identification see Dabbs 2009, 83 n. 14. Even though the contract stipulated a completion date in March of 1604, work on the altarpiece still had not begun in April of that year. For the details surrounding this commission, see Cantaro 1989, 208–9. Here is a transcription of this letter in Italian: "La Signora Lavinia Pittora Bolognese, che alloggia nel palazzo di V.S. Ill.ma fa un Quadro che ha da servire per la chiesa di S. Paolo di Roma, et desidera farlo con tutto lo studio possibile, et perché le sue stanze sono tante basse che non ci cape il Quadro, desideraria per doi mesi, sin che ha finite detta opera poter lavorare in una stanza grande e capace, di quelle però che adesso non servono a alcuno né hanno servitor. Però attese à fare i suoi ritratti, à quali col genio inclinava, e assai comodamente bene li faceva." See Cantaro 1989, 209.

4. Some scholars believe the *Head of a Youth* now in the Borghese Gallery (Galleria Borghese, Rome, inv. 81) is related to the figure in the left foreground of this altarpiece. See Graziani 2007, 162.

5. "Doveasi dare a dipingere un quadro grande in S. Paolo fuori delle mura sù la via Ostiense, e benché vi fussero molti buoni maestri, furono lasciati indietro i migliori soggetti, che in quel tempo esercitavano, e fu l'opera solamente conceduta a Lavinia, e vi dipinse la Lapidazione di S. Stefano Protomartire con quantità di figure, e con una gloria nell'alto, che rappresenta i cieli aperti; ben'egli è vero che, per esser le figure maggiori del naturale, si confuse, e si felicemente come pensava, non riuscille; poiché è gran differenza da quadro ordinario, a machine di quella grandezza, che spaventano ogni grande

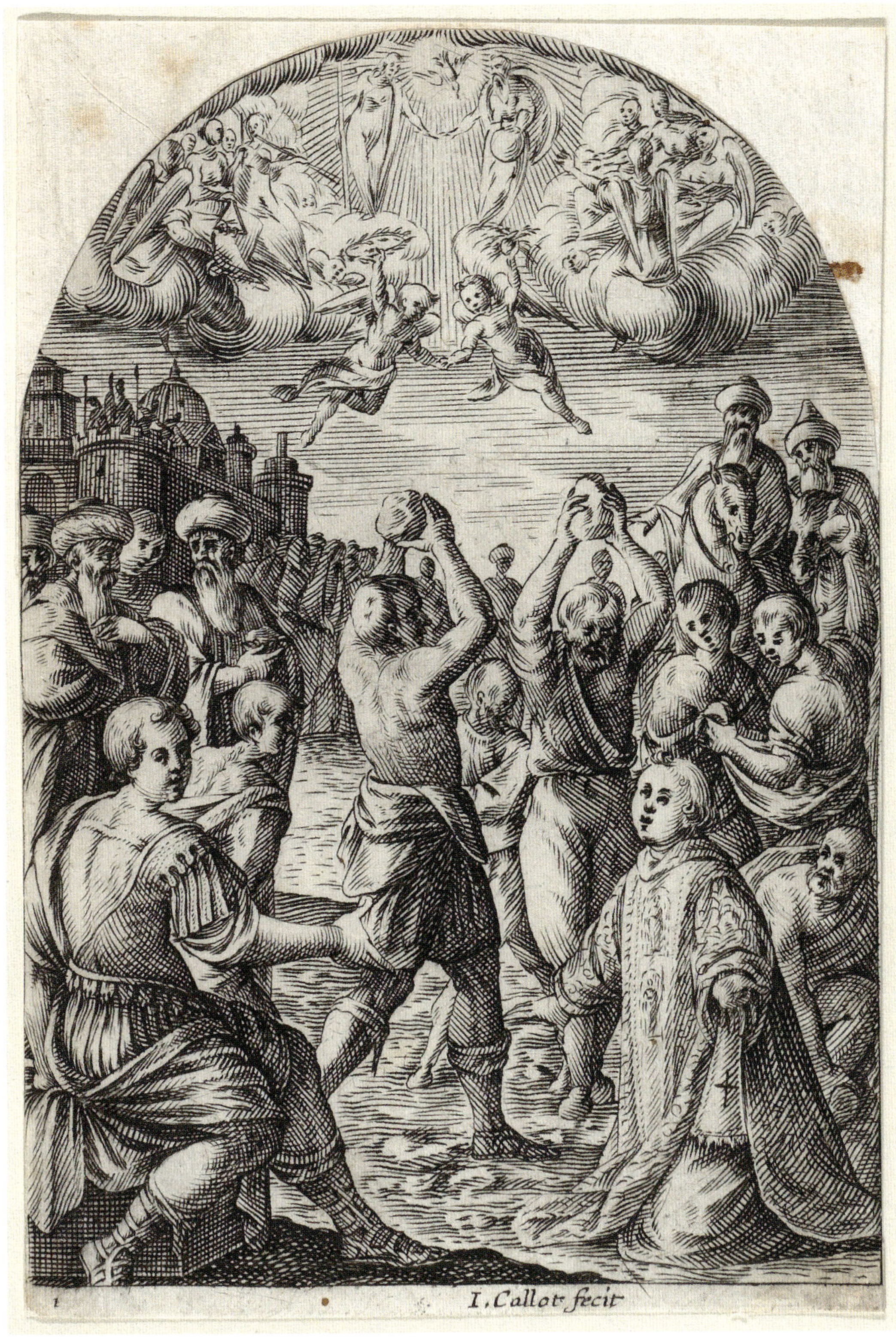

ingegno . . ." Cantaro 1989, 208. A partial English translation of this passage is given in Fortunati 1998, 29. A full English translation can be found in Sutherland Harris 1976, 30.

6. Cantaro 1989, 20; Murphy 2003, 195.

7. Murphy 2003, 195.

PROVENANCE

1959–present, sold by (R. E. Lewis) to the Metropolitan Museum of Art (New York, New York).

SELECTED PUBLICATIONS

Baglione 1733, 136; Lieure 1924, vol. 2, 13, no. 33; Mancini 1956–1957, vol. 1, 234; vol. 2, 132; Los Angeles 1976, 111–12; Sutherland Harris 1976, 30; Ghirardi 1984, 153–55; Bologna 1986, 132; Fortunati Pietrantonio 1986, vol. 2, 734, 773; Cantaro 1989, 15–16, 20, 22 n. 62, 49–50, 208–9, no. 4a.97, 212, 312–13, 319–22, 326–28; Nancy 1992, 134–35, no. 11; Fortunati 1998, 29; Washington, D.C. 1998, 104 under cat. 28; Graziani 2007, 162; Chadwick 2012, 94–95; Rocco 2017, 32; Madrid 2019, 186 under cat. 44.

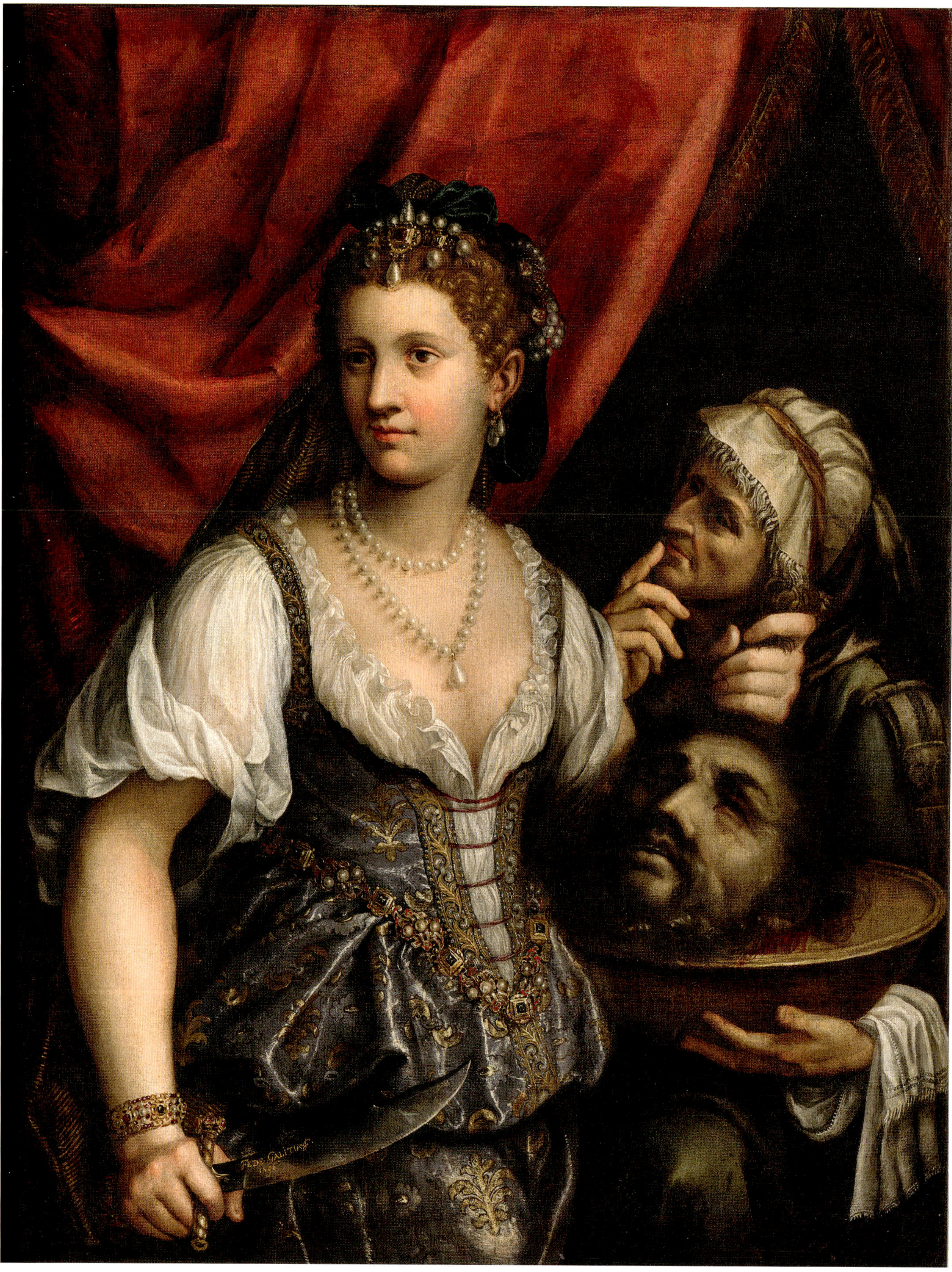

FEDE GALIZIA

Trent (?), ca. 1574–Milan, ca. 1630

DAUGHTER AND STUDENT of the Northern Lombard miniaturist and metalworker Nunzio Galizia (1550–1621), Fede Galizia was likely born in Trent and later moved to Milan. A painter of portraits, religious subjects, and still lifes of exquisite detail, she was known by contemporaries for her precocious artistic talent. Never married, in 1610 she was still living in her father's household and working on still life painting, a young genre in Italy; her first surviving and dated effort is from 1602. Her entire oeuvre is based on acute observation, and she imbued her still lifes in particular with astounding naturalism and spiritual energy.

20

Judith with the Head of Holofernes

1596
Oil on canvas, 47½ × 37 in. (120.7 × 94 cm)
Signed and dated (on the sword blade): FEDE GALITIA./1596
John and Mable Ringling Museum of Art, Sarasota, Gift of Mr. and Mrs. Jacob Polak, 1969, SN684

IN 1596 FEDE GALIZIA, trained by her father, the painter and illuminator Nunzio Galizia (active 1573–1595), created this stoic representation of Judith with the head of Holofernes accompanied by her maidservant Abra.[1] As the story is told in the Old Testament Apocrypha (12:10–20; 13:1–12), Judith—the beautiful widow of Bethulia—beheads the Assyrian general Holofernes, who is intent on annihilating the Jewish people. One of the most popular subjects for early modern artists, it is approached by Galizia with a reserve and finish fitting of late sixteenth-century Milan.[2] The painting is as much about Judith's allure and regalia—the cost, refinement, and exoticism of her gown and jewels—as it is about the biblical subject.

Judith is shown in Holofernes's tent in the moments after his execution. As she gazes confidently over her right shoulder, her white chemise falls open enticingly; this points both to Judith's efforts to seduce Holofernes prior to slaying him as well as to Fede Galizia's intent to beguile the viewer.

The luxury of her attire—a dress of dark grayish-purple silk with brilliant gold brocade, fastened with a jewel-encrusted belt that matches the style of her bejeweled bracelet—is emblematic of the importance of her deed. Her sword is a fantastical falchion with a jeweled, finely wrought hilt, which Galizia proudly signs and dates.[3] Costly pearls dominate the composition—two strands with a large drop pearl adorn her neck, and two drop pearls hang from gold hoop earrings. Pearls also embellish Judith's hair and the dark blue velvet headdress from which cascades a veil extending past her waist, shot through with golden threads. In contrast to Judith's pale skin and elegance of feature, Abra's skin tone is darker and her features broader, and her large, thick hands, which hold the trencher upon which Judith places Holofernes's severed head, were possibly meant to be perceived as more masculine.[4]

Attesting to the popularity of Fede Galizia's rendition of the Judith subject are two surviving later versions of it—one in the Borghese Gallery, Rome (fig. 1), signed and dated 1601 on the washbasin, and another, in a private collection in Milan, that Flavio Caroli dates to 1620.[5] A 1635 inventory of paintings owned by Carlo Emanuele I of Savoy (1562–1630) in the Palazzo Reale in Turin lists "a bejeweled Judith with the head of Holofernes in a basin, by Fede Galizia of Milan. Mediocre."[6] It remains unclear whether this is the picture described in the inventory, as Ann Sutherland Harris suggested in 1976, or if it is another version of

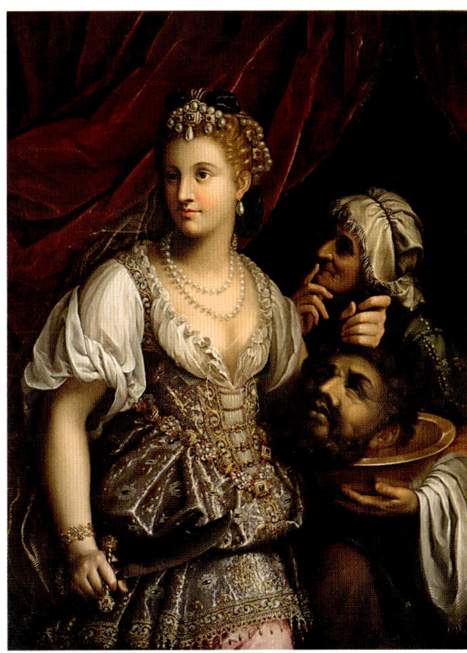

FIGURE 1 Fede Galizia, *Judith with the Head of Holofernes*, 1601, oil on canvas, 55½ × 42½ in. (141 × 108 cm). Galleria Borghese, Rome, inv. 165

the picture, the present location of which is unknown.[7] Given the descriptor "mediocre" after the entry and the fact that this painting depicts a trencher rather than a washbasin, the latter seems more likely.[8]

Infrared reflectography (IRR) further supports the theory that this is the prime version (fig. 2). From the IRR, we see four significant changes. Judith's entire head was originally shifted farther to the viewer's left and she had a thinner neck. The heroine's veil of golden thread was originally over her right forearm, and the right strap of her dress was lower on her white *camicia*.[9] Abra's face has been shifted and may initially have been tilted back even farther. In addition, Galizia used reddish-brown underpainting around Abra's left hand to block in the form.[10]

Like Artemisia Gentileschi's (1593–1654 or after) *Judith* in this exhibition (cat. 27), Fede Galizia chose to depict the moment after the decapitation. But while Gentileschi's Judith is active and anticipatory, Galizia's is stalwart and symbolic.—ESP

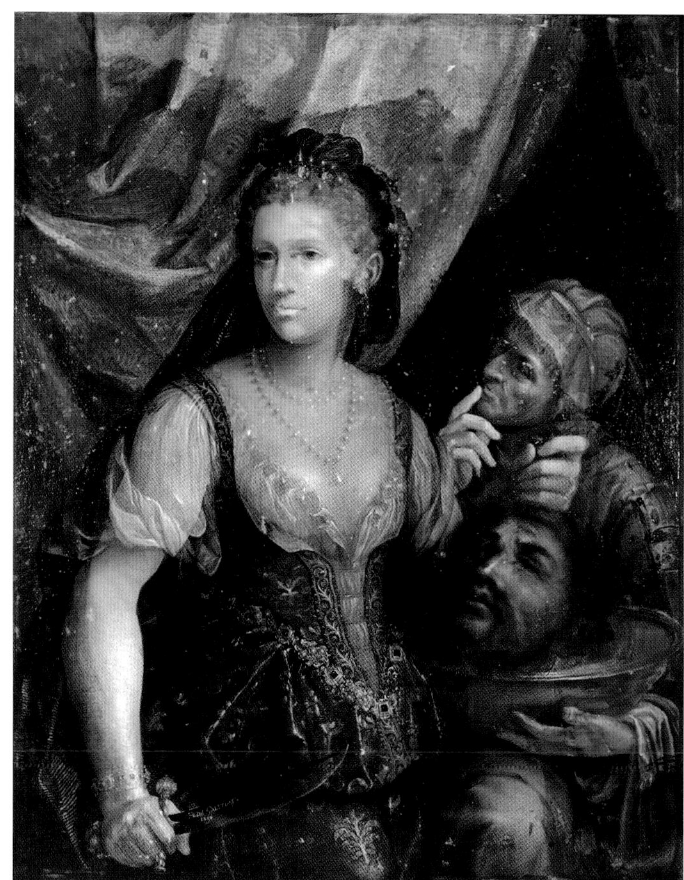

FIGURE 2 Infrared reflectogram (IRR), Fede Galizia, *Judith with the Head of Holofernes*. John and Mable Ringling Museum of Art

NOTES

1. Though Fede Galizia is largely absent from primary sources of the period, the painter and writer Giovanni Paolo Lomazzo (1538–1592) includes her in his 1590 treatise on painting, published when she was likely only twelve years old. He writes: "La Fede, figliuola di Anuncio Galizij da Trento, dandosi all'imitazion de i più eccelenti dell'arte nostra"—meaning that at this young age she made copies of works by other artists. Lomazzo 1590, 163. The city of her birth is unconfirmed.

2. On the theme of Judith, see Capozzi 1975 and Brine and Ciletti 2010.

3. The sword is part historicizing and part Orientalizing. I am grateful for the insights of Chassica Kirchhoff, assistant curator of European Sculpture and Decorative Arts, Detroit Institute of Arts, into the type of sword represented and what it might mean for the interpretation of this picture.

4. In this period it was most common to see Judith placing the head of Holofernes into a sack. Fede Galizia was one of the first artists to employ a trencher instead. The trencher was likely borrowed from the iconography associated with Salome. For more on this topic, see Joannides 1992, 164, 166.

5. The variant in the Borghese Gallery was likely housed by the Salviati family. It is wooden in execution and details such as the pearls around Judith's neck have been simplified. The physiognomies of the two Judiths also differ considerably, with the Ringling museum's Judith stoic and severe in comparison to the more youthful and expectant Judith in the Borghese Gallery version, which may have been a portrait. Caroli 1989, 82, no. 3. For the Milan picture see Caroli 1989, 82.

6. Vesme 1897, 53 (translation mine).

7. Sutherland Harris 1979, 115 n. 3.

8. A workshop copy was sold at Finarte auction house in Milan on April 21, 1988. Caroli 1989, 81.

9. I want to thank Sarah Cartwright, curator of collections at the John and Mable Ringling Museum of Art, for her help in getting an IRR of this picture taken and to Elizabeth Robson, intern in painting conservation at the Ringling, for taking and supplying this image, which teaches us so much about Fede Galizia's early painting practice. I am grateful also to Blair Bailey, former Andrew W. Mellon fellow in painting conservation at the DIA, for her help in interpreting this IRR.

10. For this technical information on the underpainting see Brilliant 2017, 95.

PROVENANCE

Possibly Galleria Sabauda or Palazzo Reale (Turin, Italy). Possibly Hinman (Maine). Possibly Logan Smith (Sarasota, Florida). Jacob and Eva Polak (Sarasota, Florida); 1969–present, gift to the John and Mable Ringling Museum of Art (Sarasota, Florida).

SELECTED EXHIBITIONS

Worcester Art Museum, 1972; Wildenstein Galleries, New York, 1981; Joslyn Art Museum, Omaha, 1997–1998; University of Michigan Museum of Art, Ann Arbor, 2002; National Museum of Women in the Arts, Washington, D.C., 2007; Patricia and Phillip Frost Art Museum, Miami, 2018.

SELECTED PUBLICATIONS

Vesme 1897, 53, no. 469; Worcester 1972, 5, 28, cat. 11, 29 illus.; Los Angeles 1976, 115; Petersen and Wilson 1976, 29, fig. III.17; Tomory 1976, 54, no. 46, illus.; New York 1981, 20, cat. 29, 41, pl. 9; Caroli 1989, 19, 27, 81–82, no. 2, fig. 2; Garrard 1989, 313, 315, fig. 279; Zeri and Porzio 1989, vol. 1, 222–23, fig. 253; Berra 1990, 58; Joannides 1992, 164, 166–67, fig. 4; Omaha 1997, 110, cat. 39, 111 illus.; Segal 1998, 164; Borzello 2000, 16 illus., 44, 46 illus.; De Girolami Cheney, Faxon, and Russo 2000, 81, pl. XV; Ann Arbor 2002, 8 illus., 86, cat. 32, 87 illus.; Murphy 2003, 154–55, fig. 136; Vigué 2003, 59 illus., 61 illus., 63; Uppenkamp 2004, 94–95, 237, no. 49; Washington, D.C. 2007, 71, 172 illus., 173, 176, cat. 36, 177 illus.; Quérat 2013; Brilliant 2017, 95–97, no. I.55, 96 illus.; Ghent 2018, 102, 104 under cat. 21; Cole 2019b, 113–14, fig. 79.

21

Glass Tazza with Peaches, Jasmine Flowers, and Quinces

ca. 1607
Oil on panel, $11^{15}/_{16} \times 16^{7}/_{16}$ in. (30.3 × 41.7 cm)
Montreal Museum of Fine Arts, Gift of Mr. and Mrs. Michal Hornstein, 2015.19

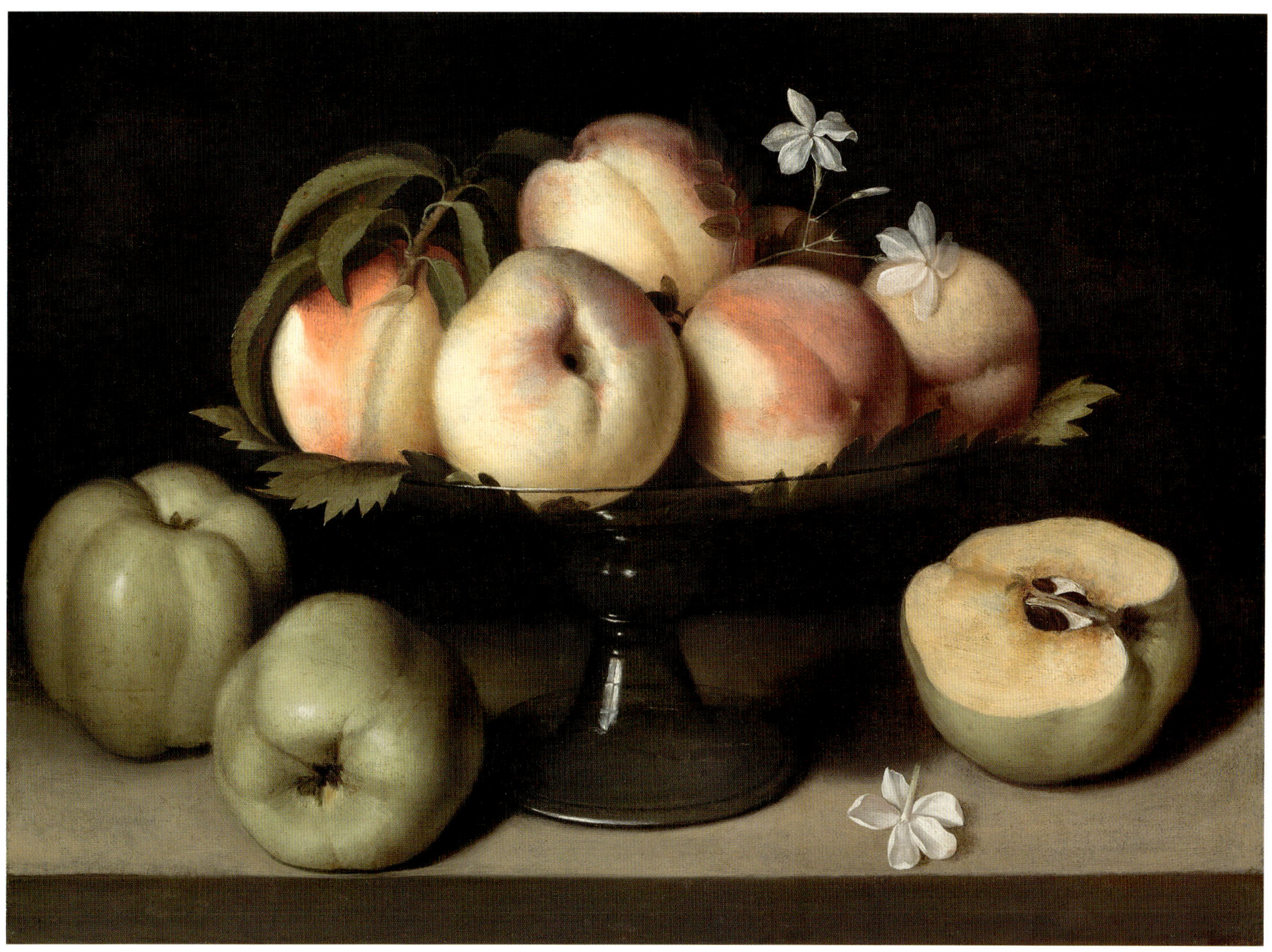

In **1590** the celebrated painter and historian Giovanni Paolo Lomazzo (1538–1592) recognized the artistic abilities of twelve-year-old Fede Galizia in his *Idea del tempio della pittura* (Idea of the Temple of Painting), a testament to her prodigious talent.[1] By age twenty she was an esteemed portraitist. Her prestigious commissions include the high altarpiece for Santa Maria

Maddalena in Milan and works for Emperor Rudolph II (reigned 1576–1612).

Likely trained by her father, a miniaturist painter, Fede Galizia's talent as a still life painter was unknown to art historians until 1938, when Curt Benedict published a still life by the artist with a date of 1602 written on the back, making it the earliest dated still life by an Italian artist. It was not until the

1960s, however, that Galizia truly emerged as a master of still life painting, featured in a series of exhibitions and publications. Today she is renowned as one of the most important still life artists in early seventeenth-century Italy.

The Montreal painting was first featured at the Royal Academy in London in 1950 and in Charles Sterling's historic 1952 exhibition *La nature morte de l'antiquité à nos jours* at the Musée de l'Orangerie, Paris, and its related publication of 1959. It is an autograph near-replica of her *Glass Tazza with Peaches, Jasmine Flowers and Quinces*, formerly on loan at the Cleveland Museum of Fine Arts (current location unknown), signed and dated 1607.[2] Two other variants of the painting are known in Bassano (private collection) and the Museo Civico, Cremona.

The balance of the composition, the play of light and shadow, and the slightly elevated viewpoint demonstrate an exemplary understanding of form, space, line, and light. The dramatic use of chiaroscuro defines the forms, giving the fruit an almost sculptural appearance. Each fruit and flower is strategically placed so as to complement the other objects in the picture. The glass tazza is primarily distinguished through reflective light. The golden and ripe peaches contrast effectively with the browning half quince in the lower right of the painting. Some scholars have read the picture as a *memento mori*, with the aging fruit symbolizing the passage of time and the inevitability of death. The painting showcases Galizia's masterful ability to naturalistically depict her subject without overly focusing on surface detailing.

The picture clearly belongs to an earlier Lombard tradition of still life painting exemplified by Caravaggio's (1571–1610) *Basket of Fruit* from about 1595 (Biblioteca Ambrosiana, Milan). Another influence on Galizia's work might be found in the only still life by Milanese artist Ambrogio Figino (1553–1608), *Still Life with Peaches on a Plate* from around 1595 (Lorenzelli Collection, Milan), which may have inspired her to maintain simplicity in her compositions and fill the pictorial space with the subject. Stefano Bottari writes of our panel that it is a work of a "delicatezza estrema, per la sbocciante freschezza dei colori, per l'integrità dei valori" ("an extreme delicacy, for the blossoming freshness of colors, for the integrity of its objects").[3]—HG

NOTES

1. Lomazzo 1973, 369.
2. Segal 1998, 166–67, figs. 2–5.
3. Bottari 1963, 311 (translation mine).

PROVENANCE

Before 1938 [when cited in an article by Curt Benedict]–1964, Vitale Bloch (The Hague, the Netherlands); 1964–1985, E. Zurstrassen (Heusy, Belgium), and by descent; 1985, (French & Company, Inc., New York, New York); 1985–2015, Michal and Renata Hornstein (Montreal, Quebec, Canada); 2015–present, Montreal Museum of Fine Arts (Montreal, Quebec, Canada).

SELECTED EXHIBITIONS

Royal Academy, London, 1950–1951, no. 325; Musée de l'Orangerie, Paris, 1952; Palazzo Reale, Naples, 1964; Kunsthaus Zurich, 1964–1965.

SELECTED PUBLICATIONS

Benedict 1938, 309 n. 1; Paris 1952, 9 illus., 89, no. 67; Sterling 1959, frontispiece, 2, 62; Bottari 1963, 311, 313, pl. 120b; Naples 1964, 28; Bottari 1965, 21, 33, 74, pl. 20; Zurich 1965, 33, no. 17; Longhi 1967, 22, pl. 47; Bergamo 1968, pl. 12; Bergamo 1985, 133, 140–43; Caroli 1989, 84, no. 11, pl. 11; Zeri and Porzio 1989, vol. 1, 222, 228, fig. 258; Segal 1998, 166–67, fig. 5; Cremona 2000, 222 under cat. 44; Florence 2003, 97; New York 2004, 184 under cat. 77; Marubbi 2007, 38; Bondil 2016, 58, illus., 122.

ISABELLA CATANEA PARASOLE

active 1585–1625

ISABELLA CATANEA PARASOLE worked as a printmaker and designer in Rome throughout her career. Little is known about her origins, upbringing, and education. She described herself as Roman and was married to the local printmaker Leonardo Parasole (ca. 1570–1612). They had two children. She may have received some training from her husband and his brothers. Together with her husband she illustrated the elaborate *Herbario nuovo* (1585) by the botanist Castor Durante (1529–1590). Later Parasole became well known through her innovative model books for needlework. Her books on lace design, aimed towards a female readership, were reprinted many times across Europe during the early seventeenth century. She was also connected with the patron Federico Cesi (1585–1630), who founded the scientific Accademia dei Lincei (Academy of the Lynx-Eyed) in Rome in 1603. Around the same time, she illustrated herbals conceived by Cesi and other leading scientists of her time. A sister, Geronima (1564–1622), also practiced as a printmaker in Rome.

22

Pretiosa gemma delle virtuose donne [Precious Gems of Virtuous Women], published by Lucchino Gargano, Venice

1600
Woodcut, overall: 4¾ × 6¹¹⁄₁₆ in. (12 × 17 cm)
The Metropolitan Museum of Art, New York, Harris Brisbane Fund, 1929.59.2

23

Teatro delle nobili et virtuose donne [Theater of Noble and Virtuous Women], published by Mauritio Bona, Rome

1616
Woodcut, engraving
Overall: 7½ × 10⁷⁄₁₆ in. (19 × 26.5 cm)
The Metropolitan Museum of Art, New York, Rogers Fund, 19.51

NEEDLEWORK BECAME POPULAR among women over the course of the 1500s, and it remained a female domain for centuries. While it was still practiced by male professionals, an increasing number of amateur women began to dedicate their time to decorating fabrics. Girls, especially from the middle and upper classes, were taught different techniques of embroidery and lacemaking from a young age to practice throughout their lives. These activities were seen to instill positive traits such as diligence, chastity, and domesticity in women, and needlework was favored over other pastimes, such as playing games, which were considered idle, if not lascivious.[1] Lace was still relatively new by the second half of the sixteenth century, but it quickly became fashionable and was worn as a conspicuous element of the aristocratic outfit. For many women artists from Irene di Spilimbergo (1538–1559) to Rosalba Carriera (1673–1757), needlework probably served as a springboard into the arts.

The Roman woodcarver Isabella Parasole exploited these new developments by creating pattern books for needlework that addressed an amateur female audience. She was the first Italian woman to specialize in this genre. Parasole gave her publications flowery titles that reflect the trend of female needlework practiced at home. *Specchio delle Virtuose Donne* (Mirror of Virtuous Women, 1593) was followed by the two exhibited here: *Pretiosa Gemma delle Virtuose Donne* (Precious Gems of Virtuous Women) and *Teatro delle Nobili et Virtuose Donne* (Theater of Noble and Virtuous Women).

On the title page of the *Teatro*, Isabella's name was changed to Elisabetta, a shrewd move to conflate her with Princess Elisabeth of France (1602–1644), to whom the book was dedicated. Similarly, the portrait below shows an elegant woman in a high collar made of lace. Although dressed as a princess, the mature woman is closer to Parasole's age. This strategy of ambiguity points to Parasole's marketing skills, while also asserting the virtue of needlepoint work.[2] Over the course of her career, Isabella Parasole designed and cut patterns for six successful books, each reprinted in several editions in and outside of Italy. Married to the engraver Leonardo Parasole, she played a considerable role in the Roman printing business, and also worked on herbal books for important patrons such as the papal physician Castor Durante, and most likely

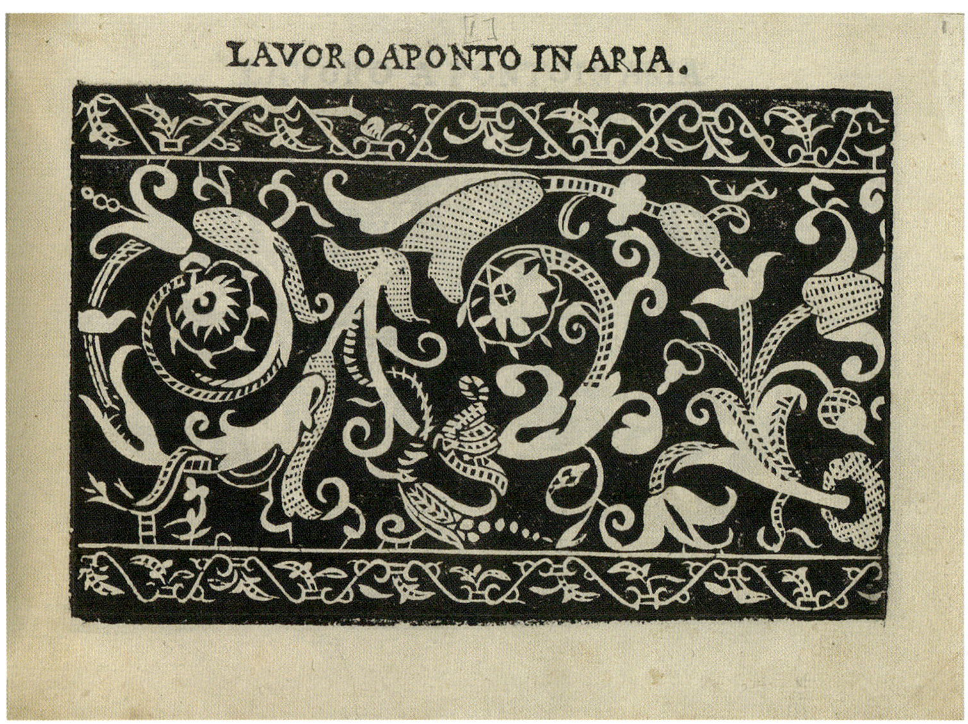

22 Page 1.

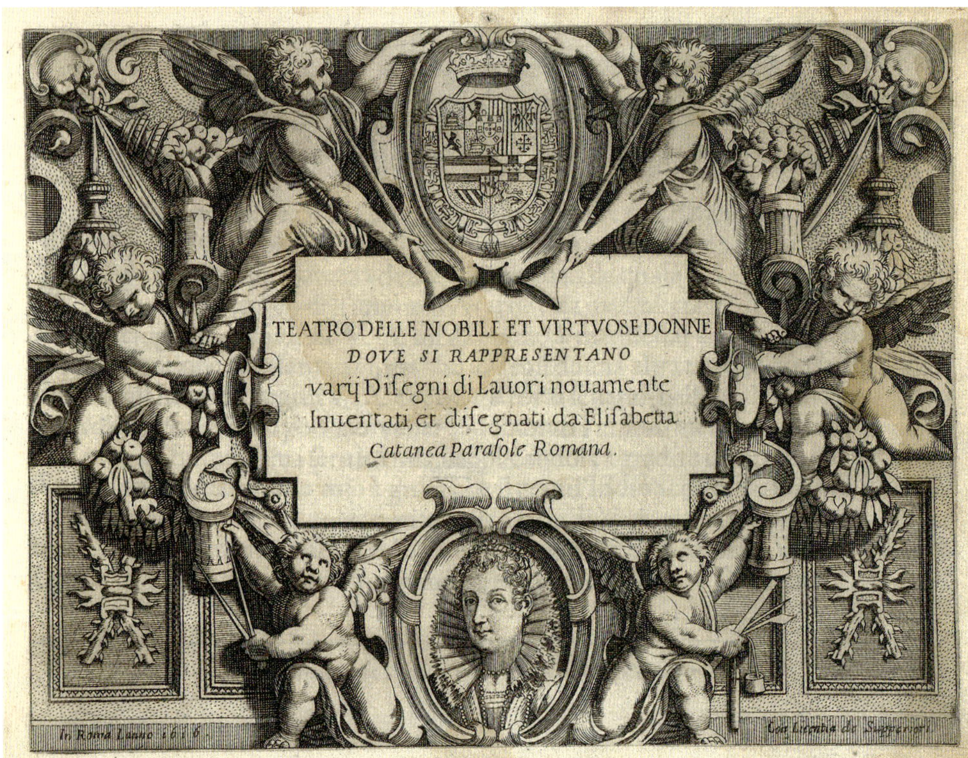

23 Title page, attributed to Francesco Villamena (1564–1624).

Federico Cesi (1585–1630), the founder of the Accademia dei Lincei, the scientific academy in Rome.[3]

Isabella Parasole's name quickly became synonymous with manuals for needlework in Italy, and beyond. Her designs reveal a deep understanding of lacework techniques and materials. Thanks to her talents in wood carving, Parasole was able to show the breadth of lacemaking skills, including the sophisticated *punto in aria* (lace without backing) with its ornamental floral borders, and *merletti a piombino* (bobbin lace), a technique that required the lacemaker to employ up to eighty-eight bobbins.[4] Her decorative patterns in white stand out against a dark background. According to Evelyn Lincoln, this method proved to be an efficient way of carving and was beneficial to the longevity of the blocks.[5] It also highlights once more Parasole's inventiveness and business acumen, and her pioneering role in the Roman printmaking business around 1600.—OT

NOTES

1. Wiesner-Hanks 2016, 177.

2. Its title page was engraved by another hand. Speelberg attributes it to Francesco Villamena (1564–1624) in Speelberg 2015, 44.

3. Castor Durante, *Herbario nuovo*, first edition 1585. Tongiorgi Tomasi 2008, 163–64. See also Lincoln 1997.

4. See Lincoln 2001, 20.

5. Lincoln 1997, 1069.

Pretiosa gemma delle virtuose donne

PROVENANCE

Edward Arnold (The Grove, Dorking, Surrey, UK); May 7, 1929, sold at Library of Edward Arnold sale at (Sotheby's, London, UK), lot 283; 1929–present, purchased from (Bernard Quaritch, Ltd., UK) by the Metropolitan Museum of Art (New York, New York).

SELECTED EXHIBITIONS

Metropolitan Museum of Art, New York, 2015–2016.

SELECTED PUBLICATIONS

Lotz 1933, 135b; Jacobs 1997b, 105–6, 110–11; Lincoln 2001, 1–35.

Teatro delle nobili et virtuose donne

PROVENANCE

1919–present, purchased from (Bernard Quaritch, Ltd., UK) by the Metropolitan Museum of Art (New York, New York).

SELECTED EXHIBITIONS

Metropolitan Museum of Art, New York, 2015–2016.

SELECTED PUBLICATIONS

Baglione 1733, 278; Lotz 1933, 143b; Lincoln 2001, 1–35; Washington, D.C. 2007, 195–97; Tongiorgi Tomasi 2010, 163; Speelberg 2015, 44–45, fig. 54.

ARTEMISIA GENTILESCHI

Rome, 1593–Naples, 1654 or later

ARTEMISIA GENTILESCHI received early training in the Roman studio of her father, the painter Orazio Gentileschi (1563–1639). In 1611 she was sexually assaulted in her home by her father's colleague, the artist Agostino Tassi (1578–1644). After his trial, she married the painter Pierantonio Stiattesi (born 1584) and together they moved to Florence. In the following years, she gave birth to five children and she enjoyed a fame that brought her back to Rome, as well as to Venice, London, and Naples. By 1616 her talents were already widely recognized, and she became one of the first women to be elected a member of the Florentine Accademia delle Arti del Disegno (Academy of the Arts of Drawing). Throughout her career, she won the patronage of numerous nobles and leading collectors, and she was celebrated for her paintings of bold and powerful women.

24

Self-Portrait as a Lute Player

1615–1617
Oil on canvas, 30½ × 28¼ in. (77.5 × 71.8 cm)
The Wadsworth Atheneum Museum of Art, Hartford, Charles H. Schwartz Endowment Fund, 2014.4.1

SINCE ITS REDISCOVERY in 1998, Artemisia Gentileschi's *Self-Portrait as a Lute Player* has been universally acknowledged to be a rare self-representation of the artist, painted at a crucial time in her career. With her self-assured pose, vigilant gaze, and strumming of the lute, the young Gentileschi presents herself as the multi-talented performer that she was striving to become. In depicting herself as a musician and not a painter, she may have been inspired by famous women artists such as Sofonisba Anguissola (ca. 1535–1625) and Lavinia Fontana (1552–1614), both of whom capitalized on their musical skills, youth, and beauty in groundbreaking self-portraits.[1] Such musical-themed depictions allowed women painters to highlight their refined education and, more broadly, their virtues. According to Catherine King, women painters were the first artists to depict themselves as musicians, beginning in the second half of the sixteenth century, when such portraits were sought after by collectors in Italy and beyond.[2] Yet, with the low-cut bodice and red makeup on her cheeks, which lend the image a strong erotic character, Gentileschi's likeness is far more sensual than those of her predecessors. This is the earliest known portrait of any woman artist that fully embraces and openly promotes her sexual attractiveness.

Various scholars have demonstrated how the Hartford self-portrait is firmly embedded in the cultural environment of Florence, where Artemisia Gentileschi lived from 1612/13 to 1620.[3] There she became a fully independent artist, embarking on a successful career fueled by her skills in self-promotion. *Self-Portrait as a Lute Player* is believed to have been painted between 1615 and 1617, and in 1638 it appeared in the inventory of the Medici Villa Artimino.[4] Together with two contemporaneous self-representations (cats. 25 and 26), the Hartford portrait conveys Gentileschi's playfulness and poise during a period when she enjoyed the patronage of the Medici and other high-ranking local collectors. At the same time, she was a wife and mother, an easily overlooked aspect of this portrait.[5] The dynamic but harmonious composition with sumptuous colors, such as the expensive ultramarine of the satin dress, lend her a luxurious, if not courtly appearance. These artistic choices corresponded well with local tastes. Florentine painters such as Lodovico Cigoli (1559–1613) and Cristofano Allori (1577–1621) preferred rich colors and muted, refined effects, often in theatrical settings.

The Hartford portrait's slightly tilted head is influenced by Artemisia Gentileschi's earlier *Self-Portrait as a Female Martyr*, believed to have been painted in 1613–1614 (cat. 25, fig. 1).[6] About two years later, Gentileschi used her own features again for the *Allegory of Inclination*, painted for Michelangelo Buonarroti the Younger (ca. 1568–1646). Like the Hartford *Self-Portrait as a Lute Player*, she rendered herself with her characteristic traits, such as a high forehead, chestnut hair, and almond-shaped eyes (fig. 1).

The circumstances of the creation of the Hartford portrait and its meaning are still under discussion. Judith Mann interpreted the picture as a self-depiction in the guise of a courtesan, an opinion that has been refuted.[7] Based on an exchange of letters between Artemisia Gentileschi and her Florentine lover Francesco Maria Maringhi

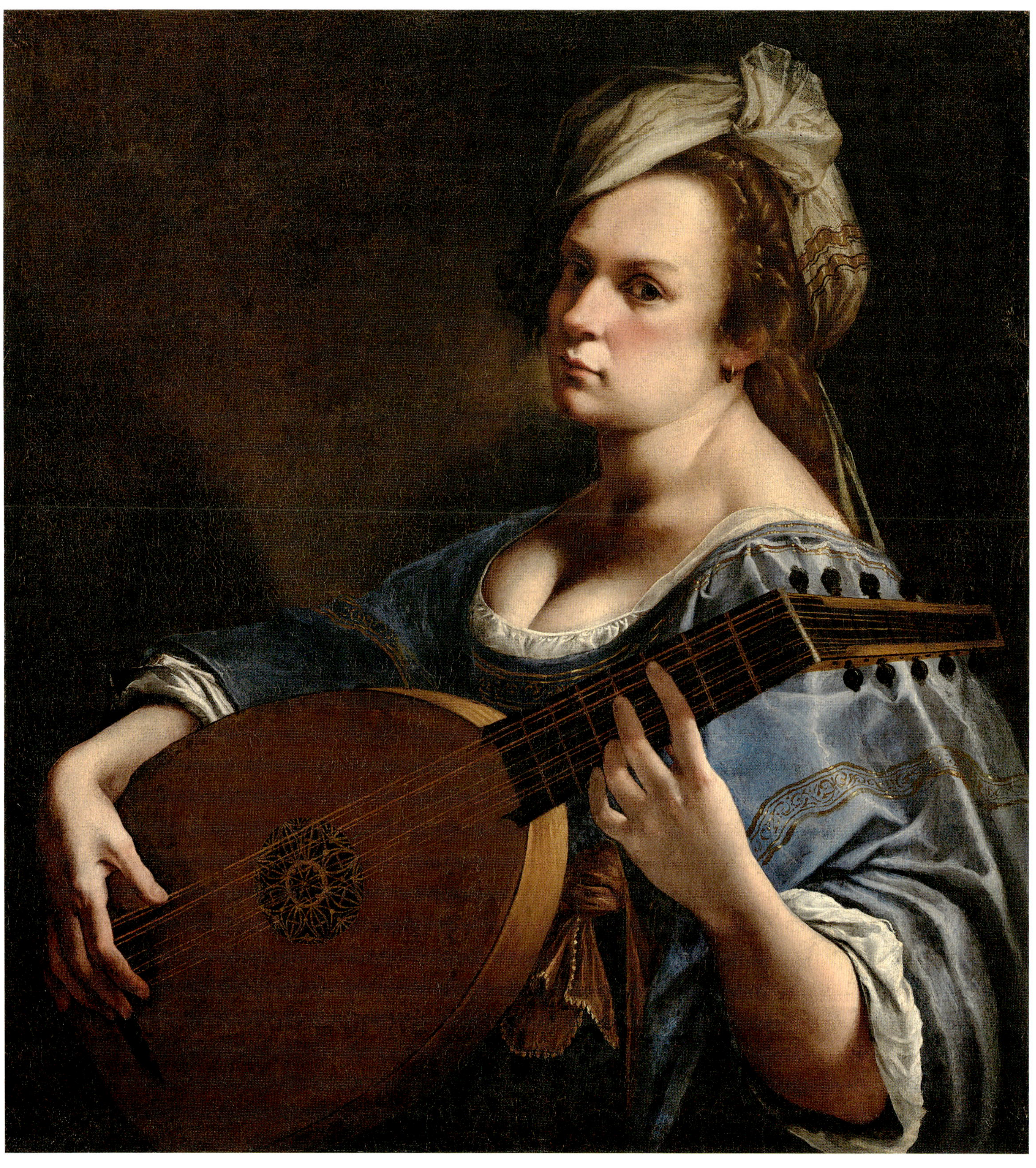

(1593–after 1653), Francesco Solinas suggested that it was painted for her paramour.[8] Elisabeth Oy-Marra supported this hypothesis.[9] Jesse Locker, Francesca Baldassari, and Letizia Treves, however, relate the portrait to a musical performance at the Medici court in 1615, the *Ball of the Gypsy Women*, in which a "Sig.ra Artimisia" participated.[10] As gypsies were stereotypically depicted with turbans, Gentileschi's elegant headscarf supports this proposal, but participants in this ball also wore black masks, and Sig.ra

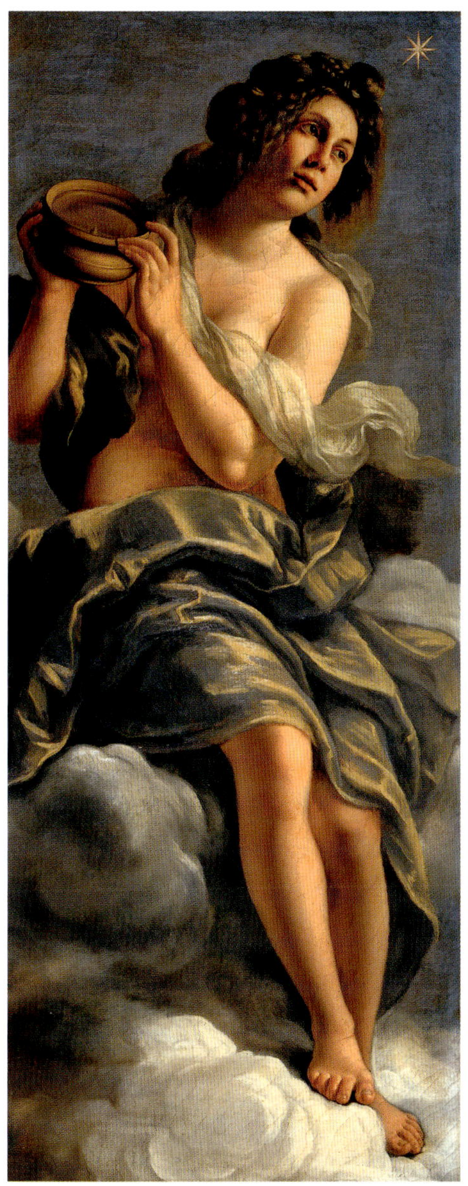

FIGURE 1 Artemisia Gentileschi, *Allegory of Inclination*, 1615–1616, oil on canvas, 59¹³⁄₁₆ × 24 in. (152 × 61 cm). Casa Buonarroti, Florence

Artimisia is highlighted in the records of the event as a singer, not a lute player.[11] It is true, however, that Gentileschi's appearance in this portrait has a pronounced theatrical character, as if she were playing a role. It is thus possible it was created for a member of the Medici family, perhaps Grand Duke Cosimo II (1590–1621).[12] As much as Gentileschi's scarf could allude to a gypsy, it may also suggest a sibyl—both are associated with magical and seductive abilities.[13] In this novel portrait, Gentileschi created a persona that emphatically uses her power as a woman to engage with the viewer, fashioning herself as a femme fatale *avant la lettre*.—OT

NOTES

1. Sofonisba Anguissola, *Self-Portrait at the Keyboard*, 1556–1557, oil on canvas, 22¹³⁄₁₆ × 18⅞ in. (58 × 48 cm), Museo di Capodimonte, Naples (two more versions are known); Lavinia Fontana, *Self-Portrait at a Spinet*, 1577, oil on canvas, 10⅝ × 9⅜ in. (27 × 23.8 cm), Accademia Nazionale di San Luca, Rome. In one of her earliest works, Giovanna Garzoni (1600–1670) depicts herself with a stringed instrument as well: *Self-Portrait as Apollo*, ca. 1618–1620, tempera on parchment, laid down on linen, 16⁹⁄₁₆ × 33 in. (42 × 33 cm), Palazzo del Quirinale, Rome. At the time this portrait was painted in Florence, Garzoni probably knew Artemisia Gentileschi. According to Sheila Barker, Garzoni may have modelled her likeness on Gentileschi's *Self-Portrait as a Lute Player*. See Barker 2020c, 124–25. The Flemish artist Caterina van Hemessen (1528–after 1565) may have painted the earliest known portrait of this type: *Girl at a Spinet (Self-Portrait?)*, 1548, oil on oak, 12⅝ × 10¼ in. (32 × 26 cm), Wallraf-Richartz-Museum, Cologne.

2. King 1995, 388.

3. See Baldassari 2016a, 23–31; Treves 2020a, 67–70.

4. The Hartford painting has been identified by Gianni Papi with "un quadro in tela alto b. 1½ largo b. 1¼ con adornam.to nero filettato d'oro entrovi dipinto il riatto dell' artemisia di sua mano che suona il liuto." Archivio di Stato, Guardaroba Medicea 532, Inventario Artimino 1638, fol. 16v. See Papi 2000, 452.

5. In November 1618 Gentileschi gave birth to her fifth child.

6. Artemisia Gentileschi, *Self-Portrait as a Female Martyr*, ca. 1613–1614, oil on canvas, 12½ × 9¾ in. (31.8 × 24.8 cm), private collection.

7. See, for instance, Bohn 2004b, 241.

8. Solinas 2011, 164.

9. Oy-Marra 2014, 168.

10. Solerti 1905, 89–92; Locker 2015, 137; Baldassari 2016b, 130; Treves 2020b, 136.

11. See Solerti 1905, 90 and 92.

12. Locker 2015, 136; Baldassari 2016b, 130; Treves 2020b, 136.

13. Mary Garrard compares the scarf with similar headgear worn by male Renaissance artists such as Michelangelo. Garrard 2020a, 98–100.

PROVENANCE

By 1638 until at least 1683, Medici collection, Villa Artimino (Artimino, Italy); private collection (Europe); July 9, 1998, sold anonymously at (Sotheby's, London, UK), lot 68; Curtis Galleries (Minneapolis, Minnesota); January 29, 2014, offered anonymously for sale at (Christie's, New York, New York), lot 36; February 2014–present, privately sold to the Wadsworth Atheneum Museum of Art (Hartford, Connecticut).

SELECTED EXHIBITIONS

Metropolitan Museum of Art, New York, 2001–2002; Galleria Palatina, Palazzo Pitti, Florence, 2010–2011; Palazzo Reale, Milan, 2011–2012; Musée Maillol, Paris, 2012; Museo di Roma, Palazzo Braschi, Rome, 2016–2017; National Gallery, London, 2020–2021.

SELECTED PUBLICATIONS

Papi 2000, 452, fig. 33; Mann 2001a, 251; Mann 2001d, 420; New York 2001–2002, 322–25, cat. 57, 322–23 illus., 328 under cat. 59, 353 under cat. 64; Bohn 2004b, 241; Garrard 2005, 99, 103–5, fig. 1; Mann 2005c, 53–54, fig. 4; Sutherland Harris 2005a, 140, fig. 11; Washington, D.C. 2007, 56, 70–71, 208 under cat. 47, fig. 7; Florence 2010b, 160–61, cat. 25; Milan 2011, 63 illus., 72, 164, cat. 15, 165 illus.; Paris 2012, 62, 70 illus., 71, cat. 11; Zutter 2013, 137, 139, fig. 4; Oy-Marra 2014, 167; Locker 2015, 125–42, fig. 5.1; Baldassari 2016a, 31; Baldassari 2016b, 130, cat. 25, 131 illus.; Locker 2017, 94–95, fig. 8; Keith et al. 2019, 4–17; Florence 2020, 124 under cat. 3; Garrard 2020a, 95–112; London 2020, frontispiece, 94–95, 94 illus., 129 under cat. 6, 140 under cat. 11, 173 under cat. 21; Treves 2020a, 69 illus., 70, 76 n. 5; Treves 2020b, 136–39, cat. 10, 137–38 illus.

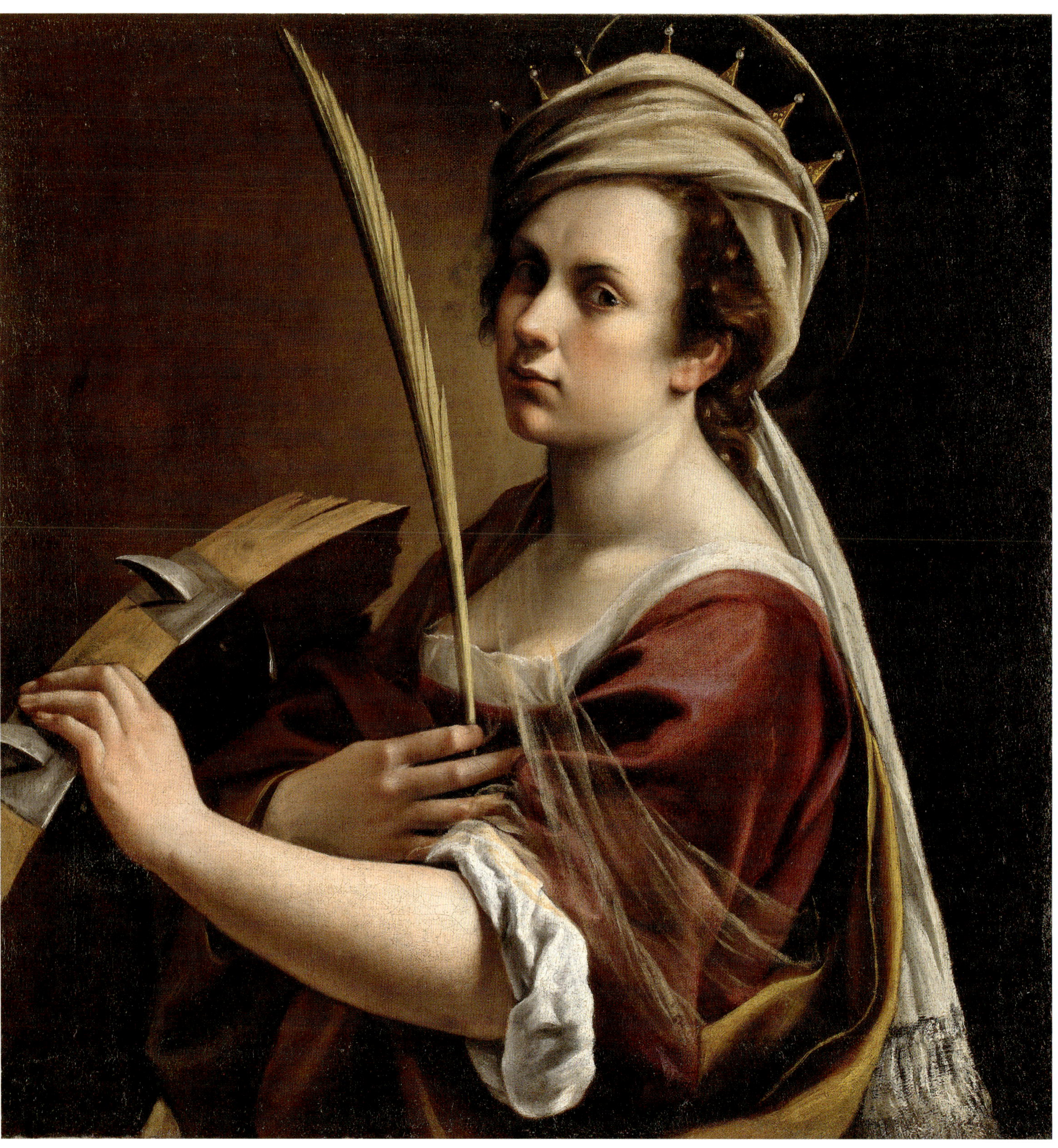

Self-Portrait as Saint Catherine of Alexandria

1615–1617
Oil on canvas, 28⅛ × 27³⁄₁₆ in. (71.4 × 69 cm)
The National Gallery, London, NG6671

DISCOVERED IN 2017, *Self-Portrait as Saint Catherine of Alexandria* is a significant addition to Artemisia Gentileschi's oeuvre. It shares formal and stylistic features with two related paintings: *Self-Portrait as a Lute Player* in Hartford and *Saint Catherine of Alexandria* in Florence (cats. 24 and 26). All three portraits were painted in Florence around the same time, all exhibit the artist's features, and all illustrate her desire for self-promotion. As demonstrated by recent technical investigations on the London and Florence pictures, Gentileschi probably created all three simultaneously or in quick succession at some point from around 1615 to 1617.[1] The paintings find a prototype in the small *Self-Portrait as a Female Martyr*, painted shortly after her arrival in Florence, around 1613–1614 (fig. 1).

Throughout her career, Artemisia Gentileschi specialized in depicting powerful women. She is easily recognized in this picture as the early fourth-century Christian martyr Catherine of Alexandria, whose attributes are a broken spiked wheel and a crown.[2] Catherine was a popular saint around 1600, especially in Florence. The arched eyebrows, pursed lips, and wavy chestnut hair are identical to those in other images of Gentileschi, most notably the Hartford self-portrait. The pose and the three-quarter view are nearly identical to those in both the Hartford and Florence paintings. Gentileschi must have traced the outlines and principal attributes such as the nose and the position of eyes and mouth and transferred them from one painting to another. She probably learned this technique from her father Orazio Gentileschi (1563–1639). In contrast to the Hartford and Florence paintings, she idealized her features in the London picture by giving herself

a slightly elongated neck, shortening her forehead, and straightening her nose. For reasons of decorum, she covered the saint's décolletage.

Recent technical studies in London and Florence have highlighted Artemisia Gentileschi's use of her likeness in images of Saint Catherine. Letizia Treves convincingly argues that the London picture started out as a self-portrait, to which the artist later added the crown, broken wheel, and palm. The turban, an unusual attribute for the saint, may have originally been an artist's garment similar to that in the Hartford painting, or it may have been an indication of a different subject, such as a sibyl. Possibly a keen marketing strategy to advance her career, and in reaction to the high demand for pictures of Saint Catherine, Gentileschi

FIGURE 1 Artemisia Gentileschi, *Self-Portrait as a Female Martyr*, ca. 1613–1614, oil on panel, 12½ × 9¾ in. (31.8 × 24.8 cm). Private collection

fused her own countenance with the likeness of the saint.

Self-portraits in the guise of someone else were popular among Italian artists beginning in the early sixteenth century. In Florence there was an avid market for such images.[3] Shortly after 1600, Caravaggio (1571–1610) and Cristofano Allori (1577–1621) painted celebrated self-representations as biblical characters that Gentileschi may have known.[4] Yet, until Artemisia Gentileschi, the practice of painting a disguised version of oneself had been rare among women artists.[5] In this case, however, only a woman could impersonate the saint and Gentileschi fully capitalized on her status as a young and attractive woman. By presenting herself as Saint Catherine, she may have aimed to associate herself with the saint's legendary courage, virtuosity, and popularity.—OT

NOTES
1. On the Uffizi painting, see Frosinini and Reginella 2019.
2. "Life of Saint Catherine," in de Voragine 1969, 708–16.
3. Treves 2020a, 69.
4. Caravaggio, *David with the Head of Goliath*, ca. 1610, oil on canvas, 49³⁄₁₆ × 39¾ in. (125 × 101 cm), Galleria Borghese, Rome; Cristofano Allori, *Judith with the Head of Holofernes*, 1613, oil on canvas, 47⅜ × 39½ in. (120.4 × 100.3 cm), Royal Collection Trust, London.
5. Lavinia Fontana's *Judith* from 1599, in the Museo Davia Bargellini, Bologna, may be an early self-portrait of the artist in the guise of Judith.

PROVENANCE
Charles Marie Boudeville (Châtenois, Vosges, France); Georges Boudeville [1930–1984]; Nicolas Boudeville [b. 1966]; December 19, 2017, sold at (Drouot, Paris, France), lot 69; 2018–present, sold by (Marco Voena and Fabrizio Moretti) to the National Gallery (London, UK).

SELECTED EXHIBITIONS
National Gallery, London, 2020–2021.

SELECTED PUBLICATIONS
Keith et al. 2019, 4–17; Garrard 2020a, 100–104; London 2020, 95, 129 under cat. 6, 134 under cat. 9, 140, cat. 11, 141–42 illus., 173 under cat. 21, fig. 40; Treves 2020a, 69–70, 69 illus., 77 n. 26; Treves 2020b, 136 under cat. 10; Treves 2020c, 144.

Saint Catherine of Alexandria

1615–1617
Oil on canvas, 30 × 24½ in. (77 × 62 cm)
Gallerie degli Uffizi, Florence, inv. 1890 no. 8032

THIS STRIKING PICTURE of Saint Catherine of Alexandria was exhibited for the first time as an autograph work by Artemisia Gentileschi in 1970. Since then, all leading scholars have accepted it as such. It was painted in Florence after the *Self-Portrait as a Female Martyr* (cat. 25, fig. 1) and the 1616 *Allegory of Inclination* (cat. 24, fig. 1).[1] The portrait has formal and stylistic similarities with closely related paintings in Hartford and London (cats. 25 and 26), both dated 1615–1617, and recent technical investigations confirm its dependence on these works.[2] Without knowing the London painting, Judith Mann dated *Saint Catherine of Alexandria* to ca. 1618–1619, while other scholars, such as Roberto Contini, dated it slightly earlier. The sequence of the three paintings is still unclear.

Artemisia Gentileschi depicts Saint Catherine in luxurious garments with her usual attributes, the spiked wheel and crown, looking towards heaven. The saint's individualized features, however, differentiate this portrait from standard interpretations of the subject. As in the London painting, they are based on Gentileschi's own distinctive features, including her uneven nose, high forehead, and slight double chin. The face appears as full and the neckline as robust as in the Hartford *Self-Portrait as a Lute Player*, in which she similarly wears a lavish gown embroidered with an elegant design in gold. The tone of the hair, however, is darker here.

Recent technical examinations have revealed another composition beneath the saint. Like the London painting, *Saint Catherine of Alexandria* started out as a self-portrait. The pose of the underpainted figure is similar to that in the London painting—she looks at the viewer and wears a turban. In light of these discoveries, Larry Keith and Letizia Treves suspect the figure may have been transferred from the original design of the London painting, which began as a self-portrait.[3] Mary Garrard, however, proposes that Gentileschi started with this portrait, before she painted the London and later the Hartford pictures.[4]

What prompted Artemisia Gentileschi to change a self-portrait into a religious subject is uncertain. It may have been a response to the high demand for such images in Florence. Mary Garrard suspects that the presence in the city of Caterina de' Medici (1593–1629), the sister of the grand duke, may be one reason for the large number of images of Saint Catherine at the time. The saint's elaborate crown may be reminiscent of the grand ducal crown designed by the Dutch goldsmith Jacques Bylivelt (1550–1603).[5] The sumptuous colors in this painting and the artist's close contacts with the Medici family make it possible that *Saint Catherine of Alexandria* was either made for that family or for another elite collector.

Despite the similarity of Saint Catherine's features to the artist's, the identification of the subject is contested. In lieu of using a model, Gentileschi could have started with her own image and then moderated her features to better align the face with that of her patron. While Garrard, Gianni Papi, and Jesse Locker see a self-portrait of Artemisia Gentileschi, Mann and Treves interpret the painting as a portrait of Caterina de' Medici, and Francesco Solinas sees it as a portrait of the Grand Duchess Maria Maddalena of Austria (1589–1631).—OT

NOTES

1. Bissell, however, places it before the two works and dates it ca. 1614–1615. Bissell 1999.

2. On the Uffizi painting, see Frosinini and Reginella 2019, 109–21.

3. Keith et al. 2019, 8–9.

4. Garrard 2020a, 102–5.

5. Treves 2020c, 144.

PROVENANCE

By 1683, Medici collection, Villa Artimino (Artimino, Italy); by 1890, Galleria dell'Accademia (Florence, Italy); until at least 1989, Soprintendenza alle Gallerie (Florence, Italy); Gallerie degli Uffizi (Florence, Italy).

SELECTED EXHIBITIONS

Palazzo Pitti, Florence, 1970; Casa Buonarroti, Florence, 1991; Metropolitan Museum of Art, New York, 2001–2002; National Museum of Women in the Arts, Washington, D.C., 2007; Palazzo Reale, Milan, 2011–2012; Musée Maillol, Paris, 2012; Museum voor Schone Kunsten, Ghent, 2018–2019; National Gallery, London, 2020–2021.

SELECTED PUBLICATIONS

Bissell 1968, 167; Florence 1970, 72–73, cat. 44, 180, pl. 44; Naples 1984, vol. 1, 147; Garrard 1989, 48–49, fig. 34; Florence 1991, 25, 45, 129 under cat. 12, 132 under cat. 13, 141 under cat. 16, 145 under cat. 17, 147–49, cat. 18, 148 illus., 171 under cat. 25, 187; Bissell 1999, 24, 203–4, no. 6, fig. 54; New York 2001–2002, 313–15, 318, 320 under cat. 56, 324 under cat. 57, 328–30, cat. 59, 329 illus., 333 under cat. 60, 352 under cat. 63; Garrard 2005, 104–5, fig. 10; Lattuada and Nappi 2005, 79, 81, fig. 2; Mann 2005c, 54–55, fig. 5; Washington, D.C. 2007, 208, cat. 47, 209 illus.; Florence 2010a, 25, fig. 4; Milan 2011, 72, 166, cat. 16, 167 illus.; Paris 2012, 60–62, 63 illus., 72, cat. 12, 73 illus.; Zutter 2013, 136; Fortune 2014, 188, 160–61, 211; Locker 2015, 134–35, fig. 5.11; Baldassari 2016a, 29, 31, fig. 9; Baldassari 2016b, 130; Ghent 2018, 136 under cat. 30, 140, cat. 32, 141 illus.; Garrard 2020a, 100–105; London 2020, 82, 83 illus., 87, 94–95, 95 illus., 115 under cat. 2, 129 under cat. 6, 140 under cat. 11, 143 illus., 209 under cat. 30; Treves 2020b, 136, 139; Treves 2020c, 144–45, cat. 12, 145 illus.

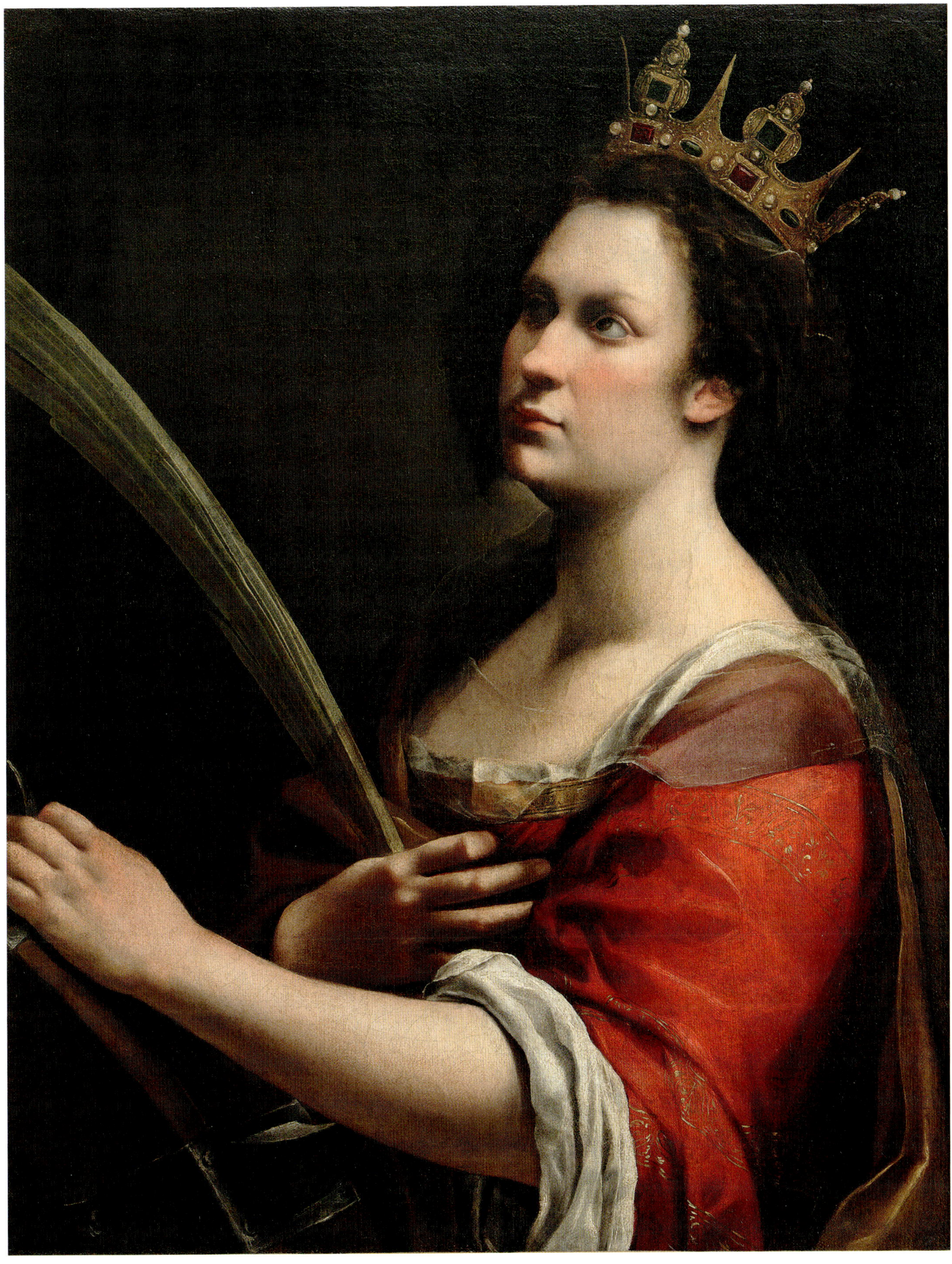

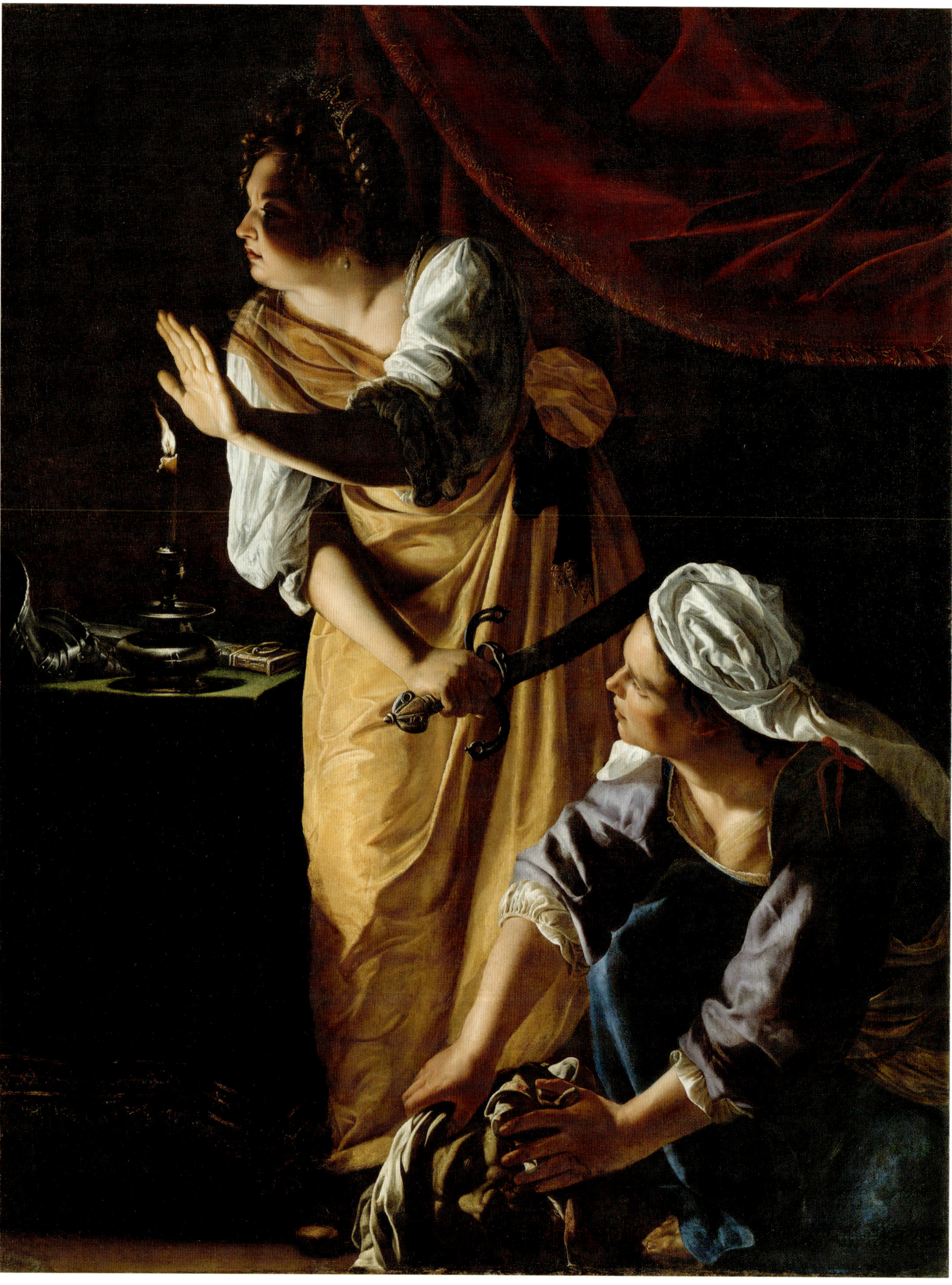

27

Judith and Her Maidservant with the Head of Holofernes

ca. 1623–1625
Oil on canvas, 72⁷⁄₁₆ × 55¾ in. (184 × 141.6 cm)
Detroit Institute of Arts, Gift of Mr. Leslie H. Green, 52.253

THERE IS NOT a grander, more elegantly powerful depiction of Judith created by a follower of Caravaggio (1571–1610) in Rome in the 1620s than this painting. With its bold, large-scale composition and mastery of light and shadow, it numbers among a small group of Artemisia Gentileschi's masterpieces.[1] Here she has depicted the biblical Jewish heroine Judith with fresh drops of blood poised to fall from the edge of her blade, just after she has beheaded the Assyrian general Holofernes with the help of her maidservant Abra. As recorded in the book of Judith (12:10–20; 13:1–12) in the Old Testament Apocrypha, Holofernes was intent on annihilating the Jewish people; dressed in her finery, Judith, a widow from Bethulia, entered the general's tent bent on beguiling and then beheading him.

A strong contrast of light and dark animates the scene, leading the spectator through a narrative that zigzags diagonally across the canvas. A yellowish light guides the eye to Judith's left palm, paused in anticipation of an imminent departure from Holofernes's tent. A warmer hue illumes Abra, equally preoccupied with determining the best moment to exit and bring the general's head—loosely bound in a bloodied, white cloth—back to the Jewish people as proof of his demise. The candlelight illumination suggests Gentileschi must have been familiar with the Dutch painter Gerrit van Honthorst's (1592–1656) nocturnal subjects.[2] The strength of the light, however, suggests an additional light source coming from beyond the lower left side of the painting—a technique employed by Caravaggio and adopted by his followers.

The tenor of this powerful tale of women's strength and bravery is matched by Artemisia Gentileschi's robust composition

and paint handling. The youthful Judith and Abra assuredly fill the space of the canvas. The depiction of Abra calls to mind a contemporary Roman model with a darker-hued complexion, incipient moustache, and unmanicured eyebrows, of the type closely associated with Caravaggesque naturalism. Judith's paler visage is idealized. The women's dress, actions, and positions within the picture underscore their inequality. Whereas Judith is resplendent in a gold silk gown, Abra is clad in humble fabrics; Judith wears elaborate shoes, while Abra is unshod; and Judith stands upright, her bloody sword unsheathed, while Abra kneels on the ground, her left hand streaked with blood as she steadies Holofernes's head. Judith's gaze is largely obscured by the shadow cast by her right hand, while Abra mirrors the viewer's intent curiosity.

Artemisia Gentileschi's virtuosic facility in painting white fabric reaches its pinnacle in this picture. One sees it in the bold, playful impasto of brushstrokes in Judith's sleeves and in the lace edge of Abra's chemise and the artful folds of her head scarf. The artist's skill is also evident in the lavish purple strokes of Abra's sleeves and the meticulous detail of Judith's diadem.[3] The same attention to crisp form and painstaking detail characterizes the still life sitting on the malachite green, velvet textile shot with gold filigree at bottom. This still life consists of an unadorned gauntlet for the right hand, a silver scabbard decorated with gold and an archer in relief, what Mary Garrard evocatively describes as "remnants of his [Holofernes's] former power."[4] Atop the table, there is also a plain, perfectly realized candle in a holder, burning with an incandescent flame.

Conservation analysis and treatment of the picture have uncovered several

noteworthy aspects.[5] The dark reddish-brown ground, for example, provides the base color of the shadows on Judith's face.[6] And the painting is confident—one does not see indecision in the handling of brushstrokes or a significant number of compositional changes (fig. 1). Most noteworthy are Judith's left ear and its pearl drop earring, which were originally farther to the viewer's left (fig. 2). The placement of Judith's and Abra's faces was also changed marginally—with Judith's entire face originally almost imperceptibly forward and Abra's showing minor changes in the positioning of her chin, lip, and nose.[7] Lastly, the artist did not economize in her use of paint, which in most areas is opaque and thick.[8] This is most in evidence where she has painted one element over another, rather than leaving it initially in reserve; the grip of Judith's hand on the sword and the sword itself were executed directly on top of the yellow dress, just as the still life was painted over the green tablecloth.[9]

As for the pigments used in this work, evidence has been found of cochineal—a red pigment derived from beetles in the Americas—in Abra's sleeves and the women's lips, and ultramarine blue—the costliest of blue pigments—in Abra's skirt.[10] The lead-tin antimonate yellow was in common use in the period in Rome and Venice, confirming the long-held belief that this picture was almost certainly executed in Rome in the 1620s.[11]

Despite the majesty, skill, and complexity of this picture—what R. Ward Bissell calls the "riveting force" of the composition—the patron or recipient remains unknown.[12] Even though Artemisia Gentileschi, like her father Orazio Gentileschi (1563–1639), often gifted her best pictures in an effort to gain privilege

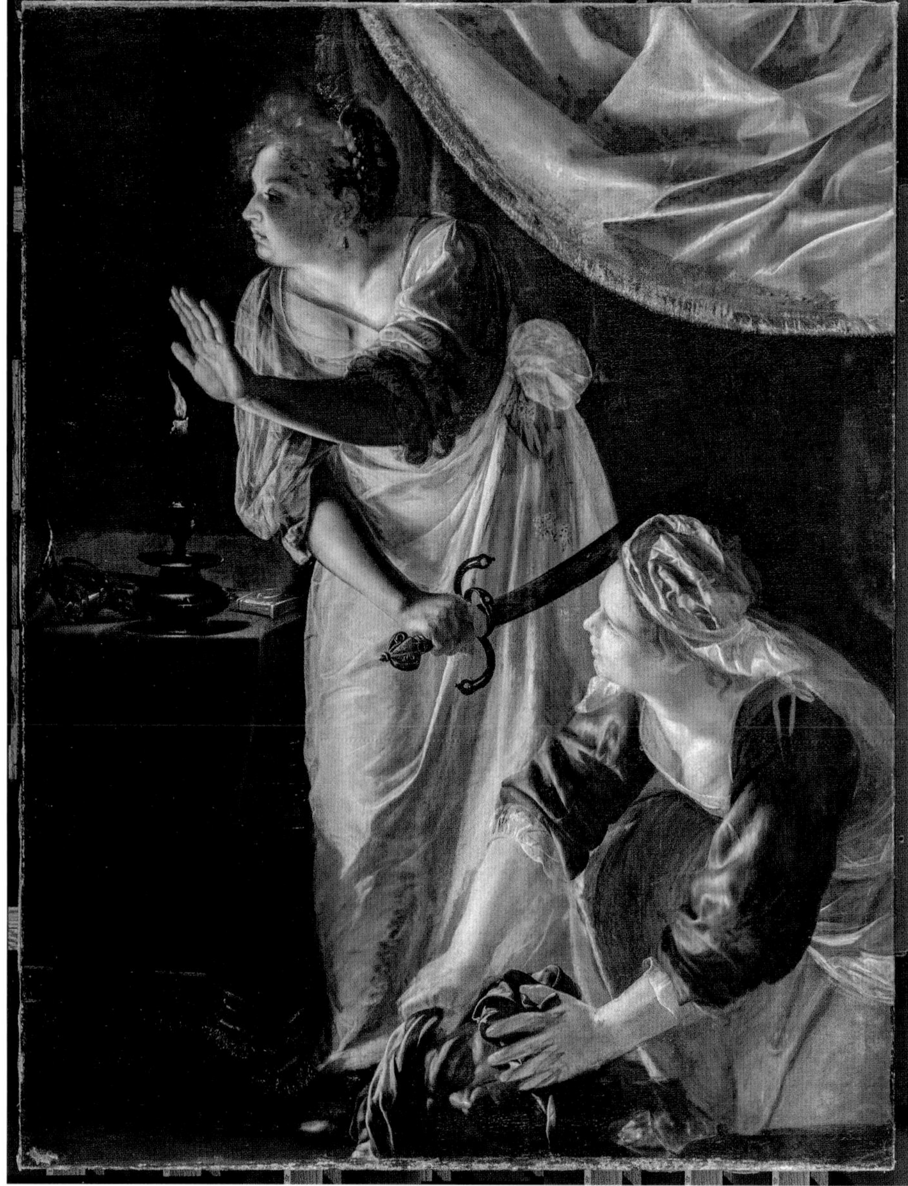

FIGURE 1 Infrared reflectogram (IRR), Artemisia Gentileschi, *Judith and Her Maidservant with the Head of Holofernes*. Detroit Institute of Arts

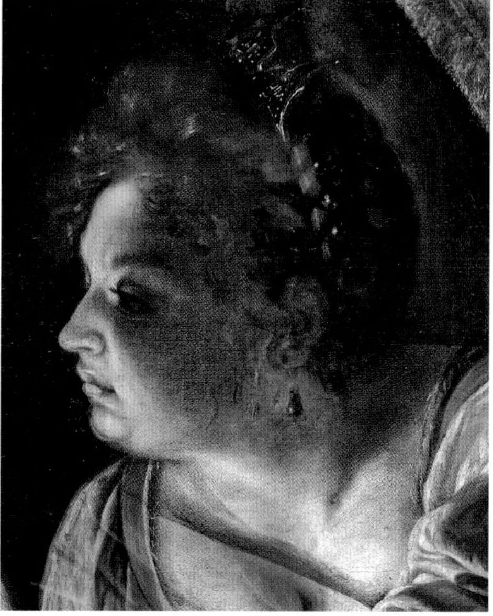

FIGURE 2 Detail of Judith's face, infrared reflectogram (IRR), Artemisia Gentileschi *Judith and Her Maidservant with the Head of Holofernes*. Detroit Institute of Arts

at court or in a particular household, our first recorded provenance for this painting comes from the mid-twentieth century.[13] An inferior version is housed in the Museo di Capodimonte, Naples (fig. 3). The DIA picture shows the biblical heroine Judith at the height of her personal power and Artemisia Gentileschi at the zenith of her painterly prowess.—ESP

NOTES

1. This work dates from Artemisia Gentileschi's second Roman period, after a prolonged stay in Florence. Among the most important sources on the picture are: Bissell 1999, 219–20, no. 14; Mann 2001b, 368–70, cat. 69; Bissell 2005, 84–87, cat. 28.

2. Mann 2001b, 368; Bissell 2005, 84. As Bissell notes, "Before returning to Utrecht in 1620, Gerrit van Honthorst had left in Italy a body of night pictures . . ."

3. Mary Garrard considers this to be a crown—a diadem is, in fact, a type of crown—which she notes is unusual iconography. She suggests it may reference Queen Marie de' Medici (1575–1642), "whose wary dodging of her political enemies assimilates her story to that of Judith, with whom she avowedly identified." She continues, "Judith alludes simultaneously to Marie de' Medici and Queen Artemisia of Caria, the artist's namesake, and is thus a homage to heroic queenship in both ancient and modern examples." Garrard 2020a, 43–44, 155–57.

4. Garrard 2020a, 155.

5. I am grateful to Blair Bailey, former Andrew W. Mellon Fellow in painting conservation at the Detroit Institute of Arts, for not only treating this picture to spectacular effect, but also for her thoughts on Artemisia Gentileschi's execution of it.

6. In the 2005 DIA catalogue the ground is described as "a dark brown." Bissell 2005, 85.

7. As recounted by Bailey, surprisingly, no significant *pentimenti* are seen in the figures' hands and feet. In all instances, they are assuredly placed—a rare feat for a seventeenth-century Italian painter. Bailey also noted Gentileschi's wonderful way of rendering knuckles, toes, and palms to make them appear three-dimensional.

8. Due to the thickness of the paint in certain areas, such as Judith's proper left sleeve, we see traction cracks that occurred when it was drying.

9. In addition to the thoughts shared in this paragraph, Bailey also suggested to me that Gentileschi was a "tidy painter." There is no paint spattered on the tacking margins and the work is painted on a good piece of well-made canvas, not inexpensive cloth. Though it is thick, the threads are still soft and supple.

10. Pigments: lead tin antimony yellow (XRF & SEM-EDX; yellow dress; light green tabletop), red insect dye, probably cochineal (field spec 4; Abra lips), lead white (XRF), iron based earth colors in reds and browns (XRF; FORS for Abra cheek), copper based green, probably malachite (XRF& SEM-EDX, microscopy; tablecloth), vermilion red (XRF; pink ribbon on Abra only vermilion no cochineal present, red curtain), ultramarine (blues and purples). From an email from Christina Bisulca, Andrew W. Mellon Scientist, Department of Conservation,

Detroit Institute of Arts, on March 23, 2020. For this information see the conservation file for this picture at the Detroit Institute of Arts.

11. As noted, "Scholars have been unanimous in assigning the Detroit picture to the 1620s, with Spear, Harris, Garrard, and Papi supporting my view." Bissell 1999, 219.

12. Bissell 2005, 86.

13. The picture was once in Naples, as a detail of a photograph taken before the relining of the canvas reads: "Napoli, Ufficio Esportazione, Ignoto secolo XVII, Giuditta e Oloferne (particolare)." For this inscription and the provenance of the picture, see Bissell 2005, 86–87. I went to Naples on March 17, 2019, to search the uncatalogued Brancaccio archival records surviving in the Biblioteca di San Lorenzo Maggiore. Special thanks are due to Carlo Caccavale and his team for accommodating my request. Unfortunately, no documents pertaining to the DIA's painting were found during this research trip.

PROVENANCE

1952, Prince Brancaccio (Rome, Italy); (Alessandro Morandotti, Rome, Italy) and (Adolph Loewi, New York, New York) co-owners; 1952, purchased by Leslie H. Green [d. 1973] (Bloomfield, Michigan); 1952–present, gift to the Detroit Institute of Arts (Detroit, Michigan).

SELECTED EXHIBITIONS

Detroit Institute of Arts, 1965; Cleveland Museum of Art, 1971–1972; Walters Art Gallery, Baltimore, 1972; Los Angeles County Museum of Art, 1976–1977; Metropolitan Museum of Art, New York, 2001–2002; National Gallery, London, 2020–2021.

SELECTED PUBLICATIONS

Richardson 1952–1953, 81–83, 82 illus.; Whitcomb et al. 1952–1953, 46, 52; Richardson 1953, 90–92, fig. 1; Grigaut 1960, 93 illus.; Detroit 1965, 29–30, cat. 8, 30 illus.; Richardson 1966, 98 illus.; Bissell 1967, 75; Moir 1967, vol. 1, 101, 126, 199 n. 19; vol. 2, 37, fig. 129; Bissell 1968, 157–58, fig. 9; Gregori 1968, vol. 1, 417; vol. 2, pl. CLXXXII.4; Davidson Reid 1969, 383 n. 46; Myers 1970, 194, pl. 77; Cleveland 1971, 96, cat. 28, 97 illus.; Baltimore 1972, cat. 7; Fredericksen and Zeri 1972, 80, 266, 580; Rome 1973, 224 under cat. 68; Tufts 1974b, 60, 66, fig. 29; Los Angeles 1976, 70, 122, cat. 13, 342, pl. 13; Alf 1977, 1 illus., 20; Greer 1979, 196, 197 illus.; Nicolson 1979, 51; *Selected Works from the Detroit Institute of Arts* 1979, 143, no. 116, illus.; Garrard 1980, 111; Gorsen 1980, 77–78, fig. 6; Bissell 1981, 63–64, fig. 171; Pointon 1981, 366; Broude and Garrard 1982, 158–59, fig. 17; Nagle 1982, 123–25, fig. 4-12; Christ 1983, 709; Naples 1984, vol. 1, 147; Grabski 1985, 38; Henshaw 1985, 15–16, fig. 8; Slap 1985, 342 n. 1; Gardner 1986, 729, fig. 19-29; Garrard 1989, 67–72, 200, 204, 295, 303–7, 313, 316, 328–36, figs. 53, 291, pl. 12–13; Lippincott 1990, 447; Nicolson and Vertova 1990, vol. 1, 111; vol. 2, fig. 225; Slatkin 1990, 52–53, fig. 13; Florence 1991, 52–53, 65, 96 under cat. 3, 141 under cat. 16, 162 under cat. 22, 175 under cat. 26, fig. 35; Spike 1991, 732; Perlingieri 1992, 187, 189, pl. 109; Garrard 1993, 34; Hartt 1993, 775, fig. 26-9; Bal 1995, 277–80, fig. 10; Cassani 1995, 95; Henshaw 1995, 184, illus.; Earls 1996, 159; Sutherland Harris 1996, 307–8, fig. 1; Topper and Gillis 1996, 11–12; Mann 1997, 178; Roberts 1998, vol. 1, 123, 453; Stocker 1998, 18; Benedetti 1999, 45–46 n. 8; Bissell 1999, 45–48, 52, 93, 123–24, 133, 179–80, 215, 219–20, no. 14, 221–22, 280, figs. 83–84, 93, pl. XIII; Lemay 1999, 92–95, 92 illus.; Vaizey 1999, 140; Adams 2000, 46–47, fig. 3.6; Papi 2000, 452; Spear 2000, 578 n. 6; Wilkin 2000, 47; Garrard 2001, 27, 33, 87, 112, 117, 132 n. 7, 143 n. 92, 157 n. 3; Mann 2001a, 249, 256; Mann 2001b, 368–70, cat. 69, 369 illus.; New York 2001–2002, 12, 97 under cat. 17, 334 illus., 336, 338, 341–42, 366 under cat. 68, 372 under cat. 70, 404 under cat. 76, 413 under cat. 79; Berti and Magherini 2002, 28; Bohlen 2002, B3 illus.; Even 2002, 38; Langdon 2002, 319; Loughery 2002, 296; Bartolena 2003, 211, 216; Christiansen 2004, 107–8, 120, fig. 15; Dewald 2004, 35; ffolliott 2004, 53, pl. 16; Uppenkamp 2004, 177–81, 238, no. 54, fig. 88, pl. VIII; Bissell 2005, 84–87, cat. 28, 85–86 illus.; Bissell, Derstine, and Miller 2005, 10; Ciletti 2005, 97–102; Garrard 2005, 100–102, 108, figs. 4–5; Getlein 2005, 410, no. 17.5; Mann 2005b, 3, 6, fig. 6; Mann 2005c, 55, 74 n. 6, fig. 7; Salomon 2005, 58–61, fig. 5; Sutherland Harris 2005a, 140–41, fig. 12; Sutherland Harris 2005b, 53–54, fig. 1.54; Phillippy 2006, 82–83, fig. 13; Mann 2009, 81; Philpot 2009, 211 n. 90; Pisa 2009, 204 illus., 206, 208; Sutherland Harris 2010, 7, pl. 5; Bissell 2011, 64–65, 69, fig. 10; Milan 2011, 40, 42–43, 45, 142 under cat. 7, 200 under cat. 29, 242 under cat. 47, 244 under cat. 48; Papi 2011, 846; Papi 2012, 831; Paris 2012, 150 under cat. 35, 181 under cat. 50, 182 under cat. 51; Chicago 2013, 36 n. 58; Zutter 2013, 136; Hottle 2014, 202; Llewellyn 2014, 3–4, fig. 1.1; Locker 2015, 4, 74, 77, 90, 94–96, fig. 3.7; Rome 2016, 34 illus., 35–36, fig. 1, 38–39, 44, 136, 186; Stokstad 2016, 379, fig. 14-13; Derstine 2017, 98; Garrard 2017, 22; Papi 2017, 148–49, fig. 4; Ghent 2018, 132, 152 under cat. 37, 154 under cat. 38; Papi, Bischoff, and Ford 2019, 542; Garrard 2020a, 43–44, 153–55, 156–57, 159, figs. 10, 42; London 2020, 106–7 illus., 124 under cat. 5, 173 under cat. 21, 178–81, cat. 23, 179 illus., 182 under cat. 24, 186.

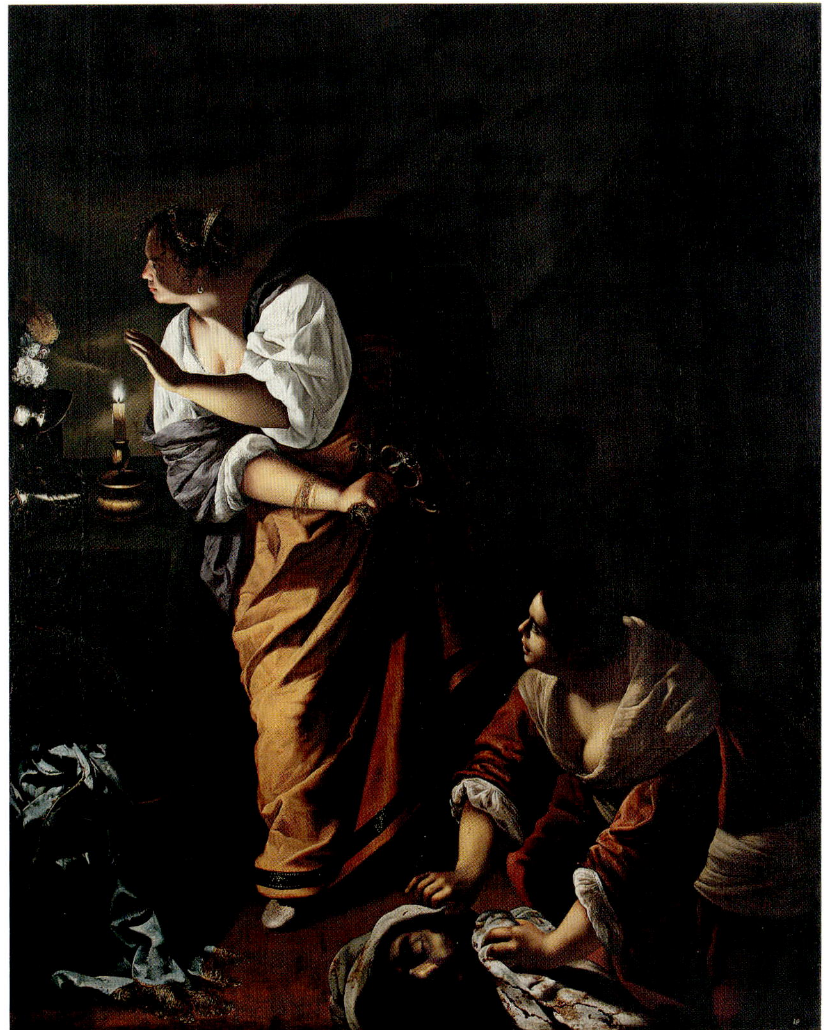

FIGURE 3 Copy after Artemisia Gentileschi, *Judith and her Maidservant*, ca. 1645–1650, oil on canvas, 107⅛ × 87 in. (272 × 221 cm). Museo Nazionale di Capodimonte, Naples, inv. Q377

28

Mary Magdalene in Ecstasy

ca. 1620–1625

Oil on canvas, 31⅞ × 41⁵⁄₁₆ in. (81 × 105 cm)

Venice, Fondazione Musei Civici, Palazzo Ducale, on long-term loan from a private collection

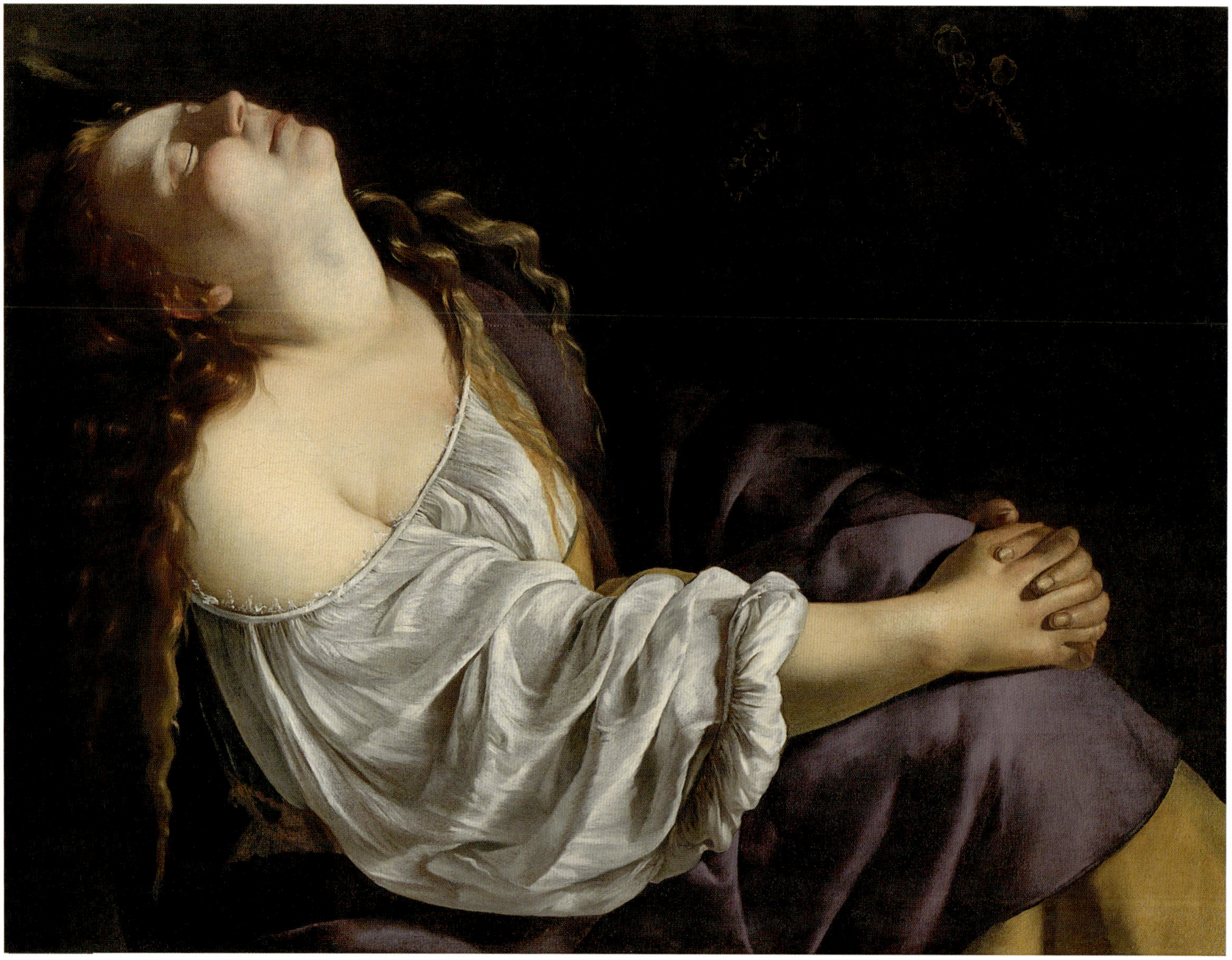

ARTEMISIA GENTILESCHI'S remarkable talent lies in her ability to infuse her subjects with drama and passion. She often shows us famous women imbued with great emotional depth, psychological nuance, and physical force. She also brings a sense of originality to her storytelling, casting a fresh light on well-known subjects, such as the reformed sinner Mary Magdalene.

Unlike generations of artists before her, Artemisia Gentileschi does not show the Magdalene repentant or suffering in a landscape setting. Nor does she include any of her customary attributes, such as a crucifix, ointment jar, and skull.[1] For other artists, the moment of the Magdalene's conversion was usually illustrated by dramatic lighting in the sky and was reinforced by her vivid pose and facial expression (see Orsola Maddalena Caccia, cat. 34). Here the conversion is represented as an internalized process, with the heroine sitting alone in a dark space lit by strong light, her head thrown back in rapture and her hands clasped around her knees. Her expression, with eyes and mouth closed, is serene, even blissful, as if she is completely at peace after surrendering to her spiritual calling.

The figure of the Magdalene is life size and fills almost the entire horizontal picture. This proximity helps the viewer to identify with her. She is not an idealized young saint, but rather an individualized, plebeian woman with curly brown hair, puffy features, and a distinctive nose. These traits find their origin in Gentileschi's own likeness.[2] While not a self-portrait in the strict sense, this depiction is another example of her practice of including her own features in portraits of heroines. Also typical for Gentileschi is the erotic character of the Magdalene, with her flowing hair and bare right shoulder. Her left breast was originally more prominent, but Gentileschi ultimately covered it with the purple blanket and lock of hair.[3] Nevertheless, the elegant neckline of the chemise and its delicate lace trim reveal an effort to convey the Magdalene's not so subtle erotic charms.

Artemisia Gentileschi painted the Magdalene numerous times over the course of her career, but none of these versions expresses the saint's newfound peace as succinctly as this one.[4] Gianni Papi has noted that Gentileschi may have been inspired by an ancient Roman statue of the sleeping Ariadne that shows a similarly recumbent heroine with her head tipped back.[5] Caravaggio (1571–1610) may have provided another inspiration, as his *Mary Magdalene in Ecstasy* from 1606 (now probably lost, but known through copies) shows the saint in a dark space with clasped hands and a tilted head (fig. 1).[6]

This Mary Magdalene was only rediscovered in 2014, and while scholars unanimously agree it is authentic, there is less certainty about its date. Judith Mann initially placed it around 1613, the moment before Gentileschi left Rome for Florence.[7] Now she sees it as a mature work, either from Gentileschi's sojourn in Rome from

1620 to 1625 or from her first stay in Naples from 1630 to 1635.[8] Papi and Letizia Treves both date it to her Roman period. With its preference for saturated colors such as plum and ochre, as well as the fluidity of the handling of the flesh colors and the white and grays in the chemise, this painting can indeed be best compared with works from Gentileschi's Roman period,[9] such as *Judith and Her Maidservant with the Head of Holofernes* in Detroit (cat. 27).—OT

NOTES

1. An overview of the various traditions of depicting Mary Magdalene is provided in Florence 1986.

2. Treves points out the technical difficulties of portraying oneself from this angle. Treves 2020e, 182.

3. See the results of the technical investigation in Currie et al. 2017, 226–28.

4. Gentileschi painted at least three more versions of Mary Magdalene: *Conversion of the Magdalene (Penitent Magdalene)*, ca. 1617–1620, oil on canvas, 57 11/16 × 42 1/2 in. (146.5 × 108 cm), Palazzo Pitti, Florence; *Penitent Magdalene*, oil on canvas, 25 9/16 × 20 in. (65 × 50.8 cm), ex-Marc A. Seidner collection, Los Angeles; *Penitent Magdalene*, 1625/26, oil on canvas, 48 × 37 13/16 in. (122 × 96 cm), Seville Cathedral. For later versions see Lattuada 2017, 201–5.

5. Roman, 2nd century, *Sleeping Ariadne*, marble, Gallerie degli Uffizi, Florence. See Papi 2017, 149.

6. Papi 2017, 149; Mann 2017, 182. According to Mary Garrard, Caravaggio's *Penitent Magdalene*, Rome, Galleria Doria Pamphili, influenced this painting as much as his *Mary Magdalene in Ecstasy*. Garrard 2017, 16–17.

7. Mann 2017, 180. See also *Tableaux et dessins anciens* 2014, lot 24.

8. Mann 2019, 155.

9. Papi 2017, 148; Treves 2020e, 182.

PROVENANCE

Private collection (Southern France); June 26, 2014–present, sold at (Sotheby's, Paris, France), lot 24, as by Artemisia Gentileschi, to a private collection (Europe).

SELECTED EXHIBITIONS

Kunsthistorisches Museum, Vienna 2019–2020; National Gallery, London, 2020–2021.

SELECTED PUBLICATIONS

Currie et al. 2017, 217–35; Garrard 2017, 11–40; Mann 2017, 167–86; Papi 2017, 147–66; Garrard 2020a, 122–26; Treves 2020e, 182–83.

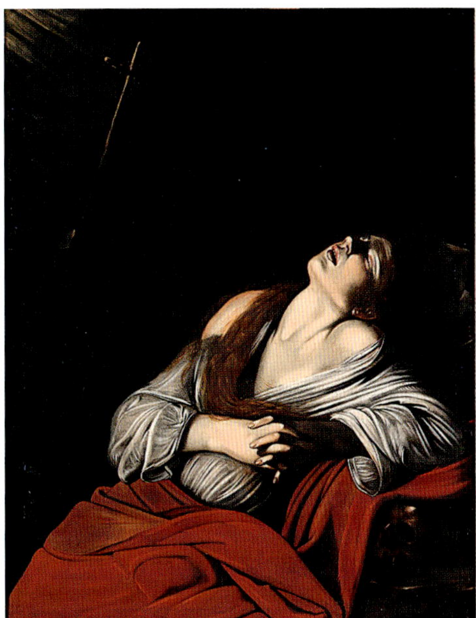

FIGURE 1 Louis Finson (Flemish, 1580/85–1617) after Michelangelo Merisi da Caravaggio (1571–1610), *Mary Magdalene in Ecstasy*, 1612, oil on canvas, 47 1/4 × 39 3/8 in. (120 × 100 cm). Musée des Beaux-Arts, Marseille

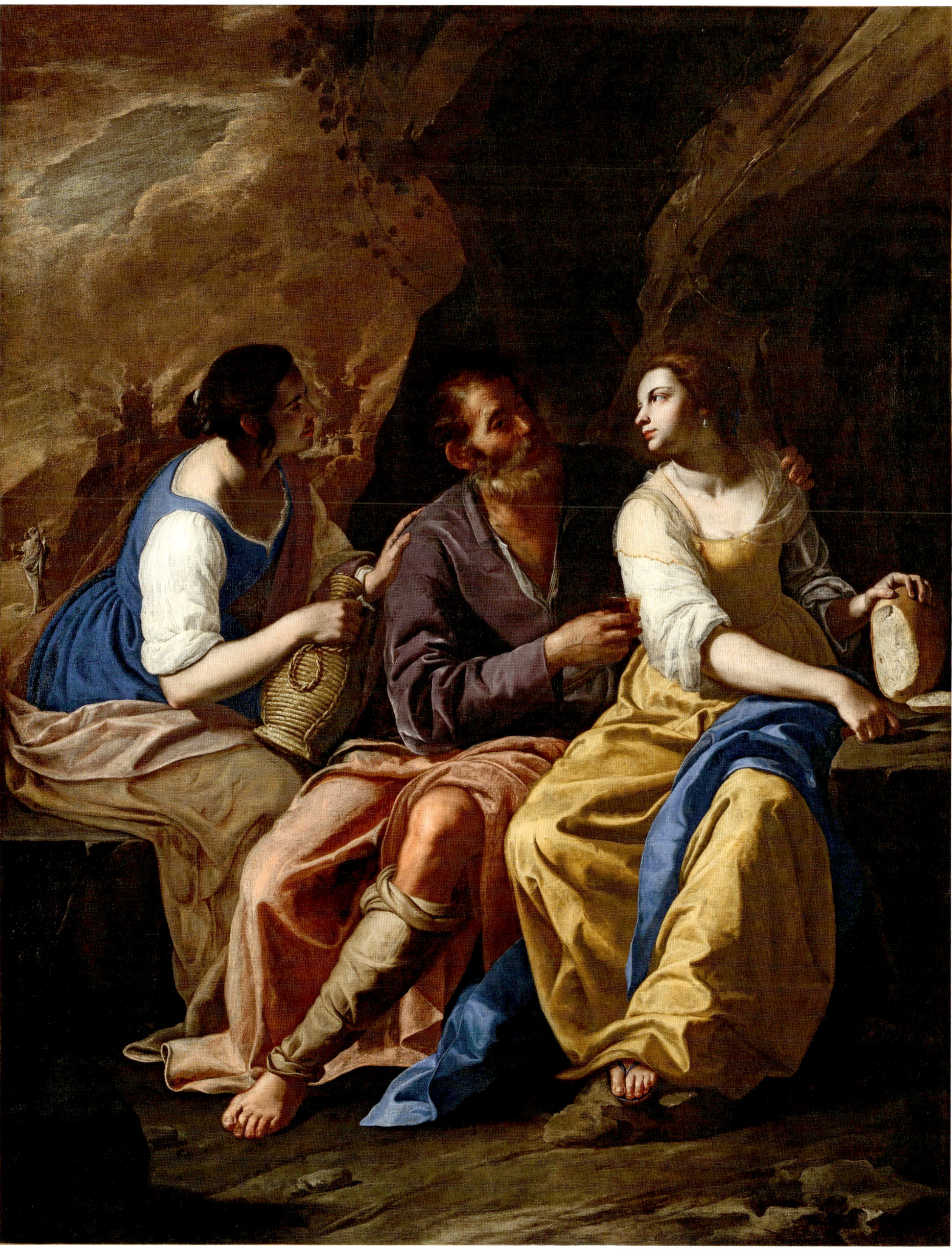

Lot and His Daughters

1636–1638
Oil on canvas, 90¾ × 72 in. (230.5 × 182.9 cm)
The Toledo Museum of Art, Clarence Brown Fund, 1983.107

WITH ITS GRAND FORMAT, multiple life-size figures, and biblical story, *Lot and His Daughters* is precisely the kind of painting that was most hailed by Artemisia Gentileschi's contemporaries. Gentileschi created many such paintings as she strove to be ranked among the most important artists in Europe. The story of Lot and his Daughters was a popular subject during the Counter-Reformation. As narrated in Genesis (19:15–38), God destroyed the cities of Sodom and Gomorrah for their sins, but spared Lot and his family. During their flight from Sodom, Lot's wife, disobeying God's command, looked back at the city and was transformed into a pillar of salt. Isolated and believing themselves to be the only survivors, Lot's daughters inebriated their father and became impregnated by him. Each gave birth to a son and the family line continued.

Artemisia Gentileschi depicts the moment when Lot and his daughters are resting in the safety of a cave. Lot's petrified wife can be seen to the left, with Sodom in the background. Having emptied a glass of wine, Lot turns towards one of his daughters with freshly awakened desire. Unlike other artists, Gentileschi refrains from mocking Lot's drunken state, and she does not depict his daughters in an overtly erotic manner. It is as if the group is a classical frieze; each family member is rendered with dignity and empathy. The daughters are emphasized by the strong lighting as well as their blue garments. Gentileschi effectively conveys the story by synchronizing the figures' movements, gently alluding to the incest by showing Lot's naked knee. The daughter to the left places her hand on her father's shoulder, while he takes his other daughter's arm; she pauses in her task and looks directly into his

eyes, accepting his lusty gesture. By rhyming the father's and daughters' arms and legs, Gentileschi found a simple formal solution to express their sexual union. Such subtle details showcase her remarkable talents as a storyteller.[1] With subdued yet festive colors, measured gestures, and a harmonious composition, Gentileschi used an artistic formula that had been popularized by Bolognese painters such as Guido Reni (1575–1642) and Domenichino (1581–1641).

There is now a consensus that this painting can be firmly rooted in Artemisia Gentileschi's stay in Naples. She had a significant impact on the city, where she lived for more than two decades, often collaborating with local artists and being in high demand among local collectors. R. Ward Bissell suggests this painting may be identical with one mentioned in 1742 by the biographer Bernardo De Dominici (1683–ca. 1759) together with other works by Gentileschi in the collection of Luigi Romeo (dates unknown), baron of San Luigi, Naples.[2] Some scholars have voiced reservations about this hypothesis.[3] Most, however, agree that Gentileschi was not the only artist involved with the painting. Bissell ascribes the sky and landscape to Domenico Gargiulo, called Micco Spadaro (1609/10–1675).[4] Nicola Spinosa sees Bernardo Cavallino's (1616–1656) hand in Lot's upper body, the daughter to his left, and the cave.[5] Letizia Treves, however, rightly gives all figures entirely to Gentileschi.[6]—OT

NOTES

1. Another aspect that unites the figures is the color scheme, which alternates earthy tones with blues and white. See Locker 2015, 114–16.

2. Bissell 1999, 268. De Dominici describes the paintings by Gentileschi in Romeo's Neapolitan collection. After enumerating a *Susannah* and

a *Bathsheba* (compare cat. 30, Columbus), he describes the following two paintings: "Di questa virtuosa donna è eziando un S. Michele Arcangelo, che discaccia Lucifero dal Paradiso, ed un Loth con le figliuole, e tutti alla grandezza del naturale." See "Life of Domenico Gargiulo (Micco Spadaro)" in De Dominici 1979, vol. 3, 199; for a critical reading of De Dominici's report, see Treves 2020f, 212–13.

3. Bissell 1999, 268.

4. Bissell 1999, 267–68.

5. Spinosa 2016, 266.

6. Treves 2020f, 212–13.

PROVENANCE

Luigi Romeo, Baron of San Luigi (Naples, Italy) (?); 1982, private collection (Switzerland); 1982–1983, with (Art Advice Enterprises, Inc., New York, New York); 1983–present, purchased by the Toledo Museum of Art (Toledo, Ohio) as by Bernardo Cavallino.

SELECTED EXHIBITIONS

Cleveland Museum of Art, 1984–1985; Metropolitan Museum of Art, New York, 2001–2002; Museo di Roma, Palazzo Braschi, Rome, 2016–2017; National Gallery, London, 2020–2021.

SELECTED PUBLICATIONS

De Dominici 1979, vol. 3, 199; Cleveland 1984, 107–9, cat. 29, 108 illus.; Grabski 1985, 23–40, figs. 1, 16, 17, 22; Garrard 1989, 123–27, fig. 116, pl. 24; Florence 1991, 79, 163 under cat. 23, 189, 195, fig. 65; Bissell 1999, 82–86, 267–69, no. 39, 276, 288, 335, figs. 163–66, pl. XX; Mann 2001a, 256; New York 2001–2002, 385, 389, 404 under cat. 76, 408–10, cat. 78, 409 illus., 426 under cat. 83, 427 under cat. 84; Lattuada and Nappi 2005, 87–88, fig. 16; Mann 2005b, 10, 12, fig. 15; Mann 2005c, 70–71, fig. 22; Reich and Rumsey 2009, 161, illus.; Milan 2011, 252 under cat. 52; Paris 2012, 188 under cat. 54; Rome 2016, 61; Spinosa 2016, 266, cat. 88, 267 illus.; Garrard 2017, 28; London 2020, 100; Treves 2020f, 212–13, cat. 32, 213 illus.; Treves 2020g, 216.

David and Bathsheba

ca. 1636–1637
Oil on canvas, 104½ × 82½ in. (265.43 × 209.55 cm)
Columbus Museum of Art, Schumacher Fund, 1967.006
Hartford only

THERE WAS A BURGEONING MARKET for pictures with nudes during the Counter-Reformation, and posessing a female nude painted by a woman must have had a particular *frisson* for patrons—who were almost exclusively male. Yet few women artists ventured into this area. By depicting heroines like Susanna, Lucretia, and Bathsheba as nudes, Artemisia Gentileschi successfully captured this niche market and made the subject one of her trademarks. Here she presents a moment from the biblical story of Bathsheba, the wife of Uriah, as told in the Book of Samuel (2 Samuel: 11–12). In the foreground Bathsheba is finishing her bath near the royal palace, observed by King David from a balcony. Distracted by her jewels, she is unaware of a messenger bearing a letter summoning her to join the enamored king. After Bathsheba complies and becomes pregnant, David sends Uriah to perish in battle. The couple then marries, but God punishes their adultery and their first child dies.

This grand painting of David and Bathsheba is one of Artemisia Gentileschi's most successful compositions, and at least six other versions are known.[1] Unique among the versions, here the life-size Bathsheba is rendered as a passive heroine, absorbed in her great beauty.[2] Oriented towards the viewer, she is presented as an object of desire with a radiant body, pearl white skin, and long wavy hair. Holding the back of her chair, she covers her breasts with her arm, a pose that references the ancient *Crouching Venus* sculpture (fig. 1). While Venus turns her head in a moment of surprise, Bathsheba stares at a pearl necklace and other jewels handed to her on a plate by the maid. In Gentileschi's painting, Venus

becomes the template for Bathsheba's beauty and obsession with mundane luxury goods.[3] Gentileschi has cleverly expanded the biblical story, devising a stage-like setting in which Bathsheba's realm is separated from David's by a balustrade, the messenger bridging their spheres. The letter she extends towards Bathsheba, not mentioned in the biblical text and not included in the other versions, may foreshadow David's letter

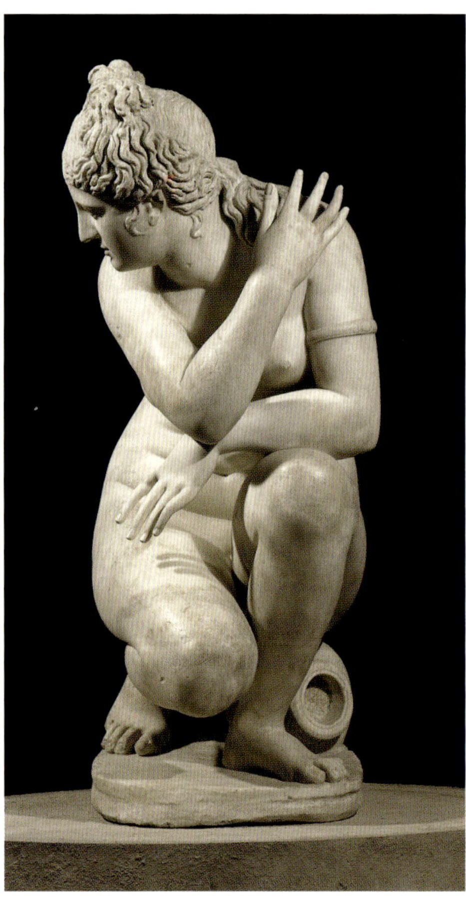

FIGURE 1 *Crouching Venus*, Roman version of a Hellenistic sculpture, 2nd century, marble, height: 49³⁄₁₆ in. (125 cm). The Royal Collection, HM Queen Elizabeth II, United Kingdom

ordering Uriah to his death. Bathsheba, however, blind to the consequence of the moment, focuses on the plate of jewels, also unmentioned in the bible.[4] Here Gentileschi sends a stark warning to viewers to avoid worldly vanity.

One reason for Artemisia Gentileschi's spirited interpretation may lie in the original pairing of this picture. Bernardo De Dominici (1683–ca. 1759) saw *David and Bathsheba* in Naples in 1742 together with a lost painting of the apocryphal biblical heroine Susanna. He described them as "two large paintings with life size figures" by the "famous" Artemisia Gentileschi in the collection of Luigi Romeo (dates unknown), baron of San Luigi, in Naples.[5] While we cannot be certain of the original owner, we know from other commissions that Susanna and Bathsheba were often displayed together.[6] Both stories provide a pretext to depict female nudes, but while Susanna resisted male advances, Bathsheba yielded to them, and the paintings may thus have been originally conceived as complements.

Scholars agree that *David and Bathsheba* was painted by Artemisia Gentileschi in Naples with some additional help. Artistic collaborations were common in Naples in the mid-seventeenth century. De Dominici mentioned two Neapolitan painters for this painting, Viviano Codazzi (1604–1672), who painted the architecture, and Domenico Gargiulo, called Micco Spadaro (1609/10–1675), who painted the trees and minor architectural elements.[7] Most scholars accept this account. There is less consensus on the date, although Judith Mann, Letizia Treves, and others rightly place it in the late 1630s.[8]—OT

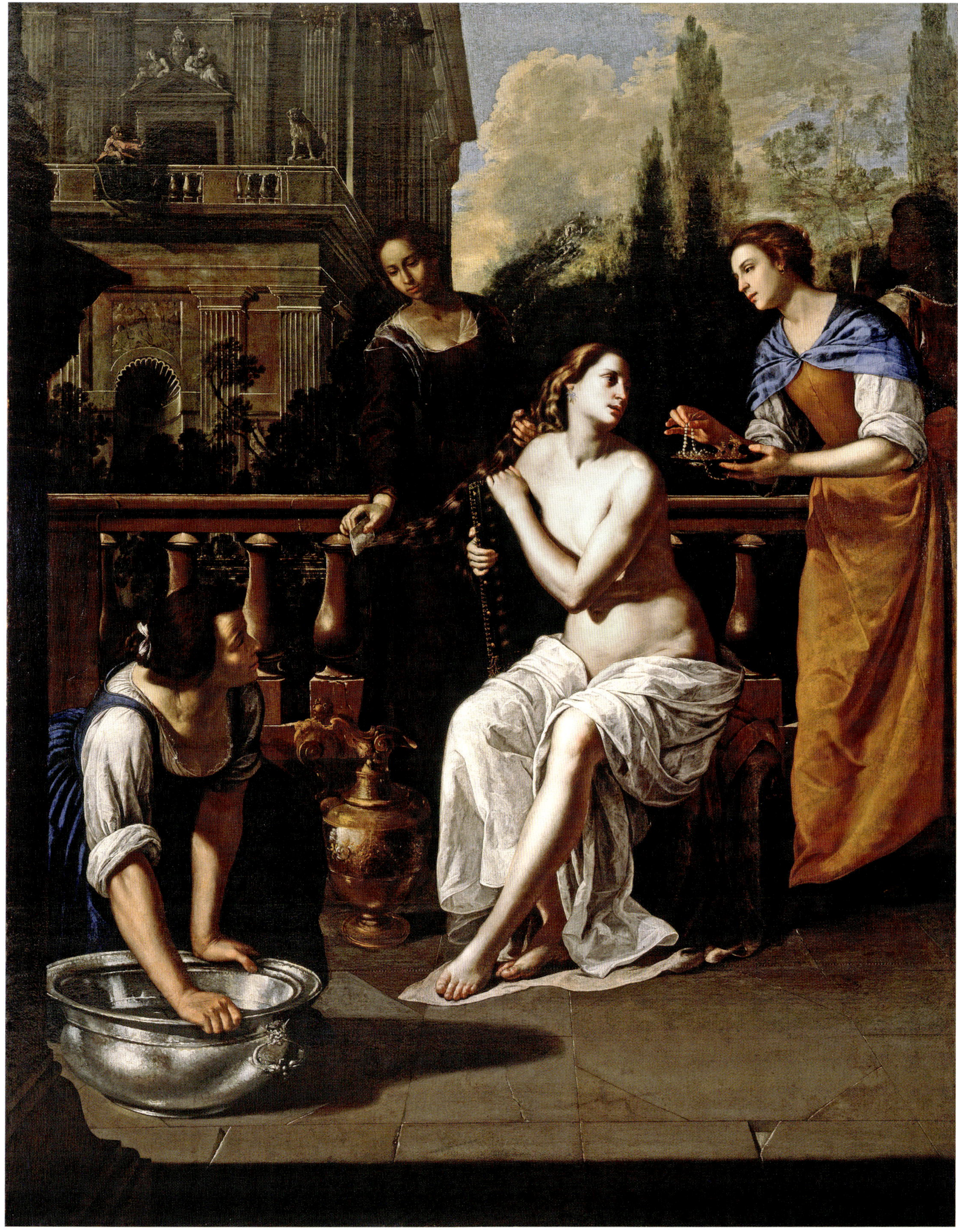

NOTES

1. Artemisia Gentileschi, *Bathsheba*, ex-Museum der Bildenden Künste, Leipzig; *Bathsheba*, ex-Castello di Coversano, Bari; *Bathsheba*, Neues Palais Potsdam; *Bathsheba*, Gallerie degli Uffizi, Florence; *Bathsheba*, Haas collection, Vienna; *Bathsheba*, ex-Gosford House, Scotland, destroyed.

2. Unlike other versions, Bathsheba is not holding anything, such as a mirror. Elisabeth Oy-Marra has rightfully noted Bathsheba's unusual passiveness in comparison with Gentileschi's other known versions of the subject. Oy-Marra 2016, 336.

3. By contrast, in an earlier depiction of Susanna, Gentileschi used Venus's pose to convey the heroine's modesty: Artemisia Gentileschi, *Susannah and the Elders*, 1622, oil on canvas, 63⁹⁄₁₆ × 48⁷⁄₁₆ in. (161.5 × 123 cm), Burghley House Collection, UK. On this painting see Treves 2020d, 174–77.

4. Judith Mann and Letizia Treves, however, stress Bathsheba's contemplative state of mind. See Mann 2001c, 416; Treves 2020g, 214–16. It should be noted that Bathsheba's eyes are directed to the plate with jewels.

5. "Due quadri grandi con figure al naturale, che esprimono le storie di Bersabea, e Susanna, che sembran di mano di Guido son dipinti dalla famosa Artemisia Gentileschi, (. . .)." "Life of Domenico Gargiulo (Micco Spadaro)," in De Dominici 1979, vol. 3, 199 (translation mine).

6. Bissell argues it was commissioned by the Romeo family, as he sees the family's coat of arms on the crest, close to King David. Bissell 1999, 264. For the pairing of Bathsheba with other heroines, see Treves 2020g, 214–16.

7. De Dominici 1979, vol. 3, 199.

8. Most recently Riccardo Lattuada argued for a date in the mid-1640s. See Lattuada 2017, 187. For a discussion of the date, see Treves 2020g, 214–16.

PROVENANCE

By 1742, Luigi Romeo, Baron of San Luigi (Naples, Italy); with (Antiquario Tarchini, Rome, Italy); around 1960, purchased by Carlo Sestieri (Rome, Italy); June 1962, with (P. and D. Colnaghi, London, UK); February 1967–present, purchased by the Columbus Museum of Art (Columbus, Ohio).

SELECTED EXHIBITIONS

Los Angeles County Museum of Art, 1976–1977; Metropolitan Museum of Art, New York, 2001–2002; Museum Wiesbaden, 2016–2017; National Gallery, London, 2020–2021.

SELECTED PUBLICATIONS

Bissell 1968, 161, 163, fig. 21; Los Angeles 1976, 123, cat. 15, 124 illus.; De Dominici 1979, vol. 3, 199; Greer 1979, 205–6, 205 illus.; Grabski 1985, 26, 37–38, 46, 59, fig. 3; Garrard 1989, 104, 121–24, 128–29, 134, fig. 115, pl. 23; Florence 1991, 69, 71, 79, 163 under cat. 23, 178–79 under cat. 27, 195, fig. 56; Bissell 1999, 82–86, 92, 248, 263–66, no. 37, 267–68, 270, 285, 288, 335, figs. 132, 157, 159, pl. XXIII; Garrard 2001, 117–18, 152 n. 67, 157 n. 5; Mann 2001a, 256, 259; Mann 2001c, 414–17, cat. 80, 415 illus.; New York 2001–2002, 384–85, 387, 404 under cat. 76, 408 under cat. 78, 414 under cat. 79, 422 under cat. 82, 426 under cat. 83, 427 under cat. 84; Garrard 2005, 109–11, fig. 19; Lattuada and Nappi 2005, 87, 89, fig. 17; Mann 2005b, 11–12, 14, fig. 17; Marshall 2005, 41–42, fig. 35; Mann 2009, 99–100, fig. 17; Milan 2011, 218 under cat. 37, 228 under cat. 41, 234 under cat. 43, 236 under cat. 44, 240 under cat. 46, 252 under cat. 52; Paris 2012, 176 under cat. 48, 185 under cat. 52, 188 under cat. 54; Rome 2016, 61–62, fig. 6; Wiesbaden 2016, 336–37, cat. 79; Garrard 2017, 24; London 2020, 100, 222 under cat. 36; Treves 2020f, 212; Treves 2020g, 214–16, cat. 33, 215 illus.

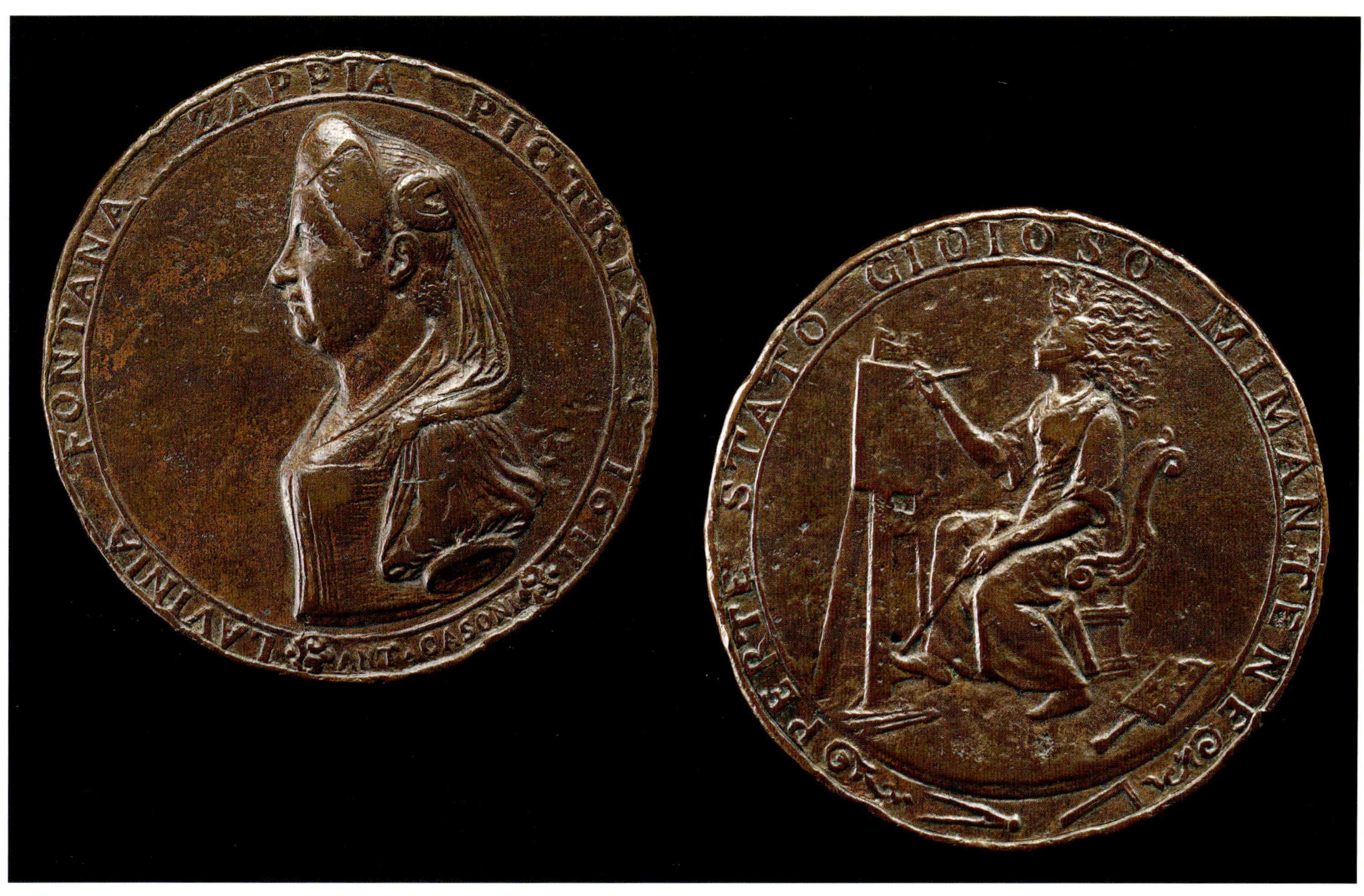

31

Portrait Medal of Lavinia Fontana

Felice Antonio Casoni (Ancona, 1559–Rome, 1634)
1611
Bronze, diameter: 2⁹⁄₁₆ in. (6.55 cm)
Inscribed (on obverse, around border): LAVINIA FONTANA ZAPPIA PICTRIX 1611 [Lavinia Fontana Zappi Painter 1611];
and: ANT. CASONI [Antonio Casoni]; (on reverse): PER TE STATO GIOIOSO MI MANTENE [Because of you (painting) I am
in a constant state of joy, or Through you, joyous state, I am maintained]
National Gallery of Art, Washington, D.C., Samuel H. Kress Collection, 1957.14.1071

32

Portrait Medal of Artemisia Gentileschi

Unknown artist active in Rome in the 1620s
Mid-1620s
Bronze with traces of gilding, diameter: 2⅛ in. (5.35 cm)
Inscribed: ARTHEMISIA GENTILESCA PICTRIX CELEBRIS [Artemisia Gentileschi, the celebrated painter]
The Stephen K. and Janie Woo Scher Collection, New York

DURING THE SECOND HALF of the sixteenth century the first portrait medals
commemorating female artists appeared in
Italy. The genre had existed for more than
a century for male artists, dating back to
Leon Battista Alberti (1404–1472) and his
self-portrait medal of around 1435 (National
Gallery of Art, Washington, D.C.). Sofonisba
Anguissola (ca. 1535–1625) was the first
woman to be recognized for her artistic
achievements in medal form.[1] Manufactured
at the height of her career around 1559, the
medal was followed by one honoring the
engraver Diana Scultori (ca. 1547–1612) from
the 1570s and the two that are the focus here:
one celebrating Lavinia Fontana (1552–1614)
and the other Artemisia Gentileschi.[2]

In the medal of Lavinia Fontana, the
painter is depicted in profile in the dress
of a noblewoman. An inscription running
around the portrait identifies Fontana; her
profession as painter; the year the medal
was made, 1611; and the medalist, Felice
Antonio Casoni. The reverse bears an allegorical representation of Painting (Pittura)
working at an easel in a long dress, with
wild hair, her mouth covered and a mahlstick at her feet. The iconography follows
the description of Pittura in Cesare Ripa's
(1555–1622) *Iconologia*, first published in
1593.[3] Ripa explains that good painters are
always in a state of frenzied thought—hence
the disheveled hair—and that the band over
the mouth signifies that painting is a silent
art, unlike poetry. An inscription around
the allegory also references the intellectual
rewards of being a painter: "PER TE STATO
GIOIOSO MI MANTENE" ("Because of you
[painting] I am in a constant state of joy"
or "Through you, joyous state, I am maintained").[4] Whatever the precise translation, Casoni expresses here how Fontana's
achievements as an artist are tied to the
vitality of her imagination.

The medal of Artemisia Gentileschi
is one sided. Her portrait appears on the
obverse with the inscription "ARTHEMISIA
GENTILESCA PICTRIX CELEBRIS"
("Artemisia Gentileschi, the celebrated
painter"). Although the medal lacks an

explicit allegorical reference on its reverse,
one may be imbedded in the portrait, as
Gentileschi's hair is far from being perfectly
kempt, especially at the peak of her forehead, where several locks spring errantly
forward. This is also how her hair appears
in a work that is widely agreed to be a
self-portrait in the guise of Pittura (Royal
Collection Trust, London).[5] The painting's iconography follows Ripa's description closely, which strongly suggests the
loose hair falling to the side of her face was
meant to serve as an attribute of Pittura. It
bears noting, however, that this was apparently Gentileschi's natural hairstyle. In a
print by Jérôme David (ca. 1605–ca. 1670)
from around 1627 after a lost self-portrait
by Gentileschi (fig. 1), one of her most distinctive features is her wiry hair, almost a
tamped-down version of the electrified hair
seen on the reverse of Fontana's medal.[6]
Gentileschi must have been conscious that
she was in many ways the perfect emblem of
Pittura—successful, talented, and able to the

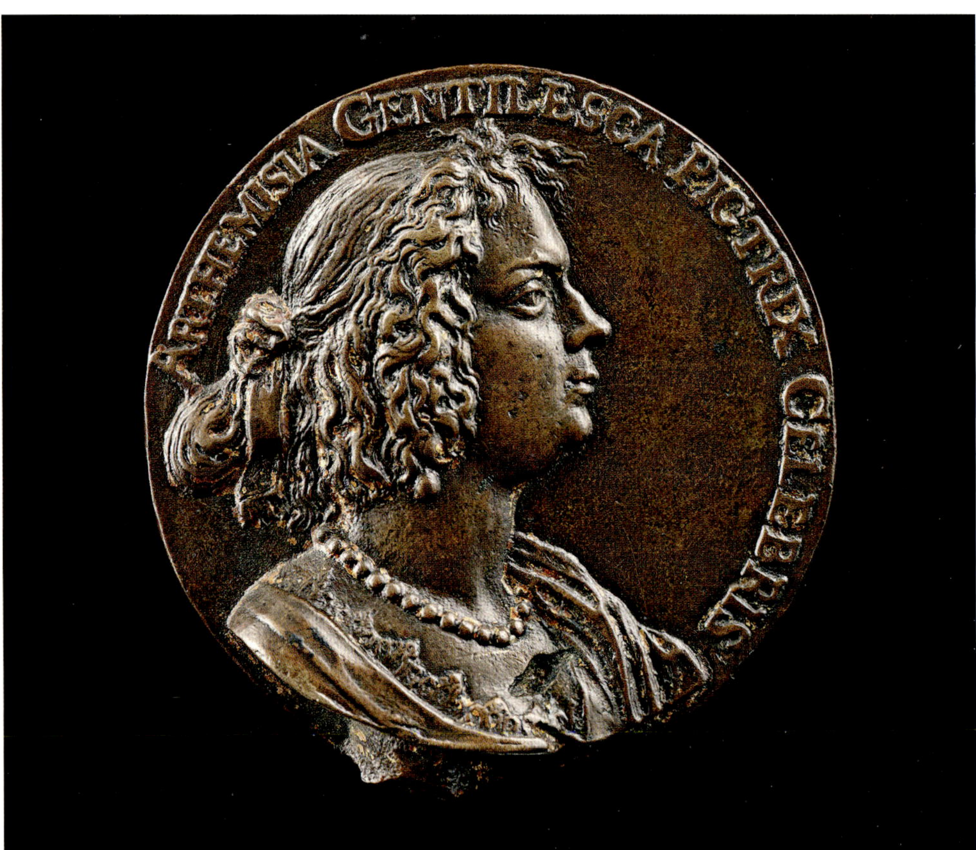

32 Obverse

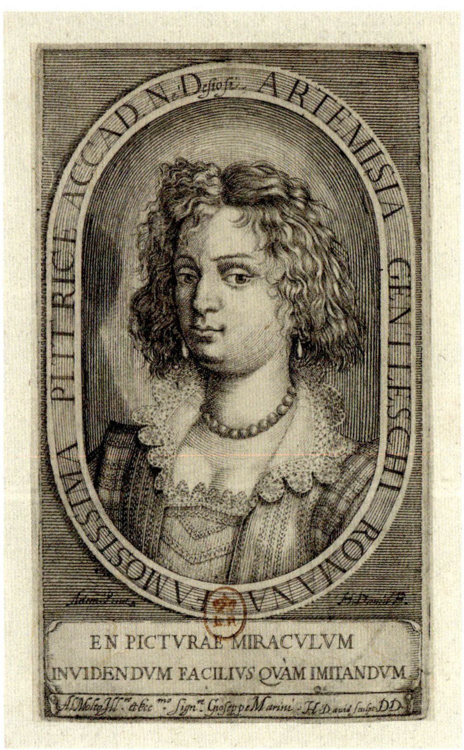

FIGURE 1 Jérôme David, *Artemisia Gentileschi*,
ca. 1627, engraving. Bibliothèque Nationale de
France, Paris

look the part. Her medalist seems to have recognized that her hair was an important element of her identity.

Based on the similarities with David's print, the Gentileschi medal probably dates to the mid-1620s, when the painter was working in Rome. Like the Fontana medal, which was also made in Rome, it is extremely rare, with only two known examples. There are three examples of Fontana's medal. The audience for these medals must have been limited. Who commissioned them and why? Both artists had reasons for wanting to promote their fame, and the medals may have functioned as deluxe calling cards. It is also possible that admiring patrons took the initiative and had the medals made to share with friends. Curiously, no medals celebrating famous male artists were produced in Rome during these decades—not for Annibale Carracci (1560–1609), Caravaggio (1571–1610), the Cavaliere d'Arpino (1568–1640), Guido Reni (1575–1642), or any others. The medals may represent acts of self-promotion, recognition on the part of these women artists that in order for them to be as famous as their male colleagues, they had to be more proactive in shaping their professional image. If so, linking themselves to Pittura through the venerable medium of the portrait medal was a highly savvy maneuver.—CDD

NOTES

1. For the medal of Sofonisba, see Lozano 2019b.

2. For the medal of Diana Scultori, see Attwood 2003, 401.

3. Ripa 2012, 478–80.

4. For some of the ways the inscription has been translated, see De Girolami Cheney 2020, 56; Marro 1998, 114; and Graziani 2019, 132, who also discusses the inscription's source in a poem by Petrarch (1304–1374).

5. For the painting see Mann 2001d.

6. For the print see Mann 2001a, 250, fig. 95.

Portrait Medal of Lavinia Fontana

PROVENANCE

Gustave Dreyfus [1837–1914] (Paris, France); his heirs; July 9, 1930, purchased with the entire Dreyfus collection by (Duveen Brothers, Inc., London, UK, New York, New York, and Paris, France); January 31, 1944, sold to the Samuel H. Kress Foundation (New York, New York); 1957–present, gift to the National Gallery of Art (Washington, D.C.).

SELECTED EXHIBITIONS

National Museum of Women in the Arts, Washington, D.C., 1998; Hood Museum of Art, Dartmouth College, Hanover, 2000; Museo Nacional del Prado, Madrid, 2019–2020.

SELECTED PUBLICATIONS

Pollard 1967, 91, no. 477; Owens Schaefer 1984, 232–34; Fortunati 1998, 30; Marro 1998, 114, cat. 33, 115 illus.; Washington, D.C. 1998, 35–36; Lacas 2015, 71, 73, fig. 17; Cole 2019a, 48; Graziani 2019, 132, cat. 21, 133 illus.; Lozano 2019b, 130; Madrid 2019, 33–34.

Portrait Medal of Artemisia Gentileschi

PROVENANCE

Arthur Löbbecke collection (Braunschweig, Germany); November 26, 1908, sold at his sale through (Jacob Hirsch, Munich, Germany), lot 154; private collection; April 18, 2002–present, sold at (Morton & Eden Ltd., London, UK), lot 626, to the Stephen K. and Janie Woo Scher Collection (New York, New York).

SELECTED EXHIBITIONS

Metropolitan Museum of Art, New York, 2001–2002, (St. Louis venue only); National Gallery, London, 2020–2021.

SELECTED PUBLICATIONS

Sammlung Arthur Löbbecke 1908, 20, no. 154, pl. X; *Ancient, Islamic, British and Foreign Coins* 2002, no. 626, illus.; Mann 2005c, 52, 58, fig. 2; Locker 2015, 19–20, fig. 1.4; Rome 2016, 40, 41 n. 19; Modesti 2017, 133, fig. 4; Scher 2019, 145, no. 231, illus.; London 2020, 162, cat. 18, 162–63 illus.

ORSOLA MADDALENA CACCIA

Moncalvo, 1596–1676

THEODORA CACCIA was born in the small Piedmontese town of Moncalvo to Guglielmo Caccia (1568–1625), a successful painter in Piedmont and Lombardy. Along with her sisters, she received a thorough education and initial training in the arts by her father. In 1620 she entered the convent of the Ursuline sisters in nearby Bianzè, adopting the name Orsola Maddalena. In 1625 she moved back to Moncalvo, where her father had built a small convent in the family house. Soon after she became its abbess, she began to oversee its busy art studio. Orsola Maddalena painted for the rest of her life, producing large altarpieces, smaller devotional paintings, and still lifes to support the convent in Moncalvo.

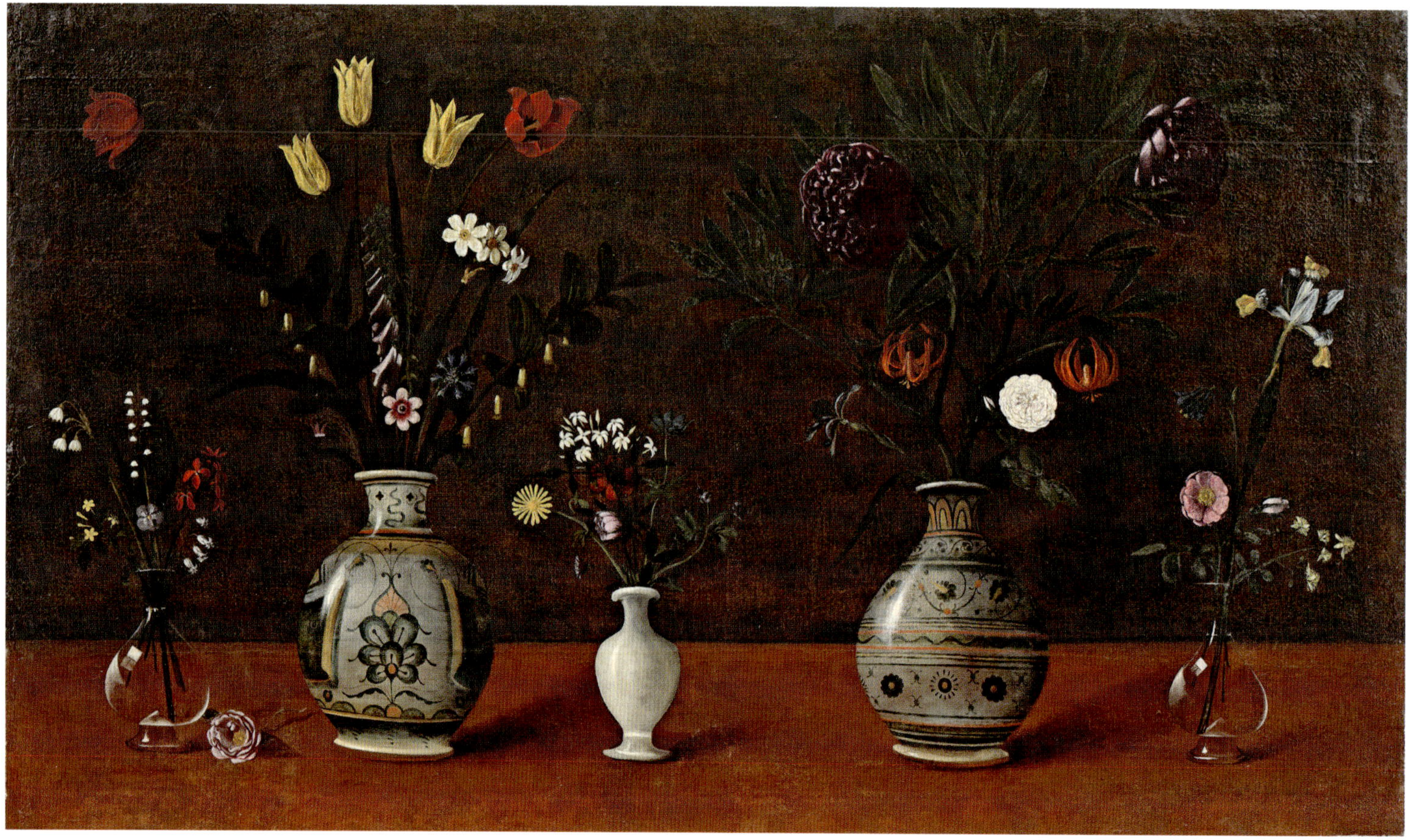

33

Vases of Flowers on a Table

1615–1625
Oil on canvas, 37¾ × 64⅜ in. (95.5 × 163.4 cm)
Yale University Art Gallery, New Haven, Leonard C. Hanna, Jr., Class of 1913,
Fund, 2018.157.1

ORSOLA MADDALENA CACCIA has recently emerged as a fascinating nun-artist. As most of her works are dispersed in institutions in her home region of Monferrat, situated on the eastern fringes of the Piedmont region, she is hardly known to the broader public. Traditionally many of her works have been ascribed to her father, the better-known painter Guglielmo Caccia, making it difficult to differentiate between the two. A prolific artist, Orsola Maddalena Caccia produced many large-scale religious paintings for churches and convents around Moncalvo.[1] The scholar Luigi Lanzi (1732–1810) speculated that together with her little-known sister Francesca Caccia (1608–1628), she painted more altarpieces than any other woman artist in Italy.[2] She was also one of the first, if not the first, painters in the Piedmont region to specialize in still lifes.

Lanzi also reports that Caccia adopted the symbol of a flower as a signature to distinguish her work. Indeed, flowers play a significant role in Caccia's oeuvre. She inserted them in the majority of her altarpieces and pictures of saints, and she painted numerous still lifes with flowers. The writer Guglielmo della Valle (1740–1794) used the adjective *fiorito* ("flowery") to describe the artist's style, with its propensity for delicate forms and attention to detail, and, more broadly, her close association with the motif.[3] Scholars agree that flowers had an enormous spiritual value to Caccia, who regarded them as metaphors for the sacred.

Caccia's still lifes are generally distinguished by their symmetrical and harmonious arrangements.[4] In *Vases of Flowers on a Table* she chose an unusual horizontal format. By spreading the five glass and ceramic vases equally over the table, and by arranging them in an alternating pattern, she created an almost rhythmic composition, which is reinforced by details such as the light reflections on each vase. The vases are filled with small bouquets of tulips, jasmine, peonies, and other types of flowers, each painted with great precision. For this geometrical composition, Caccia may have been inspired by prints such as the frontispiece of Adriaen Collaert's (ca. 1560–1618) *Florilegium* from ca. 1589 (fig. 1).[5] Yet she may also have studied the plants from nature.

Because *Vases of Flowers on a Table* stands out from the dozen known still lifes by Caccia, who usually mixed flowers with fruits and animals, its attribution to the artist is contested.[6] Her accepted still lifes are also distinguished by a greater quantity of flowers and a denser composition.[7] In addition, the two distinctive pottery vases from Faenza, as well as the white *lattimo* vase in the center, do not reoccur, to my knowledge, in any other work.[8]

If the painting is indeed by Caccia, its proposed date of 1615–1625 would explain the many incongruities with still lifes dated to her later period. Scholars such as Angela Ghirardi assumed that Caccia started painting still lifes only during the 1630s, so if the attribution is correct, the painting would shed light on her early career, when she assisted her father, followed by her first period at the convent of Bianzè.[9] —OT

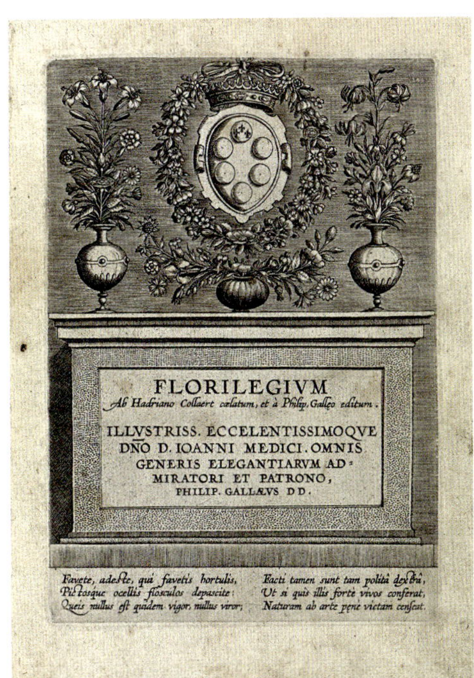

FIGURE 1 Adriaen Collaert, *Florilegium*, frontispiece, ca. 1589, engraving, sheet: 10 7/16 × 6 15/16 in. (26.4 × 17.6 cm). The Museum of Fine Arts Houston, Sarah Campbell Blaffer Foundation, BF.2014.7

NOTES

1. On the artist see Ghirardi 2002; San Secondo di Pinerolo 2012; and Solinas 2018, 114–28.

2. "(. . .), cd ebbe in ajuto de' suoi lavori anche due figlie, che sono le Gentilesche o le Fontane del Monferrato, ove sempre stettero lavorando non pur quadri da camera, ma tavole d'altare in più numero forse che altra donne." Lanzi 1795–1796, 362.

3. For a discussion of Caccia's career and the term "fiorito," see Caretta 2015, 178.

4. On Caccia's still lifes, see particularly Cottino 2012.

5. For a discussion of Caccia's use of prints, see Ghirardi 2002, 121–23. Cottino discusses the influence of Collaert's *Florilegium* on Caccia in Cottino 2012, 39.

6. The attribution to Caccia is endorsed by Francesco Solinas and Filippo Maria Ferro, while Alberto Cottino refutes it. See *Old Master Paintings, Part II* 2016, lot 229.

7. See Caccia's three still lifes dated ca. 1630 at the Museo Civico, Moncalvo, for instance *Vase of Flowers with a White Lily*.

8. I thank Justin Raccanello, London, for this information.

9. Ghirardi 2019.

PROVENANCE

A noble Piedmontese family (Italy), then by descent; October 18, 2016, sold at (Dorotheum, Vienna, Austria), lot 229, to (Richard L. Feigen, New York, New York); 2018–present, purchased by the Yale University Art Gallery as Orsola Maddalena Caccia (New Haven, Connecticut).

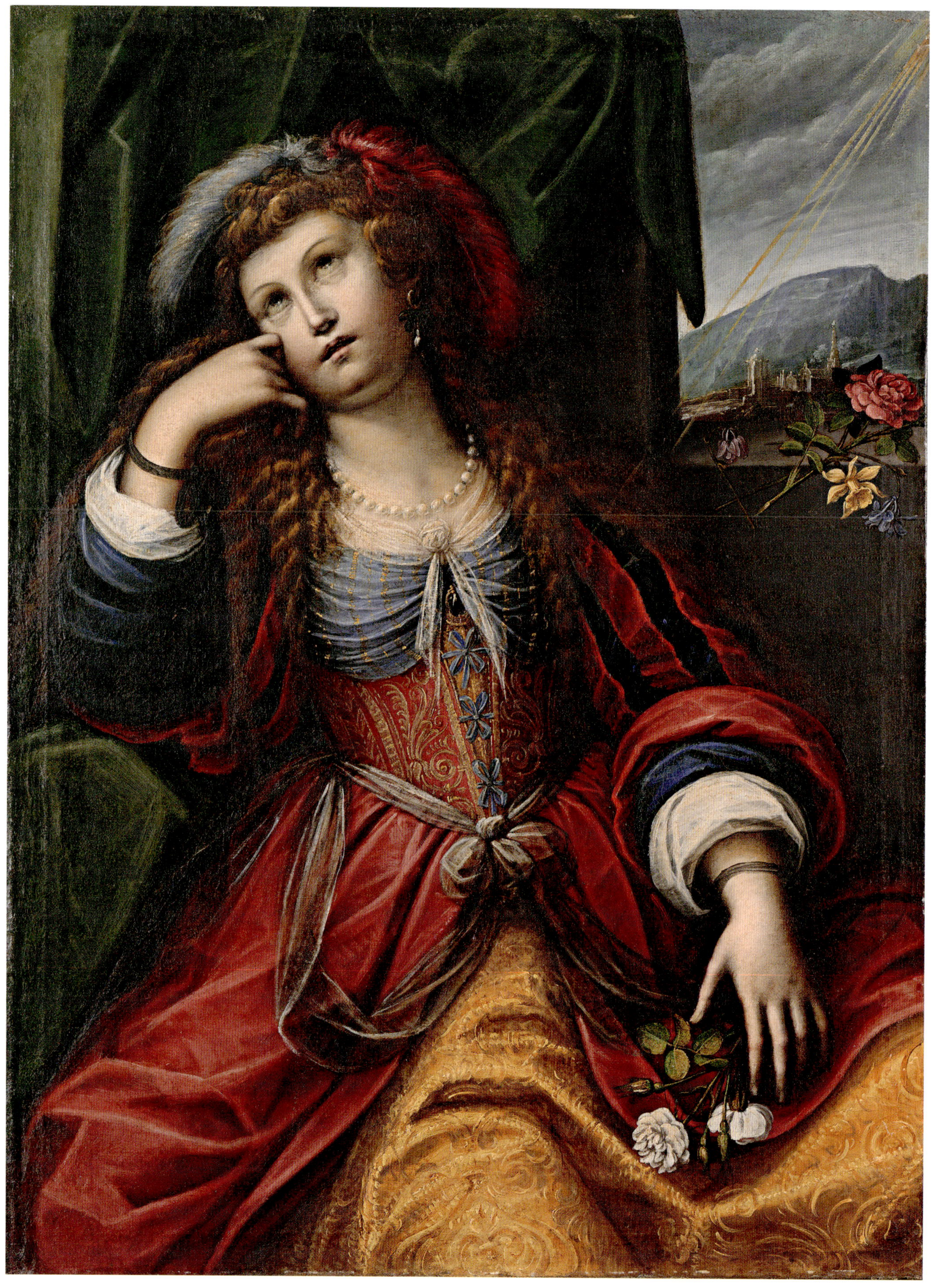

34

Mary Magdalene

1620–1630 (?)
Oil on canvas, $46\frac{5}{8} \times 35\frac{1}{16}$ in. (118.5 × 89 cm)
Private collection, Connecticut

LIKE A NUMBER of other Italian women artists, Orsola Maddalena Caccia spent most of her artistic career as a nun in convents, and religious subjects constituted a major component of her output. This little-known painting stands out with its sparkling colors and unusual iconography. The powerful themes of penance and redemption made the life of Mary Magdalene highly significant for Counter-Reformation spirituality. Painters usually presented the saint passionately praying or traveling with Jesus Christ, but Caccia chose the moment of the Magdalene's conversion from an earthly sinner to a humble follower of Christ. This subject was famously depicted in 1606 by Caravaggio (1571–1610) in his now lost *Mary Magdalene in Ecstasy* (cat. 28, fig. 1).[1] Artemisia Gentileschi (1593–1654 or later) painted a similarly rapturous Mary Magdalene in ca. 1620–1625 (cat. 28).[2]

Unlike Caravaggio and Gentileschi, Caccia shows Mary Magdalene amidst an abundance of worldly riches, enhanced by bright colors. Luxuriously clad in a brocade dress, pearl necklace, and gaudy feathers, she is seated in a barely defined interior, covered with a green drape, and surrounded by flowers. Absent are the usual ointment jar, crucifix, and skull. The view onto a landscape with a church and the golden rays piercing through the sky into her room leave no doubt about her spiritual awakening. With her head resting on her right hand and watery eyes directed upwards, she is deeply stirred by her calling. The moment of conversion is also reflected in the choice of flowers in her lap and on the window frame—identified as white and pink thornless roses, a yellow jonquil, and a blue columbine, they serve as spiritual metaphors and allude to the mystery of Christ's life.[3]

This *Mary Magdalene* surfaced only in 2017. It has been ascribed to Orsola Maddalena Caccia by Alberto Cottino, Filippo Ferri, and Alessandro Morandotti.[4] Morandotti cautiously suggests that Caccia painted the picture around 1620–1625,[5] a time when she stepped out of the shadow of her father, the painter Guglielmo Caccia (1568–1625), to become a more independent artist. In 1620 she also left her family home to join the order of the Ursulines in Bianzè, before returning in 1625. The Magdalene's lengthened fingers and neck and the angular creases of her dress betray a geometrical style typical of Caccia's father's work. The tilted head and mask-like features also bear a striking similarity to his depictions of female saints.[6] Educated in her father's workshop in the 1610s, Caccia was deeply influenced by his works and continued to use his drawings and patterns throughout her career.[7] The awkward position of the Magdalene's legs suggests her inexperience with depicting the human body. Yet, the painting's originality lies in the prominent role of the precisely rendered and carefully orchestrated flowers, which is typical of her work.

Mary Magdalene was a popular subject among women artists of the early 1600s. In addition to Artemisia Gentileschi, Lavinia Fontana (1552–1614) depicted the saint in 1581, Anna Maria Vaiani (1604–ca. 1655) in 1627, and Giovanna Garzoni (1600–1670) in 1642, to name just a few.[8] While whether Gentileschi depicted herself as the Magdalene in the painting of ca. 1620–1625 is contested, the artist Virginia da Vezzo (1600–1638) was portrayed as the Magdalene around 1626 by her husband Simon Vouet (1590–1649) (cat. 38). Because Caccia adopted the name of Magdalene (together with that of Orsola)

when she took her vows in 1620, the subject probably had a personal relevance for her. This notion is reinforced by the flowers, which were also used as a signature by Caccia.[9] We can therefore conclude that the subject had a strong quality of self-projection and poignancy for the artist, one that is echoed in the works of her female peers.—OT

NOTES

1. Caravaggio's painting is known through various copies.

2. Gentileschi painted at least three more versions of Mary Magdalene: *Conversion of the Magdalene (Penitent Magdalene)*, ca. 1617–1620, oil on canvas, $57\frac{11}{16} \times 42\frac{1}{2}$ in. (146.5 × 108 cm), Palazzo Pitti, Florence; *Penitent Magdalene*, oil on canvas, $25\frac{9}{16} \times 20$ in. (65 × 50.8 cm), ex-Marc A. Seidner collection, Los Angeles; *Penitent Magdalene*, 1625/26, oil on canvas, $48 \times 37\frac{13}{16}$ in. (122 × 96 cm), Seville Cathedral.

3. For the importance of flowers in Caccia's paintings, see Cottino 2012.

4. In emails to Maurizio Canesso, Paris, shared with the author.

5. Email Alessandro Morandotti to Maurizio Canesso, September 8, 2020.

6. See, for example, Guglielmo Caccia, *Martyrdom of Saint Orsola* altarpiece in the Church of Saint Francis, Moncalvo.

7. Solinas 2018, 117–18.

8. Lavinia Fontana, *Noli me tangere*, 1581, oil on canvas, $31\frac{1}{2} \times 25\frac{13}{16}$ in. (80 × 65.5 cm), Gallerie degli Uffizi, Florence; Anna Maria Vaiani, *Saint Mary Magdalene*, 1627, etching and engraving, plate: $7\frac{5}{16} \times 5\frac{9}{16}$ in. (18.5 × 14.1 cm), Philadelphia Museum of Art; Giovanna Garzoni, *Mary Magdalene in the Desert*, after Orazio Gentileschi, 1642, bodycolor and gum arabic on vellum laid down on panel, $6\frac{5}{8} \times 8\frac{1}{2}$ in. (16.8 × 21.6 cm), oval, private collection.

9. Lanzi 1795–1796, 362.

PROVENANCE

Private collection (Cuneo, Piedmont, Italy); May 23, 2017, sold at (Della Rocca, Turin, Italy), lot 273, as by Orsola Maddalena Caccia; private collection (Italy); October 2020–present, sold by (Galerie Canesso, Paris, France), as by Orsola Maddalena Caccia, to a private collection (Connecticut).

GIOVANNA GARZONI

Ascoli Piceno, 1600–Rome, 1670

BORN INTO A FAMILY of Venetian origins, Giovanna Garzoni received a broad education and was trained in music, calligraphy, and oil painting. She pursued a career that brought her to far-flung Italian cities and to Paris. In 1651 she settled in Rome. Garzoni attracted distinguished patrons, working for the Duke of Alcalá (1583–1637) in Naples, the Savoy family in Turin, as well as the Medici family in Florence and Rome. Equally important were her connections to artistic and learned circles, especially those attached to the Accademia di San Luca (Academy of Saint Luke), an association of artists, and the Accademia dei Lincei (Academy of the Lynx-Eyed), a scientific association, in Rome. She worked primarily as a miniaturist and specialized in portraits and botanical still lifes.

35

A Hedgehog in a Landscape

ca. 1643–1651 (?)
Tempera with graphite on parchment, 9¼ × 14¹⁵⁄₁₆ in. (23.5 × 38 cm)
Private collection

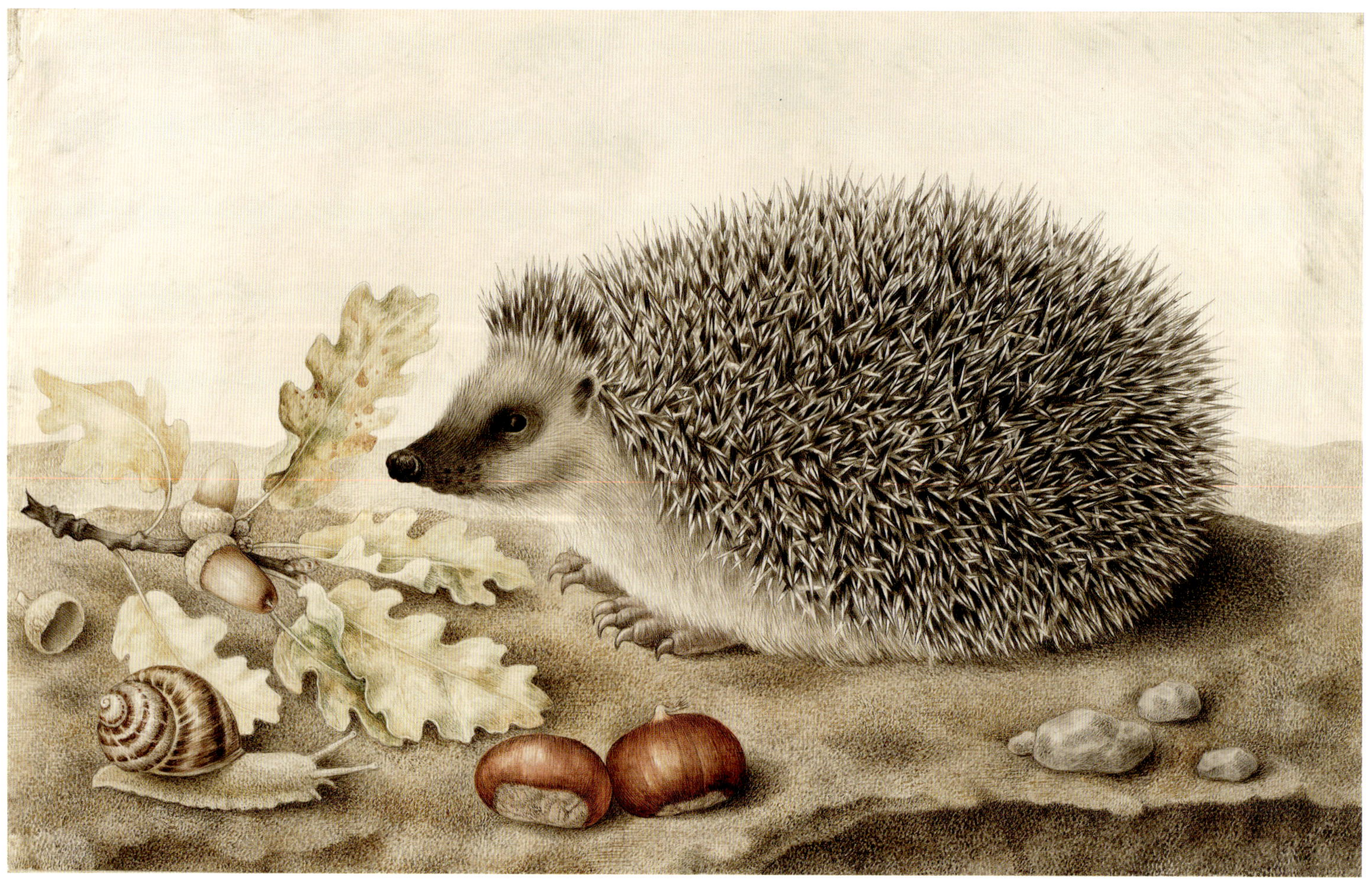

CALLED "INSIGNE MINIATRICE" (distinguished miniaturist) by her contemporaries, Giovanna Garzoni became one of the most famous artists of the mid-seventeenth century.[1] Rare for a woman artist of her time, she was affiliated with the prestigious Accademia di San Luca in Rome. Despite being trained in oil painting, she quickly found her niche in the Italian art market by specializing in miniatures. Stand-alone miniature painting produced as medallions, in boxes, or as small pictures had developed out of the medieval practice of manuscript illumination in the sixteenth century. Garzoni painted small, jewel-like portrait miniatures early in her career and focused later on larger, rectangular pictures, called *quadretti di miniatura* or cabinet miniatures, which are discussed here.[2]

Miniatures, which beguile with their brilliant color effects and minute details, require a diligent and painstaking technique. Garzoni often used a thin piece of animal skin as a support since it provided a smooth surface. To give the parchment greater stability, it was attached to pasteboard. After placing the support on an even surface, such as a simple desk, she outlined the objects in pencil. Traces of graphite can be seen on the oak leaves in *A Hedgehog in a Landscape*. Afterwards, she applied thin layers of tempera and watercolor on the parchment.[3] These colors lend Garzoni's works their typical textural and transparent qualities. Layers of mid-tone colors were applied first with broad brushstrokes, and details were then added in lighter and darker colors. The most intricate details, such as the quills of the hedgehog or the characteristic irregular dots creating the foreground in most of her miniatures, were added last.

To enliven her pictures, Garzoni regularly included small animals among the fruits and vegetables, continuing a well-established tradition that reaches back to illuminated Books of Hours. She usually drew and painted her objects from life, and while working for the Medici she is said to have had a steady supply of fresh fruits, vegetables, and animals.[4] To better study smaller objects up close, she may have used lenses or a microscope. Creatures in well-known prints by Jacob Hoefnagel (1573–ca. 1632), or works by the Florentine artist Jacopo Ligozzi (1547–1627), may have inspired her as well.

Occasionally, Garzoni made birds, dogs, or insects the prime subjects of her pictures.[5] The animals are often shown in small groups in barren landscapes, as in *A Hedgehog*.[6] Joined by a Roman snail (Helix pomatia), the European hedgehog (Erinaceus europaeus) captivates with its delicately executed soft hair and the geometrical precision of its sharp spikes. To my knowledge, this is the only known picture of a hedgehog by Garzoni, though examples of miniatures with Roman snails at the bottom exist.[7] Together with the wilted oak leaves and chestnuts, it may allegorically reference the autumn season, and it could have belonged to a larger series of the seasons. Depictions like this might have impressed her contemporary, the art writer Carlo Ridolfi (1594–1658), who praised the artist for her "perspicuity," by which he may have meant her skill in bringing to life even the smallest subjects.[8]

While we do not have any specific information about the early provenance of this miniature, we know that Giovanna Garzoni was popular among an international circle of elite collectors. The biographer Lione Pascoli (1674–1744) noted that because of the high demand for her artwork, she could get any price she asked for it.[9] Garzoni enjoyed the patronage of some of the most discerning collectors of her time, such as Fernando Afán de Ribera (1583–1637), the Spanish viceroy of Naples; Christine of France (1606–1663), the Duchess of Savoy; and various members of the Medici family in Florence and Rome. It is likely Garzoni painted this intriguing picture for one such distinguished collector.—OT

NOTES

1. For Garzoni's biography see Casale 1991, 1–32; Meloni Trkulja 2000, 4–11; Barker 2020a, 16–29. The writer Pellegrino Antonio Orlandi (1660–1727), among others, praised Garzoni as "insigne Miniatrice" in his entry on her life in his *Abecedario pittorico*. Orlandi 1753, 241.

2. See Simari 2014, 9; Colding 1953, 26.

3. See Policicchio 2018a, 195.

4. Meloni Trkulja 2000, 9.

5. See Giovanna Garzoni, *Still Life with Birds and Fruits*, ca. 1650, tempera on vellum, $9^{11}/_{16} × 16^{3}/_{8}$ in. (25.1 × 41.6 cm), Cleveland Museum of Art (Casale 1991, A35); *The Old Man from Artimino*, ca. 1648, tempera on parchment, $15 × 23^{1}/_{2}$ in. (38.6 × 60 cm), Galleria Palatina, Florence (Casale 1991, A54); *A Dog*, ca. 1648, tempera on parchment, $10^{5}/_{8} × 15^{3}/_{8}$ in. (27 × 39 cm), Galleria Palatina, Florence (Casale 1991, A55).

6. Gerardo Casale supports the attribution of *A Hedgehog* to Garzoni. He dates it to her Florentine period, ca. 1643–1651. See *Important Old Master Paintings Part I* 2007, 106.

7. See Giovanna Garzoni, *Grapes, Pears and a Snail*, ca. 1655–1662, tempera on parchment, $9^{5}/_{8} × 13^{9}/_{16}$ in. (24.5 × 34.5 cm), Galleria Palatina, Florence, inv. 1890 no. 4769.

8. Ridolfi includes Garzoni in an encomium about the distinctions of women artists: "(. . .) da quali esempij chiaramente si comprende, à quale segno arrivi la perspicaccia donnesca, all'hor, che viene erudite negli studij." See Ridolfi 1648, vol. 2, 71.

9. Pascoli 1933, vol. 2, 451.

PROVENANCE

Silvano Lodi Collection (Campione d'Italia, Italy); (Simon Dickinson, London, UK); (Trinity Fine Arts, London, UK); April 19, 2007–present, sold at (Christie's, New York, New York), lot 88, to a private collection.

36

Still Life of Quinces, Almonds, and Figs with a Mouse

ca. 1632–1637
Tempera on parchment, 9¹³⁄₁₆ × 14⁹⁄₁₆ in. (25 × 37 cm)
On the back side, lower left corner: old paper clip with the name: Auguste de Mus(g/y . . .).
Private collection

A Plate of Figs

ca. 1661–1662
Tempera on parchment, laid on board, vellum, 9¾ × 13⅞ in. (24 × 35 cm)
W. Graham Arader III collection, New York

GIOVANNA GARZONI began her career as a painter of religious scenes and portraits but soon specialized in still lifes, a genre to which she greatly contributed with her sensitivity for the natural world and her meticulous technique. A highly skilled painter of miniatures, Garzoni aims to balance naturalistic details with a decorative composition. Most of her still lifes feature in the central foreground a single dish, plate, or vase filled with fruits, flowers, or vegetables. Her compositions were possibly inspired by the Lombard painter Fede Galizia (ca. 1574–ca. 1630) and her circle, as well as by painters from the Northern school such as Balthasar van der Ast (1593/94–1657) and Jan Brueghel the Elder (1568–1625). Garzoni did not, however, merely translate their formulas into miniatures; she experimented with, varied, and manipulated her subjects to create some of the most captivating and original still lifes of her time.

In both *Still Life of Quinces, Almonds, and Figs with a Mouse* and *A Plate of Figs*, the uneven surfaces of the painting resemble rocks or patches of mud. These amorphous, semi-abstract grounds, which became one of Giovanna Garzoni's trademarks, add a touch of somberness to the otherwise luminous pictures. Garzoni also experimented with backgrounds, using the polished shine of a sheet of vellum or, more rarely, painting it black. In *Still Life of Quinces*, she executed the dark background with her characteristic pointillist technique, stippling dots close to one another. The effect is a wafting softness that contrasts with the sharp outlines of the fruits and dishes.

Because of her meticulous working process and the need to satisfy the pressing demands of her patrons, Garzoni effectively reused elements in similar compositions while playing with viewers' expectations. In *Still Life of Quinces*, she presents a ceramic dish that appears in at least two other pictures.[1] In each case, this Chinese export dish, seemingly of the *kraak* type, with a distinctive geometric pattern and delicate rim, is depicted from the same perspective. The colors, however, differ. Here, a radiant coral color creates a vibrant contrast with the yellow-green tones of the quinces. In this instance Garzoni seems to have used her artistic license to color the dish in a way that enhanced the quinces.[2] While the overwhelming majority of Chinese ceramics were produced in white and cobalt blue at the time, some porcelain was colored red, yet characteristically a brownish copper red. With its simplified composition, slight incongruities in the depiction of the fruits, and skillful use of color, this enchanting still life can best be compared with similar works from Garzoni's stay in Turin from 1632 to 1637.[3]

Giovanna Garzoni painted several plates of figs during her career, all piled high with delicate fruit. Except that it lacks two small pomegranates, *A Plate of Figs* is similar to a version at the Pitti Palace, Florence.[4] The carefully executed figs are arranged nearly identically, and placed in a simple, well-used maiolica bowl, topped by a corona of leaves. While the Florentine miniature belongs to a well-documented series of twenty still lifes painted by Garzoni for Grand Duke Ferdinando II de' Medici (1610–1670) between ca. 1655 and 1662, little is certain about the date and provenance of this picture. Because of its luminosity and fluid execution, Gerardo Casale and Stefania Biancani place it in Garzoni's mature period and date it ca. 1661–1662, while Mary Garrard proposes a date of 1655–1662. Lucia Tongiorgi Tomasi suggests that it was painted for an important patron, perhaps a member of the Medici family.[5] Despite these open questions, *Plate of Figs* exemplifies the high degree of quality in Giovanna Garzoni's production of still lifes.—OT

NOTES

1. Compare with Giovanna Garzoni, *Still Life with Artichokes, a Rose, and Strawberries*, ca. 1655–1662, 9⁵⁄₁₆ × 12⅝ in. (24 × 32 cm), Galleria Palatina, Florence, inv. no. 1890/4760 (Casale 1991, A18); *Plate with Apples and Almonds*, 8¹¹⁄₁₆ × 13 in. (22.9 × 33.3 cm), Accademia Nazionale di San Luca, Rome (Casale 1991, A78). Teresa Canepa, in an email to the author, identifies it as a dish produced for the export market in the kilns in Jingdezhen in the late Ming dynasty, probably during the Chongzhen reign.
2. I am thankful to Kee Il Choi Jr. and Teresa Canepa for their suggestions on the dish.
3. See Casale 1991, 86–87 (A32), 133 (A78); Policicchio 2018c, 224.
4. Giovanna Garzoni, *Plate with Figs*, 1655–1662, tempera on parchment, 9¹³⁄₁₆ × 12¹³⁄₁₆ in. (25 × 32.5 cm), Galleria Palatina, Florence (Casale 1991, A25).
5. Letter Lucia Tongiorgi Tomasi, Pisa, to Graham Arader, New York, July 30, 2012, Arader archives.

Still Life of Quinces, Almonds, and Figs with a Mouse

PROVENANCE

Private collection (France); 2005–present, sold by (Didier Aaron) to a private collection.

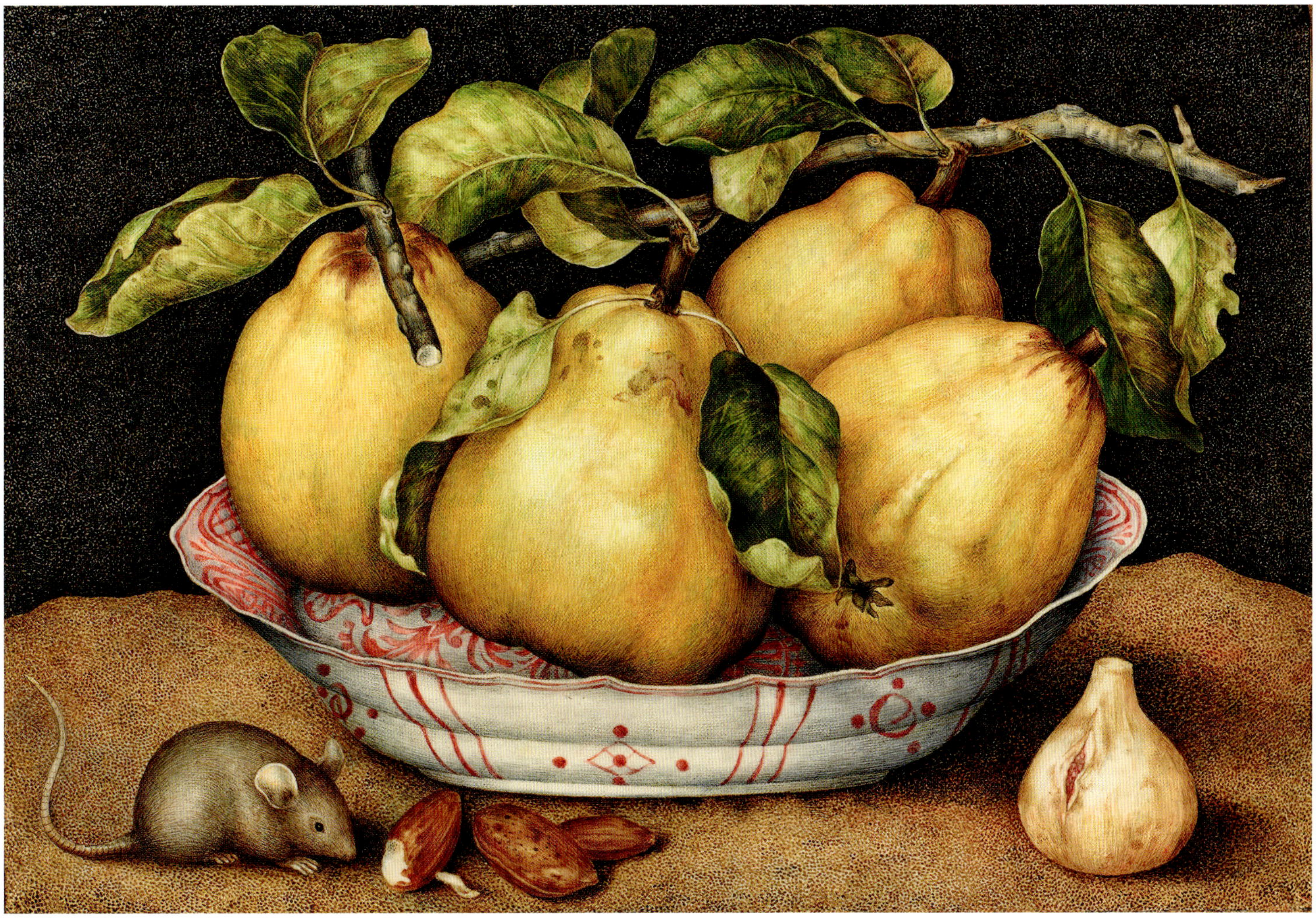

36

A Plate of Figs

PROVENANCE

Silvano Lodi Collection (Campione d'Italia, Italy);
April 6, 2006–present, sold at (Christie's, New York,
New York), lot 56, to the W. Graham Arader III col-
lection (New York, New York).

SELECTED EXHIBITIONS

Westfälisches Landesmuseum für Kunst und
Kulturgeschichte, Münster, 1979–1980, no. 152;
Bayerische Staatsgemäldesammlungen, Alte
Pinakothek, Munich, 1984–1985; Israel Museum,
Jerusalem, 1994; National Museum of Women in the
Arts, Washington, D.C., 2007.

SELECTED PUBLICATIONS

Munich 1984, 103–4, no. 41; Casale 1991, 89, no. A34,
illus.; Jerusalem 1994, 50, cat. 18, 51 illus.; *Important
Old Master Paintings Part I* 2006, no. 56; Pomeroy
2007, 22; Washington, D.C. 2007, 228, cat. 55, 229
illus.; Florence 2020, 62–63, 65, fig. 1.

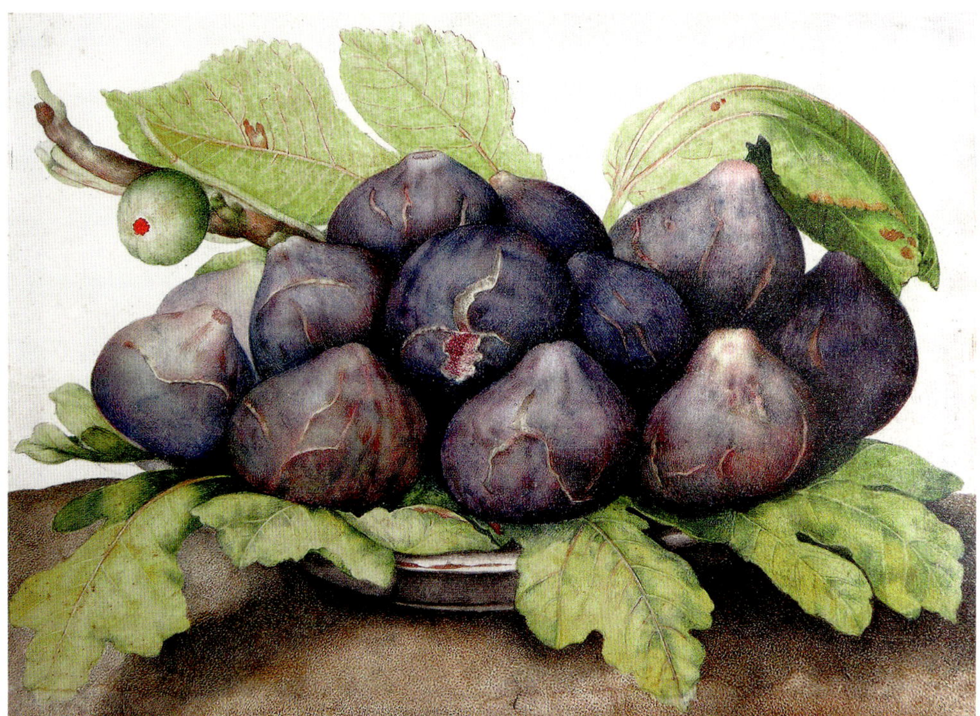

37

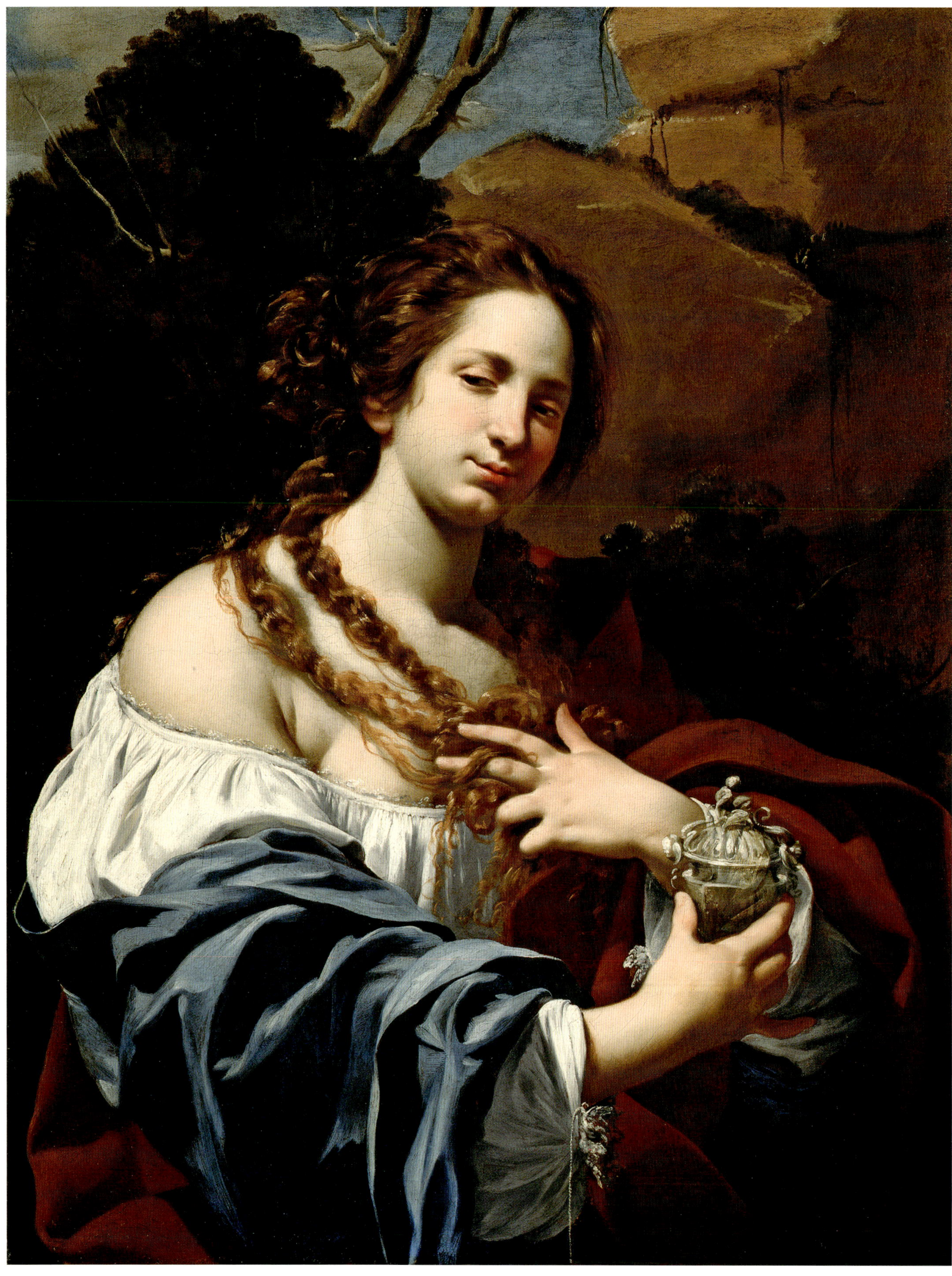

VIRGINIA DA VEZZO

Velletri, 1600–Paris, 1638

VIRGINIA DA VEZZO was the second daughter of three children born to Pompeo da Vezzo, a landowner, and Plinia Ferri, a midwife, in Velletri, outside of Rome. The family transferred permanently to the city in 1611. She may have received her early training from the painter Marco Tullio Montagna (ca. 1594–1649), from her hometown. In Rome she attended the life drawing classes of the French-born painter Simon Vouet (1590–1649) in her building on the Strada Ferratina. She married him in 1626 and accompanied him soon after to Paris, where she continued to paint and started a life drawing course for women of the French court. Da Vezzo worked closely with her husband, and many pictures in the "style of Vouet" are inconclusively attributed to her.

38

Virginia da Vezzo, the Artist's Wife, as the Magdalene

Simon Vouet (Paris, 1590–1649)

ca. 1626

Oil on canvas, 40 × 31 in. (101.6 × 78.74 cm)

Los Angeles County Museum of Art, Gift of the Ahmanson Foundation, M.83.201

THIS EVOCATIVE AND SENSUAL half-length image of Saint Mary Magdalene by Simon Vouet—the French-born artist and pre-eminent follower of Caravaggio (1571–1610) in 1620s Rome—is also a tenderly naturalistic portrait of his wife, the little-known Italian artist Virginia da Vezzo, who served as the model. This blurring of the line between saintly subjects and models plucked from the streets of Rome and painted from life lends pictures by Caravaggio and his followers their piquancy and persuasive power. The fact that the model was a painter in her own right adds a further layer of complexity to this image.[1] Virginia da Vezzo embodies the roles of saint, wife, and artist—a rare combination in the seventeenth century.

Although there is only one definitive attribution to Virginia da Vezzo, a growing body of works are ascribed to her hand.[2] The most widely accepted attribution is a *Judith*, possibly painted as her reception piece for the Accademia di San Luca (Academy of Saint Luke) in Rome (fig. 1).[3] As Simon Vouet and Virginia da Vezzo married in 1626, the picture does not date much before that year.

In 1626 Claude Mellan (1598–1688) also made an engraving of Virginia da Vezzo (fig. 2), and her physiognomy and apparent age are aligned in painting and print, further

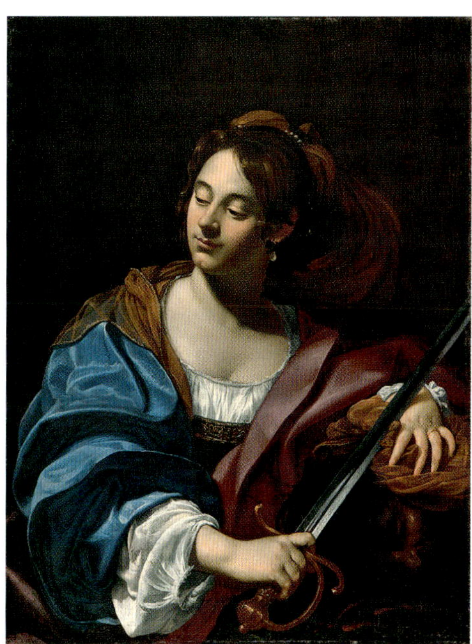

FIGURE 1 Virginia da Vezzo, *Judith*, ca. 1624–1626, oil on canvas, 38½ × 29⁵⁄₁₆ in. (97.8 × 74.5 cm). Musée d'Arts de Nantes, inv. 09.1.1.P

suggesting a date of around 1626 for *Judith*.[4] The couple likely met at Vouet's Roman drawing academy sometime between 1621, when he opened it, and 1626, when they wed. In 1627 they moved to Paris, where the French art critic and official court historian to King Louis XIV (1638–1715), André Félibien (1619–1695), records that Virginia da Vezzo "was intelligent in the profession of painting."[5] Like Elisabetta Sirani (1638–1665) a few decades later in Bologna, she ran an art academy for female pupils in Paris.[6]

Set in a rocky outcropping meant to evoke the grotto to which Mary Magdalene is believed to have retreated to devote herself to a life of prayer, Simon Vouet's painting captures both the saint's worldly ways and her act of repentance. Yet the erotic energy of the scene overpowers. Her left hand, held to her bosom in a gesture of penitence, is also intertwined in her cascading auburn hair in a manner so enticing that the viewer experiences it tactilely.[7] With her coy gaze, bared right shoulder, and partially exposed right breast, the unguent jar—a reference to Mary's washing and anointing of Christ's feet

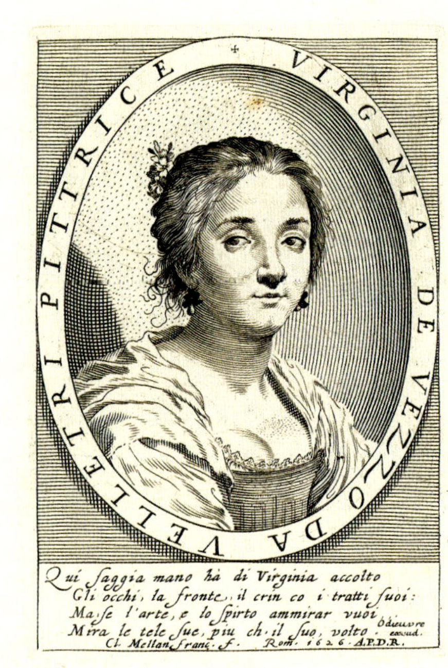

FIGURE 2 Claude Mellan, *Virginia da Vezzo*, 1626, engraving on laid paper, plate: 4¾ × 3³⁄₁₆ in. (12 × 8.1 cm); sheet: 5³⁄₁₆ × 3¹¹⁄₁₆ in. (13.2 × 9.3 cm). National Gallery of Art, Washington, D.C., Gift of John O'Brien, 1991.164.8

in the house of Simon of Pharisee—hardly registers. Vouet's voluptuous handling of paint in her flesh tones, white chemise, and voluminous drapery compete with the picture's penitential theme.

In seventeenth-century Italy, it was a popular conceit to depict a sitter in the guise of a saint. Giusto Sustermans' (1597–1681) portrait of Medici Grand Duchess Maria Maddalena of Austria (1589–1631) in the Pitti Palace, Florence, is a striking example of a painting in which the sitter was certainly supposed to be both recognized as herself and identified as the penitent Saint Mary Magdalene.[8] Was this true of Simon Vouet's picture? As is often the case with the naturalistic approach of Caravaggio's followers, the line between life and painted subject is artfully obscured.—ESP

NOTES

1. As the historian of French art Jacques Thullier wrote in his 1992 exhibition catalogue, "The problem of Virginia da Vezzo is complex" (translation mine). See Paris 1990, 32.

2. Michel 1991, 123–33; Lollobrigida 2011, 64–69.

3. This picture is attributed to Virginia da Vezzo based on a print of the Nantes painting by Claude Mellan, which is inscribed in Latin *Virginia de Vezzo pinx* ["Virginia da Vezzo painted it"].

4. The painting was previously thought to date to after Vouet's return to Paris in 1627, where he was called by King Louis XIII (1601–1643), but scholars now commonly accept that he executed it at the end of his Roman sojourn, when his palette was more saturated and tenebrist, around 1626 or 1627. Conisbee, Levkoff, and Rand 1991, 122–24. See also Bissell 1999, 224.

5. "Elle étoit jeune & intelligente dans la Peintre." Félibien 1725, 394.

6. Cavazzini 2008, 43.

7. This interweaving of hand and hair recalls an earlier depiction of the penitent saint by Titian (1488/90–1576), a prime version of which is in the Pitti Palace, Florence.

8. For this picture by Sustermans, see Pizzorusso 1986, 235–36, no. 99.

PROVENANCE

November 15, 1836, possibly sold by (Foster, London, UK), "Portrait of a Lady of Quality in the figure of a Magdalen," for £1.3, to Golding. Around 1860, "Alderman" T. Holroyd. Unidentified religious institution (UK); sold at auction (Lancaster, UK). 1982, (art market, London, UK). (Trafalgar Galleries, London, UK); 1983–present, sold to the Los Angeles County Museum of Art (Los Angeles, California).

SELECTED EXHIBITIONS

Royal Academy, London, 1983; Musée des Beaux-Arts de Nantes, 2008–2009.

SELECTED PUBLICATIONS

Brejon de Lavergnée 1982, 686–89, fig. 34; *Apollo* 1983, 449, fig. 1; London 1983, 8–11, cat. 3, 9 illus.; *Burlington Magazine* 1985, 492, fig. 86; Florence 1986, 231, fig. 1; Schaefer and Fusco 1987, 99, illus.; Conisbee, Levkoff, and Rand 1991, 122–24, cat. 31, 123 illus.; Tzeutschler Lurie 1993, 160–61, fig. 5; Bissell 1999, 47, 223–24, fig. 91; Marandel and Einecke 2006, 44, fig. 46; Schleier 2006, fig. 20; Nantes 2008, 90 illus., 167, cat. 51, illus.; Loire 2011, 218; Marandel 2017, 52, 55 illus., 56; Antwerp 2018, 194, fig. A; Walsh 2019a, 46–49, no. 12, 46 illus., 184–85.

ANNA MARIA VAIANI

Florence (or Milan?), 1604–Rome, ca. 1655

BORN TO THE FLORENTINE PAINTER Alessandro Vaiani (dates unknown), Anna Maria Vaiani had moved to Rome before 1626 and stayed in the city for the rest of her life. She quickly made a name for herself as an engraver and painter of flower still lifes. She also worked as a fresco painter in one of the papal chapels at the Vatican. In 1630 she befriended the polymath Galileo Galilei (1564–1642), who introduced her to the powerful Barberini family. At the same time, she became associated with the Accademia di San Luca (Academy of Saint Luke), as well as the scientific Accademia dei Lincei (Academy of the Lynx-Eyed). During her career, Vaiani participated in some of the most ambitious printing projects of her time, such as Giovanni Battista Ferrari's (1584–1685) *De Florum Cultura* (1633) and the *Galleria Giustiniani* (1635 and 1636), the catalogue of Vincenzo Giustiniani's (1564–1637) famous art collection.

39

Bouquet of Flowers in Giovanni Battista Ferrari (1584–1655), *De Florum Cultura*

Rome, 1633
Engraving on paper, overall: 9¹³⁄₁₆ × 6¹¹⁄₁₆ × 1¹³⁄₁₆ in. (25 × 17 × 4.6 cm)
Inscribed: Anna M[ari]a Vaiani delin[eavit] et p[ropria] m[anu] incid[it].
[Anna Maria Vaiani drew and incised it with her own hand.]
The Metropolitan Museum of Art, New York, 21.36.8

IN THE SIXTEENTH CENTURY the study of plants rapidly developed into a modern science, and the systematic exploration of flowers and their classification offered numerous opportunities for artists to collaborate with botanists. About a century later, women artists, particularly from Northern Europe, such as Maria Sibylla Merian (1647–1717), became famous for their botanical, floral, and zoological illustrations. The study of natural specimens afforded them intellectual and artistic liberties they did not have with other subjects. In Italy the number of women practicing botanical illustration was smaller, but one important artist was the painter and engraver Anna Maria Vaiani. She was connected to patrons such as Cassiano dal Pozzo (1588–1657) and other members of Europe's first scientific academy, the Accademia dei Lincei, founded in Rome in 1603. Its members comprised scholars and scientists, and many of them fostered an exchange with artists, whose drawings and prints played an increasingly important role in classifying and documenting the visual world. The picture under discussion here was probably produced in Rome during the early 1630s, when the city was the center of scientific debates in Italy.

Too little is known about Anna Maria Vaiani (fig. 1). She was close to the scientist Galileo Galilei and must have been well connected with artistic and scientific circles in Rome, as she contributed in 1633 to the remarkable *De Florum Cultura*, published by the Jesuit Giovanni Battista Ferrari. Dedicated to the cultivation and planning of flower gardens, this book is considered one of the most significant publications on gardening of the seventeenth century. Leading artists such as Guido Reni (1575–1642), Giovanni Lanfranco (1582–1647), and Pietro da Cortona (1596–1669) contributed to it as well. Vaiani probably designed and engraved many of the illustrations, but she actually signed only one plate, *Bouquet of Flowers.*

She based the symmetrical composition on earlier flower still lifes by Northern artists such as Jan Brueghel the Elder (1568–1625). By placing flowers with smaller stems close to the foreground, backed by those with longer stems, she achieves a harmonious effect of forms that accords with Ferrari's theories about designing an ideal flower garden. Vaiani rendered the bouquet in a precise and naturalistic way and she largely eschewed dramatic effects, with the exception of the

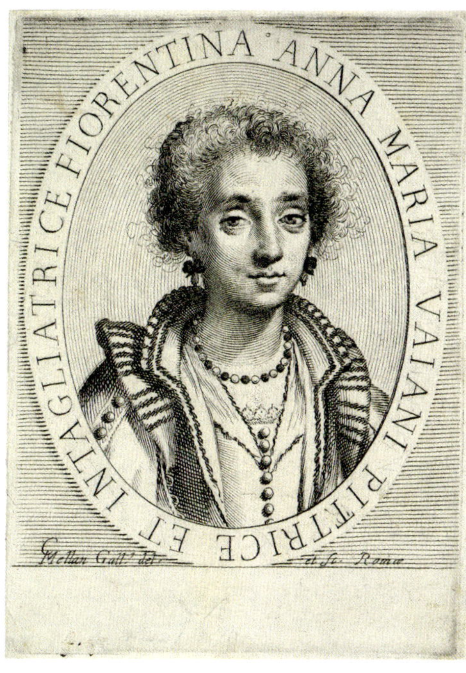

FIGURE 1 Claude Mellan (French, 1598–1688), *Portrait of Anna Maria Vaiani*, 1624–1636, engraving, sheet: 4¹⁵⁄₁₆ × 3⅝ in. (12.6 × 9.2 cm). The Metropolitan Museum of Art, New York

421
Anna Mª Vaiana
delin et pᵐ incid
IDẼ VAS ORDINATIS FLORIBVS CONSPICVVM Dd 3

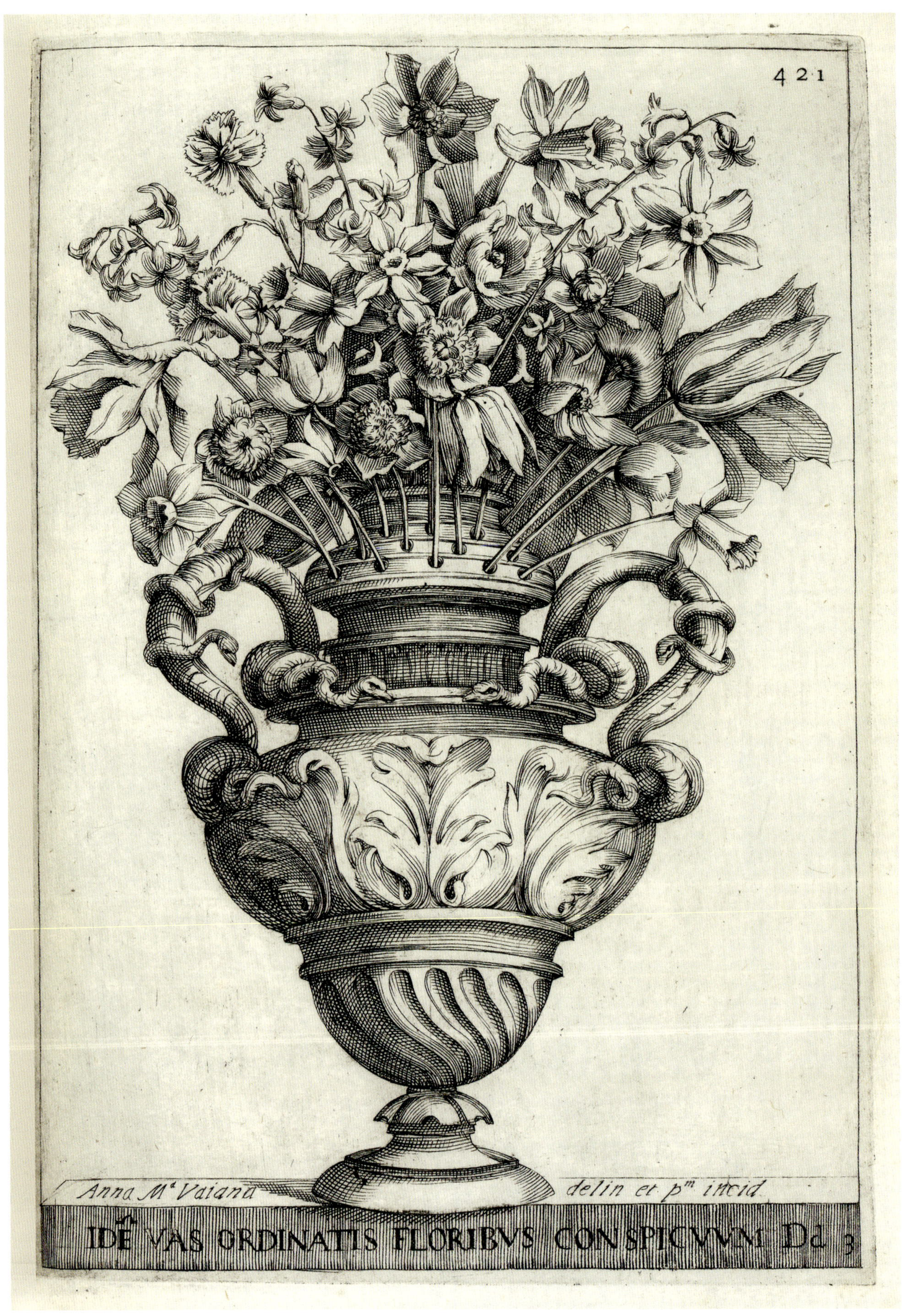

134

spectacular ornamental vase. The sinuous contours of the flowers, however, mirror features such as the vase's snake-shaped handles. Vaiani's fine balance between attention to detail and naturalism on the one hand, and a sense of aesthetic delight on the other, perfectly suits this artistically ambitious florilegium.—OT

PROVENANCE

1921–present, accessioned by the Metropolitan Museum of Art (New York, New York) [transferred from the Library].

SELECTED EXHIBITIONS

Metropolitan Museum of Art, New York, 1995; Metropolitan Museum of Art, New York, 1999.

SELECTED PUBLICATIONS

The Illustrated Bartsch 1978–, vol. 200, 127, no. 5, 421; Tongiorgi Tomasi 1990, 10; Tongiorgi Tomasi 1997, 116–21; Pisa 2009, 256, 260; Tongiorgi Tomasi 2010, 164–66; Bredekamp 2019, 275–79

ELISABETTA SIRANI

Bologna, 1638–1665

WHEN THE LEARNED BOLOGNESE PAINTER Elisabetta Sirani died in 1665, at the age of twenty-seven, she had painted over 200 pictures and created ten prints. Trained by her father Giovanni Andrea Sirani (1610–1670), a follower of Guido Reni (1575–1642), Elisabetta Sirani executed a substantial number of original compositions, often privileging female protagonists. Unlike most artists in Bologna, who did not typically sign their pictures, Sirani identified many works with her distinctive signature. Although she executed portraits, she painted more religious and secular narrative subjects than any other woman artist before the eighteenth century.

40

Cupid Triumphant in the Sea (Medici Cupid)

1661
Oil on canvas, 35 × 27⁹⁄₁₆ in. (89 × 70 cm)
Private collection, Bologna

ALTHOUGH THE BOLOGNESE artist Elisabetta Sirani was primarily a religious painter, she included twenty-six allegorical pictures in her *Notes of the Paintings Made by Me Elisabetta Sirani*, published by scholar Carlo Cesare Malvasia (1616–1693) in his 1678 biographies of Bolognese artists, which constitutes about thirteen percent of her total painted production.[1] The *Cupid Triumphant* was made on the occasion of Marguerite Louise d'Orléans de Bourbon's (1645–1721) marriage to Cosimo de' Medici (1642–1723), which took place in Paris on April 17, 1661. In her list, Sirani describes the picture as a Cupid in the sea, raising his bow with one hand and holding in the other a shell containing pearls arranged to suggest the Medici coat of arms.[2] Sirani repeated this clever heraldic reference to the Medici two years later, in a painting of Galatea (private collection, 1663). Although Sirani did not identify the patron for *Cupid Triumphant* in her list, Adelina Modesti has suggested it may have been commissioned by the groom's mother, Vittoria della Rovere (1622–1695), then grand duchess of Tuscany.[3] Her son Cosimo became Grand Duke Cosimo III of Tuscany in 1670. His bride Marguerite, daughter of Gaston duc d' Orléans (1608–1660) and Marguerite of Lorraine (1615–1672), was also related to the reigning French king, Louis XIV (1638–1715). When Marguerite returned to France in 1675, she took this painting with her.

Sirani painted two other pictures for members of the Medici family in 1664, and both are signed, as is true for most of the artist's paintings. It seems very likely that *Cupid Triumphant* was also originally signed, but perhaps the signature was accidentally removed in a restoration.

This charming work seems to have been one of Elisabetta Sirani's best-known allegorical paintings. It was celebrated in contemporary poems, including one by Gasparo Bombacci (dates unknown), who compared its delicate coloring to the works of the great Guido Reni (1575–1642), the most celebrated Bolognese painter of the seventeenth century.[3] Sirani's graceful design focuses on the central figure of the plump, blond Cupid. He is seated on a red cushion on a large seashell, silhouetted against sea and sky and surrounded by the curvilinear arc of lavender drapery that emphasizes the engaging figure even more eloquently. Although no drawings for this picture have been identified, the artist must surely have prepared the harmoniously constructed composition in preliminary studies. Although Sirani made several other paintings depicting Cupid, this example was the most successful and celebrated of these works.—BB

NOTES
1. Malvasia 1678, vol. 2, 470; Malvasia 1841, vol. 2, 395.
2. Modesti 2014, 283.
3. Published in Malvasia 1678, vol. 2, 470; Malvasia 1841, vol. 2, 395.

PROVENANCE
Grand Duchess Marguerite Louise d'Orléans de Bourbon de' Medici (Florence, Italy, from 1661–1675, then Paris, France, until 1721); June 29, 1989, (art market, Paris, France); 1990, (Drouot, Paris, France); private collection (France); 1990, Wildenstein Foundation (New York, New York); 1995, (Galleria Altomani, Pesaro, Italy); ca. 1997–2004, Collezione GMB (Vignola, Italy); May 26, 2004–present, sold by (Porro & Co., Milan, Italy), lot 29, to a private collection (Bologna, Italy).

SELECTED EXHIBITIONS
Galleria degli Uffizi, Florence, 1975; Chiesa di San Carlo, Modena, 1998–1999; Museo Civico Archeologico, Bologna, 2004–2005; Palazzo Reale, Milan, 2007–2008; Palazzo Fava, Palazzo delle Esposizioni, Pinacoteca Nazionale, Bologna, 2015.

SELECTED PUBLICATIONS
Piccinardi 1665, 18; Masini 1666, 619; Malvasia 1678, vol. 2, 470; "Nota delle pitture fatte da me Elisabetta Sirani" 1841, 395–96; Manaresi 1898, 126; Florence 1975, 160; Goldberg 1983, 42, 44; Frisoni 1992, 344, 346 n. 17, 347, 359, fig. 340; Modena 1998, 136, cat. 40, 137 illus.; Modesti 2001a, 196 n. 124;

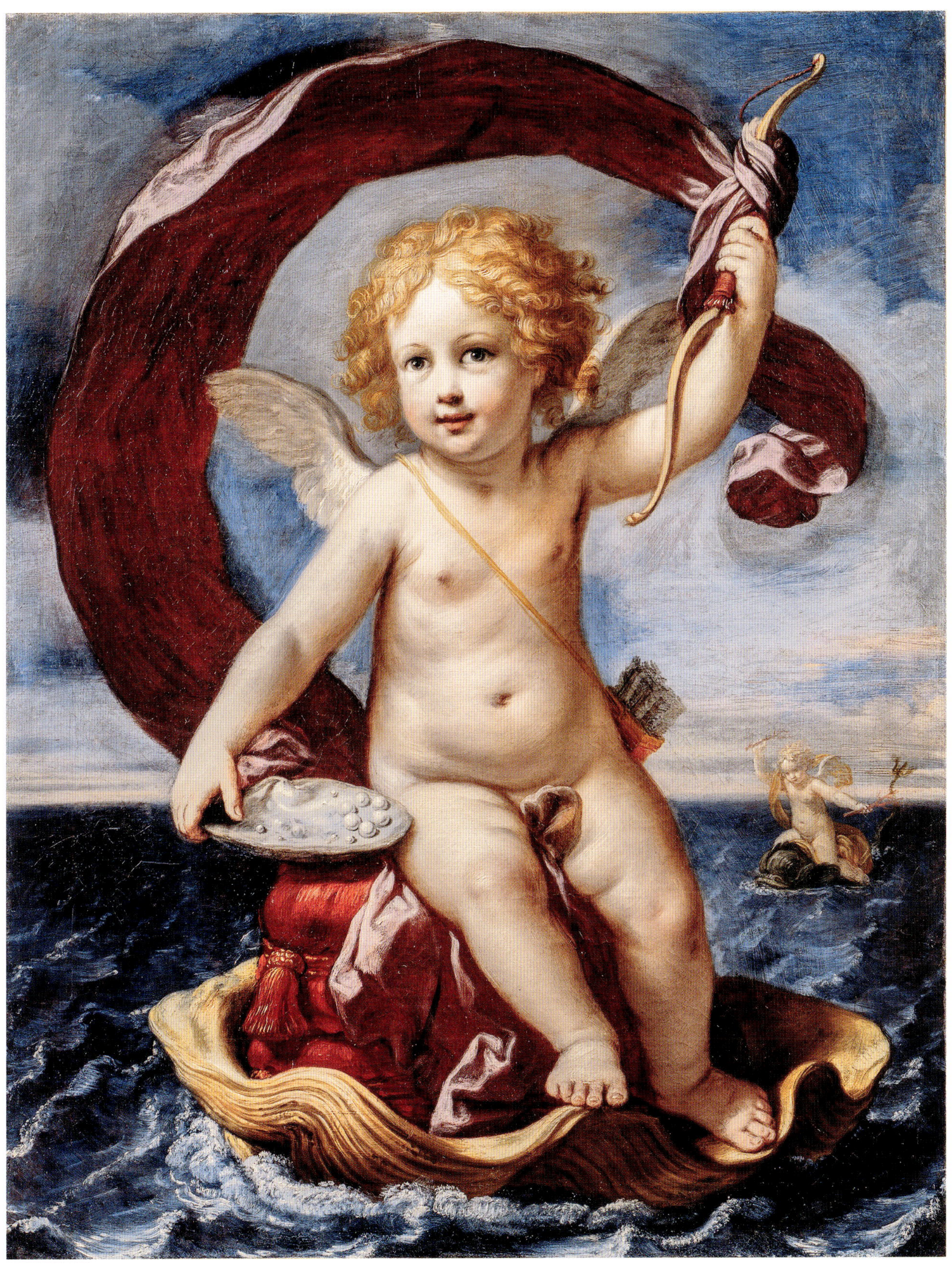

Modesti 2003, 372–73, 376–78, 387 nn. 95–96, fig. XXVIII-8; Bologna 2004, 28–29, 230–31, cat. 84, 230 illus.; Galli 2004, 52, no. 29, 53 illus.; Modesti 2004, 24, 27, 208, 306, fig. 12; Milan 2007, 98 illus., 363; Lollobrigida 2012, 18; Bohn 2013, 119; Modesti 2014, 20, 81 n. 124, 128, 186 n. 110, 283–84, no. 60, 283 illus., 285 under no. 62, 288 under no. 65, 293 under no. 71, 307 under no. 86, pl. 19; Bologna 2015, 250, cat. 83, 251 illus.; Modesti 2018, 88; Bohn 2021, 77–78, fig. 41.

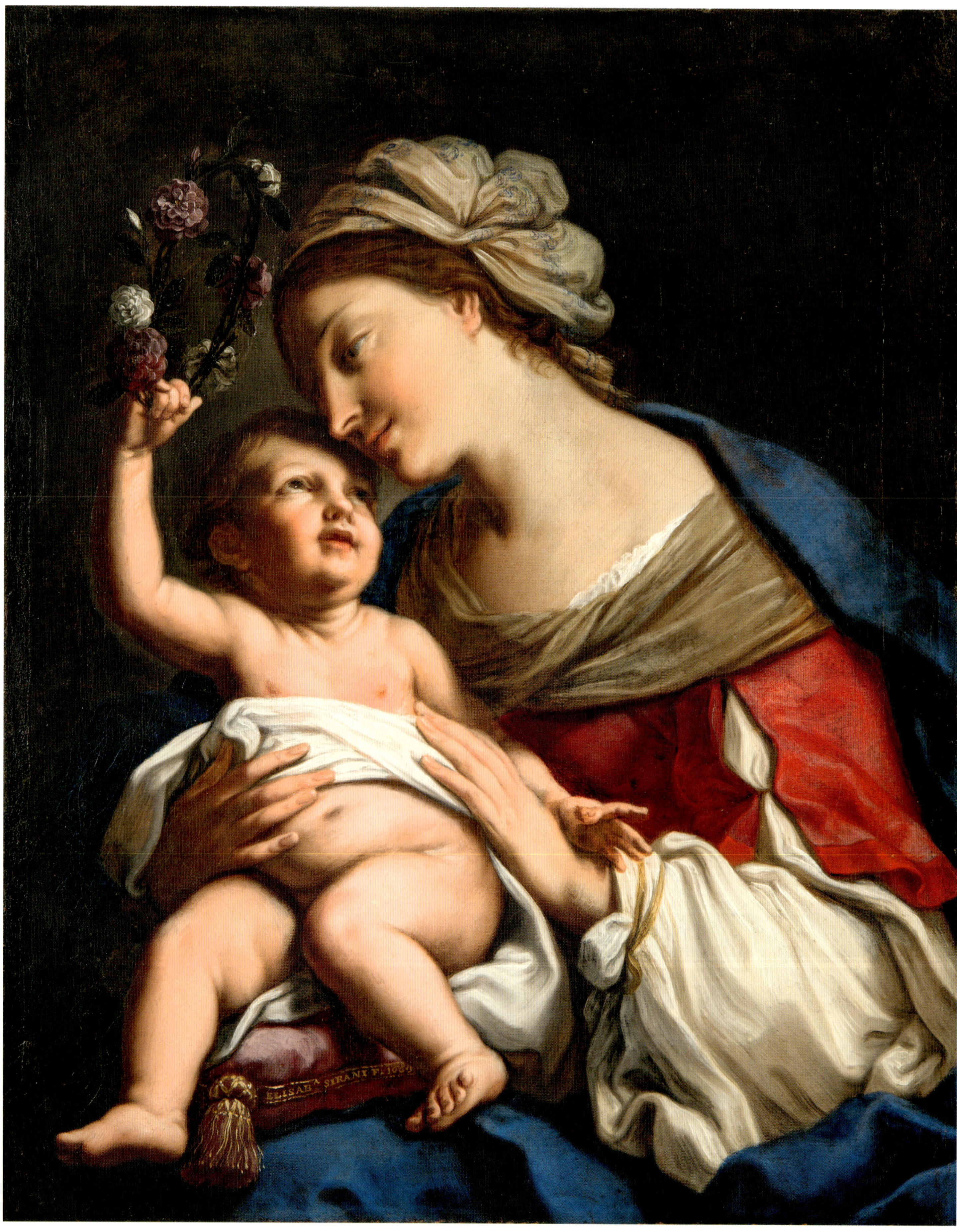
ELISABA SIRANI F. 1660

41

Madonna and Child

1663
Oil on canvas, 34 × 27½ in. (86.4 × 70 cm)
Signed and dated (on the cushion braid): ELISAB.ᴬ SIRANI F. 1663 [Elisabetta Sirani made it 1663]
National Museum of Women in the Arts, Washington, D.C.

THIS MADONNA AND CHILD—of the highest level of painterly facility and imbued with a moving tenderness—was executed by famed painter and printmaker Elisabetta Sirani for a prominent patron. Cleverly signed and dated on the cushion, it is described in the artist's notes, published by scholar and close associate Carlo Cesare Malvasia (1616–1693) in his 1678 biographies of Bolognese artists, as "A Blessed Virgin half figure, with Child, who is in the act of placing a crown of roses on her head, as she sustains him seated on a cushion which she has on her lap, for Don Mario brother of the Pope."[1]

Like every artist in the period, Elisabetta Sirani executed numerous private devotional pictures of the Madonna and Child—the challenge was to infuse this common subject with *invenzione*, or an innovative compositional as well as devotional sway. By some accounts, all households in Bologna possessed at least one image of the Madonna and Child.[2] Given this demand, the quality of such works ranged from the pedestrian to the exemplary, such as this moving, pious picture. Sirani's Madonna and Child pictures can be organized into four types: Madonna Lactans; Madonna of the Swaddling; Madonna of the Veil; and Madonna of the Rose/Rosary, which includes this picture and five additional recorded or extant works.[3]

Equal attention and care are expressed in all aspects of the picture, from the crown of white and pink roses, which evokes Christ's crown of thorns, to the sensual and creamy application of whites in the Madonna's left sleeve and the Christ child's swaddling cloth—a tour de force of virtuosic impasto—to the sense of human connection between mother and child. As her Bolognese biographer Malvasia concludes with the highest praise, Elisabetta Sirani "always had a particular propensity" for Madonnas and "showed divinity in making them, that after those of the great Guido [Reni], they are the most beautiful ever seen."[4]

A preparatory study in red chalk with brownish wash, now in the Walker Gallery, Liverpool, differs in one key respect—the figures' heads are less intimately aligned (fig. 1). The absence of red chalk and brown wash on the faces demonstrates Sirani's "interest in luminescent passages," which plays out in the painted work with an intense light from the upper left illuminating this intimate, maternal moment.[5] With her gentle, downward gaze and the delicate yet reassuring placement of her slender hands around Christ's pleasantly plump midsection, the female figure represents motherly

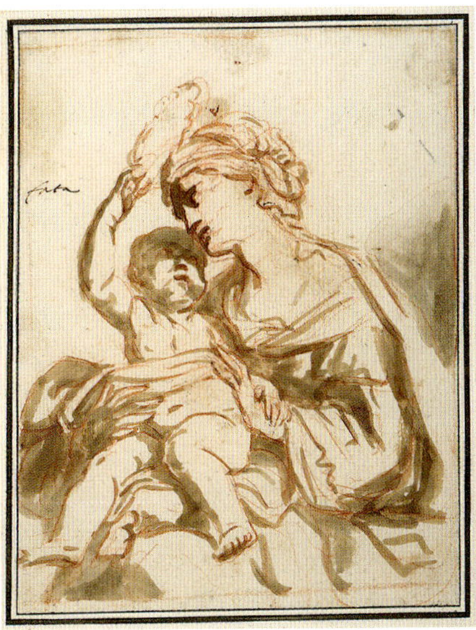

FIGURE 1 Elisabetta Sirani, *Study for the Madonna Crowned by Christ Child with Roses*, 1663, gray-brown wash and red chalk on paper, 8¼ × 6½ in. (21 × 16.2 cm). National Museums Liverpool, Walker Art Gallery, 1995.76

warmth and kindness.[6] With its humble and more relatable Madonna, complete with a turban typical of seventeenth-century Bolognese peasant attire, this is a post-Tridentine Bolognese religious picture par excellence.—ESP

NOTES

1. A *Madonna and Child* from 1665 in a private collection is also signed and dated on the cushion. As Malvasia records: "Una B. Vergine mezza figura, con il Bambino, quale sta in atto di porle una corona di rose in capo, sostenendolo ella a sedere sopra d'un cuscino che ha in grembo, per D. Mario fratello del Papa." For the English translation and original Italian see Modesti 2014, 320. Don Mario Chigi (1594–1669) was the brother of Pope Alexander VII (1599–1667).

2. Modesti 2014, 321.

3. "The artist was famed for her ever-inventive variations on imagery of the Holy Family, especially the Virgin and Child, in which a strong maternal sensibility dominates expressed through intimate and tender exchanges of glances and gestures." Modesti 2014, 5 and 320. The other five Madonna of the Rose/Rosary pictures were painted for: Panina Malvezzi Bentivoglio in 1661; Paolo Poggi in 1663; Carlo Gerini in 1664; Andrea Cattalani in 1664; Cardinal Pietro Vidoni in 1665. Modesti 2014, 320. In her recent book, Babette Bohn identifies this picture as the "Queen of heaven crowned by Christ" type. Bohn 2021, 62.

4. Dabbs 2009, 128–29.

5. Frisoni 2007, 246, cat. 63.

6. This Madonna and Child picture captures the *Mater Amabilis*—the loving and down-to-earth mother. Modesti 2014, 320; Pomeroy 2007, 21.

PROVENANCE

May 16, 1984, sold at (Sotheby's, London, UK); Paolo Brisigotti (London, UK); September 27, 1984, sold by Brisigotti to Wallace and Wilhelmina Holladay; 1986–present, gift to the National Museum of Women in the Arts (Washington, D.C.).

SELECTED EXHIBITIONS

National Museum of Women in the Arts, Washington, D.C., 1998; National Museum of Women in the Arts, Washington, D.C., 2007; National Museum of Women in the Arts, Washington, D.C., 2014–2015.

SELECTED PUBLICATIONS

Vincenzo Maria Marescalchi in Piccinardi 1666, 73–74; "Nota delle pitture fatte da me Elisabetta Sirani" 1841, 398; Rennolds 1987, 19; Frisoni 1992, 347; Brooke 1998, 103–4 under cat. 51; Washington, D.C. 1998, 126, cat. 38, 127 illus.; Heller 2000, 36–37; Modesti 2001a, 174 n. 76; Bartolena 2003, 25; Bohn 2004a, 221, 223, fig. 30; Bohn 2004c, 110, 112, fig. 4; Modesti 2004, 55, fig. 21; Frisoni 2007, 246; Pomeroy 2007, 21; Washington, D.C. 2007, 240 illus., 248, cat. 64, 249 illus.; Holladay 2008, 81–82, 82 illus.; Fortune 2014, 121, 126; Modesti 2014, 320–21, no. 98, fig. 72; Washington, D.C. 2014, 142, cat. 66, 143 illus; Bohn 2021, 62 , 64, 148, 196, fig. 27.

42

Berenice

1664

Oil on canvas, 21⅝ × 17½ in. (55 × 44.5 cm)

Signed and dated (on the trim of both shoulders): ELISABETTA | SIRANI F. 1664

[Elisabetta Sirani made it 1664]

Private collection, Connecticut

IN THIS PAINTING, Elisabetta Sirani depicts a bust-length woman at a three-quarter angle gazing expectantly over her right shoulder and holding a lock of brown hair in her left hand. She is dressed in a chemise with voluminous sleeves that demonstrates the Bolognese artist's tremendous facility in rendering whites. In line with Sirani's prominent placement of her signature on almost seventy percent of her works, "ELISABETTA" and "SIRANI F. 1664" are cleverly embroidered in gold thread on the sleeve's inner edge.[1]

Does this painting represent the biblical heroine Delilah, who drains Samson's strength by cutting his hair, or the Egyptian Queen Berenice II, who vowed to sacrifice her locks if her husband Ptolemy III Euergetes returned safely from battle?[2] When it reappeared in 2011 at auction in Paris, the subject was given as "Queen Berenice II of Egypt."[3] As Elisabetta Sirani describes in her record book of painted works for 1664 a "testa di Dalida" ("head of Delilah") painted for Andrea de' Buoi (dates unknown) to gift to a Florentine cavalier, and no such entry exists for a Berenice,[4] the scholarly literature favors Delilah.[5] As noted by her biographer Carlo Cesare Malvasia (1616–1693), however, Sirani "remained silent about many other pictures in her record book."[6]

It is likely the subject of this picture is Berenice, not Delilah. As noted by several scholars, Sirani was an iconographic innovator, especially in the realm of *femmes fortes*, or strong women, and "some of her subjects seem to have never previously been represented."[7] To my eye, the reddish-brown color and thick, wavy texture of the lock of hair in the figure's left hand matches the color and texture of the sitter's own hair; there is no visual evidence to suggest it comes from another head. In addition, her pose is directly related to that in a painting attributed to Elisabetta Sirani's father, Giovanni Andrea Sirani (1610–1670), the subject of which is identified as "Absalom Weighing Hair with Another Figure" (fig. 1).[8] Massimo Pulini attributes the so-called Absalom picture to both Giovanni Andrea Sirani and Elisabetta Sirani and believes it to represent Berenice.[9] That Berenice is portrayed in the Connecticut painting is further substantiated when one compares it to Rosalba Carriera's (1673–1737) version from the next century, which employs almost identical iconography (cat. 57).—ESP

NOTES

1. Bohn 2004c, 109. More recently, Bohn has identified the subject as Delilah and compares it with an earlier version from 1657 in a private collection. Bohn 2021, 67–70.

2. For Delilah see Judges 16:17–18; for Berenice see Clayman 2014.

3. Sale, Paris, Brissoneau-Daguerre, November 4, 2011, lot 24: Elisabetta Sirani, 1664, *Queen Berenice II of Egypt*.

4. Malvasia 1841, vol. 2, 399. "Una testa di una Dalida per il sig. Andrea de' Buoi, che le donò ad un Cavaliere Fiorentino."

5. Adelina Modesti fully accepts the subject as Delilah. See Modesti 2014, 324, no. 118, fig. 90.

6. For Malvasia's comment see Frisoni 1978, 10.

7. Golahny 2011, 41. "Some of her subjects seem to have never previously been represented, such as *Portia Wounding Her Thigh* and *Berenice Cutting Her Hair*." As Modesti—an expert on Elisabetta Sirani—remarks, "Elisabetta also painted innovative representations of famous women from ancient classical and biblical history, which she depicted as virile, majestic, dignified, intelligent, and courageous, virtues usually associated with men." Modesti 2014, 5.

8. The title in Italian reads: "Absalone che pesa delli cappelli con un'altra figura."

9. Pulini 2020, 54–55.

PROVENANCE

Private collection (France); November 4, 2011, sold at (Brissoneau-Daguerre, Paris, France), lot 24, as by Elisabetta Sirani, depicting Queen Berenice II of Egypt. Private collection (Italy); (Robert Simon Fine Art, New York, New York); private collection (Connecticut).

SELECTED EXHIBITIONS

Fiera dell'Antiquariato, Modena, 2012.

SELECTED PUBLICATIONS

Frisoni 1992, 347 (as *Delilah*, identified with the 1664 painting made for Andrea de' Buoi); Modesti 2014, 223, 342, no. 118, fig. 90 (as *Delilah*, identified with the 1664 painting made for Andrea de' Buoi); Pulini 2020, 54; Bohn 2021, 67, 71, 148, fig. 35 (as *Delilah*).

FIGURE 1 Giovanni Andrea Sirani and/or Elisabetta Sirani, *Absalom Weighing His Hair* or *Berenice*, 1664, oil on canvas, 42¹⁵⁄₁₆ × 59¼ in. (109 × 150.5 cm). Altomani & Sons, Pesaro

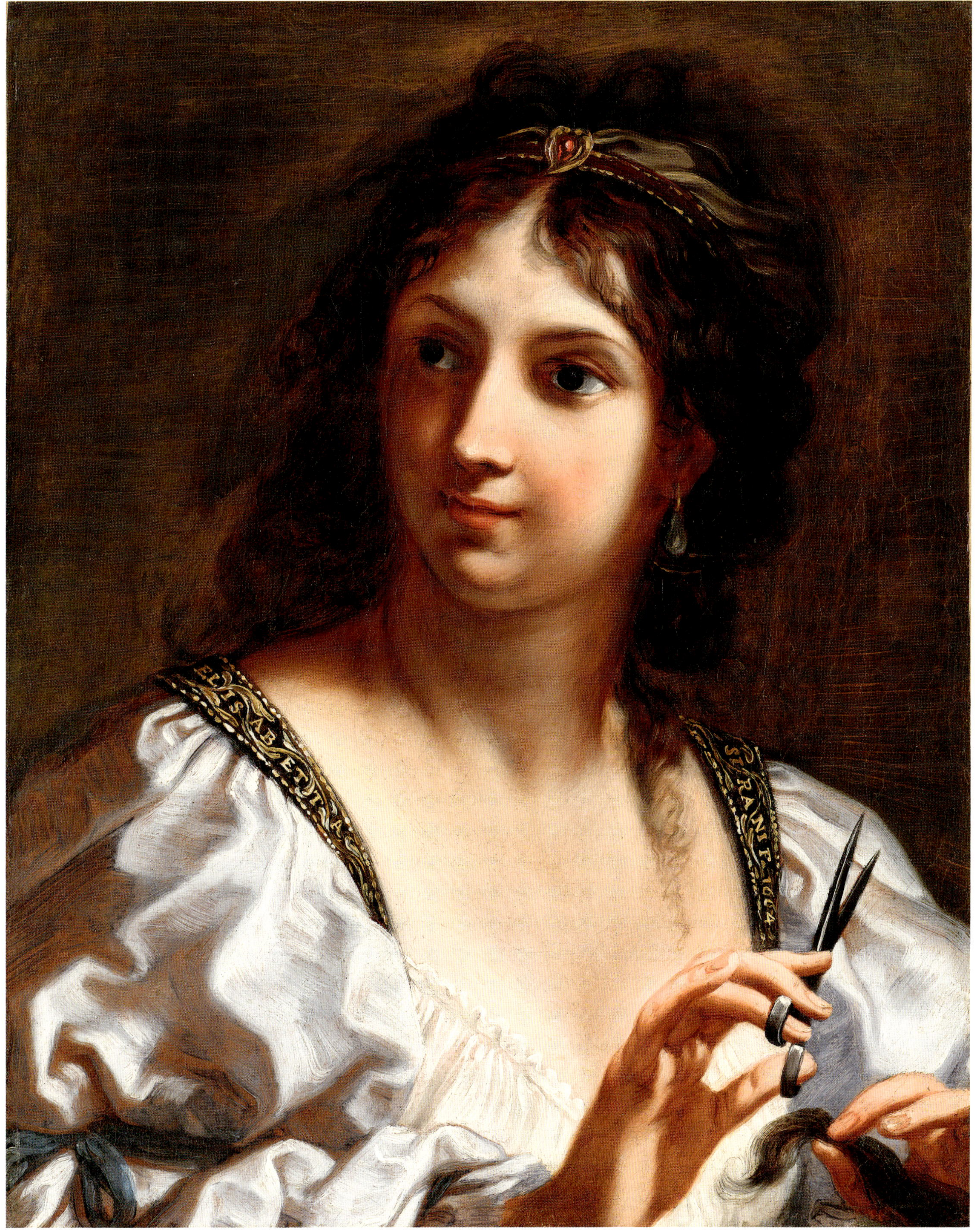

43

Portia Wounding Her Thigh

1664

Oil on canvas, 39¾ × 54¾ in. (101 × 138 cm)

Signed and dated (on the base of the chair back): ELISAB.ᴬ SIRANI F. 1664 [Elisabetta Sirani made it 1664]

Collezioni d'Arte e di Storia della Fondazione della Cassa di Risparmio di Bologna

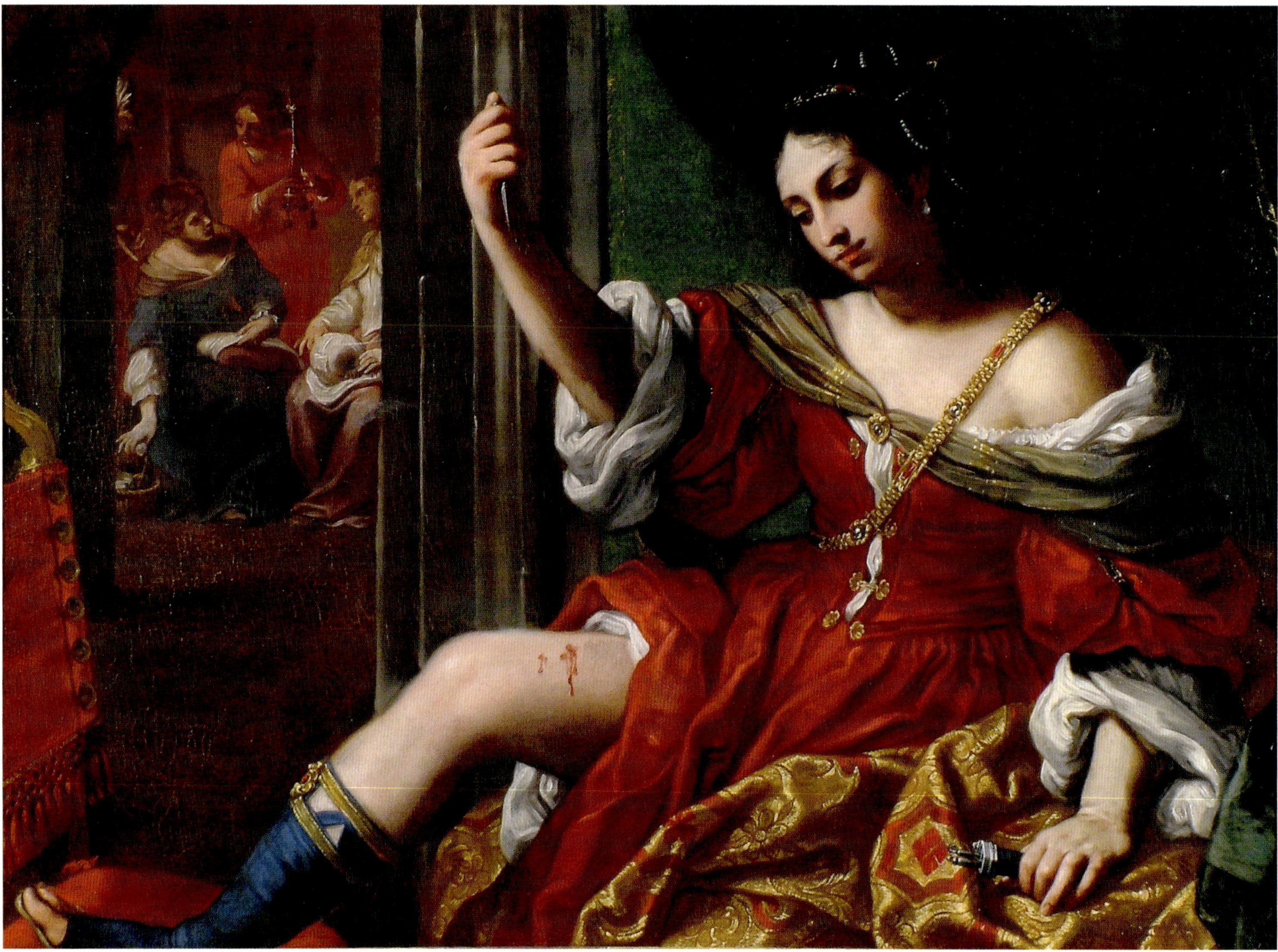

ELISABETTA SIRANI'S novel depiction of the ancient Roman subject of Portia piercing her thigh to prove her bravery to her husband Brutus—the Roman senator who assassinated Julius Caesar—represents the painter's invention and mastery of multifigure narrative pictures.[1] It is described in her compiled *Notes*, published in 1678 by her biographer Carlo Cesare Malvasia (1616–1693), as "Portia in the act of stabbing her thigh, when she wished to know the conspiracy troubling her husband; an overdoor canvas, and in the background in another room young women are working, for Signor Tassi."[2] The painting was made in 1664 for Simone Tassi (died 1675), a wealthy silk merchant in Bologna for whom Sirani had already painted *Saint Anthony of Padua in Adoration of the Christ Child* in 1662 and a *Madonna of the Book* in 1660.[3] According to Malvasia, it was commissioned by Tassi as a companion to a work by Giovanni Andrea Sirani (1610–1670), Elisabetta's father and teacher, depicting another rare and erudite subject, *Absalom Weighing His Hair* (cat. 42, fig. 1).[4] By the time of his death, Tassi had acquired at least four pictures by Elisabetta Sirani, more than any other artist in his posthumous inventory.[5] This picture was second in value to a *Madonna and Child with Saints* by fellow Bolognese artist Ludovico Carracci (1555–1619), attesting to its monetary and artistic worth.[6]

Executed at the highest level of creativity and skill, the painting ranks as one of Elisabetta Sirani's most accomplished and important works. Her patron's trade was the silk industry, and she renders the symphony of red and gold fabrics in exquisite and shimmering detail—particularly the gold and red brocade cloak with voluminous, undulating folds that Portia has cast off to accomplish her bold act. The subject is taken from Plutarch's *Lives*, a copy of which was in Giovanni Andrea Sirani's 1666 household inventory. As told in the Life of Brutus (18–26), Portia

> resolved not to inquire into Brutus's secrets before she had made this trial of herself. She turned all her attendants out of her chamber, and, taking a little knife, such as they use to cut nails with, she gave herself a deep gash in the thigh.[7]

One admires Sirani's close adherence to the textual source: Portia brandishes the small knife, recently removed from an early modern Italian toilet or embroidery set and still dripping with fresh droplets of blood (fig. 1).[8] Sirani adopts the Flemish (Pieter Aertsen, 1508–1575) and later Spanish (Diego Velázquez, 1599–1660) visual conceit of depicting multiple scenes in one picture to powerful narrative effect. The attendants are seen at back left engaging in the domestic duties of yarn winding, sewing, and apparently idle chat, while Portia performs her heroic act in an adjacent room.

Does Sirani eroticize Portia by exposing her thigh for the male gaze?[9] According to Malvasia, she painted outside the confines of her gender by "working in a style that had virility and greatness."[10] Also suggesting the ambiguous gender position of the

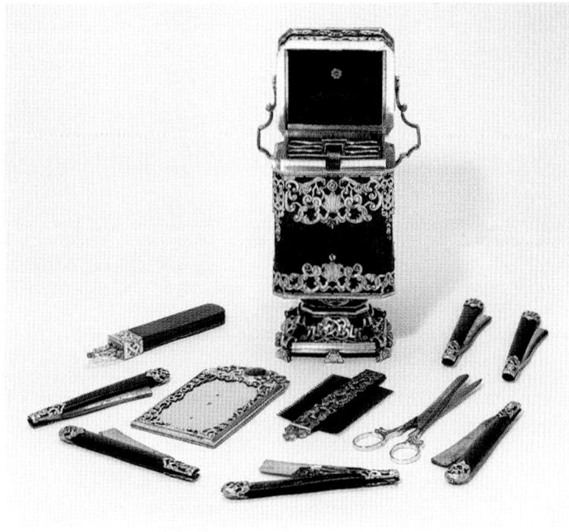

FIGURE 1 Shaving set, early 17th century, silver, tortoiseshell, steel. Victoria and Albert Museum, London, inv. 192:1-1881

protagonist, Portia realizes an act typically associated with male courage.[11] With this picture, Elisabetta Sirani displays a painterly prowess and ingenuity of subject that defies easy gender classification.—ESP

NOTES

1. Portia was typically depicted committing suicide by swallowing hot coals after Brutus's death. See, for instance, Pierre Mignard, *The Suicide of Portia*, Musée des Beaux-Arts de Rennes.

2. Malvasia 1841, vol. 2, 399.

3. Unlike the nobility to whom Lavinia Fontana and Artemisia Gentileschi catered, Simone Tassi was part of the "emerging commercial and merchant middleclass, who became the Sirani's [father and daughter] most committed patrons." Modesti 2014, 16. For Portia and Sirani, see Modesti 2014, 149. Tassi's 1671 inventory lists three additional pictures by Sirani. Morselli and Sones 1998, 420. According to Modesti, Sirani painted four pictures for Tassi: *Portia Wounding her Thigh*, 1664; *Saint Anthony of Padua in Adoration of the Christ Child*, 1662; two untraced *Madonnas*, 1660, 1664. Modesti, 2014, 16.

4. Malvasia 1961, 95. Mis-recorded in the 1671 Tassi inventory as a Semiramis. See Morselli and Sones 1998, 420.

5. For the entire 1671 Tassi inventory, see Morselli and Sones 1998, 420, no. 74.

6. The *Madonna with Saints* by Ludovico Carracci (1555–1619) was valued at 800 lire and the Sirani *Portia* at 500 lire. See Morselli and Sones 1998, 420.

7. Plutarch 2018, 558.

8. For the toilet set, see Phillippy 2006, 54–55. According to Babette Bohn, Portia stabs herself with a stiletto, an embroidery tool: she "uses a woman's instrument to perform a man's task." The tool can be related to the textile business of the work's patron, Simone Tassi. Bohn 2021, 90–92.

9. Bohn points out that Portia and other *femmes fortes* by Sirani were portrayed "not as eroticized subjects presented to the male gaze but as exceptional females who had transcended the conventional limits of their gender in possessing the masculine-identified virtue of fortitude." Bohn 2011, 532.

10. Dabbs 2009, 127.

11. "As the painting woman inscribes her identity on the female body, she undertakes an act of self-authorship that recreates the world in her own image." Phillippy 2006, 60.

PROVENANCE

1664, commissioned by Simone Tassi [d. 1671] (Bologna, Italy), remaining in his collection until 1671; July 1671, collection of Lodovico Foschi (Bologna, Italy); collection of Domenico Maria Riva (Bologna, Italy) (?); 1757, Bonfiglioli collection (Bologna, Italy); Carlo Sestieri (Rome, Italy); 1968, (Wildenstein & Co., New York, New York); Wildenstein Foundation (New York, New York); December 11, 1984, sold at (Christie's, London, UK), lot 80; 1985, (Spencer A. Samuels Gallery, New York, New York); 1988, Herbert F. Johnson Museum of Art, Cornell University (Ithaca, New York) [Stephen Warren Miles and Marilyn Rose Miles Foundation Purchase Fund]; Stephen Warren Miles and Marilyn Rose Miles Foundation (Houston, Texas); January 24, 2008–present, sold at (Sotheby's, New York, New York), lot 44, to the Collezioni d'Arte e di Storia della Fondazione della Cassa di Risparmio di Bologna (Bologna, Italy).

SELECTED EXHIBITIONS

L'Oeil Galerie d'Art, Paris, 1973, no. 19; Los Angeles County Museum of Art, 1976–1977; Herbert F. Johnson Museum of Art, 1990–1996; Museo Civico Archeologico, Bologna, 2004–2005; National Museum of Women in the Arts, Washington, D.C., 2007.

SELECTED PUBLICATIONS

"Nota delle pitture fatte da me Elisabetta Sirani" 1841, 399; Campori 1870, 619; Manaresi 1898, 129; Cantalamessa 1922, 43; della Pergola 1955, vol. 1, 68–69; Malvasia 1961, 95; Los Angeles 1976, 77, 150, cat. 31, 344, pl. 31; Alf 1977, 20; Butterfield 1977, 43; Frisoni 1978, 12–13, fig. 25; Cornell University Department of the History of Art 1983, 85; Mason Rinaldi 1985, 248, illus.; Heller 1987, 33–34, fig. 17; Frisoni 1992, 345, 347, 349, fig. 333; Modesti 1995, 753; Modesti 1997, 1274–75; Morselli and Sones 1998, 417–18, 420, no. 49, fig. 75; Minor 1999, 163–64, fig. 5.4; Modesti 2001b, 401–2; Bohn 2002, 66–70, fig. 3; Modesti 2003, 381 n. 36; Bohn 2004c, 117 n. 44; Bologna 2004, 35–36, fig. 12, 86, 217, cat. 67, illus.; Modesti 2004, 248–56, fig. 142; Phillippy 2006, 26–27, 51–60, figs. 5–6; Milan 2007, 37–38, 37 illus.; Pomeroy 2007, 21; Washington, D.C. 2007, 28, 250, cat. 65, 251 illus.; *Important Old Master Paintings and Sculpture* 2008, no. 44, illus.; Morselli 2010, 161, fig. 50; Bohn 2011, 532; Chadwick 2012, 101–4, fig. 42; Bohn 2013, 120–21, 261, pl. 22; Modesti 2014, 16, 95, 142, 149–55, 160, 169, 193, 337–38, no. 113, 337 illus., 357, pl. 26; Lacas 2015, 188; Rocco 2017, 130, 133; Bohn 2021, 90–92, 138–39, fig. 50.

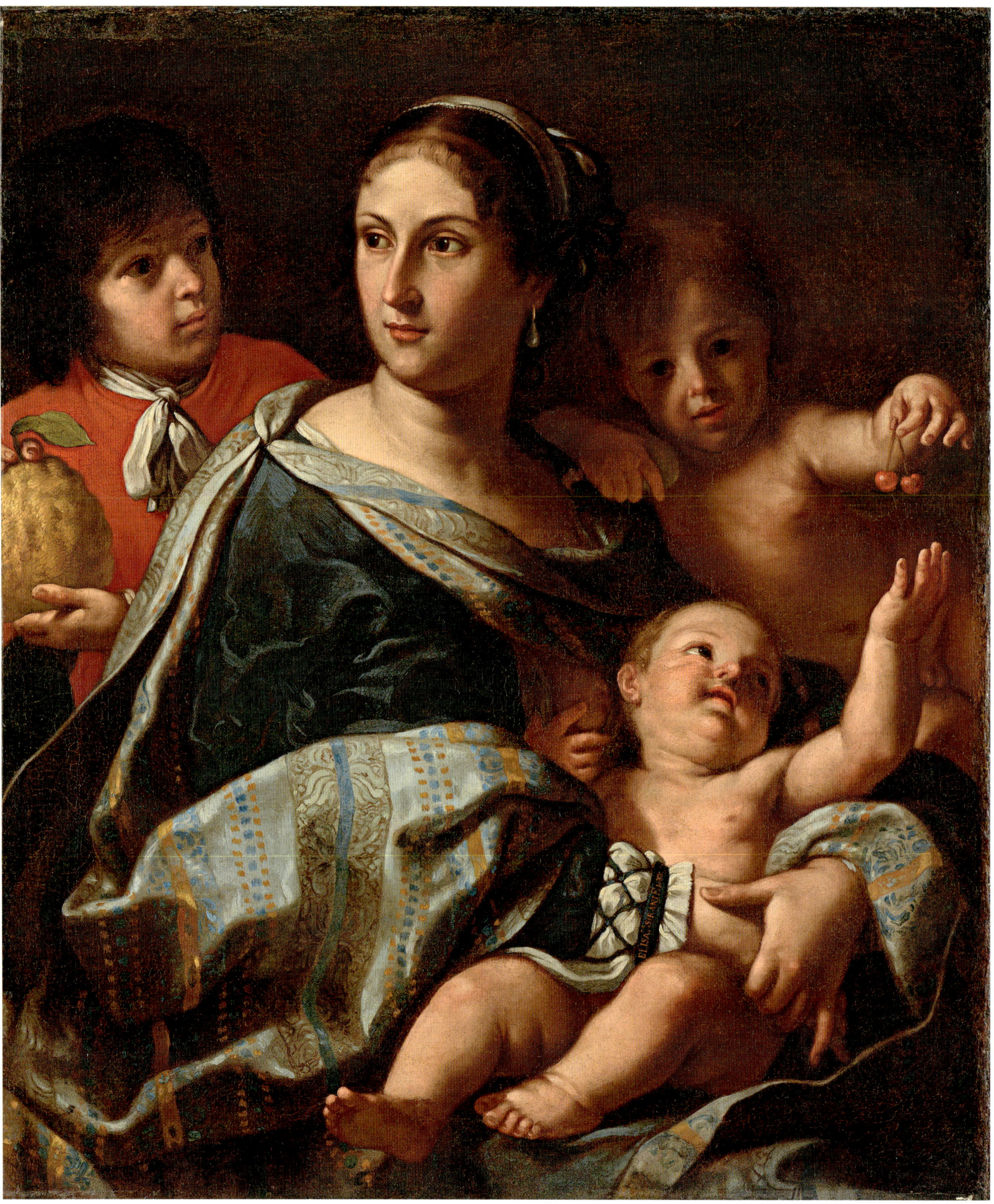

44

Portrait of Anna Maria Ranuzzi as Charity

1665

Oil on canvas, 35⅜ × 30½ in. (90.5 × 77.5 cm)

Signed and dated (on the woman's right sleeve): "ELISA.^{TA} SIRANI. F. 1665." [Elisabetta Sirani made it 1665]

Private collection, Connecticut

ELISABETTA SIRANI specialized in religious pictures, also producing some allegorical, mythological, and historical subjects. In contrast to most women artists in early modern Italy, she painted relatively few portraits—only thirteen are included in a list of her works compiled by Sirani and published by her biographer Carlo Cesare Malvasia (1616–1693) in 1678. Consistent with her interest in historicized iconographies, most of Sirani's portraits employ allegorical, mythological, or religious associations. This work is no exception. It represents the Bolognese noblewoman Anna Maria Ranuzzi (1634–1683) as the allegory of

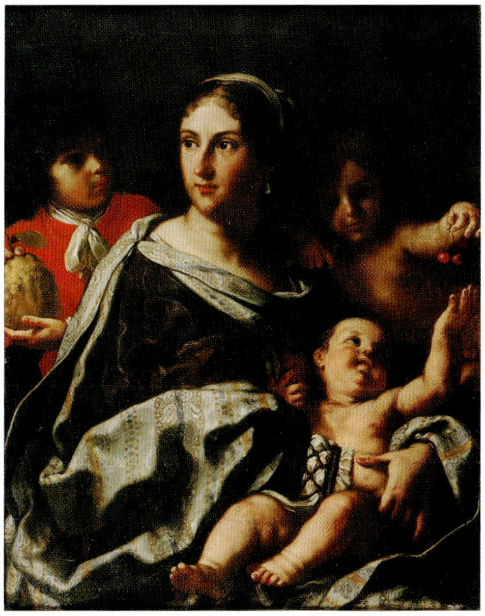

FIGURE 1 Elisabetta Sirani, *Portrait of Anna Maria Ranuzzi as Charity*, signed and dated 1665, oil on canvas, 38 × 30¾ in. (96 × 78 cm). Collezioni d'Arte e di Storia della Fondazione Cassa di Risparmio, Bologna

Charity, posing with two of her children and an allegorical figure holding a piece of fruit. Signed and dated 1665, the year of Sirani's death, the painting is one of two autograph versions of the subject that were probably the artist's last portraits. The other version, now in the art collection of the Cassa di Risparmio, Bologna (fig. 1), is identical to this picture, including even such fine details as the signature in the sleeve. Sirani signed most of her paintings, about seventy percent, and she often positioned her signatures in clothing or other areas that subtly incorporated these inscriptions into the illusionistic fabric of the picture.[1] This is the only known example, however, of a painting by the artist that exists in two autograph versions, both signed and dated in identical fashion.

Sirani's allegorical portrait is one of only ten works listed by the artist during the last year of her life (she died on August 28). She records that the work depicts the beautiful Anna Maria Ranuzzi and her children Silvio and Francesco, noting that the painting was commissioned by the sitter's brother, Count Annibale Ranuzzi (1625–1697), a Bolognese senator and one of the artist's major Bolognese patrons.[2] Perhaps this second version was made for Anna Maria and her husband, Cesare Marsigli (1633–1690). Sirani's description also explains the iconography as the allegory of Charity, traditionally represented in Italian art as a woman with three children. Angela Ghirardi identifies the large piece of fruit as a citrus, which, together with the cherries held by one of the children, symbolizes virtue.[3] Three preparatory drawings for the painting are known, in the Louvre Museum, Paris; the Royal Collection at Windsor Castle; and the Ashmolean Museum, Oxford.[4]—BB

NOTES

1. See Bohn 2004c.

2. Malvasia 1678, vol. 2, 475; Malvasia 1841, vol. 2, 400. The Bologna painting is listed in the 1698 inventory of Ranuzzi's large art collection; see Bohn 2021, app. 3.

3. Ghirardi 2004b.

4. Frisoni 1992, fig. 127; Modesti 2014, 360–61, no. 132; Bohn 2004a, 225–27, figs. 37–38; Bohn 2021, fig. 124.

PROVENANCE

Durst Family (Budapest, Hungary, until 1919, then Vienna, Austria); by descent to Robert and Paula Zalaudek Durst (Vienna, Austria, until 1936, then New York, New York, until 1985); 1985–2016, by descent to her niece, Gertrude Hounsell (New York, New York); April 2016, (Robert Simon, New York, New York); October 2016–present, private collection (Connecticut).

SELECTED PUBLICATIONS

Bohn 2021, 83, 85, fig. 47.

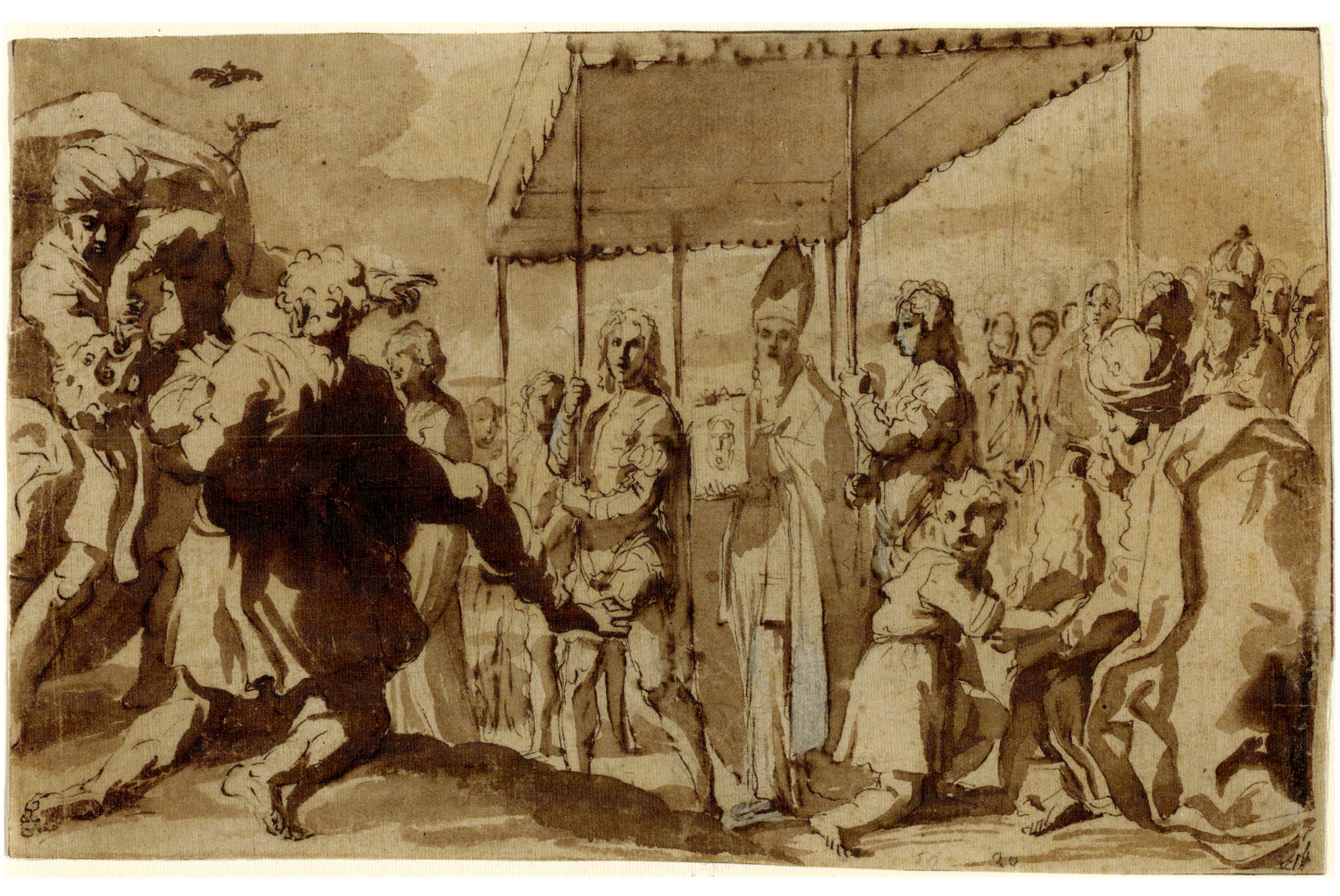

45

The Healing of the Possessed Boy in a Procession of the Volto Santo

1659

Pen and brown ink with brown washes heightened with white over graphite on laid paper, 5⅞ × 9⁷⁄₁₆ in. (14.9 × 23.9 cm)

Inscribed (lower right in graphite, in a later hand): 50 20

National Gallery of Art, Washington, D.C., 1991.102.1, Gift of Sydney J. Freedberg, in Honor of the 50th Anniversary of the National Gallery of Art

ELISABETTA SIRANI was more celebrated for her drawings than any other woman artist in early modern Italy. Indeed, she seems to have been the only woman of the period who was renowned explicitly for her drawings. This fame is reflected in the frequent appearances of her drawings in Bolognese inventories of the seventeenth and eighteenth centuries. Her popularity in these early collections in her native city contributed to the large number of sheets that are still known today: perhaps as many as 150, far more than any of her female contemporaries. Many of these are preparatory studies for her paintings, making her the first woman artist whose preparatory procedures are fully elucidated by extant preliminary studies. Sirani was most famous for her wash drawings, such as this study. In 1678 her first biographer, Carlo Cesare Malvasia (1616–1693), praised Sirani's virtuosity and speed of execution in this medium, observing that he had seen the process firsthand, when the artist "dipped a small brush in ink wash; from this quickly appeared a spirited invention that seemed to be without drawn or shaded strokes, and heightened together all at once."[1]

The Washington drawing exemplifies Sirani's command of this technique. The sheet is one of two known preparatory studies for a painting commissioned by the Genoese preacher Romolo Marchelli (dates unknown) for the choir of San Bartolomeo degli Armeni, Genoa (fig. 1). This church honored the famous relic of the Volto Santo, or Holy Face of Christ, which had been housed in the church since 1384.[2] Sirani depicts this relic miraculously healing a young boy possessed by demons. Whereas the first sheet (École des Beaux-Arts, Paris, inv. no. 2302) is still some distance from the painting and relies largely on pen lines,[3] in this later study, Sirani is closer to her final solution and uses wash more extensively, creating dramatic patterns in chiaroscuro. This technique is particularly striking at the left, where two men and the possessed boy are described vividly, their dynamic shadows setting them off against the background and other figures. This treatment exemplifies the virtuosity with wash for which the artist was justly celebrated.—BB

NOTES

1. Malvasia 1678, vol. 2, 478–79; Malvasia 1841, vol. 2, 402.

2. See further Modesti 2014, 251–53.

3. Loisel 2006.

PROVENANCE

December 7, 1976, sold at (Sotheby Parke-Bernet, London, UK), lot 11; Professor Sydney J. Freedberg [1914–1997] (Washington, D.C.); 1991–present, gift to the National Gallery of Art (Washington, D.C.).

SELECTED EXHBITIONS

National Gallery of Art, Washington, D.C., 1992, no. 21.

SELECTED PUBLICATIONS

Modesti 2004, 185–86, fig. 101; Bohn 2017–2018, 64; Bohn 2021, 188–91, fig. 109.

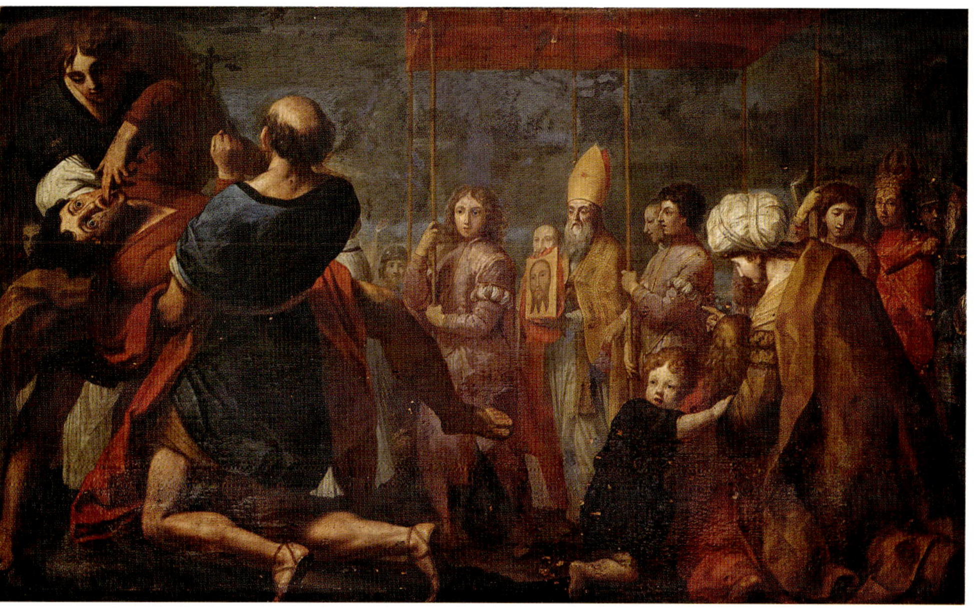

FIGURE 1 Elisabetta Sirani, *The Healing of the Possessed Boy in a Procession of the Volto Santo*, signed and dated 1659, oil on canvas, 98⁷⁄₁₆ × 59⁷⁄₁₆ in. (250 × 150 cm). San Bartolomeo degli Armeni, Genoa

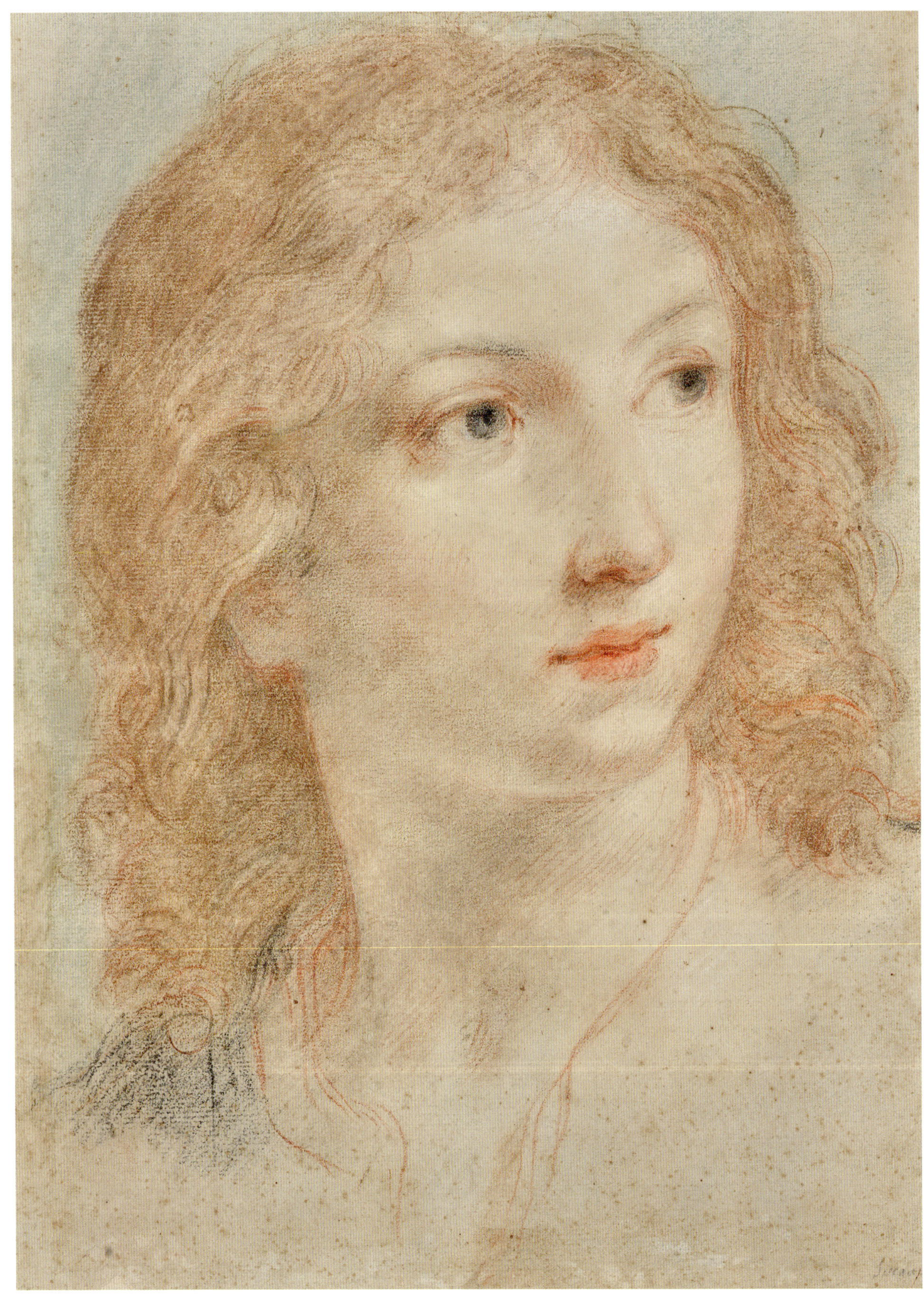

Head of a Youth

1662 or later
Red, black, brown, and blue chalks with white chalk heightening on cream-colored paper, 12⅝ × 9³⁄₁₆ in. (32.07 × 23.34 cm)
Inscribed (in graphite, lower right): Sirani.
Collection of Linda Cheverton Wick and Walter Wick

PRAISED BY CONTEMPORARIES for her skills, Elisabetta Sirani was among the most prolific draftswomen in early modern Italy. Over one hundred of her drawings, executed in a variety of media, have survived.[1] Apart from her paintings, Sirani is probably best known today for her lavish pen and ink drawings with striking chiaroscuro effects, created with her spirited use of brown wash. Lesser known are her chalk drawings. While she usually worked in red and black chalk, she sometimes added more colors, as in *Head of a Youth* exhibited here for the first time. Sirani's authorship of this drawing has not been questioned.[2]

Of uncertain gender, but probably male, the youth has a striking presence thanks to the turned head and the gaze, which is focused outside the picture plane. Sirani's concern for the play of light is evident in the fine modeling of the face and the swirling, soft hair. With light falling from the right, she used darker chalks to give the face its contours. Soft hatchings accentuate a few details, such as parts of the chin or the eye socket, and red, white, and brown chalks heighten the rest of the face. Eventually, she went over some areas, perhaps with a piece of cloth or a finger, to stump the colors and to create subtle gradations of shadows. Quick and loosely applied lines in red and brown give the face its vivacity. She finished the drawing by adding a subtle blue halo. With this intricate technique, Sirani achieved a decidedly painterly effect that has retained an attractive freshness and a subtlety similar to that of pastel.[3] Sirani's practice of using multiple colors is rooted in a Bolognese tradition that reached its apogee with Guido Reni (1575–1642). Such colored drawings were in high demand, especially among local collectors.

The subject and technique of *Head of a Youth* can be compared with two bust-length portraits by Sirani. All three sheets show youthful sitters, each with an affecting expression, emphasized by well-placed thin, sinuous lines in red and brown. In all three works Sirani created expressive heads through a broad rendering of light, amplified by a wide range of colors. Despite important differences, the *Head of a Youth* at the Uffizi Gallery shows a similar understanding of

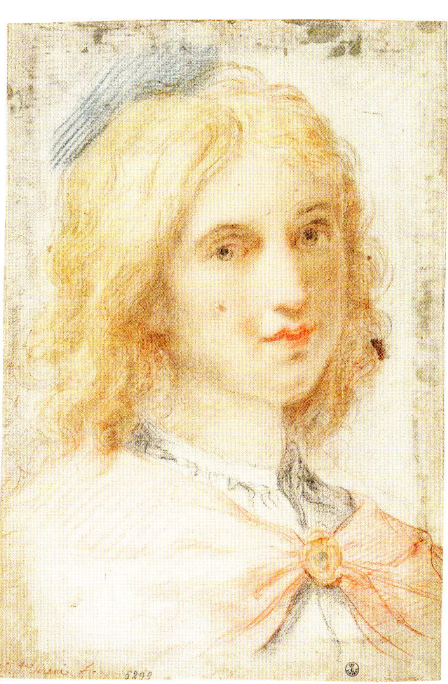

FIGURE 1 Elisabetta Sirani, *Head of a Youth*, undated, black and red chalk, subsequent additions in colored pastels on paper, 15¹³⁄₁₆ × 11 in. (40.2 × 28 cm). Gabinetto dei Disegni e delle Stampe, Gallerie degli Uffizi, Florence, inv. no. 6299F

form and light (fig. 1).[3] While its fuller coloration and vividly drawn blouse and reddish cape suggest retouching by an unknown artist, probably during the eighteenth century, the colors in the Wick *Head of a Youth* seem to be entirely by Sirani's hand. A third head study at the Louvre Museum, Paris, this time of a young woman, also shows ample use of different colors.[4]

Because both the Uffizi and the Wick drawings show idealized youths, they are probably not portraits in the strict sense, but rather idealized heads or *teste ideate*. The Wick head could have been an independent presentation drawing, like the Uffizi sheet, which was given to Cardinal Leopoldo de' Medici (1617–1675) in August 1662 by his Bolognese agent Ferdinando Cospi (1606–1686). Recently, however, Babette Bohn identified the Wick sheet as a preparatory drawing for Sirani's painting *The Redeemer*.[5]—OT

NOTES

1. For Sirani's drawings see Bohn 2004a. Compare with Modesti 2004.

2. The ascription of this drawing to Elisabetta Sirani has been confirmed by Adelina Modesti and Babette Bohn. See Modesti 2014, 121; Bohn 2021, 195.

3. Both Adelina Modesti (Modesti 2014, 379) and Babette Bohn (Bohn 2021, 195) identify this drawing as a pastel.

4. On the drawing see Faietti 2004, 200–201. See also Da Rin Bettina 2018.

4. Elisabetta Sirani, *Head of a Woman*, undated, brown, red, yellow, and blue pastels, 13¹¹⁄₁₆ × 11 in. (34.7 × 28 cm), Musée du Louvre, Cabinet des dessins, Paris, inv. 8967, recto. This drawing has been ascribed to Sirani by Adelina Modesti and Catherine Loisel. See Loisel 2013, 516, no. 947.

5. Bohn 2021, 195. Bohn does not provide further information about the painting.

PROVENANCE

Private collection (New York, New York); 2009–present, sold by (Mia N. Weiner, Norfolk, Connecticut) to current private collection as Elisabetta Sirani.

SELECTED PUBLICATIONS

Modesti 2014, 121, 379, fig. 117; Jeffares 2020a, 1, no. J.68.102; Bohn 2021, 195–96, fig. 117.

Allegory of Justice, Charity, and Prudence

ca. 1664

Brush and brown wash, over traces of red chalk, 5⁵⁄₁₆ × 7³⁄₈ in. (13.5 × 18.7 cm)

RISD Museum, Providence, Esther Mauran Acquisitions Fund, 2018.101

Hartford only

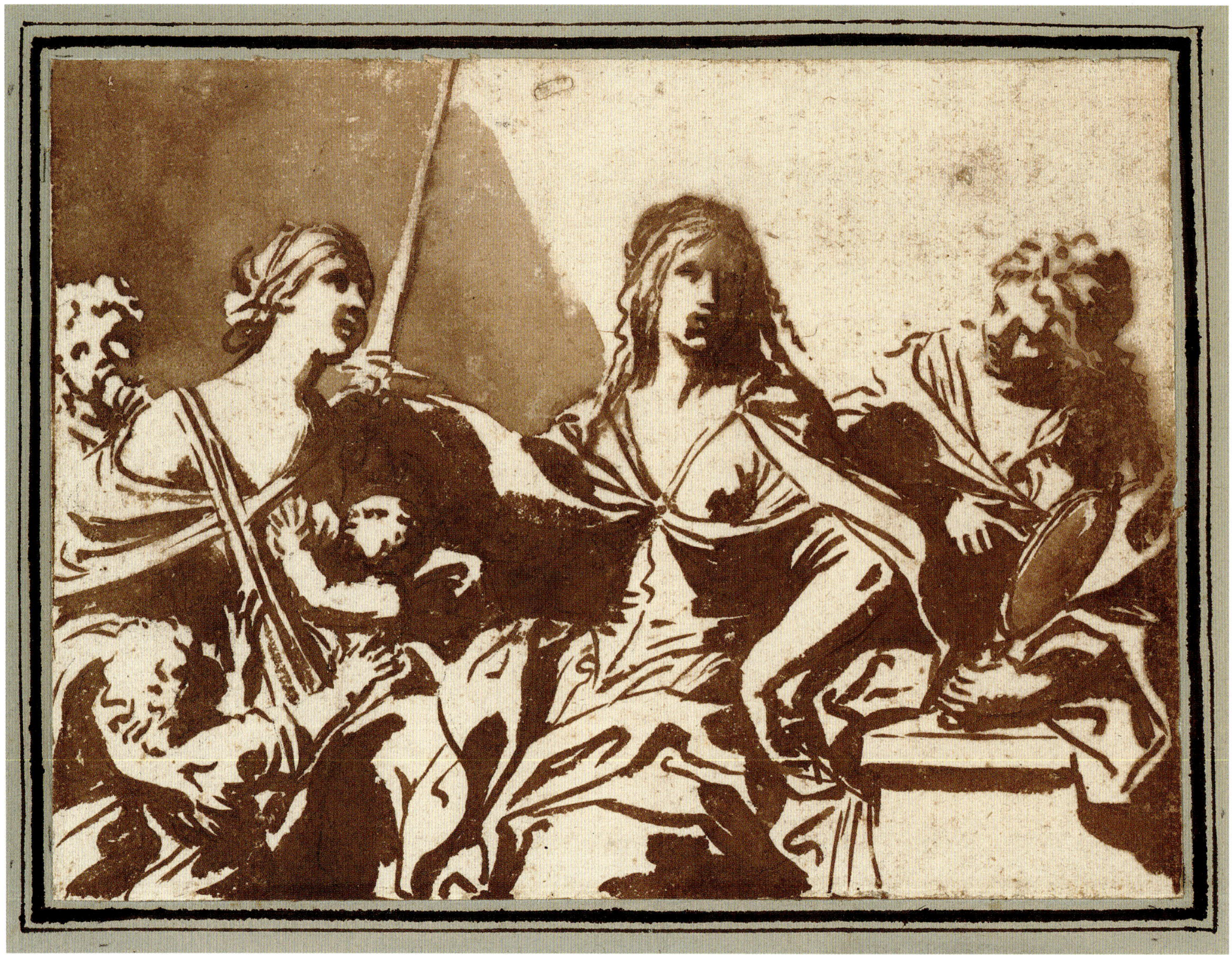

EXECUTED ALMOST ENTIRELY with ink wash over the faintest traces of chalk, this drawing of the personifications of the virtues associated with the Medici household is a splendid example of Elisabetta Sirani's idiosyncratic draftsmanship. Boldly doing away with line work altogether, Sirani depicts a complex, harmoniously balanced composition in considerable detail by deftly employing a brush, judiciously contrasting the fluid brown ink against the white reserve of the paper. In spite of its economy of means and its relatively small scale, the drawing is powerful and lively, strongly conveying a convincing sense of volume, texture, and the dramatic play of light on the figures.

This sheet is an advanced compositional study for one of Elisabetta Sirani's most prestigious commissions (fig. 1).[1] In late 1663 the renowned collector Prince Leopoldo de' Medici (1617–1675) asked Sirani through

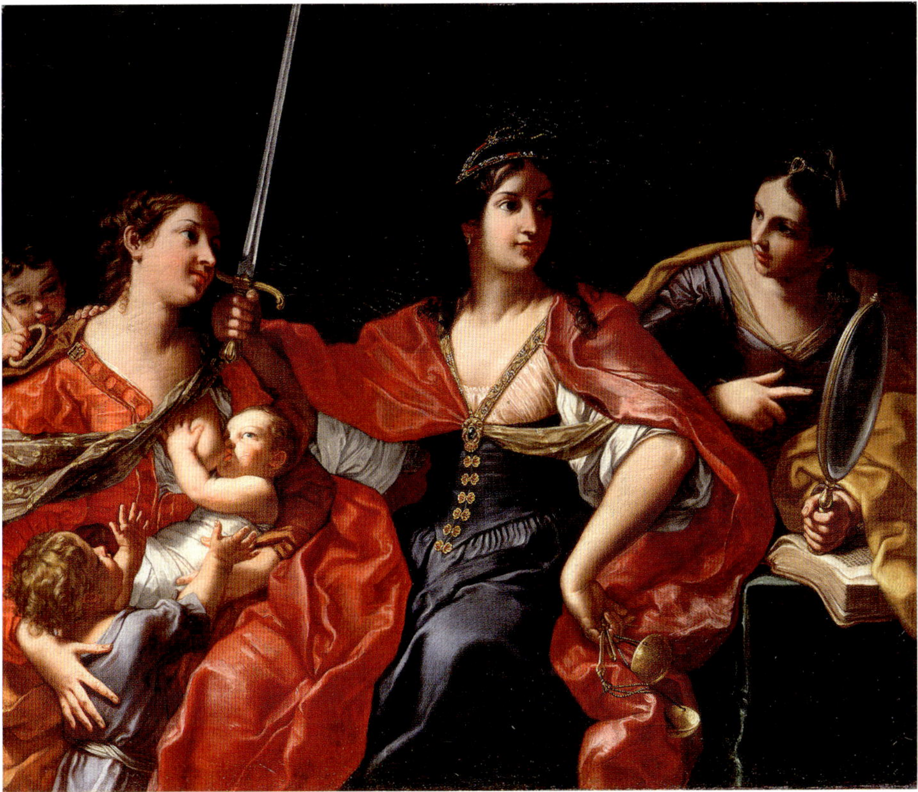

FIGURE 1 Elisabetta Sirani, *Allegory of Justice, Charity, and Prudence*, 1664, oil on canvas, 54¾ × 64¹⁵⁄₁₆ in. (139 × 165 cm). Comune di Vignola (Modena)

paint."[5] Leopoldo must have been satisfied, since, according to Sirani's entry, he regaled her with a cross adorned with fifty-six diamonds. Elisabetta Sirani was dubbed "the best brush" in Bologna and widely admired by her contemporaries, but her remarkable career was cut short by her premature death at the age of twenty-seven.—JG

NOTES

1. Bohn 2004a, 222.
2. Modesti 2014, 334.
3. Modesti 2014, 335.
4. Malvasia 1841, vol. 2, 399.
5. Modesti 2014, 335.

PROVENANCE

Leopoldo de' Medici [1617–1675] (?); before 1985, Giuseppe Giusti; January 16, 1985, sold at (Sotheby's, New York, New York), lot 257; private collection (New York, New York); 2018–present, RISD Museum (Providence, Rhode Island).

SELECTED PUBLICATIONS

Modesti 2003, 371, fig. XXVIII-2; Bohn 2004a, 222, 226, fig. 35; Bologna 2004, 232 under cat. 85; Modesti 2004, 118, fig. 56; Modesti 2014, 334–36, 382, fig. 125; Bohn 2021, 196, 200, fig. 123.

his Bolognese intermediaries to paint an allegory of Medici rule, giving visual form to its principal virtues.[2] In early January 1664, Ferdinando Cospi (1606–1686), Leopoldo's agent in Bologna, informed him that Sirani was busy "making sketches for the painting," and a few days later her patron Annibale Ranuzzi (1625–1697) sent a compositional sketch to Leopoldo in Florence for approval.[3] While an individual study in the same technique for the figure of Charity at left is in the National Gallery of Canada, Ottawa (fig. 2), the Providence sheet is the only known full compositional study for the *Allegory*. It seems probable, therefore, given that the painting follows it very closely, that the present drawing was indeed the one that Ranuzzi sent to Leopoldo.

In the records she kept of her work, Sirani noted with pride that in May 1664 Prince Cosimo de' Medici (the future Grand Duke Cosimo III) (1642–1723) visited her studio and saw her working on the canvas commissioned by his uncle.[4] By September of that year the painting was completed,

and Ranuzzi suggested to Leopoldo that Sirani would gladly receive something that would make her look "more magnificent in front of the noblewomen who go watch her

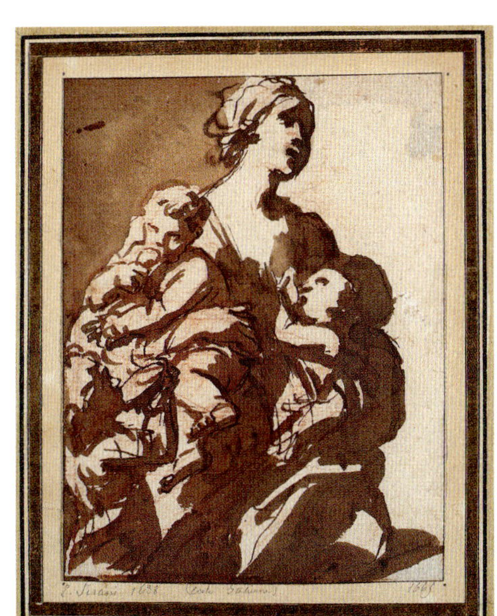

FIGURE 2 Elisabetta Sirani, *Charity*, ca. 1664, pen and brown wash over red chalk, 4⅜ × 3⁷⁄₁₆ in. (11.1 × 8.7 cm). The National Gallery of Canada, Ottawa, inv. no. 6856

48

The Holy Family with Saint Elizabeth and the Young Saint John the Baptist, second state

ca. 1661
Etching on laid paper
Plate: 11⁹⁄₁₆ × 8⅝ in. (29.4 × 21.9 cm), sheet: 12³⁄₁₆ × 9¼ in. (31 × 23.5 cm)
Inscribed (lower right, printed within the image): Siranus Inv. [Sirani invented it]; (lower left in graphite): 7586.
National Gallery of Art, Washington, D.C., Print Purchase Fund (Rosenwald Collection), 1968.5.1

ELISABETTA SIRANI was one of the first Italian women recorded as a *peintre-graveur* (painter-printmaker), and she is probably the earliest whose prints are still extant. Although she was not a prolific printmaker, all ten of the etchings she created are still known. Whereas some portray designs that she also painted, and one reproduces the work of another artist, a few seem to represent independent designs that were never intended to be painted. *The Holy Family with Saint Elizabeth and the Young Saint John the Baptist* is an example of this third type. Sirani's father and teacher, Giovanni Andrea Sirani (1610–1670), was also a painter-printmaker who produced etchings, and the young Elisabetta probably learned the technique from him. Her earliest etchings date to 1657, when she was only twenty years old. The present work, however, seems more sophisticated than the artist's initial forays into etching and probably dates a few years later. The print contains strong contrasts, ranging from areas of bright illumination conveyed by the white of the paper to deep shadows, an effect achieved by staged biting to expand the tonal range of the image.[1] Such contrasts add to the drama of the scene and enhance the sense of both depth and volume. Adam von Bartsch first distinguished between two different states of this print.[2] This fine, second-state impression includes the inscription with Sirani's name.

The subject is a common one in Elisabetta Sirani's oeuvre throughout her career: the Holy Family, represented here in an interior setting with their cousins Saint Elizabeth and her young son, Saint John the Baptist. While the Virgin Mary nurses her son, observed by the young John, who reaches out to receive a cherry from the Virgin, Elizabeth winds up swaddling cloths and Joseph applies himself to his carpenter's trade in the background. All of Sirani's etchings, including this one, depict religious subjects, and all were probably intended for private devotion. Most of her paintings were also religious, and she was especially well known for her painted depictions of the Virgin and Child.—BB

NOTES

1. As was first observed in Wallace 1989, cat. 64, where the print was dated somewhat earlier than I have suggested here.

2. Bartsch 1802–1821, vol. 19, 156, no. 8.

PROVENANCE

1967, (C.G. Boerner, Düsseldorf, Germany), cat. 46, no. 189; (Robert M. Light, Santa Barbara, California); 1967, purchased by Lessing J. Rosenwald [1891–1979]; 1968–present, gift to the National Gallery of Art (Washington, D.C.).

SELECTED EXHIBITIONS

Museum of Fine Arts, Boston, 1989.

SELECTED PUBLICATIONS

Bartsch 1802–1821, vol. 19, 156, no. 8; Bellini 1976, 11, no. 8; Wallace 1989, 131, cat. 64, 132 illus.; Bohn 2021, 206–7, fig. 132.

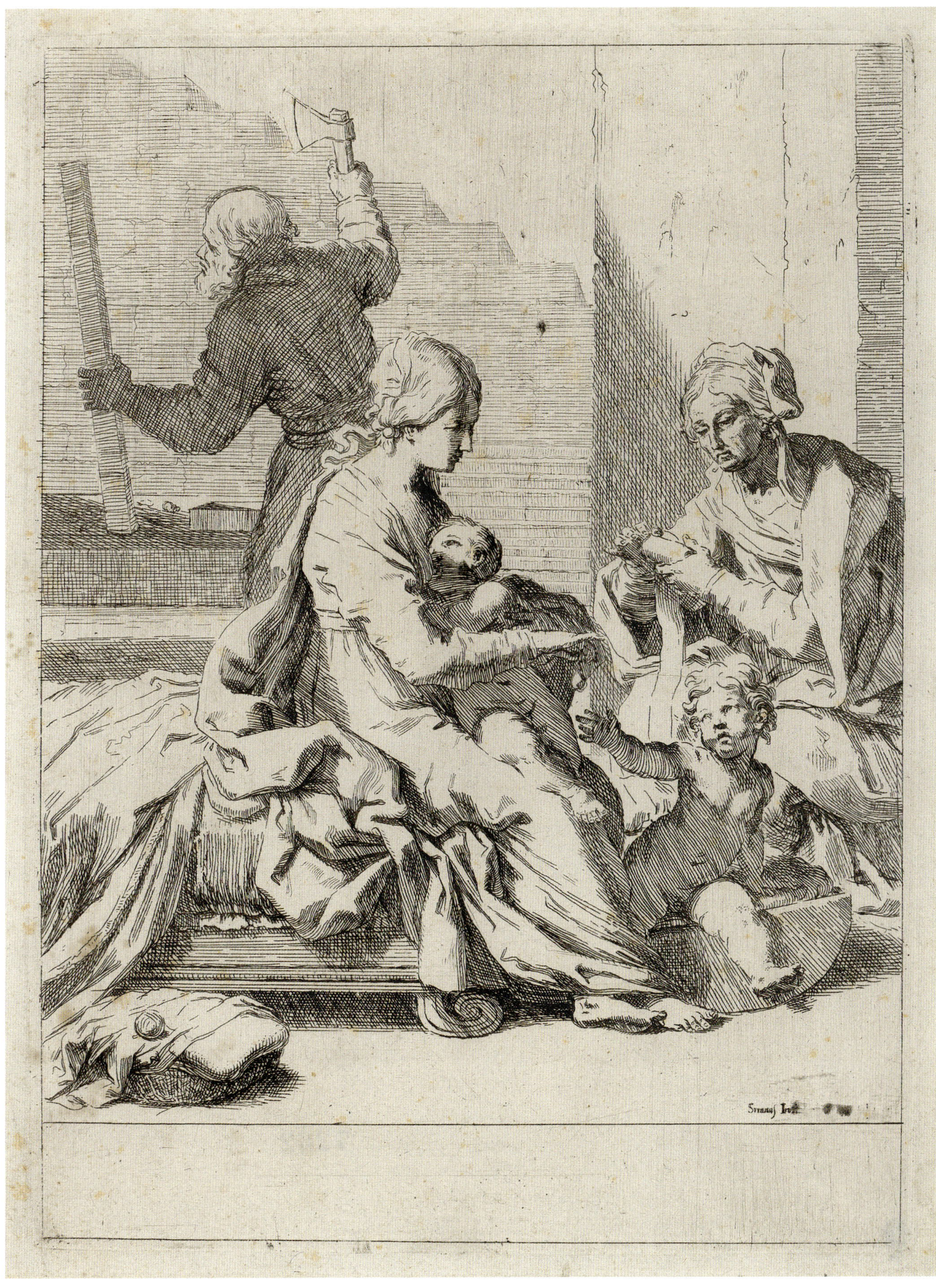

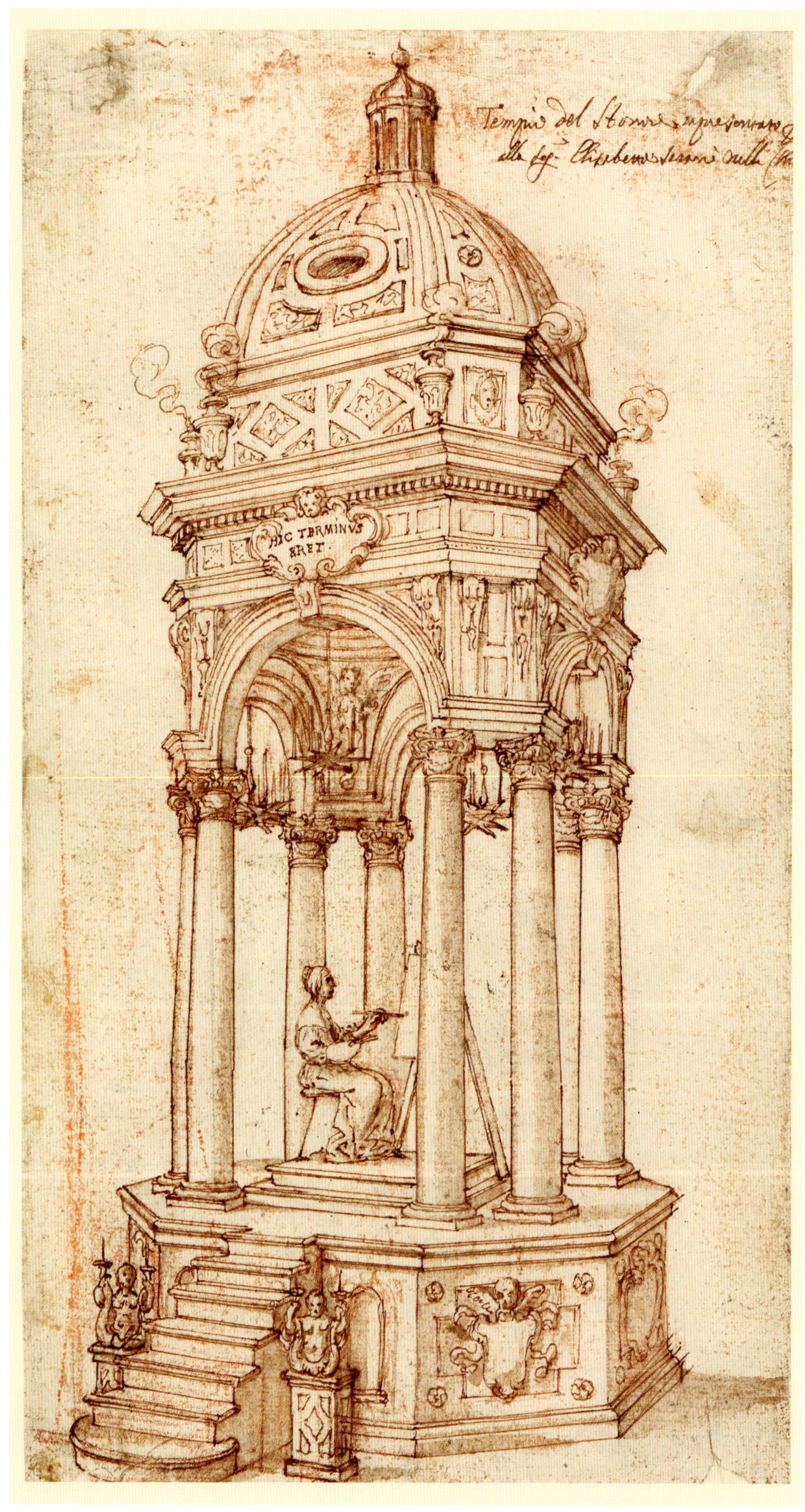

49

Catafalque of the Bolognese Artist Elisabetta Sirani (1638–1665)

Matteo Borboni (Bologna, ca. 1610–ca. 1678)

1665

Pen and brown ink, brush and brown wash, and red chalk on off-white laid paper, 11¾ × 6⁷⁄₁₆ in. (29.9 × 16.3 cm)

Inscribed in pen and brown ink (in an escutcheon over the front): HIC TERMINUS/ ERET [This is the end]; in pen and brown ink (upper right): Tempio del Honore rapresentato p[er] alla Sig. Elisabetta Sirani nella Chie[sa] [Temple of Honor created for Elisabetta Sirani in the Church]

Cooper Hewitt, Smithsonian Design Museum, New York, 1938-88-2503

ON NOVEMBER 14, 1665, a towering catafalque almost thirteen-feet high, painted to resemble marble and mounted by eight columns of pseudo-porphyry, was displayed in the Basilica of San Domenico in Bologna at the funeral of the renowned Bolognese painter and printmaker Elisabetta Sirani (1638–1665), who died at age twenty-seven from peritonitis due to a ruptured peptic ulcer.[1] So beloved was the artist that on August 29, 1665, one of her most devoted patrons, Marchese Ferdinando Cospi (1606–1686), wrote to Cardinal Leopoldo de' Medici (1617–1675): "The painter Sirani is dead, the entire City [of Bologna] being bereft of a *Virtuosa*."[2] The ephemeral monument was designed by the painter Matteo Borboni to honor Sirani's short and prolific career. Borboni's "machine of excellent architecture" was accompanied by a moving sung liturgy by Maurizio Cazzati (1616–1678) and a rousing funeral oration by Giovanni Luigi Piccinardi (active 1660s and early 1670s). The Temple of Honor (*Tempio del Honore*) was the most ambitious part of his decorative funeral ensemble. We know from Piccinardi's oration that inside this *tempietto* of fictitious marble, adorned with trophies and cartouches, was a statue "from life [*al naturale*] of the so-called Signora Sirani majestically seated in the middle . . . in the act of painting."[3]

The catafalque was one of the most popular ephemeral creations in the seventeenth century. We are left to piece together the original appearance of these temporary commemorative monuments from drawings, prints, and written descriptions. Immortalizing the "heroine painter" ("*pittrice eroina*") Elisabetta Sirani at her easel, this refined and virtuosic pen and brown ink drawing would appear to be preparatory for a rare engraving, designed by Borboni and incised by Lorenzo Tinti (1626–1672), that commemorated Sirani's catafalque (fig. 1).[4] The drawing and print are similar in almost every detail, including the pair of sirens—a play on the artist's surname—flanking the steps, the smoke emanating from the urns adorning the cupola, and the star-shaped candelabra hanging from the dome. However, the print bears the inscription "VELOX NON TARDA" ["Fast not Late"] in the cartouche on the pedestal, left blank in this drawing.[5] The drawing carries the inscription: HIC TERMINUS [HA]ERET ["This is the End"], which was uttered by Dido upon her death in Virgil's *The Aeneid*—a fitting tribute to the passing of one of early modern Bologna's leading painters.[6] —ESP

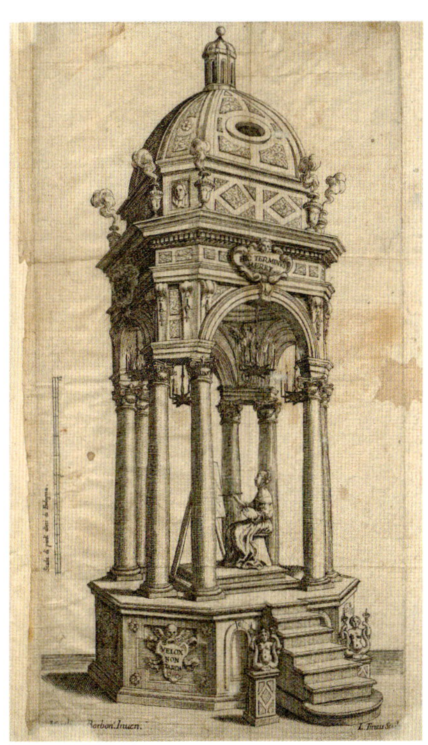

FIGURE 1 Designed by Matteo Borboni; incised by Lorenzo Tinti (1626–1672), *Tempietto per il funerale di Elisabetta Sirani*, undated, engraving, 13 × 6⅞ in. (33 × 17.4 cm). Biblioteca Comunale dell'Archiginnasio, Bologna, ms. Gozzadini 270

NOTES

1. Modesti 2014, 1. The myth of her death due to poisoning persisted for many years.

2. For this letter see Modesti 2001b, 402.

3. Piccinardi 1665, 393.

4. Malvasia 1841, vol. 2, 386. In 1678 a woodcut was published as an engraving, either by one of the two illustrators in Malvasia's service or by Giovan Francesco Cassioni (1636–after 1706), or, more probably, by Veronica Fontana (1651–1690), one of Elisabetta Sirani's own pupils. Ghirardi 2004a, 169, cat. 6. The other drawing in the Cooper Hewitt's collection appears to have been made earlier and is possibly preparatory for the construction of this architectural structure: Matteo Borboni, *Catafalque of the Bolognese Artist Elisabetta Sirani*, pen and brown ink, brush and brown wash over graphite on off-white laid paper, Cooper Hewitt, Smithsonian Design Museum, New York, 1901-39-2493.

5. This phrase may be borrowed from Murcia de la Llana 1619, 70. Was this a volume in Sirani's extensive library?

6. On the drawing the inscription is truncated to "HIC TERMINUS ERET," while on the print it reads correctly: "HIC TERMINUS HAERET." *The Aeneid of Virgil* 1900, 300.

PROVENANCE

1938–present, purchased by the Cooper Hewitt, Smithsonian Design Museum (New York, New York).

SELECTED EXHIBITIONS

Cooper Union Museum for the Arts of Decoration, New York, 1962.

SELECTED PUBLICATIONS

Cooper Union Museum Chronicle 1962, 16, cat. 35; *Summary Catalogue of Drawings* 1964, 2; Morselli and Sones 1998, 115 n. 2; Modesti 2004, 347 n. 12; Modesti 2014, 201–3, 202 n. 20; Siemon 2018.

GINEVRA CANTOFOLI

Bologna, 1618–1672

GINEVRA CANTOFOLI, born to Ottavia Buldrini and Francesco Cantofoli, came from a wealthy but not artistic family. In 1653 she married Francesco Facchini (dates unknown) and had two children. In 1656 she met the renowned artist Elisabetta Sirani (1638–1665) and became her student, but she had almost certainly begun painting earlier in her life. A 1668 household inventory, penned after the death of her husband, lists fifty-one artworks by Cantofoli, including portraits and allegorical, mythological, and religious paintings, some on crystal. Best known as Sirani's pupil, the contours of Cantofoli's life and work have only come into sharper focus in the last fifteen years, with a now sizable corpus of paintings that continues to grow.

50

Cleopatra

1650s/1660s

Oil on canvas, 29¾ × 23½ in. (75.6 × 59.7 cm)

Private collection, Connecticut

AS THE BEST-KNOWN PUPIL of the Bolognese painter and printmaker Elisabetta Sirani, Ginevra Cantofoli has slowly been gaining recognition since the publication of Massimo Pulini's 2006 monograph.[1] Although she is mentioned in passing in Carlo Cesare Malvasia's (1616–1693) life of Sirani from 1678, it is only in the last fifteen years that a compelling and persuasive group of works can be ascribed to her hand, among which this delicate and richly colored Cleopatra most certainly numbers.[2]

Malvasia writes "Ginevra Cantofoli, who first, it is true, painted, but who then supported and assisted by Sirani, made great progress, at least, in going from small scale works to works on a larger scale."[3] Cantofoli was, in other words, already a practicing artist before meeting Sirani. It was, however, under Sirani's tutelage, according to Malvasia, that she was able to advance from executing small cabinet pictures—such as this *Cleopatra*—to altarpieces. His assessment is borne out by the score of small format pictures attributed to Cantofoli, as well as by her six recorded altarpieces, of which only two can be located today: *Saint Thomas of Villanova*, 1658, in San Giacomo, Bologna, and the *Immaculate Virgin with the Child*, now in the Franciscan Institute of the Immaculate Conception, Bologna.[4]

Ginevra Cantofoli's oeuvre is characterized by female figures presented in allegorical or mythological guises with a trademark physiognomy that includes long, aquiline noses; relatively close-set, ovoid eyes; and pallid complexions. The first picture to be firmly attributed to her is the *Allegory of Painting* from the 1660s (Pinacoteca di Brera, Milan), followed by her painting (often attributed to Guido Reni (1575–1642) of Beatrice Cenci (1577–1599), notorious for patricide, in the 1650s (Palazzo Barberini, Rome) (fig. 1).[5] The distinctive features of these two figures coalesce in the depiction of Cleopatra.

The Egyptian queen has just removed an earring and is about to drop "the pearl in the vinegar," to melt into a poisonous concoction.[6] Depicted at half-length and at a three-quarter angle, Cleopatra wears a mauve silk dress with a richly brocaded neckline that displays her décolletage as she gingerly places the earring in a gold chalice. An embroidered gold cape; her auburn hair, braided and interwoven into her crown and elaborate headdress; and her beguiling yet languid gaze, all speak to the artist's interest in creating an exotic and intoxicating effect—transporting the viewer far from the

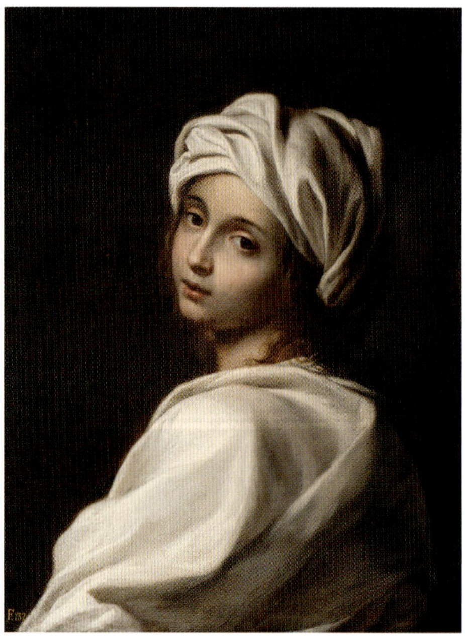

FIGURE 1 Guido Reni (here attributed to Ginevra Cantofoli), *Beatrice Cenci*, 1630s, oil on canvas, 25⅜ × 19⁵⁄₁₆ in. (64.5 × 49 cm). Palazzo Barberini, Rome, inv. 1944

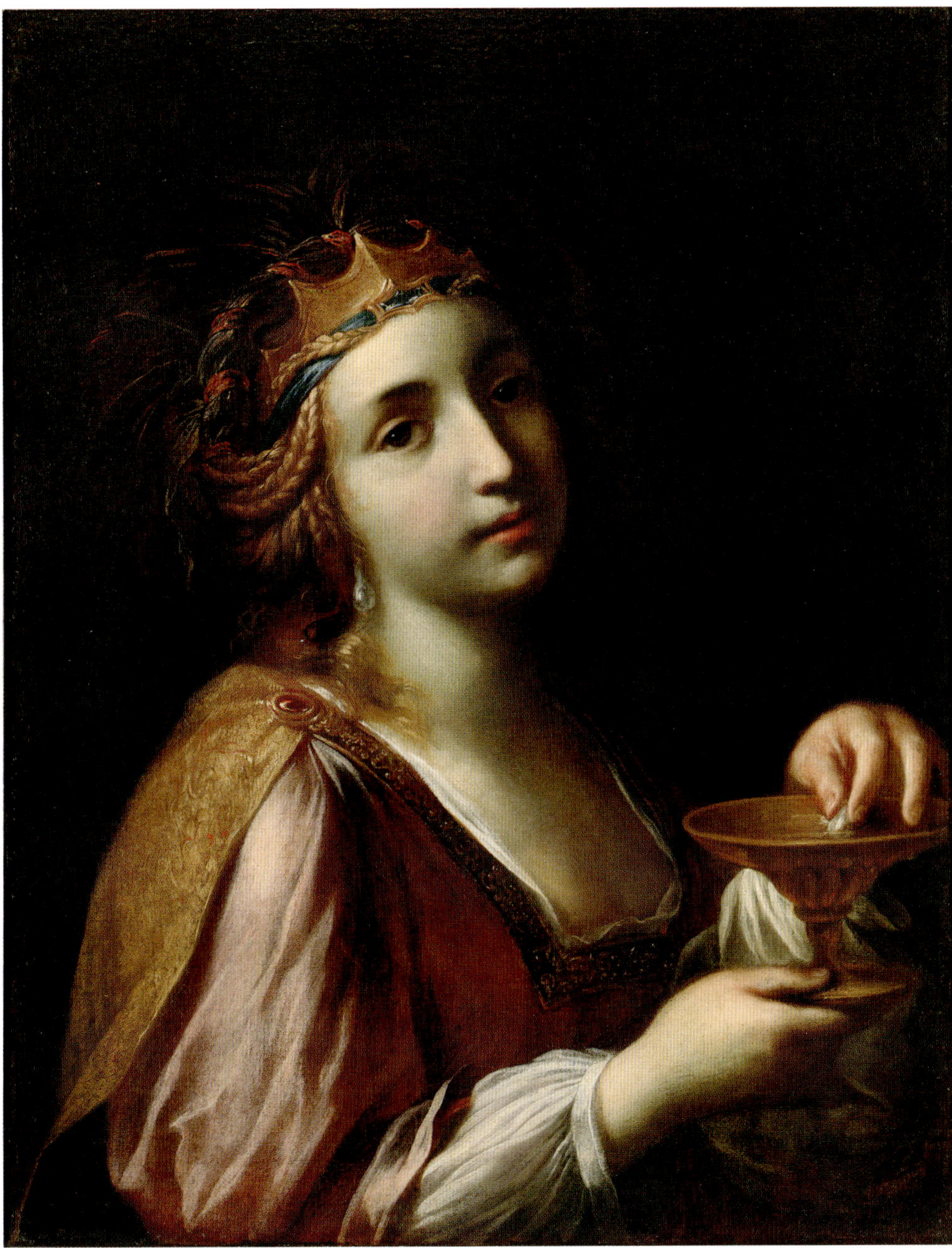

passare da picciolo quadretti ad opre grandiose . . ." Malvasia 1841, vol. 2, 407 (translation mine).

4. For *Saint Thomas of Villanova*: "1659 adì 5 genaro—Il sabato dopo nel pomeriggio si chiusero tutte le botteghe della città. Mons. Ill.mo Arcivescovo Boncompagni benedì l'imagine di S. Tomaso di Villanova dipinta dalla sig.ra Ginevra Cantofoli, posta alla destra dell'altar maggiore della metropolitana di San Pietro con musiche, e dapoi processionalmente fu portato alla nostra chiesa." These words of Marcello Oretti (1714–1787), the eighteenth-century Bolognese writer on art, were reported in Astengo 1923, 59. *The Immaculate Virgin with the Child* was first attributed to Ginevra Cantofoli by Massimo Pulini in Pulini 2004, 138–39.

5. Pulini 2004, 141 n. 3.

6. Pliny the Elder 2004, Book IX, part 121.

7. Pulini 2006, 139. For this inventory see ASB (Archivio di Stato Bologna) Notarile, Lorenzo Pellegrini, 26 gennaio, prot. 8, f. 99.

8. Bohn 2002, 77.

PROVENANCE

July 16, 1992, sold at (Sotheby's, New York, New York), lot 190, as attributed to Lorenzo Pasinelli; 1992–2014, David Abbate (New York, New York, and Jersey City, New Jersey); (Robert Simon Fine Art, New York, New York); private collection (Connecticut).

banality of Bologna to the time of Anthony and Cleopatra.

In 1668, following the death of her son and husband, Ginevra Cantofoli bequeathed to her daughter Orsola Caterina (dates unknown) fifty-one paintings, largely by her hand, that included a Cleopatra—perhaps this very picture.[7] Unlike the Cleopatras of Lavinia Fontana (1552–1614) and Elisabetta Sirani, who are depicted as "unemotional, heroic figures without erotic overtones,"[8] Cantofoli relishes the seductive aspects of the subject. Also, in keeping with period representations by early modern Italian artists, Cleopatra is represented as white, with no indication of her African origins.—ESP

NOTES

1. In fact, one of the first works that Sirani notes in her record book of her art is a "Portrait of the Signora Ginevra Cantofoli, Painter," which has yet to materialize. See Malvasia 1841, vol. 2, 393; Pulini 2006.

2. Another Cleopatra attributed to Ginevra Cantofoli is housed in the Museo Civico, Padua. See Pulini 2006, 76–77.

3. "Ginevra Cantofoli, che prima, è vero, pingeva, ma che poi dalla Sirani sostenuta ed aiutata, avea fatto maggior progresso, se non altro, in arricharsi a

CATERINA DE JULIANIS

Naples (?), ca. 1670–ca. 1742

CATERINA DE JULIANIS was a Neapolitan artist known, according to early sources, as a sculptor, particularly of wax, as well as a landscape and figure painter. She likely became a master of modeling wax under the tutelage of Gaetano Giulio Zumbo (1656–1701), a Sicilian sculptor. De Julianis created macabre scenes with wax as her primary medium and other elements in paper, paint, feathers, and glass. In addition to these morbid scenes, she fabricated a large number of religious subjects in wax and mixed media, and according to a contemporary source, she was esteemed in the region for her modeling. The majority of her works remain in Italy.

51

Penitent Magdalene

1717

Beeswax, pigments, paint, paper, glass, vellum, silk, feathers, wire, burlap, and varnish, unframed: 10⁹⁄₁₆ × 10⅝ in. (26.9 × 27 cm); framed: 23⁵⁄₁₆ × 20¹⁵⁄₁₆ × 4½ in. (59.2 × 53.2 × 11.5 cm)

Signed and dated (on banderole, lower left): Caterina de Julianis F. 1717 [Caterina de Julianis made it 1717]

Detroit Institute of Arts, Museum Purchase, Robert H. Tannahill Foundation Fund, 2019.44

Detroit only

CATERINA DE JULIANIS is known today primarily as a sculptor, particularly of wax.[1] A strand of literature posits that she was a nun, but I can find no primary evidence to support this assertion. Even though her teacher Gaetano Giulio Zumbo made both anatomical models and religious subjects in wax, Caterina de Julianis appears to have made only religious models, and possibly portraits.[2] The great majority of her extant works can be found in religious institutions in Naples.[3]

This multimedia diorama depicts the repentant Mary Magdalene on bended knee with her right hand at her heart and her left stretched towards a white unguent jar. Her head is tilted towards the heavens and Christ is on the cross behind her. At center are the book and skull typically used by the saint for her meditations. Having retreated from human society to repent, she finds respite in nature and the animal kingdom. Caterina de Julianis has rendered the flora and fauna surrounding the Magdalene in astounding variety and detail, fabricating the ducks with real feathers, modeling the snail in pigmented beeswax, and using mirrors to mimic water, reflect light, establish depth, and delight the eye.[4] There is a variant of this work in the Cavallini Sgarbi Collection (fig. 1). The iconography departs from standard Italian depictions of the subject, which often show the Magdalene half naked. Perhaps this is because the original setting for the work was a religious institution, but it is also possible that the artist could not abide this more common representation. Most likely, given Spanish control of Naples around this period, the iconography responds to the conservative, religious interpretation of the subject favored by Spanish patrons. The curious addition of a metal chain around the Magdalene's right arm might symbolize that she—or humanity more generally—is chained to base or earthly desires.[5]

The longest and most valuable early modern account of Caterina de Julianis is found in Bernardo De Dominici's (1683–ca. 1759) 1743 biographies of Neapolitan painters, sculptors, and architects, which devotes a passage in the life of the male painter Francesco Solimena (1657–1747) to praise the artist's multimedia creations and paintings of both secular and religious subjects.[6] Although modern scholarship on the artist is also scant, the literature on early

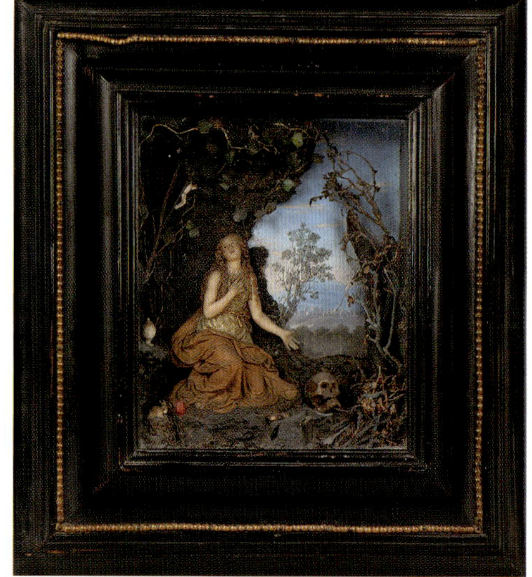

FIGURE 1 Caterina de Julianis, *Saint Mary Magdalene (possibly Mary of Egypt)*, 1717, polychrome wax, painted paper, glass, tempera on paper, and other materials, 15¾ × 14⁹⁄₁₆ in. (40 × 37 cm). Cavallini Sgarbi collection

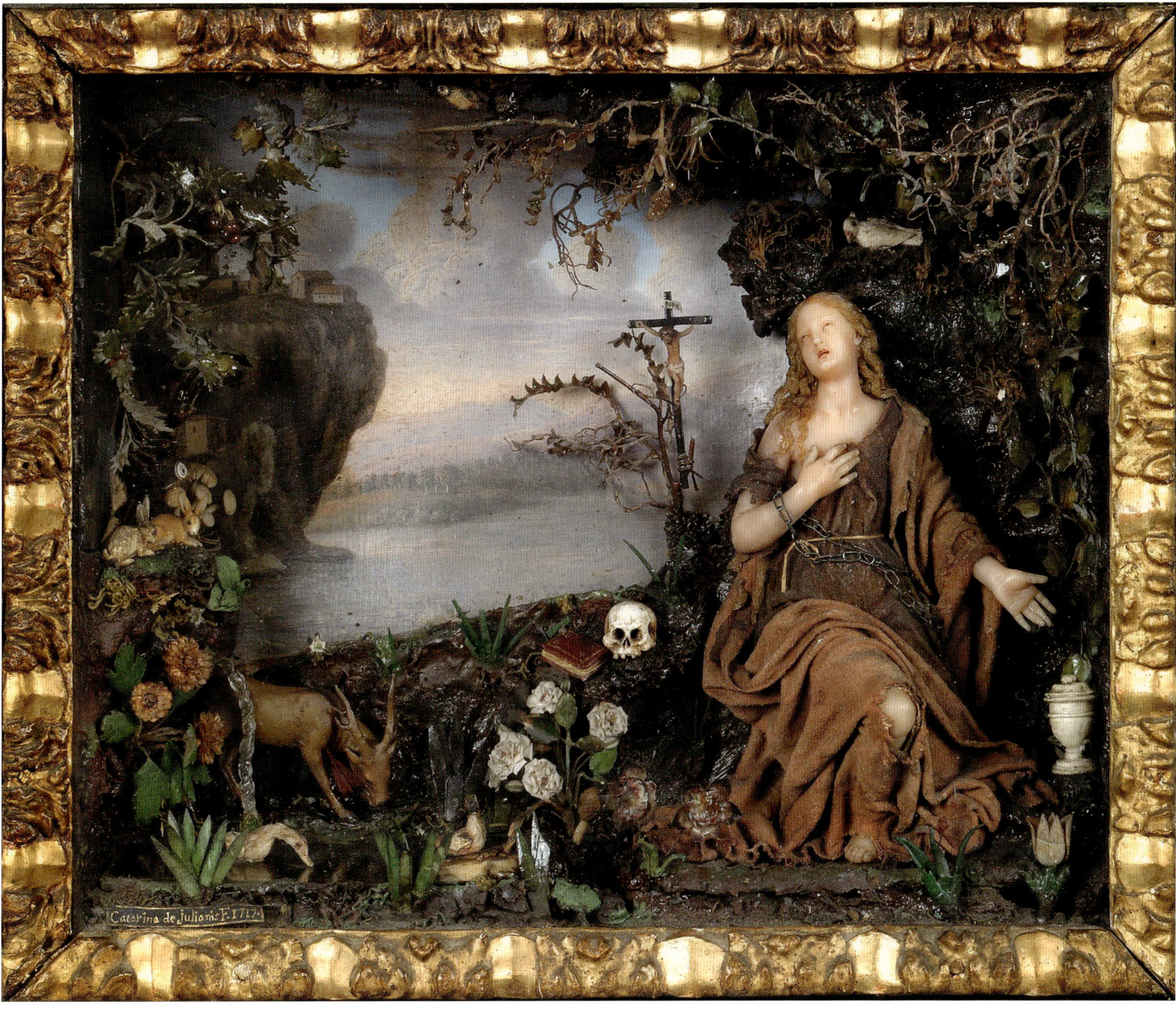

modern wax sculpture, particularly the role of women artists working in this medium, is a burgeoning field of intellectual inquiry.[7] Although wax modeling was practiced by women and men in the 1600s and 1700s, it took on decidedly feminine connotations in the period, when, as scholar Marjan Sterckx writes, it "provided an appropriately feminine means through which women could enter the masculine world of sculpture."[8] In his 1901 *Little Memoirs of the Eighteenth Century*, George Paxton wrote: "To model well in clay is considered as strong minded and anti-feminine, but to model badly in wax or bread is quite a feminine occupation."[9] The gendered associations of working in certain media still haunt the field.—ESP

NOTES

1. Pyke 1973, 149.

2. Francesco de Ceglia has written three important articles on Italian wax modelers: de Ceglia 2006; de Ceglia 2011; de Ceglia 2014.

3. Beyond Italy, the Victoria and Albert Museum in London houses *Time and Death*, before 1727, and the Harvard Art Museums hold *Saint Jerome in the Desert*, no date. There has only been one work attributed to the artist on the recent market: *Portrait of Carlo Spinello (1579–1614)*, ca. 1700, which sold for €3,750 ($4264.27 on June 25, 2019) as lot 52 on April 17, 2019, at Sotheby's Paris.

4. Elizabeth Homberger, objects conservator at the Detroit Institute of Arts, wrote that *The Penitent Magdalene* by Caterina de Julianis is in "fair condition considering the fragility of the materials and the age of the work," in the conservation report, located in the Objects Conservation Lab at the Detroit Institute of Arts.

5. A version of *The Penitent Magdalene* by Caterina de Julianis in the collection of art historian Vittorio Sgarbi is vertical in format and does not have nearly the expanse of flora and fauna as the present work.

6. Of the approximately 200 artists whose lives Bernardo De Dominici describes, only three are

exclusively devoted to women artists: Mariangela Criscuolo (ca. 1548–1630), Luisa Capomazza (ca. 1600–1646), and Diana de' Rosa (1602–1643). For a discussion of Bernardo De Dominici and women artists, see Dabbs 2009, 220–25. De Dominici says: "In this region [Naples], Caterina de Julianis was very esteemed for her ability to model. [She was] famous and also appreciated by foreigners for her very beautiful and naturalistic flowers made of silk, which also had the odors specific to their type. But, the aspect most rare, for which she was praised by [Francesco] Solimena, was her ability to model divinely several small babies in wax with such a beautiful conception of likeness, and perfection of all parts that it is impossible to surpass them in this material, just like it would seem impossible to equal her cemetery scenes, representing cadavers, and exhumed bones, one of which you can find in the Sacristy of S. Severo de' PP. Predicatori, in which she has represented most vividly cadavers that are rotting, those that are already without flesh, and exhumed/excavated skulls, of which there is a marvelous one situated farther ahead, that certainly admiring this cemetery arouses horror and fear in those regarding it. One sees in the same Sacristy five other works by this virtuous woman. They are: a full Madonna with the Christ Child in her arms, in the act of saying grace and her devotions; another half-length Madonna similarly with the Christ Child in her arms sleeping, which is very beautiful, presented at an earlier age than the aforementioned. A half-figure of an Ecce Homo excellently designed, and with a visage truly of a Savior very gentle and expressive in his passion. A figure of Saint Rose of Lima with Baby Jesus, who has picked a lily from the garden, where they are seen, and presents it to her. The companion to this nice small, modeled sculpture is a Saint Dominic, who disputes with the Heretics in favor of our Saint Fede, who throws her book into the fire—it emerges from the same flame lifted up unscathed towards Heaven. In the house of the Valletta family, one finds by this famous woman several paintings with small figures, and little landscapes; for many rare virtues she is highly esteemed by every class of people, and from Solimena she was given a picture with the Blessed Virgin and Child, a very beautiful work of his hands. Therefore done with all his genius as a subject of so much virtue, and which adorns our Fatherland, all that presently has long since been rendered almost incapacitated to form her marvelous works, on account of a continuous indisposition, caused, I believe, by the weight of the years." De Dominici 1743, vol. 3, 621–22 (translation mine).

7. In Italy two centers were famous for wax modelers—Bologna, with the anatomical modelers Ercole Lelli (1702–1766), Giovanni Manzolini (1700–1755), and Anna Morandi Manzolini (1714–1774), and Naples and its environs, with Gaetano Giulio Zumbo, Caterina de Julianis, and the virtually unknown Anna Fortino (1673–1749) from Palermo. For an overview of Bolognese and Neapolitan wax modelers see Dacome 2017, 216–53.

8. Sterckx continues, "Approximately 80 percent of sculptresses active after 1660 and born before 1700 worked in wax, a total that is almost exactly equivalent to the number of all recorded sculptresses working before 1660." Sterckx 2007, 86–102.

9. Sterckx 2007, 94.

PROVENANCE

Private collection (Rome, Italy); by October 27, 2018, (Galleria Carlo Virgilio & Co., Rome, Italy); by March 2018, (Jaime Eguiguren Arts & Antiques, Buenos Aires, Argentina); 2019–present, purchased by the Detroit Institute of Arts (Detroit, Michigan).

SELECTED EXHIBITIONS

Palais de Tokyo, Paris, 2017–2018; TEFAF, New York, 2018, with Galleria Carlo Virgilio & Co.

SELECTED PUBLICATIONS

Che 2017; Étienne 2017; Nechvatal 2017; Paris 2017, 17, 22 illus.; Phasis 2017; Étienne 2018, 128–29, fig. 3; Kinsella and Neuendorf 2018; New York 2018, 42–44, cat. 4, 43 illus., 45 illus.; Ruotolo 2018, 2–6, fig. 2; Grifol 2019.

ROSALBA CARRIERA

Venice, 1673–1757

ROSALBA CARRIERA—often referenced in her time solely as Rosalba—began her career painting miniature portraits on small oval pieces of ivory, which could be fitted inside snuffbox lids. She turned her hand to pastel portraits in the first decade of the eighteenth century. In 1720 she visited Paris, where she executed portraits of royalty, including the young Louis XV (1710–1774). Her later years were spent fulfilling commissions for distinguished collectors such as Augustus II the Strong, king of Poland (1670–1733), who devoted a whole room to her pastels in his Dresden palace. Carriera also taught a group of women artists, including Marianna Carlevarijs (1703–after 1750), Margherita Terzi (active ca. 1756), and Felicità Sartori (ca. 1714–1760). Her Venetian studio, located along the Grand Canal, attracted patrons and tourists from across Europe.

52

The Muse Calliope (A Sibyl?)

Early to mid-1720s
Pastel on paper, laid down on canvas, 24⁷⁄₁₆ × 20¹⁄₁₆ in. (62 × 51 cm)
Private collection, Connecticut
Hartford only

53

Allegory of Faith (A Sibyl?)

Early to mid-1720s
Pastel on paper, laid down on canvas, 24⁷⁄₁₆ × 20¹⁄₁₆ in. (62 × 51 cm)
Private collection, Connecticut
Hartford only

ROSALBA CARRIERA was not only one of the first Italian artists to work consistently in pastel, but also the most famous and commercially most successful. Hailed by her contemporaries as "la prima pittrice de l'Europa" (the "first woman painter of Europe"), she quickly became a celebrity.[1] While artists during the sixteenth and seventeenth centuries had occasionally painted pastels, it was the Venetian Carriera who fully exploited the artistic possibilities of the medium during the early eighteenth century.[2] Remarkably, many women were among the few artists painting pastels at that time. Giovanna Fratellini (1666–1731) in Florence and Teresa del Pò (1649–1713) in Rome and Naples were the best-known pastellists besides Carriera.

Pastels showing contemporaneous beauties, international Grand Tour sitters, and elegant allegories became almost synonymous with Rosalba Carriera's name in Italy and beyond. Today, some 360 pastels by her hand have survived.[3] Hundreds more replicating her most successful works were executed by her busy workshop and imitators. While during the seventeenth century pastels had been classified somewhere between drawings and paintings, the medium significantly gained in stature as an independent art form during Carriera's lifetime. After being admitted to the Roman Accademia di San Luca (Academy of Saint Luke) in 1705 with a miniature as a reception piece, she entered the prestigious Académie Royale in Paris as a pastel painter in 1720. Because pastels convey a unique sense of intimacy and immediacy, they had become fashionable during the early eighteenth century. Recent technical innovations, such as readymade crayons and large sheets of glass to protect fragile works, helped this practice to proliferate among artists.

The two pastels discussed here are believed to belong to a series of four allegories, all showing young, idealized women. Since their discovery in 1976, the attribution to Rosalba Carriera has never been questioned, and the pictures have been included in subsequent catalogues of the artist's oeuvre. *The Muse Calliope* and *Allegory of Faith* came on the market only in 2020, and this exhibition offers an opportunity to discuss them in greater detail, as they were previously known only through crude black and white images.

Both pictures show bust-length female figures depicted from a low vantage point. Holding a book, her gaze directed upwards towards a star, Calliope has a nearly sculptural presence. Her full face, with its broad features, and her blond hair are idealized, painted in the most radiant colors Carriera's

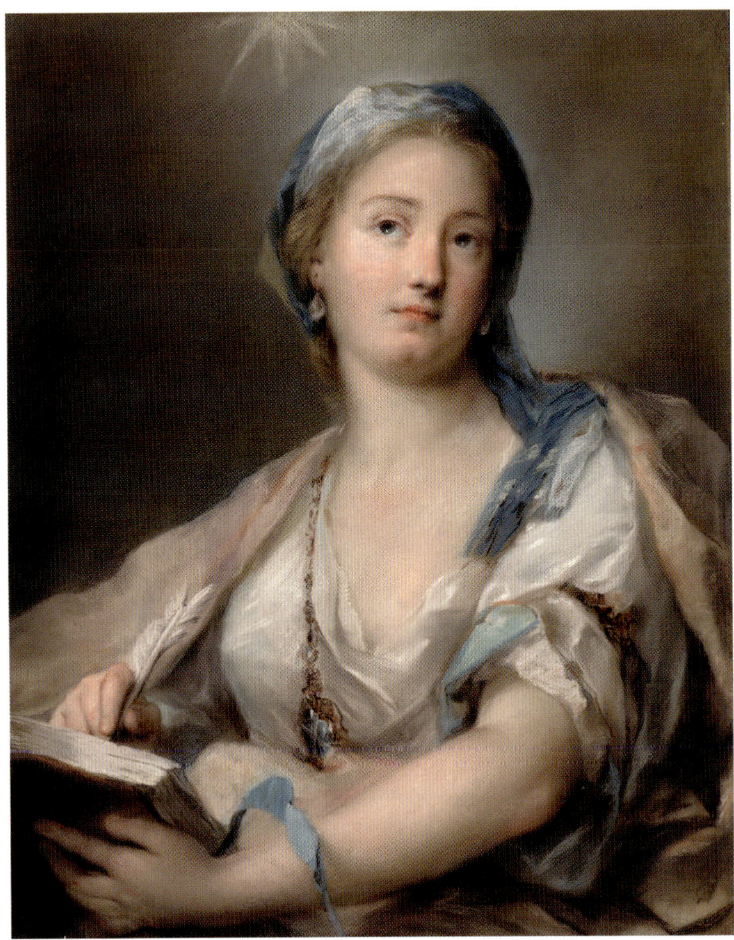

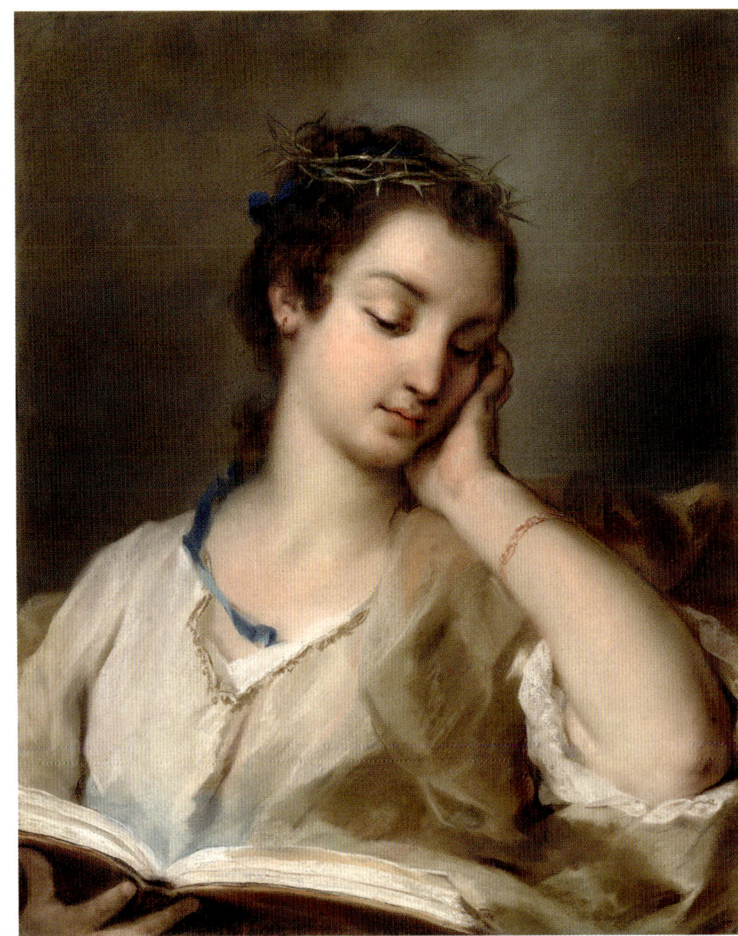

palette offered. By contrast, the *Allegory of Faith* has a stronger inward presence, emphasized by the figure leaning her head on her hand and a limited but nuanced palette of browns, whites, and blues. By stumping over the flesh tones, Carriera attained remarkably soft shadows, especially in the face, hair, and diaphanous garment.

Two more allegories, identified as *The Muse Polymnia* (fig. 1) and *The Muse Urania* (fig. 2), have been linked to these two works, and because of their similar size, pose, and shared allegorical subjects, the four pastels are believed to form a set. Despite being largely unknown, their early provenance seems to corroborate this theory. The four pictures were replicated by an unidentified hand before 1806, when they appeared for the first time in an inventory of the Villa Reale di Stra, owned by the noble Pisani dal Banco family in Venice. Another inventory from 1808 describes the replicas as sibyls.[4] While Giuseppe Maria Pilo called

them simply allegories, Neil Jeffares tentatively interpreted them as Mary Magdalene with three liberal arts (history, poetry, and philosophy). Bernardina Sani identified them as personifications of faith and astrology, together with the muses Calliope and Polymnia.[5] More recently, Jeffares changed his opinion and now titles the works an *Allegory of Faith* and the muses Calliope, Polymnia, and Urania/Astrology.[6]

In the absence of any firm information about the circumstances of the commissioning of this ambitious series, various questions remain open. As already noted by Sani, Carriera did not follow a particular text for the iconography—the combination of one religious with three secular figures is unusual—and the identifications of the individual allegories are contested.[7] By contrast, all other known series in Carriera's oeuvre consist of well-established iconographical themes, such as the four seasons, the four elements, and the four continents. And if

Carriera did depict three muses, she deviated from her usual repertoire of bare-breasted female figures crowned with a laurel.[8]

All four figures appear chaste—they avoid direct eye contact. Since they are depicted with books, they can perhaps be better interpreted as sibyls, who are usually shown writing or reading. As the figure wears a thin blue haircloth and stares at a star, *Calliope* is better understood as a sibyl writing down her celestial vision. Similarly, the wreath of thorns in the *Allegory of Faith* can be associated with the Samian Sibyl. Moreover, given the apparition of a face in the sky, one can interpret *The Muse Polymnia* as a third sibyl, seeing a light-filled vision of what appears to be an angel. In *The Muse Urania*, what is likely the fourth sibyl holds a metallic bar surrounded by stars, pointing to her powers as a seer. This set may thus present the ancient seers announcing the coming of Christ and his Passion, a well-known typological conceit from the Renaissance to the late Baroque periods. Further research will have to test this hypothesis. No other figures by Rosalba Carriera have been identified as sibyls, which makes the cycle rare in her oeuvre.[9] Pilo suggests that it was strongly influenced by her brother-in-law, Giovanni Antonio Pellegrini (1675–1741), but he does not provide further details.[10] While Pilo placed the series before Carriera's stay in Paris in 1720/21, Sani dated it shortly afterwards.[11] The *sfumato* effects together with the motif of a pensive young woman in the *Allegory of Faith* are reminiscent of Antonio da Correggio's (1489–1534) work and may point to a date in the early to mid 1720s, a period when Carriera was strongly influenced by the Emilian artist.[12]

Although religious subjects form only a small group within Carriera's body of work, they were highly appreciated by her contemporaries. More than at any other time during her career, Carriera devoted herself to religious subjects during the 1720s, most noticeably with a group of works later acquired by Augustus III, prince elector of Saxony and later king of Poland (1696–1763).[13] In the following years Carriera also painted several allegorical cycles for the cardinals Melchior de Polignac (1661–1742) and Alessandro Albani (1692–1779).

Despite our lack of knowledge about its first owner and possible commissioner, this series elucidates an important moment and occupies a unique place in Rosalba Carriera's career. With its sophisticated allegorical subjects and technical bravura, it stands out and deserves to be better known.—OT

NOTES

1. See letter from Christian Cole to Rosalba Carriera dated May 2, 1705, in Sani 1985, vol. 1, 89, no. 44.

2. Carriera's first pastel is dated ca. 1700. Rosalba Carriera, *Portrait of Anton Maria Zanetti*, pastel, 17¾ × 12⅜ in. (45 × 31.5 cm), Nationalmuseum, Stockholm, NMB 2102. See Sani 2007, 59, no. 1.

3. According to Sani 2007.

4. Two unrelated profane allegories showing the seasons winter and summer were thought to be part of the circle. On the replicas see Basso 2009; Tormen 2009, 247.

5. Sani 2007, 196.

6. See Jeffares 2020c, J.21.1783; J.21.1803; J.21.1809; J.21.1813.

7. Sani 1988, 299, no. 174.

8. See, for example, Rosalba Carriera, *The Muse Clio*, mid-1720s, pastel on blue laid paper, 12³⁄₁₆ × 10¼ in. (31 × 26 cm), formerly Gemäldegalerie Alte Meister, Dresden, now J. Paul Getty Museum, Los Angeles, 2003.17, in Sani 2007, 328, no. 373.

9. In 1738, however, Carriera was asked by Giuseppe Pollaroli (dates unknown) to paint the Eritraean and Cumaean Sybills. If these pastels were executed, they are now lost. See Sani 2007, 56.

10. Pilo 1976, 110.

11. Sani 2007, 196.

12. See, for instance, Correggio's celebrated *The Magdalene Reading in the Wilderness*, formerly Gemäldegalerie Alte Meister, Dresden. Carriera may have seen the work during her visit to Modena in 1723. Sani has noted a strong influence of Correggio on Carriera at this time in Sani 2007, 231. On Correggio's influence on Carriera's religious works see Oberer 2020, 213–15.

13. Sani 2007, 233.

PROVENANCE

Private collection (Venice/Friuli, Italy); 2020–present, sold at TEFAF Maastricht 2020 by (Salamon Old Masters, Milan, Italy), as *Allegory of Grammar* and *Allegory of Faith by Rosalba Carriera*, to a private collection (Connecticut).

SELECTED EXHIBITIONS

Biblioteca Antica del Convento del Santo, Sant'Antonio di Padova, 2019.

SELECTED PUBLICATIONS

Pilo 1976, 110–16; Sani 1988, 299, no. 174, figs. 148–49; Jeffares 2006, 107; Sani 2007, 196, nos. 194a–b, illus.; Padua 2019, 32–35, 33 illus., 35 illus.; Jeffares 2020c, 5–6, nos. J.21.1783, J.21.1803.

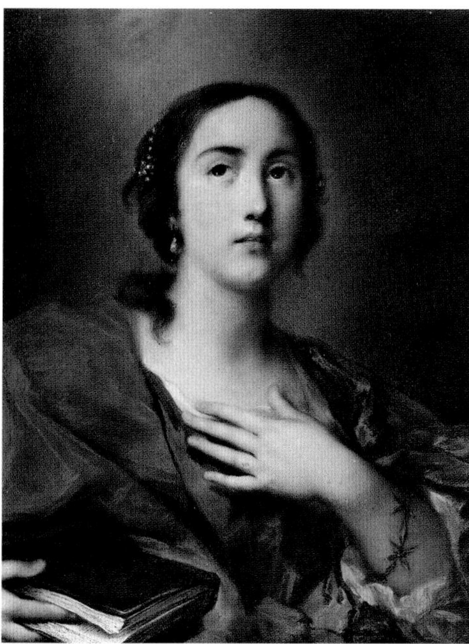

FIGURE 1 Rosalba Carriera, *The Muse Polymnia*, early to mid-1720s, pastel on paper, 24⁷⁄₁₆ × 20¹⁄₁₆ in. (62 × 51 cm). Private collection, Venice/Friuli

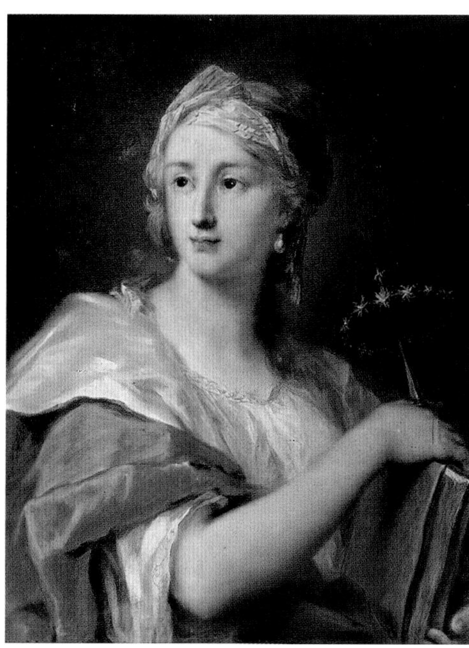

FIGURE 2 Rosalba Carriera, *The Muse Urania*, early to mid-1720s, pastel on paper, 24⁷⁄₁₆ × 20¹⁄₁₆ in. (62 × 51 cm). Private collection, Venice/Friuli

Portrait of a Man

ca. 1720
Gouache and watercolor on ivory, 3 × 2¼ in. (7.6 × 5.9 cm)
The Metropolitan Museum of Art, New York, Rogers Fund, 1949, 49.122.2

A Woman Putting Flowers in Her Hair

ca. 1710
Gouache and watercolor on ivory, unframed: 3⅜ × 4⅛ in. (8.6 × 10.5 cm);
framed: 4³⁄₁₆ × 5 in. (10.6 × 12.7 cm)
The Cleveland Museum of Art, The Edward B. Greene Collection, 1940.1203

Woman with a Dog

1710–1720
Gouache and watercolor on ivory, framed: 2¹⁵⁄₁₆ × 2³⁄₁₆ in. (7.5 × 5.5 cm)
The Cleveland Museum of Art, Bequest of Muriel Butkin, 2008.291

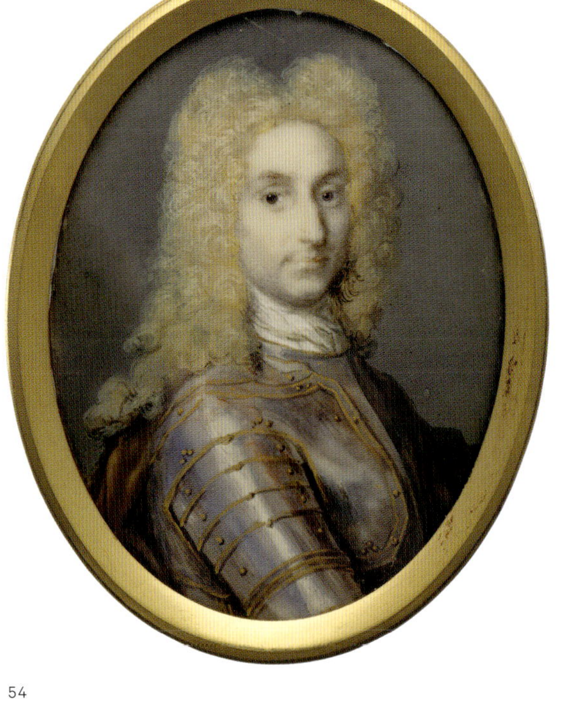

54

HARDLY ANY OTHER art object embodies the visual qualities of the Rococo period as brilliantly as miniatures, and Rosalba Carriera's pictures stand out among the works of her contemporaries as dazzling, precious, and full of spirit. While she is better known today for her pastels, it was thanks to her outstanding talents as a miniaturist that she quickly rose to fame and became the most successful international woman artist of her era. Known to her contemporaries simply as Rosalba, she exerted an extensive influence on European artists during the eighteenth century. The three miniatures discussed here are exemplary in terms of their subjects, technique, and superb quality. Little known, and shown for the first time together, they provide a representative overview of Carriera's characteristic artistic traits in this medium. Perhaps more than any other miniaturist before her, she experimented with subjects and innovative techniques. She also successfully translated some of the latest trends in oil painting into her diminutive works.

In *A Woman Putting Flowers in Her Hair*, Carriera avoided narrow categorizations of her subject, creating a picture that combines a genre scene with allegorical elements. Such hybrid pictures became one of her trademarks, not only in miniatures, but also in her larger pastels. Here she shows an idealized young woman in contemporary dress, leaning on a console table and looking at a mirror. The scene is reminiscent of Venus at her toilet—a popular subject in Venice since the Renaissance—as well as fashionable boudoir scenes. The woman's bare underarm, curved fingers, and low-cut bodice create an atmosphere of erotically charged intimacy.[1] Carriera used a comparable strategy in *Woman with a Dog*, in which a similar and equally beautified young woman seems to have abruptly moved, perhaps because of the frisky pug, revealing her naked shoulder—the question of whether it was uncovered accidentally adds to the picture's sensuous allure, which is reinforced by the woman's direct eye contact with the viewer. Such playful eroticism is typical of

Carriera's miniatures, which were meant for private use.

Portrait of a Man reveals a different facet of Carriera's oeuvre. Throughout her career she depicted male sitters—often posed similarly, formally clad in armor, and wearing double-peaked wigs—in surprisingly lifelike portraits in either miniature or pastel. Indeed, no other contemporaneous miniaturist in Italy painted as many portraits in this genre as Carriera. By turning the unknown sitter's body to the right and his head to face the viewer, she has translated a popular formula for official portraits into miniature. The head is effectively modeled with soft shading, subtle coloring, and differently accentuated brushstrokes. According to Bernardo Falconi, Carriera depicted her sitters from life, a novel approach in the often-arduous process of miniature painting.[2]

Carriera's vividly painted miniatures are distinguished by their fluidity, brilliance, and translucency of colors. As seen in these three examples, she worked with

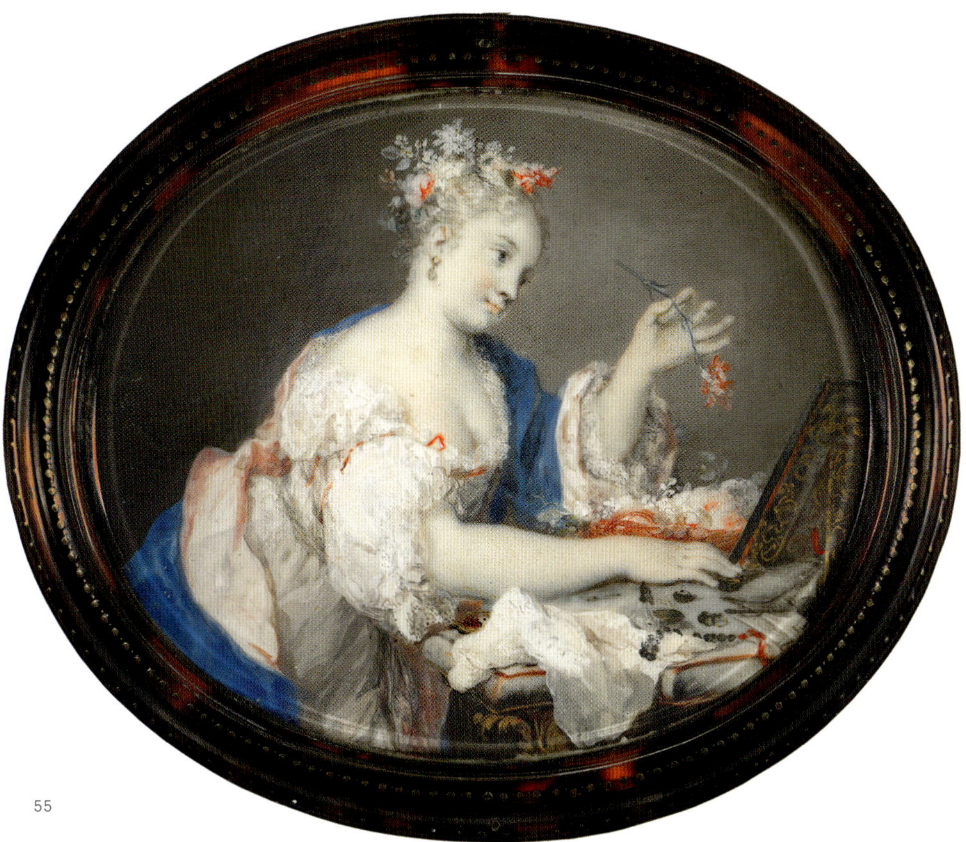

55

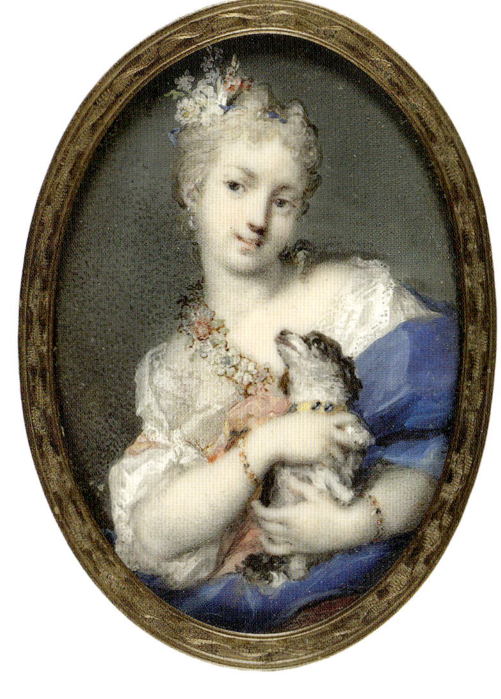

56

the warm natural tone of the ivory support when painting flesh. The subtle shadows, indicated by tiny dots, are often painted in a soft blue that contributes to the harmonious distribution of colors. She used a thicker gouache to apply impasto next to or on top of thin layers of watercolors. Traditionally, miniaturists used vellum as their support, but Carriera was the first artist to systematically and fully exploit ivory, considered notoriously difficult because it does not absorb watercolors.[3] Carriera, however, experimented with a combination of watercolors and gum arabic as a fixative to produce an opaque gouache that adheres to the slick surface. While ivory was difficult to procure for artists in most European cities, Carriera had the advantage of living in the trade center of Venice. In addition, she occasionally used silver—in *A Woman Putting Flowers in Her Hair* it may be seen in the now-tarnished paraphernalia on the dressing table, which once would have emphasized the jewel-like character of the miniature.[4]

As a young adult, Carriera started her career as a painter of ivory snuffboxes; however, she soon began to use the small ivory tablets to create independent pictures and thus placed her work into a more exclusive art market. She called her tiny pictures *fondelli*, a name that probably refers to the bottom of snuffboxes.[5] Covered with glass or crystal, her independent miniatures were set into medallions of metal and tortoiseshell. When Carriera was admitted to the prestigious Roman Accademia di San Luca (Academy of Saint Luke) in 1705, the painting academy's president, Carlo Maratti (1625–1713), praised the variety of white colors in her small reception piece, *Allegory of Innocence* or *Girl with a Dove* (Tostmann, "The Advantages of Painting Small," fig. 8), an effect that she achieved in large part because of her choice of ivory as a support.[6] Because of Carriera's unprecedented success, numerous contemporaneous and later artists chose ivory as a support and adopted her technique.

Dating Carriera's miniatures is exceedingly difficult. Because she painted the *Allegory of Innocence* as a reception piece for the Roman art academy, it is well documented and the only miniature in her oeuvre that can be dated safely. We know that she started painting independent miniatures in the mid-1690s and continued so until the mid to late 1720s, when her deteriorating eyesight and increasing popularity as a pastel artist led her to give them up. While Henry Wehle dated *Woman Putting Flowers in Her Hair* to ca. 1730, Bernardina Sani objected rightfully that Carriera had probably stopped painting miniatures by that time. Sani compared the painting to another miniature, *A Woman Cutting Her Hair* (fig. 1), now at the Hermitage Museum, Saint Petersburg, and dated both to ca. 1710.[7] *Woman with a Dog* seems to belong to the same time period. The fluidity of the brushstrokes and choice of colors is similar to *Woman Putting Flowers in Her Hair*. Moreover, *Woman with a Dog* can be compared with two miniatures from the Hermitage Museum, Saint Petersburg—the

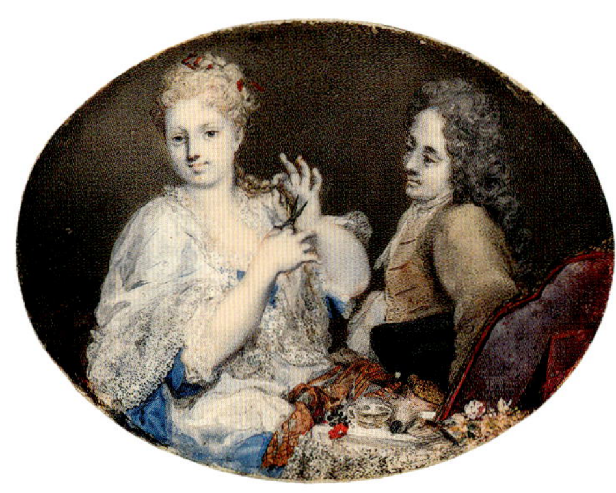

FIGURE 1 Rosalba Carriera, *A Woman Cutting Her Hair*, Gouache and watercolor on ivory, 2⅜ × 2¹⁵⁄₁₆ in. (6 × 7.5 cm). Hermitage Museum, Saint Petersburg

figure's pose is similar to that in the *Portrait of a Young Lady as Cleopatra*, and the motif can be compared with *Portrait of a Lady with a Dog*,[8] which Assia Kantor-Gukovskaya places in Carriera's early period.[9] The pug, with its distinctive collar, reappears in two other related miniatures in which it lounges on a young lady's lap.[10]

With its more subdued palette and delicate brushstrokes, *Portrait of a Man* differs from the two other miniatures. Although dated by art historian Graham Reynolds to ca. 1710, its palette and subtle light effects, such as the blued armor, make a date around Carriera's sojourn in Paris from 1720 to 1721 more reasonable.[11] Pastels by Carriera from this time feature a similar palette. *Portrait of a Man* can be compared with other portraits of male sitters in ceremonial armor, such as the contemporaneous *Portrait of a Prince*, now at the Musée Condé, Chantilly.[12]

We do not yet know anything about the early provenance of these three miniatures, but it is worth pointing out that at least two, if not all three, were once in the possession of the legendary Austrian connoisseur and dealer of miniatures Leo R. Schidlof (1886–1966).

International clients from France, Germany, and England traveled to Rosalba Carriera's hometown of Venice and vied for her precious artworks. Copyists forged her miniatures as early as 1709.[13] It is no surprise then that her contemporary, the writer Pellegrino Antonio Orlandi (1660–1727), praised the artist in his *Abecedario pittorico* as "a virtuosa who achieved outstanding success in her profession as a miniaturist, unsurpassed by anybody else."[14]—OT

NOTES

1. On the sensuously charged aspects of the picture, see Oberer 2020, 86–87.

2. Falconi 2009.

3. See Falconi 2009, 216.

4. The silver is now tarnished. I am grateful to Cory Korkow for her observations.

5. For a discussion of the term, see Sani 1981, 392–95. See also Falconi 2009, 223.

6. Johns 2003, 20 and 40–41.

7. Wehle 1951, 20–21. *A Woman Cutting her Hair*, Hermitage Museum, Saint Petersburg, is dated by Assia Kantor-Gukovskaya to Carriera's early-mature phase. See Kantor-Gukovskaya 2009, 364; Sani 2007, 71, no. 19. An undated copy of *Woman Putting Flowers in Her Hair* attests to the appeal of this miniature. This version is painted in a vertical oval format. Rosalba Carriera, *A Young Lady Putting Flowers in Her Hair*, ex-Comerford Collection, Dublin; Ellison Fine Art, London. Sani also mentions a drawing, attributed to Antoine Watteau (1684–1721), now at the Rijksmuseum, Amsterdam, being partially inspired by the Cleveland *Woman Putting Flowers in Her Hair*. Sani 2007, 71.

8. Sani 2007, 82, no. 42; 105, no. 77.

9. See Kantor-Gukovskaya 2009, 364, with color illustration, 16.

10. See Sani 2007, 124, nos. 114 and 115, both undated.

11. See New York 1996, 117, no. 97. For a later date around Carriera's stay in Paris, see Sani 2007, 113.

12. See Sani 2007, 133, no. 126.

13. Oberer 2020, 60–61.

14. Orlandi 1753, 448: "Questa virtuosa col disegno è giunta a tale eccellenza nella miniatura, che si è resa singolare, ed ha oltrepassato tutti gli altri professori dei nostri tempi."

A Woman Putting Flowers in Her Hair

PROVENANCE

Collection of Viktor Emmanuel Pollak (Vienna, Austria); (Leo R. Schidlof [1886–1966], Vienna, Austria, and Paris, France) (?); Edward B. Greene (Cleveland, Ohio); 1940–present, bequest to the Cleveland Museum of Art (Cleveland, Ohio).

SELECTED EXHIBITIONS

Albertina Museum, Vienna, 1924, no. 133; Los Angeles County Museum of Art, 1976–1977; Cleveland Museum of Art, 2013–2014.

SELECTED PUBLICATIONS

Wehle 1951, 20–21, 38, no. 84, pl. XXXVII; Schidlof 1964, vol. 1, 130; Los Angeles 1976, 164, cat. 42, illus., 345; Sani 1988, 277, no. 17, fig. 15; Sani 2007, 71, no. 18; Oberer 2020, 86–88.

Woman with a Dog

PROVENANCE

Edouard Warneck Collection (Paris, France); November 19, 1924, sold by (Leo R. Schidlof, Vienna, Austria), no. 40; collection of Muriel and Noah Butkin (Cleveland, Ohio); 2008–present, bequest to the Cleveland Museum of Art (Cleveland, Ohio).

SELECTED EXHIBITIONS

Cleveland Museum of Art, 2013–2014.

SELECTED PUBLICATIONS

Schidlof 1964, vol, 1, 130; Sani 1988, 284, no. 69 (?).

Portrait of a Man

PROVENANCE

Until 1949, collection of Leo R. Schidlof [1886–1966]; 1949–present, sold to the Metropolitan Museum of Art (New York, New York).

SELECTED EXHIBITIONS

Metropolitan Museum of Art, New York, 1950; Metropolitan Museum of Art, New York, 1981–1982; Metropolitan Museum of Art, New York, 1996–1997.

SELECTED PUBLICATIONS

New York 1996, 12–13, 40, 116 illus., 117, no. 97, pl. 97; Baetjer 1999, 23, illus.; Sani 2007, 113, no. 97, illus.

57

Berenice

ca. 1741
Pastel on blue laid paper adhered to fine, plain weave canvas stretched onto a wooden strainer
Labels: No signature. Partially covered stenciled numbering on the verso top stretcher member. Partial red wax
seal at upper right on top frame member, verso, sheet: 18 × 9¹⁄₁₆ in. (45.7 × 23 cm)
Detroit Institute of Arts, Gift of Mrs. William D. Vogel in memory of her mother Mrs. Ralph Harman Booth, 56.264
Detroit only

IN ACCORD with eighteenth-century aesthetic standards that often privileged lighter compositions in terms of tonality and tenor, Rosalba Carriera's pastel portraits have a vivacity and freshness. Since its acquisition in 1956 by the Detroit Institute of Arts, this pastel has been documented as a portrait of Caterina Sagredo Barbarigo (1715–1772)—a Venetian woman renowned for her intellect and beauty—in the guise of the Egyptian Queen Berenice II.[1] This identification is based on visual precedents such as Elisabetta Sirani's (1638–1665) painting in this exhibition (cat. 42), as well as iconographic details.[2] Having sworn she would cut her hair—a beloved asset—if her husband returned safely from battle, Berenice is depicted fulfilling her promise, poised with scissors in her left hand to remove the first lustrous lock. The particularity of the sitter's features suggests this is a portrait of a specific individual. Whether the young woman is Caterina Sagredo Barbarigo, however, requires further consideration.

Rosalba Carriera executed around 361 works in her career,[3] the majority of which are pastel portraits, though she also executed portrait miniatures (cats. 53–55) and began her career making lace patterns.[4] The Prince Elector of Saxony, later Augustus III of Poland (1696–1763), was Carriera's greatest patron, acquiring 150 of her pastels for his residence in Dresden, including a portrait of Caterina Sagredo Barbarigo that also dates to around 1740 (fig. 1).[5] There are notable differences in the shapes of the sitters' noses, eyes, and eyebrows in these two portraits. In the Dresden work, for example, the nose has a particular angularity about the nostrils, but they are rounded in the Detroit work. Given such pronounced visual differences, it is hard to maintain that Detroit's pastel represents Caterina Sagredo Barbarigo. To my eye, this work is an allegorical portrait of a female sitter in the guise of Berenice; however, the identity of the sitter remains an open question.

Like most of Rosalba Carriera's surviving pastels, this one is executed on blue paper adhered to a canvas support.[6] The thickness of the pastel application varies across the surface of the composition, heaviest in the flesh tones, and a wide range of pigments is used—from the earth tones in the sitter's dress to the azurite stroke in the handle of the scissors.[7] Infrared reflectology (IRR) of the portrait did not reveal any evidence of underdrawing, which is consistent with "the dearth of underdrawings hitherto discovered under Carriera's pastels."[8] The IRR did, however, reveal a change in the position of Berenice's left thumb as it holds the scissors (fig. 2), indicating that it is the prime, autograph version of the subject.[9]

This work was acquired by Henry Fiennes Pelham-Clinton, Earl of Lincoln, later 2nd Duke of Newcastle-under-Lyne (1720–1794) in 1741 at around the age of twenty-one, when most British men of means went abroad on the Grand Tour.[10]—ESP

NOTES

1. There are three main sources on the work: Sani 1988, 322, no. 342; Jeffares 2020d; Knox 1992, 98, cat. 43. For the subject of Berenice see Clayman 2014.

2. Berenice gained in popularity as a subject in European art in the seventeenth and into the eighteenth century. See, for example, Bernardo Strozzi (1581–1644), *Berenice, Wife of Ptolemy III*, ca. 1640, El Paso Museum of Art.

3. Modesti 2014, 4.

4. For a biographical sketch of Rosalba Carriera see Sani 1988, 9–31.

5. Giacometti 1997, 355.

6. For her typical technique see Burns 2007, 102, 111–13. According to Detroit Institute of Arts paper conservator Christopher Foster, "The pastel is executed on a blue handmade laid paper, applied to the wire side of the sheet. The chain and laid lines are apparent with raking light, with the chain lines running vertically. No watermark is apparent" and "The blue paper may have faded and yellowed slightly; the paper color is brighter and bluer at the covered tacking edges where it was protected from light. There are radial draws at the upper right corner, related to two tears there. One tear, which has been repaired, is located along the fold at the vertical tacking edge and extends downward for four inches from the upper right corner." Behind the canvas, "There are two faint strokes (possibly chalk) at center that form a double slash, and a smaller sideways 'V' shape in graphite below and to the right of center." Foster 2020.

7. Fiber optic reflectance spectroscopy (FORS) was performed by Christina Bisulca at the Detroit Institute of Arts' Conservation Department on March 3, 2020. Comparison of the observed spectra with known spectra revealed the following: "Blue paper: indigo (indicating denim rags used in papermaking); Yellows, reds and browns: iron oxides (earth pigments); Reds in flesh tones: iron oxide; Two areas of brighter red at lower edge: vermillion; Blue stroke in scissor handle: possibly azurite (copper carbonate); White: not determined; Black: not determined; White inpainting pigment, center of forehead and raised area above and left of mouth: titanium dioxide." See Foster 2020.

8. Burns 2007, 114.

9. There is a copy after the work by another hand in the Worcester Art Museum, Massachusetts, as well as an oil painting of the same subject once in the Suida-Manning collection, New York. Knox 1992, 98.

10. Listed in Hipkin 1923, no. 315. After graduating from university, Lord Lincoln was sent abroad to complete his education. At Turin, Italy, where he was studying fencing, he was joined by his school friend,

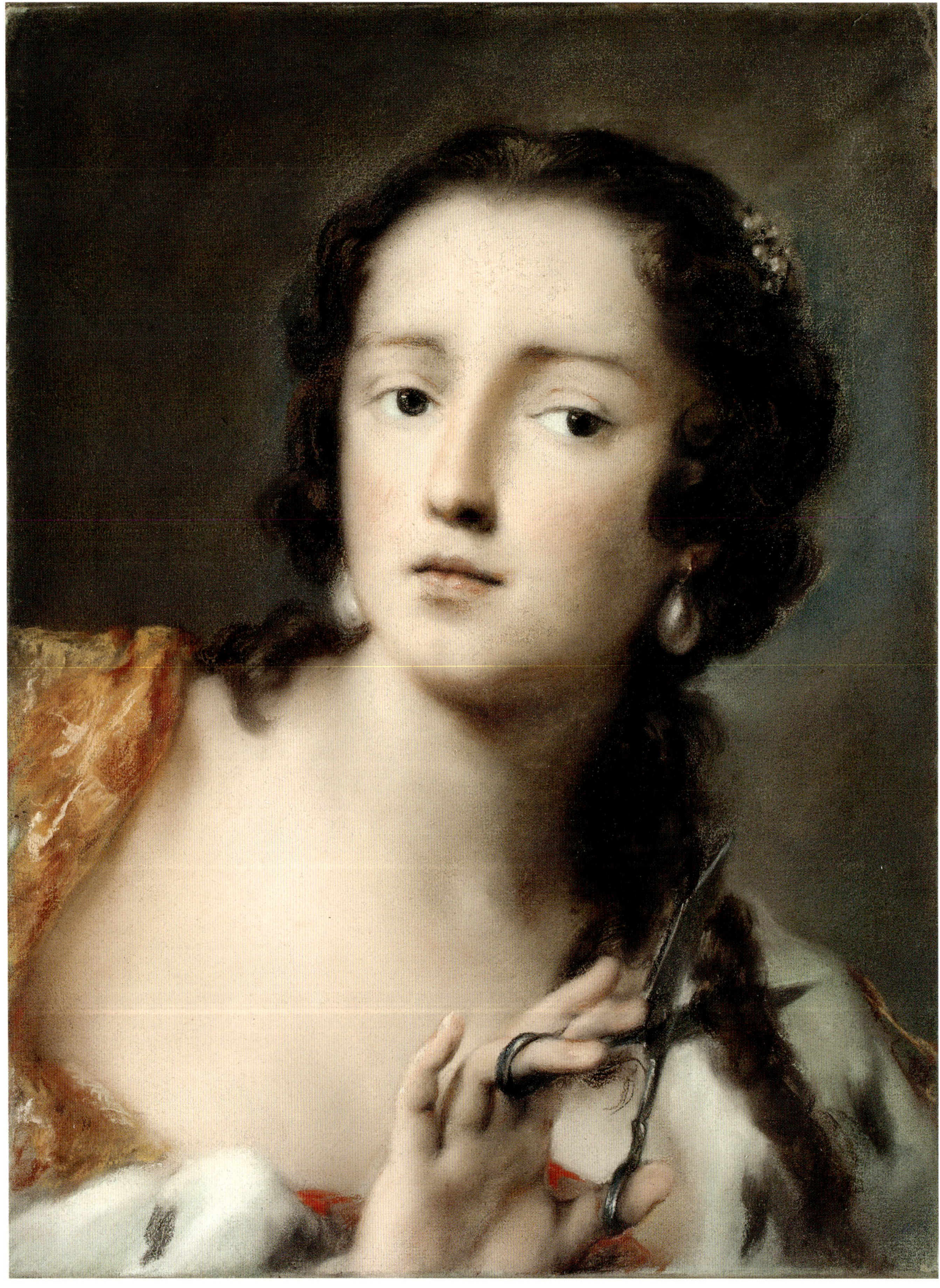

FIGURE 1 Rosalba Carriera, *Portrait of Caterina Sagredo Barbarigo*, ca. 1735/40, pastel on paper, 16⅞6 × 13 in. (42 × 33 cm). Staatliche Kunstsammlungen, Gemäldegalerie Alte Meister, Dresden, Gal.-Nr. P 16

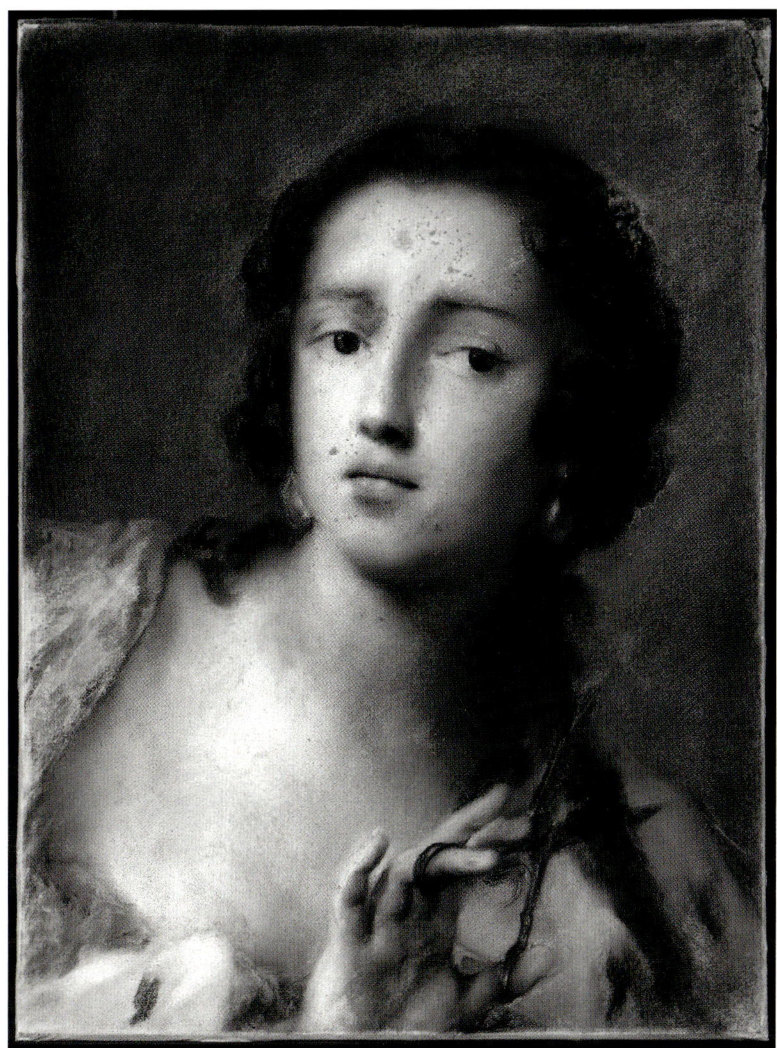

FIGURE 2 Infrared reflectogram (IRR), Rosalba Carriera, *Berenice*. Detroit Institute of Arts

Horace Walpole (1717–1797), who was in love with Lord Lincoln; Walpole biographer Timothy Mowl believes the two men were lovers. Lord Lincoln was exceedingly good-looking, and would later be considered the most handsome man in England. As Mowl writes, "If Horace and Lord Lincoln's slow return to Paris could be accurately retold, it would read like the happy ending for a romantic novel for older homosexuals." Mowl 2011, 41. "I left off compliments when I began loving you, and am now only Yours most sincerely," Letter from Horace Walpole to Lord Lincoln on January 3, 1741, NS, http://images.library.yale.edu/hwcorrespondence/page.asp?vol=30&page=9.

PROVENANCE

1741, probably sold in (Venice, Italy); June–July 1741, purchased by Henry Fiennes Pelham-Clinton, Earl of Lincoln, later 2nd Duke of Newcastle-under-Lyne [1720–1794] (UK) [listed in the catalogue of the Newcastle collection at Clumber, 1914/23, no. 315]; October 25, 1946, sold at (Christie's, London, UK), lot 59C; Arturo Grassi (New York, New York); Ralph H. Booth (Detroit, Michigan); Mrs. Ralph H. Booth (Detroit, Michigan); gift to her daughter, Mrs. Virginia Booth Vogel (Detroit, Michigan); 1956–present, gift to the Detroit Institute of Arts (Detroit, Michigan).

SELECTED EXHIBITIONS

Detroit Institute of Arts, 1952; Finch College Museum of Art, New York, 1961; Detroit Institute of Arts, 1993; Detroit Institute of Arts, 2009.

SELECTED PUBLICATIONS

Hipkin 1923, no. 315; Detroit 1952, 26–27, cat. 21, fig. 21; *Art Quarterly* 1957, 206, 212 illus.; Payne 1957–1958, 4–5, 4 illus.; New York 1961, no. 9; Sani 1988, 322, no. 342, fig. 300; *Collections of the Detroit Institute of Arts* 1992, 141, pl. XIII; Knox 1992, 98, cat. 43, 99 illus.; Sani 2007, no. 398, illus.; Detroit 2009, 5, 13, fig. 4; van Oppen de Ruiter 2015, 67–70, pl. 3.15; Jeffares 2020d, 2, no. J.21.0231.

58

Saint Cecilia

Circle of Rosalba Carriera (Venice, 1673–1757)

1730s/1740s

Pastel on blue laid paper adhered to fine, plain weave canvas stretched onto a wooden strainer

Labels: Gummed paper label with trimmed corners and blue inked border lines adhered to top strainer member; the center of the label is scraped away, unframed: 16¾ × 13⁵⁄₁₆ in. (42.5 × 33.8 cm)

Collection of Anne G Fredericks

Detroit only

THIS PASTEL REPRESENTS Saint Cecilia, the third-century Roman martyr and patron saint of music, her head tilted back, attuned to the heavens. According to legend, as a child Cecilia had vowed her virginity to God; set to be married to the future saint Valerian, she informed him of God's plan for her, eventually converting him and her brother Tiburtius to Christianity. During her wedding, Cecilia, here identified by the organ at her back and her upturned gaze, sat apart and engaged with a divine, internal music. The pastel captures this moment of lyrical solitude. After Saint Cecelia's body was exhumed below the high altar of the Roman church of Santa Cecilia in Trastevere in October 1599, interest in representations of her increased dramatically throughout the seventeenth and eighteenth centuries.[1]

Even though this work was not in the 1988 or the updated 2007 catalogue raisonné of the work of Rosalba Carriera, Bernardina Sani—a leading expert on Carriera—subsequently included it in an article on the artist, noting that it appears to be of "good quality," with coloring typical of the eighteenth century and a composition that draws on seventeenth-century prototypes.[2] This assessment of quality is borne out in the work's sound state of conservation.[3] Sani compares the figure's upturned gaze to those of various saints in seventeenth-century works by the Bolognese artist Guercino (1591–1666), as well as a Saint Catherine of Alexandria by the eighteenth-century Venetian painter Francesco Fontebasso

(1707–1769) in the Hermitage Museum, Saint Petersburg.[4] To my eye this *Saint Cecilia* owes a debt to Raphael's (1483–1520) Bolognese depiction of the saint (now in the Pinacoteca Nazionale, Bologna), as well as to Domenichino's (1581–1641) painted and frescoed representations of her in the Church of San Luigi dei Francesi in Rome.

Given the loose execution of the pastel—which is more characteristic of the latter part of Rosalba Carriera's career—this work likely dates to the 1730s or 1740s. Like the majority of her pastels, it is adhered to a canvas support.[5] For now, until we can get a firmer purchase on her religious representations, which are largely housed in the Gemäldegalerie Alte Meister Museum in Dresden, it should be attributed to the circle of Rosalba Carriera. The artist shared her talents with her sisters Giovanna Carriera (1675–1737) and Angela Carriera Pellegrini (1677–1760) and, later in life, had female pupils such as Margherita Terzi (active ca. 1756), and Felicità Sartori (ca. 1714–1760). Might this work be the product of such matrilineal dissemination of artistic knowledge?—ESP

NOTES

1. For Saint Cecilia in art of these periods, see Hanning 2004, 91–103.

2. Sani 2009, 99–100. It is also published in Jeffares 2006, 109.

3. "The pastel is in good condition. The pastel surface appears to be largely intact, with only a few minor losses related to losses of the paper support. Most of the losses are at the right edge, and extend irregularly into the sheet, ranging from a quarter-inch to a half-inch. The majority of these

losses have been toned with pastel directly onto the exposed canvas support to disguise them. There are also a few similar losses at the upper third of the left edge. Within the composition's interior, there are a few minor disturbed areas." For the conservation report, written by paper conservator Christopher Foster, see the conservation files at the Detroit Institute of Arts.

4. Sani 2009, 100.

5. Burns 2007, 102, 111–13.

PROVENANCE

December 5, 1984, sold at (Drouot, Paris, France), lot 66. (Succi Limited, London, UK); (DuMouchelles, Detroit, Michigan); 2005, purchased by Anne G Fredericks (Massachusetts); 2018–present, on loan to the Detroit Institute of Arts (Detroit, Michigan).

SELECTED PUBLICATIONS

Jeffares 2006, 109, illus.; Sani 2009, 99–100, fig. 3; Jeffares 2020c, 13, no. J.21.201.

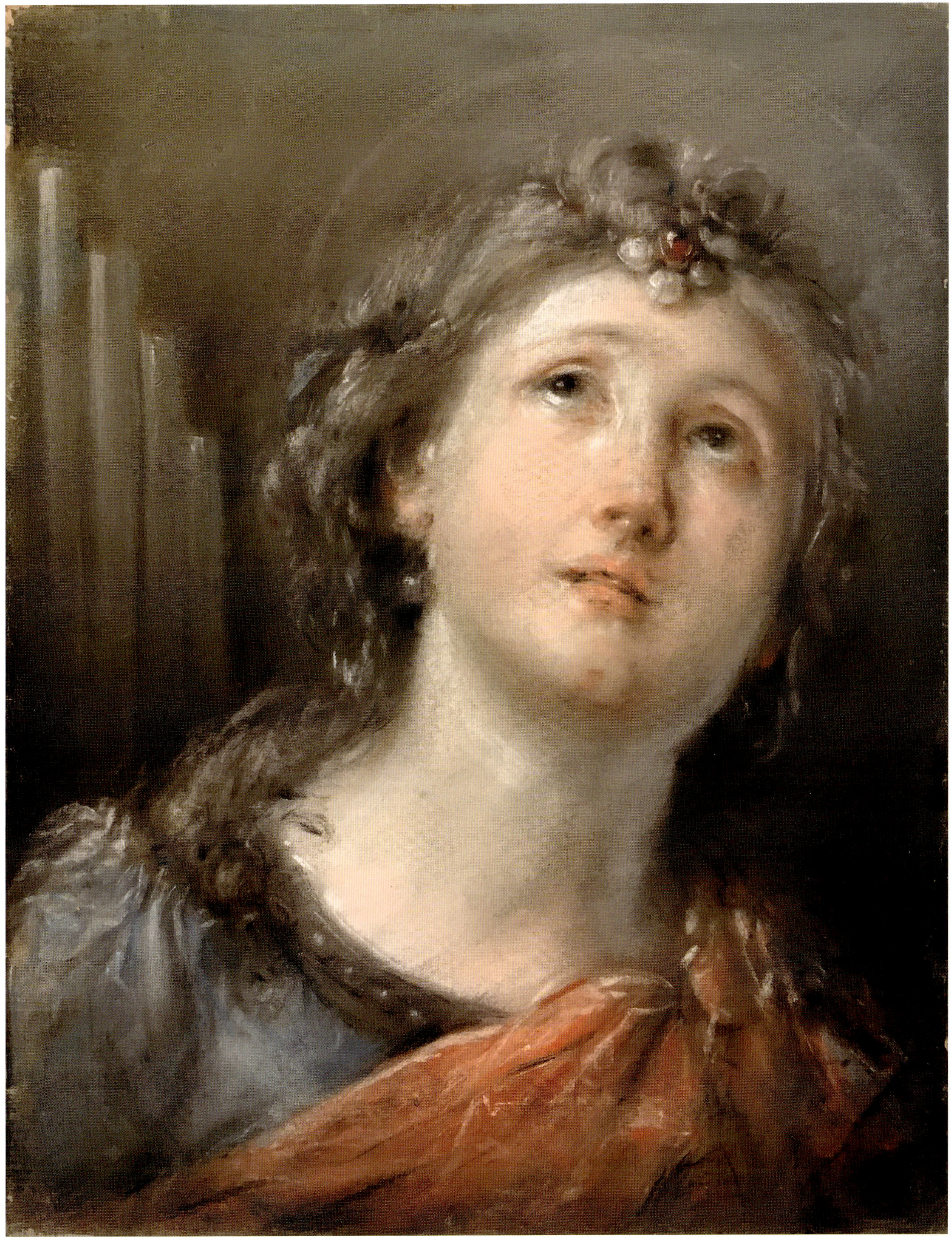

MARIANNA CARLEVARIJS

Venice, 1703–after 1750

MARIANNA CARLEVARIJS'S career is still overshadowed by that of her father, the distinguished *vedute* (views) painter Luca Carlevarijs (1663–1770). It is likely she received her first lessons in her father's workshop. She was later trained by and then worked with Rosalba Carriera (1673–1757), the most famous woman artist of her time, specializing in portraits in pastel and miniature. Since Carlevarijs's technique is similar to Carriera's, only a small group of pastel portraits has been convincingly ascribed to her. Carlevarijs was patronized by the eminent Venetian Zenobio and Balbi families.

59

Portrait of a Young Lady

After 1741

Pastel on blue paper, mounted on canvas, 17⁵⁄₁₆ × 13 in. (44 × 33 cm)

Private collection, Connecticut

Hartford only

BEFORE ITS RECENT attribution to Marianna Carlevarijs, this portrait was ascribed to her teacher, the Venetian pastellist Rosalba Carriera. This confusion about works from Carlevarijs's hand is typical given our scant knowledge of the artist and the organization of Carriera's workshop. Carlevarijs probably entered the studio during the 1720s or early 1730s, when "Rosalba" was a celebrity in Venice and required the help of students and assistants to satisfy the demand for her work. The busy Venetian workshop consisted mostly, if not exclusively, of female students.[1] The portrait under discussion here both demonstrates Marianna Carlevarijs's considerable technical skills and serves as an example of Carriera's distinctive influence on numerous artists working in Venice during the second quarter of the eighteenth century. One sees in it traces of Carriera's technical virtuosity and her typical working process, such as the choice of blue paper and the use of thin strainers. Carlevarijs learned how to emulate her teacher's style and thus contributed to the international success of the Carriera brand.

While little is known about her early years, Marianna Carlevarijs must have learned to work in pastel and miniatures in Carriera's highly specialized workshop.[2] In 1738, she is mentioned in Tomaso Temanza's (1705–1789) *Zibaldon* as an independent painter of portraits, distinguished by her earlier apprenticeship with Carriera.[3] According to Neil Jeffares, she was supported by the important Zenobio family of Venice.[4] No extant signed works by Carlevarijs have survived, but a small group of portraits in pastels has been convincingly ascribed to her. These pastels, now at the Ca' Rezzonico in Venice, demonstrate Carlevarijs's indebtedness to Carriera.[5]

Because of the close affinities with Rosalba Carriera's style, this work was ascribed to her until 2018. The metallic shine of the dress, slightly enlarged eyes, and small mouth, however, are typical of Marianna Carlevarijs's known portraits, particularly her *Portrait of Caterina Balbi* from 1735–1740 (fig. 1).[6] The portraits are similar in size and, more importantly, present young sitters in a more formal, less relaxed manner than portraits of youth by Carriera.

In this portrait of a still-unidentified sitter, the skin of the face and neck is remarkably fresh, a feat accomplished by the skillful handling of the pastel medium. Using only a small selection of crayons, Carlevarijs achieved an impeccably fair skin color, highly desired by her contemporaries. Splendidly dressed, with neatly coiffed hair and sizable pearl earrings, this young lady has the accoutrements of distinction, but her large eyes and small nose and mouth betray her youth. The vaporous qualities of pastel colors also greatly enhance the young

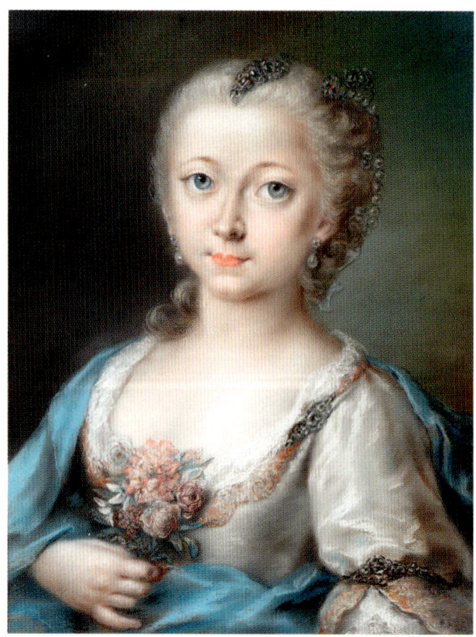

FIGURE 1 Marianna Carlevarijs, *Portrait of Caterina Balbi*, 1735–1740, pastel on paper, 18½ × 14¹⁵⁄₁₆ in. (47 × 38 cm). Ca' Rezzonico, Venice, Cl. I n. 1456

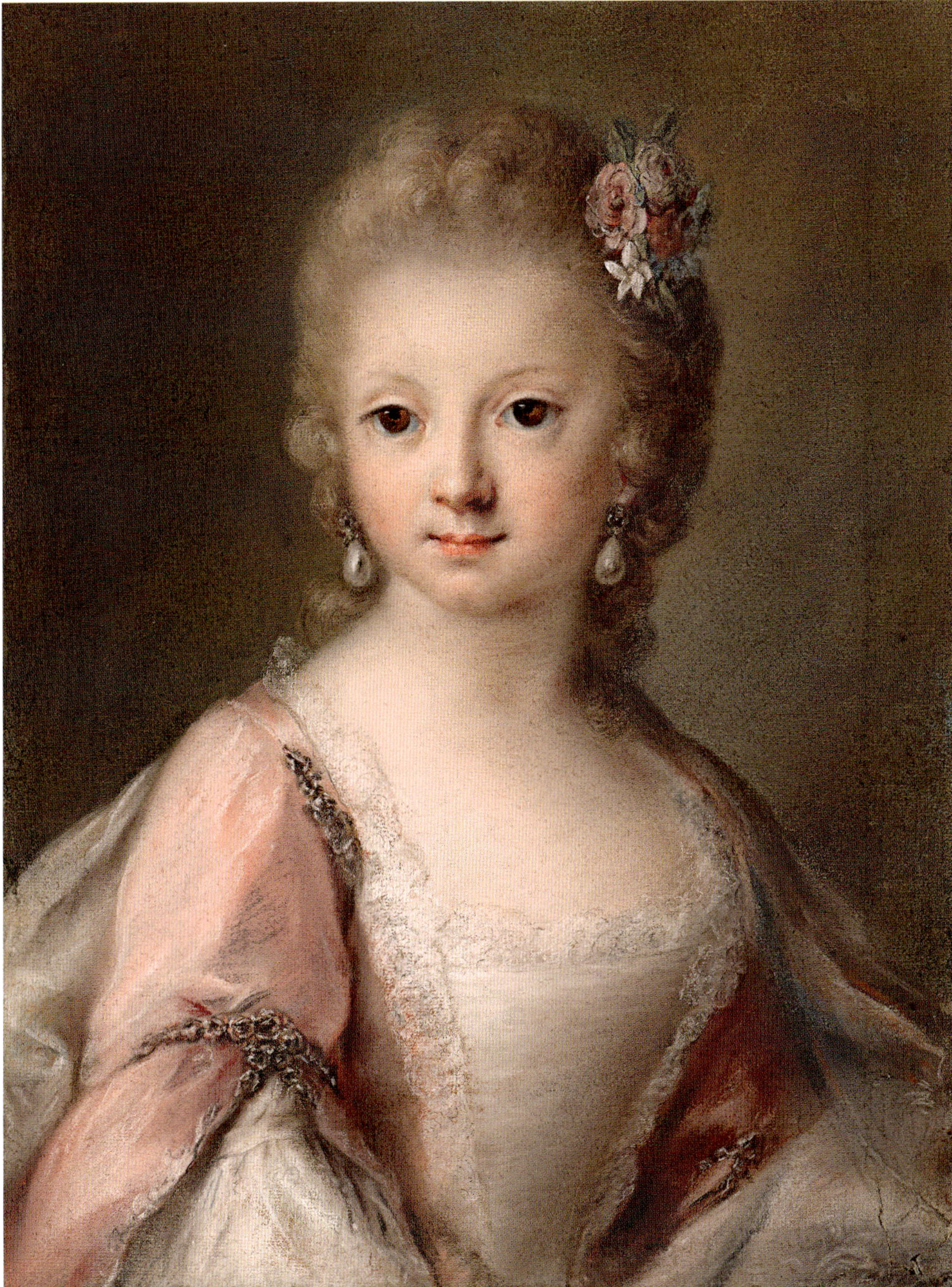

3. "Marianna è brava Pittrice di ritratti, e fu allieva di Rosalba Carriera." See Temanza 1993, 57, here quoted after Bottacin 1996, 156–163, 159.

4. Jeffares 2020b, 1.

5. This set of four pastels was gifted with an old attribution to Carlevarijs by the Balbi Valier family in 1906 to the Ca' Rezzonico. See Bottacin 1996, 159. See also Jeffares 2020b, J.198.101; J.198.102; J.198.105; J.198.107.

6. Jeffares 2020b, J.198.107.

7. On Carriera's working process, see Burns 2007, 111–13.

PROVENANCE
November 9, 2003, sold by (Semenzato, Venice, Italy), lot 75, as attributed to Rosalba Carriera; May 30, 2018, sold by (Cambi Casa d'Aste, Genoa, Italy), lot 131, as attributed to Rosalba Carriera; private collection (Venice, Italy); March 2020–present, sold at TEFAF Maastricht 2020 by (Tomasso Brothers Fine Art, London, UK) to a private collection (Connecticut) as Marianna Carlevarijs.

SELECTED PUBLICATIONS
Jeffares 2020b, 1–2, no. J.198.116.

sitter's appeal. With fluid strokes and a nuanced palette, Carlevarijs hints at the contrast between role and age. Carefully built up on blue paper, the shimmering effects of the satin dress contrast with the crisp forms of the jewelry.

This pastel is mounted on a canvas with a thin wooden strainer similar to those used by Rosalba Carriera.[7] It is lined with pages from a book published in Venice in 1741 and was likely painted shortly afterwards.—OT

NOTES

1. A few members of Rosalba Carriera's workshop are known in addition to Carlevarijs: her sisters, Angela (1677–1760) and Giovanna Carriera (1675–1737); Felicità Sartori (ca. 1714–1760); Margherita Terzi (mentioned in Venice in the year 1756); and Luisa Bergalli (1703–1779). On Marianna Carlevarijs see Bottacin 1996, 155–63. For Sartori see Puhlmann 2003.

2. No miniature by Carlevarijs has survived, but Moschini describes her as an artist practicing in pastel and miniatures. Moschini 1806, vol. 3/4, 88.

MARIA FELICE TIBALDI

Rome, 1707–1770

BORN INTO A CULTIVATED family, Maria Felice Tibaldi was one of the most successful women artists in Rome in the mid-eighteenth century. After an early beginning in oil painting, Tibaldi switched to miniatures and the occasional pastel. She was trained by the famed miniaturist Giovanni Felice Ramelli (1666–1740). In 1739 Tibaldi married the French painter Pierre Subleyras (1699–1749). In 1742 she was elected into the Accademia di San Luca (Academy of Saint Luke) in Rome. Her miniature copy of a work by Subleyras was acquired by Pope Benedict XIV (1740–1758) for the Capitoline Museums in 1752. This is one of the first pictures—if not the first—by a contemporary artist purchased by a public art museum.

60

Madame Subleyras, née Maria Felice Tibaldi

Pierre Subleyras (Saint-Gilles, France, 1699–Rome, 1749)
1739 (?)
Oil on canvas, 39 × 29¼ in. (99.1 × 74.3 cm)
Worcester Art Museum, Massachusetts, Gift of Helen Bigelow Merriman, 1901.54

A SPECIALIST IN MINIATURES, Maria Felice Tibaldi was admitted as a professional woman artist into the prestigious Accademia di San Luca in Rome in 1742, having been preceded by the famed Venetian miniaturist and pastellist Rosalba Carriera (1673–1757) in 1705. Despite her professional accomplishments, Tibaldi is only indirectly shown to be an artist in this portrait by her husband, the French painter Pierre Subleyras, who has largely followed the conventions of society portraits and rendered his wife as the attractive socialite that, according to contemporaneous sources, she was.

Tibaldi is seated in a luxurious space that can hardly be described as an artist's studio, despite the easel with a picture in the background. It resembles instead a salon or boudoir.[1] Sporting a floral corsage at her décolletage, she wears an elegant dress with rich trimmings and precious stones. As the daughter of the famous violinist Giovanni Battista Tibaldi (1660–1750), she came from a successful family that was well connected in Rome. Tibaldi and Subleyras had already met around 1735, but

to match his future wife's financial standing, Subleyras had to delay his marriage proposal until 1739. If it is true that he painted this portrait on the occasion of their wedding in March 1739, it emphasizes Tibaldi's social prominence at an important moment in their lives.[2] The unframed painting of a young woman, typical of Subleyras's production, may be understood as a reference to his artistic profession.[3] It should be mentioned that Subleyras painted his wife with a remarkable, if not unprecedented softness, not unlike a pastel. As if he had caressed Tibaldi's skin with soft touches of his brush, Subleyras created a powdery looking surface that epitomizes his wife's youthful nature.

This portrait confirms that miniatures played an important role in Tibaldi's career. Making eye contact with the viewer, she plays with an oval miniature. The motif of an artist or collector presenting one of his or her pictures to the viewer had been popular in representations of painters since the Renaissance.[4] According to Olivier Michel and Pierre Rosenberg, the second miniature, standing on the console table, is a copy after Francesco Mancini's (1679–1758) *Amor and Pan*.[5] Precious miniatures like this were associated closely with the courtly sphere in the eighteenth century and earlier. These avidly collected luxury objects were painted not only by professional artists who specialized in them, but also by a growing number of amateurs, especially female aristocrats. At the time, painting miniatures was considered perfectly legitimate for women of rank.[6] By showing Tibaldi with miniatures in a salon-like setting, Subleyras obfuscates her professional status—she might easily be mistaken for a socialite rather than a miniaturist, or she may be taken for both. Tibaldi was portrayed contemporaneously at least two more times.[7] In each case, she is shown as an artist working on miniatures. It is therefore noteworthy that Subleyras rejected this formula in his portrait of his wife. By contrast, however, Subleyras depicted many male artists performing their professional work. In a portrait of Giovanni Felice Ramelli from 1735, he shows the miniaturist seated with his palette, small pots, and a brush on the table (fig. 1).

Nonetheless, unlike any other contemporaneous portrait, this likeness of Maria Felice Tibaldi broadly reflects the importance and allure of miniatures for women artists during the eighteenth century. By specializing in this genre, women artists like Tibaldi profited from its association with the courtly sphere and were able to advance their careers.—OT

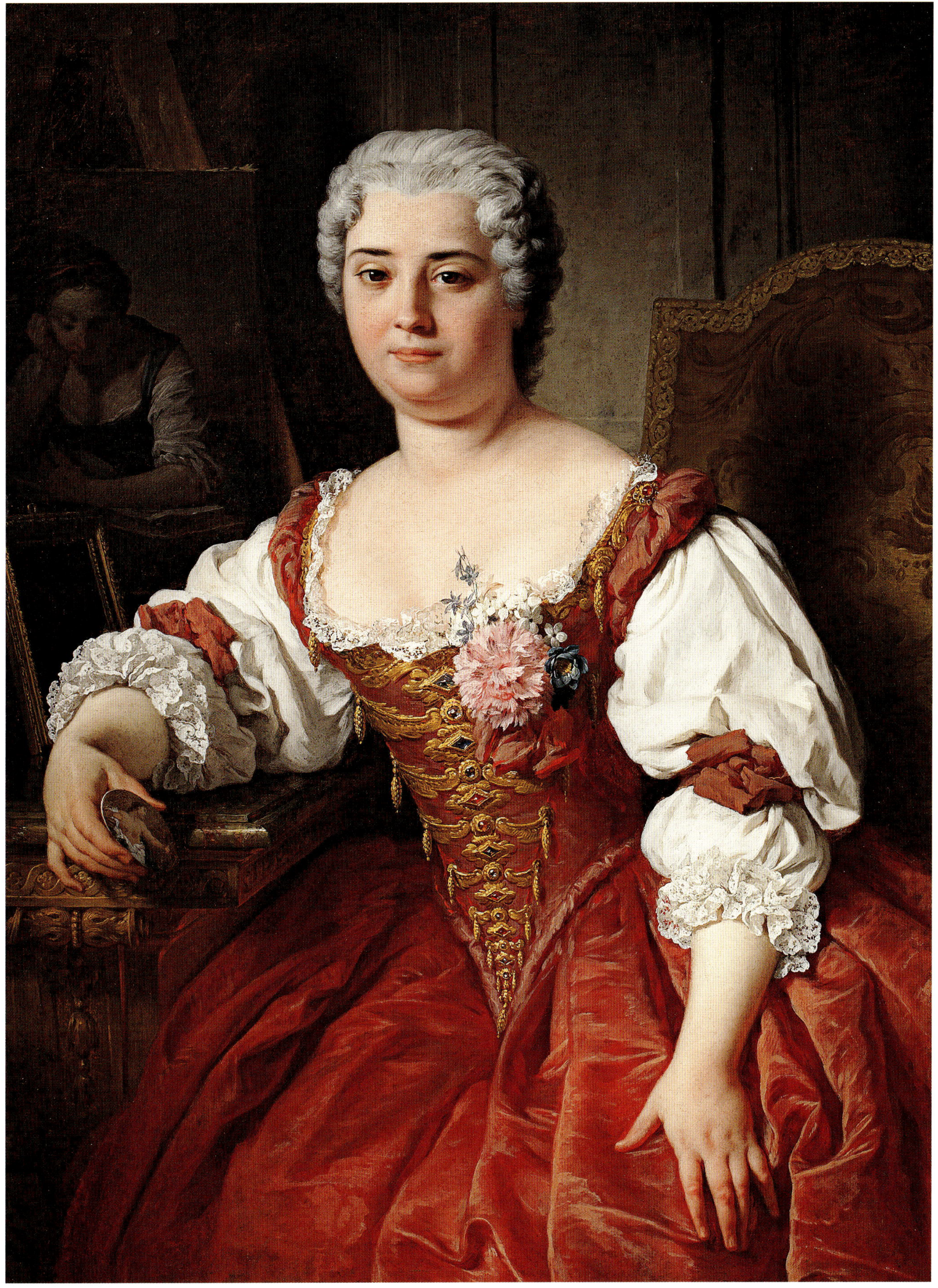

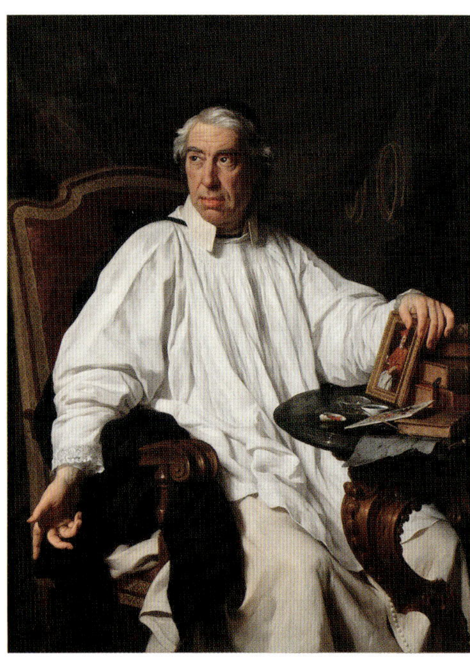

NOTES

1. Johns, however, describes it as a studio space in Johns 2019, 171 n. 1.

2. Rosenberg and Michel 1987b, Rosenberg 2000, and Johns 2019 date this painting ca. 1739.

3. Rosenberg and Michel 1987b suggested that this easel painting, now lost, was painted by Subleyras. Is it possible that it depicts Tibaldi at an earlier moment in her life?

4. In addition, this motif was occasionally used by artists to depict their wives. Carlo Maratti's (1625–1713) portrait of his mistress and later wife Francesca Gommi (1660–1711) set an important precedent in Roman portraiture for Subleyras. See Carlo Maratti, *Portrait of Francesca Gommi Maratti*, ca. 1701, oil on canvas, 38¾ × 29⁵⁄₁₆ in. (98.5 × 74.5 cm), Cleveland Museum of Art.

5. See Rosenberg and Michel 1987b, and Rosenberg 2000.

6. See, for instance, Catherine Perrot's (ca. 1620–after 1693) influential manual on miniature painting from 1686 and 1693 that addresses foremost a female readership.

7. Unknown artist, *Portrait of Maria Felice Tibaldi*, pen and black chalk, 7¹³⁄₁₆ × 6¹³⁄₁₆ in. (19.8 × 17.3 cm), Gallerie degli Uffizi, Gabinetto dei Disegni e delle stampe, Florence, inv. 8414 S. Pierre Rosenberg suggests this is a self-portrait by Tibaldi and dates it ca. 1740. See Rosenberg and Michel 1987a, 134–35. Pier Luigi Ghezzi, *Signora Subleyras*, March 18, 1739, black ink on paper, Biblioteca Vaticana, Ottoboni Lat. 3318, fol. 59.

PROVENANCE

Purchased from (Müller, Amsterdam, the Netherlands) by Helen Bigelow Merriman; 1901–present, gift to the Worcester Art Museum (Massachusetts).

SELECTED EXHIBITIONS

Copley Hall, Boston, 1902; Royal Academy, London, 1968, no. 647; Musée du Luxembourg, Paris, 1987; Philadelphia Museum of Art, 2000.

SELECTED PUBLICATIONS

Boston 1902, 37, no. 25; Arnaud 1928–1930, 84, no. 155; Juynboll 1934, 186; Clark 1964–1965, 48–50, fig. 1; Wilenski 1973, 119; Rich 1974, 288, 601 illus.; Paris 1987, 37, 77–81, pl. IX; Rosenberg and Michel 1987b, 238–39, cat. 63, illus.; Philadelphia 2000, 439; Rosenberg 2000, 436, cat. 283, illus.; Morandotti 2018, 13–31; Johns 2019, 167–68, fig. 1.

VERONICA STERN TELLI

Rome, 1717–1801

DURING HER LIFETIME, which she spent entirely in Rome, Veronica Stern Telli was a well-known miniaturist. Little is known about her work, life, and career, but in May 1742 she was admitted to the Accademia di San Luca (Academy of Saint Luke) in Rome, where she was listed as a miniaturist. Around that time, she married. Thanks to her artistic family, she had close connections to the exiled Stuart court and other high-ranking circles in Rome, for which she primarily painted portraits. She also made miniature copies of portraits by fashionable painters such as Pompeo Batoni (1708–1787).

61

A Lady Playing the Lute (Allegory of Music?)

1740s
Signed on the obverse: Veronica/****n
Gouache and watercolor on ivory miniature, rectangular, height: 2⅛ in. (5.4 cm)
Private collection, Connecticut

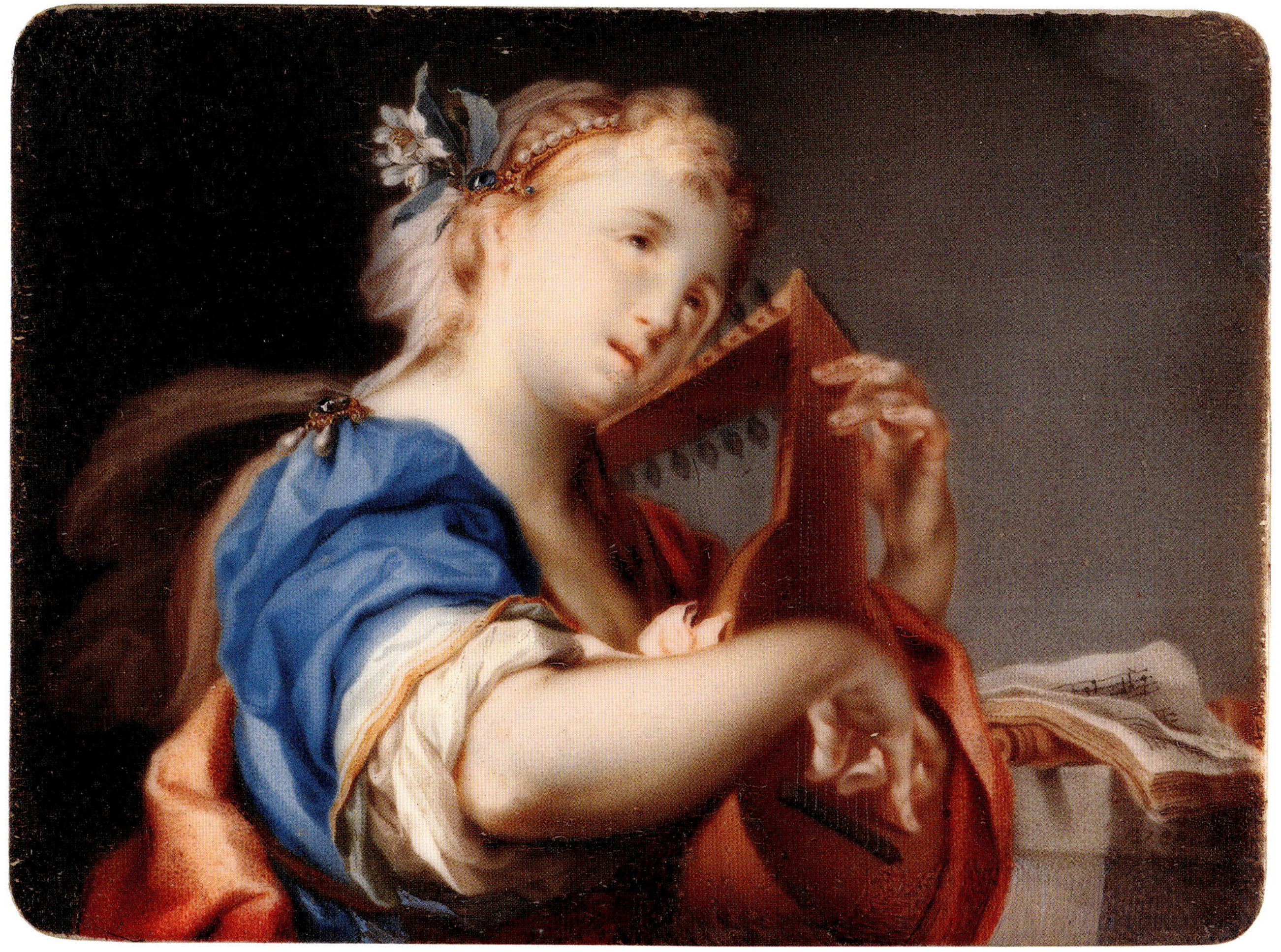

ROME WAS A LEADING CENTER in miniature making in the eighteenth century. The intimate scale of these diminutive artworks attracted local collectors as well as visiting tourists. Many women practiced in this genre and the most successful among them were able to sell their works for considerable prices. Indeed, miniatures provided women a highly respected niche in the Roman art world. By 1796 the Accademia di San Luca (Academy of Saint Luke) had accepted numerous women as professional members, the majority of whom were miniaturists.[1] By that year, Veronica Stern Telli was the oldest member of the academy, which she had entered more than fifty years earlier in 1742, directly following the admission of Maria Felice Tibaldi (1707–1770) (cat. 60), another Roman miniaturist. It is worth noting that Stern Telli and Tibaldi followed the Venetian Rosalba Carriera (1673–1757), who had entered the academy in 1705 with a miniature as a reception piece (Tostmann "The Advantages of Painting Small," fig. 8). Carriera had a marked influence on Roman miniaturists of the following generations.

Veronica Stern Telli spent her life in Rome.[2] She was recognized for her portraits and considered by contemporaries to be "the best painter of miniatures in Italy."[3] This ravishing miniature, exhibited for the first time, presents an important addition to her known oeuvre.

Occasionally, Stern Telli painted miniature copies after larger oil paintings. Many miniaturists practiced this lucrative side-business. Here she worked from a now-lost model by the sought-after Roman painter Giuseppe Bartolomeo Chiari (1654–1727). A drawing by him that survives in the collection of the Albertina Museum in Vienna shows a young woman playing an unseen stringed instrument (fig. 1).[4] Its connection with this miniature has not been recognized thus far. The figure is in a similar pose as in Stern Telli's miniature and wears a comparable classicizing dress, but Stern Telli emphasizes the subject's sensuous allure, showing the richly adorned player from below with her head tilted and her gaze directed upwards. Her idealized young musician is highly focused, animated, and fully devoted to her music; she may, indeed, be an allegorical depiction of music.

Stern Telli makes ample use of the natural white tone of the ivory tablet in the flesh colors. She may have seen this technique in earlier miniatures by Rosalba Carriera. Unlike Carriera, however, she uses a muted palette that is evenly applied in a highly finished manner. This polished style had become popular in Rome, especially in the wake of the painter Carlo Maratti (1625–1713), and it was also practiced by his pupil Chiari. *A Lady Playing the Lute* reflects Carriera's distinctive influence on miniaturists in the eighteenth century while showcasing a refined technique that was fashionable in Rome during the first half of the eighteenth century.—OT

NOTES

1. Out of fourteen women, eleven are listed as professional artists in the statutes of the art academy in 1796. Six of them specialized in miniatures. While five are identified as miniaturists, the sixth, Caterina Cherubini (1730–1811) is listed as a painter. Today she is only known as a miniaturist. *Statuti* 1796, 52–54.

2. Noack 1920. See also Corp 2011, 297–301.

3. Quoted in Clark 1985, vol. 1, 56.

4. On this drawing and Chiari, see Kerber 1968, 80.

PROVENANCE

November 19, 2008, sold at (Bonhams Knightsbridge, London, UK), lot 37; 2010–present, sold at TEFAF Maastricht 2010 by (Rafael Valls Limited, London, UK) to a private collection (Connecticut) as Veronica Stern Telli.

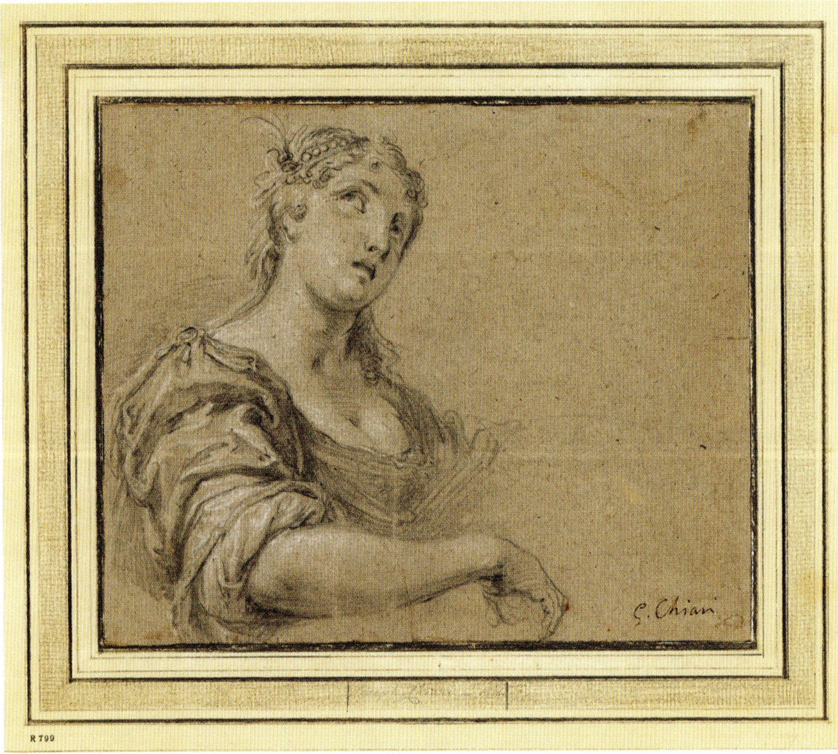

FIGURE 1 Giuseppe Bartolomeo Chiari, *Woman Looking Upward (Allegory of Music?)*, black and white chalk, 8½ × 10⅜ in. (21.6 × 26.4 cm). Albertina Museum, Vienna, no. 1146

ANNA BACHERINI PIATTOLI

Florence, 1720–1788

IN 1741 ANNA BACHERINI married the painter Gaetano Piattoli (1703–1774) and her earliest commissioned works are signed "Anna Piattoli." She studied with Francesco Ciaminghi (died 1736), Francesco Conti (1681–1760), and Violante Beatrice Siries Cerroti (1709–1783), another Italian woman artist in Florence. Although Piattoli worked mostly in that city, she spent several years as the official portrait painter for the Verrazzano family in the Prato region. In addition to the self-portrait for which she is most famous, she created portraits of nobility and religious figures and is credited with the designs for prints by Pier Antonio Pazzi (1706–1768), Francesco Bartolozzi (1727–1815), and Carlo Faucci (1729–1784). After her husband's death she lived out her years in relative solitude and poverty.

62

Self-Portrait at the Age of Fifty-Six

1776

Oil on canvas, 30¹³⁄₁₆ × 23⅝ in. (78.2 × 60 cm)

Signed: Anna Bacherini/Piattoli nata 1720/d'anni 56 [Anna Piattoli born 1720 56 years old]

Gallerie degli Uffizi, Florence, inv. 1890 no. 2032

THIS DEEPLY EXPRESSIVE and poignant self-portrait of artist Anna Bacherini Piattoli at age fifty-six serves as a bookend to the exhibition.[1] The three-quarter length portrayal shows the sitter at a three-quarter angle before a primed but unpainted canvas. Dressed in an ochre dress and white bonnet, both decorated with light blue ribbons, her hands resting decorously atop her workstation like a patrician posing for her portrait, the artist pauses from her work to confront the viewer with an alert and unprepossessing countenance. On the easel before her is a partially executed copy in miniature—in oil with the color palette and appearance of pastel—of the Florentine Renaissance artist Andrea del Sarto's (1486–1530) *Madonna of the Sack* (*Madonna del Sacco*), a lunette fresco from 1525 in the cloister of the Basilica of Santissima Annunziata in Florence (fig. 1).[2] Piattoli thus presents herself as a painter of multiple genres in myriad media—miniatures, pastels, copies, and portraits, in this case a self-portrait.[3] As attested to by the scene she copies, she also executed religious subjects, including religious portraits (fig. 2).[4]

As we know from the eighteenth-century Florentine diplomat, art collector, and biographer Niccolò Gabburri (1676–1742), Anna Bacherini Piattoli, who was born in Florence, and lived the majority of her life there, studied with Francesco Ciaminghi, Francesco Conti, and with another woman artist, Violante Beatrice Siries Cerroti—pointing to the matrilineal dissemination of artistic knowledge that began in Bologna in the seventeenth century with Elisabetta Sirani (1638–1665) and became more common in the eighteenth century.[5] In 1741 she married the painter Gaetano Piattoli; they had two children, Gaetano Piattoli (1748–1834), who was a painter and engraver, and Scipione Piattoli (1749–1809), who was a priest, educator, and political activist.[6]

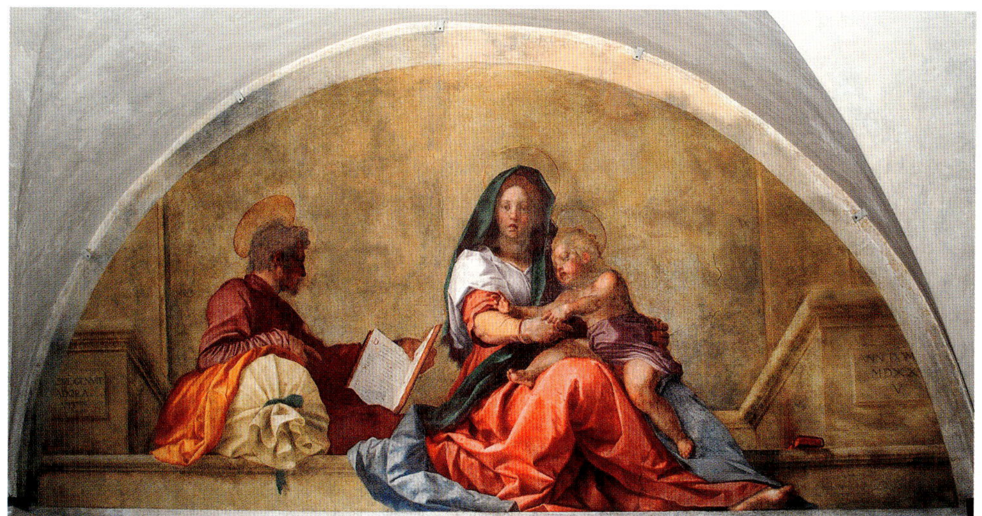

FIGURE 1 Andrea del Sarto, *Madonna of the Sack* (*Madonna del Sacco*), 1525, fresco, 75³⁄₁₆ × 158¹¹⁄₁₆ in. (191 × 403 cm). Cloister of the Santissima Annunziata, Florence

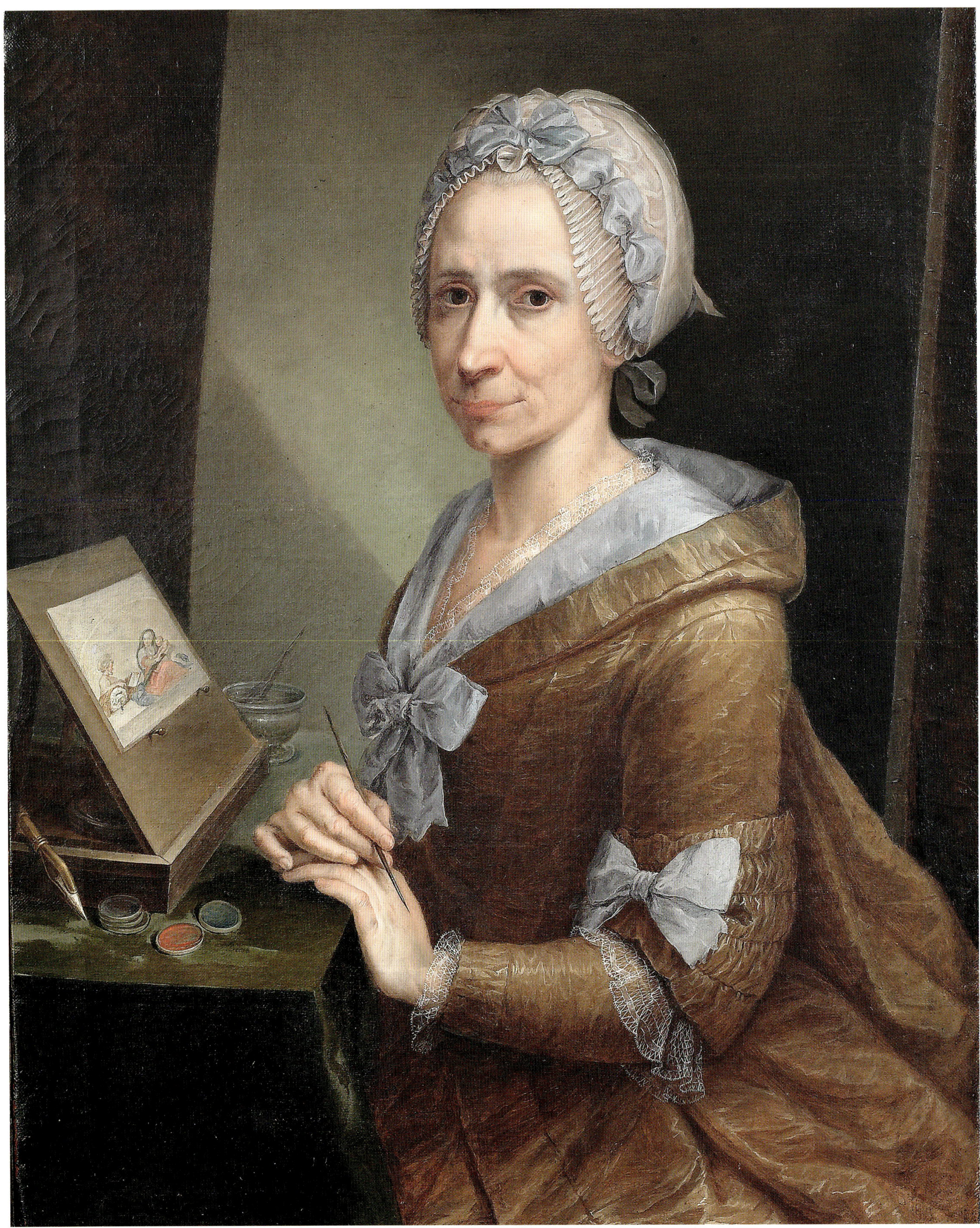

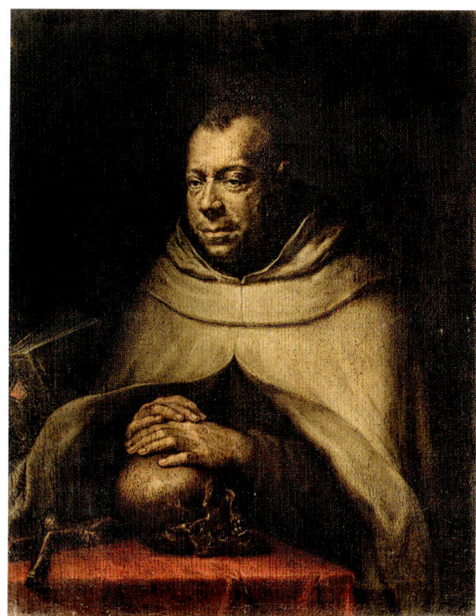

FIGURE 2 Anna Bacherini Piattoli, *Portrait of Father Ildefonso Gonzaga*, 1750, oil on canvas, 38⁹⁄₁₆ × 30⁵⁄₁₆ in. (98 × 77 cm). Gallerie degli Uffizi, Florence, deposito, inv. 5142

When her husband died in 1774, the artist found herself in financial difficulties. By all accounts, she gifted this self-portrait to Grand Duke Pietro Leopoldo (1747–1792) in 1776 with the hope of receiving monies in exchange—she eventually received fifteen zecchini.[7] This celebration of the power and pathos of aging is Anna Bacherini Piattoli's best-known work—the rest of her artistic output has yet to come into full focus.[8]—ESP

NOTES

1. Another self-portrait of the artist once existed in the collection of Marchese Giuseppe Riccardi (1744–1789), as listed in his 1776 inventory, ASF (Archivio di Stato, Florence), Riccardi 272: "A di 27 settembre 1776 Nota dei ritratti de' pittori che si ritrovano in questa villa del Terrafino del Illustrissimo Signore Marchese Giuseppe Riccardi." See Barker 2016a, 14 n. 31.

2. There are numerous copies in all media after this popular lunette fresco by Andrea del Sarto. See, for example, Cesare Mariannecci (active 1850s–1870), *Copy after the Madonna del Sacco, Andrea del Sarto in the Cloister of Santissima Annunziata (Florence)*, 1861, watercolor and pencil on paper, 17⁷⁄₈ × 29⁹⁄₁₆ in. (45.4 × 67.4 cm), Arundel Society (commissioned and published), Victoria and Albert Museum, London, 4591; and unknown artist, *After Andrea del Sarto's The Madonna del Sacco*, 1600–1699, oil on canvas, 78¼ × 135½ in. (198.8 × 344.2 cm), Royal Collection Trust, England, RCIN 406129.

3. Portraits by Piattoli of Teresa Vai (dates unknown) survive in the Galleria del Palazzo Communale, Prato, as well as portraits of the Medici Grand Duchess Anna Maria Luisa (1667–1743) and other members of the Medici court. Badino 2010, 58, cat. 13. See also Ferraiuolo 2020, fig. 53 and fig. 55 (*Portrait of Father Ildefonso Gonzaga*, 1750, Gallerie degli Uffizi, Florence, deposits); fig. 61 (*Father Giovanni Maria di Gesù*, 1769, Gallerie degli Uffizi, Florence); fig. 64 (*Saint Teresa Margherita del Sacro Cuore di Gesù*, 1770, Ex-Convent of the Carmelites, Florence).

4. There is a signed painting by Piattoli of a praying Saint Francis, in need of conservation, in storage at the San Salvi museum, Florence. For the Church of Santa Marta in Montughi, the artist created the *Blessed Margherita del Caccia in Florence*. Fortune 2009, 49; Ferraiuolo 2020, 150, fig. 53. In addition, Piattoli created portraits of nobility and religious figures and is credited with the "disegno," or designs, for prints by Francesco Bartolozzi (1727–1815), Pier Antonio Pazzi (1706–1768), and Carlo Faucci (1729–1784). For the portraits see Ferraiuolo 2020, 144–47, and for the prints see 159, fig. 62; 160, fig. 63; 162, fig. 65.

5. Piattoli spent several years working as the official portrait painter for the Verrazzano family in the Prato region in the early 1770s. Ferraiuolo 2020, 142.

6. For a biographical sketch of Anna Bacherini Piattoli, see Gabburri ca. 1730–1742. For information on her children, see Ferraiuolo 2020, 148.

7. Berti 1979, 957, no. A693.

8. Ferraiuolo's 2020 essay is a move in this direction.

PROVENANCE

1776, gift of the artist to Pietro Leopoldo, Grand Duke of Tuscany [1747–1792] (Florence, Italy); Gallerie degli Uffizi (Florence, Italy).

SELECTED EXHIBITIONS

Galleria degli Uffizi, Florence, 2010–2011.

SELECTED PUBLICATIONS

Ademollo 1887, 99–100; Pera 1888, 349–50, 526; Viallet 1923, 73–74, illus.; Pera 1971, 8–9; Prinz 1971, 53; Berti 1979, 957, no. A693, illus.; Greer 1979, 79, illus.; Badino 2010, 58, cat. 13, illus.; Charles and Carl 2010, 319, no. 601, illus.; Gaze 2011, 37; Fortune 2014, 49, 52, 213; Jeffares 2019, 1; Ferraiuolo 2020, 141–43, 155, fig. 58.

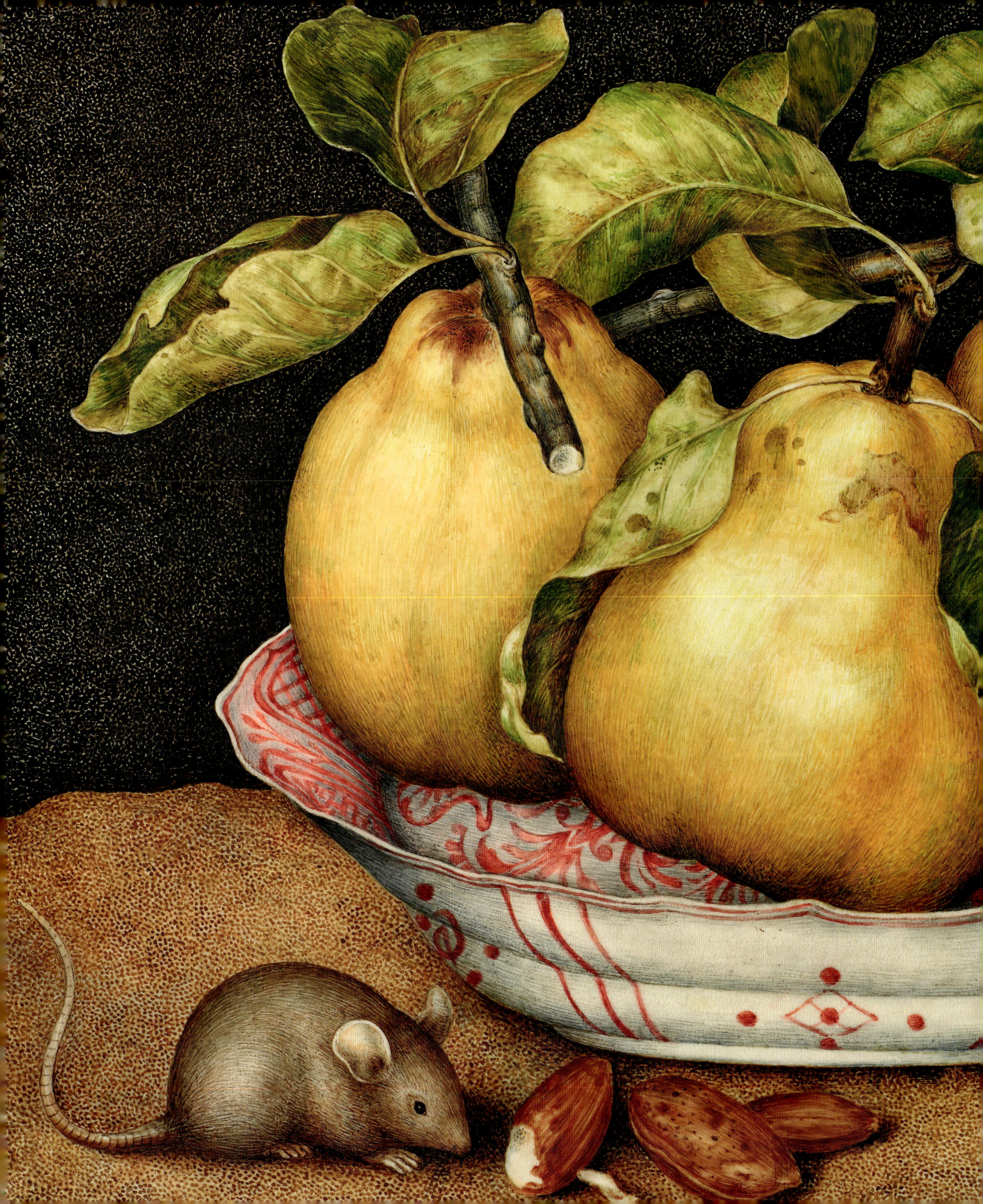

EXHIBITIONS

ALBERTINA MUSEUM, VIENNA, 1924
International Exhibition of Miniatures, Albertina Museum, Vienna, May–June 1924.

ALBUQUERQUE MUSEUM, 2005
El Alma de España/The Soul of Spain, Albuquerque Museum, April 17–July 31, 2005.

ANTIOCH COLLEGE, YELLOW SPRINGS, 1963–1964
Antioch College, Yellow Springs, Ohio, 1963–1964.

BAYERISCHE STAATSGEMÄLDESAMMLUNGEN, ALTE PINAKOTHEK, MUNICH, 1984–1985
Italian Still Life Painting from Three Centuries: The Silvano Lodi Collection, Bayerische Staatsgemäldesammlungen, Alte Pinakothek, Munich, November 27, 1984–February 22, 1985.

BIBLIOTECA ANTICA DEL CONVENTO DEL SANTO, SANT'ANTONIO DI PADOVA, 2019
700 Veneziano: Opere dalla Collezione Gallo Fine Art, Biblioteca Antica del Convento del Santo, Sant'Antonio di Padova, June 15–July 6, 2019.

CASA BUONARROTI, FLORENCE, 1991
Artemisia, Casa Buonarroti, Florence, June 18–November 4, 1991.

CENTRO CULTURALE "CITTÀ DI CREMONA," 1994
Sofonisba Anguissola e le sue sorelle, Centro culturale "Città di Cremona," September 17–December 11, 1994.

CHIESA DI SAN CARLO, MODENA, 1998–1999
Tesori ritrovati: La pittura del ducato estense nel collezionismo privato, Chiesa di San Carlo, Modena, October 24, 1998–January 10, 1999.

CLEVELAND MUSEUM OF ART, 1971–1972
Caravaggio and His Followers, Cleveland Museum of Art, October 30, 1971–January 2, 1972.

CLEVELAND MUSEUM OF ART, 1984–1985
Bernardo Cavallino of Naples, 1616–1656, Cleveland Museum of Art, November 14–December 30, 1984; Kimbell Art Museum, Fort Worth, January 26–March 24, 1985; Museo Pignatelli Cortes, Naples, April 24–June 26, 1985.

CLEVELAND MUSEUM OF ART, 2013–2014
Disembodied: Portrait Miniatures and Their Contemporary Relatives, Cleveland Museum of Art, November 10, 2013–February 16, 2014.

COOPER UNION MUSEUM FOR THE ARTS OF DECORATION, NEW YORK, 1962
The Architect's Eye, Cooper Union Museum for the Arts of Decoration, New York, 1962.

COPLEY HALL, BOSTON, 1902
A Loan Collection of Portraits and Pictures of Fair Women, Copley Hall, Boston, February 27–March 27, 1902.

CORNELL FINE ARTS MUSEUM AT ROLLINS COLLEGE, WINTER PARK, 1991
Italian Renaissance and Baroque Paintings in Florida Museums, Cornell Fine Arts Museum at Rollins College, Winter Park, Fla., March 14–May 5, 1991.

CORNELL FINE ARTS MUSEUM AT ROLLINS COLLEGE, WINTER PARK, 1993–1996
Treasures of the Cornell Fine Arts Museum, Cornell Fine Arts Museum at Rollins College, Winter Park, Fla., June 5–September 26, 1993; Center for the Arts, Vero Beach, Fla.; Samuel P. Harn Museum of Art, University of Florida, Gainesville; Polk Museum of Art, Lakeland, Fla.; Center for the Fine Arts, Miami, 1994–1996.

DETROIT INSTITUTE OF ARTS, 1952
Venice, 1700–1800: An Exhibition of Venice and the Eighteenth Century, Detroit Institute of Arts, September 30–November 2, 1952; John Herron Art Museum, Indianapolis, November 14–December 31, 1952.

DETROIT INSTITUTE OF ARTS, 1965
Art in Italy, 1600–1700, Detroit Institute of Arts, April 6–May 9, 1965.

DETROIT INSTITUTE OF ARTS, 1993
Master Drawings from the Permanent Collection, 1500–1800, Detroit Institute of Arts, June 10–September 5, 1993.

DETROIT INSTITUTE OF ARTS, 2009
Learning by Line: The Role of Drawing in the Eighteenth Century, Detroit Institute of Arts, February 18–June 15, 2009.

FIERA DELL'ANTIQUARIATO, MODENA, 2012
Fiera dell'Antiquariato, Modena, 2012.

FINCH COLLEGE MUSEUM OF ART, NEW YORK, 1961
A Loan Exhibition of Venetian Paintings of the 18th Century, Finch College Museum of Art, New York, October 31–December 16, 1961.

GALLERIA DEGLI UFFIZI, FLORENCE, 1975
Pittori bolognesi del Seicento nelle gallerie di Firenze, Galleria degli Uffizi, Florence, February–April 1975.

GALLERIA DEGLI UFFIZI, FLORENCE, 2010–2011
Autoritratte: "Artiste di capriccioso e destrissimo ingegno," Galleria degli Uffizi, Florence, December 17, 2010–January 30, 2011.

GALLERIA PALATINA, PALAZZO PITTI, FLORENCE, 2010–2011
Caravaggio e Caravaggeschi a Firenze, Galleria Palatina, Palazzo Pitti, Florence, May 22, 2010–January 9, 2011.

HERBERT F. JOHNSON MUSEUM OF ART, 1990–1996
Herbert F. Johnson Museum of Art, Cornell University, Ithaca, New York, 1990–1996.

HOOD MUSEUM OF ART, DARTMOUTH COLLEGE, HANOVER, 2000
The Power of Appearances: Renaissance and Reformation Portrait Prints, Hood Museum of Art, Dartmouth College, Hanover, N.H., October 7–December 3, 2000.

ISRAEL MUSEUM, JERUSALEM, 1994
Natura Morta Italiana: Italian Still Life Painting from Four Centuries: The Silvano Lodi Collection/Natura morta italiana: Quattro secoli di natura morta italiana: La raccolta Silvano Lodi, Israel Museum, Jerusalem, June–October 1994.

JOSLYN ART MUSEUM, OMAHA, 1997–1998
Hot Dry Men and Cold Wet Women: The Theory of Humors in Western European Art 1575–1700, Joslyn Art Museum, Omaha, September 13–November 2, 1997; Arkansas Arts Center, Little Rock, November 20, 1997–February 6, 1998; John and Mable Ringling Museum of Art, Sarasota, February 27–April 24, 1998.

KUNSTHAUS ZURICH, 1964–1965
Das italienische Stilleben von den Anfängen bis zur Gegenwart, Kunsthaus Zurich, December 1964–February 1965; Museum Boymans-Van Beuningen, Rotterdam, March–April 1965.

KUNSTHISTORISCHES MUSEUM, VIENNA, 1995
La prima donna pittrice Sofonisba Anguissola: Die Malerin der Renaissance (um 1535–1625), Kunsthistorisches Museum, Vienna, January 17–March 26, 1995.

KUNSTHISTORISCHES MUSEUM, VIENNA, 2019–2020
Caravaggio and Bernini, Kunsthistorisches Museum, Vienna, October 15, 2019–January 19, 2020; *Caravaggio-Bernini: Baroque in Rome*, Rijksmuseum, Amsterdam, February 14–September 13, 2020.

LEEDS GENERAL INFIRMARY, 1868
National Exhibition of Works of Art, at Leeds, 1868, Leeds General Infirmary, May 19–October 31, 1868.

L'OEIL GALERIE D'ART, PARIS, 1973
Tableaux italiens: XIVe–XVIIe siècle, L'Oeil Galerie d'Art, Paris, June–July 1973.

LOS ANGELES COUNTY MUSEUM OF ART, 1976–1977
Women Artists: 1550–1950, Los Angeles County Museum of Art, December 21, 1976–March 13, 1977; University Art Museum, University of Texas, Austin, April 12–June 12, 1977; Museum of Art, Carnegie Institute, Pittsburgh, July 14–September 4, 1977; Brooklyn Museum, October 8–November 27, 1977.

MAISON D'ART, MONTE CARLO, 2005
Le Meraviglie dell'arte: Important Old Master Paintings, Maison d'Art, Monte Carlo, March 25–April 25, 2005.

METROPOLITAN MUSEUM OF ART, NEW YORK, 1923
Loan Exhibition of the Arts of the Italian Renaissance, Metropolitan Museum of Art, New York, May 7–September 9, 1923.

METROPOLITAN MUSEUM OF ART, NEW YORK, 1950
Four Centuries of Miniature Painting, Metropolitan Museum of Art, New York, January 18–March 19, 1950.

METROPOLITAN MUSEUM OF ART, NEW YORK, 1965–1966
Drawings from New York Collections I: The Italian Renaissance, Metropolitan Museum of Art, New York, November 8, 1965–January 9, 1966.

METROPOLITAN MUSEUM OF ART, NEW YORK, 1981–1982
The Eighteenth-Century Woman, Metropolitan Museum of Art, New York, December 12, 1981–September 5, 1982.

METROPOLITAN MUSEUM OF ART, NEW YORK, 1995
Drawings and Prints: Selections from the Permanent Collection, Metropolitan Museum of Art, New York, February 6–April 16, 1995.

METROPOLITAN MUSEUM OF ART, NEW YORK, 1996–1997
European Miniatures in the Metropolitan Museum of Art, Metropolitan Museum of Art, New York, November 5, 1996–January 5, 1997.

METROPOLITAN MUSEUM OF ART, NEW YORK, 1999
Drawings and Prints: Selections from the Permanent Collection, Metropolitan Museum of Art, New York, May 3–July 25, 1999.

METROPOLITAN MUSEUM OF ART, NEW YORK, 2001–2002
Orazio and Artemisia Gentileschi: Father and Daughter Painters in Baroque Italy, Museo del Palazzo di Venezia, Rome, October 15, 2001–January 6, 2002; Metropolitan Museum of Art, New York, February 11–May 12, 2002; Saint Louis Art Museum, June 17–September 15, 2002.

METROPOLITAN MUSEUM OF ART, NEW YORK, 2004
Painters of Reality: The Legacy of Leonardo and Caravaggio in Lombardy, Metropolitan Museum of Art, New York, May 27–August 15, 2004.

METROPOLITAN MUSEUM OF ART, NEW YORK, 2015–2016
Fashion and Virtue: Textile Patterns and the Print Revolution, 1520–1620, Metropolitan Museum of Art, New York, October 20, 2015–January 10, 2016.

MUSÉE DE L'ORANGERIE, PARIS, 1952
La nature morte de l'antiquité à nos jours, Musée de l'Orangerie, Paris, April–September 1952.

MUSÉE DES BEAUX-ARTS DE NANTES, 2008–2009
Simon Vouet (les années italiennes 1613/1627), Musée des Beaux-Arts de Nantes, November 21, 2008–February 23, 2009; Musée des Beaux-Arts et d'Archéologie de Besançon, March 27–June 29, 2009.

MUSÉE DU LUXEMBOURG, PARIS, 1987
Subleyras, 1699–1749, Musée du Luxembourg, Paris, February 20–April 26, 1987; Académie de France, Villa Médicis, Rome, May 18–July 19, 1987.

MUSÉE MAILLOL, PARIS, 2012
Artemisia: Pouvoir, gloire et passions d'une femme peintre, Musée Maillol, Paris, March 14–July 15, 2012.

MUSEO CIVICO, CREMONA, 1985
I Campi e la cultura artistica cremonese del Cinquecento, Museo Civico, Cremona, April 27–July 28, 1985.

MUSEO CIVICO ALA PONZONE, CREMONA, 2004
Pittori della realtà: Le Ragioni di una Rivoluzione da Foppa e Leonardo a Caravaggio e Ceruti, Museo Civico Ala Ponzone, Cremona, February 14–May 2, 2004.

MUSEO CIVICO ARCHEOLOGICO, BOLOGNA, 1994
Lavinia Fontana (1552–1614), Museo Civico Archeologico, Bologna, October 1–December 4, 1994.

MUSEO CIVICO ARCHEOLOGICO, BOLOGNA, 2004–2005
Elisabetta Sirani "pittrice eroina" 1638–1665, Museo Civico Archeologico, Bologna, December 4, 2004–February 27, 2005.

MUSEO DI ROMA, PALAZZO BRASCHI, ROME, 2016–2017
Artemisia Gentileschi e il suo tempo, Museo di Roma, Palazzo Braschi, Rome, November 30, 2016–May 8, 2017.

MUSEO NACIONAL DEL PRADO, MADRID, 2019–2020
Historia de dos pintoras: Sofonisba Anguissola y Lavinia Fontana/A Tale of Two Women Painters: Sofonisba Anguissola and Lavinia Fontana, Museo Nacional del Prado, Madrid, October 22, 2019–February 2, 2020.

MUSEUM OF FINE ARTS, BOSTON, 1989
Italian Etchers of the Renaissance and Baroque: Parmigianino to Giordano, Museum of Fine Arts, Boston, January 24–April 2, 1989; Cleveland Museum of Art, April 25–June 25, 1989; National Gallery of Art, Washington, D.C., September 24–November 26, 1989.

MUSEUM OF FINE ARTS, ST. PETERSBURG, FLA., 1992
Hidden Treasures: Selections from the George D. and Harriet W. Cornell Fine Arts Museum, Museum of Fine Arts, St. Petersburg, Fla., March 1–May 10, 1992.

MUSEUM VOOR SCHONE KUNSTEN, GHENT, 2018–2019
De dames van de barok: Vrouwelijke schilders in het Italië van de 16de en 17de eeuw, Museum voor Schone Kunsten, Ghent, October 20, 2018–January 20, 2019.

MUSEUM WIESBADEN, 2016–2017
Caravaggios Erben: Barock in Neapel, Museum Wiesbaden, October 14, 2016–February 12, 2017.

NATIONAL GALLERY, LONDON, 2020–2021
Artemisia, National Gallery, London, October 3, 2020–January 24, 2021.

NATIONAL GALLERY OF ART, WASHINGTON, D.C., 1985
Landscape Prints from the National Gallery's Collection, National Gallery of Art, Washington, D.C., February 3–August 4, 1985.

NATIONAL GALLERY OF ART, WASHINGTON, D.C., 1992
Dürer to Diebenkorn: Recent Acquisitions of Art on Paper, National Gallery of Art, Washington, D.C., May 10–September 7, 1992.

NATIONAL MUSEUM OF WOMEN IN THE ARTS, WASHINGTON, D.C., 1995
Sofonisba Anguissola: A Renaissance Woman, National Museum of Women in the Arts, Washington, D.C., April 7–June 15, 1995.

NATIONAL MUSEUM OF WOMEN IN THE ARTS, WASHINGTON, D.C., 1998
Lavinia Fontana of Bologna, 1552–1614, National Museum of Women in the Arts, Washington, D.C., February 5–June 7, 1998.

NATIONAL MUSEUM OF WOMEN IN THE ARTS, WASHINGTON, D.C., 2007
Italian Women Artists from Renaissance to Baroque, National Museum of Women in the Arts, Washington, D.C., March 16–July 15, 2007.

NATIONAL MUSEUM OF WOMEN IN THE ARTS, WASHINGTON, D.C., 2014–2015
Picturing Mary: Woman, Mother, Idea, National Museum of Women in the Arts, Washington, D.C., December 5, 2014–April 12, 2015.

PALAIS DE TOKYO, PARIS, 2017–2018
Dioramas, Palais de Tokyo, Paris, June 14–September 10, 2017; *Diorama: Erfindung einer Illusion*, Schirn Kunsthalle, Frankfurt, October 6, 2017–January 21, 2018.

PALAZZO DUCALE, MANTUA, 1937
Mostra iconografica Gonzaghesca, Palazzo Ducale, Mantua, May 16–September 19, 1937.

PALAZZO FAVA, PALAZZO DELLE ESPOSIZIONI, PINACOTECA NAZIONALE, BOLOGNA, 2015
Da Cimabue a Morandi: Felsina Pittrice, Palazzo Fava, Palazzo delle Esposizioni, Pinacoteca Nazionale, Bologna, February 14–May 17, 2015.

PALAZZO PITTI, FLORENCE, 1970
Caravaggio e Caravaggeschi nelle gallerie di Firenze, Palazzo Pitti, Florence, July 8–September 30, 1970.

PALAZZO REALE, MILAN, 2007–2008
L'Arte delle donne dal Rinascimento al Surrealismo, Palazzo Reale, Milan, December 5, 2007–March 9, 2008.

PALAZZO REALE, MILAN, 2011–2012
Artemisia Gentileschi: Storia di una passione/Artemisia Gentileschi: The Story of a Passion, Palazzo Reale, Milan, September 23, 2011–January 29, 2012.

PALAZZO REALE, NAPLES, 1964
La natura morta italiana, Palazzo Reale, Naples, October–November 1964.

PATRICIA AND PHILLIP FROST ART MUSEUM, MIAMI, 2018
Dangerous Women: Selections from the John and Mable Ringling Museum of Art, Patricia and Phillip Frost Art Museum, Florida International University, Miami, February 1–May 27, 2018; Cornell Fine Arts Museum at Rollins College, Winter Park, Fla., September 8–December 30, 2018.

PHILADELPHIA MUSEUM OF ART, 2000
Art in Rome in the Eighteenth Century, Philadelphia Museum of Art, March 16–May 28, 2000; Museum of Fine Arts, Houston, June 25–September 17, 2000.

PINACOTECA NAZIONALE DI BOLOGNA, 1986–1987
Nell'età di Correggio e dei Carracci: Pittura in Emilia dei secoli XVI e XVII, Pinacoteca Nazionale di Bologna, September 10–November 10, 1986; *The Age of Correggio and the Carracci: Emilian Painting of the Sixteenth and Seventeenth Centuries*, National Gallery of Art, Washington, D.C., December 19, 1986–February 16, 1987; Metropolitan Museum of Art, New York, March 26–May 24, 1987.

ROYAL ACADEMY, LONDON, 1950–1951
Exhibition of Works by Holbein and Other Masters of the 16th and 17th Century, Royal Academy, London, December 9, 1950–March 7, 1951.

ROYAL ACADEMY, LONDON, 1962
Primitives to Picasso: An Exhibition from Municipal and University Collections in Great Britain, Royal Academy, London, January 6–March 7, 1962.

ROYAL ACADEMY, LONDON, 1968
France in the Eighteenth Century, Royal Academy, London, January 6–March 3, 1968.

ROYAL ACADEMY, LONDON, 1983
Trafalgar Galleries at the Royal Academy III, Royal Academy, London, October 10–29, 1983.

TEFAF, MAASTRICHT, 2012
The European Fine Art Fair, Maastricht, March 16–25, 2012.

TEFAF, NEW YORK, 2018
The European Fine Art Fair, New York, October 27–31, 2018.

UNIVERSITY OF MICHIGAN MUSEUM OF ART, ANN ARBOR, 2002
Women Who Ruled: Queens, Goddesses, Amazons in Renaissance and Baroque Art, University of Michigan Museum of Art, Ann Arbor, February 17–May 5, 2002; Davis Museum at Wellesley College, September 14–December 8, 2002.

WALTERS ART GALLERY, BALTIMORE, 1972
Old Mistresses: Women Artists of the Past, Walters Art Gallery, Baltimore, April 17–June 18, 1972.

WALTERS ART GALLERY, BALTIMORE, 1995–1996
Going for Baroque: 18 Contemporary Artists Fascinated with the Baroque and Rococo, Walters Art Gallery, Baltimore, September 24, 1995–February 4, 1996.

WESTFÄLISCHES LANDESMUSEUM FÜR KUNST UND KULTURGESCHICHTE, MÜNSTER, 1979–1980
Stilleben in Europa, Westfälisches Landesmuseum für Kunst und Kulturgeschichte, Münster, November 25, 1979–February 24, 1980; Staatliche Kunsthalle, Baden-Baden, March 15–June 15, 1980.

WILDENSTEIN GALLERIES, NEW YORK, 1981
Masterworks from the John and Mable Ringling Museum of Art, The State Art Museum of Florida, Wildenstein Galleries, New York, April 1–May 8, 1981; Tampa Museum, June 14–September 6, 1981.

WILDENSTEIN GALLERY, LONDON, 1970
Pictures from Southampton, Wildenstein Gallery, London, June 11–July 18, 1970.

WORCESTER ART MUSEUM, 1972
Woman as Heroine, Worcester Art Museum, Mass., September 15–October 22, 1972.

BIBLIOGRAPHY

ACANFORA 2014
Acanfora, Elisa. "'Si disegna, si minia e si dipigne': La pittura su pergamena nelle fonti e la sua fortuna a Firenze tra Sei e Settecento." In Poggio a Caiano 2014, 23–37.

ADAMS 2000
Adams, Laurie Schneider. *Key Monuments of the Baroque*. Boulder, Col., 2000.

ADAMS ET AL. 2017
Adams, Renée B., Roman Kräussl, Marco A. Navone, and Patrick Verwijmeren. "Is Gender in the Eye of the Beholder? Identifying Cultural Attitudes with Art Auction Prices." SSRN.com (December 6, 2017). http://dx.doi.org/10.2139/ssrn.3083500.

ADEMOLLO 1887
Ademollo, Alessandro. *Corilla Olimpica*. Florence, 1887.

THE AENEID OF VIRGIL 1900
The Aeneid of Virgil. Edited by Charles Knapp. Chicago and New York, 1900.

AJMAR-WOLLHEIM 2006
Ajmar-Wollheim, Marta. "Housework." In *At Home in Renaissance Italy*, edited by Marta Ajmar-Wollheim and Flora Dennis, 152–63. Exh. cat., Victoria and Albert Museum, London, 2006–2007. London, 2006.

ALBRICCI 1975
Albricci, Gioconda. "Prints by Diana Scultori." *Print Collector* 12 (1975): 17–23.

ALBUQUERQUE 2005
El Alma de España/The Soul of Spain. Exh. cat., Albuquerque Museum, N.M., 2005. Catalogue contributions by Marcus Burke, Selma Holo, and Mari-Tere Alvarez. Albuquerque, 2005.

ALEXANDER 1997
Alexander, David. "Printmakers." In Gaze 1997, vol. 1, 61–66.

ALF 1977
Alf, Martha. "Women Artists Throughout History." *Artweek* 8, no. 4 (January 22, 1977): 1, 20.

ANCIENT, ISLAMIC, BRITISH AND FOREIGN COINS 2002
Ancient, Islamic, British and Foreign Coins, War Medals, Orders and Decoration, Important Renaissance Plaquettes, Historic Medals, Banknotes. Sales cat., Morton and Eden, London, April 18, 2002.

ANDREW W. MELLON FOUNDATION 2019
Andrew W. Mellon Foundation News and Blog. "Latest Art Museum Staff Demographic Survey Shows Increases in African American Curators and Women in Leadership Roles." mellon.org (January 28, 2019). https://mellon.org/news-blog/articles/latest-art-museum-staff-demographic-survey-shows-increases-african-american-curators-and-women-leadership-roles/.

ANDREWS 1947
Andrews, Julia Gethman. *A Catalogue of European Paintings, 1300–1870: The Fine Arts Gallery, Balboa Park*. San Diego, 1947.

ANN ARBOR 2002
Women Who Ruled: Queens, Goddesses, Amazons in Renaissance and Baroque Art. Exh. cat., University of Michigan Museum of Art, Ann Arbor, 2002. Catalogue edited by Annette Dixon. London, 2002.

ANTWERP 2018
Michaelina Wautier 1604–1689: Glorifying a Forgotten Talent. Exh. cat., Museum aan de Stroom, Antwerp, 2018. Catalogue by Katlijne Van der Stighelen and others. Kontich, 2018.

APOLLO 1983
"Round the Galleries: A November Selection." *Apollo* 118, no. 261 (November 1983): 449.

APOLLO 2012
"Galerie Canesso. Tableaux anciens." *Apollo* 175, no. 595 (February 2012): 10.

APOLLODORUS 1921
Apollodorus: The Library. Translated by Sir James George Frazer. 2 vols. London, 1921.

ARNAUD 1928–1930
Arnaud, Odette. "Subleyras, 1699 à 1749." In *Les peintres français du XVIIIe siècle: Histoire des vies et catalogue des oeuvres*, edited by M. Louis Dimier, vol. 2, 49–92. 2 vols. Paris, 1928–1930.

ART QUARTERLY 1957
"Accessions of American and Canadian Museums: January–March, 1957." *Art Quarterly* 20, no. 2 (Summer 1957): 204–14.

ASTENGO 1923
Astengo, Stefano Luigi. *Gli Agostiniani a Bologna e il tempio di San Giacomo*. Bologna, 1923.

ATTWOOD 2003
Attwood, Philip. *Italian Medals c. 1530–1600 in British Public Collections*. London, 2003.

BADINO 2010
Badino, Grazia. "13. Anna Bacherini Piattoli, *Autoritratto*." In Florence 2010a, 58.

BAETJER 1995
Baetjer, Katharine. *European Paintings in The Metropolitan Museum of Art by Artists Born before 1865: A Summary Catalogue*. New York, 1995.

BAETJER 1999
Baetjer, Katharine. "British Portraits in the Metropolitan Museum of Art." *Metropolitan Museum of Art Bulletin* 57, no. 1 (Summer, 1999): 1, 5–72.

BAETJER 2016
Baetjer, Katharine. "The Women of the French Royal Academy." In *Vigée Le Brun*, edited by Joseph Baillio, Katharine Baetjer, and Paul Lang, 33–45. Exh. cat., Metropolitan Museum of Art, New York; National Gallery of Art, Ottawa, 2016. New York and New Haven, 2016.

BAGLIONE 1733
Baglione, Giovanni. *Le Vite de' pittori, scultori et architetti dal Pontificato di Gregorio XIII del 1572 fino a tutto quello d'Urbano VIII nel 1642*. Rome, 1642. Reprint. Naples, 1733.

BAL 1995
Bal, Mieke. "Head Hunting: 'Judith' on the Cutting Edge of Knowledge." In *A Feminist Companion to Esther, Judith and Susanna*, edited by Athalya Brenner, 253–85. Sheffield, 1995.

BAL 2005
Bal, Mieke, ed. *The Artemisia Files: Artemisia Gentileschi for Feminists and Other Thinking People*. Chicago, 2005.

BALDASSARI 2016A
Baldassari, Francesca. "Artemisia nel milieu del Seicento fiorentino." In Rome 2016, 23–33.

BALDASSARI 2016B
Baldassari, Francesca. "25. Artemisia Gentileschi, *Autoritratto come suonatrice di liuto*." In Rome 2016, 130–31.

BALDINUCCI 1845–1847
Baldinucci, Filippo. *Notizie dei professori del disegno da Cimabue in qua*. Edited by Ferdinando Ranalli. 9 vols. Florence, 1845–1847.

BALDINUCCI 1975
Baldinucci, Filippo. *Notizie de' professori del disegno da Cimabue in qua*. 6 vols. Florence, 1681–1728. Reprint. Florence, 1975.

BALTIMORE 1972
Old Mistresses: Women Artists of the Past. Exh. cat., Walters Art Gallery, Baltimore. Catalogue by Ann Gabhart and Elizabeth Broun. Baltimore, 1972.

BALTIMORE 1995
Going for Baroque: 18 Contemporary Artists Fascinated with the Baroque and Rococo. Exh. cat., Walters Art Gallery. Catalogue edited by Lisa G. Corrin and Joaneath Spicer. Baltimore, 1995.

BARKER 2015A
Barker, Sheila, ed. *Artiste nel chiostro: Produzione artistica nei monasteri femminili in età moderna*. Special issue of *Memorie domenicane*, 46 (2015).

BARKER 2015B
Barker, Sheila. "Painting and Humanism in Early Modern Florentine Convents." In Barker 2015a, 105–39.

BARKER 2016A
Barker, Sheila. "Introduction." In Barker 2016c, 5–14.

BARKER 2016B
Barker, Sheila. "Lucrezia Quistelli (1541–94), a Woman Artist in Vasari's Florence." In Barker 2016c, 47–80.

BARKER 2016C
Barker, Sheila, ed. *Women Artists in Early Modern Italy: Careers, Fame, and Collectors*. Turnhout, 2016.

BARKER 2017A
Barker, Sheila, ed. *Artemisia Gentileschi in a Changing Light*. Turnhout, 2017.

BARKER 2017B
Barker, Sheila. "Artemisia's Money: The Entrepreneurship of a Woman Artist in Seventeenth-Century Florence." In Barker 2017a, 59–88.

BARKER 2017C
Barker, Sheila. "1. Plautilla Nelli, *Initial A: The Presentation of Jesus in the Temple with Two Nuns*." In Florence 2017, 70–73.

BARKER 2018
Barker, Sheila. "The First Biography of Artemisia Gentileschi." *Mitteilungen des Kunsthistorischen Institutes in Florenz* 60, no. 3 (2018): 404–35.

BARKER 2020A
Barker, Sheila. "The Universe of Giovanna Garzoni: Art, Mobility, and the Global Turn in the Geographical Imaginary." In Florence 2020, 16–29.

BARKER 2020B
Barker, Sheila. "Women Artists and Their Contended Place in Public History." artherstory. net (April 14, 2020). https://artherstory.net/the-politics-of-exhibiting-female-old-masters/.

BARKER 2020C
Barker, Sheila. "3. Giovanna Garzoni, *Self-Portrait as Apollo*." In Florence 2020, 124–25.

BARKER 2020D
Barker, Sheila. "12. Angelo Rossini, *View of the Church of Santi Luca e Martina, and Garzoni's House*." In Florence 2020, 142–43.

BARKER 2020E
Barker, Sheila. "13. Carlo Maratti, *Portrait of Giovanna Garzoni*." In Florence 2020, 144–45.

BARKER AND JAMES 2020
Barker, Sheila, and Julie James. "Art as a Conduit for Nuns' Networks: The Case of Suor Teresa Berenice Vitelli at S. Apollonia in Florence." In *Convent Networks in Early Modern Europe*, edited by Saundra Weddle and Marilyn Dunn, 303–30. Turnhout, 2020.

BAROCCHI 1979
Barocchi, Paola. "Storiografia e collezionismo dal Vasari al Lanzi." In *Storia dell'arte italiana*. Vol. 2, *L'artista e il pubblico*, edited by Giulio Bollati and Paolo Fossati, 6–81. Turin, 1979.

BARTOLENA 2003
Bartolena, Simona. *Arte al femminile: Donne artiste dal rinascimento al XXI secolo*. Milan, 2003.

BARTSCH 1802–1821
Bartsch, Adam. *Le peintre graveur*. 21 vols. Vienna, 1802–1821.

BASSANI 1816
Bassani, Petronio. *Guida agli amatori delle belle arti, architettura, pittura, e scultura per la città di Bologna, suoi sobborghi, e circondario*. Bologna, 1816.

BASSO 2009
Basso, Amalia Donatella. "Otto 'mezze figure a pastella' nella collezione del Palazzo Reale di Venezia." In Pavanello 2009, 255–71.

BAUMAN 1998
Bauman, Jennifer Marie. "Miniature Painting and Its Role at the Medici Court in Florence, 1537–1627." Ph.D. diss., Johns Hopkins University, 1998.

BAYER 2003
Bayer, Andrea. "North of the Apennines: Sixteenth-Century Italian Painting in Lombardy and Emilia-Romagna." *Metropolitan Museum of Art Bulletin* 60, no. 4 (Spring 2003): 4–64.

BELLINI 1976
Bellini, Paolo. "Elisabetta Sirani: Catalogue des gravures." *Nouvelles de l'estampe* 30 (November–December 1976): 7–12.

BELLINI 1991
Bellini, Paolo, ed. *L'opera incisa di Adamo e Diana Scultori*. Milan, 1991.

BENEDETTI 1999
Benedetti, Laura. "Reconstructing Artemisia: Twentieth-Century Images of a Woman Artist." *Comparative Literature* 51, no. 1 (Winter 1999): 42–61.

BENEDICT 1938
Benedict, Curt. "Osias Beert." *L'Amour de l'art* (October 1938): 307–14.

BERENSON 1932
Berenson, Bernard. *Italian Pictures of the Renaissance*. Oxford, 1932.

BERENSON 1936
Berenson, Bernard. *Pitture italiane del Rinascimento*. Translated by Emilio Cecchi. Milan, 1936.

BERENSON 1968
Berenson, Bernard. *Italian Pictures of the Renaissance: Central and North Italian Schools*. 3 vols. London, 1968.

BERGAMO 1968
Natura in posa: Aspetti dell'antica natura morta italiana. Exh. cat., Galleria Lorenzelli, Bergamo, 1968. Catalogue edited by Ferdinando Bologna. Bergamo, 1968.

BERGAMO 1985
Forma vera: Contributi a una storia della natura morta italiana. Exh. cat., Galleria Lorenzelli, Bergamo, 1985. Catalogue by Pietro Lorenzelli and Alberto Veca. Bergamo, 1985.

BERMINGHAM 2000
Bermingham, Ann. *Learning to Draw: Studies in the Cultural History of a Polite and Useful Art*. New Haven and London, 2000.

BERRA 1990
Berra, Giacomo. "La natura morta nella bottega di Fede Galizia." *Osservatorio delle arti* 5 (1990): 55–62.

BERTI 1979
Berti, Luciano, ed. *Gli Uffizi: Catalogo generale*. Florence, 1979.

BERTI AND MAGHERINI 2002
Berti, Luciano, and Graziella Magherini. *Artemisia Gentileschi: Nostra Contemporanea/Artemisia Gentileschi: Our Contemporary*. Florence, 2002.

BISSELL 1967
Bissell, R. Ward. "Orazio Gentileschi's 'Young Woman with a Violin.'" *Bulletin of the Detroit Institute of Arts* 46, no. 4 (1967): 71–79.

BISSELL 1968
Bissell, R. Ward. "Artemisia Gentileschi: A New Documented Chronology." *Art Bulletin* 50, no. 2 (June 1968): 153–68.

BISSELL 1981
Bissell, R. Ward. *Orazio Gentileschi and the Poetic Tradition in Caravaggesque Painting*. University Park, Penn., 1981.

BISSELL 1999
Bissell, R. Ward. *Artemisia Gentileschi and the Authority of Art: Critical Reading and Catalogue Raisonné*. University Park, Penn., 1999.

BISSELL 2005
Bissell, R. Ward. "28. Artemisia Lomi Gentileschi, *Judith and Her Maidservant with the Head of Holofernes*." In Bissell, Derstine, and Miller 2005, 84–87.

BISSELL 2011
Bissell, R. Ward. "Simon Vouet, Raphael, and the Accademia Di San Luca in Rome." *Artibus et historiae* 32, no. 63 (2011): 55–72.

BISSELL, DERSTINE, AND MILLER 2005
Bissell, R. Ward, Andria Derstine, and Dwight Miller. *Masters of Italian Baroque Painting: The Detroit Institute of Arts*. Detroit and London, 2005.

BOHLEN 2002
Bohlen, Celestine. "Elusive Heroine of the Baroque." *New York Times* (February 18, 2002).

BOHN 2002
Bohn, Babette. "The Antique Heroines of Elisabetta Sirani." *Renaissance Studies* 16, no. 1 (March 2002): 52–79.

BOHN 2004A
Bohn, Babette. "Elisabetta Sirani and Drawing Practices in Early Modern Bologna." *Master Drawings* 42, no. 3 (Autumn 2004): 207–36.

BOHN 2004B
Bohn, Babette. "Female Self-Portraiture in Early Modern Bologna." *Renaissance Studies* 18, no. 2 (June 2004): 239–86.

BOHN 2004C
Bohn, Babette. "Il fenomeno della firma: Elisabetta Sirani e le firme dei pittori a Bologna." In Bologna 2004, 107–17.

BOHN 2011
Bohn, Babette. "The Construction of Artistic Reputation in Seicento Bologna: Guido Reni and the Sirani." *Renaissance Studies* 25, no. 4 (September 2011): 511–37.

BOHN 2013
Bohn, Babette. "Patronizing *pittrici* in Early Modern Bologna." In *Bologna: Cultural Crossroads from the Medieval to the Baroque. Recent Anglo-American Scholarship*, edited by Gian Mario Anselmi, Angela De Benedictis, and Nicholas Terpstra, 113–26. Bologna, 2013.

BOHN 2017–2018
Bohn, Babette. "Women Artists, Their Patrons, and Their Publics in Early Modern Bologna." In *Center 38: National Gallery of Art, Center for Advanced Study in the Visual Arts, Research Reports*, 64–67. Washington, D.C., 2017–2018.

BOHN 2021
Bohn, Babette. *Women Artists, Their Patrons, and Their Publics in Early Modern Bologna*. University Park, Penn., 2021.

BOLOGNA 1986
The Age of Correggio and the Carracci: Emilian Painting of the Sixteenth and Seventeenth Centuries/Nell'età di Correggio e dei Carracci: Pittura in Emilia dei secoli XVI e XVII. Exh. cat., Pinacoteca Nazionale, Bologna; National Gallery of Art, Washington, D.C.; Metropolitan Museum of Art, New York, 1986–1987. Catalogue contributions by Giuliano Briganti and others. Washington, D.C. and Bologna, 1986.

BOLOGNA 1994
Lavinia Fontana (1552–1614). Exh. cat., Museo Civico Archeologico, Bologna, 1994. Catalogue edited by Vera Fortunati. Milan, 1994.

BOLOGNA 2004
Elisabetta Sirani "pittrice eroina" 1638–1665. Exh. cat., Museo Civico Archeologico, Bologna, 2005. Catalogue edited by Jadranka Bentini and Vera Fortunati. Bologna, 2004.

BOLOGNA 2015
Da Cimabue a Morandi: Felsina Pittrice. Exh. cat., Palazzo Fava, Palazzo delle Esposizioni, Pinacoteca Nazionale, Bologna, 2015. Catalogue edited by Vittorio Sgarbi and Pietro Di Natale. Bologna, 2015.

BONDIL 2016
Bondil, Nathalie, ed. *The Montreal Museum of Fine Arts Michal and Renata Hornstein Pavilion for Peace: International Art and Education*. Montreal, 2016.

BOORSCH AND SPIKE 1986
Boorsch, Suzanne, and John T. Spike. *The Illustrated Bartsch*. Vol. 31, *Italian Artists of the Sixteenth Century*. New York, 1986.

BORENIUS 1913
Borenius, Tancred. *A Catalogue of the Paintings at Doughty House Richmond and Elsewhere in the Collection of Sir Frederick Cook*. Vol. 1, *Italian Schools*. London, 1913.

BORRONI SALVADORI 1974
Borroni Salvadori, Fabia. "Le esposizioni d'arte a Firenze dal 1674 al 1767." *Mitteilungen des Kunsthistorischen Institutes in Florenz* 18 (1974): 1–166.

BORZELLO 1998
Borzello, Frances. *Seeing Ourselves: Women's Self-Portraits*. New York, 1998.

BORZELLO 2000
Borzello, Frances. *A World of Our Own: Women as Artists since the Renaissance*. New York and London, 2000.

BOSTON 1902
A Loan Collection of Portraits and Pictures of Fair Women. Exh. cat., Copley Hall, Boston, 1902. Catalogue by The Copley Society. Boston, 1902.

BOSTON 1989
Italian Etchers of the Renaissance and Baroque: Parmigianino to Giordano. Exh. cat., Museum of Fine Arts, Boston; Cleveland Museum of Art; National Gallery of Art, Washington, D.C., 1989. Catalogue by Sue Welsh Reed, Richard Wallace, and others. Boston, 1989.

BOTTACIN 1996
Bottacin, Francesca. "Marianna Carlevarijs." In *"Le tele svelate": Antologia di pittrici venete dal Cinquecento al Novecento*, edited by Caterina Limentani Virdis, 155–63. Mirano, 1996.

BOTTARI 1963
Bottari, Stefano. "Fede Galizia." *Arte antica e moderna* 24 (1963): 309–18.

BOTTARI 1965
Bottari, Stefano. *Fede Galizia pittrice 1578–1630*. Trento, 1965.

BRAESEL 2009
Braesel, Michaela. *Buchmalerei in der Kunstgeschichte zur Rezeption in England, Frankreich und Italien*. Cologne and Weimar, 2009.

BREDEKAMP 2019
Bredekamp, Horst. *Galileo's Thinking Hand: Mannerism, Anti-Mannerism, and the Virtue of Drawing in the Foundation of Early Modern Science*. Berlin and Boston, 2019.

BREJON DE LAVERGNÉE 1982
Brejon de Lavergnée, Arnauld. "Four New Paintings by Simon Vouet." *Burlington Magazine* 124, no. 956 (November 1982): 685–89.

BRESCIA 2020
Donne nell'arte da Tiziano a Boldoni. Exh. cat., Palazzo Martinego, Brescia, 2020. Catalogue edited by Davide Dotti. Milan, 2020.

BRILLIANT 2017
Brilliant, Virginia. *Italian, Spanish, and French Paintings in the Ringling Museum of Art*. Sarasota and New York, 2017.

BRINE AND CILETTI 2010
Brine, Kevin R., and Elena Ciletti, eds. *The Sword of Judith: Judith Studies Across the Disciplines*. Cambridge, 2010.

BROOKE 1998
Brooke, Xanthe. *Mantegna to Rubens: The Weld-Blundell Drawings Collection*. London, 1998.

BROUDE AND GARRARD 1982
Broude, Norma, and Mary D. Garrard, eds. *Feminism and Art History: Questioning the Litany*. New York, 1982.

BRULLIOT 1832–1834
Brulliot, Francois. *Dictionnaire des monogrammes, marques figures, lettres initiales, noms abrégés etc. avec lesquels les peintres, dessinateurs, graveurs et sculpteurs ont désigné leurs noms*. 3 vols. Munich, 1832–1834.

BULLETIN OF THE DETROIT INSTITUTE OF ARTS 1969
"Appendix VII: Accessions." *Bulletin of the Detroit Institute of Arts* 48, no. 1 (1969): 17–22.

BULLETIN OF THE DETROIT INSTITUTE OF ARTS 1970
"Appendix VI: Conservation of Works of Art–1969." *Bulletin of the Detroit Institute of Arts* 49, no. 1 (1970): 15.

BURLINGTON MAGAZINE 1985
"Some Acquisitions of Seventeenth-Century Art in American Museums." *Burlington Magazine* 127, no. 988 (July 1985): 489–92.

BURLINGTON MAGAZINE 2012
"Galerie Canesso: Tableaux anciens." *Burlington Magazine* 154, no. 1307 (February 2012): unpaginated.

BURNS 2007
Burns, Thea. *The Invention of Pastel Painting*. London, 2007.

BURROUGHS, BRECK, AND IVINS 1923
Burroughs, Bryson, Joseph Breck, and William M. Ivins, Jr. "Loan Exhibition of the Arts of the Italian Renaissance." *Metropolitan Museum of Art Bulletin* 18, no. 5 (May 1923): 105, 107–14.

BUTTERFIELD 1977
Butterfield, Jan. "Replacing Women Artists in History." *Art News* 76, no. 3 (March 1977): 40–44.

CALABRESE 2006
Calabrese, Omar. *Artists' Self-Portraits*. New York, 2006.

CAMPORI 1870
Campori, Giuseppe, ed. *Raccolta di cataloghi ed inventarii inediti di quadri, statue, disegni, bronzi, dorerie, smalti, medaglie, avorii, ecc. dal secolo XV al secolo XIX*. Modena, 1870.

CANTALAMESSA 1922
Cantalamessa, Giulio. "David, Saul o Astolfo? . . ." *Bollettino d'arte* 1 (July 1922): 37–43.

CANTARO 1989
Cantaro, Maria Teresa. *Lavinia Fontana bolognese, "pittora singolare," 1552–1614*. Milan, 1989.

CANTARO 1993
Cantaro, Maria Teresa. "Aggiornamenti e precisazioni sul catalogo di Lavinia Fontana." *Bollettino d'arte* 79 (May–June 1993): 85–102.

CANTARO 2014
Cantaro, Maria Teresa. "Lavinia Fontana: Il primo 'Autoritratto alla spinetta' ritrovato e una breve disamina sugli autoritratti della pittrice." *Bollettino d'arte* 24 (October–December 2014): 99–110.

CAPOZZI 1975
Capozzi, Frank. "The Evolution and Transformation of the Judith and Holofernes Theme in Italian Drama and Art before 1627." Ph.D. diss., University of Wisconsin-Madison, 1975.

CARETTA 2015
Caretta, Paola. "Orizzonti figurativi e riferimenti culturali nell'opera di Orsola Maddalena Caccia." In Barker 2015a, 179–89.

CAROLI 1987
Caroli, Flavio. *Sofonisba Anguissola e le sue sorelle*. Milan, 1987.

CAROLI 1989
Caroli, Flavio. *Fede Galizia*. Turin, 1989.

CASALE 1991
Casale, Gerardo, with contributions by Paola Lanzara. *Giovanna Garzoni: "Insigne miniatrice," 1600–1670*. Milan, 1991.

CASSANI 1995
Cassani, Silvia, ed. *La Collezione Farnese: I dipinti lombardi, liguri, veneti, toscani, umbri, romani, fiamminghi: Altre scuole: Fasti Farnesiani*. Naples, 1995.

CASTIGLIONE 1976
Castiglione, Baldassare. *The Book of the Courtier*. Translated and introduction by George Bull. Revised ed. Harmondsworth, 1976.

CATALOGUE OF ANCIENT AND MODERN PICTURES 1925
Catalogue of Ancient and Modern Pictures and Drawings from Various Sources. Sales cat., Christie, Manson, and Woods, London, May 4, 1925.

CAVAZZINI 2008
Cavazzini, Patrizia. *Painting as Business in Early Seventeenth-Century Rome*. University Park, Penn., 2008.

CHADWICK 1990
Chadwick, Whitney. *Women, Art, and Society*. London, 1990.

CHADWICK 2012
Chadwick, Whitney. *Women, Art, and Society*. 5th ed. London, 2012.

CHAPPELL 2003
Chappell, Miles. "The Artistic Education of Maria de' Medici." In *Le siècle de Marie de Medicis: Actes du Séminaire de la chaire rhétorique et société en Europe (XVIe – XVIIe siècles)*, 13–25. Special issue of *Franco-italica*, 21–22, Alessandria, 2003.

CHARLES AND CARL 2010
Charles, Victoria, and Klaus H. Carl. *One Thousand Portraits of Genius*. New York, 2010.

CHE 2017
Che, Jenny. "The Enduring Delight of the Diorama." hyperallergic.com (August 4, 2017). https://hyperallergic.com/394021/the-enduring-delight-of-the-diorama/.

CHICAGO 2013
Violence and Virtue: Artemisia Gentileschi's "Judith Slaying Holofernes." Exh. cat., Art Institute of Chicago, 2013–2014. Catalogue by Eve Straussman-Pflanzer. Chicago, 2013.

CHRIST 1983
Christ, Yvan. "L'art dans la cité." *Revue des deux mondes* (June 1983): 705–10.

CHRISTADLER 2000
Christadler, Maike. *Kreativität und Geschlecht: Giorgio Vasaris "Vite" und Sofonisba Anguissolas Selbstbilder*. Berlin, 2000.

CHRISTIANSEN 2004
Christiansen, Keith. "Becoming Artemisia: Afterthoughts on the Gentileschi Exhibition." *Metropolitan Museum Journal* 39 (2004): 101–26.

CILETTI 2005
Ciletti, Elena. "'Gran Macchina è Bellezza': Looking at the Gentileschi *Judiths*." In Bal 2005, 63–105.

CLARK 1964–1965
Clark, Anthony M. "Three Roman Eighteenth-Century Portraits." *Journal of the Walters Art Gallery* 27/28 (1964–1965): 48–56.

CLARK 1985
Clark, Anthony M. *Pompeo Batoni: A Complete Catalogue of His Works with an Introductory Text*. Edited by Edgar Peters Bowron. 2 vols. New York, 1985.

CLAYMAN 2014
Clayman, Dee L. *Berenice II and the Golden Age of Ptolemaic Egypt*. New York, 2014.

CLEVELAND 1971
Caravaggio and His Followers. Exh. cat., Cleveland Museum of Art, 1971–1972. Catalogue edited by Richard E. Spear. Cleveland, 1971.

CLEVELAND 1984
Bernardo Cavallino of Naples, 1616–1656. Exh. cat., Cleveland Museum of Art; Kimbell Art Museum, Fort Worth; Museo Pignatelli Cortes, Naples, 1984–1985. Catalogue by Ann T. Lurie, Ann Percy and others. Cleveland and Fort Worth, 1984.

COHN 1998
Cohn, Samuel Kline. "Women and Work in Renaissance Italy." In *Gender and Society in Renaissance Italy*, edited by Judith C. Brown and Robert C. Davis, 107–26. London and New York, 1998.

COLDING 1953
Colding, Torben Holck. *Aspects of Miniature Painting: Its Origins and Development*. Copenhagen, 1953.

COLE 2019A
Cole, Michael. "Sister Arts." In Madrid 2019, 39–51.

COLE 2019B
Cole, Michael. *Sofonisba's Lesson: A Renaissance Artist and Her Work*. Princeton, 2019.

COLLECTIONS OF THE DETROIT INSTITUTE OF ARTS 1992
The Collections of the Detroit Institute of Arts: Italian, French, English, and Spanish Drawings and Watercolors, Sixteenth through Eighteenth Centuries. New York, 1992.

CONIGLIELLO 1992
Conigliello, Lucilla. *Jacopo Ligozzi: Le vedute del Sacro Monte della Verna*. Poppi, 1992.

CONISBEE, LEVKOFF, AND RAND 1991
Conisbee, Philip, Mary L. Levkoff, and Richard Rand. *The Ahmanson Gifts: European Masterpieces in the Collection of the Los Angeles County Museum of Art*. Los Angeles, 1991.

COOMBS 2005
Coombs, Katherine. *The Portrait Miniature in England*. London, 2005.

COOPER UNION MUSEUM CHRONICLE 1962
"The Architect's Eye." *Cooper Union Museum Chronicle* 3, no. 4 (September 1962): 3–52.

CORNELL UNIVERSITY DEPARTMENT OF THE HISTORY OF ART 1983
Cornell University Department of the History of Art. *Women Artists: Selected Works from the Collection*. Ithaca, N.Y., 1983.

CORP 2011
Corp, Edward. *The Stuarts in Italy, 1719–1766: A Royal Court in Permanent Exile*. Cambridge, 2011.

COSGROVE 2020
Cosgrove, Aiofe. "'E scrittrice, e pittrice': Giovanna Garzoni and the Art of Calligraphy." In Florence 2020, 30–35.

COSMOPOLITAN ART JOURNAL 1958
"Women-Artists." *Cosmopolitan Art Journal* 3, no. 1 (December 1958): 47–48.

COSTA 1999
Costa, Patrizia. "Sofonisba Anguissola's Self-portrait in the Boston Museum of Fine Arts." *Arte lombarda* 125 (1999): 54–62.

COTTINO 2012
Cottino, Alberto. "Metafore dipinte: Le nature morte 'devote' di Orsola Maddalena Caccia." In San Secondo di Pinerolo 2012, 37–46.

CRAIK 1853
Craik, Dinah. "The Story of Elisabetta Sirani." In *Avillion and Other Tales*, vol. 3, 317–34. 3 vols. London, 1853.

CREMONA 1985
I Campi e la cultura artistica cremonese del Cinquecento. Exh. cat., Museo Civico, Cremona, 1985. Catalogue edited by Mina Gregori. Milan, 1985.

CREMONA 1994
Sofonisba Anguissola e le sue sorelle. Exh. cat., Centro culturale "Città di Cremona," 1994. Catalogue contributions by Mina Gregori and others. Milan, 1994.

CREMONA 2000
Vincenzo Campi: Scene del quotidiano. Exh. cat., Museo Civico Ala Ponzone, Cremona, 2000. Catalogue edited by Franco Paliaga. Milan, 2000.

CREMONA 2004
Pittori della realtà: Le ragioni di una rivoluzione da Foppa e Leonardo a Caravaggio e Coruti. Exh. cat., Museo Civico Ala Ponzone, Cremona, 2004. Catalogue edited by Andrea Bayer and Mina Gregori. Milan, 2004.

CURRIE ET AL. 2017
Currie, Christina, Livia Depuydt-Elbaum, Valentine Handeriks, Steven Saverwyns, and Ina Vanden Berghe. "*Mary Magdalene in Ecstasy* by Artemisia Gentileschi: A Technical Study." In Barker 2017a, 217–35.

DABBS 2009
Dabbs, Julia K. *Life Stories of Women Artists, 1550–1800: An Anthology*. Farnham, 2009.

DACOME 2017
Dacome, Lucia. *Malleable Anatomies: Models, Makers, and Material Culture in Eighteenth-Century Italy*. Oxford, 2017.

D'ARCO 1840
D'Arco, Carlo. *Di cinque valenti incisori mantovani*. Mantua, 1840.

DA RIN BETTINA 2018
Da Rin Bettina, Laura. "Scheda Catalogo '6299 F.'" euploos.uffizi.it (2018). https://euploos.uffizi.it/scheda-catalogo.php?invn=6299+F.

DAVIDSON REID 1969
Davidson Reid, Jane. "The True Judith." *Art Journal* 28, no. 4 (Summer 1969): 376–87.

DE CEGLIA 2006
de Ceglia, Francesco. "Rotten Corpses, a Disembowelled Woman, a Flayed Man: Images of the Body from the End of the 17th to the Beginning of the 19th Century; Florentine Wax Models in the First-Hand Accounts of Visitors." *Perspectives on Science* 14, no. 4 (Winter 2006): 417–56.

DE CEGLIA 2011
de Ceglia, Francesco. "The Importance of Being Florentine: A Journey around the World for Wax Anatomical Venuses." *Nuncius* 26 (2011): 83–108.

DE CEGLIA 2014
de Ceglia, Francesco. "Thinking with the Saint: The Miracle of Saint Januarius of Naples and Science in Early Modern Europe." *Early Science and Medicine* 19, no. 2 (2014): 133–73.

DE DOMINICI 1743
De Dominici, Bernardo. *Vite de' pittori, scultori, ed architetti napoletani*. 3 vols. Naples, 1743.

DE DOMINICI 1979
De Dominici, Bernardo. *Vite de' pittori, scultori, ed architetti napoletani*. 3 vols. Naples, 1742. Reprint. Bologna, 1979.

DE GIROLAMI CHENEY 2017
De Girolami Cheney, Liana. "Giulia Lama: A Luminous Painter and a Tenebrist Poet." *Artibus et historiae* 75, no. 38 (2017): 225–52.

DE GIROLAMI CHENEY 2020
De Girolami Cheney, Liana. *Lavinia Fontana's Mythological Paintings: Art, Beauty, and Wisdom*. Newcastle upon Tyne, 2020.

DE GIROLAMI CHENEY, FAXON, AND RUSSO 2000
De Girolami Cheney, Liana, Alicia Craig Faxon, and Kathleen Lucey Russo. *Self-Portraits by Women Painters*. Aldershot, 2000.

DE KLERCK 1994
de Klerck, Bram. "39. Sofonisba Anguissola, *Ragazzo morso da un gambero*." In Cremona 1994, 274–77.

DELLA PERGOLA 1955
della Pergola, Paola. *Galleria Borghese: I dipinti*. 2 vols. Rome, 1955.

DELLE DONNE ILLUSTRI ITALIANE 1840
Delle donne illustri italiane dal XIII al XIX secolo. Rome, 1840.

DEMPSEY 1980
Dempsey, Charles. "Some Observations on the Education of Artists in Florence and Bologna during the Later Sixteenth Century." *Art Bulletin* 62, no. 4 (1980): 552–69.

DERSTINE 2017
Derstine, Andria. "The Detroit Institute of Arts and Italian Baroque Painting." In *Buying Baroque: Italian Seventeenth-Century Paintings Come to America*, ed. Edgar Peters Bowron, 92–103. University Park, Penn., 2017.

DE TOLNAY 1941
De Tolnay, Charles. "Sofonisba Anguissola and Her Relations with Michelangelo." *Journal of the Walters Art Gallery* 4 (1941): 114–19.

DETROIT 1952
Venice, 1700–1800: An Exhibition of Venice and the Eighteenth Century. Exh. cat., Detroit Institute of Arts; John Herron Art Museum, Indianapolis, 1952. Catalogue by E. P. Richardson. Detroit, 1952.

DETROIT 1965
Art in Italy, 1600–1700. Exh. cat., Detroit Institute of Arts, 1965. Catalogue contributions by Robert Enggass and others. Detroit, 1965.

DETROIT 2009
Learning by Line: The Role of Drawing in the Eighteenth Century. Exh. cat., Detroit Institute of Arts, 2009. Catalogue by Hope Saska. Detroit, 2009.

DE VORAGINE 1969
de Voragine, Jacobus. *The Golden Legend*. Translated by Granger Ryan and Helmut Ripperger. New York, 1969.

DEWALD 2004
Dewald, Jonathan. *Encyclopedia of the Early Modern World: Europe 1450 to 1789; Gabrieli to Lyon*. New York, 2004.

DOCAMPO 2019
Docampo, Javier. "16. Sofonisba Anguissola, *Giulio Clovio*." In Madrid 2019, 122–23.

DOLFI 1670
Dolfi, Pompeo Scipione. *Cronologia delle famiglie nobili di Bologna*. 2 vols. Bologna, 1670.

DUNN 1993
Dunn, Julie, ed. *San Diego Museum of Art: Selections from the Permanent Collection*. San Diego, 1993.

DUNN 1997
Dunn, Marilyn. "Spiritual Philanthropists: Women as Convent Patrons in Seicento Rome." In *Women and Art in Early Modern Europe: Patrons, Collectors and Connoisseurs*, ed. Cynthia Lawrence, 154–88. University Park, Penn., 1997.

EARLS 1996
Earls, Irene. B*aroque Art: A Topical Dictionary*. Westport, Conn., 1996.

EISNER ELEY 2017
Eisner Eley, Susan. "Gender Imbalance in the Art Museum and Gallery Worlds." huffpost.com (October 25, 2017; updated December 6, 2017). https://www.huffpost.com/entry/gender-imbalance-in-museu_b_12508666.

ELIAS 1969
Elias, Norbert. *Die höfische Gesellschaft: Untersuchungen zur Soziologie des Königtums und der höfischen Aristokratie*. Neuwied and Berlin, 1969.

ELLET 1859
Ellet, Elizabeth F. *Women Artists in All Ages and Countries*. London, 1859.

ELLET 1904
Ellet, Clara Erskine. *Women in the Fine Arts, from the 7th Century B.C. to the 20th Century A.D.* Boston and New York, 1904.

ÉTIENNE 2017
Étienne, Noémie. "Dioramas, Before and After." journal18.org (September 15, 2017). https://www.journal18.org/nq/dioramas-before-and-after-by-noemie-etienne/.

ÉTIENNE 2018
Étienne, Noémie. "Le diorama, par-delà l'espace et le temps: un média transhistorique et transcultural." In *D'une rive à l'autre: Patrimoines croisés, mélanges en l'honneur de Leïla el-Wakil*, edited by Silvia Naef, Nadia Radwan, and Pauline Nerfin, 125–32. Geneva, 2018.

EVEN 2002
Even, Yael. "Reviewed Works: *Artemisia Gentileschi and the Authority of Art* by R. Ward Bissell; *Artemisia Gentileschi around 1620–22: The Shaping and Reshaping of an Artistic Identity* by Mary D. Garrard." *Woman's Art Journal* 23, no. 1 (Spring–Summer 2002): 37–39.

FAIETTI 2004
Faietti, Marzia. "47. Elisabetta Sirani e ignoto autore presumibilmente del sec. XVIII, *Ritratto di giovinetto a mezzo busto*." In Bologna 2004, 200–201.

FALCONI 2008
Falconi, Bernardo. "Rosalba Carriera (1673–1757) und die Miniaturmalerei auf Elfenbein." In *Miniaturen des Rokoko aus der Sammlung Tansey*, edited by Bernd Pappe and Juliane Schmieglitz-Otten, 14–23. Munich, 2008.

FALCONI 2009
Falconi, Bernardo. "Rosalba Carriera e la miniatura su avorio." In Pavanello 2009, 215–36.

FANTONI, MATTHEW, AND MATTHEWS-GRIECO 2003
Fantoni, Marcello, Louisa Chevalier Matthew, and Sara F. Matthews-Grieco, eds. *The Art Market in Italy: 15th–17th Centuries/Il mercato dell'arte in Italia secc. XV–XVII*. Modena, 2003.

FARAGO 1992
Farago, Claire. *Leonardo da Vinci's Paragone: A Critical Interpretation with a New Edition of the Text in the Codex Urbinas*. Leiden, 1992.

FÉLIBIEN 1725
Félibien, André. *Entretiens sur les vies et sur les ouvrages des plus excellens peintres anciens et modernes*. Trevoux, 1725.

FERINO-PAGDEN 1995
Ferino-Pagden, Sylvia. "2. Sofonisba Anguissola, *Selbstbildnis in Miniatur*." In Vienna 1995, 62.

FERRAIUOLO 2020
Ferraiuolo, Serena. "La pittrice fiorentina Anna Piattoli Bacherini 'opera meravigliosamente in ritratti ed altre cose, facendo stupire chiunque veda le sue pitture.'" In *Oltre il "diletto del bel colorire": Nuovi sguardi sull'arte fiorentina del Settecento*, 133–67. Florence, 2020.

FERRANTE AND SIMON 2019
Ferrante, Dominic, and Robert B. Simon. *1380–1830: Important European Paintings*. New York, 2019.

FFOLLIOTT 2004
ffolliott, Sheila. "Reviewed Work: *Orazio and Artemisia Gentileschi* by Keith Christiansen and Judith W. Mann." *Woman's Art Journal* 24, no. 2 (Autumn 2003–Winter 2004): 53–55.

FFOLLIOTT 2016
ffolliott, Sheila. "'Più che famose': Some Thoughts on Women Artists in Early Modern Europe." In Barker 2016c, 15–27.

FFOLLIOTT 2020
ffolliott, Sheila. "Do We Have Any Great Women Artists Yet?" artherstory.net (April 16, 2020). https://artherstory.net/do-we-have-any-great-women-artists-yet/.

FIDIÈRE 1885
Fidière, Octave. *Les femmes artistes à l'Académie royale de peinture et de sculpture*. Paris, 1885.

FINDLEN 2020
Findlen, Paula. "With a Letter in Hand: Writing, Communication, and Representation in Renaissance Italy." In *The Renaissance of Letters: Knowledge and Community in Italy, 1300–1650*, ed. Paula Findlen and Susan Sutherland, 1–27. London and New York, 2020.

FINE ARTS SOCIETY 1960
Catalogue: A Selective Listing of All the Collections of the Fine Arts Society. San Diego, 1960.

FLORENCE 1970
Caravaggio e Caravaggeschi nelle gallerie di Firenze. Exh. cat., Palazzo Pitti, Florence, 1970. Catalogue edited by Evelina Borea. Florence, 1970.

FLORENCE 1975
Pittori bolognesi del Seicento nelle gallerie di Firenze. Exh. cat., Galleria degli Uffizi, Florence, 1975. Catalogue edited by Evelina Borea. Florence, 1975.

FLORENCE 1986
La Maddalena tra sacro e profano: Da Giotto a De Chirico. Exh. cat., Palazzo Pitti, Florence, 1986. Catalogue edited by Marilena Mosco. Milan and Florence, 1986.

FLORENCE 1991
Artemisia. Exh. cat., Casa Buonarroti, Florence, 1991. Catalogue edited by Roberto Contini and Gianni Papi. Rome, 1991.

FLORENCE 2003
La natura morta italiana: Da Caravaggio al Settecento. Exh. cat., Palazzo Strozzi, Florence, 2003. Catalogue edited by Mina Gregori. Milan, 2003.

FLORENCE 2010A
Autoritratte: "Artiste di capriccioso e destrissimo ingegno." Exh. cat., Galleria degli Uffizi, 2010–2011. Catalogue edited by Giovanna Giusti. Florence, 2010.

FLORENCE 2010B
Caravaggio e Caravaggeschi a Firenze. Exh. cat., Galleria Palatina, Palazzo Pitti, Florence, 2010–2011. Catalogue edited by Gianni Papi. Florence and Livorno, 2010.

FLORENCE 2017
Plautilla Nelli: Art and Devotion in Savonarola's Footsteps. Exh. cat., Gallerie degli Uffizi, Florence, 2017. Catalogue edited by Fausta Navarro. Livorno, 2017.

FLORENCE 2020
"The Immensity of the Universe" in the Art of Giovanna Garzoni. Exh. cat., Palazzo Pitti, Florence, 2020. Catalogue edited by Sheila Barker. Florence, 2020.

FORTUNATI 1997
Fortunati, Vera. "Fontana, Lavinia." In *Dizionario biografico degli italiani*, vol. 48, 694–98. Rome, 1997.

FORTUNATI 1998
Fortunati, Vera. "Lavinia Fontana: A Woman Artist in the Age of the Counter-Reformation." In Washington, D.C. 1998, 13–31.

FORTUNATI AND GRAZIANI 2008
Fortunati, Vera, and Irene Graziani. *Properzia de' Rossi: Una scultrice a Bologna nell'età di Carlo V*. Bologna, 2008.

FORTUNATI PIETRANTONIO 1986
Fortunati Pietrantonio, Vera, ed. *Pittura Bolognese del '500*. 2 vols. Bologna, 1986.

FORTUNE 2009
Fortune, Jane. *Invisible Women: Forgotten Artists of Florence*. Florence, 2009.

FORTUNE 2014
Fortune, Jane. *Invisible Women: Forgotten Artists of Florence*. 3rd ed. Florence, 2014.

FOSTER 2020
Foster, Christopher. "Technical Examination and Conservation Report." March 5, 2020. Unpublished. Paper Conservation, Detroit Institute of Arts.

FOX HOFRICHTER 2005
Fox Hofrichter, Frima. "An Intimate Look at Baroque Women Artists: Births, Babies, and Biography." In *Framing the Family: Narrative and Representation in the Medieval and Early Modern Periods*, edited by Rosalynn Voaden and Diane Wolfthal, 139–58. Tempe, 2005.

FREDERICKSEN AND ZERI 1972
Fredericksen, Burton B., and Federico Zeri, eds. *Census of Pre-Nineteenth-Century Italian Paintings in North American Public Collections*. Cambridge, Mass., 1972.

FRISONI 1978
Frisoni, Fiorella. "La vera Sirani." *Paragone* 29, no. 335 (1978): 3–18.

FRISONI 1992
Frisoni, Fiorella. "Elisabetta Sirani." In *La scuola di Guido Reni*, ed. Emilio Negro and Massimo Pirondini, 343–64. Modena, 1992.

FRISONI 2007
Frisoni, Fiorella. "63. Elisabetta Sirani, *Study for the Madonna Crowned by Christ Child with Roses*." In Washington, D.C. 2007, 246–47.

FROSININI AND REGINELLA 2019
Frosinini, Cecilia, and Maria Luisa Reginella. "Artemisia Gentileschi, la Santa Caterina d'Alessandria delle Gallerie degli Uffizi: Nuove acquisizioni dalle indagini diagnostiche." *Rivista dell'Opificio delle Pietre Dure e Laboratori di Restauro di Firenze* 31 (2019): 109–21.

FUMAGALLI 2010
Fumagalli, Elena. "Florence." In Spear and Sohm 2010, 172–203.

FUMAGALLI 2020
Fumagalli, Elena. "Miniature Painters at the Medici Court in the Seventeenth Century." In Florence 2020, 54–61.

GABBURRI CA. 1730–1742
Gabburri, Niccolò. *Vite dei pittori*. Vol. 4. Unpublished manuscript, MS Palatino E.B.9. Biblioteca Nazionale Centrale, Florence.

GABHART AND BROUN 1972
Gabhart, Ann, and Elizabeth Broun. "Old Mistresses: Women Artists of the Past." *Walters Art Gallery Bulletin* 24, no. 7 (April 1972): unpaginated.

GALLI 1940
Galli, Romeo. *Lavinia Fontana pittrice 1552–1614*. Imola, 1940.

GALLI 2004
Galli, Alessandro, ed. *Dipinti antichi*. Sales cat., Porro & C., Milan, May 26, 2004.

GAMBERINI 2019A
Gamberini, Cecilia. "10. Sofonisba Anguissola, *The Artist's Sister in the Garb of a Nun*." In Madrid 2019, 108–109.

GAMBERINI 2019B
Gamberini, Cecilia. "15. Sofonisba Anguissola, *Marquis Massimiliano Stampa*." In Madrid 2019, 120–21.

GARCÍA-FRÍAS CHECA 2019
García-Frías Checa, Carmen. "50. Sofonisba Anguissola, *Holy Family with Saints Anne and John the Baptist*." In Madrid 2019, 200–201.

GARDNER 1948
Gardner, Albert Ten Eyck. "A Century of Women." *Metropolitan Museum of Art Bulletin* 7, no. 4 (December 1948): 110–18.

GARDNER 1986
Gardner, Helen. *Art through the Ages*. 8th ed. New York, 1986.

GARRARD 1977
Garrard, Mary D. "Review of 'Women Artists' in Los Angeles." *Burlington Magazine* 119, no. 892 (July 1977): 530–32.

GARRARD 1980
Garrard, Mary D. "Artemisia Gentileschi's Self-Portrait as the Allegory of Painting." *Art Bulletin* 62, no. 1 (March 1980): 97–112.

GARRARD 1989
Garrard, Mary D. *Artemisia Gentileschi: The Image of the Female Hero in Italian Baroque Art*. Princeton, 1989.

GARRARD 1993
Garrard, Mary D. "Artemisia Gentileschi's 'Corisca and the Satyr.'" *Burlington Magazine* 135, no. 1078 (January 1993): 34–38.

GARRARD 1994
Garrard, Mary D. "Here's Looking at Me: Sofonisba Anguissola and the Problem of the Woman Artist." *Renaissance Quarterly* 47, no. 3 (Autumn 1994): 556–622.

GARRARD 2001
Garrard, Mary D. *Artemisia Gentileschi Around 1622: The Shaping and Reshaping of an Artistic Identity*. Berkeley, 2001.

GARRARD 2005
Garrard, Mary D. "Artemisia's Hand." In Mann 2005a, 99–120.

GARRARD 2017
Garrard, Mary D. "Identifying Artemisia: The Archive and the Eye." In Barker 2017a, 11–40.

GARRARD 2020A
Garrard, Mary D. *Artemisia Gentileschi and Feminism in Early Modern Europe*. London, 2020.

GARRARD 2020B
Garrard, Mary D. "The Not-So-Still Lifes of Giovanna Garzoni." In Florence 2020, 62–77.

GARRIDO 1990
Garrido, Carmen. "Estudio técnico." In Madrid 1990, 215–43.

GARZONI 1605
Garzoni, Tomaso. *La piazza universale di tutte le professioni del mondo . . .* Venice, 1605.

GAYA NUÑO 1958
Gaya Nuño, Juan Antonio. *La pintura Española fuera de España (historia y catálogo)*. Madrid, 1958.

GAYLARD 2015
Gaylard, Susan. "*De mulieribus claris* and the Disappearance of Women from Illustrated Print Biographies." *I Tatti Studies in the Italian Renaissance* 18, no. 2 (September 2015): 287–318.

GAZE 1997
Gaze, Delia, ed. *Dictionary of Women Artists*. 2 vols. London and Chicago, 1997.

GAZE 2011
Gaze, Delia, ed. *Concise Dictionary of Women Artists*. New York, 2011.

GAZZETTA 1995
Gazzetta, Liviana. "La rivoluzione pacifica: Istruzione, lavoro ed emancipazione femminile nella rivista *La Donna*." *Bollettino del Museo Civico di Padova* 84 (1995): 249–70.

GAZZETTA AND SEGA 2006
Gazzetta, Liviana, and Maria Teresa Sega. "Movimenti di emancipazione: Reti, iniziative, rivendicazioni (1866–1914)." In *Donne sulla scena pubblica: Società e politica in Veneto tra Sette e Ottocento*, edited by Nadia Maria Filippini, 138–217. Milan, 2006.

GERHARD AND SIMON 1901
Gerhard, Adele, and Helene Simon. *Mutterschaft und geistige Arbeit*. Berlin, 1901.

GETLEIN 2005
Getlein, Mark. *Gilbert's Living with Art*. 7th ed. Boston, 2005.

GHELFI 2007
Ghelfi, Barbara. "Un nuovo inventario della galleria Hercolani nella Biblioteca dell'Archiginnasio." *L'Archiginnasio* 102 (2007): 405–69.

GHENT 2018
De dames van de barok: Vrouwelijke schilders in het Italië van de 16de en 17de eeuw/Les dames du baroque: Femmes peintres dans l'Italie du XVIe et XVIIe siècle. Exh. cat., Museum voor Schone Kunsten, Ghent, 2018–2019. Catalogue edited by Valentine De Beir, Francesco Solinas, and Alain Tapié. Ghent, 2018.

GHEZZI 1696
Ghezzi, Giuseppe. *Il centesimo dell'anno MDCXCV celebrato in Roma dall'Accademia del Disegno*. Rome, 1696.

GHIRARDI 1984
Ghirardi, Angela. "Una pittrice Bolognese nella Roma del primo Seicento: Lavinia Fontana." *Il Carrobbio* 10 (1984): 150–61.

GHIRARDI 2002
Ghirardi, Angela. "Dipingere in lode del Cielo: Suor Orsola Maddalena Caccia e la vocazione artistica delle Orsoline de Moncalvo." In *Vita artistica nel monastero femminile*, edited by Vera Fortunati, 114–29. Bologna, 2002.

GHIRARDI 2004A
Ghirardi, Angela. "6. Matteo Borboni e Lorenzo Tinti, *Tempietto per il funerale di Elisabetta Sirani*." In Bologna 2004, 169.

GHIRARDI 2004B
Ghirardi, Angela. "51. Elisabetta Sirani, *Ritratto di Anna Maria Ranuzzi Marsigli come Carità*." In Bologna 2004, 204–5.

GHIRARDI 2019
Ghirardi, Angela. "Suor Orsola Maddalena Caccia (1596–1676), Convent Artist." artherstory.net (November 25, 2019). https://artherstory.net/orsola-maddalena-caccia-convent-artist/.

GIACOMETTI 1997
Giacometti, Margherita. "Carriera, Rosalba." In Gaze 1997, vol. 1, 354–59.

GIANSANTE 2017
Giansante, Massimo. "Rossi, Properzia de'." In *Dizionario biografico degli Italiani*, vol. 88, 715–19. Rome, 2017.

GOLAHNY 2011
Golahny, Amy. "Elisabetta Sirani's 'Timoclea' and Visual Precedent." *Notes in the History of Art* 30, no. 4 (Summer 2011): 37–42.

GOLDBERG 1983
Goldberg, Edward L. *Patterns in Late Medici Art Patronage*. Princeton, 1983.

GOLDENBERG STOPPATO 2016
Goldenberg Stoppato, Lisa. "Arcangela Paladini and the Medici." In Barker 2016c, 81–97.

GORSEN 1980
Gorsen, Peter. "Venus Oder Judith? Zur Heroisierung Des Weiblichkeitsbildes bei Lucas Cranach und Artemisia Gentileschi." *Artibus et historiae* 1, no. 1 (1980): 77–78.

GÖTTLER 2013
Göttler, Christine. "The Temptation of the Senses at the Sacra Monte di Varallo." In *Religion and the Senses in Early Modern Europe*, edited by Wietse de Boer and Christine Göttler, 393–451. Leiden and Boston, 2013.

GRABSKI 1985
Grabski, Jósef. "On Seicento Painting in Naples: Some Observations on Bernardo Cavallino, Artemisia Gentileschi and Others." *Artibus et historiae* 6, no. 11 (1985): 23–63.

GRASSI AND PEPE 1994
Grassi, Luigi, and Mario Pepe. *Dizionario dei termini artistici*. Milan, 1994.

GRAZIANI 2007
Graziani, Irene. "31. Lavinia Fontana, *Head of a Youth*." In Washington, D.C. 2007, 162–63.

GRAZIANI 2019
Graziani, Irene. "21. Felice Antonio Casoni, Commemorative Medal of Lavinia Fontana." In Madrid 2019, 132–33.

GREER 1979
Greer, Germaine. *The Obstacle Race: The Fortunes of Women Painters and Their Work*. New York, 1979.

GREGORI 1968
Gregori, Mina. "Su due quadri caravaggeschi a Burghley House." In *Festschrift Ulrich Middeldorf*, ed. Antje Kosegarten and Peter Tigler, vol. 1, 414–21. 2 vols. Berlin, 1968.

GREGORI 2005
Gregori, Mina. "7. Lucia Anguissola, *Autoritratto*." In *Le Meraviglie dell'Arte: Important Old Master Paintings*, edited by Frank Dabell and Tiziana Zennaro, 39–41. Exh. cat., Maison d'Art, Monte Carlo, 2005. Monte Carlo, 2005.

GRIFOL 2019
Grifol, Pedro. "Maastricht y su TEFAF, la feria de arte por excelencia." *El Economista* (March 18, 2019). https://www.eleconomista.es/turismo-viajes/noticias/9766696/03/19/Maastricht-y-su-TEFAF-la-feria-de-arte-por-excelencia-.html.

GRIGAUT 1960
Grigaut, Paul L., ed. *Treasures from the Detroit Institute of Arts*. Detroit, 1960.

GRISOLIA 2019
Grisolia, Francesco. *Die Zeichnungen des Giovan Battista Beinaschi: Aus der Sammlung der Kunstakademie Düsseldorf am Kunstpalast*. Petersberg, 2019.

GUHL 1858
Guhl, Ernst. *Die Frauen in der Kunstgeschichte*. Berlin, 1858.

GUICCIARDINI 1588
Guicciardini, Lodovico. *Descrittione di M. Lodovico Guicciardini . . . de tutti i Paesi Bassi, altrimenti detti Germania Inferiore . . . .* Antwerp, 1588.

GUICHARD 2015
Guichard, Charlotte. "'Amatrice': Die Rolle der 'Amateurin' im Europa der Aufklärung." In *Aufgeklärter Kunstdiskurs und höfische Sammelpraxis: Karoline Luise von Baden im europäischen Kontext*, edited by Christoph Frank and Wolfgang Zimmermann, 80–89. Exh. cat., Staatlich Kunsthalle Karlsruhe, 2015. Berlin, 2015.

GUZMAN 2019
Guzman, Alissa. "Baltimore Museum of Art Will Only Acquire Works by Female-Identifying Artists in 2020." hyperallergic.com (November 18, 2019). https://hyperallergic.com/528984/baltimore-museum-of-art-will-only-acquire-works-by-female-identifying-artists-in-2020/.

HAMBURGER 1997
Hamburger, Jeffrey F. *Nuns as Artists: The Visual Culture of a Medieval Convent*. Berkeley, 1997.

HANNING 2004
Hanning, Barbara Russano. "From Saint to Muse: Representations of Saint Cecilia in Florence." *Music in Art* 29, no. 1/2 (Spring–Fall 2004): 91–103.

HANSEN AND SPICER 2005
Hansen, Morten Steen, and Joaneath A. Spicer, eds. *Masterpieces of Italian Painting: The Walters Art Museum*. Baltimore, 2005.

HARTT 1993
Hartt, Frederick. *Art: A History of Painting, Sculpture and Architecture*. 4th ed. New York, 1993.

HATT AND KLONK 2006
Hatt, Michael, and Charlotte Klonk. "Hegel and the Birth of Art History." In *Art History: A Critical Introduction to Its Methods*, 21–64. Manchester and New York, 2006.

HEIL 1930
Heil, Walter. "The Lawrence P. Fisher Collection in Detroit." *Antiquarian* (December 1930): 45–50, 108–12.

HELLER 1987
Heller, Nancy G. *Women Artists: An Illustrated History*. New York, 1987.

HELLER 2000
Heller, Nancy G. *Women Artists: Works from the National Museum of Women in the Arts*. New York, 2000.

HENSHAW 1985
Henshaw, Julia P., ed. *100 Masterworks from the Detroit Institute of Arts*. New York, 1985.

HENSHAW 1995
Henshaw, Julia P., ed. *The Detroit Institute of Arts: A Visitor's Guide*. Detroit, 1995.

HILL 1972
Hill, M. Brawley. "Introduction." In *Women: A Historical Survey of Works by Women Artists*, vii–xiv. Exh. cat., North Carolina Museum of Art, Raleigh; Salem Fine Arts Center, Winston-Salem, 1972. Raleigh, 1972.

HIPKIN 1923
Hipkin, William John. *Descriptive catalogue of the pictures, pastel drawings, water-colour drawings, engravings, & c: belonging to his Grace the Duke of Newcastle at Clumber House, Workshop in the county of Nottingham, 1914*. London, 1923.

HIRSCH 1905
Hirsch, Anton. *Die bildenden Künstlerinnen der Neuzeit*. Stuttgart, 1905.

HOEFNAGEL 1630
Hoefnagel, Jacob. *Diversae insectarum volatilium: Icones ad vivum accuratissimè depictae per celeberrimum pictorem*. Amsterdam, 1630.

HOLCOMB 1987–1988
Holcomb, Adele M. "Anna Jameson on Women Artists." *Woman's Art Journal* 8, no. 2 (Autumn 1987–Winter 1988): 15–24.

HOLLADAY 2008
Holladay, Wilhelmina Cole. *A Museum of Their Own: National Museum of Women in the Arts*. Washington, D.C., and New York, 2008.

HONIG 2001–2002
Honig, Elizabeth Alice. "The Art of Being 'Artistic': Dutch Women's Creative Practices in the 17th Century." *Woman's Art Journal* 22, no. 2 (Autumn 2001–Winter 2002): 31–39.

HONIG 2016
Honig, Elizabeth Alice. *Jan Brueghel and the Senses of Scale*. University Park, Penn., 2016.

HOTTLE 2014
Hottle, Andrew D. *The Art of the Sister Chapel: Exemplary Women, Visionary Creators, and Feminist Collaboration*. Farnham, 2014.

HUBER 1800
Huber, Michel. *Manuel des curieux et des amateurs de l'art*. Vol. 3, *L'ecole Italienne*. Zurich, 1800.

HUFTON 1998
Hufton, Olwen. *The Prospect Before Her: A History of Women in Western Europe*. Vol. 1, *1500–1800*. New York, 1998.

THE ILLUSTRATED BARTSCH 1978–
The Illustrated Bartsch. Norwalk, Conn., 1978–ongoing.

IMPORTANT OLD MASTER PAINTINGS AND SCULPTURE 2008
Important Old Master Paintings and Sculpture. Sales cat., Sotheby's New York, January 24, 2008.

IMPORTANT OLD MASTER PAINTINGS PART I 2006
Important Old Master Paintings Part I. Sales cat., Christie's New York, April 6, 2006.

IMPORTANT OLD MASTER PAINTINGS PART I 2007
Important Old Master Paintings Part I. Sales cat., Christie's New York, April 19, 2007.

IMPORTANT PAINTINGS BY OLD AND MODERN MASTERS 1927
Important Paintings by Old and Modern Masters from the Estate of the Late James Stillman, and from the Collection of the Late C.C. Stillman. Sales cat., American Art Association, New York, 1927.

JACOBS 1997A
Jacobs, Fredrika H. "Anguissola, Sofonisba." In Gaze 1997, vol. 1, 188–91.

JACOBS 1997B
Jacobs, Fredrika Herman. *Defining the Renaissance Virtuosa: Women Artists and the Language of Art History and Criticism.* Cambridge, 1997.

JACOBS 2019
Jacobs, Julia. "Female Artists Made Little Progress in Museums since 2008, Survey Finds." *New York Times* (September 19, 2019; updated September 25, 2019).

JACOBSON SCHUTTE 1991
Jacobson Schutte, Anne. "Irene di Spilimbergo: The Image of a Creative Woman in Late Renaissance Italy." *Renaissance Quarterly* 44, no. 1 (Spring 1991): 42–61.

JAMES 2016
James, Susan E. *The Feminine Dynamic in English Art, 1485–1603: Women as Consumers, Patrons and Painters.* New York and London, 2016.

JAMESON 1834
Jameson, Anna. *Visit and Sketches at Home and Abroad.* 4 vols. London, 1834.

JEFFARES 2006
Jeffares, Neil. *Dictionary of Pastellists before 1800.* London, 2006.

JEFFARES 2019
Jeffares, Neil. "Anna Piattoli." *Pastels and Pastellists before 1800.* http://www.pastellists.com/Articles/PIATTOLIa.pdf (updated January 11, 2019).

JEFFARES 2020A
Jeffares, Neil. "Elisabetta Sirani." *Pastels and Pastellists before 1800.* http://www.pastellists.com/Articles/SIRANIe.pdf (updated August 14, 2020).

JEFFARES 2020B
Jeffares, Neil. "Marianna Carlevarijs." *Pastels and Pastellists before 1800.* http://www.pastellists.com/Articles/Carlevarijs.pdf (updated June 29, 2020).

JEFFARES 2020C
Jeffares, Neil. "Rosalba Carriera: Mythological Subjects II." *Pastels and Pastellists before 1800.* http://www.pastellists.com/Articles/Carriera2a.pdf (updated December 1, 2020).

JEFFARES 2020D
Jeffares, Neil. "Rosalba Carriera: Named Sitters A–K." *Pastels and Pastellists before 1800.* http://www.pastellists.com/Articles/Carriera1.pdf (updated November 29, 2020).

JEFFARES 2020E
Jeffares, Neil. "Teresa del Po." *Pastels and Pastellists before 1800.* http://www.pastellists.com/Articles/PO.pdf (updated August 10, 2020).

JERUSALEM 1994
Natura Morta Italiana: Italian Still Life Painting from Four Centuries: The Silvano Lodi Collection. Exh. cat., Israel Museum, Jersualem, 1994. Catalogue introduction by Luigi Salerno. Milan, 1994.

JOANNIDES 1992
Joannides, Paul. "Titian's *Judith* and its Context: The Iconography of Decapitation." *Apollo* 135, no. 361 (March 1992): 163–70.

JOHNS 2003
Johns, Christopher M.S. "'An Ornament of Italy and the Premier Female Painter of Europe': Rosalba Carriera and the Roman Academy." In *Women, Art and the Politics of Identity in Eighteenth-Century Europe*, edited by Melissa Lee Hyde and Jennifer Dawn Milam, 20–45. Aldershot and Burlington, Vt., 2003.

JOHNS 2019
Johns, Christopher M.S. "Making History at the Capitoline Museum: Maria Tibaldi Subleyras's *Christ in the House of Simon the Pharisee.*" *Eighteenth-Century Studies* 52, no. 2 (Winter 2019): 167–71.

JOHNSON AND MATTHEWS-GRIECO 1997
Johnson, Geraldine A., and Sara F. Matthews-Grieco, eds. *Picturing Women in Renaissance and Baroque Italy.* Cambridge, 1997.

JOHNSTON 1997
Johnston, Judith. *Anna Jameson: Victorian, Feminist, Woman of Letters.* Hants, 1997.

JOVER DE CELIS, GARCÍA, AND CARCELÉN 2019
Jover de Celis, Maite, M.ª Dolores Gayo García, and Laura Alba Carcelén. "Sofonisba Anguissola in the Museo del Prado: An Approach to her Technique." In Madrid 2019, 71–87.

JUYNBOLL 1934
Juynboll, Willem Rudolf. *Het komische genre in de italiaansche schilderkunst gedurende de zeventiende en de achttiende eeuw.* Leiden, 1934.

KANTOR-GUKOVSKAYA 2009
Kantor-Gukovskaya, Assia. "La collezione delle opere di Rosalba Carriera in Russia." In Pavanello 2009, 361–72.

KEITH ET AL. 2019
Keith, Larry, Letizia Treves, Marta Melchiorre di Crescenzo, and Joanna Russell. "Artemisia Gentileschi's *Self Portrait as Saint Catherine of Alexandria.*" *National Gallery Technical Bulletin* 40 (2019): 4–17.

KERBER 1968
Kerber, Bernhard. "Giuseppe Bartolomeo Chiari." *Art Bulletin* 50, no. 1 (March 1968): 75–86.

KING 1995
King, Catherine. "Looking a Sight: Sixteenth-Century Portraits of Woman Artists." *Zeitschrift für Kunstgeschichte* 58, no. 3 (1995): 381–406.

KINSELLA AND NEUENDORF 2018
Kinsella, Eileen, and Henri Neuendorf. "From a Portrait by a Teenage Picasso to Artemisia Gentileschi's 'Allegory,' Here are 5 Standout Works at TEFAF New York." *Artnet News* (October 29, 2018). https://news.artnet.com/market/6-must-see-masterpieces-tefaf-new-york-1381510.

KNOX 1992
Knox, George. "43. Rosalba Carriera, *Caterina Sagredo Barbarigo as Berenice.*" In *Collections of the Detroit Institute of Arts* 1992, 98–99.

KÜHNEL-KUNZE 1962
Kühnel-Kunze, Irene. "Zur Bildniskunst der Sofonisba und Lucia Anguisciola." *Pantheon* 20 (1962): 83–96.

KUSCHE 1995
Kusche, Maria. "Sofonisba Anguissola—Leben und Werk." In Vienna 1995, 23–57.

LACAS 2015
Lacas, Martine. *Des femmes peintres du XVe à l'aube du XIXe siècle.* Paris, 2015.

LANGDON 2002
Langdon, Helen. "*Orazio and Artemisia Gentileschi*: Rome, New York, and Saint Louis." *Burlington Magazine* 144, no. 1190 (May 2002): 318–21.

LANGER 1980–1981
Langer, Sandra L. "Review: *Women Artists in All Ages and Countries* by Elizabeth Fries Lummis Ellet." *Woman's Art Journal* 1, no. 2 (Autumn 1980–Winter 1981): 55–58.

LANZI 1795–1796
Lanzi, Luigi. *Storia pittorica della Italia.* Vol. 2, *Ove descrivono altre scuole della Italia superiore, la Bolognese, la Ferrarese, e quelle di Genova e del Piemonte.* Bassano, 1795–1796.

LARSON 2007
Larson, Judy L. "Introduction." In Washington, D.C. 2007, unpaginated.

LATTUADA 2017
Lattuada, Riccardo. "Unknown Paintings by Artemisia in Naples, and New Points Regarding Her Daily Life and 'Bottega.'" In Barker 2017a, 187–216.

LATTUADA AND NAPPI 2005
Lattuada, Riccardo, and Eduardo Nappi. "New Documents and Some Remarks on Artemisia's Production in Naples and Elsewhere." In Mann 2005a, 79–98.

LE BLANC 1854–1858
Le Blanc, Charles. *Manuel de l'amateur d'estampes.* Vol. 2. Paris, 1854–1858.

LEEDS 1868
National Exhibition of Works of Art, at Leeds, 1868. Exh. cat., Leeds General Infirmary, 1868. Catalogue by Ralph N. James and L. Lefèvre. Leeds, 1868.

LEHMBECK 2019
Lehmbeck, Leah, ed. *Gifts of European Art from The Ahmanson Foundation.* 3 vols. Los Angeles, 2019.

LEILANI 2020
Leilani, Raven. *Luster.* New York, 2020.

LEMAY 1999
Lemay, Shawna. "What a Woman Can Do." In *All the God-Sized Fruit*, 92–95. Montreal, 1999.

LIEURE 1924
Lieure, J. *Jacques Callot*. 5 vols. Paris, 1924.

LINCOLN 1997
Lincoln, Evelyn. "Parasole, Isabella [Elisabetta, Isabetta] Catanea." In Gaze 1997, vol. 2, 1068–70.

LINCOLN 2001
Lincoln, Evelyn. "Models for Science and Craft: Isabella Parasole's Botanical and Lace Illustrations." *Visual Resources* 17, no. 1 (2001): 1–35.

LINCOLN 2006
Lincoln, Evelyn. "Mantuana [Ghisi; Mantovana; Scultori], Diana." oxfordartonline.com (October 20, 2006). https://doi.org/10.1093/gao/9781884446054.article.T2021811.

LIPPINCOTT 1990
Lippincott, Kristen. "Review: *Artemisia Gentileschi: The Image of the Female Hero in Italian Baroque Art* by Mary D. Garrard." *Renaissance Studies* 4, no. 4 (December 1990): 444–48.

LLEWELLYN 2014
Llewellyn, Kathleen M. *Representing Judith in Early Modern French Literature*. Farnham, 2014.

LOCKER 2015
Locker, Jesse M. *Artemisia Gentileschi: The Language of Painting*. New Haven, 2015.

LOCKER 2017
Locker, Jesse. "Artemisia Gentileschi: The Literary Formation of an Unlearned Artist." In Barker 2017a, 89–101.

LOIRE 2011
Loire, Stéphane. "Simon Vouet en Italie (1612–1627): Questions d'attributions et de datations." In *Simon Vouet en Italie*, edited by Olivier Bonfait and Hélène Rousteau-Chambon, 183–233. Rennes, 2011.

LOISEL 2006
Loisel, Catherine. "66. Elisabetta Sirani, *Libération du possédé de Constantinople*." In *Le génie de Bologne des Carracci aux Gandolfi: Dessins des XVIIe et XVIIIe siècles*, edited by Diederik Bakhuÿs, Luisa Berretti, and Catherine Loisel, 148–49. Exh. cat., Musée des Beaux Arts, Rouen, 2006–2007. Montreuil, 2006.

LOISEL 2013
Loisel, Catherine, ed. *Inventaire général des dessins italiens*. Vol. 10, *Dessins bolonais du XVIIe siècle, tome II*. Paris, 2013.

LOLLOBRIGIDA 2011
Lollobrigida, Consuelo. "Virginia da Vezzo: Un inedito e qualche riflessione." *Diana* 2 (2011): 64–69.

LOLLOBRIGIDA 2012
Lollobrigida, Consuelo. *Di mano donnesca: Donne artiste dal XVI al XX secolo*. Rome, 2012.

LOLLOBRIGIDA 2015
Lollobrigida, Consuelo. "Maria Luigia Raggi monaca Turchina: Pittrice di capricci e paesaggi (Genova, ante 15 febbraio 1742–25 marzo 1813)." In Barker 2015a, 191–98.

LOLLOBRIGIDA 2017
Lollobrigida, Consuelo. *Plautilla Bricci: Pictura et architectura celebris: L'architettrice del Barocco romano*. Rome, 2017.

LOLLOBRIGIDA 2018
Lollobrigida, Consuelo. "19. Lavinia Fontana, *Portret van een dame uit de familie Gonzaga of Sanvitale/Portrait d'une dame de la famille Gonzaga ou Sanvitale*." In Ghent 2018, 96–97.

LOMAZZO 1590
Lomazzo, Giovanni Paolo. *Idea del tempio della pittura*. Milan, 1590.

LOMAZZO 1844
Lomazzo, Giovanni Paolo. *Trattato dell'arte della pittura, scultura ed architettura*. 2 vols. Rome, 1844.

LOMAZZO 1973
Lomazzo, Giovanni Paolo. *Scritti sulle arti*. Vol. 1, *Libro de sogni, idea del tempio della pittura*. Edited by Roberto Paolo Ciardi. Florence, 1973.

LONDON 1983
Trafalgar Galleries at the Royal Academy III. Exh. cat., Royal Academy, London, 1983. Catalogue by Ronald Cohen, Alfred Cohen, and Edward Cohen. London, 1983.

LONDON 2020
Artemisia. Exh. cat., National Gallery, London, 2020–2021. Catalogue by Letizia Treves and others. London, 2020.

LONGHI 1916
Longhi, Roberto. "Gentileschi padre e figlia." *L'arte* 19 (1916): 245–314.

LONGHI 1967
Longhi, Roberto. "Anche Ambrogio Figino sulle soglie della natura morta." *Paragone* 209 (July 1967): 18–22.

LORDE 2007
Lorde, Audre. "The Master's Tools Will Never Dismantle the Master's House." In *Sister Outsider: Essays and Speeches*, 110–14. Berkeley, 2007.

LOS ANGELES 1976
Women Artists: 1550–1950. Exh. cat., Los Angeles County Museum of Art; University Art Museum, University of Texas, Austin; Museum of Art, Carnegie Institute, Pittsburgh, Brooklyn Museum, 1976–1977. Catalogue edited by Ann Sutherland Harris and Linda Nochlin. Los Angeles and New York, 1976.

LOS ANGELES COUNCIL OF WOMEN ARTISTS 1971
Los Angeles Council of Women Artists Report. June 15, 1971. Getty Research Institute, 2003.M.46.

LOTZ 1933
Lotz, Arthur. *Bibliographie der Modelbücher*. Leipzig, 1933.

LOUGHERY 2002
Loughery, John. "Sexual Violence: Baroque to Surrealist." *Hudson Review* 55, no. 2 (Summer 2002): 293–300.

LOZANO 2019A
Lozano, Jorge Sebastián. "3. Sofonisba Anguissola, *Self-Portrait in Miniature*." In Madrid 2019, 94–95.

LOZANO 2019B
Lozano, Jorge Sebastián. "20. Commemorative Medal of Sofonisba Anguissola." In Madrid 2019, 130–31.

LUKEHART 2020
Lukehart, Peter M. "Giovanna Garzoni, 'Accademica.'" In Florence 2020, 96–105.

MADRID 1990
Alonso Sánchez Coello y el retrato en la corte de Felipe II. Exh. cat., Museo Nacional del Prado, 1990. Catalogue contributions by Alfonso E. Pérez Sánchez and others. Madrid, 1990.

MADRID 2019
A Tale of Two Women Painters: Sofonisba Anguissola and Lavinia Fontana. Exh. cat., Museo Nacional del Prado, 2019–2020. Catalogue edited by Leticia Ruiz Gómez. Madrid, 2019.

MALAMANI 1910
Malamani, Vittorio. *Rosalba Carriera*. Bergamo, 1910.

MALVASIA 1678
Malvasia, Carlo Cesare. *Felsina pittrice: Vite de' pittori bolognesi*. 2 vols. Bologna, 1678.

MALVASIA 1841
Malvasia, Carlo Cesare. *Felsina pittrice: Vite de' pittori bolognesi del Conte Carlo Cesare Malvasia con aggiunte, correzioni e note inedite del medesimo autore*. Edited by Giampietro Zanotti and Vicente Victoria. 2 vols. Bologna, 1841.

MALVASIA 1961
Malvasia, Carlo Cesare. *Vite di pittori bolognesi: Appunti inediti*. Edited by Adriana Arfelli. Bologna, 1961.

MANARESI 1898
Manaresi, Antonio. *Elisabetta Sirani*. Bologna, 1898.

MANCINI 1956–1957
Mancini, Giulio. *Considerazioni sulla pittura*. Edited by Adriana Marucchi. 2 vols. Rome, 1956–1957.

MANN 1997
Mann, Judith W. "Caravaggio and Artemisia: Testing the Limits of Caravaggism." *Studies in Iconography* 18 (1997): 161–85.

MANN 2001A
Mann, Judith W. "Artemisia and Orazio Gentileschi." In New York 2001–2002, 249–61.

MANN 2001B
Mann, Judith W. "69. Artemisia Gentileschi, *Judith and Her Maidservant*." In New York 2001–2002, 368–70.

MANN 2001C
Mann, Judith W. "80. Artemisia Gentileschi, *David and Bathsheba*." In New York 2001–2002, 414–17.

MANN 2001D
Mann, Judith W. "81. Artemisia Gentileschi, *Self-Portrait as the Allegory of Painting (La Pittura)*." In New York 2001–2002, 417–21.

MANN 2005A
Mann, Judith W., ed. *Artemisia Gentileschi: Taking Stock*. Turnhout, 2005.

MANN 2005B
Mann, Judith W. "Introduction: Taking Stock of Artemisia and Her Symposium." In Mann 2005a, 1–18.

MANN 2005C
Mann, Judith W. "The Myth of Artemisia as Chameleon: A New Look at the London *Allegory of Painting*." In Mann 2005a, 51–77.

MANN 2009
Mann, Judith W. "Identity Signs: Meanings and Methods in Artemisia Gentileschi's Signatures." *Renaissance Studies* 23, no. 1 (February 2009): 71–107.

MANN 2016
Mann, Judith W. "Artemisia a Roma 1606–1613: Inizi strategici e stilistici." In Rome 2016, 13–21.

MANN 2017
Mann, Judith W. "Deciphering Artemisia: Three New Narratives and How They Expand Our Understanding." In Barker 2017a, 167–86.

MANN 2019
Mann, Judith W. "26. Artemisia Gentileschi, *Mary Magdalen in Ecstasy*." In *Caravaggio, Bernini: Early Baroque in Rome*, edited by Frits Scholten, 154–55. Exh. cat., Kunsthistorisches Museum, Vienna; Rijksmuseum, Amsterdam, 2019–2020. New York and London, 2019.

MANNARINO 2018
Mannarino, Amy. "What the Data Tell Us about the Challenges Facing Female Artists of Color." hyperallergic.com (March 1, 2018). https://hyperallergic.com/429885/what-the-data-tell-us-about-the-challenges-facing-female-artists-of-color/.

MANTUA 1937
Mostra iconografica Gonzaghesca. Exh. cat., Palazzo Ducale, Mantua, 1937. Mantua, 1937.

MARANDEL 2017
Marandel, J. Patrice. *Abecedario: Collecting and Recollecting*. Los Angeles, 2017.

MARANDEL AND EINECKE 2006
Marandel, J. Patrice, and Claudia Einecke, eds. *Los Angeles County Museum of Art: European Art*. Paris, 2006.

MARCIARI 2015
Marciari, John. *Italian, Spanish and French Paintings before 1850 in the San Diego Museum of Art*. San Diego, 2015.

MARRO 1998
Marro, Lucia. "33. Felice Antonio Casoni, *Lavinia Fontana, 1552–1614, Bolognese Painter*." In Washington, D.C. 1998, 114–15.

MARSHALL 2005
Marshall, Christopher R. "An Early Inventory Reference and New Technical Information for Bernardo Cavallino's 'Triumph of Galatea.'" *Burlington Magazine* 147, no. 1222 (January 2005): 40–44.

MARUBBI 2007
Marubbi, Mario. *La Pinacoteca Ala Ponzone: Il Seicento: Catalogo delle collezione del museo civico di Cremona*. Milan, 2007.

MASINI 1666
Masini, Antonio di Paolo. *Bologna perlustrata*. Bologna, 1666.

MASON RINALDI 1985
Mason Rinaldi, Stefania, ed. *Il valore dei dipinti antichi: L'analisi critica, storica, ed economica*. Turin, 1985.

MASSARI 1980
Massari, Stefania. *Incisori mantovani del '500: Giovan Battista, Adamo, Diana Scultori e Giorgio Ghisi*. Rome, 1980.

MATTHEWS-GRIECO 2017
Matthews-Grieco, Sara F. "Self-Portraits, Self-Fashioning and the Language of Things: Sofonisba Anguissola and Lavinia Fontana." In *Archetipi del femminile: Rappresentazioni di genere, identità e ruoli sociali nell'arte dalle origini a oggi*, edited by Alessandra Buccheri, Giulia Ingarao, and Emilia Valenza, 23–39. Milan, 2017.

MATZAT 2001
Matzat, Wolfgang. "Leidenschaft." In *Historisches Wörterbuch der Rhetorik*, edited by Gert Ueding, vol. 5, 151–64. 10 vols. Darmstadt, 2001.

MCGLONE 2019
McGlone, Peggy. "Women Are Increasingly Getting the Top Museum Jobs: Will More of Them Finally Get Equal Pay?" *Washington Post* (July 2, 2019). https://www.washingtonpost.com/entertainment/museums/women-are-increasingly-getting-the-top-museum-jobs-will-more-of-them-finally-get-equal-pay/2019/07/01/d85717fa-9682-11e9-8d0a-5edd7e2025b1_story.html.

MEIJER 1994
Meijer, Bert W. "38. Jacob Bos, *La vecchia rimbambita muove il riso alla fanciulletta*." In Cremona 1994, 272–73.

MELONI TRKULJA 1979
Meloni Trkulja, Silvia. "Le miniature degli Uffizi." In Berti 1979, 1167–71.

MELONI TRKULJA 2000
Meloni Trkulja, Silvia. "Giovanna Garzoni and 'The Great Theatre of Nature.'" In *Still Lifes: Giovanna Garzoni*, edited by Silvia Meloni Trkulja and Elena Fumagalli, 4–11. Paris, 2000.

MICHEL 1991
Michel, Olivier. "Virginia Vezzi et l'entourage de Simon Vouet à Rome." In *Simon Vouet: Actes du colloque international, Grand Palais, 5–7 February 1991*, edited by Stéphane Loire, 123–33. Paris, 1992.

MIDDELDORF 1978
Middeldorf, Ulrich. "The Dilettante Sculptor." *Apollo* 107 (1978): 310–22.

MILAN 2007
L'arte delle donne dal Rinascimento al Surrealismo. Exh. cat., Palazzo Reale, Milan, 2007–2008. Catalogue contributions by Vittorio Sgarbi and others. Milan, 2007.

MILAN 2011
Artemisia Gentileschi: The Story of a Passion. Exh. cat., Palazzo Reale, Milan, 2011–2012. Catalogue edited by Roberto Contini and Francesco Solinas. Milan, 2011.

MINGHETTI 1877
Minghetti, Marco. "Le donne italiane nelle belle arti al secolo XV e XVI." *Nuova antologia* (June 1877): 1–42.

MINOR 1999
Minor, Vernon Hyde. *Baroque and Rococo: Art and Culture*. Upper Saddle River, N.J., 1999.

MODENA 1998
Tesori ritrovati: La pittura del ducato estense nel collezionismo privato. Exh. cat., Chiese di San Carlo, Modena, 1998–1999. Catalogue contributions by Daniele Benati and others. Milan, 1998.

MODESTI 1995
Modesti, Adelina. "Elisabetta Sirani 'Pittrice Eroina': A Portrait of the Artist as a Young Woman." In *Identità e appartenenza: Donne e relazioni di genere dal mondo classico all'età contemporanea*, vol. 3, 745–68. 3 vols. Bologna, 1995.

MODESTI 1997
Modesti, Adelina. "Sirani, Elisabetta." In Gaze 1997, vol. 2, 1272–75.

MODESTI 2001A
Modesti, Adelina. "Alcune riflessioni sulle opere grafiche della pittrice Elisabetta Sirani nelle raccolte dell'Archiginnasio." *L'Archiginnasio* 94 (2001): 151–215.

MODESTI 2001B
Modesti, Adelina. "The Making of a Cultural Heroine: Elisabetta Sirani 'Pittrice Celebrissima' di Bologna (1638–1665)." In *Per l'arte da Venezia all'Europa: Studi in onore di Giuseppe Maria Pilo*, edited by Mario Piantoni and Laura De Rossi, vol. 2, 399–404. 2 vols. Monfalcone, 2001.

MODESTI 2003
Modesti, Adelina. "Patrons as Agents and Artists as Dealers in Seicento Bologna." In Fantoni, Matthew, and Matthews-Grieco 2003, 367–88.

MODESTI 2004
Modesti, Adelina. *Elisabetta Sirani: Una virtuosa del Seicento bolognese*. Bologna, 2004.

MODESTI 2014
Modesti, Adelina. *Elisabetta Sirani 'virtuosa': Women's Cultural Production in Early Modern Bologna*. Turnhout, 2014.

MODESTI 2017
Modesti, Adelina. "'Il Pennello Virile': Elisabetta Sirani and Artemisia Gentileschi as Masculinized Painters?" In Barker 2017a, 131–46.

MODESTI 2018
Modesti, Adelina. "Maestra Elisabetta Sirani, 'Virtuosa del Pennello.'" *Imagines* 2 (August 2018): 84–97.

MOIR 1967
Moir, Alfred. *The Italian Followers of Caravaggio*. 2 vols. Cambridge, Mass., 1967.

MORANDINI 1956
Morandini, Francesca, ed. *Statuti delle arti dei fornai e dei vinattieri di Firenze (1337–1339)*. Florence, 1956.

MORANDOTTI 2018
Morandotti, Alessandro. "Pierre Subleyras e il ritratto a Roma nel Settecento." In *Pierre Subleyras e l'abate miniatore Felice Ramelli*, edited by Alessandro Morandotti and Gelsomina Spione, 13–31. Milan, 2018.

MORSELLI 2010
Morselli, Raffaella. "Bologna." In Spear and Sohm 2010, 145–72.

MORSELLI AND SONES 1998
Morselli, Raffaella, and Anna Cera Sones, eds. *Collezioni e quadrerie nella Bologna del Seicento: Inventari 1640–1707*. Documents for the History of Collecting: Italian Inventories, 3. Los Angeles, 1998.

MOSCHINI 1806
Moschini, Giannantonio. *Della letteratura veneziana dal secolo XVIII fino a' nostri giorni*. 4 vols. Venice, 1806.

MOÜCKE 1752–1762
Moücke, Francesco. *Serie di ritratti degli eccellenti pittori dipinti di propria mano che esistono nell'imperial galleria di Firenze colle vite in compendio de' medesimi descritte da Francesco Moücke*. 4 vols. Florence, 1752–1762.

MOWL 2011
Mowl, Timothy. *Horace Walpole: The Great Outsider*. London, 2011.

MUNICH 1984
Italian Still Life Painting from Three Centuries: The Silvano Lodi Collection. Exh. cat., Bayerische Staatsgemäldesammlungen, Alte Pinakothek, Munich, 1984–1985. Catalogue by Luigi Salerno. Florence, 1984.

MURCIA DE LA LLANA 1619
Murcia de la Llana, Francisco. *Rhetoricorum tomus primus in duas partes diuisus, quarum prima breui stylo artis praecepta continet, & multiplicat, secunda artis exercitamenta complecititur, selectus ex doctoribus magistris Societatis Iesu*. Madrid, 1619.

MURPHY 1997A
Murphy, Caroline P. "Fontana, Lavinia." In Gaze 1997, vol. 1, 534–37.

MURPHY 1997B
Murphy, Caroline P. "Lavinia Fontana and the Female Life Cycle Experience in Late Sixteenth-Century Bologna." In Johnson and Matthews-Grieco 1997, 111–38.

MURPHY 2003
Murphy, Caroline P. *Lavinia Fontana: A Painter and Her Patrons in Sixteenth-Century Bologna*. New Haven, 2003.

MUSACCHIO 2001
Musacchio, Jacqueline Marie. "Weasels and Pregnancy in Renaissance Italy." *Renaissance Studies* 15, no. 2 (June 2001): 172–87.

MYERS 1970
Myers, Bernard S., ed. *Encyclopedia of Painting: Painters and Painting of the World from Prehistoric Times to the Present Day*. 3rd ed. New York, 1970.

NAGLE 1982
Nagle, Judy. *The Responsive Arts*. Palo Alto, 1982.

NANCARROW 2003
Nancarrow, Mindy. "The Artistic Activity of Spanish Nuns During the Golden Age." In *Essays on Women Artists: "The Most Excellent,"* edited by Liana De Girolami Cheney, vol. 1, 41–52. 2 vols. Lewiston, 2003.

NANCY 1992
Jacques Callot 1592–1635. Exh. cat., Musée Historique Lorrain, Nancy, 1992. Catalogue by Brigitte Heckel. Paris, 1992.

NANTES 2008
Simon Vouet (les années italiennes 1613/1627). Exh. cat., Musée des Beaux Arts de Nantes, 2008. Catalogue contributions by Adeline Collange and others. Paris, 2008.

NAPLES 1964
La natura morta italiana. Exh. cat., Palazzo Reale, Naples, 1964. Catalogue introduction by Stefano Bottari. Milan, 1964.

NAPLES 1984
Civiltà del Seicento a Napoli. Exh. cat., Museo di Capodimonti, Naples, 1984. Catalogue edited by Silvia Cassani. 2 vols. Naples, 1984.

NAPPI 2005
Nappi, Eduardo. "Appendix: New Documents Concerning Artemisia Gentileschi in the Archivio Storico del Banco di Napoli." In Mann 2005a, 97–98.

NECHVATAL 2017
Nechvatal, Joseph. "Review: *Dioramas–Palais de Tokyo*." whitehotmagazine.com (September 2017). https://whitehotmagazine.com/articles/dioramas-at-palais-de-tokyo/3746.

NEW YORK 1961
A Loan Exhibition of Venetian Paintings of the 18th Century. Exh. cat., Finch College Museum of Art, New York, 1961. Catalogue by Robert L. Manning. New York, 1961.

NEW YORK 1965
Drawings from New York Collections I: The Italian Renaissance. Exh. cat., Metropolitan Museum of Art, New York, 1965–1966. Catalogue by Jacob Bean and Felice Stampfle. New York, 1965.

NEW YORK 1981
Masterworks from the John and Mable Ringling Museum of Art, The State Art Museum of Florida. Exh. cat., Wildenstein Galleries, New York, 1981. Catalogue by Denys Sutton. Sarasota, 1981.

NEW YORK 1996
European Miniatures in the Metropolitan Museum of Art. Exh. cat., Metropolitain Museum of Art, New York, 1996–1997. Catalogue by Graham Reynolds and Katharine Baetjer. New York, 1996.

NEW YORK 2001–2002
Orazio and Artemisia Gentileschi. Exh. cat., Museo del Palazzo di Venezia, Rome; Metropolitan Museum of Art, New York; Saint Louis Art Museum, 2001–2002. Catalogue by Keith Christiansen, Judith W. Mann, and others. New York and New Haven, 2001.

NEW YORK 2004
Painters of Reality: The Legacy of Leonardo and Caravaggio in Lombardy. Exh. cat., Metropolitan Museum of Art, New York, 2004. Catalogue edited by Andrea Bayer. New York, 2004.

NEW YORK 2018
Selected Works from 17th to 20th Century: TEFAF New York Fall, October 27–31, 2018. Exh. cat., New York, 2018. Catalogue edited by Giuseppe Porzio. London and Rome, 2018.

NICOLSON 1979
Nicolson, Benedict. *The International Caravaggesque Movement*. Oxford, 1979.

NICOLSON AND VERTOVA 1990
Nicolson, Benedict, and Luisa Vertova. *Caravaggism in Europe*. 2nd ed. 3 vols. Turin, 1990.

NOACK 1920
Noack, Friedrich. "Die Künstlerfamilie Stern in Rom." *Monatshefte für Kunstwissenschaft* 13, no. 2 (1920): 166–73.

NOCHLIN 1971
Nochlin, Linda. "Why Have There Been No Great Women Artists?" *Art News* 69, no. 9 (January 1971): 22–39.

NOCHLIN 1972
Nochlin, Linda. "Eroticism and Female Imagery in Nineteenth-Century Art." In *Woman as Sex Object: Studies in Erotic Art, 1730–1970*, edited by Thomas B. Hess and Linda Nochlin, 9–15. Art News Annual, 38. New York, 1972.

NOCHLIN 1999
Nochlin, Linda. "Memoirs of an Ad Hoc Art Historian." In *Representing Women*. New York, 1999, 6–33.

NOCHLIN 2017
Nochlin, Linda. "From the Archives: Linda Nochlin on Black Male." *ARTnews* (February 6, 2017). https://www.artnews.com/art-in-america/features/from-the-archive-linda-nochlin-on-black-male-63243/.

NOCHLIN AND GARB 1996
Nochlin, Linda, and Tamar Garb, eds. *The Jew in the Text: Modernity and the Construction of Identity*. London, 1996.

NORRIS 2019
Norris, Mary. "Female Trouble: The Debate Over 'Woman' as an Adjective." *New Yorker* (May 30, 2019). https://www.newyorker.com/culture/comma-queen/female-trouble-the-debate-over-woman-as-an-adjective.

"NOTA DELLE PITTURE FATTE DA ME ELISABETTA SIRANI" 1841
"Nota delle pitture fatte da me Elisabetta Sirani." In Malvasia 1841, vol. 2, 393–96.

OBERER 2020
Oberer, Angela. *The Life and Work of Rosalba Carriera (1673–1757): The Queen of Pastel*. Amsterdam, 2020.

OLD MASTER PAINTINGS, PART II 2016
Old Master Paintings, Part II. Sales cat., Dorotheum, Vienna, October 18, 2016.

OMAHA 1997
Hot Dry Men, Cold Wet Women: The Theory of Humors in Western European Art, 1575–1700. Exh. cat., Joslyn Art Museum, Omaha; Arkansas Arts Center, Little Rock; John and Mable Ringling Museum of Art, Sarasota, 1997–1998. Catalogue by Zirka Z. Filipczak. New York, 1997.

ORLANDI 1753
Orlandi, Pellegrino Antonio. *Abecedario pittorico*. Venice, 1753.

OWENS SCHAEFER 1984
Owens Schaefer, Jean. "A Note on the Iconography of a Medal of Lavinia Fontana." *Journal of the Warburg and Courtauld Institutes* 47 (1984): 232–34.

OY-MARRA 2014
Oy-Marra, Elisabeth. "Maskierung einer Malerin: Die Selbstporträts der Artemisia Gentileschi." In *Maske, Maskerade und die Kunst der Verstellung: Vom Barock bis zur Moderne*, edited by Christiane Kruse, 151–72. Wolfenbütteler Arbeiten zur Barockforschung, vol. 52. Wiesbaden, 2014.

OY-MARRA 2016
Oy-Marra, Elisabeth. "79. Artemisia Gentileschi, *David and Bathsheba*." In Wiesbaden 2016, 336–37.

PADUA 2019
700 Veneziano. Exh. cat., Biblioteca Antica del Convento del Santo, Sant'Antonio di Padova, 2019. Catalogue edited by Fabrizio Magani. Milan, 2019.

PAINE 1960
Paine, Edward Grosvenor. *Inventory of the Miniatures in the Fredrick Collection*. Unpublished, 1960.

PAINTINGS IN THE DETROIT INSTITUTE OF ARTS 1970
Paintings in the Detroit Institute of Arts: A Check List of the Paintings Acquired before May, 1970. Detroit, 1970.

PANIGAROLA 1585
Panigarola, Francesco. *Cento ragionamenti sopra la passione di Nostro Signore*. Venice, 1585.

PAPI 2000
Papi, Gianni. "Review: *Artemisia Gentileschi and the Authority of Art* by Roger Ward Bissell." *Burlington Magazine* 142, no. 1168 (July 2000): 450–53.

PAPI 2011
Papi, Gianni. "Artemisia Gentileschi: Milan." *Burlington Magazine* 153, no. 1305 (December 2011): 846–47.

PAPI 2012
Papi, Gianni. "Artemisia Gentileschi's 'Suffer the Little Children to Come unto Me.'" *Burlington Magazine* 154, no. 1317 (December 2012): 828–31.

PAPI 2017
Papi, Gianni. "*Mary Magdalene in Ecstasy* and the *Madonna of the Svezzamento*: Two Masterpieces by Artemisia." In Barker 2017a, 147–66.

PAPI, BISCHOFF, AND FORD 2019
Papi, Gianni, Nina Gram Bischoff, and Thierry Ford. "Orazio and Artemisia Gentileschi and 'Judith and her Maidservant' in Oslo." *Burlington Magazine* 161, no. 1396 (July 2019): 532–43.

PARIS 1952
La nature morte de l'antiquité à nos jours. Exh. cat., Musée de l'Orangerie, Paris, 1952. Catalogue by Charles Sterling. Paris, 1952.

PARIS 1987
Subleyras, 1699–1749. Exh. cat., Musée de Luxembourg, Paris; Académie de France, Villa Médicis, Rome, 1987. Catalogue edited by Olivier Michel and Pierre Rosenberg. Paris, 1987.

PARIS 1990
Vouet. Exh. cat., Grand Palais, Paris, 1990–1991. Catalogue by Jacques Thullier, Barbara Brejon de Lavergnée, and Denis Lavalle. Paris, 1990.

PARIS 2012
Artemisia: Pouvoir, gloire et passions d'une femme peintre. Exh. cat., Musée Maillol, Paris, 2012. Catalogue edited by Roberto Contini and Francesco Solinas. Paris, 2012.

PARIS 2017
Dioramas. Exh. cat., Palais de Tokyo, Paris; Schirn Kunsthalle, Frankfurt, 2017–2018. Catalogue edited by Katharina Dohm and others. Paris, 2017.

PASCOLI 1933
Pascoli, Lione. *Vite de' pittori, scultori, ed architetti moderni*. 2 vols. Rome, 1730–1736. Reprint. Rome, 1933.

PAVANELLO 2009
Pavanello, Giuseppe, ed. *Rosalba Carriera, 1673–1757: Atti del convegno internazionale di studi 26–28 aprile 2007*. Verona, 2009.

PAYNE 1957–1958
Payne, Elizabeth H. "A Venetian Portrait in Pastel." *Bulletin of the Detroit Institute of Arts* 37, no. 1 (1957–1958): 4–5.

PERA 1888
Pera, Francesco. *Curiosità livornesi inedite o rare*. Livorno, 1888.

PERA 1971
Pera, Francesco. *Nuove curiosità livornesi inedite o rare*. Livorno, 1889. Reprint. Florence, 1971.

PÉREZ DE TUDELA 2019A
Pérez de Tudela, Almudena. "Sofonisba Anguissola at the Court of Philip II." In Madrid 2019, 53–69.

PÉREZ DE TUDELA 2019B
Pérez de Tudela, Almudena. "30. Sofonisba Anguissola, *Infanta Isabella Clara Eugenia*/31. Sofonisba Anguissola, *Infanta Catalina Micaela with a Marmoset*." In Madrid 2019, 156–59.

PERLINGIERI 1992
Perlingieri, Ilya Sandra. *Sofonisba Anguissola: The First Great Woman Artist of the Renaissance*. New York, 1992.

PERROT 1693
Perrot, Catherine. *Traité de la mignature*. Paris, 1693.

PETERSEN AND WILSON 1976
Petersen, Karen, and J. J. Wilson. *Women Artists: Recognition and Reappraisal from the Early Middle Ages to the Twentieth Century*. New York, 1976.

PHASIS 2017
"Schirin Kunsthalle Frankfurt, Diorama—Inventing Illusion." phasisgallery.com. (December 2, 2017). https://phasisgallery.com/en/schirn-diorama/.

PHILADELPHIA 2000
Art in Rome in the Eighteenth Century. Exh. cat., Philadelphia Museum of Art; Museum of Fine Arts Houston, 2000. Catalogue edited by Edgar Peters Bowron and Joseph J. Rishel. London, 2000.

PHILLIPPY 2006
Phillippy, Patricia. *Painting Women: Cosmetics, Canvases, and Early Modern Culture*. Baltimore, 2006.

PHILPOT 2009
Philpot, Elizabeth. *Old Testament Apocryphal Images in European Art*. Gothenburg, 2009.

PICCINARDI 1665
Piccinardi, Giovani Luigi. *Il pennello lagrimato: Orazione funebre del signor Gio. Luigi Piccinardi dignissimo Priore de' Signori Leggisti nello Studio di Bologna, con varie poesie: In morte della Signora Elisabetta Sirani pittrice famosissima*. Bologna, 1665.

PICCINARDI 1666
Piccinardi, Giovanni Luigi, ed. *La poesia muta celebrata dalla pittura loquace: Applausi di nobili ingegni al pennello immortale della Signora Elisabetta Sirani pittrice Bolognese*. Bologna, 1666.

PILO 1976
Pilo, Giuseppe Maria. *Sebastiano Ricci e la pittura veneziana del Settecento*. Pordenone, 1976.

PISA 2009
Il cannocchiale e il pennello: Nuova scienza e nuova arte nell'età di Galileo. Exh. cat., Palazzo Blu, Pisa, 2009. Catalogue edited by Lucia Tongiorgi Tomasi and Alessandro Tosi. Florence, 2009.

PIZZORUSSO 1986
Pizzorusso, Claudio. "99. Justus Sustermans, *Maria Maddalena d'Austria come Santa Maria Maddalena*." In Florence 1986, 235–36.

PLINY THE ELDER 2004
Pliny the Elder. *Natural History: A Selection*. Translation and introduction by John F. Healy. London, 2004.

PLUTARCH 2018
Plutarch. *Lives*. Translated by A. H. Clough. Frankfurt, 2018.

POGGIO A CAIANO 2014
Pergamene fiorite: Pitture di fiori dalle collezioni medicee. Exh. cat., Villa Medicea, Poggio a Caiano, 2014. Catalogue edited by Maria Matilde Simari and Elisa Acanfora. Livorno, 2014.

POINTON 1981
Pointon, Marcia. "Artemisia Gentileschi's 'The Murder of Holofernes.'" *American Imago* 38, no. 4 (Winter 1981): 343–67.

POINTON 2001
Pointon, Marcia. "'Surrounded with Brilliants': Miniature Portraits in Eighteenth-Century England." *Art Bulletin* 83, no. 1 (March 2001): 48–71.

POLICICCHIO 2018A
Policicchio, Giada. "Het album met miniaturen en tekeningen van Giovanna Garzoni uit de Accademia di San Luca/L'album de miniatures et dessins de Giovanna Garzoni à l'Accademia di San Luca." In Ghent 2018, 188–97.

POLICICCHIO 2018B
Policicchio, Giada. "2. Sofonisba Anguissola, *Zelfportret/Autoportrait*." In Ghent 2018, 54–55.

POLICICCHIO 2018C
Policicchio, Giada. "48.22. Giovanna Garzoni, *Schotel met kweeappelen en amandelen/Assiette avec des coings et des amandes*." In Ghent 2018, 224–25.

POLLARD 1967
Renaissance Medals from the Samuel H. Kress Collection at the National Gallery of Art. Revised by Graham Pollard. London, 1967.

POLONSKY 2019
Polonsky, Naomi. "Female Artists Are Finally in Our Galleries—Let's Keep Them There." *Guardian* (January 31, 2019). https://www.theguardian.com/artanddesign/2019/jan/31/female-artists-are-finally-in-our-galleries-lets-keep-them-there.

POMEROY 2007
Pomeroy, Jordana. "Italian Women Artists from Renaissance to Baroque." In Washington, D.C. 2007, 19–22.

POPE-HENNESSY 1989
Pope-Hennessy, John. "The Study of Italian Plaquettes." In *Italian Plaquettes*, edited by Alison Luchs, 19–32. Studies in the History of Art, 22; CASVA Symposium Papers, 9. Washington, D.C., 1989.

PRAAMSTRA 2010
Praamstra, Olf. "A Woman Warrior: Mina Kruseman, 1839–1922." In *Women's Writing from the Low Countries 1880–2010: An Anthology*, edited by Jacqueline Bel and Thomas Vaessens, 23–25. Amsterdam, 2010.

PRIMAROSA 2014
Primarosa, Yuri. "Nuova luce su Plautilla Bricci, pittrice e architettrice." *Studi di storia dell'arte* 25 (2014): 145–61.

PRINZ 1971
Prinz, Wolfram. *Die Sammlung der Selbstbildnisse in den Uffizien*. Vol. 1, *Geschichte der Sammlung*. Berlin, 1971.

PROHASKA 1995
Prohaska, Wolfgang. "28. Elena Anguissola (?), *Portrait einer Dominikanerin als hl. Katharina von Siena*." In Vienna 1995, 99–100.

PUHLMANN 2003
Puhlmann, Helga. "Eine Karriere im Schatten von Rosalba Carriera—Felicita Sartori/Hoffmann in Venedig und Dresden." *Zeitenblicke* 2, no. 3, (2003). http://www.zeitenblicke.de/2003/03/pdf/Puhlmann.pdf.

PULINI 2004
Pulini, Massimo. "1656: Ritratto di Ginevra Cantofoli pittrice." In Bologna 2004, 136–41.

PULINI 2006
Pulini, Massimo. *Ginevra Cantofoli: La nuova nascita di una pittrice nella Bologna del Seicento*. Bologna, 2006.

PULINI 2020
Pulini, Massimo. "20. Giovanni Andrea Sirani, Elisabetta Sirani, *Berenice*." In Brescia 2020, 54–55.

PYKE 1973
Pyke, E. J. *A Biographical Dictionary of Wax Modellers*. Oxford, 1973.

QUÉRAT 2013
Quérat, Lisa. "Les représentations italiennes du mythe de Judith en peinture et au théâtre de la Renaissance au Baroque." *Cahiers d'études romanes* 27 (2013). http://journals.openedition.org/etudesromanes/4153.

RABINER 1984
Rabiner, Donald. "Teresa del Pò: A Pre-Rosalba Pastel Portraitist." *Woman's Art Journal* 5, no. 1 (Spring–Summer 1984): 16–22.

RAGG 1907
Ragg, Laura M. *The Women Artists of Bologna*. London, 1907.

REICH AND RUMSEY 2009
Reich, Paula, and Monica S. Rumsey, eds. *Toledo Museum of Art Masterworks*. Toledo, 2009.

REILLY 2015
Reilly, Maura. "Taking the Measure of Sexism: Facts, Figures, and Fixes." *ARTnews* (May 26, 2015). https://www.artnews.com/art-news/news/taking-the-measure-of-sexism-facts-figures-and-fixes-4111/.

RENNOLDS 1987
Rennolds, Margaret B. *The National Museum of Women in the Arts*. New York, 1987.

REPORT OF THE WOMAN'S RIGHTS CONVENTION 1848
Report of the Woman's Rights Convention. Rochester, 1848.

REYNOLDS 2003
Reynolds, Catherine. "Illuminators and the Painters' Guilds." In *Illuminating the Renaissance: The Triumph of Flemish Manuscript Painting in Europe*, edited by Thomas Kren and Scot McKendrick, 15–33. Exh. cat., J. Paul Getty Museum, Los Angeles; Royal Academy of Arts, London, 2003–2004. Los Angeles, 2003.

RICH 1974
Rich, Daniel Catton, ed. *European Paintings in the Collection of the Worcester Art Museum*. Worcester, Mass., 1974.

RICHARDSON 1952–1953
Richardson, E. P. "A Masterpiece of Baroque Drama." *Bulletin of the Detroit Institute of Arts* 32, no. 4 (1952–1953): 81–83.

RICHARDSON 1953
Richardson, E. P. "A Masterpiece of Baroque Drama." *Art Quarterly* 16, no. 2 (1953): 90–92.

RICHARDSON 1966
Richardson, E. P., ed. *Treasures from the Detroit Institute of Arts*. 3rd ed. Detroit, 1966.

RIDOLFI 1648
Ridolfi, Carlo. *Le maraviglie dell'arte, overo Le vite de gl'illustri pittori veneti e dello stato*. 2 vols. Venice, 1648.

RIPA 2012
Ripa, Cesare. *Iconologia*. Edited by Sonia Maffei. Turin, 2012.

ROBERTS 1998
Roberts, Helene E., ed. *Encyclopedia of Comparative Iconography: Themes Depicted in Works of Art*. 2 vols. Chicago, 1998.

ROCCO 2017
Rocco, Patricia. *The Devout Hand: Women, Virtue, and Visual Culture in Early Modern Italy*. Montreal and Kingston, 2017.

ROME 1973
I Caravaggeschi Francesi. Exh. cat., Académie de France, Villa Médicis, Rome, 1973. Catalogue edited by Arnauld Brejon de Lavergnée and Jean-Pierre Cuzin. Rome, 1973.

ROME 2016
Artemisia Gentileschi e il suo tempo. Exh. cat., Museo di Roma, Palazzo Braschi, Rome, 2016–2017. Catalogue contributions by Francesca Baldassari and others. Milan, 2016.

ROSENBERG 2000
Rosenberg, Pierre. "283. Pierre Subleyras, *Madame Subleyras, née Maria Felice Tibaldi*." In Philadelphia 2000, 436.

ROSENBERG AND MICHEL 1987A
Rosenberg, Pierre, and Olivier Michel. "H.C. 3. *Portrait de Madame Subleyras née Maria Felice Tibaldi*." In Paris 1987, 134–35.

ROSENBERG AND MICHEL 1987B
Rosenberg, Pierre, and Olivier Michel. "63. Pierre Subleyras, *Portrait de Madame Subleyras née Maria Felice Tibaldi*." In Paris 1987, 238–39.

RUOTOLO 2018
Ruotolo, Renato. *Caterina De Julianis, Naples ca. 1670–1743, Penitent Magdalene 1717*. Buenos Aires, 2018.

SACCHI 1872
Sacchi, Federico. *Notizie pittoriche cremonesi*. Cremona, 1872.

SACCHI 1994A
Sacchi, Rossana. "1. Sofonisba Anguissola, *Ritratto di monaca (Ritratto di Elena?)*. In Cremona 1994, 186–87.

SACCHI 1994B
Sacchi, Rossana. "6. Sofonisba Anguissola, *Autoritratto in miniatura*." In Cremona 1994, 196–97.

SACCHI 1994C
Sacchi, Rossana. "7. Sofonisba Anguissola, *Autoritratto al cavalletto*." In Cremona 1994, 198–99.

SACCHI 1994D
Sacchi, Rossana. "11. Sofonisba Anguissola, *Ritratto di Massimiliano Stampa*." In Cremona 1994, 206–7.

SACCHI 1994E
Sacchi, Rossana. "12. Cerchia delle sorelle Anguissola, da Sofonisba Anguissola, *Ritratto di Massimiliano Stampa*/13. Cerchia delle sorelle Anguissola? da Sofonisba Anguissola. *Ritratto di Massimiliano Stampa*." In Cremona 1994, 208–11.

SALOMON 2005
Salomon, Nanette. "Judging Artemisia: A Baroque Woman in Modern Art History." In Bal 2005, 33–61.

SAMMLUNG ARTHUR LÖBBECKE 1908
Sammlung Arthur Löbbecke Braunschweig, Kunstmedaillen und Plaketten des XV. bis XVII. Jahrhunderts. Sales cat., Jacob Hirsch, Munich, November 26, 1908.

SANI 1981
Sani, Bernardina. "La terminologia della pittura a pastello e in miniatura nel carteggio di Rosalba Carriera." In *Convegno nazionale sui lessici tecnici del Sei e Settecento, Pisa, Scuola Normale Superiore, 1–3 dicembre 1980: Contributi*, edited by Gabriella Cantini Guidotti, vol. 2, 385–417. 2 vols. Florence, 1981.

SANI 1985
Sani, Bernardina. *Rosalba Carriera: Lettere, diari, frammenti*. 2 vols. Florence, 1985.

SANI 1988
Sani, Bernardina. *Rosalba Carriera*. Turin, 1988.

SANI 2007
Sani, Bernardina. *Rosalba Carriera (1673–1757): Maestra del pastello nell'Europa ancien régime*. Turin, 2007.

SANI 2009
Sani, Bernardina. "Precisazioni su Rosalba Carriera, i suoi maestri e la sua scuola: Un percorso europeo tra Rococò e Illuminismo." In Pavanello 2009, 97–113.

SAN SECONDO DI PINEROLO 2012
Orsola Maddalena Caccia. Exh. cat., Castello di Miradolo, San Secondo di Pinerolo, 2012. Catalogue edited by Paola Caretta and Daniela Magnetti. Savigliano, 2012.

SCHAEFER AND FUSCO 1987
Schaefer, Scott, and Peter Fusco. *European Painting and Sculpture in the Los Angeles County Museum of Art: An Illustrated Summary Catalogue*. Los Angeles, 1987.

SCHER 2019
Scher, Stephen K., ed. *The Scher Collection of Commemorative Medals*. New York, 2019.

SCHIDLOF 1964
Schidlof, Leo R. *The Miniature in Europe in the 16th, 17th, 18th and 19th Centuries*. 2 vols. Graz, 1964.

SCHLEIER 2006
Schleier, Erich. *Simon Vouet 1590–Paris–1649*. London, 2006.

SCHWEIKHART 1992
Schweikhart, Gunter. "Boccaccios *De claris mulieribus* und die Selbstdarstellungen von Malerinnen im 16. Jahrhundert." In *Der Künstler über sich in seinem Werk: Internationales Symposium der Bibliotheca Hertziana, Rom, 1989*, edited by Matthias Winner, 113–36. Weinheim, 1992.

SEGAL 1998
Segal, Sam. "An Early Still Life by Fede Galizia." *Burlington Magazine* 140, no. 1140 (March 1998): 164–71.

SELECTED WORKS FROM THE DETROIT INSTITUTE OF ARTS 1979
Selected Works from the Detroit Institute of Arts. Detroit, 1979.

SHAPLEY 1973
Shapley, Fern Rusk. *Paintings from the Samuel H. Kress Collection, Italian Schools, XVI–XVIII Century*. London, 1973.

SHEETS 2017
Sheets, Hilarie M. "Gender Gap Persists at Largest Museums." *New York Times* (March 22, 2017).

SHELLEY 2011
Shelley, Marjorie. "Painting in the Dry Manner: The Flourishing of Pastel in 18th-Century Europe." In *Pastel Portraits: Images of 18th-Century Europe*, edited by Katharine Baetjer and Marjorie Shelley, 5–60. Exh. cat., Metropolitan Museum of Art, New York, 2011. New Haven and London, 2011.

SIEMON 2018
Siemon, Julia. "Elisabetta Sirani, 'Gem of Italy.'" cooperhewitt.org (June 23, 2018). https://www.cooperhewitt.org/2018/06/23/elisabetta-sirani-gem-of-italy/.

SIMARI 2014
Simari, Maria Matilde. "Pittori e pittrici di 'quadretti di miniatura' a Firenze." In Poggio a Caiano 2014, 8–22.

SIMON 1986
Simon, Robert B. "The Identity of Sofonisba Anguissola's 'Young Man.'" *Journal of the Walters Art Gallery* 44 (1986): 117–22.

SLAP 1985
Slap, Joseph. "Artemisia Gentileschi: Further Notes." *American Imago* 42, no. 3 (Fall 1985): 335–42.

SLATKIN 1990
Slatkin, Wendy. *Women Artists in History: From Antiquity to the 20th century*. 2nd ed. Englewood Cliffs, N.J., 1990.

SMITH 1964
Smith, Webster. "Giulio Clovio and the 'Maniera di Figure Piccole.'" *Art Bulletin* 46, no. 3 (September 1964): 395–401.

SOHM 1995
Sohm, Philip. "Gendered Style in Italian Art Criticism from Michelangelo to Malvasia." *Renaissance Quarterly* 48, no. 4 (Winter 1995): 759–808.

SOLERTI 1905
Solerti, Angelo. *Musica, ballo, e drammatica alla corte Medicea dal 1600 al 1637*. Florence, 1905.

SOLINAS 2011
Solinas, Francesco, ed. *Lettere di Artemisia: Edizione critica e annotata con quarantatre documenti inediti*. Rome, 2011.

SOLINAS 2018
Solinas, Francesco. "Orsola Maddalena Caccia. Moncalvo nel Montferrato 1596–1676." In Ghent 2018, 114–28.

SOPRANI AND RATTI 1768
Soprani, Raffaello, and Carlo Giuseppe Ratti. *Vite de' pittori, scultori ed architetti genovesi*. Genoa, 1768.

SORRENTINO 1931
Sorrentino, Antonino. "La Rocca di Fontanellato." *Emporium* 74 (1931): 21–35.

SPARROW 1905
Sparrow, Walter Shaw, ed. *Women Painters of the World from the Time of Caterina Vigri, 1413–1463, to Rosa Bonheur and the Present Day*. New York, 1905.

SPEAR 2000
Spear, Richard E. "Reviewed Work: *Artemisia Gentileschi: Ten Years of Fact and Fiction.*" *Art Bulletin* 82, no. 3 (September 2000): 568–79.

SPEAR AND SOHM 2010
Spear, Richard E., and Philip Sohm, eds. *Painting for Profit: The Economic Lives of Seventeenth-Century Italian Painters*. New Haven and London, 2010.

SPEELBERG 2015
Speelberg, Femke. "Fashion and Virtue: Textile Patterns and the Print Revolution, 1520–1620." *Metropolitan Museum of Art Bulletin* 73, no. 2 (Fall 2015): 5–48.

SPIKE 1991
Spike, John T. "Exhibition Review: *Artemisia Gentileschi*, Florence, Casa Buonarroti." *Burlington Magazine* 133, no. 1063 (October 1991): 732–34.

SPINOSA 2016
Spinosa, Nicola. "88. Artemisia Gentileschi and Bernardo Cavallino. *Loth e le figlie.*" In Rome 2016, 266–67.

STATUTI 1796
Statuti dell'insigne Accademia del disegno di Roma detta di San Luca evangelista. Rome, 1796.

STERCKX 2007
Sterckx, Marjan. "Pride and Prejudice: Eighteenth-Century Women Sculptors and their Material Practices." In *Women and Material Culture, 1660–1830*, edited by Jennie Batchelor and Cora Kaplan, 86–102. London, 2007.

STERLING 1959
Sterling, Charles. *Still Life Painting: From Antiquity to the Present Time*. Paris, 1959.

STOCKER 1998
Stocker, Margarita. *Judith Sexual Warrior: Women and Power in Western Culture*. New Haven, 1998.

STOKSTAD 2016
Stokstad, Marilyn. *Art: A Brief History*. 6th ed. Boston, 2016.

STROCCHIA 1999
Strocchia, Sharon. "Learning the Virtues: Convent Schools and Female Virtue in the Renaissance." In *Women's Education in Early Modern Europe: A History, 1500–1800*, edited by Barbara J. Whitehead, 3–46. New York and London, 1999.

STROCCHIA 2011
Strocchia, Sharon. "The Nun Apothecaries of Renaissance Florence: Marketing Medicines in the Convent." *Renaissance Studies* 25, no. 5 (November 2011): 627–47.

STRUNCK 2017
Strunck, Christina. "Hofkünstlerinnen: Weibliche Karrierestrategien an den Höfen der Frühen Neuzeit." In *Künstlerinnen: Neue Perspektiven auf ein Forschungsfeld der Vormoderne*, edited by Birgit Ulrike Münch, Andreas Tacke, Markwart Herzog, and Sylvia Heudecker, 20–37. Kunsthistorisches Forum Irsee, 4. Petersberg, 2017.

SUMMARY CATALOGUE OF DRAWINGS 1964
Summary Catalogue of Drawings by Identified Italian Architects in The Cooper Union Museum. New York, 1964.

SUTHERLAND HARRIS 1976
Sutherland Harris, Ann. "Introduction." In Los Angeles 1976, 13–44.

SUTHERLAND HARRIS 1979
Sutherland Harris, Ann. "Fede Galizia." In *Women Artists: 1550–1950*, edited by Ann Sutherland Harris and Linda Nochlin, 115. Exh. Cat., Los Angeles County Museum of Art; University Art Museum, University of Texas, Austin; Museum of Art, Carnegie Institute, Pittsburgh, Brooklyn Museum, 1976–1977. 4th printing. Los Angeles and New York, 1979.

SUTHERLAND HARRIS 1996
Sutherland Harris, Ann. "Artemisia Gentileschi." In *The Dictionary of Art*, edited by Jane Turner, vol. 12, 306–9. 34 vols. London: Grove, 1996.

SUTHERLAND HARRIS 2005A
Sutherland Harris, Ann. "Artemisia and Orazio: Drawing Conclusions." In Mann 2005a, 131–46.

SUTHERLAND HARRIS 2005B
Sutherland Harris, Ann. *Seventeenth-Century Art and Architecture*. London, 2005.

SUTHERLAND HARRIS 2010
Sutherland Harris, Ann. "Artemisia Gentileschi and Elisabetta Sirani: Rivals or Strangers?" *Woman's Art Journal* 31, no. 1 (2010): 3–12.

SUTHERLAND HARRIS AND NOCHLIN 1976
Sutherland Harris, Ann, and Linda Nochlin. "Preface." In Los Angeles 1976, 11–12.

TABLEAUX ET DESSINS ANCIENS 2014
Tableaux et dessins anciens et du XIXe siècle. Sales cat., Sotheby's Paris, June 26, 2014.

TANZI 2019
Tanzi, Marco. *Antonio Campi: The Portrait of a Gentleman*. London, 2019.

TEMANZA 1993
Temanza, Tomaso. *Zibaldon: Di memorie storiche appartenenti a' professori delle belle arti del disegno 1738*. Edited by Nicola Ivanoff. Venice, 1993.

TICKNER 1988
Tickner, Lisa. *The Spectacle of Women: Imagery of the Suffrage Campaign, 1907–14*. Chicago, 1988.

TICOZZI 1831
Ticozzi, Stefano. *Dizionario degli architetti, scultori, pittori intagliatori in rame, pietre preziose, in acciaio per medaglie e per caratteri, niellatori, intarsiatori musaicisti d'ogni età e d'ogni nazione, tomo secondo*. Milan, 1831.

TOMORY 1976
Tomory, Peter. *Catalogue of the Italian Paintings before 1800*. Sarasota, 1976.

TONGIORGI TOMASI 1990
Tongiorgi Tomasi, Lucia. "The Visual Arts and the Science of Horticulture in Tuscany from the 16th to the 18th Century." *Advances in Horticultural Science* 4, no. 1 (1990): 3–18.

TONGIORGI TOMASI 1997
Tongiorgi Tomasi, Lucia. *An Oak Spring Flora: Flower Illustration from the Fifteenth Century to the Present Time: A Selection of the Rare Books, Manuscripts, and Works of Art in the Collection of Rachel Lambert Mellon*. Upperville, Va., 1997.

TONGIORGI TOMASI 2008
Tongiorgi Tomasi, Lucia. "'La femminil pazienza': Women Painters and Natural History in the Seventeenth and Early Eighteenth Centuries." In *The Art of Natural History: Illustrated Treatises and Botanical Paintings, 1400–1850*, edited by Therese O'Malley and Amy R.W. Meyers, 158–85. New Haven, 2008.

TONGIORGI TOMASI 2010
Tongiorgi Tomasi, Lucia. "'La femminil pazienza': Women Painters and Natural History in the Seventeenth and Early Eighteenth Centuries." In *The Art of Natural History: Illustrated Treatises and Botanical Paintings, 1400–1850*, edited by Therese O' Malley and Amy R.W. Meyers, 159–85. 2nd ed. Washington, D.C., 2010.

TOPAZ ET AL. 2019
Topaz, Chad M., Bernhard Klingenberg, Daniel Turek, Brianna Heggeseth, Pamela E. Harris, Julie C. Blackwood, C. Ondine Chavoya, Steven Nelson, and Kevin M. Murphy. "Diversity of Artists in Major U.S. Museums." *PLOS ONE* 14, no. 3 (2019). https://doi.org/10.1371/journal.pone.0212852.

TOPPER AND GILLIS 1996
Topper, David, and Cynthia Gillis. "Trajectories of Blood: Artemisia Gentileschi and Galileo's Parabolic Path." *Woman's Art Journal* 17, no. 1 (Spring–Summer 1996): 10–13.

TORMEN 2009
Tormen, Gianluca. "Rosalba negli inventari delle collezioni venete del Settecento." In Pavanello 2009, 237–54.

TOZZI 2005
Tozzi, Ileana. "Suor Eufrasia Burlamacchi: I corali del Monastero di San Domenico a Lucca." *Alumina* 3, no. 11 (2005): 20–25.

TREVES 2020A
Treves, Letizia. "Artemisia Portraying Her Self." In London 2020, 64–77.

TREVES 2020B
Treves, Letizia. "10. Artemisia Gentileschi, *Self Portrait as a Lute Player*." In London 2020, 136–39.

TREVES 2020C
Treves, Letizia. "12. Artemisia Gentileschi, *Saint Catherine of Alexandria*." In London 2020, 144–45.

TREVES 2020D
Treves, Letizia. "22. Artemisia Gentileschi, *Susannah and the Elders*." In London 2020, 174–77.

TREVES 2020E
Treves, Letizia. "24. Artemisia Gentileschi, *Mary Magdalene in Ecstasy*." In London 2020, 182–83.

TREVES 2020F
Treves, Letizia. "32. Artemisia Gentileschi, *Lot and his Daughters*." In London 2020, 212–13.

TREVES 2020G
Treves, Letizia. "33. Artemisia Gentileschi, *David and Bathsheba*." In London 2020, 214–16.

TSCHUDY 1932
Tschudy, Herbert B. "Women in Art." *Brooklyn Museum Quarterly* 19, no. 1 (January 1932): 12–16.

TUFTS 1972
Tufts, Eleanor. "Sofonisba Anguissola, Renaissance Woman." *Art News* 71, no. 6 (1972): 50–62.

TUFTS 1974A
Tufts, Eleanor M. "A Successful 16th-century Portraitist: Ms. Lavinia Fontana from Bologna." *Art News* 73, no. 2 (February 1974): 60–64.

TUFTS 1974B
Tufts, Eleanor. *Our Hidden Heritage: Five Centuries of Women Artists*. New York, 1974.

TUFTS 1982
Tufts, Eleanor. "Lavinia Fontana, Bolognese Humanist." In *Le arti a Bologna e in Emilia dal XVI al XVII secolo*, edited by Andrea Emiliani, 129–34. Bologna, 1982.

TURRILL 2003
Turrill, Catherine. "Parenti, clienti, e conoscenti: The Nun-Artisans of Santa Caterina da Siena and Their Clients." In Fantoni, Matthew, and Matthews-Grieco 2003, 95–103.

TURRILL 2017
Turrill, Catherine. "Reviewing the Life and Literature of Plautilla Nelli." In Florence 2017, 19–33.

TZEUTSCHLER LURIE 1993
Tzeutschler Lurie, Ann. "'The Repentant Magdalene' by Simon Vouet." *Bulletin of the Cleveland Museum of Art* 80, no. 4 (April 1993): 158–63.

UPPENKAMP 2004
Uppenkamp, Bettina. *Judith und Holofernes in der italienischen Malerei des Barock*. Berlin, 2004.

VAIZEY 1999
Vaizey, Marina, ed. *Art: The Critic's Choice: 150 Masterpieces of Western Art Selected and Defined by the Experts*. New York, 1999.

VAN DER STIGHELEN 1999
Van der Stighelen, Katlijne. "Ravissantes ou cassantes, féminines ou indociles? Les femmes artistes des Pays-Bas méridionaux entre 1500 et 1800." In *A chacun sa grâce: Femmes artistes en Belgique et aux Pays-Bas 1500–1950*, edited by Katlijne Van der Stighelen and Mirjam Westen, 27–42. Exh. cat., Koninklijk Museum voor Schone Kunsten, Antwerp; Museum voor Moderne Kunst, Arnhem, 1999–2000. Brussels, 1999.

VANDI 2007
Vandi, Loretta. "The Eternal Flame: Eufrasia Burlamacchi and Savonarolan Art in the Lucchese Convent of San Domenico." In *Four Essays*, 19–39. Umeå, 2007.

VANDI 2015
Vandi, Loretta. "Sister Eufrasia Burlamacchi and the Art of the Wayside." In Barker 2015a, 89–104.

VAN OPPEN DE RUITER 2015
van Oppen de Ruiter, Branko. *Berenice II Euergetis: Essays in Early Hellenistic Queenship*. New York, 2015.

VASARI 1568
Vasari, Giorgio. *Le vite de' più eccellenti pittori, scultori, et architettori . . .* 3 vols. Florence, 1568.

VERTOVA 1995
Vertova, Luisa. "Lavinia versus Sofonisba." *Apollo* 140, no. 395 (January 1995): 43–46.

VESME 1897
Vesme, Alessandro. "La regia Pinacoteca di Torino." In *Le gallerie nazionali italiane: Notizie e documenti, anno III*, 3–68. Rome, 1897.

VIALLET 1923
Viallet, Bice. *Gli autoritratti femminili delle R.R. Gallerie degli Uffizi in Firenze*. Rome, 1923.

VICIOSO 2016
Vicioso, Julia. "Costanza Francini: A Painter in the Shadow of Artemisia Gentileschi." In Barker 2016c, 99–120.

VIENNA 1995
La prima donna pittrice Sofonisba Anguissola: Die Malerin der Renaissance (um 1535–1625). Exh. cat., Kunsthistorisches Museum, Vienna, 1995. Catalogue contributions by Sylvia Ferino-Pagden, Maria Kusche, and others. Vienna, 1995.

VIGUÉ 2003
Vigué, Jordi. *Great Women Masters of Art*. New York, 2003.

VOCABOLARIO 1612
Vocabolario degli accademici della Crusca. Venice, 1612.

VON HOERSCHELMANN 1908
von Hoerschelmann, Emilie. *Rosalba Carriera, die Meisterin der Pastellmalerei: Studien und Bilder aus der Kunst und Kulturgeschichte des 18. Jahrhunderts*. Leipzig, 1908.

VULLO 2017
Vullo, Daniela. "Il matrimonio tra Sofonisba Anguissola e il nobile siciliano Fabrizio Moncada." In *Voci d'artiste: Sofonisba Anguissola, Rosalia Novelli, Anna Fortino*, edited by Luana Lupo, 23–35. Palermo, 2017.

WAAGEN 1857
Waagen, Gustav Friedrich. *Galleries and Cabinets of Art in Great Britain: Supplemental Volume to The Treasures of Art in Great Britain*. London, 1857.

WALLACE 1989
Wallace, Richard. "64. Elisabetta Sirani, *The Holy Family with Saint Elizabeth and Saint John the Baptist*." In Boston 1989, 131–32.

WALSH 2019A
Walsh, Amy. "12. Simon Vouet, *Virginia da Vezzo, the Artist's Wife, as the Magdalen*." In Lehmbeck 2019, vol. 2, 46–49, 184–85.

WALSH 2019B
Walsh, Amy. "22. Lavinia Fontana, *The Holy Family with Saint Catherine of Alexandria*." In Lehmbeck 2019, vol. 1, 76–77, 140–41.

WASHINGTON, D.C. 1995
Sofonisba Anguissola: A Renaissance Woman. Exh cat., National Museum of Women in the Arts, Washington, D.C., 1995. Catalogue by Sylvia Ferino-Pagden and Maria Kusche. Washington, D.C., 1995.

WASHINGTON, D.C. 1998
Lavinia Fontana of Bologna, 1552–1614. Exh. cat., National Museum of Women in the Arts, Washington, D.C., 1998. Catalogue edited by Vera Fortunati. Milan, 1998.

WASHINGTON, D.C. 2007
Italian Women Artists from Renaissance to Baroque. Exh. cat., National Museum of Women in the Arts, Washington, D.C., 2007. Catalogue contributions by Carole Collier Frick, Sheila ffolliott, Vera Fortunati and others. Milan, 2007.

WASHINGTON, D.C. 2014
Picturing Mary: Woman, Mother, Idea. Exh. cat., National Museum of Women in the Arts, Washington, D.C., 2014–2015. Catalogue contributions by Timothy Verdon and others. New York, 2014.

WASSYNG ROWORTH 1997
Wassyng Roworth, Wendy. "Academies of Art: Italy." In Gaze 1997, vol. 1, 43–45.

WEHLE 1951
Wehle, Harry B. "Portrait Miniatures, Their History." In *Portrait Miniatures: The Edward B. Greene Collection*, edited by Herry Wehle and Louise Burchfield, 9–24. Cleveland, 1951.

WESTMINSTER REVIEW 1858
"Art. VI.–Women Artists: *Die Frauen in die Kunstgeschichte* von Ernst Guhl, Berlin, 1858." *Westminster Review* 70 (July 1858): 91–104.

WEY 1854
Wey, Francis. *Les Anglais chez eux: Esquisses de moeurs et de voyage*. Paris, 1854.

WHITCOMB ET AL. 1952–1953
Whitcomb, Edgar, et al. "The Arts Commission Annual Report for the Year 1952." *Bulletin of the Detroit Institute of Arts* 32, no. 2 (1952–1953): 32–57.

WIED 1995A
Wied, Alexander. "15. Sofonisba Anguissola, *Portrait des Giulio Clovio*." In Vienna 1995, 81–82.

WIED 1995B
Wied, Alexander. "17. Sofonisba Anguissola, *Portrait des Massimiliano Stampa*." In Vienna 1995, 84–85.

WIED 1995C
Wied, Alexander. "18. Nach Sofonisba Anguissola, *Portrait des Massimiliano Stampa*." In Vienna 1995, 84–85.

WIESBADEN 2016
Caravaggios Erben: Barock in Neapel. Exh. cat.,
Museum Wiesbaden, 2016–2017. Catalogue edited
by Peter Forster, Elisabeth Oy-Marra, and Heiko
Damm. Munich, 2016.

WIESNER-HANKS 2009
Wiesner-Hanks, Merry. *The Marvelous Hairy Girls:
The Gonzales Sisters and Their World*. New Haven,
2009.

WIESNER-HANKS 2016
Wiesner-Hanks, Merry E. *Women and Gender
in Early Modern Europe*. 3rd ed, 8th printing.
Cambridge, 2016.

WILENSKI 1973
Wilenski, Reginald Howard. *French Painting*. 3rd
revised ed. New York, 1973.

WILKIN 2000
Wilkin, Karen. "Father and Daughter at the Met."
New Criterion 20, no. 8 (April 2000): 46–51.

WINTER PARK 1991
*Italian Renaissance and Baroque Paintings in
Florida Museums*. Exh. cat., Cornell Fine Arts
Museum at Rollins College, Winter Park, Fla., 1991.
Catalogue by Arthur R. Blumenthal. Winter Park,
Fla., 1991.

WINTER PARK 1993
Treasures of the Cornell Fine Arts Museum. Exh.
cat., Cornell Fine Arts Museum at Rollins College,
Winter Park, Fla.; Center for the Arts, Vero Beach,
Fla.; Samuel P. Harn Museum of Art, University
of Florida, Gainesville; Polk Museum of Art,
Lakeland, Fla.; Center for the Fine Arts, Miami,
1993–1996. Catalogue by Arthur R. Blumenthal
and others. Winter Park, Fla., 1993.

WOODS-MARSDEN 1998
Woods-Marsden, Joanna. *Renaissance Self-
Portraiture: The Visual Construction of Identity
and the Social Status of the Artist*. New Haven,
1998.

WORCESTER 1972
Woman as Heroine. Exh. cat., Worcester Art
Museum, 1972. Catalogue introduction by D.
Denise Minault. Worcester, Mass., 1972.

ZANETTI 1837
Zanetti, Alexandre. *Le premier siècle de la
Chalcographie ou catalogue raisonné des estampes
du cabinet de feu M. le Comte Léopold Cigognara*.
Venice, 1837.

ZANOBONI 2016A
Zanoboni, Maria Paola. *Donne al lavoro nell'Italia
e nell'Europa medievali (secoli XIII–XV)*. Milan,
2016.

ZANOBONI 2016B
Zanoboni, Maria Paola. "Mobilità sociale e lavoro
femminile nelle grandi città italiane." In *La mobilità sociale nel Medioevo italiano: Competenze,
conoscenze e saperi tra professioni e ruoli sociali
(secc. XII–XV)*, edited by Lorenzo Tanzini and
Sergio Tognetti, 51–76. Rome, 2016.

ZAPPERI 2004
Zapperi, Roberto. *Il selvaggio gentiluomo:
L'incredibile storia di Pedro Gonzalez e dei suoi
figli*. Rome, 2004.

ZERI 1976
Zeri, Federico. *Italian Paintings in the Walters Art
Gallery*. 2 vols. Baltimore, 1976.

ZERI AND PORZIO 1989
Zeri, Federico, and Francesco Porzio, eds. *La
natura morta in Italia*. 2 vols. Milan, 1989.

ZURICH 1965
*Das italienische Stilleben von den Anfängen bis zur
Gegenwart*. Exh. cat., Kunsthaus Zurich; Museum
Boymans-Van Beuningen, Rotterdam, 1964–1965.
Catalogue contributions by Stefano Bottari, Franco
Russoli, and Vitale Bloch. Milan, 1965.

ZUTTER 2013
Zutter, Jörg. "Review: *Artemisia Gentileschi:
Storia di una passione* (Milano, Palazzo Reale, 23
September 2011–29 January 2012)." *Renaissance
Studies* 27, no. 1 (February 2013): 133–40.

INDEX

Page numbers in *italics* refer to illustrations.

A

Académie Royale, 41n96, 161
Accademia dei Lincei, 99, 100, 126, 133
Accademia delle Arti del Disegno, 41n103, 46, 47, 51n23, 101
Accademia di San Luca, 39, 47, 127, 133, 174, 177, 178, 178n1; "accademica di merito," 41n100, 47; reception pieces, 131, 161, 165
Albani, Cardinal Alessandro, 163
Alberti, Leon Battista, 40n6, 120
Aldrovandi, Ulisse, 89
Alexander VII, Pope, 139n1
allegory: Charity, 145, 151; of Medici rule, 151; Music, 178; Painting, 120; portraits in the guise of, 14, 39n2, 120, 145, 167; of the seasons, 127, 162, 163n4
Allori, Alessandro, 40n39, 49, 58n1
Allori, Cristofano, 101, 105
altarpieces, 35, 48; by Caccia, 122, 123, 125n6; by Cantofoli, 156; by Fontana, 38, 76, 92, 92nn1–4; by Galizia, 97
amateur artists, 15, 37, 47–49, 51n24, 99, 174
Anguissola, Amilcare, 61
Anguissola, Annamaria, 53
Anguissola, Elena, 34, 53, 55n4; *Portrait of a Nun as Saint Catherine of Alexandria*, 55n2
Anguissola, Europa, 21, 53, 64n2
Anguissola, Lucia, 21, 53, 61, 61n8, 64n2
Anguissola, Minerva, 61, 61n8, 64n2
Anguissola, Sofonisba, 14, 15, 27, 53; artistic training, 34, 53, 64n6; in Cremona, 36, 47, 56, 61, 67, 70, 71n10; earlier sources on, 21, 45, 47–48; fame of, 31, 37, 53, 56, 120; in Genoa, 53, 69; miniature techniques, 56; portrait medal of, 120; portraits, 36, 41n61, 53, 61, 64, 64n6, 67, 70; questions of attribution, 70, 70nn3–4, 71n8, 71nn10–11; religious paintings, 69, 69n2; self-portraits, 14, 31, 36, 39n2, 41n57, 53, 56, 58, 69, 101; Spanish court and, 37, 41n74, 41n83, 53, 67, 70n2, 71n7
Anguissola, Sofonisba, works: *Artist's Sister in the Garb of a Nun* (cat. 1 and cat. 1, fig. 1), 53–55, *54*, *55*; *Boy Bitten by a Crayfish* (cat. 5, fig. 1), 63, *63*; *Chess Game*, 63, 64n2; *Childish Old Woman Makes the Young Woman Laugh* (cat. 5), Jacob Bos after, 62–63, *62*; *Giulio Clovio* (Tostmann, fig. 6), *37*; *Giulio Clovio* (unfinished), 36; *Holy Family with Saints Anne and John the Baptist* (cat. 8), *68*, 69; *Philip II*, 67, 70; *Portrait of a Spanish Prince, Probably the Infante Don Fernando* (cat. 7), *66*, 67; *Portrait of Marchese Massimiliano Stampa* (cat. 6), 64–65, *65*, 70; *Queen Anna of Austria*, 67; *Saint Ursula*, 41n67; *Self-Portrait* (cat. 2), 36, 55n5, 56–57, *57*; *Self-Portrait* (cat. 4), *60*, 61; *Self-Portrait* (cat. 4, fig. 1), 61, *61*; *Self-Portrait* (Tostmann, fig. 1), 31, *32*, 39n1; *Self-Portrait at the Easel* (cat. 3), 58, *59*; *Self-Portrait at the Easel* (cat. 3, fig. 1), 58, *58*
Anna of Austria, queen of Spain, 37, 41n83, 53, 67
Arpino, Cavaliere d', 121
art market, 15, 18, 24–25
Aspertini, Amico, 50
Ast, Balthasar van der, 128
Augustus III, prince elector of Saxony, 163, 167

B

Baglione, Giovanni, 13, 14, 38, 92
Baillie, William, 58

Balbi, Caterina: portrait of (cat. 59, fig. 1), 172, *172*
Balbi family, 172, 173n5
Baldacci, Maria Maddalena Gozzi, 47
Baldinucci, Filippo, 40n16, 63, 69
Bandinelli, Baccio, 40n39
Barbarigo, Caterina Sagredo: portraits of (cat. 57 and cat. 57, fig. 1), 167–69, *168*, *169*
Barberini family, 133
Bartolozzi, Francesco, 179, 181n4
Bartsch, Adam von, 152
Basso, Ercole, 38
Bathsheba. *See* Gentileschi, Artemisia: works
Batoni, Pompeo, 177
Beccari, Gualberta Alaide, 19, *19*
Beinaschi, Angela Maria, 40n38
Bellori, Giovanni Pietro, 13
Benedict XIV, Pope, 174
Berenice. *See* Carriera, Rosalba: works; Sirani, Elisabetta: works
Bernerio, Cardinal Girolamo, 92
Boccaccio, Giovanni: *Des cleres et nobles femmes* (Tostmann, fig. 2), 33, *33*, 56n4
Bologna: *La Donna*, 19; Fontana in, 76, 78n8, 79, 83, 84, 87, 89, 92; nobility of, 44, 84, 87, 89, 145; post-Tridentine, 76, 83, 139; Sirani in, 131, 136, 139, 142, 145, 147, 149, 151, 155, 179; University of Bologna, 21, 84, 89; Vigri's influence in, 34; wax modeling in, 160n7; *Women Artists of Bologna*, 21–22
Bombacci, Gasparo, 136
Bona, Mauritio, 99
Bonasone, Giulio, 83
Borboni, Matteo: *Catafalque of the Bolognese Artist Elisabetta Sirani (1638–1665)* (cat. 49), 14, *154*, 155; *Tempietto per il funerale di Elisabetta Sirani* (cat. 49, fig. 1), 155, *155*
Borghese, Camilla Orsini, 49
Bos, Jacob, after Anguissola: *Childish Old Woman Makes the Young Woman Laugh* (cat. 5), 62–63, *62*
botanical illustrations, 48, 89, 133
Bourbon, Marguerite Louise d'Orléans d', 136
Bricci, Plautilla, 35, 37
Bronzini, Cristoforo, 48
Bronzino, Agnolo, 45–46, 47, 49
Brooklyn Museum, 23, *23*, 28n19
Broun, Elizabeth, 58
Brueghel, Jan, the Elder, 128, 133
Bufalo, Claudia del: *Portrait of Faustina del Bufalo* (Barker, fig. 8), 49, *49*
Bufalo, Faustino del: portrait of (Barker, fig. 8), 49, *49*
Buoi, Andrea de', 140
Buonarroti, Michelangelo, 40n4, 63, 81, 83, 103n13
Buonarroti, Michelangelo, the Younger, 44, 50n3, 101
Burlamacchi, Sister Eufrasia, 48; *Saint Peter* (Barker, fig. 5), *48*
Bylivelt, Jacques, 106

C

Caccia, Francesca, 123
Caccia, Guglielmo, 122, 123, 125; *Martyrdom of Saint Orsola*, 125n6
Caccia, Orsola Maddalena, 15, 27, 122–23; *Mary Magdalene* (cat. 34), 112, *124*, 125; *Vases of Flowers on a Table* (cat. 33), *122*, 123
Caffi, Margherita, 29n36, 46–47
calligraphy, 34–35, 44, 126

Callot, Jacques, after Fontana: *Stoning of Saint Stephen* (cat. 19), 92–93, *93*
Calvaert, Denis, 78n8; *Annunciation* (cat. 12, fig. 1), *76*, 78
Cambiaso, Luca: *Madonna of the Candle* (cat. 8, fig. 1), 69, *69*
Camelli, Sister Beatrice, 45, 48
Campi, Antonio, 71n10
Campi, Bernardino, 34, 53, 64n6, 71n10
Campi, Giulio, 71n10
candle painting, *44*, 45
Cantofoli, Ginevra, 156; *Allegory of Painting*, 156; *Beatrice Cenci* (cat. 50, fig. 1), 156, *156*; *Cleopatra* (cat. 50), 156–57, *157*; *Immaculate Virgin with the Child*, 156, 157n4; *Saint Thomas of Villanova*, 156, 157n4
Caravaggio, Michelangelo Merisi da, 24, 25, 109, 121, 131, 132; *Basket of Fruit*, 98; *David with the Head of Goliath*, 105; *Mary Magdalene in Ecstasy* (cat. 28, fig. 1), 113, *113*, 113n6, 125, 125n1; *Penitent Magdalene*, 113n6
Carlevarijs, Luca, 172
Carlevarijs, Marianna, 14, 15, 161, 172; *Portrait of a Young Lady* (cat. 59), 172–73, *173*; *Portrait of Caterina Balbi* (cat. 59, fig. 1), 172, *172*
Carlo Emanuele I, duke of Savoy, 95
Caro, Annibale, 56
Carracci, Agostino, 83
Carracci, Annibale, 25, 121
Carracci, Ludovico: *Madonna and Child with Saints*, 143, 143n6
Carriera, Giovanna, 170, 173n1
Carriera, Rosalba, 15, 21, 27, 29n36, 32, 36, 38, 40n6, 47, 161; Accademia di San Luca, 39, 41n98, 41n100, 161, 165, 174, 178; drawings, 34, 40nn39–40; earlier sources on, 22, 29n41; fame of, 161, 164, 174; ivory, 161, 165; letters, 15, 35, 161, 164–67, 178; needlework, 35, 99; in Paris, 36, 41n52, 161, 163, 166; pastels, 15, 21, 35, 39n2, 161, 163n2, 164–67, 170, 172, 173; self-portraits, 34, 39n2, 40n39; in Venice, 161, 165, 166, 172, 174, 178; workshop, 161, 172, 173n1
Carriera, Rosalba, works: *Allegory of Faith* (cat. 53), 161–63, *162*; *Allegory of Innocence* (Tostmann, fig. 8), *38*, 39, 41n100, 165; *Berenice* (cat. 57), 167–69, *168*, *169*; *Muse Calliope* (cat. 52), 161–63, *162*; *Muse Clio*, 163n8; *Muse Polymnia* (cat. 52–53, fig. 1), 162, *163*; *Muse Urania* (cat. 52–53, fig. 2), 162, *163*; *Portrait of a Man* (cat. 54), 164–66, *164*; *Portrait of Anton Maria Zanetti*, 163n2; *Portrait of a Young Lady as Cleopatra*, 165; *Portrait of Caterina Sagredo Barbarigo* (cat. 57, fig. 1), 167, *169*; *Saint Cecilia* (cat. 58) (circle of Carriera), 170, *171*; *Self-Portrait* (Tostmann, fig. 4), 34, *35*; *Woman Cutting Her Hair* (cat. 54–56, fig. 1), 165, *166*, 166n7; *Woman Putting Flowers in Her Hair* (cat. 55), 164–66, *165*, 166n7; *Woman with a Dog* (cat. 56), *165*, 164–66
Casoni, Felice Antonio: *Portrait Medal of Lavinia Fontana* (cat. 32), *119*, 119–21
Castiglione, Baldassare, 51n39
Catalina Micaela of Spain, Infanta, 67, 67n1
Catani, Caterina, 47
Catherine of Alexandria, Saint. *See* Fontana, Lavinia: works; Gentileschi, Artemisia: works; Quistelli, Lucrezia
Cavalieri, Tommaso, 63
Cavallino, Bernardo, 115

Cazzati, Maurizio, 155
Cecilia, Saint, 170
Cerroti, Violante Beatrice Siries, 21, 29n36, 46, 179
Cesi, Federico, 99, 100
Chacón, Alonso, 36
Champaigne, Philippe de, 49
Cherubini, Caterina, 39, 178n1
Chiari, Giuseppe Bartolomeo: *Woman Looking Upward* (cat. 61, fig. 1), 178, *178*
Chigi, Maria Virginia Borghese, princess of Farnese, 49
Christine of France, duchess of Savoy, 127
Ciaminghi, Francesco, 179
Cigoli, Lodovico, 101
Cleopatra. *See* Cantofoli, Ginevra; Carriera, Rosalba: works
Clovio, Giulio, 31, 32, 40n12, 56; portraits of, 36, *37*
Codazzi, Viviano, 116
Cole, Christian, 41n100
Cole, Michael, 29n45, 35, 58, 61, 70n3, 71n8, 71n11
Collaert, Adriaen: *Florilegium* (cat. 33, fig. 1), 123, *123*
Colonna, Vittoria, 83
Compagnia dei Pittori di San Luca, 45–46, *45*, 50n15
confraternities, 40n23, 45–46, 47, 50n15
Conti, Francesco, 179
convents, 33–35, 48, 51n41, 53, 76, 84; Caccia and, 122, 123, 125
copper, 32, 76, 78nn8–9, 79, 80
Correggio, Antonio da, 69, 79, 163; *Magdalene Reading in the Wilderness*, 163n12
Cort, Cornelius, Scultori after: *Spinario* (cat. 11), 72–75, *74*
Cortona, Pietro da, 133
Cospi, Marchese Ferdinando, 149, 151, 155
Counter-Reformation, 115, 125; devotional art during, 45, 76, 81, 83, 115, 125, 139; the nude during, 116
courts, 21–22, 36–38, 44, 56; d'Este, 36; Farnese, 36; Gonzaga, 36, 72; Medici, 34, 37, 40n34, 44, 45, 49, 103, 181n3; Spanish, 36, 37, 41n74, 41n83, 56, 67, 70n2
Craik, Dinah, 29n40
Crouching Venus (cat. 30, fig. 1), 116, *116*
Crozat, Pierre, 32

D

David, Jérôme: *Artemisia Gentileschi* (cat. 31–32, fig. 1), *120*, 120–21
De Dominici, Bernardo, 35, 115, 115n2, 116, 158, 159–60n6
Delle donne illustri italiane dal XIII al XIX secolo, 28n15
Detroit Institute of Arts, 13, 17, *18*, 70, 167
devotional painting, 35, 58, 81, 83, 122, 139
Domenichino, 115, 170
Donahue, Kenneth, 23, 29n55
La Donna, 19, 28n15
drawing: in a humanist education, 34, 48, 51n39; from life, 34, 35, 40n38, 63, 89, 127, 131
Duchetti, Claudio, 72
Durante, Castor, 99
Dürer, Albrecht, 33, 41n57, 56
Dyck, Anthony van, 87, 89

E

early modern women artists: aristocratic amateurs, 15, 37, 47, 48, 49, 51n24, 99, 174; artistic training, 34–36; critical and market appraisal of, 24–27;

exhibitions, 17–18, 22–24, 27; nun-artists, 15, 29n36, 34, 45, 48, 123; professional artists, 15, 37, 40n34, 41n100, 43–50, 121, 174, 178n1
Elisabeth of France, queen of Spain, 99
Elisabeth of Valois, queen of Spain, 37, 41n83, 53, 67
Elizabeth I, queen of England, 37
Ellet, Elizabeth F.: *Women Artists in All Ages and Countries*, 20, 28n24
embroidery, 34–35, 40nn41–42, 99, 143, 143n8
Encarnación, Estefanía de la, 51n41
Este, Alessandro d', 92
Este, Ercole II d', 39n1
Este family, 36

F

Facchinetti, Marchese Alessandro, 89
Farnese, Ottavio, 36
Farnese family, 36
Faucci, Carlo, 179, 181n4
Fedeli, Sister Ortenisia, 48
Félibien, André, 131
feminism, 18; International Council of Women, *19*; Seneca Falls Convention, 18, *19*; as a term, 28n9
feminist art history, 17–22, 26, 28n4, 28n10, 29n43, 29n45
Fernando, Infante: portrait of (cat. 7), *66*, 67
Ferrari, Giovanni Battista: *De Florum Cultura* (cat. 39), 133–35, *134*
Figino, Ambrogio, 98
Finson, Louis, after Caravaggio: *Mary Magdalene in Ecstasy* (cat. 28, fig. 1), *113*
Flemish art and artists, 41n74, 56, 58, 78, 81, 81n7, 103n1, 143
Florence, 15; Fratellini in, 36, 161; Garzoni in, 103n1, 126, 127, 127n6; Gentileschi in, 29n67, 43–44, 46, 101, 105, 106, 110n1, 113; Nelli in, 15, 34, 47; Piattoli in, 14, 179. *See also* Accademia delle Arti del Disegno; Compagnia dei Pittori di San Luca; Medici family
flower painting, 38, 98, 123, 125, 128, 133
Fontana, Lavinia, 15, 22, 27, 38, 76; altarpieces, 38, 76, 92, 92nn1–4; artistic training, 34, 35, 76, 83; in Bologna, 76, 78n8, 79, 83, 84, 87, 89, 92; drawings, 14, 76, 89–91; earlier sources on, 21, 28n15, 29n36; fame of, 14, 28n15, 47, 76, 79, 84, 87, 89, 121; marriage, 76, 80, 83, 84, 87; noblewomen and, 44, 76, 79, 84, 87, 89, 143n3; portrait medal (cat. 31), 14, 119–21, *119*; portraits, 76, 79, 84, 84n2, 87, 89–91; religious paintings, 15, 34, 41n91, 76, 83; in Rome, 87, 92, 92n2; self-portraits, 15, 33–34, 36, 39n2, 39n40, 44, 89, 101; small-scale works, 34, 35, 40n27, 41n98; workshop, 48
Fontana, Lavinia, works: *Album of Portrait Studies* (cat. 18 and cat. 18, figs. 1–3), *88*, 89–90, *89*, *90*; *Annunciation* (cat. 12), 76–78, *77*; *Christ in the House of Martha and Mary*, 92n2; *Christ with the Symbols of the Passion* (cat. 14, fig. 1), 80, *81*; *Dead Christ with Symbols of the Passion* (cat. 14), 80–81, *80*; *Holy Family with Saint Catherine of Alexandria* (cat. 15), *82*, 83; *Portrait of a Lady of the Gonzaga or Sanvitale Family* (cat. 16), 84–85, *85*; *Portrait of a Lady of the Gonzaga or Sanvitale Family* (cat. 16, fig. 1), 84, *84*; *Portrait of a Prelate* (cat. 13), 79, *79*; *Portrait of Ginevra Aldrovandi Hercolani* (cat. 17), *86*, 87; *Portrait of Isabella Ruini*, 89; *Self-Portrait at a Spinet* (Tostmann, fig. 3), 33, *33*, 40n26; *Self-Portrait in a Studio* (Tostmann, fig. 5), 36, *36*, 41n64,

79; *Stoning of Saint Stephen* (cat. 19), Jacques Callot after, 38, 92–93, *93*; *Virgin Appearing to Saint Hyacinth*, 92n3; *Vision of Saint Hyacinth*, 38
Fontana, Prospero, 76, 78n8, 81, 83, 92n2
Fontebasso, Francesco, 170
Fortunati, Vera, 13, 81n1
Francini, Costanza, 45
Fratellini, Giovanna, 35, 36, 161; Accademia delle Arti del Disegno, 41n103, 46–47, 51n20, 51n23; Medici court and, 34, 37, 40n34; *Self-Portrait* (Barker, fig. 4), *46*
frescoes, 32, 35, 40n4, 133, 170, 179, 179n2

G

Gabburri, Niccolò, 179
Gabhart, Ann, 23
Galantini, Ippolito, 40n34
Galileo Galilei, 50n3, 133
Galizia, Fede, 22, 27, 29n41, 35, 95, 96n1, 97, 128; *Glass Tazza with Peaches, Jasmine Flowers, and Quinces* (cat. 21), 97–98, *97*; *Judith with the Head of Holofernes* (cat. 20 and cat. 20, fig. 2), *94*, 95–96, *96*; *Judith with the Head of Holofernes* (cat. 20, fig. 1), 95, *95*
Galizia, Nunzio, 95
Gargano, Lucchino, 99
Gargiulo, Domenico, 115, 116
Garrard, Mary, 13, 24, 29n43, 103n13, 106, 109, 110n3, 111n11, 113n6, 128
Garzoni, Giovanna, 27, 34, 35, 41n98, 126, 127, 127n8, 128; Accademia di San Luca, 5n25, 47, 126, 127; Dumbarton Oaks album, 89; fame of, 127, 127n1; letters, 44, 50n5; Medici court and, 37, 126, 127, 128; miniatures, 35, 127, 127n1, 128
Garzoni, Giovanna, works: *Hedgehog in a Landscape* (cat. 35), 126–27, *126*; *Mary Magdalene in the Desert*, 125; *Plate of Figs* (cat. 37), 128–29, *129*; *Self-Portrait as Apollo*, 39n2, 103n1; *Still Life of Quinces, Almonds, and Figs with a Mouse* (cat. 36), 128, *129*
Garzoni, Tommaso, 32
Gatti, Bernardino, 34, 53
Gentile, Fabio, 50n3
Gentileschi, Artemisia, 13, 14, 15, 43–44, 101; Accademia delle Arti del Disegno, 43–44, 46, 101; artistic training, 34, 43, 101, 105; earlier sources on, 21, 22, 25, 28n15, 28n30, 29n36, 29n41; earnings and modern-day prices for, 25, 29n67–68, 45, 50; exhibitions, 25, 27, 28n2, 29n55, 29n62–63; fame of, 23, 24, 28, 29n61, 101, 116, 121; in Florence, 29n67, 43–44, 46, 101, 105, 106, 110n1, 113; marriage, 43, 101; in Naples, 101, 113, 115, 116; portrait medal of (cat. 32), 14, 119–21, *120*; portrait of (cat. 31–32, fig. 1), 120; in Rome, 29n63, 101, 109, 110n1, 112, 121; self-portraits, 14, 15, 101, 105, 106, 113, 120, 125; self-promotion, 44, 101, 105, 121; sexual assault of, 50, 101
Gentileschi, Artemisia, works: *Allegory of Inclination* (cat. 24, fig. 1), 101, *103*, 106; *Allegory of Painting*, 39n2; *David and Bathsheba* (cat. 30), 116–18, *117*; *Judith and Her Maidservant with the Head of Holofernes* (cat. 27 and cat. 27, figs. 1–3), *108*, 109–11, 113; *Lot and His Daughters* (cat. 29), *114*, 115; *Lucretia* (Straussman-Pflanzer, fig. 8), 25, *25*; *Mary Magdalene in Ecstasy* (cat. 28), 14, 112–13, *112*, 125, 125n2; *Saint Catherine of Alexandria* (cat. 26), 106, *107*; *Self-Portrait as a Female Martyr* (cat. 25, fig. 1), 101, 105, *105*, 106; *Self-Portrait as a Lute Player*

(cat. 24), 101–3, *102*, 105, 106; *Self-Portrait as Saint Catherine of Alexandria* (cat. 25), 14, 25, *104*, 105
Gentileschi, Orazio, 22, 34, 43, 101, 105, 109; *Orazio and Artemisia Gentileschi*, 24, 28n2, 29nn62–63
Ghezzi, Giuseppe, 39
Giambologna, 38, 47
Giancarli, Campaspe, 49
Ginnasi, Caterina, 47
Giorgio, Maria di, 46
Giustiniani, Vincenzo, 133
Goethe, Ottilie von, 21
Gonzaga, Ildefonso: portrait of (cat. 62, fig. 2), *181*
Gonzaga, Isabella, 84
Gonzaga, Laura, 84
Gonzaga family, 36, 72, 84
Gonzalez, Petrus, 89
gran maniera, 32, 40n6
Gregory XIII, Pope, 72
Guercino, 170
Guerrilla Girls, 22
Guhl, Ernst: *Women in the History of Art*, 19–20
Guicciardini, Lodovico, 33
guilds, 38, 40n23, 47, 50n14; of the Accademia delle Arti del Disegno, 43–44, 46, 51n23; women artists' avoidance of, 47, 50, 51n30

H

Habsburg family, 37, 67
Haensen, Caterine, 41n74
Hemessen, Caterina van, 15, 39n2, 41n74; *Girl at a Spinet*, 103n1; *Self-Portrait at the Easel*, 39n2, 58
Henry VIII, king of England, 37
Hercolani, Ginevra Aldrovandi, 87; portrait of (cat. 17), *86*, 87
Hilliard, Nicholas: *Art of Limning*, 35, 40n16
Hoefnagel, Jacob, 127
Honthorst, Gerrit van, 109, 110n2
Horenbout, Susanna, 33, 37

I

Iaia (Marcia), 33, *33*, 56, 56n4
Ignatius of Loyola, 80
intersectionality, 22
Isabella Clara Eugenia, Infanta, 67, 67n1
Italian Women Artists from Renaissance to Baroque (2007), 24, 29n60
ivory, 32, 33, 34, 39, 161; *fondelli*, 35, 165

J

Jameson, Anna, *20*, 21, 28nn30–31
Judith and Holofernes. *See* Galizia, Fede; Gentileschi, Artemisia: works; Vezzo, Virginia, da
Julianis, Caterina de, 158–60; *Penitent Magdalene* (cat. 51), 158–60, *159*; *Saint Mary Magdalene* (cat. 51, fig. 1), 158, *158*

L

Ladies of the Baroque (2018–2019), 24
Lama, Giulia, 15, 34, 35, 40n38
Lanfranco, Giovanni, 133
Lanzi, Luigi, 123
Leonardo da Vinci, 25, 26, 63, 69
Ligozzi, Jacopo, 37, 49, 127; *Portrait of a Woman Traditionally Identified as Maria de' Medici* (Barker, fig. 7), 49, *49*
Liotard, Jean-Étienne, 41n53; *Portrait of Archduchess Maria Christina Habsburg* (Tostmann, fig. 7), *37*
Lomazzo, Giovanni Paolo, 32, 56, 63, 96n1, 97
Lombardy, art and artists in, 46, 53, 64, 95, 98, 122, 128

Longhi, Roberto, 22, 29n41
Lorde, Audre, 22
Los Angeles County Museum of Art (LACMA), 23–24

M

male artists: as creators of small works, 31, 40n34, 41n53; prices for, 25–26; training of, 14, 34
Malvasia, Carlo Cesare, 78n8; on Cantofoli, 156; on Fontana, 87, 89; on Sirani, 139, 140, 142–43, 147, 155n4; Sirani's list of works published by, 136, 142, 145
Mancini, Francesco, 174
Mancini, Giulio, 32, 36, 41n56
Man of Sorrows (anonymous candlepainter) (Barker, fig. 2), *44*
Mantovano, Giovanni Battista, 72
manuscript illumination, 35, 48, 127
Maratti, Carlo, 39, 41n100, 165, 176n4, 178
Marchelli, Romolo, 147
Marcia (Iaia), 33, *33*, 56, 56n4
Margaret of Parma, 36
Maria Christina, archduchess of Austria, 37, *37*
Maria Maddalena of Austria, Medici grand duchess, 106, 132
Maria of Austria, Holy Roman Empress, 69
Marie Louise d'Orléans, queen of Spain, 37
Maringhi, Francesco Maria, 101–3
Maron, Theresa Concordia, 39
Marsigli, Cesare, 145
Marten's head (cat. 16, fig. 2), 84, *84*
Mary Magdalene: as popular theme, 125. *See also* Caccia, Orsola Maddalena; Gentileschi, Artemisia: works; Julianis, Caterina de; Vouet, Simon
Mazzolari, Giuseppe Maria, 38
Medici, Caterina de', 106
Medici, Cosimo I de', 63
Medici, Cosimo II de', 103
Medici, Cosimo III de', 136, 151
Medici, Ferdinando II de', 128
Medici, Leopoldo de', 149, 150–51, 155
Medici, Maria Cristina de', 49
Medici, Maria de', 110n3; *Portrait of a Woman Traditionally Identified as Maria de' Medici* (Barker, fig. 7), 49, *49*
Medici family, 37, 38, 45, 46, 49, 132, 181n3; Fratellini and, 34, 37, 40n34; Garzoni and, 37, 126, 127, 128; Gentileschi and, 44, 101, 103, 106; miniatures and, 37, 40n34; Sirani and, 136, 149, 150–51, 155; Villa Artimino, 101
Mellan, Claude, 132n3; *Portrait of Anna Maria Vaiani* (cat. 39, fig. 1), *133*; *Virginia da Vezzo* (cat. 38, fig. 2), 131, *132*
Mengs, Anton Raphael, 41n53
Merian, Maria Sibylla, 34, 133
Metropolitan Museum of Art, 24, 27, 29nn62–63, 79
Michelangelo, 40n4, 63, 81, 83, 103n13
Michele, Lisabetta di, 46
Mills, John Stuart, 19
miniatures: by Carriera, 15, 35, 161, 164–67, 178; definitions and terminology, 32, 40n16; by Garzoni, 35, 127, 127n1, 128; manuals and treatises on, 35, 40n7, 40n16, 41n73, 176n6; Medici and, 37, 40n34; portraits, 35, 36, 79, 127, 161, 167
Montagna, Marco Tullio, 131
Moroni, Giovanni Battista, 64; *Portrait of a Gentleman* (cat. 6, fig. 1), 64, *64*
Mozzoni, Anna Maria, 18–19
Museum of Fine Arts, Ghent, 24
museums, 17–18; gender and racial disparities in, 17, 22, 24–26, 28nn7–8

N

Naples, 40n38, 116, 158; Del Pò in, 32, 36, 161; Garzoni in, 126, 127; Gentileschi in, 101, 113, 115, 116; De Julianis in, 158, 160n6; Spanish control of, 127, 158; wax modeling in, 160nn6–7
Nati, Camilla Guerrieri, 37
National Gallery, London, 14, 24, 25, 27, 29n62
National Gallery of Art, Washington, D.C., 26
National Museum of Women in the Arts, 24, 27, 29n60
needlework/stitching, 34–35, 99–100
Nelli, Sister Plautilla, 15, 27, 29n36, 34, 45, 47–48
noblewomen: as amateur artists, 15, 37, 47, 48–49; Fontana's portraits of, 76, 84, 87, 89; as lenders to exhibitions, 46–47
Nochlin, Linda, 17, *20*, 28n4; "Why Have There Been No Great Women Artists?," 17, 22, 26, 51n47; *Women Artists: 1550–1950*, 14, 23–24, 29n55
nude, the, 69, 76, 116; drawing from, 14, 34
nun-artists, 15, 29n36, 34, 45, 48, 123

O

Offner, Richard, 70, 70n4
oil paintings, 41n53, 126, 127, 174, 178; frescoes vs., 40n4; miniatures vs., 40n16; small, 32, 35, 40n12, 164
O'Keeffe, Georgia, 26
Old Mistresses: Women Artists of the Past (1972), 23, 76
Orlandi, Pellegrino Antonio, 127n1, 166
Orsini, Eleanora, 49

P

Paladini, Arcangela, 35, 37
Paleotti, Cardinal Gabriele, 63, 76, 83
Panciroli, Ottavio, 92
Panigarola, Minor Francesco, 80
Parasole, Isabella Catanea, 75, 99; *Herbario nuovo*, 99; *Pretiosa gemma delle virtuose donne* (cat. 22), 99–100, *100*; *Teatro delle nobili et virtuose donne* (cat. 23), 99–100, *100*
Parasole, Leonardo, 99
Parmigianino, 81n4
Pascoli, Lione, 127
pastels, 14, 15, 27, 32, 34–36, 37, 174, 179; by Carlevarijs, 172–73; by Carriera, 15, 21, 35, 39n2, 161, 163n2, 164–67, 170, 172, 173; by Fratellini, 36, 47, 161; by Del Pò, 32, 35, 36, 40n19, 161; as specialty for male artists, 41n53
Pazzi, Pier Antonio, 179, 181n4
Pelham-Clinton, Henry Fiennes, Earl of Lincoln, 167, 167n10
Pellegrini, Angela Carriera, 170
Pellegrini, Giovanni Antonio, 163
Perrot, Catherine, 40n7, 176n6
Philip II, king of Spain, 36, 37, 53, 67, 70, 70n2, 92n2
Piattoli, Anna Bacherini, 14, 28n15, 179–81; *Portrait of Father Ildefonso Gonzaga* (cat. 62, fig. 2), *181*; *Self-Portrait at the Age of Fifty-Six* (cat. 62), 14, 39n2, 179–81, *180*
Piccinardi, Giovanni Luigi, 155
Piccini, Sister Isabella, 75n9
Pinelli, Antonia Bertusi, 28n15
Pisani dal Banco family, 162
pitture ridicule, 63
Pizan, Christine de, 20, 28n20
Pliny the Elder, 33, 56n4
Plutarch, 143
Pò, Teresa del, 34, 35, 36, 41n98, 75n9; pastels, 32, 35, 36, 40n19, 161
Polignac, Cardinal Melchior de, 163
Pollaroli, Giuseppe, 163n9

portrait medals, 120; of Fontana (cat. 31), 14, 119–21, *119*; of Gentileschi (cat. 32), 14, 119–21, *120*
portraits: of courtly and royal figures, 37, 41n83, 64, 67, 181n3; exchanges of, 36; as gifts, 36; miniature, 35, 36, 79, 127, 161, 167; of noblewomen, 76, 84, 87, 89; of religious figures, 79, 91, 179; of scholars, 76, 79, 84, 84n2; as self-promotion, 36, 56
Pozzo, Cassiano dal, 50n3, 133

Q

Quistelli, Lucrezia, 45, 47–48, 49; *Enthroned Madonna and the Christ Child with Saint Catherine of Alexandria and an Apostle* (Barker, fig. 6), *48*, 49

R

Ragg, Laura: *Women Artists of Bologna*, 21–22
Raggi, Sister Maria Luigia, 48
Ramelli, Giovanni Felice, 174; portrait of (cat. 60, fig. 1), 174, *176*
Ranuzzi, Anna Maria: portraits of (cat. 44 and cat. 44, fig. 1), *144*, 145, *145*
Ranuzzi, Annibale, 145, 151
Raphael, 25, 83, 170
Ratti, Carlo Giuseppe, 25
Razzi, Fra' Serafino, 48
Razzi, Silvano, 49
Rembrandt, 41n57, 56
Reni, Guido, 41n100, 115, 121, 136, 139, 149; *Beatrice Cenci* (cat. 50, fig. 1), 156, *156*; *De Florum Cultura*, 133
Ribera, Fernando Afán de, 127
Ribera, Pietro Paolo da, 69
Riccardi, Marchesa Cassandra Capponi, 46
Riccardi, Marchese Giuseppe, 181n1
Ridolfi, Carlo, 127, 127n8
Ripa, Cesare, 120
Roberto, Virginio, 92
Romano, Giulio: *Latona Giving Birth to Apollo and Diana on the Island of Delos* (cat. 10, fig. 1), 72, *73*; *Latona Giving Birth to Apollo and Diana on the Island of Delos* (cat. 10), Scultori after, 72–75, *73*
Rome, 14, 15, 33, 35, 72, 99, 133, 161, 174, 177, 178; Fontana in, 87, 92, 92n2; Garzoni in, 126, 127; Gentileschi in, 29n63, 101, 109, 110n1, 112, 121. *See also* Accademia dei Lincei; Accademia di San Luca
Romeo, Luigi, baron of San Luigi, 115, 115n2, 116, 118n6
Rossi, Properzia de', 13, 15, 35, 45, 47, 50
Rovere, Vittoria della, 46–47, 136
Rovere family, 37
Rudolph II, Holy Roman Emperor, 97

S

Saint Louis Art Museum, 24, 27, 29nn62–63
Salem Fine Arts Center, 22–23
Sánchez Coello, Alonso, 67, 67n5, 71n8
Sánchez Coello, Isabel, 41n74
Sangallo, Francesco da, 43
Sanvitale, Count Giovanni, 84
Sanvitale family, 84
Sarto, Andrea del: *Madonna of the Sack* (cat. 62, fig. 1), 179, *179*, 181n2
Savoy family, 37, 126
Schidlof, Leo R., 166
Scultori, Diana, 29n36, 72, 120; *Latona Giving Birth to Apollo and Diana on the Island of Delos* (cat. 10), after Giulio Romano, 72–75, *73*; *Spinario* (cat. 11), after Cornelius Cort, 72–75, *74*
self-portraits: allegorical, 14, 39n2, 120, 145, 167; disguised, 14, 15, 39n2, 58, 101, 105, 105n5, 113, 120, 125, 132, 145, 167; as draftswoman, 34, 40n39; as humanist or scholar, 36, 41n64, 56; mirror used for, 33, 41n58, 56, 89; and self-promotion, 14, 36, 105
Sigonio, Carlo, 79
Sirani, Elisabetta, 22, 27, 136; allegorical paintings, 136, 145, 150–51; artistic training, 34, 136; in Bologna, 131, 136, 139, 142, 145, 147, 149, 151, 155, 179; catafalque for (cat. 49), 14, *154*, 155; drawings, 14, 34, 147, 149; earlier sources on, 21, 28n15, 29n36, 136, 139, 140, 142–43, 145, 147, 155n4; fame of, 28n15, 29n40, 139, 139n3, 147; iconographic innovations, 139n3, 140, 140n7, 142–43, 143n9; Medici and, 136, 149, 150–51, 155; prints, 75, 136, 152; self-portraits, 44; signing of works, 136, 139, 139n1, 140, 145; workshop, 131, 156, 179
Sirani, Elisabetta, works: *Absalom Weighing His Hair* or *Berenice* (cat. 42, fig. 1), *140*, 143; *Allegory of Justice, Charity, and Prudence* (cat. 47), 150–51, *150*; *Allegory of Justice, Charity, and Prudence* (cat. 47, fig. 1), 150–51, *151*; *Berenice* (cat. 42), 140, *141*; *Charity* (cat. 47, fig. 2), 151, *151*; *Cupid Triumphant in the Sea* (cat. 40), 136–37, *137*; *Head of a Youth* (cat. 46), *148*, 149; *Head of a Youth* (cat. 46, fig. 1), 149, *149*; *Healing of the Possessed Boy in a Procession of the Volto Santo* (cat. 45), *146*, 147; *Healing of the Possessed Boy in a Procession of the Volto Santo* (cat. 45, fig. 1), 147, *147*; *Holy Family with Saint Elizabeth and the Young Saint John the Baptist* (cat. 48), 152, *153*; *Madonna and Child* (cat. 41), *138*, 139; *Madonna of the Book*, 142; *Portia Wounding Her Thigh* (cat. 43), 140n7, 142–143, *142*; *Portrait of Anna Maria Ranuzzi as Charity* (cat. 44), *144*, 145; *Portrait of Anna Maria Ranuzzi as Charity* (cat. 44, fig. 1), 145, *145*; "Portrait of the Signora Ginevra Cantofoli, Painter," 157n1; *Saint Anthony of Padua in Adoration of the Christ Child*, 142, 143n3; *Self-Portrait as the Allegory of Painting* (Barker, fig. 1), 44, *44*; *Study for the Madonna Crowned by Christ Child with Roses* (cat. 41, fig. 1), 139, *139*
Sirani, Giovanni Andrea, 136; *Absalom Weighing His Hair* or *Berenice* (cat. 42, fig. 1), *140*, 143
small-scale works, 31–41; courts and, 36–37; critical denigration of, 31–32; market for, 39, 45; portraits, 32, 33, 35, 36, 41n69, 58, 61, 79; as self-promotion, 36; terminology, 32. *See also* miniatures
Soldani, Isabella, 46
Solimena, Francesco, 158, 160n6
Soprani, Raffaele, 25
Sotheby's, 25, 26, 28n7
Sparrow, Walter Shaw: *Women Painters of the World*, 21, 29nn36–37
Spilimbergo, Irene di, 49, 99
Spinario (cat. 11, fig. 2), 75, *75*; Scultori after (cat. 11), 72–75, *74*
Stampa, Ermete, second marchese of Soncino, 64
Stampa, Massimiliano, 64; portrait of (cat. 6), 64–65, *65*, 70
Stern Telli, Veronica, 39, 177, 178; *Lady Playing the Lute* (cat. 61), 177–78, *177*
Stiattesi, Pierantonio, 44, 101
still lifes, 14, 34, 38, 46, 133; by Caccia, 122, 123; by Galizia, 95, 97, 98; by Garzoni, 35, 126, 128
Subleyras, Pierre, 174; *Madame Subleyras, née Maria Felice Tibaldi* (cat. 60), 14, 29n64 174–76, *175*; *Portrait of the Abbot Miniaturist Giovanni Felice Ramelli* (cat. 60, fig. 1), 174, *176*
Sustermans, Giusto, 132
Sutherland Harris, Ann, 14, 23–24, 29n55, 40n38, 40n42, 41n57, 95

T

Tassi, Agostino, 45, 101
Tassi, Simone, 142–43, 143n3, 143n8
Teerlinc, Levina, 15, 36, 37, 41n66, 41n73, 56
Temanza, Tomaso, 172
Tibaldi, Maria Felice, 14, 29n36, 39, 174, 178; portrait of (cat. 60), 14, 29n64, 174–76, *175*
Tinti, Lorenzo, 155, *155*
Tintoretto, Jacopo, 47
Tintoretto, Marietta, 21
Titian, 25, 40n39, 49, 49n1, 132n7
toilet or embroidery set (cat. 43, fig. 1), 143, *143*
Tschudy, Herbert, 28n19

U

Ulrika Eleonora, queen of Sweden, 37

V

Vaiana, Caterina, 47
Vaiani, Anna Maria, 41n98, 75, 133; *Bouquet of Flowers* (cat. 39), 133–35, *134*; portrait of (cat. 39, fig. 1), *133*; *Saint Mary Magdalene*, 125
Valle, Guglielmo della, 123
Vasari, Giorgio, *Lives of the Most Excellent Painters, Sculptors, and Architects*, 13, 50, 56; gender disparity in, 13, 14, 31–32; *gran maniera*, 32; de' Rossi in, 13, 50; on small oil paintings, 32, 40n12; *variazione*, 80; women artists in second edition, 45, 47–48, 49, 50n13, 72, 75
Velli, Teresa Raimondi, 41n98
Venice, 15, 35, 126; Carlevarijs in, 14, 172, 173; Carriera in, 161, 165, 166, 172, 174, 178; Gentileschi in, 101
Vezzo, Virginia da, 14, 15, 41n98, 131, 132n1; *Judith* (cat. 38, fig. 1), 131, *131*, 132n3; portrait of (cat. 38), 14, 29n64, 125, *130*, 131–32; portrait of (cat. 38, fig. 2), 131, *132*
Vigée Le Brun, Elisabeth-Louise, 26
Vigri, Caterina, 29n36, 34
Violante Beatrice, duchess of Bavaria, 46–47
Vitelli, Sister Teresa Berenice, 47, 48
Volterra, Francesco da, 72
Vouet, Simon, 131; *Virginia da Vezzo, the Artist's Wife, as the Magdalene* (cat. 38), 14, 29n64, 125, *130*, 131–32

W

Wadsworth Atheneum Museum of Art, 13, 17, *18*
Walters Art Gallery, 23, 76
Watteau, Antoine, 166n7
wax modeling, 45, 49, 158–59, 160nn1–3
Women: A Historical Survey of Works by Women Artists (1972), 22–23
women artists, early modern: *See* early modern women artists
Women Artists: 1550–1950 (1976/1977), 14, 23–24, *23*, 29n55
Worlidge, Thomas, 58

Y

Young Man (unknown Northern Italian artist) (cat. 9 and cat. 9, fig. 1), 70–71, *70*, *71*

Z

Zappi, Gian Paolo, 76, 80, 92
Zenobio family, 172
Zuccari, Taddeo: *Pietà* (cat. 14, fig. 2), 81, *81*
Zumbo, Gaetano Giulio, 158, 160n7

PHOTOGRAPHY CREDITS

Unless otherwise noted, all photographs of artworks and archival documents appear by permission of the lenders mentioned in their captions. Every effort has been made to contact copyright holders and to ensure that all the information presented is correct. If proper copyright acknowledgment has not been made, or for clarification and corrections, please contact the publishers and we will correct the information in future reprinting, if any.

© Accademia Nazionale di San Luca, Roma, p. 33 (fig. 3)

AKG-Images, p. 44 (fig. 1)

The Albertina Museum, Vienna, p. 178

Album/Art Resource, NY, pp. 105, 145

Allen Phillips/Wadsworth Atheneum, cover (cat. 24, detail); pp. 2 (cat. 42, detail), 12 (cat. 50, detail), 18 (fig. 1), 59, 60, 85, 102, 124, 126, 129 (cat. 36), 141, 144, 148, 157, 162 (cat. 52), 162 (cat. 53), 173, 177, 182 (cat. 36, detail)

Altomani & Sons, pp. 137, 140

Arader Galleries, p. 129 (cat. 37)

Archbishop Alemany Library, Dominican University of California, p. 48 (fig. 5)

© Artcurial, Paris, p. 25

Arthemisia, Milan, pp. 48 (fig. 6), 49 (fig. 8)

Associazione Metamorfosi, Rome/Photo Scala, Florence/Art Resource, NY, p. 103

Biblioteca Comunale dell'Archiginnasio, p. 155

Bibliothèque Nationale de France, Paris, pp. 33 (fig. 2), 120 (fig. 1)

Bridgeman Images, p. 37 (fig. 6)

Brooklyn Museum Archives, Records of the Department of Photography, p. 23

© 2021 Christie's Images Limited, p. 49 (fig. 7)

The Cleveland Museum of Art, pp. 10 (cat. 54, detail), 165 (cats. 55 and 56)

Collezioni d'Arte e di Storia della Fondazione Casa di Risparmio in Bologna, p. 142

Columbus Museum of Art, p. 117

Comune di Padova—Settore Cultura, Turismo, Musei e Biblioteche, p. 19 (fig. 4)

Comune di Vignola, p. 151 (fig. 1)

Cornell Fine Arts Museum, Rollins College, p. 80

Detroit Institute of Arts, pp. 16 (cat. 27, detail), 71, 108, 159, 168, 171; back cover (cat. 27, detail)

DIA Conservation Department Imaging Lab, pp. 70, 110 (fig. 1, fig. 2), 169 (fig. 2)

Dominique Provost Art Photography—Bruges, Belgium, pp. 52 (cat. 28, detail), 112

Donato Pineider, p. 45

© Dumbarton Oaks Research Library and Collection, Rare Book Collection, Trustees for Harvard University, Washington, D.C., p. 134

El Paso Museum of Art, p. 81 (fig. 1)

Matt Flynn, Smithsonian Institution, p. 154

Fondazione Federico Zeri, pp. 58, 163 (fig. 1, fig. 2)

Fondazione Musei Civici di Venezia, p. 172

The Frick Collection, p. 120 (cat. 32)

Galleria Borghese, p. 95

Galleria Carlo Virgilio & C., p. 158

Galleria Colonna, Rome, p. 61

Gallerie degli Uffizi, pp. 36, 46, 107, 149, 180, 181

Galleria Nazionale Delle Marche—Urbino, p. 81 (fig. 2)

Gallerie Nazionali di Arte Antica, MIBACT—Bibliotheca Hertziana, Istituto Max Planck for the Histoy of Art/Enrico Fontolan, p. 156

Richard Goodbody Inc., New York, p. 114

HIP/Art Resource, NY, p. 111

Sid Hoeltzell, p. 68

Paola Ircani Menichini, p. 179

The John and Mable Ringling Museum of Art, pp. 94, 96

KHM—Museumsverband, p. 32

Library of Congress, LC-DIG-det-4a03650, p. 18 (fig. 2),

Library of Congress, LC-DIG-npcc-27027, p. 19 (fig. 3)

Marie-Lan Nguyen, p. 75

Massimo Capaldi, p. 76

© The Metropolitan Museum of Art/Art Resource, NY, pp. 79, 93, 100 (cat. 22), 100 (cat. 23), 133, 164 (cat. 54)

© MiBACT—Musei Reali, Galleria Sabauda, p. 176

Mondadori Portfolio/Electa/Antonio Quattrone/Bridgeman Images, p. 63

Montreal Museum of Fine Arts, pp. 8 (cat. 21, detail), 97

The Morgan Library & Museum, pp. 88, 89 (fig. 2, fig. 3), 90

© Musée d'arts de Nantes—Photographie: CECILE CLOS, p. 131

© Museum Associates/LACMA, by Annie Appel, p. 20 (fig. 6)

© 2021 Museum Associates/LACMA. Licensed by Art Resource, NY, pp. 82, 130

© Museums of Art and History, City of Geneva, p. 37 (fig. 7)

© 2021 Museum of Fine Arts, Boston, pp. 30, 57, 62

Muzeul National Brukenhtal, Sibiu, Romania, p. 35

National Gallery of Art, Washington, D.C., pp. 73 (cat. 10), 74, 119, 132, 146, 153

National Gallery of Canada, p. 151 (fig. 2)

© The National Gallery, London, pp. 55, 64, 104

National Museums Liverpool, p. 139

National Portrait Gallery, London, p. 20 (fig. 5)

RISD Museum, Providence, p. 150

© RMN—Grand Palais/Art Resource, NY, pp. 73, 113

Robert Simon Fine Art, p. 84 (fig. 1)

Royal Collection Trust/© Her Majesty Queen Elizabeth II 2021, pp. 38, 116

© San Diego Museum of Art/Gift of Anne R. and Amy Putnam/Bridgeman Images, p. 66

Sarah Campbell Blaffer Foundation, Houston, p. 123

Scala/Art Resource, NY, p. 69

© Southampton City Art Gallery/Bridgeman Images, pp. 42 (cat. 1, detail), 54

Lee Stalsworth, p. 138

© The State Hermitage Museum/photo by Darya Bobrova, p. 166

Julia Vicioso, p. 44 (fig. 2)

Victoria and Albert Museum, London, p. 143

Daria Vinco, dell'Archivio Fotografico della Soprintendenza Archeologia, Belle Arti Paesaggio per la Città Metropolitana di Genova e per la provincia di La Spezia, p. 147

The Walters Art Museum, Baltimore, pp. 65, 77, 84 (fig. 2), 86

© Worcester Art Museum/Gift of Helen Bigelow Merriman/Bridgeman Images, p. 175

Yale University Art Gallery, p. 122